THE COURSE OF MEXICAN HISTORY

The Course of Mexican History

Fifth Edition

MICHAEL C. MEYER
University of Arizona

WILLIAM L. SHERMAN
University of Nebraska

New York   Oxford
OXFORD UNIVERSITY PRESS
1995

Oxford University Press

Oxford   New York
Athens   Auckland   Bangkok   Bombay
Calcutta   Cape Town   Dar es Salaam   Delhi
Florence   Hong Kong   Istanbul   Karachi
Kuala Lumpur   Madras   Madrid   Melbourne
Mexico City   Nairobi   Paris   Singapore
Taipei   Tokyo   Toronto

and associated companies in
Berlin   Ibadan

Published by Oxford University Press, Inc.,
198 Madison Avenue, New York, New York 10016-4314

Oxford is a registered trademark of Oxford University Press

Library of Congress Cataloging-in-Publication Data
Meyer, Michael C.
    The course of Mexican history / Michael C. Meyer,
William L. Sherman. — 5th ed.
        p.   cm.   Includes bibliographical references (p.   ) and index.
    ISBN 0-19-508979-0.
    ISBN 0-19-508980-4 (pbk.)
    1. Mexico—History.   I. Sherman, William L.   II. Title.
F1226.M54   1995   972—dc20   94-6727

5 7 9 8 6 4

Printed in the United States of America
on acid-free paper

PREFACE

Since we completed the first draft of the first edition of *The Course of Mexican History* Mexico has recorded some successes and has suffered some setbacks, and we have tried to document the most important of them in subsequent editions. The historical literature upon which we now rely to form our own judgments has grown immeasurably richer, and we have profited from the diligence and scholarship of many others as we undertook the revisions for this edition. The path of Mexican history might not yet be strewn with the rubbish of discarded hypotheses, but a substantial body of new scholarship continues to bring into question many commonly held assumptions about the Mexican past.

Our original purpose has not changed. The challenge still is to present an up-to-date, interesting, and informative synthesis of Mexican history. While we naturally hope that our colleagues in both Mexico and the United States will find merit in our approach, we have directed our history not to them but to their students and the general reader. Like all survey texts, ours is intended to throw open the subject of Mexican history, certainly not to close it. Those wishing to pursue a topic in greater depth will find that we have updated the list of English-language works appended to each chapter. We have included works now considered standard with more recent interpretations that we found perceptive and interesting, including those whose conclusions differ from our own.

The understanding of Mexican history logically begins with an understanding of major political themes. These we have dutifully reconstructed, but we view them as a means to an end. They are, in effect, a foundation upon which to build. Political decisions influence the direction of the economy, the social structure, and even the cultural vitality of a country. Because we are persuaded that history properly encompasses the entire human experience, we have directed special attention to social and cultural developments, including population trends, life styles, the special role of women, literature, art, music, and intellectual life. We recognize that social and cultural patterns seldom fit neatly into political or economic periods, but as in the past, we have included a chapter on society and culture within each major chronological division in the belief that these sections help to provide a broader and more accurate representation of Mexican life in the crucial eras of Mexico's historical development.

The fifth edition has afforded us the opportunity to address an entire series of emerging themes. Naturally, the most timely developments, such as NAFTA, the Salinas administration, the Chiapas rebellion, and the acknowledged shortcomings of the Revolution required the most extensive additions and changes. Finally, in response to helpful suggestions from our students and our colleagues, we have also reorganized some of the chapters, corrected some inadvertent errors, and undertaken a series of minor revisions.

Mexico's experience in the world community continues to be remarkable and unique. On some occasions, a national consensus has emerged, facilitating the tasks of exposition and interpretation; but on other occasions, uncompromising ideologies, differing views of national purpose, and competing articulations of problems and solutions render difficult our accounting of the Mexican experience. At those times where the air is not yet clear, where polemic threatens to offend our sensibilities, we can think of no better response than to offer the tempering context of historical perspective. Mexico's future inevitably will be tied to Mexico's past.

We gratefully acknowledge our debt to Nancy Lane of Oxford University Press for her support and wise counsel over the past sixteen years.

Tuscon, Arizona   M. C. M.
Lincoln, Nebraska   W. L. S.
May 1994

CONTENTS

MAPS AND CHARTS

THE COURSE OF MEXICAN HISTORY

I PRE-COLUMBIAN MEXICO

1

The First Mexicans

There is in Mexican society a pervasive awareness of the ancients. The Indian presence intrudes on the national psyche; it suffuses the art, philosophy, and literature. It is stamped on the face of Mexico, in the racial features of the sturdy mestizo. It lies within the marvelous prehistoric ruins among whose haunted piles the Mexican seeks his origins. It has not always been so. Following the Spanish conquest of the sixteenth century, a combination of the conquerors' ethnocentrism and excessive Christian zeal reduced all things Indian to a level of shame. During the subsequent four centuries, until the cultural phase of the Revolution during the 1920s, the indigenous past lurked in the background as a mild embarrassment, save to a few enlightened scholars. This paradox existed among a people, the majority of whom had at least some Indian blood, because the minority of whites, insensitive to historical realities, looked to a European model. But the maturing Revolution sought the spirit of a Mexican cultural identity—*mexicanidad*—and what emerged was indeed revolutionary in its cultural implications. In the past several decades anthropologists, historians, painters, musicians, novelists, and craftsmen have bent their talents toward an exaltation of native values. If in its enthusiasm the movement took some liberties, it may be excused as following the natural path of cultural nationalism. More important, it revealed the stunning achievements of the past, for when, in 1519, Fernando Cortés and the Spanish host invaded, advanced civilization in Mexico was more than a thousand years old.

Pre-Agricultural and Proto-Agricultural Mexico

At what point the first Mexican appeared on the scene we shall, of course, never know. He was no doubt one of an obscure band of nomads descended from the intrepid hunters who crossed from the Asian mainland to Alaska. There appear to have been successive waves of migrants, the first perhaps as early as 50,000 B.C., with the beginning of the Wisconsin (Pleistocene) Ice Age. At this time much of the earth's water formed into gigantic ice caps, and the level of the oceans was reduced. Consequently, a land bridge over the Bering Straits facilitated the passage. When a melting trend began around 8000 B.C., the migrations very likely ceased.

"The story of Indian America," Pablo Martínez del Río used to tell his classes, "must be written with soft chalk, easily erased and corrected." Thus reference was made to our tenuous hold on knowledge of ancient Mexico. With increasing interest in anthropology, however, we may expect that many of our present conceptions will be altered, perhaps radically, in years ahead. For the moment, it is convenient to divide the history of pre-Hispanic Mexico into periods, which vary somewhat both in chronology and terminology according to the authority one consults. It will be noted that not all cultures fit within this chart, and there is inevitable overlapping on some dates.

STAGES OF PRE-HISPANIC INDIAN DEVELOPMENT

40,000–5000 B.C.	*Pre-Agricultural:* Nomadic hunters and food gatherers.
5000–1500 B.C.	*Proto-Agricultural* or *Archaic:* Agricultural beginnings; formation of crude but permanent villages; appearance of rudimentary political and social organization; development of primitive skills.
1500–200 B.C.	*Formative* or *Pre-Classic:* Elaboration of Proto-Agricultural achievements and refinement of techniques; artistry in ceramics; planned ceremonial sites, anticipating the Classic period.
200 B.C.–A.D. 900	*Classic:* The florescence of ancient Mexican civilization, with cities ruled by priests and kings; the apogee of artistic expression; monumental architecture; advancement in literacy and science.
A.D. 900–1521	*Post-Classic* or *Historical:* Societies increasingly yield to rule by warriors; emergence of conquest states; appearance of metallurgy; origin of authentic historical sources; an excess of human sacrifice; final destruction of the Indian states by Spanish Conquest.

Early man in America was a hunter, a food gatherer, and sometimes a fisherman. Contrary to recent popular assertions, his prominent trait was not aggressiveness but insecurity. It must be supposed that man spent an inordinate amount of his time merely struggling to survive and was almost constantly on the search for food. For thousands of years the Indian led a precarious existence, with no perceptible improvement in his condition.

Recent finds indicate that humans roamed northern Mexico at least forty thousand years ago, but our ignorance of their society is almost complete. We must, therefore, pass over at least twenty-five or thirty thousand years, during which time man's prospects remained essentially static. Although scattered indications of his presence in the interval exist, there is little substantive evidence of the nature of his society until the period of 10,000–8000 B.C. By these times of moist conditions, lush grasslands and full foliage provided ample fodder for strange animals—hairy mammoths, mastodons, giant armadillos, and early ancestors of the bison, camel, and horse. A large lake covered the floor of the Valley of Mexico, and to that watering place came the prehistoric beasts. In the congenial environment of the Valley man also lived. When animals became mired in the lakeshore marshes, primitive warriors assailed their prey with missiles—stone-tipped lances or darts propelled by the *atl-atl*, or spear thrower, the extension of which gave added velocity. Evidence of successful hunts was preserved in the muck. In the 1940s, the remains of a human were discovered at the village of Tepexpan, situated a few miles north of today's Mexico City on what was the edge of the old lake. The bones lay at a depth corresponding to a layer that also contained the bones of a mammoth, giving fragmentary evidence that the two were contemporaries. "Tepexpan Man" (who, it turned out, was a woman) is the first tangible clue to the early race. In 1952, not far distant at Santa Isabel Iztápan, another important discovery was unearthed: mammoth bones were found with a stone point lodged in the ribs, and there were clear indications that the beast had been butchered with flint knives that lay nearby. There is some dispute about the exact dating of these finds, but they seem to be from ten to twelve thousand years old.

Changes in climatic conditions reordered ancient man's routine. Around 7500 B.C. a drying-up phase began: rainfall was less frequent, and the rich plant life gradually yielded to sparse vegetation; the lake shriveled up; and the huge beasts that had provided a plentiful supply of meat eventually became extinct as their sources of food and water disappeared. Man was again back to eating insects, lizards, snakes, rodents, and anything else remotely edible, to supplement his diet of seeds, roots, nuts, berries, eggs, and shellfish. The audacious killer of mammoths gave way to the hunter of small game.

It appears that about the time large animals vanished—around 7000 B.C.—crude experimentations with agriculture began. It would be thousands of years before domesticated plants provided a reliable source of food, but no discovery of man in his long quest for security was more momentous than that of agriculture. The most important plant was maize, or corn, which responded well to human care and grew almost anywhere. It became the basis of the Mexican diet. As far as we know, the earliest successful planting was at Tehuacán in the modern state of Puebla; perhaps as early as 5000 B.C. primitive farmers there practiced the most rudimentary form of agriculture. In the many centuries that followed, other plants were domesticated to form the essential staples of the Mexican diet—corn, beans, and squash. It may be said that by at least 2500 B.C. they contributed an important part of man's sustenance, as indicated by the presence of grinding stones for the making of meal.

By the passage of the next millennium, when more moisture had returned to the land, the authentic farmer had evolved. Now, barring disasters common to all tillers of the soil, there was a fairly reliable source of food. The impact of this achievement can hardly be exaggerated. From having to devote almost all of his efforts to the desperate search for something to eat, man finally found some leisure time for experimentation, to develop and refine his skills and talents. Long a weaver of baskets and mats, he now—around 2000 B.C.—began to shape clay, a most important development.

The Formative Period

Ancient garbage dumps are to the archaeologist what documents are to the historian. From those piles of refuse scientific investigators patiently assemble pictures of primitive societies with a sophistication astonishing to the layman. Much has, of course, long been reduced to dust, and whatever use early man made of wood, hides, and woven reeds must be left to speculation. But instruments of flint, obsidian, and various kinds of stone survive, and when man began to fashion pottery he left behind indelible

Ceramic figurine of a dancer from Tlatilco, near Mexico City. The swollen thighs suggest an association with fertility.

traces of his culture. More often than not the vessels are found smashed, but these potsherds provide key links with the past. According to the way pots are made, shaped, and decorated, the archaeologist reconstructs and defines a way of life.

By 1500 B.C. the rough outlines of an existence with which we can identify had formed. Agriculture had enabled man to settle down and support larger population clusters, and he built huts of branches, reeds, and mud. A simple village life with incipient political and social orders evolved. Subsequently, cliques emerged to control both power and wealth. Increased exchange of goods among different cultures developed as a result of the distinctive techniques and specialties of local artisans. In addition, varied climate and geography yielded regional fruits, vegetables, woods, stone, and other items of value, such as shells, jade, cotton, and turquoise. This spreading trade naturally led to cultural exchanges as well.

Artists began to create ceramics that were both esthetically pleasing and functional. Clay figurines, usually of females and more often than not naked, were produced in great numbers. The most unusual were those of Tlatilco, in the Valley of Mexico, where, artists rendered charming figurines of the type known as "pretty lady," with delicate and beautiful faces. The eyes are almost Oriental and the hairdos sometimes elaborate. The figures have tiny waists, and their bulging thighs suggest that they were symbols of fertility. At the same time, a fascination with the deformed manifested early the Mexican idea of duality, for other small clay figures represented dwarfs, hunchbacks, and the diseased. Some figurines are of interest for their depiction of everyday life—nursing babies, dancing, playing, and performing acrobatics. Through them we gain some idea of popular pastimes, the use of jewelry, and clothing. Still other pieces were made in the forms of animals, birds, and fish. Art at this point was still an expression of curiosity, of the frivolous and innocent, devoid of the serious religious connotations it later acquired.

Agriculture advanced during the Formative period with the use of terracing and *chinampas*, or floating gardens. The chinampas were rafts made of branches onto which fertile mud from the lake bottom was piled. These made rich gardens for the raising of food, and irrigation was no problem. Farming implements of stone, horn, bone, and probably wood facilitated cultivation of fields.

Although textile manufacturing had evolved, it is likely that, in the more temperate zones anyway, people went about nude, or almost so. Clothing was apparently worn more among the upper classes than the lower, as were sandals, jewelry, and other adornments. Individual expression and vanity were evident in the dyed hair and elaborate coiffures of aristocratic women.

As villages grew in size and society became more complex, serious decisions had to be made by those who were most knowledgeable. Increasing reliance on agriculture made people aware that their security depended upon the blessings of nature. The mysteries of the universe were associated with the supernatural, and, as in other ancient cultures, gods of nature came to be worshipped. Vagaries of the elements were equated with capricious gods. When rain failed, for example, supplication was made to the angry deity through the agency of the priesthood. Among a **credulous people, the priest, with his special powers, acquired a predominant position. This presumed special relationship with the gods, astutely cultivated by the priests, gave them a certain** mystique and a hold over the community. In order to pay due reverence to the gods and to ensure their cooperation in providing rain and sunshine, priests ordered the construction of mounds, on top of which offerings were made. As the structures became larger and more elaborate, advanced permanent architecture evolved. By the late Formative, or Pre-Classic period, some impressive sites were already in evidence.

La Venta and Monte Albán

Because of the great diversity in aboriginal Mexico, it is perhaps misleading to refer to any group as the "mother culture." But the people with the best claim to being the first emerging civilization in Mexico are the Olmecs. "Civilization" here is meant to imply an urban, literate society. If La Venta, the main Olmec center, was not a true city, it at least displayed the pristine characteristics of urbanism; if its people were not truly literate, they at least drew hieroglyphs, the first step in writing. By 1200 B.C. the Olmecs flourished in western Tabasco and southern Veracruz. They reached the height of their development between 700 and 400 B.C., during which time they carved hieroglyphs and devised an early calendar. The most impressive of the Olmec sites, La Venta, was built in a swampy area in Tabasco, where a large pyramid, along with other painted structures, formed part of a ceremonial center. It served a nearby population of perhaps eighteen thousand.[1] La Venta was apparently destroyed around 400 B.C., having been subjected to violent desecrations.

Olmec origins are obscure; little, in fact, is known of the Olmecs except through their distinctive art. During this springtime of the Mexican world Olmec sculptors fashioned jade figurines whose elegance is unsurpassed. Their most spectacular pieces are colossal carved stone heads, some of which are over nine feet high and weigh up to forty tons. The facial features are strikingly Negroid, and the heads are covered with what seem to be helmets. Smaller pieces have facial characteristics designated as "baby face" and pudgy bodies that suggest infants or eunuchs.

Strongly established among the Olmecs was the jaguar cult, identified in some way with the rain god and fertility. Manifestations of the cult appear frequently in Olmec stone carvings, figures, and other artifacts. The obsession with feline forms, or "were-jaguars," was such that jaguars are even depicted in sexual union with women. The down-turned, snarling jaguar mouth is often seen in the sculptured faces of human forms, and it is

1. Michael D. Coe, *Mexico* (New York, 1967), p. 88.

This handsome basalt stone carving from the Gulf Coast Olmec culture is known as "The Wrestler."

possible that these strange faces actually represent masks. The mysterious Olmec civilization gradually declined, perhaps because of cultural pressures from the rising Maya to the south and the incipient Teotihuacán complex in the central highlands.

Developing at a time roughly parallel with La Venta was the important center at Monte Albán, situated on a mountain top outside of today's city of Oaxaca. Sometime before 200 B.C. the Indians of the Oaxacan civilization devised a calendar and a rudimentary form of writing expressed in carvings on stone markers. Both La Venta and Monte Albán anticipated the great civilizations to follow, having by the late Formative period already exhibited many of the characteristics associated with the Classic. There was unquestionably contact between the two sites. But while the Olmec influence was on the wane by the end of the Formative period, Monte Albán emerged as one of the great centers of the Classic world in Mexico.

It may be noted briefly that in the southern area of Chiapas and Yucatán, where the impressive Maya civilization would eventually rise, there were signs of advancing culture. These were, however, behind the development at La Venta and Monte Albán. Early achievement in the Valley of Mexico lagged somewhat; at Cuicuilco, located on the outskirts of Mexico City, the

Several colossal Olmec stone heads have been discovered. This one, more than eight feet high, is covered with what appears to be a helmet.

An Olmec jade figurine illustrates the skill of ancient artists.

Representing a pudgy baby, or perhaps a eunuch, this Olmec piece is 13½ inches in height.

oldest extant structure dates from approximately 600 B.C. A curious conical pyramid, it was built to a height of sixty feet, only to be buried in a later volcanic eruption.

Destined to become the most influential site of all was the developing center of Teotihuacán in the Valley of Mexico. By at least 200 B.C. the Teotihuacanos were formulating plans for what would later become a vast city. Before the birth of Christ work had begun on the great pyramids and mural paintings that may be seen today. A complicated polytheistic religion evolved. By the end of the Formative period there had emerged in that large civic-religious complex the technology and central authority necessary for the creation of one of the splendors of the ancient world.

Recommended for Further Study

Benson, Elizabeth P., ed. *The Olmec and Their Neighbors.* New York: Crowell, 1977.

Bernal, Ignacio. *The Olmec World.* Translated by Doris Heyden and Fernando Horcasitas. Berkeley: University of California Press, 1969.

Coe, Michael. *America's First Civilization: Discovering the Olmecs.* New York: Van Nostrand, 1968.

———. *The Jaguar's Children: Pre-Classic Central Mexico.* New York: Museum of Primitive Art, 1965.

———. *Mexico.* New York: Praeger, 1967.

Huddleston, Lee E. *Origins of the American Indians: European Concepts, 1492–1729.* Austin: University of Texas Press, 1970.

Litvak-King, Jaime. *Ancient Mexico, an Overview.* Albuquerque: University of New Mexico Press, 1985.

Miller, Mary Ellen. *The Art of Mesoamerica, from Olmec to Aztec.* London: Thames and Hudson, 1986.

Soustelle, Jacques. *The Olmecs: The Oldest Civilization in Mexico.* Translated by Helen R. Lane. Norman: University of Oklahoma Press, 1985.

Terra, Helmut de. *Man and Mammoth in Mexico.* Translated by Alan H. Brodrick. London: Hutchinson, 1957.

Wauchope, Robert. *They Found the Buried Cities: Exploration and Excavation in the American Tropics.* Chicago: University of Chicago Press, 1965.

Wicke, Charles R. *Olmec: An Early Art Style of Precolumbian Mexico.* Tucson: University of Arizona Press, 1971.

Willey, Gordon R., ed. *Prehistoric Settlement Patterns in the New World.* New York: Johnson Reprint, 1963.

Wolf, Eric. *Sons of the Shaking Earth: The People of Mexico and Guatemala—Their Land, History, and Culture.* Chicago: University of Chicago Press, 1974.

2

Mexico's Golden Age: The Classic Period

When, around 200 B.C., much of the Old World was being introduced to Roman ways, there was in the New World only a glimmer of high civilization. Six centuries later, when the Roman Empire crumbled and Europe entered its Dark Ages, Middle America was resplendent.

The Golden Age

The Classic period in pre-Columbian Mexico lasted about a thousand years (200/0 B.C. to A.D. 800/1000), of which some six hundred may be viewed as a Golden Age. Because of the many cultures under consideration, the Classic cannot be put into any simple chronological framework.[1] At some sites, such as Teotihuacán and Monte Albán, a Proto-Classic style began to evolve by 200 B.C., while at others it did not appear until a couple of centuries later. That transitional stage lasted until A.D. 200/300, at which time the splendor of the Full Classic emerged, flourishing until the declining stages between A.D. 650 to 800. There was a final, decadent phase, the Late Classic (or Epi-Classic), persisting in some areas as late as A.D. 1000.

One is struck by the grandiose scale of man's work in those centuries, most notable in the monumental architecture but also by the excellence of the ceramics, sculpture, and murals. Reli-

1. With about eleven thousand known archaeological sites in Mexico, of which perhaps no more than ninety have been scientifically excavated, the complexities of charting can be appreciated.

Why is this boy laughing? Such unrestrained joy is characteristic of the thousands of ceramic pieces found at the site of Remojadas in the state of Veracruz. Unique for their expressiveness, the figurines have triangular, flattened heads, and teeth that are often filed to points.

A howling coyote, another delightful piece from the Remojadas culture, A.D. 300–900. Indian artists frequently displayed a touch of whimsy in their works.

gion was the cohesive force in an increasingly stratified society, and the hierarchy of priests commanded the power to exact both labor and tribute from the masses. It was a time of great vigor, with the proliferation of crafts and skills necessary to provide for complex communities. The leadership was dedicated to a sense of order and progress, made possible by an apparently strict adherence to regimentation. Pressures to provide sustenance for a burgeoning population led to more careful consideration of planting cycles, which in turn produced exact calculations of the seasons. Consequently there developed a very sophisticated knowledge of astronomy and mathematics, which made possible precise calendrical markings. The Maya devised the world's most accurate calendar. Farming became scientific; abstract thinking soared. The intellectuals in ancient Middle America may have arrived at the revolutionary concept of the zero cipher even before its discovery by the fifth-century Hindus. Not until A.D. 1202 did Arab mathematicians introduce this concept to Europe. Yet, oddly enough, the accomplished scientists of the New World made almost no practical use of metals, nor had they stumbled onto the utility of the wheel!

It is therefore all the more admirable that these Middle Americans were able to raise structures to the height of 230 feet that have stood for some fifteen hundred years. The magnitude of their technical limitations was equaled by their ingenuity. Massive blocks of cut stone were most likely transported on river rafts from quarries to distant cities, and for lifting the pieces high in the air some clever engineering devices, however crude in appearance, were utilized. Nature had provided Mexico no beasts of burden, so armies of laborers toiled for years on public works projects.

Though we marvel that these structures remain after so many centuries (all the more remarkable in earthquake country), excellence of construction was not these early people's strongest suit. Rather, one finds in their work the origins of a fundamental, and not unattractive, Mexican trait—the subordination of technical perfection to the irresistible propensity for the esthetic. The affinity for that which is pleasing to the eye was uppermost. Though capable of exact measurements, they avoided harsh angles. If the result was agreeable to man, the purpose, it is clear, was to please the gods.

It was long believed that these building complexes were not true cities but only ceremonial centers inhabited by priests, rulers, and their retainers. Today it is generally agreed that these centers were true cities. They contained temples, pyramids, palaces, tombs, observatories, and acropoli, as well as ball courts, steam baths, and causeways. While the upper classes lived there in luxurious chambers, the artisans, petty officials, soldiers, merchants, laborers, farmers, and others of the commoner class lived in modest huts constituting cluster communities in outlying regions. There they farmed the land, hunted, fished, carried the burdens, and performed all sorts of tasks necessary to support the aristocracy. Apparently only during festivals, usually religious in nature, or on market days, did the masses gather in the central precincts. These marvelous stone cities were conceived for an impression of grandeur and laid out in breathtaking expanses. The architects were true artists, interposing grand courtyards to offset with horizontal lines the massive vertical projections. Vladimir Kaspé writes that "the early builders treated space . . . with remarkable intelligence and sensitivity. They achieved what modern architects and town planners continually advocate: to 'compose' with space." They blended their creations with nature, he adds, and "they knew how to obtain textures and could dress stone so that it not only fulfilled its function but also reflected the Mexican sunlight."[2]

Whether or not an "urban revolution" occurred is debatable, but there is no question that concentrated populations in so many sites had an incalculable impact on culture. The arts always thrive with greatest vigor in an urban milieu, and intellectual growth is enhanced as well. At the same time, the stratification of society is inevitable. So, too, is a central administration to maintain order, promote public works, provide justice, set regulations—to perform, in short, on a more simplified scale, the functions familiar to city administrators of our own times. And although the details of how these early people of Mexico accomplished all this still evade us, there are signs of considerable efficiency. Great plazas and avenues were paved, buildings were plastered and painted, subterranean tile drainage systems were provided, waste was disposed of, domestic water supplies were channeled, and the staggering problems of food supply were met. Over the centuries central authority was maintained, it seems, in an atmosphere of progress and relative tranquility, at least in central Mexico.

Traditionally, the Classic period was viewed as having been devoted to moderation and comparative serenity, with order imposed by dominant centers such as Teotihuacán and Monte Albán. These powers, like city-states, carved out spheres of influence that were tolerated by others. Allowing for some exceptions over the centuries, this impression may have been largely true for the non-Maya cultures. Conflict is, nevertheless, part of the human condition, and it would be unrealistic to assume that the Classic peoples had risen completely above it. But for central Mexico, indications of warfare during the Classic are relatively few. Little evidence exists to indicate that cities were planned with defense in mind, until later times. Moreover, the abundant examples of art present almost no battle scenes, nor are warriors prominently depicted. Where humans are shown, it is the priests who predominate. Certain works of art, especially toward the end of the period, do show soldiers, weapons, and slaves, as well as indications of human sacrifice. Then, too, one may reasonably ask if the wide dispersion of culture was simply the result of

2. Vladimir Kaspé, preface to Henri Stierlin, *Living Architecture: Ancient Mexican* (New York, 1968), pp. 4–5.

peaceful exchange or whether it was imposed by force. No doubt
some fighting occurred in the central regions, but it appears that
in no sense did a warrior elite dominate.

However, we can no longer accept scenes of relative tranquility
for the Classic Maya. Because of important revelations as a result
of improved deciphering of Maya hieroglyphic script, the character of these people has been dramatically reassessed. The Maya
genius in art, architecture, and science remains clear; nevertheless, the romanticized version of a society ruled by a benevolent
and intellectual priesthood, shunning violence and conquest, now
rings hollow. Scholars have revealed that aggressive Maya kings
during the Classic period regularly made war on their neighbors
for both ritualistic and materialistic motives. The most valued
prize was another king, who would be humiliated over a period
of time, subjected to exquisite tortures, and finally decapitated.
These kings, with a profound sense of history, erected monuments to commemorate their victories and to record their lineage.
Nevertheless, despite their bloody campaigns, it appears that no
Maya city was ever able to impose its will on a large area, as in
the case of the more northern power centers. Instead, there were
scattered, independent sites, with no dominant capital. One authority believes that there may have been twenty cities of fifty
thousand inhabitants or more and that altogether some 2 million
Maya existed.

The unifying element in Classic societies was religion. In the
early centuries admission to the religious hierarchy seems to
have been by talent, but over the years it became increasingly
hereditary. The priestly ranks not only held political authority
but also constituted the intelligentsia. Priests were the scientists
and the cultural leaders, giving strong direction to those below.
In the pantheon of gods the most ancient was the rain god Tláloc
(Chac to the Maya). To the god of the sun and goddess of the
moon were added deities to celebrate the beneficence of fire,
corn, and the butterfly. Ultimately, however, the most powerful
of gods was Quetzalcóatl, the Feathered Serpent.

In these theocracies social cleavage was implicit. There was an
order in which everyone had his assigned place. The individual,
unless of the aristocratic sacerdotal class, counted for little. In
this respect social stratification was like that in other parts of the
world, except that perhaps the individual in Mexico had more
security. There is no reason to believe that the masses did not
perform their obligatory duties willingly, but the evidence on
which to construct a satisfactory examination of Classic society is

Small, hairless *techichi* dogs from Colima were bred for the table and were also used as foot-warmers. Molded in various poses, these ceramic pieces are usually in the form of a vessel.

Poised for action, another Colima figure may represent either a warrior or an athlete.

A bearded musician sings and keeps rhythm with rasps. The clay figure, from the state of Nayarit (A.D. 300–900) is about 20 inches in height.

lamentably slim. Enough disturbing signs exist to caution against painting a scene of pagan paradise. Still, it is not excessive to suggest that people fared well compared to their contemporaries in other parts of the world.

After a spectacular run of several centuries, the Classic world in Middle America began to deteriorate. Just why the great centers fell is still a mystery, although all sorts of theories abound. While some of the cities went into gradual decline, others, it appears, met a sudden, violent end. Pressures of various kinds impinged on ordered ways: aggressive nomadic tribes on the peripheries played a role in some cases; demand for increased food supplies, the result of population pressures, crop failures, and possibly soil exhaustion, was another cause. Perhaps an internal disruption was occasioned by a peasants' revolt against the ruling classes, bred by excessive demands or the parasitic priests' inability to mediate successfully with the all-important nature gods. Or were there plagues of some kind? Conceivably there was war between the different cultures. The reasons no doubt vary from place to place, and there may well have been a combination of factors. In any event, the Golden Age came apart after a long period that stands as one of the brightest in the history of man.

Teotihuacán and Its Successors

Classic Mexico had many important centers, but three dominant cultures exercised great influence over surrounding regions— Teotihuacán, Monte Albán, and the Maya. The most important Indian site of its time was the immense urban complex of Teotihuacán, "the Place of the Gods," as the Aztecs were to call it. The overall expanse measured at least twelve square miles, in the core of which was the ceremonial center occupying about two square miles. Surrounding this precinct were the sumptuous quarters of the priests and their retainers, and on the outer fringes the masses resided in the rude dwellings that have long since disappeared. The population of the city at its height of prosperity remains in dispute, but it probably had as many as 250,000 inhabitants, making it one of the largest cities in the world at the time. Long after its fall the site was held in reverence and awe by succeeding cultures, and owing to the grandiose dimensions of its structures, the Aztecs considered it to have been built by a race of giants.

The origins of the Teotihuacanos are unknown, but by 200 B.C. they had begun to emerge as a superior culture in the central

The Pyramid of the Sun at Teotihuacán dominates the extensive ruins of the ancient city.

Valley of Mexico. Their carefully planned city, conceived in a grid pattern, was laid out on a colossal scale. Its main thoroughfare was the Avenue of the Dead, 150 feet wide and stretching over two miles through the heart of the ceremonial center. The most striking monument is the splendid Pyramid of the Sun, measuring over 700 feet at the base lines and rising about 215 feet high. Like most Mexican pyramids, the truncated structure served merely as a base for the elevation of a temple on top. It contains no inner chambers[3] but is filled with over a million cubic yards of sun-dried bricks and rubble. The summit, reached after an ascent of 268 steps, offers the breathless viewer a commanding sweep of the surrounding Valley. Even so, what we see today is a pale replica of the former magnificence of the Pyramid of the Sun. Now stripped of its thick outer layer and violated by

3. In 1974, however, tunnels were discovered underneath the pyramid.

Carved stone images of the rain god Tláloc and Quetzalcóatl on the Temple of Quetzalcóatl at Teotihuacán.

Detail of a plumed serpent head. The eyes at one time held red jewels, long since plucked out by vandals.

a botched reconstruction many years ago, it was originally larger, its slope faced with cut stone. Its construction probably occupied ten thousand workers for two decades.

Teotihuacán must have been a bustling metropolis, teeming with porters carrying goods to the marketplace, laborers erecting temples, artisans busily engaged with their crafts, and here and there the sober presence of the elegant lords. Along the main avenue were various kinds of edifices covered with lime stucco, painted, and polished. Walkways and courts were paved. There were about one hundred palaces for priests, the largest of which had an estimated three hundred rooms. Some of the salons contained bright frescoes. A ceremonial plaza covering about thirty-eight acres, now known as the Citadel, was flanked by fifteen low pyramid mounds. Near one end is the Temple of Quetzalcóatl, its incline studded with carved stone projections of the Feathered Serpent and Tláloc that are as phantasmic as medieval gargoyles.

The dominance of Teotihuacán was so extensive that some scholars have discussed it in terms of an empire, believing its hegemony to have been as broad as that of the later Aztecs. In any event, its sway reached from parts of northern Mexico down into Guatemala. For the most part, however, Monte Albán and the Maya culture remained independent of Teotihuacán. Within its sphere the impact of that great city consisted not only in its cultural imperialism with respect to art and architecture but also in its religious dominance, for it was a shrine to which pilgrims traveled from far away. Ruling the pantheon of gods was Quetzalcóatl, by this time a deity almost universal in the Mexican world. Although there is some evidence that human sacrifice may have occurred in the city, the cult of the Feathered Serpent held that the god wished sacrifices of snakes and butterflies, not humans.

For some reason, very likely related to an agricultural debacle, decline set in, inviting incursions by barbarians on the northern frontier. About A.D. 650 a weakened Teotihuacán fell to its enemies, who desecrated and burned the city. The fall of the mightiest center was the first casualty in the gradual decay of the Classic world in Mexico.

With the Teotihuacano culture dissipated, central Mexico lost its focus. Three centers remained, however, to exert some influence: Cholula in the modern state of Puebla, Xochicalco in Morelos, and El Tajín in Veracruz. Although all three had probably been satellites of Teotihuacán, each had its own distinct character. There was almost certainly contact among them, but whether they shared power or were in conflict with each other is uncertain.

Cholula was a holy city and a large center of considerable importance. While tradition has it that 365 Christian chapels were later built over the ruins of pagan temples, the actual number is closer to seventy. The nature of the city's relationship with Teotihuacán is not entirely clear, but it seems to have been close. The center was dominated by its massive pyramid, the largest single man-made monument in Indian America. Begun in Pre-Classic times, it is now considerably reduced in size and stripped of its outer layers. Still, its total volume is greater than that of Egypt's Pyramid of Cheops. It was a sanctuary of Quetzalcóatl, and many of the refugees from Teotihuacán fled to Cholula, which continued to flourish for about another century and a half. By around A.D. 800 Cholula had fallen to invaders, and there began a five-hundred-year rule by a resurgent Olmec tyranny.

Xochicalco, first built around 200 B.C. atop small mountains, is of interest as a transition culture, exhibiting influences of both Teotihuacán and the Maya. The original purpose of its elevated

The Pyramid of the Niches, El Tajín, state of Veracruz.

site may not have been strategic, but it appears that with the
later unleashing of the Olmec despotism Xochicalco was fortified
with moats and parapets. It is the earliest known fortress
site in central Mexico and is a manifestation of the alarming
trend to militarism that developed there in the Late Classic
period.

El Tajín had extensive influence along the Gulf coast. After
the decline of Teotihuacán, it was very likely the most powerful
culture of the three sites under discussion. A dramatic example
of its unique architecture is the pyramid of niches, of which
there is one for each day of the year.

The vigorous life at Tajín included bloody rites that anticipated the terror of the Post-Classic period. The ball game, *ollama*,

A ball court at Monte Albán. The ball game of *ollama* (*tlachtli*), was played in many different cultures, although the rules and courts varied somewhat.

was an ancient tradition that became an obsession with these lowland peoples. Most of the prominent centers in Mexico had ball courts, and Tajín had no fewer than eleven. Along each side of the court (which could vary considerably in length, according to the culture) was a wall on which a stone ring was fixed. Two teams played, the object being to keep the seven- to eight-inch solid rubber ball out of the opponents' possession and, if possible, to hit the ball through one of the rings. Scoring was exceedingly difficult, not only because the ring was small and high but also because the players could not hit the ball with their hands. Often they were allowed to use only their hips, although it seems that rules differed according to time and place. The athletes wore padding in vulnerable spots, as the flying ball could kill if struck with sufficient force. Contests were played with great enthusiasm, and on some occasions large sums were wagered. Ollama was more than a game, however; it was a sacred ritual in imitation of the movement of celestial bodies and associated with man's fate. On occasion the teams represented political factions. So serious was ollama taken that the losing captain was sometimes sacrificed, as scenes on the architectural friezes depict. A variation on the agreement was that the losers became slaves of the victors.

Monte Albán

From its lofty eminence thirteen hundred feet above the valley floor, Monte Albán, the creation of the Zapotecs, dominated surrounding Oaxaca for centuries. Less grand in scale than Teotihuacán, it was nevertheless spacious, poised on a rocky shelf over three thousand feet long and half again as wide. Urban construction was carried out at great cost in human effort because all materials, and even water, had to be hauled up the mountainsides. Grouped around its great paved plaza were many temples, platforms, and low pyramids, along with sunken patios. Unlike most of the other cultures of the Classic, the Zapotecs, with some two hundred sites, had kings, but the influence of the high priests was such, at least in domestic affairs, that government was more theocracy than monarchy. Monte Albán was one of the oldest of important Classic centers, for the Zapotecs were there by 600 B.C.

After A.D. 650 Monte Albán was possibly the single most powerful force in Mexico for some time, extending its influence into some areas formerly dominated by Teotihuacán. The extent to which its authority was challenged by the expansionist Tajín state has not been satisfactorily defined. Unaccountably, Monte Albán began to lose its cohesion sometime during the ninth century A.D. Whatever the reasons, whether from economic pressures or internal political problems, by A.D. 900 the great Zapotec center was abandoned. There is no indication, however, that the general populace served by that center left their homes. The region was ultimately invaded by the neighboring Mixtecs, with whom the Zapotecs coexisted for quite some time.

An overview of Monte Albán in Oaxaca, showing its platforms and expansive plazas.

Incised on stone slabs, curious figures who seem to be dancing are a feature of Monte Albán. They are called *danzantes*.

PRINCIPAL ARCHAEOLOGICAL SITES

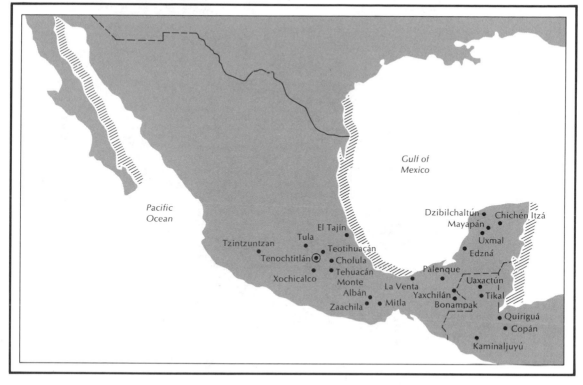

The Maya

Of all the Classic groups, the Maya have generally been considered the most brilliant. But while their luster is not diminished, it now seems clear that they were not the first great civilization in Middle America and that, in fact, their rise to greatness not only came considerably after that of the Olmecs but probably later than that of Teotihuacán and Monte Albán as well. The early history of the Maya is nebulous; however, by the beginning of our era they were evolving into an advanced state, and by A.D. 300 they were into their full Classic stage. Great expansion and the florescence of Maya culture began around A.D. 600 and lasted until about A.D. 900.

The Classic Maya had so many important centers, no one of which completely dominated the others, that they must be dealt with collectively. A good number of them, moreover, were outside of Mexico. If it can be said that Maya civilization had a

In dark hardwood, this unusual carving depicts a dignified worthy from the Tabasco Maya culture. It dates from the early Classic period.

heart, it would have to be considered the Petén, that northern-most region of Guatemala jutting up into southern Mexico. The area's isolation from the main corridors of migration allowed the Maya to achieve cultural stability with little foreign corruption. Their descendants were the last to be conquered by the Span-iards, not until 1697. But the Classic Maya also lived in the Mexi-can states of Chiapas, Tabasco, Campeche, and Yucatan, as well as in Quintana Roo.

The Petén was an unlikely region for settlement. Even today the forest, the inaccessibility, and unpleasant insects make it un-attractive, and it is very sparsely settled. But corn grew well enough in the soil, and there was an ample supply of limestone for constructing majestic buildings. Maya architecture was char-acterized by false fronts of mansard-style roofs and combs; the pyramids were more narrow and steep than those of other cul-tures. Like Teotihuacán and Monte Albán, the Maya had a vig-orous ceramic tradition and produced lovely polychrome bowls. In their exotic murals and bas-reliefs, however, they tended less to the geometric designs of central Mexico and more to the de-piction of the human form, often rendered with superb drafts-manship. Furthermore, there is an exuberance in the Maya style that stands much in contrast to the more restrained northern tra-dition. The great fluidity of Maya art gives it a baroque quality, whether in stone or stucco. Of the fascinating pictorial manu-scripts, only three survived the ravages of time, climate, insects, and the fires of Spanish clergymen.

The Maya stand as the premier scientists of ancient America, for if others invented calendars and writing, it was they who car-ried them to their highest expression. Like other Mexican calen-dars, theirs had 365 days; in addition, a ceremonial calendar had 260 days. The Maya did not, however, measure small units of time, like minutes and hours. Whereas we fix the beginning of our era with the birth of Christ, the Maya established theirs at the equivalent of 3133 B.C., apparently for mythical reasons. The preoccupation of the Maya with dates resulted in the pe-riodic chronological markings on stone pillars (stelae) that, in spite of the disputed correlations, allow us to convert them to our calendar. Because of their careful records, the descendants of the Post-Classic ruling Xiu family in Yucatán can trace their lineage back to the time of Charlemagne, that is, to about A.D. 800. Each date was assigned characteristics so distinctive that it would not recur in the records until the passage of 374,400 years. One of the Maya's mathematical units was the equivalent of 64 million.

The Temple of the Sun at Palenque is framed by thick jungle growth.

Although central Mexican pyramids are usually solid, without interior chambers, to the south temple-pyramids of the Maya sometimes contain tombs like the one shown here at Palenque's "Temple of the Inscriptions."

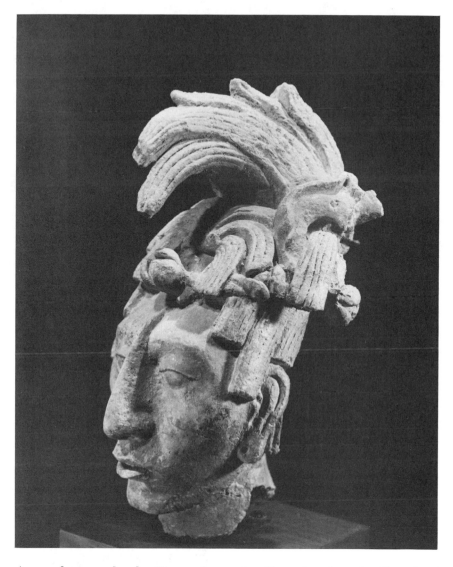

A superb stucco head with an elegant headdress found at the Temple of
the Inscriptions at Palenque.

So puzzling are their hieroglyphs that it has taken years for
scholars to master them.

The metropolis of the Maya Classic was Tikal, with a population in the nearby region estimated to have reached close to one
hundred thousand. It is one of the earliest sites, having been settled by A.D. 292, the date of the earliest inscription. Set in a clearing of Guatemala's Petén jungle, Tikal is dominated by six great
pyramids, including the tallest of any in the Maya civilization,

A pot-bellied, seed-filled ceramic rattle from the Maya culture on the small island of Jaina, off the coast of Campeche.

Of the same Maya culture is this whistle, in the form of an embracing couple.

towering 230 feet. The inner precinct covers more than a square mile, with other ceremonial edifices surrounding the core for a considerable distance. Aside from the usual temples, palaces, plazas, and ball courts, Tikal had ten reservoirs and was beautified by artificial lakes.

In a secondary category were other large cities. Uaxactún, a few miles north of Tikal, was apparently the oldest site, with a vault bearing the date A.D. 278. Yaxchilán, in the modern state of Chiapas, is known for its great central plaza, a thousand feet long. Palenque (Chiapas), though relatively small, is considered the gem of the Maya cities because of its exquisite sculpture. The bas-relief work there shows the art in its highest form. Although of minor importance in most respects, Bonampak (Chiapas) contains the most illustrious of the Maya murals. And Dzibilchaltún on the Yucatán Peninsula, long thought to be of less significance, now appears to have been one of the largest of the New World cities. With its multiple ceremonial precincts and numerous house mounds, it may have had fifty thousand structures. Dzibilchaltún was, moreover, populated continuously for three thousand years, from 1500 B.C. to the time of the Spanish conquest.

There may have been no common cause for the decline of all the Classic Maya centers, scattered as they were over considerable distances. Again, speculation suggests insufficient food supplies resulting from pestilence, locusts, earthquakes, or a confluence of these and other factors. There is also a reasonable chance that invaders from central Mexico introduced terror among the Maya, who themselves became more warlike toward the end. Equally credible is the thesis that the masses finally rose up in rebellion against the aristocracy in a social revolution. Although all sites did not fall simultaneously, by around A.D. 900 the cities were abandoned to the fecund jungle growth. They remained lost to the outside world until their lichen-mottled ruins were rediscovered almost a thousand years later. Thus the Classic world in Mexico folded, marking a turning point in history. What followed was distinctly different.

Recommended for Further Study

Adams, Richard E. W., ed. *The Origins of Maya Civilization.* Albuquerque: University of New Mexico Press, 1977.

Coe, Michael D. *The Maya.* London: Thames and Hudson, 1980.

———. *Mexico.* New York: Praeger, 1967.

Culbert, T. P., ed. *The Classic Maya Collapse.* Albuquerque: University of New Mexico Press, 1977.

Doolittle, William E. *Canal Irrigation in Prehistoric Mexico: The Sequence of Technological Change.* Austin: University of Texas Press, 1990

Hammond, Norman. *Ancient Maya Civilization.* New Brunswick, N.J.: Rutgers University Press, 1982.

Kubler, George. *Art and Architecture of Ancient America.* Harmondsworth and Baltimore: Pelican, 1984.

Marcus, Joyce. *Mesoamerican Writing Systems.* Princeton, N.J.: Princeton University Press, 1993.

Miller, Mary Ellen. *The Murals of Bonampak.* Princeton, N.J.: Princeton University Press, 1986.

Paddock, John, ed. *Ancient Oaxaca: Discoveries in Mexican Archaeology and History.* Stanford, Calif.: Stanford University Press, 1966.

Proskouriakoff, Tatiana. *Maya History.* Edited by Rosemary A. Joyce. Austin: University of Texas Press, 1993.

Scarborough, Vernon L., and David R. Wilcox. *The Mesoamerican Ballgame.* Tucson: University of Arizona Press, 1991.

Schele, Linda, and Mary Ellen Miller. *The Blood of Kings. Dynasty and Ritual in Maya Art.* Fort Worth: Kimbell Art Museum, 1986.

Weaver, Muriel Porter. *The Aztecs, Maya, and Their Predecessors. Archaeology of Mesoamerica.* New York: Academic Press, 1981.

Whitecotton, Joseph W. *The Zapotecs: Princes, Priests and Peasants.* Norman: University of Oklahoma Press, 1977.

3

Times of Trouble:
Post-Classic Mexico

The order imposed by Teotihuacán's dominance during the Classic period gave way to a fragmentation of power among the transition centers. Details of history in the Valley of Mexico are nebulous from A.D. 650 to 900, but one has the impression of confusion and a great shifting of peoples in the waning decades of the Classic, when aggressive city-states—Cholula, Xochicalco, and El Tajín—vied for control, but none succeeding in bringing about unity and order. Then gradually a new period emerges, with very different characteristics.

The Post-Classic era began about A.D. 900 and lasted until the Spanish Conquest in the early sixteenth century. Culturally a plateau had been reached; indeed, in many respects the succeeding centuries were inferior to the Classic. Nor was there significant intellectual and scientific growth. Although metallurgy was introduced, probably from South America, its use was very limited. Gold and silver were fashioned into beautiful jewelry and copper was used in the manufacture of various tools and to cover the tips of arrow shafts.

The most striking change during the Post-Classic, especially for central Mexico, can be seen in the political systems, which became depressingly similar to those of the Old World. Now there appeared militaristic societies in which the prizes of war were no longer territorial but tributes to be exacted from the subject states. Political power was seized by a warrior elite whose ascendancy checked the traditional powers of religious leaders. Religion itself was cheapened with the rising importance of frightful gods thought to require ever-increasing quantities of the "divine liquid"—human blood. This orgy of human sacrifice was played out in the last bloody rites subsequent to the fall of the final Indian rulers of Mexico, the Aztecs.

Taking A.D. 900 as the pivotal date introducing the Post-Classic, we discern the emergence of historical central Mexico; for while earlier history must be deduced cautiously from archaeological evidence alone, there are in this period the beginnings of written records in which individuals appear with more clarity. But although there are now pegs upon which to drape our historical fabric, accounts are manifestly shot through with myths; thus some details vary with the telling, and many versions are vague and fragmentary at best.

The Toltecs

The great city of Teotihuacán, situated on the northern edge of the lake, had served as a buffer between civilized Mexico and the nomadic barbarians of the north. With the fall of that stronghold, however, the frontier was breached by vigorous warriors from the lands beyond. The northern tribes, consisting of many diverse groups, were known by the generic term *Chichimecs*, which meant, literally, "People of Dog Lineage" but carried none of the pejorative implications we might assign it. The most important of these were the Tolteca-Chichimeca, or Toltecs, whose origins were probably in southern Zacatecas. At the beginning of the tenth century they swept into the central valley led by Mixcóatl (Cloud Serpent), a Mexican Ghengis Khan who swifty scattered his demoralized opponents. After establishing his capital at Culhuacán and successfully extending his power, the resourceful Mixcóatl was assassinated by his brother, who seized leadership for himself.

Mixcóatl's pregnant wife fled into exile, where she died on giving birth to a son. The boy was given the name Ce Acatl Topiltzin (Ce Acatl meaning "One Reed," the year of his birth, perhaps A.D. 947, and Topiltzin meaning "Our Prince"), and he would become the cultural hero of foremost proportions in ancient Mexico. Reared in Tepoztlán, the boy completed his education at nearby Xochicalco, where he became a devotee of the ancient god Quetzalcóatl. Later, as a high priest of the cult, he assumed the name of his deity.

Upon reaching manhood, Topiltzin-Quetzalcóatl sought his destiny. With the support of his dead father's loyal partisans,

he killed in single combat his uncle, Mixcóatl's assassin, and
made himself lord of the Toltecs. Topiltzin-Quetzalcóatl eventually removed his capital some fifty miles northwest of the present
Mexico City to a remote site on the frontier. There, around A.D.
968, he founded the splendid city of Tula, the most important
city in the long interim between the fall of Teotihuacán and the
later rise of Aztec Tenochtitlán. A semibarbarous people, the
Toltecs only gradually absorbed the more advanced ways of central Mexico. From their new capital they asserted power over
most of central Mexico and beyond. Although their hegemony
lasted only about two centuries, their prestige was such that the
name Toltec pervaded the consciousness of the land for five hundred years.

The legends of Tula that would so haunt the later Aztecs were
at least in part pure confection. They began with the incredible
benefactions attributed to Topiltzin-Quetzalcóatl, whose mythical achievements are interwoven with those of the Feathered Serpent god himself. According to tradition, Topiltzin-Quetzalcóatl,
as the great leader of infinite knowledge, showed his people how
to plant the "miraculous" corn, and under his tutelage all cultivated plant life yielded produce of gigantic size. Fields of cotton
were a marvel, as the tufts of the plant emerged naturally in a
variety of rich colors. Even the cacao trees (which, in fact, flourish in tropical lowlands) were said to be multihued. The ruler
was also responsible for writing, the ritual calendar, and the architectural wonders of Tula. He was, indeed, the author of all
benefits to mankind.

Less extensive than Teotihuacán, Tula was certainly more
grandiose than its ruins today indicate. Palace interiors were
decked with the brilliant plumage of exotic birds, while various
salons were lined with sheets of gold, jewels, and rare seashells.
Residents' ears were soothed by the sweet singing of pet birds.
This version of paradise on earth, in which there was an abundance of all things, was embellished in the retelling over the
centuries; it accounts, in part, for the curiously persistent Toltec
mystique.

This honeyed tradition notwithstanding, all was not peace and
light at Tula, for despite the undeniable prestige of Topiltzin-
Quetzalcóatl, dissident factions existed within his capital. For
one thing, diverse tribes, not yet amalgamated into a homogeneous society, lived in the city. Moreover, the ancestral supreme
deity of the Toltecs was Tezcatlipoca (Smoking Mirror, or Shining Smoke), an invisible and unpredictable god who was feared—

The ingenuous Topiltzin-Quetzalcóatl is deceived by the crafty Tezcatlipoca.

and never crossed. His adherents resented the exaltation of the foreign god Quetzalcóatl introduced by Topiltzin. The priests of Tezcatlipoca bided their time, conspiring against the heresy.

The cult of the Feathered Serpent was the higher form of religion, as may be seen in its monotheism as well as by the wish of the god to be gratified only by modest sacrifices of butterflies, birds, or snakes, and offerings of jade, incense, or merely tortillas. Tezcatlipoca, on the other hand, demanded human hearts. His followers sought by various deceits to discredit the high priest of Quetzalcóatl. According to one account, Tezcatlipoca, in disguise, gained entrance to the house of Topiltzin, who was ill. At first the ruler refused an offer of "medicine," which was, in fact, the strong drink of *pulque*, made from undistilled cactus juice. Finally persuaded to take a sip, the innocent Topiltzin found it pleasing and asked for more. At length inebriated by five cupfuls, the lord of Tula awoke the next morning on a mat beside his sister. Having broken his priestly vows and disgraced himself by the sins of drunkenness and incest, he prepared to go into exile after almost twenty years of enlightened rule.

The benevolent reign of Topiltzin-Quetzalcóatl at Tula thus came to a close, but he does not disappear from history. He and his followers traveled to the holy city of Cholula, and in 987 they sailed across the Gulf of Mexico to the land of the Maya, where their impact was sharply felt. The legendary exit of the great Topiltzin-Quetzalcóatl is appropriate, if fantastic: he coasted

Giant stone warriors at Tula were manifestations of the militaristic spirit that came to dominate the Toltecs.

down a river to the sea in a raft of serpents, after which he flashed into the heavens to become the morning star.

A more prosaic denouement, though heavily laden with the most serious implications, is the more credible version. When Topiltzin and his partisans left Tula for their long odyssey, they marked their way by shooting arrows through saplings, leaving crosslike signs. Later he sent word that he would return from where the sun rose to take back his rightful throne in the year Ce Acatl, which recurred cyclically. Now, by tradition, he was of fair complexion and bearded. All of this would be of immense significance when, five centuries later, the Spaniards—white, bearded, and wearing crosses—appeared on the eastern horizon. The year was 1519—and Ce Acatl.

Meanwhile, with the success of the militant Tezcatlipoca faction at Tula, a new order of things evolved. While the reputation of the Toltecs as great architects was secure (the Aztecs named them Toltecs, meaning "Artificers"), a new and fearsome image of them was revealed in later works. Towering statues of impassive warrior figures, sixteen to eighteen feet tall, appeared on top of temples, and friezes symbolized the military orders of the jaguar and eagle, the latter of which were shown devouring human hearts. Tula nourished two traditions that persisted until the coming of the Spaniards—an excess of human sacrifice and the forceful conquest of other states. An aggressive expansionist policy led the Toltec legions to create an empire that in size approximated that of Classic Teotihuacán.

From the late eleventh century to 1156, drought and famine struck the Toltecs. Wars further weakened the state until, in desperation, the people even turned to the worship of their enemies' alien deities. Finally they abandoned Tula in despair, and the great Toltec diaspora began, with people spreading in many directions. The collapse of Tula was very significant for Mexico: once again the northern march between the sedentary peoples of the Valley and the northern barbarians was left unguarded. Not long after, new hordes descended upon this wonder of the Post-Classic world and subjected Tula to brutal desecration.

The Zapotecs and Mixtecs

To the south, following the abandonment of Monte Albán in Oaxaca, the Zapotecs remained a vigorous culture with many important centers. Their capital was at Zaachila, but the site

A palace at Mitla.

Detail of the palace showing the intricate geometric designs formed by precision stone cutting.

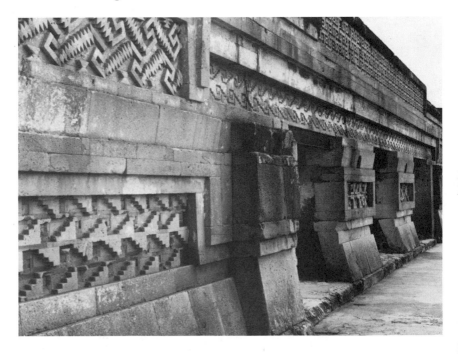

that interests us most is Mitla, built roughly the same time as Tula. Mitla was a comparatively small religious and military base. What one sees there, however, is a jewel of Mexican architecture. Surrounding a modest courtyard are white temples with walls of marvelous design—thousands of small pieces of cut stone, fitted together with a precision requiring no mortar, form mosaics of dazzling geometric patterns. Opening off the patios are subterranean passages leading to crypts. Although the site is in an exposed area, set apart some distance is the hill fortress, a grim reminder of the intense warfare that had overtaken Post-Classic Mexico.

To the areas west and north of the Zapotecs were a remarkable people who inhabited the mountainous regions, the Mixtecs, or Cloud People. The Mixtecs were certainly influenced by the Toltecs, some of whom apparently infiltrated after the fall of Tula. By the thirteenth century the Mixtecs were penetrating eastward into Zapotec territories, and, through open warfare and intermarriage, they eventually came to dominate their neighbors. At times they occupied many of the Zapotec sites, including Monte Albán and Mitla.

Mixtec artistic achievements are extraordinary. Among the treasures they gave us is the richest collection extant of picture *códices* in Mexico. These "books" are executed in brilliant colors on deerskin (the books of the Maya and others were made of vegetable fiber). They are also valuable historical sources. One gives data reaching back to A.D. 692, providing the earliest historical narrative of any society in the land. Mixtec códices also tell us that by the early years of the eighth century militaristic city-states had formed. Following the appearance of metallurgy around A.D. 1000, the Mixtecs became, in addition, the foremost jewelers in Mexico, fashioning delicate pieces in gold and silver.

The Post-Classic Maya

Coincident with the final distintegration of the Maya Classic period by around A.D. 900, there was a rising Maya cultural phenomenon on the peninsula of Yucatán. That peninsula is a limestone shelf, flat with some rolling, brush-covered hills, a land without surface rivers. With its thin soil and dependence for water on the *cenotes*, the sinkholes created by the collapse of underground caverns, it was an unlikely location for an agricultural people. Maya groups had inhabited Yucatán for many cen-

This unusual ceramic vessel, created in the Classic Period, is in the form of a stylized monkey wearing a startled expression.

A Mixtec vase from Zaachila. Representations of death were and still are common and are often treated lightly.

A Oaxacan gold pendant of a solar disk, with a bell.

turies B.C., but their achievements had not matched those of the southern Maya who flourished during the Classic era.

Beginning in the tenth century, the ancestral Yucatec Maya culture was adulterated by outside influences of peoples stigmatized as "foreigners." Some of the newcomers were undoubtedly refugees from the deserted Classic areas. But the invigorating force that gave impulse to the new hybrid style in Yucatán came from the northwest, with the dramatic appearance of Topiltzin-Quetzalcóatl and his Toltecs. Arriving in 987, the wanderers from Tula introduced the harsher traditions of the central highlands of Mexico. The Toltecs of Chichén Itzá made an alliance,

During the period of Toltec rule, curious Chacmool figures appeared at Chichén Itzá.

perhaps for mutual security, with the cities of Mayapán and Uxmal. This triple alliance, the Mayapán League, was dominated by Chichén Itzá and, according to some accounts, lasted for over two centuries.

The period of Toltec (or Mexican) rule was dynamic and prosperous, a time of great activity. The Maya region under the control of the Toltecs was much smaller than the broad dimensions of the Classic Maya sphere. Tragically, the malaise that was sweeping the northern regions of Mexico was insinuated in Yucatán. Under Toltec rule a military caste seized power, and human sacrifice among the Yucatec Maya apparently became

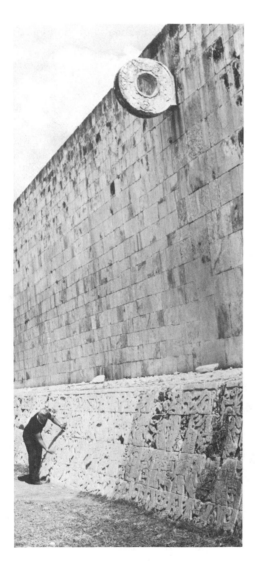

A great ball court in the Maya style at Chichén Itzá. Scores were seldom made by knocking the ball through the high ring. This city had six ball courts, one of which, the largest in Middle America, measures 480 by 120 feet.

Detail of the carved stone ring.

A heavily padded Maya ball player is portrayed in this graceful sculpture from Jaina.

more common. The new order of things was evident in the art
and architecture, both reflecting the militant spirit of the invaders: the ruins of Chichén Itzá are strikingly evocative of far-
off Tula. To the local Maya architecture dating from the sixth
century, a new style was joined. Thus, in the warrior motifs, images of the Feathered Serpent, the forest of columns, even in the
appearance of the quaint Chacmools (reclining stone figures),
an exotic cast is given to the city. Among the monuments of Post-
Classic Maya centers, those of Toltec Chichén Itzá are the most
widely known. Though distinctive, they are, in the words of
Eric Thompson, "showy, but unstable."[1] Like the sculptures, they
are esthetically less pleasing than works of the Classic Maya.
Uxmal, however, has structures of great beauty. Its Palace of the
Governor "is considered by many to be the most elegant of pre-
Hispanic architecture."[2]

With the arrival of the Toltecs in Maya lands, Quetzalcóatl
(called Kukulcán by the Maya) entered the pantheon of local
deities. Traditionally the most powerful of Maya gods was It-
zamná, while the rain god Chac and the gods of corn and the sun
were also important. Into the great Sacred Cenote, a well measuring some two hundred feet across at the mouth, victims (although infrequently the virgins so dear to modern tradition)
were cast, along with jewels and other valuables, to appease the
rain god. Human sacrifice continued to increase after the Toltec
phase had passed, but the practice never reached the excesses
that were to overtake central Mexico.

Some authorities believe that the elitist priestly class lost considerable political and cultural influence to rising utilitarian
merchants. Expanded commerce, some by sea, and increased production enhanced the peasants' lot.[3] But increasing repression by
the militarists led to rebellion. In the subsequent fighting between Chichén Itzá and Mayapán, the latter emerged the victor.
After some two centuries the Mayapán League broke apart, but
the wonder is that it lasted as long as it did, considering its conflicting economic and political interests.

Henceforth a dozen cities of northern Yucatán were dominated by Mayapán, and, from 1200 or so until about 1450, a period of general decline set in. The Toltecs were absorbed, and
their cultural influence disappeared. The new rulers established

1. J. Eric S. Thompson, *The Rise and Fall of Maya Civilization* (Norman, 1966),
    p. 141.
2. Justino Fernández, *Mexican Art* (London, 1965), p. 37.
3. Jeremy Sabloff and William Rathje, "The Rise of a Maya Merchant Class," *Sci-
    entific American* 233 (1975):72–82.

A reconstruction of Chichén Itzá shows the broad thoroughfare leading from the Temple of Kukulcán to the Sacred Cenote (well).

a strongly centralized regime maintained by Mexican mercenaries, by intermarriage, and by forcing all local chiefs from outlying areas to reside in Mayapán as hostages. Under this tyranny the capital was a walled city within which the inhabitants lived for security, while the economy was less oriented to agriculture and trade than to the parasitical dependence on tribute paid by subject towns. In the two and a half centuries there was a general lowering of standards: building construction was not only shoddy but devoid of beauty, hieroglyphic inscriptions ceased, and it seems that athletes even stopped playing the sacred ball game.

The shattering of Mayapán hegemony resulted in the decentralization of the Yucatec Maya, in which some sixteen petty city-states clung feebly to the vestiges of the distant past. Anarchy now became widespread as warfare among the various groups was almost constant. The neglected cities fell into ruin,

The Temple of Kukulcán, also known as "El Castillo."

sometimes hastened by vicious and wanton destruction by marauders. Indeed one finds few redeeming qualities in this final
crumbling phase, a melancholy time with little ennobling or
creative vitality. To the casualties of war were added, during
the last half of the fifteenth century, the victims of plagues
and a disastrous hurricane. When the first Spanish adventurers arrived in the Yucatán Peninsula a few decades later, they
found only the demoralized and impoverished descendants of
the grandeur that was the Maya civilization for so many centuries.

Despite their amazing skills, the Maya architects never developed the true arch; however, a corbeled vault of the type pictured here served much the same purpose. This is the magnificent Palace of the Governor at Uxmal, measuring more than 320 feet in length and 25 feet in height.

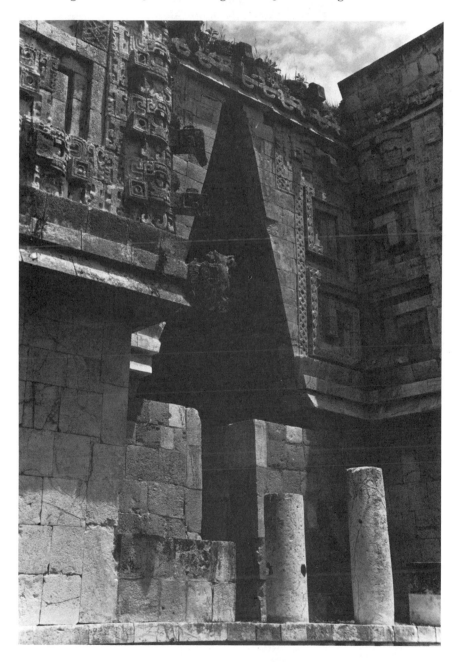

Recommended for Further Study

Castedo, Leopoldo. *A History of Latin American Art and Architecture from Precolumbian Times to the Present.* New York: Praeger, 1969.

Davies, Nigel. *The Toltecs: Until the Fall of Tula.* Norman: University of Oklahoma Press, 1977.

Fox, John W. *Maya Postclassic State Formation.* New York: Cambridge University Press, 1987.

Hardoy, Jorge. *Precolumbian Cities.* New York: Walker, 1973.

Katz, Friedrich. *The Ancient American Civilizations.* New York: Praeger, 1974.

Kelemen, Pál. *Art of the Americas, Ancient and Hispanic.* New York: Crowell, 1969.

Peterson, Frederick A. *Ancient Mexico: An Introduction to the Pre-Hispanic Cultures.* London: George Allen & Unwin, 1959.

Robertson, Donald. *Mexican Manuscript Painting of the Early Colonial Period.* New Haven, Conn.: Yale University Press, 1959.

Schroeder, Susan. *Chimalpahin & the Kingdom of Chalco.* Tucson: University of Arizona Press, 1991.

Soustelle, Jacques. *Mexico.* Translated by James Hogarth. Cleveland: World, 1967.

Spores, Ronald. *The Mixtecs in Ancient and Colonial Times.* Norman: University of Oklahoma Press, 1985.

Thompson, J. Eric S. *The Rise and Fall of Maya Civilization.* Norman: University of Oklahoma Press, 1966.

Von Hagen, Victor W. *World of the Maya.* New York: Mentor, 1960.

4

The Rise of the Barbarians

The high Valley of Anáhuac—the Indian name for the Valley of Mexico, meaning "near the water"—was a compelling lure to rootless peoples seeking a more abundant life. With its equable climate and system of interconnecting lakes bordered by forests full of wild game, it was especially attractive to the nomads of the arid north. Because of its central location the Valley had been, from ancient times, a corridor through which tribes of diverse cultures passed—and sometimes remained. This cultural mélange produced a rich environment for the exchange of ideas and skills. Moreover, traders and merchants introduced exotic products from the coasts and other regions, thereby adding to the variety of life. At the same time, alien groups were frequently hostile, so that the lake country was periodically upset by violence. While there was little danger of cultural stagnation, the continual disruptions were not conducive to the relatively more settled traditions preserved in some of the more isolated Oaxaca and Maya lands for so many centuries. In the Valley of Anáhuac there was calm and order only when a dominant center such as Teotihuacán or Tula prevailed.

The Chichimecs and Tepanecs

With the power vacuum created by the collapse of Tula in the twelfth century, primitive Chichimecs again poured into the Valley from the north. By the early thirteenth century the Valley was teeming with activity and becoming increasingly crowded, with many of the attendant pressures so familiar to us today. It was an age of anxiety and tension. The first barbarian groups quickly staked out their claims, and later arrivals found no available space. The early Chichimecs settled in the proximity of established towns populated by remnants of Toltec refugees who had kept alive some semblance of a higher civilization. The phenomenon so familiar in history occurred: the militant savages gradually adopted the more advanced ways of their sedentary neighbors.

Most prominent of the early invader chieftains was Xólotl (Monster), who led his people into the northern reaches of the Valley in 1244. The "Chichimecs of Xólotl" entrenched themselves at their capital of Tenayuca and proceeded to dominate the immediate area. Their military successes owed much to the "revolutionary" weapon of the bow and arrow, used with devastating effect against the cruder atl-atl of ancient times, which the Toltecs still employed. The Chichimec archers were as significant in their way as were the English longbowmen in the military history of Europe.

During the long reign of Xólotl (1244–1304) Chichimec hegemony was established. In 1246 the Chichimecs conquered the prestigious city of Culhuacán, and, in order to give respectability to the Chichimec dynasty, Xólotl, with sure instinct, married his son Nopaltzin (Revered Prickly Pear) to a princess of the vanquished Toltecs. In other ways, too, contact with sedentary agricultural towns mellowed the crude northerners. Though they had at first preferred living in caves, the Chichimecs gradually built dwellings; they exchanged their animal skins for woven cloth garments; they ceased eating raw meat in favor of cooked meat; and they made wider use of agricultural foods, especially corn. The Chichimecs also adopted the Náhuatl language, which was becoming the *lingua franca* of the Valley.

While the followers of Xólotl at Tenayuca were improving their lineage, becoming more refined, and broadening their political influence, other cities in the Valley were emerging to prominence as well. Atzcapotzalco, originally settled long before by refugees from the ancient Teotihuacán, was infiltrated by a nomadic group known as the Tepanecs in the year 1230. Like others in the surrounding region, the Tepanecs ultimately recognized Xólotl as overlord and received land from him, and Xólotl gave his daughters in marriage to cement alliances.

At length the stronghold of Tenayuca went into decline, and, with the passing of Xólotl, the ascending power was Atzcapotzalco. Under the extended rule of Acolhua (1304–63) the Tepanecs of that thriving metropolis wrested important cities from their rivals. But the most domineering figure of his time was Acolhua's son, Tezozómoc, who lived from 1320 to 1427. Through deceit, dynastic marriages, violence, and treachery, this great tyrant made Atzcapotzalco the most powerful center in the Valley. Using the soldiery of the petty warlords as mercenaries, he was able to crush Tenayuca and take the important city of Culhuacán. In the last quarter of the fourteenth century, Tezozómoc and his allies extended the Tepanec dominions even further, conquering many centers, including Xochimilco, and spilling over the mountains southward to seize Cuauhnáhuac (now Cuernavaca).

Paralleling the rise of Atzcapotzalco was Texcoco, founded by Quinatzin, a great-grandson of Xólotl. From its modest beginnings (ca. 1318), the city made steady progress during the founder's reign, which lasted until 1377. But Texcoco gradually fell on hard times, owing to internecine strife. Then, under the rule of Ixtlilxóchitl (1409–18), the city was attacked by the forces of Tezozómoc. Defeated in battle, Ixtlilxóchitl retreated to a remote spot where he faced his pursuers alone. After a valiant struggle, he was impaled on the spears of his enemies in full view of his young son, Nezahualcóyotl (Fasting Coyote), who was concealed in a tree. This heir to the throne of Texcoco managed to escape the henchmen of Tezozómoc and finally found sanctuary across the mountains to the east. "In order to wipe out the memory of Ixtlilxochitl," writes Frederick Peterson, "Tezozomoc had his soldiers ask every child in Texcoco under the age of seven, 'Who is your king?' When the little children answered either 'Ixtlilxochitl' or 'Nezahualcoyotl,' they were immediately struck down with obsidian-edged clubs. In this way several thousand children were put to death before parents taught their children the name of Tezozomoc."[1]

Two years later, in 1420, at age one hundred, and having reigned since 1363, the hoary tyrant finally relinquished his rule. Through politics of terror, Tezozómoc had succeeded in unifying under one government most of central Mexico. And, as Wigberto Jiménez Moreno observes, Tezozómoc invites comparison with his contemporaries, the Italian princes of the Renaissance, so

1. Frederick A. Peterson, *Ancient Mexico: An Introduction to the Pre-Hispanic Cultures* (London, 1959), p. 79.

much so that the Tepanec ruler might have been inspired by
The Prince of Machiavelli.[2] Yet, though he lived on for six or
seven years, his territories were divided and Atzcapotzalco power
vitiated.

The Aztec Rise to Power

The irruption of the Chichimecs from the dun wastelands of the
north included one group that engages our attention above all
others. While they called themselves the Mexica (pronounced
"Mesheeka"), they have become more commonly known as the
Aztecs. No tribe of record had more humble beginnings and rose
to such heights in so short a time. Over the long view of pre-
Hispanic Mexico, they must be regarded as upstarts, latecomers
on the scene. The last of the important nomadic groups to enter
the Valley, they were beginning to acquire some notoriety about
two hundred years prior to the Spanish Conquest, but their rise
to great power occurred less than a century before the advent of
Cortés in 1519.

The origins of the Aztecs are apparently found on an island
off the coast of the state of Nayarit, at Aztatlán or Aztlán, from
which many tribes wandered southward. Historical accounts for
the first decades following their departure from Aztlán, evidently in A.D. 1111, are fragmentary and unreliable, for, once secure, the Aztecs destroyed all the records and reconstructed their
history with accounts favorable to themselves. Full of symbolism
and myths, these official histories concede no Aztec defeats and
are at pains to establish (however spuriously) Toltec roots. Eventually the Aztecs came to call themselves the Culhúa-Mexica,
thus asserting a relationship with the prestigious Toltec culture
of Culhuacán.

The Aztecs' great search for the promised land logically enough
led them toward the verdant intermontane basin of Anáhuac,
but they arrived there only after many decades of wandering.
Somewhere along the way they came to conceive of themselves
as a messianic people, the chosen of the gods. They pressed on,
inspired by visions of their imperial destiny and by the persistent twitterings of their strange hummingbird god. Their su-

---

2. José Miranda et al., *Historia de México* (Mexico, 1971), p. 115. These chapters on
   Indian Mexico, especially the parts treating the Chichimecs, rely much on the
   various findings of Wigberto Jiménez Moreno.

The founding of the Aztec capital of Tenochtitlán, as depicted in the Codex Mendoza.

preme deity was the terrible Huitzilopochtli (Hummingbird of the South), god of war and the sun.

At length these nomads made their way into the Valley of Mexico, where they found a cold reception. To begin with, all the lands were already carved up into various city-states. The Aztecs became unwelcome squatters, a boorish, uncouth lot, disposed to all sorts of vulgarities. They were held in disdain by the more refined farming residents of the Valley, who encouraged the barbarians to keep moving. It seems as if the Aztecs purposely sought to anger others by their disgusting habits (which included some gruesome human sacrifices) and their outrageous practice of stealing their neighbors' wives. But however much the farming peoples of the Valley were repulsed by the interlopers, they also learned (sometimes the hard way) to entertain a healthy respect for them. The Aztecs were a young, vigorous people, hungry and ambitious. They were also superb warriors, whose fighting abilities did not go unnoticed by the ruling warlords of the Valley. Consequently, it was as mercenaries, exploiting the tenuous balance of power in Anáhuac, that the Aztecs first achieved recognition.

From the 1270s to the year 1319 the Aztecs maintained a precarious existence, occupying the hill of Chapultepec (now a park in Mexico City). They continued in their perverse ways, and the leaders of some of the principal towns decided to deal with them once and for all. They drove the intruders from Chapultepec and sacrificed the Aztec chief and his daughter. The survivors escaped by concealing themselves in the rushes along the lake shore until it was safe to come out.

Now subject to Coxcox (Pheasant), the ruler of Culhuacán, the Aztecs were given some land to settle. But what land! They found themselves living in a gully acrawl with rattlesnakes, no doubt to the amusement of their enemies. But, as it turned out, the Aztecs liked rattlesnake meat, and they devoured the vipers with gusto. Still, it was not the promised land, and the restless Aztecs bided their time. Their chance came when Coxcox agreed to give them their liberty and better land in exchange for assistance in a war against the town of Xochimilco. Aztec leaders delivered to the shocked Coxcox proof of their deeds—sacks containing eight thousand ears cut from the slain Xochimilcas.

Although the king of Culhuacán hastily gave them their freedom, the Aztecs did not go away. They asked Coxcox for his daughter, who would be made the Aztec queen and would be treated as a goddess. Coxcox—who should have known better—

agreed. The perversity of the early Aztec mentality surfaced again, as the princess was sacrificed and flayed. When her father attended the banquet in his honor, he was horrified to find that the entertainment included a dancer dressed in the skin of his daughter. Having finally had enough of the Aztecs, Coxcox raised an army that scattered the barbarians, who took refuge once more among the reeds of the lake.

Again the Aztecs showed their adaptability and turned the situation to their advantage. They found that in the marshy edges of the lake no one bothered them, for the place was considered unsuitable for dwelling. It was, however, a region abundant in waterfowl, fish, and other edible creatures. Furthermore, it was of some strategic placement, located at a point where three kingdoms merged. Huddled in those swamps, the miserable Aztecs drew on their resources, and, finding strength and unity in adversity, they stiffened their resolve.

Unmolested, in 1345 (or 1325) the Aztecs occupied a small isle and began to acquire, through trade, the materials they needed to enlarge their foothold. They dredged the lake bottom to form more surface soil. From such inauspicious beginnings, and with considerable ingenuity and great labor, they eventually created the great city of Tenochtitlán. From that island redoubt they later built connecting causeways, which could easily be defended, to the mainland. It was an inspired defensive concept, flawed only by the eventual dependence on mainland Chapultepec for drinking water. Aqueducts conveying water could be cut.

Meanwhile the furious activity of the Aztecs and the development of the island came to the attention of Tezozómoc, the strongman of Anáhuac, who brought them under his sway and used them in their traditional role of mercenaries. Tezozómoc made unreasonable demands of tribute from the Aztecs, and even humiliated them, but he was astute enough not to push them too far. Gradually they were accepted as minor partners, and in 1376 Tezozómoc allowed Tenochtitlán to institute a monarchy. In that year the young Acamapichtli became the first king of the Aztecs. By the time Tezozómoc finally died in 1426, the Aztecs, his apt disciples, were flourishing.

About this time the Aztecs elected as their king Itzcóatl (Obsidian Snake), whose energetic rule led to Aztec independence. Following a power struggle, Tenochtitlán allied itself with the cities of Texcoco and Tlacopan. This Triple Alliance would soon control central Mexico. While the three were ostensibly equal partners, in fact, Tlacopan was inferior.

Although the feverish drive of the Aztecs ultimately carried them to dominance of the alliance, Texcoco maintained its position of equality for some time. To considerable extent Texcoco's strength was owing to the brilliance of Nezahualcóyotl (ruled 1418–72), one of the most remarkable figures in the history of Mexico. While so many are remembered for their military exploits, the illustrious Nezahualcóyotl is recalled for his cultural refinement. He was too much a man of his times to be a pacifist, and he steadily increased his influence through military force, but he had more positive redeeming qualities. Renowned for his philosophical verse, this "Poet King of Texcoco" was also a wise legislator and an impartial judge; he did not hesitate to condemn to death, for example, members of his own family who broke laws. In addition, he was an engineer who was instrumental in the construction of a great aqueduct, which brought water to Tenochtitlán from the mainland, and of a long dike across the lake. A scholar and bibliophile, his Texcoco, "the Athens of Anáhuac," had libraries housing thousands of manuscripts, which were, tragically, later destroyed. The city, with its gardens, royal baths, and beautiful temples, was the finest expression of civilization in an age otherwise marred by cruelty, intrigue, and almost constant warfare. When Nezahualcóyotl died in 1472, his son Nezahualpilli, who had many of his father's qualities, became ruler of Texcoco. But the city came increasingly under the influence of Tenochtitlán.

After Itzcóatl died, in 1440, his nephew, the mighty Moctezuma I (Moctezuma Ilhuicamina) became sovereign of the Aztecs. Even before taking power, Moctezuma was a prominent general, and during his reign of twenty-eight years he launched his armies to smashing victories, as the Aztec dominions were extended to the south and northeast. Beyond this explosive territorial growth, the Aztec state took on more formal characteristics and began to achieve remarkable cohesion. At the same time, a genuine Aztec art style evolved as one manifestation of fervent nationalism. On a less positive note, the pretension and arrogance for which the Aztecs were notorious became increasingly extravagant, as former allies were bullied and cheated in the extension of imperial ambitions.

Growth of the empire was checked in the middle of the fifteenth century by the onset in 1450–51 of a catastrophic famine occasioned by heavy snowfalls and rains that caused floods, which ruined crops. The food shortage persisted, leading the Aztecs to placate the gods with human sacrifices in ever-increasing num-

PRINCIPAL LAKE CITIES IN THE VALLEY OF MEXICO DURING THE AZTEC PERIOD

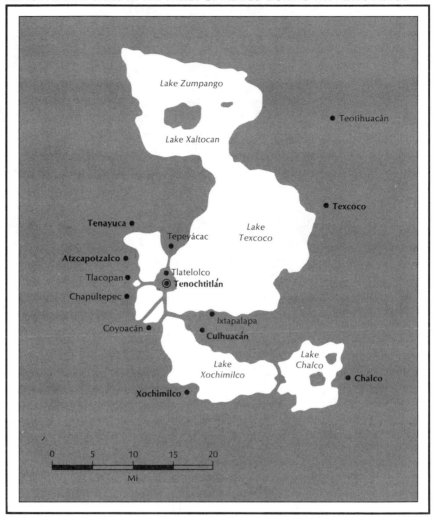

bers. Still they were not favored by nature, and the situation became even more desperate as wild beasts came out of the mountains to attack humans and vultures swarmed to feed on the dead. Great numbers of people sold themselves for a few ears of corn, becoming slaves to the Totonacs of the Gulf coast, where the famine had not occurred. When, after five years of near-starvation, food was again plentiful, the priests observed that the human sacrifices had been successful; the lesson had been learned, and the gods would never again be deprived of a regular diet of human hearts.

The sculpture of a female deity is reflected in an Aztec obsidian mirror with a wooden frame.

When Moctezuma I died in 1468, he was replaced by Axayácatl (ruled 1469–81), who faced rebellions of various tributary towns within the empire. Axayácatl cracked down on the rebels, and, in order to prevent future trouble, he established garrisons at frontier outposts. Like his predecessors he continued to conquer new provinces, and in the course of one furious battle he lost a leg. All Aztec kings were expected to be brave leaders, and one source of their immense authority derived from their presence in the thick of battle, where they shared dangers along with the lowliest common soldier.

The next lord of the Aztecs was the least distinguished of their number—Tizoc (Bloodstained Leg), brother of Axayácatl. Even though his armies enjoyed many victories (having taken a reported hundred thousand prisoners), Tizoc himself was considered a coward, anathema to the warriors of Tenochtitlán. It was no benefit to the hapless Tizoc that the armies were led by the extraordinary general Tlacaélel. This intrepid commander was the sinister power behind three different kings, and, while he never seized outright rule for himself, he had no need to, as he was in effect a king maker. It has been suggested that Tizoc's death by poisoning, after a short rule (1481–86), was contrived with the concurrence of Tlacaélel, who then saw to the election of Ahuítzotl (Water Dog), the third son of Moctezuma I to reign.

Much in contrast to his predecessor, Ahuítzotl was an extremely aggressive and fierce leader who unleashed the Aztec fury. He took his legions on wide-ranging expeditions, conquering the valley of Oaxaca, driving down the Pacific coast to Guatemala, and pushing up the Gulf coast. His merciless tactics subdued many provinces and increased the tributes paid to Tenochtitlán. Under his rule, in 1487, a great orgy of bloodletting was enacted as part of the dedication of an impressive new temple erected to honor the god Huitzilopochtli. In a ceremony lasting four days sacrificial victims taken during campaigns were formed in four columns, each stretching three miles. At least twenty thousand human hearts were torn out to please the god. Prominent guests, selected from allies and tributary towns, were invited to be impressed (and intimidated) by the might and glory of Tenochtitlán. In the frenzy of this ghastly pageant, the priests were finally overcome by exhaustion. The bloody reign of Ahuítzotl closed in 1502 when he accidentally struck his head on a stone lintel while trying to escape a flood. He had succeeded not only in knitting together a vast conglomeration of tribes under the Aztec yoke but also in imposing a tight bureaucratic control over the empire.

The Aztec Empire

By the beginning of the sixteenth century the Aztec system embraced most of central and much of southern Mexico, excluding the Maya regions. The north held little attraction, for the Aztecs were concerned with exacting tribute, not controlling land, especially not the semidesert area of the bellicose Chichimecs. There were areas along the southern Pacific coast that remained independent of the Aztec net, along with some in the northeast. Most notable among the independent states were those of the Tarascans and the Tlaxcalans.

The Tarascans lived in the scenic western state of Michoacán near Lake Pátzcuaro. Legends say that they were originally part of the Aztec migration from Aztlán. When the nomads reached the lake, some went in to bathe and came out of the water to find that their clothes and belongings had been stolen by the others,

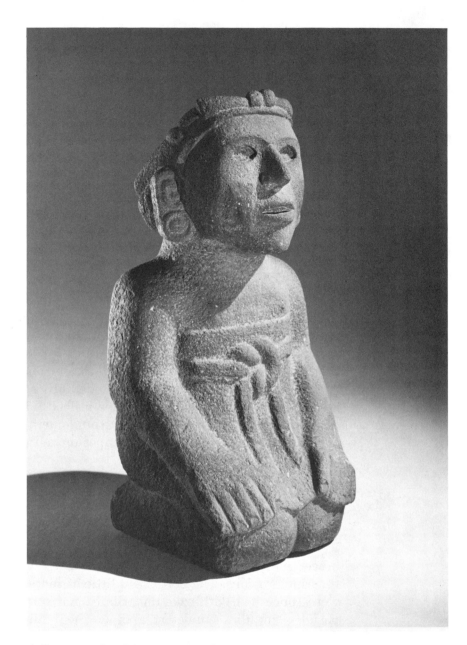

A fine example of Aztec stone sculpture.

who had departed. The thieves (or pranksters) went on to establish Tenochtitlán, and the victims remained to become the Tarascans. From those early bathers of the remote past have emerged the tall, slender, fine-featured people regarded by many today as the most handsome of the land. Over the generations they prospered in their territory, isolated from the troubles of the Valley of Mexico. They built their capital at Tzintzuntzan. Eventually the Aztecs got around to attacking them, but the powerful Tarascans gave them a taste of copper weapons. In 1479 Axayácatl invaded Michoacán with the intention of capturing sacrificial victims to celebrate the carving of the great Aztec calendar stone, and of course to get tribute. His army of twenty-four thousand met a large Tarascan force, with disastrous consequences: the Aztecs left twenty thousand dead on the field. Thereafter few bothered the Tarascans.

The independent state of Tlaxcala was founded by one of the early Chichimec tribes in the region east of the mountains lining the Valley of Mexico. At various times the Tlaxcalans were allies of the Aztecs, but trouble erupted between the two in a curious way. During the great famine of the 1450s the Aztecs ran short of sacrificial victims to propitiate the gods. They dared not keep the gods waiting by undertaking campaigns in distant provinces, so they made an ingenious, if macabre, arrangement with the Tlaxcalans, who also needed victims. It was agreed that limited war would be waged for the precise purpose of taking live prisoners. It had a grim sort of logic, for lives would not be "wasted" in battlefield deaths but rather would be spent for the higher, "useful" purpose of pleasing the gods in order to lift the famine. Moreover, it would have the incidental goal of training young warriors. This concept of *Xochiyaoyotl* (Flowery Wars), which may have existed in earlier times, demonstrates the expediency of the Aztecs and their neighbors. But there was a ritualistic aspect to it as well; a Flowery War was defined by rules and had overseers. It began and ended by mutual consent. It appears, however, that such engagements, which had the ceremonial airs of a tournament, gradually got out of hand. Whatever the precise nature of the misunderstanding, the Aztecs and Tlaxcalans eventually got down to the real thing. They became exceedingly bitter enemies, a turn of events that would have ominous consequences with the arrival of the Spaniards in 1519.

The Aztecs never gained control of the Tlaxcalans, whose state was an island surrounded by Aztec dominions. But the Tlaxcalans were contained, and they were seriously disadvantaged when their trading was restricted, especially with the interdiction of their supplies of salt and cotton. Some speculate that the Aztecs purposely did not conquer the Tlaxcalans in order to maintain a state of war in which fledgling warriors could be tested and captives taken.

In 1502 the ill-starred Moctezuma II (Moctezuma Xocoyótzin), a son of Axayácatl, was elected to succeed Ahuítzotl. He reigned as the most absolute of Aztec lords, governing with great authority and enjoying the deference due a demigod. He was educated to be a high priest, but he later proved his valor on the field of battle. Moctezuma II undertook further expeditions to expand his suzerainty, and he laid the groundwork for an invasion of Central America. With the Aztec empire enjoying power and prosperity, there was a bustling commerce, a vigorous artistic style, and an advanced, well-organized society. From the brutish and pitiful beginnings, the Aztecs had created an astonishing capital city with a complex, sophisticated society. For seventeen years Moctezuma II ruled in splendor; then, quite suddenly, the Aztec world was turned upside down.

Recommended for Further Study

Bernal, Ignacio. *Mexico before Cortez: Art, History and Legend*. Translated by Willis Barnstone. Garden City, N.Y.: Doubleday, 1975.

Brundage, Burr C. *A Rain of Darts: The Mexica Aztecs*. Austin: University of Texas Press, 1972.

Caso, Alfonso. *The Aztecs: People of the Sun*. Norman: University of Oklahoma Press, 1958.

Clendinnen, Inga. *Aztecs: An Interpretation*. New York: Cambridge University Press, 1991.

Davies, Nigel. *The Aztec Empire: The Toltec Resurgence*. Norman: University of Oklahoma Press, 1987.

———. *The Aztecs: A History*. London: Macmillan, 1973.

Duran, Fr. Diego. *The Aztecs: The History of the Indians of New Spain*. Translated, with notes, by Doris Heyden and Fernando Horcasitas. New York: Orion Press, 1964.

Gillespie, Susan D. *The Aztec Kings: The Construction of Rulership in Mexican History*. Tucson: University of Arizona Press, 1989.

Hodge, Mary G., and Michael E. Smith, eds. *Economies and Polities in the Aztec Realm*. Austin: University of Texas Press, 1993.

León-Portilla, Miguel. *The Aztec Image of Self and Society: An Introduction to Nahua Culture*. Edited by José Jorge Klor de Alva. Salt Lake City: University of Utah Press, 1992.

Rojas, Pedro. *The Art and Architecture of Mexico, from 10,000 B.C. to the Present Day*. Feltham, Eng.: Hamlyn, 1968.

Von Hagen, Victor W. *The Aztec: Man and Tribe*. New York: New American Library, 1961.

5

Aztec Society and Culture

It is one of the paradoxes of history that violence and artistic development are entirely compatible within the same society; brutality coexists with refinement and justice. Aztec society is a good case in point. We have seen the emergence of a state committed to a policy of war and hostage to a bloodthirsty religion; it is also true that Aztec society and culture embodied some remarkably enlightened codes of conduct and justice, sensitive accomplishments in the arts, an orderly administration, and behavior that was strangely puritanical in outlook. In some respects it was civilization of the highest order.

Aztec Religion

The negative aspects of late Aztec life bear some examination, not by way of apologia but rather because they inform a facet of thought central to Aztec policy. The rationale for human sacrifice finds its origin in a cosmic view of things. When the early Aztecs wandered in search of their homeland, they carried with them an effigy of their god Huitzilopochtli, lord of the sun and god of war. They believed that the sun and earth had been destroyed in a cataclysm and recreated four times, and that in their age of the fifth sun, final destruction was imminent. That fate was, understandably, to be avoided as long as possible, and the Aztecs believed that special intervention through Huitzilopochtli would serve their interests.

Furthermore, the Aztecs accepted the view of a natural cycle:

Modern re-enactment at Teotihuacán of the Aztec Fifth Sun Festival.

the sun, along with the rain, nourished the plant life that sustained man, and therefore man, in turn, should give sustenance to the sun and rain gods. Ancient deities had sacrificed themselves to the sun, and mere mortals could hardly decline the same honor. The greatest offering that could be made, the highest expression of piety, was the giving of life itself. In practice, the ritual offering to the sun god involved the removal of a palpitating human heart for presentation to Huitzilopochtli. Without such expressions of reverence, it was feared that the sun might not rise to make its way across the sky. Having accepted that warped premise, Aztec thought then progressed with considerable logic.

Human sacrifice was a stage through which many ancient cultures of the Old World passed on the way to becoming great civilizations. In many respects the New World schedule of development lagged centuries behind, so the practice persisted until a much later age. Sacrifice was to the Aztecs a solemn, and necessary, religious ceremony for the purpose of averting disaster. Victims were sent as messengers to the gods to demonstrate the reverence of the people, and it was often considered an honor to make the trip. With the same pious convictions priests occasionally indulged in ritual cannibalism[1] as a kind of pagan communion through which they might acquire the attributes of the enemy.

All was done in accordance with a strictly prescribed procedure. The most familiar sacrificial ceremony took place atop a high temple, where the victim was spread-eagled over a rounded stone, his back arched. While his limbs were held by four assistants, the priest went in under the rib cage with an obsidian knife to remove the heart. There were variations, according to the god to be honored. Those dispatched for Xipe Totec, the god of fertility, were bound and shot full of arrows, the falling drops of blood symbolizing the falling of spring rain. Those honoring the fire god were drugged with hashish and then placed in fire. There was also a kind of gladiatorial combat that amounted to sacrifice, in which a captured warrior, usually one who had shown great skill and bravery, was tied by the ankle to a great round, flat stone. He was given dull wooden weapons to face a series of well-armed Aztec warriors, one at a time. In the unlikely event that the captive survived, he could have his freedom, but, in at least one notable case, a survivor insisted that he be honored as a warrior with a sacrificial death.

Aztec successes seemed to justify their practices. Reversals in fortunes simply called for more sacrifices, which eventually brought about a shortage of the "god food." Hence the resort to Flowery Wars. In order to supply victims, an almost constant state of war was maintained; thus, for religious reasons, militarism was elevated to virtue.

1. Will Durant, *Our Oriental Heritage* (New York, 1935), p. 10, writes, "Cannibalism was at one time practically universal; it has been found in nearly all primitive tribes, and among such later peoples as the Irish, the Iberians, the Picts, and the eleventh-century Danes."

At the end of every fifty-two year cycle (the Indians' "century"), there was always the doubt that the sun would rise to begin a new cycle. Therefore, in fatalistic anticipation, on the last night of the cycle all dishes were broken and all fires put out. Then the priests assembled on a mountaintop to pray. When the sun did rise, a victim was sacrificed in appreciation and a New Fire ceremony was held; a new fire was kindled from which torches were carried to light all other fires.

The Aztecs perceived themselves as living in an insecure world, at the mercy of the elements and at the edge of doom. Natural calamities in their fragile universe were occasioned by the gods'

A temple is burned in this Indian painting, signifying the end of a 52-year cycle. From the Codex Telleriano-Remensis.

The New Fire ceremony is portrayed here much like a May Day frolic. The European artist had probably never seen an Indian in his native habitat.

displeasure. The Indians believed themselves surrounded by strange and harmful forces: as human beings were at one with nature, a person could suddenly be transformed into a hawk, a coyote, a fish, or even a tree or a rock. In such forms those who had passed on could haunt the living. There were demons and other strange apparitions in the nighttime, and in the dark one had to be especially careful of the noxious "airs." In an atmosphere heavy with symbolism, the apprehensive Aztec took no chances.

Huitzilopochtli was the predominant god, but there were many others to whom homage was paid. The ancient deities of Tláloc, Tezcatlipoca (the favorite of the warriors), and Quetzalcóatl (revered by the intellectual priests), were only a few of the more prominent gods worshipped for their special benefactions. Favored gods of conquered peoples were readily incorporated into a swelling Aztec pantheon of deities.

There was a version of afterlife, but it was not the same for all. Mothers who died in childbirth went to a special heaven. Warriors who fell in battle or who were sacrificed by the enemy went to a paradise with perfumed clouds, to accompany the sun in its daily passage; or they could find a new life as a hummingbird,

In old age the Aztecs confessed to the goddess Tlazoltéotl, whose effigy is shown here giving birth to the God of Corn.

destined to spend eternity among fragrant blossoms. Thus the warrior did not fear death any more than later Spanish priests feared the martyrdom that assured them a place in their heaven. Unless one was surprised by death, it was customary to confess late in life. Sins were related to the goddess Tlazoltéotl, "the Eater of Filth [sins]." After satisfying a penance imposed by a priest, the sinner was then cleansed.

Religion was all-pervasive in Tenochtitlán, and from birth to death there was daily religious observance. The Indians had many holy days during which celebrations, both solemn and joyful, took place. Some festivities included singing and dancing, along with children parading in garlands of flowers. Although religious fanaticism led to excesses among the Aztecs, the same can be said for their contemporaries in other parts of the world. If the Spanish Inquisition offers the most convenient comparison, we do not have to look far to find others.

Aztec Society

The early tribal society of the Aztecs was somewhat democratic. While they were nomadic and relatively few in number, Aztec social structure was simple; the majority were peasants or warriors, and the handful of priests and war leaders enjoyed comparatively few perquisites. Following the settlement of Tenochtitlán, however, a rapidly expanding population, a diversified economy, and the organizational demands of the imperial system led to a more complex class structure.

Naturally, the royal family was the most noble of all, and it was a large group. While the emperor had one principal (or "legitimate") wife, he had many others as well. The royal offspring were numerous, and they proliferated greatly. It is said that Nezahualpilli of Texcoco had two thousand wives and 144 children. Moctezuma II, with one thousand women, once had 150 pregnant at the same time. The royal wives had position and respect, and some were highly accomplished women whose views and talents were appreciated at court. Over a period of several generations the ruling dynasty had sufficient relations to be considered almost as a class apart. Emperors were always chosen from the royal family, but, unlike most monarchies, the heir apparent was not fixed. The best male candidate was chosen, whether he was a brother, nephew, or younger son of the previous emperor, a policy in keeping with Aztec recognition of merit over birth. Members of the royal family bore great responsibility; they were expected to serve as examples, to maintain dignity, and to lead warriors. Consequently, the moral fiber of Aztec leadership was strong. As Ignacio Bernal observes, "Excessive well-being had not made the imperial family either effeminate or degenerate,"[2] which was often the case with European royalty.

Others in the noble category included high priests, prominent military officers, and influential government leaders. Sons of nobles were in an advantageous position to achieve their fathers' rank, but nobility (outside of the royal family) was not an inherited right. One had to distinguish himself in service in order to enjoy the privileges of the aristocracy. Nobles wore fine clothing, had commodious houses, servants, jewelry, and prestige—in sum, the best of everything that was available. Such luxuries went with the office, however; they were a consequence of achievement and were not sought for their own sake. Little wealth could be passed on to children. In the late Aztec period, however, an elite class with landed estates, a kind of incipient feudal aristocracy, was apparently in process of formation. Whereas the noble had traditionally valued his reputation above all, it

2. Ignacio Bernal, "Mexico-Tenochtitlan," in *Cities of Destiny*, ed. Arnold Toynbee (New York, 1968), p. 208.

seems probable (had the Spanish Conquest not intervened) that within two or three generations a more materialistic class of nobility would have evolved.

Nobles had an acute sense of *noblesse oblige*; obligations and moral duties were not taken lightly, and commoners were treated with consideration, compassion, and mercy. The aristocratic tradition was hostile to open displays of frivolity; but, in spite of a public image of austerity, frugality, and modesty, in private the nobles were allowed some ostentation. The so-called Precepts of the Elders reflected a concern for courtly manners and behavior. One finds in it a startling similarity to the famous Renaissance manual, *The Courtier*, written by the Italian humanist Baldassare Castiglione at precisely the time Aztec nobility flowered in its most civilized state. The genteel Aztec courtier of the early sixteenth century was a far cry from his antecedents who had entered the Valley of Mexico several generations earlier. In Tenochtitlán, Leopoldo Castedo reminds, the "nobles were so extraordinarily refined that when they were forced to come near the Spaniards, they screened their nasal passages with branches of fragrant flowers."[3]

All able-bodied males were expected to bear arms, but soldiers came primarily from the lower class. Distinction in battle was one way in which a commoner might rise to the nobility. In order to achieve the cherished rank of warrior, a youth had to take a prisoner. If he succeeded in capturing or killing four of the enemy he was entitled to share in the booty. Perhaps more important, he was allowed to dress in the distinctive adornments of the military elite. Conceivably, he could become a member of the prestigious military orders—the Eagle Knights or Jaguar Knights—and thus enjoy the luxuries of noble status. By encouraging upward mobility through performance, Aztec society remained flexible and vigorous.

Access to high status might also be gained through the priesthood. However, there were a great many priests (five thousand were assigned to the main temple of Tenochtitlán alone), and most of them remained in minor positions. The sacerdotal life began with training young boys (or girls destined to be priestesses) in a monastery school, or *calmécac*. If suited to the life, a youth made the decision to enter the priesthood at about the age of twenty-one. Priests were expected to lead exemplary lives, and they spent long hours in prayer, fasting, and penance. The latter

3. Leopoldo Castedo, *A History of Latin American Art and Architecture from Precolumbian Times to the Present* (New York, 1969), pp. 38–39.

included scarification of the body, usually by drawing drops of blood with a thorn passed through the ear, tongue, or penis. Most of the priests led modest lives of service; those who advanced through the hierarchy, however, enjoyed the status of nobles and many of the perquisites that went with it. Like their European counterparts, the Aztec priests commanded the greatest knowledge, which gave them extraordinary power. Aside from routine religious duties, each priest had a specialty, such as music, painting, teaching, dancing, or assisting at sacrificial rites. Priests were the guardians of morality, and some of their admonitions are not unlike Scriptural injunctions: "He who looks too curiously on a woman commits adultery with his eyes."

Even though Tenochtitlán produced little for export, the merchants of that city ranged far and wide. These traders, the *pochteca*, were one of the most interesting groups in Aztec society. They organized and led caravans as far as Central America, often passing through hostile country. The pochteca were as brave as they were shrewd and often depended on both their wits and courage to evade dangers. Some of them knew foreign languages and customs and served as spies for the Aztec militarists.

The pochteca imported to the capital exotic and profitable goods, which were displayed in the markets. But while these merchants were prosperous, they took great care to avoid any show of opulence. Unlike any other groups in Aztec society, they were incipient capitalists; unlike Aztec nobles, they were little concerned about their reputations. They lived in their own district and formed a separate group altogether. They had their own guild, their special deities, and their own courts. Within their section of the city they frequently gave sumptuous banquets and enjoyed other luxuries. Not of the nobility, they nevertheless had influence and respect.

The great majority of the people formed the class of commoners (*maceguales*). These farmers, laborers, minor craftsmen, servants, vendors, and petty functionaries of the state were organized into wards or districts called *calpullis* (*barrios* to the Spaniards). A clan made up of many families, the calpulli was the basic social unit. It was a close-knit organization with loyalties much like those of an extended family. Each calpulli had lands apportioned to family heads who could use fields but did not own them. Members of the calpulli worked together, played together, and, in times of war, fought together as a unit. The people elected a captain who served as military commander of the district and was responsible for their welfare and good order.

Another group occupied still a lower position: those who rented their services out to the upper classes, to work their fields or to perform other labor for wages, were called *mayeques*. Though technically free, they were neither citizens nor identified with a calpulli and were considered socially and economically inferior to the commoners. These mayeques were often much like sharecroppers, without real roots or traditions. In all probability they were conquered people from other areas.

At the bottom of the socioeconomic scale were the slaves. Aztec slavery differed from the slave system most familiar to us inasmuch as slaves had certain rights and bondage was not passed from parent to child. Some, in fact, served as slaves only for a specified term, either in payment of a debt or as punishment for a crime. In bad times people sometimes sold themselves or their children into slavery to avoid starvation. A gambler might bet his freedom on a ball game and end up as a slave. Some of the slaves were favored as concubines, and all slaves could intermarry with free persons. Little stigma was attached to some conditions of slavery; the mother of the emperor Itzcóatl, in fact, had been a slave. In a different category were those captured in war and destined for sacrifice. The class of slaves was increasing at the time of the Spanish Conquest, another sign of the widening social gap.

Aztec society's concern with education was singular for its time—school was compulsory for children. There were two main types of schools, and attendance at one or the other determined social and economic status. Children of the nobility usually attended the calmécac, run by the scholarly priests, in preparation for the priesthood or some high office in the state. Occasionally a talented son of a commoner gained entrance. To prepare students for future responsibilities, discipline was very strict and hours of study were long. In a vigorous intellectual regimen young boys studied religion, astronomy, philosophy, history, poetry, rhetoric, and oratory, among other disciplines. Although the spoken language was rich and expressive and lent itself to fine subtleties, the picture writing was limited. History was passed on by oral traditions committed to memory. Written accounts depicted certain dramatic scenes that gave continuity and jogged the memory, but the fine details were transmitted from one generation to another by the retelling.

Most of the children attended one of the *telpochcallis* and found a more relaxed, less intellectual atmosphere. These students would become the class of commoners, or workers. Lay

Prehispanic Mexican women ground their corn with stone *mano* and *metate*, and made tortillas much as many do today. From the Florentine Codex.

persons gave both boys and girls practical instruction in basic subjects. Here boys learned the rudiments of warfare, and those who went on to excel in the profession of arms could do very well for themselves; others had to be content with learning trades or lesser skills. Girls were instructed in the responsibilities of the household and motherhood. All were taught modesty, courtesy, and conformity.[4] The humility and courtesy of so many Mexican Indians today are deeply rooted in the Aztec concept of virtue.

In the home parents imposed strict discipline. The birth of a child occasioned celebration and florid speeches. A child was named in hopeful anticipation of its character—the boys usually given names indicating military prowess and the girls names denoting beauty and delicacy, such as Rain Flower or Water Bird. In the home children were taught not only proper deportment but also the performance of daily tasks: girls learned to cook, sew, and embroider, while boys were taught agriculture and crafts. While children were very young some indiscretions were tolerated; but by the age of eight they were considered to be responsible, and infractions brought harsh punishment. Although

4. For more on women, see María J. Rodríguez-Shadow, *La mujer azteca* (Toluca, 1991).

parents were ordinarily tender and loving, wayward children
were castigated by whippings, scratching with thorns, or by being forced to inhale the smoke of a fire into which chile peppers
had been placed. It is reasonable to suppose that most children
behaved themselves. Girls worked in the household until they
were sixteen to eighteen, when they married; boys took mates in
their early twenties.

Aztec society was curiously puritanical. Drunkenness could be
a capital offense, although older people were allowed to become
inebriated. The rule prohibiting excessive use of the strong pulque was rooted in the conviction that drunken behavior would
undermine the good order of society and the economy. Oddly
enough, there was no similar ban on drugs. Various kinds of hal-
lucinogens were used, one of which was a fungus that produced
powerful and graphic visions, to either the delight or the horror
of the consumer. It appears, however, that such drugs were taken
primarily by the upper classes, who did so privately and who
could afford the luxury of the consequences. Both pulque and
drugs were believed to have magical properties because they
changed the personality.

Aztec society demanded moral conformity, and violators of the
code, as well as criminal offenders, were dealt with firmly. For
minor offenses punishment was correspondingly light. But since
personal dignity was highly prized, any public humiliation, such
as the cutting of one's hair, was a great insult to pride. Several
offenses, including lying, theft, and treason, brought the death
penalty. The heads of adulterers were crushed between stones,
homosexuals were hanged, and the lips of slanderers were cut off.
Such penalties may seem unduly harsh to us, but it must be recalled that sentences in other parts of the world at that time were
also excessive.

The Aztec legal system was complex, with high judges seated
at both Texcoco and Tenochtitlán and lesser judges in localities.
The legalistic society had need for many judicial officials to prepare the multitude of carefully documented lawsuits. There were
judges in the great marketplaces to maintain fairness in business
transactions and to settle disputes. Appointed by the emperor,
judges were selected for their integrity and virtue. They had
great authority and could arrest even the highest dignitaries, for
under the law all were equal. The judge was expected to be absolutely impartial; if he accepted a bribe or favored a noble over
a plebeian he could be executed.

Duty and responsibility, as well as danger, increased with

one's rank, and they imposed special restraints. Because self-control was considered a mark of good breeding and nobility, the upper classes were subject to standards different from those of the lower classes. In contrast to most systems, where the upper classes have a favored position before the law, Aztec aristocrats were dealt with more harshly than plebeians. An offense that might bring a whipping or public humiliation for a commoner often brought death to a noble. Tax collectors, who had considerable rank, were executed for embezzlement, and the same fate awaited the lascivious priest. A salient example of justice for the wayward nobility may be observed in the notorious case of one of Nezahualpilli's wives (a daughter of Axayácatl) who was unfaithful. She and three of her lovers were publicly executed.

Aztec medical practices were generally on a par with those in Europe, and were in some respects superior. Doctors knew how to set broken bones and dislocations and to treat dental cavities. They even performed brain operations. Like their European counterparts, Aztec healers were ill informed on the causes of disease but adept at effecting cures. The bleeding of patients, accepted medical practice in Europe until the end of the eighteenth century, was practiced by Aztec physicians as well. Aztec medicines were essentially extractions from plant life (and some animal life), from which were prepared a bewildering variety of brews, powders, poultices, purges, and pastes. Years after the Conquest a Spanish physician cataloged some fifteen hundred different plants whose medicinal properties were utilized by the Indians. The conquerors adopted native medicines, many of which are still popular in rural Mexico today.

Because Aztec society was largely agricultural in character, the daily routine of most people was directly involved in the growing of food. Aside from the many floating gardens that ringed the island city, there were extensive plantings along the shores of the lakes. The diet remained much as it had been for centuries, with a base of corn, beans, chile, and squash. It also included a wide variety of other vegetables and melons, cactus fruit, and amaranth, in addition to many fruits imported from tropical regions. Commoners seldom ate meat, but the nobles, who liked to hunt for sport, consumed venison, peccary, pheasant, and turkey. A special treat was the small hairless dog fattened for the table. Cacao from the tropics was made into a chocolate drink, and avocados and many other exotic delicacies were brought in by the traders. Fish was a favorite when available.

A girl has been put to death for drunkenness and a thief has been executed by stoning. Adulterers are shown wrapped together in a sheet and then stoned to death. From the Codex Mendoza.

An older woman is legally allowed to partake of the intoxicant *octli* (pulque). From the Codex Mendoza.

Aztec justice was strict, and it often imposed the harshest punishment on high officials. Here an erring functionary is being strangled. From the Florentine Codex.

The Aztec Political System

The limited resources of the Valley were not sufficient to meet the needs of Tenochtitlán, Texcoco, Tlacopan, and other Valley communities. Moreover, there was an increasing demand for luxuries from other provinces. To satisfy the necessities and desires for both raw materials and consumer goods, Aztec realms were extended. The so-called Aztec empire was really a loose coalition of subject city-states that paid tribute to the imperial center. The lords of Anáhuac were not particularly desirous of colonizing conquered areas with their own people or of imposing their own political system; nor were they cultural imperialists. Rather, the collection of tribute, which kept the Valley culture prosperous, was their main concern.

Tributes included a wide variety of commodities, among which were cacao, cotton, feathers, precious stones, jaguar skins, eagles, shells, dyes, cloth, gold, silver, sandals, and corn and other foodstuffs, as well as jewelry. Imperial tax collectors (*calpixquis*) were stationed in tributary towns to ensure prompt payment. Towns conquered by the Aztecs were expected to provide soldiers and slaves and were required to recognize the imperial courts of appeal. But they were also allowed considerable autonomy. If the conquered peoples agreed to submit to Aztec sovereignty, the Aztecs did not much interfere with their internal affairs and their customs. Huitzilopochtli had to be recognized as the supreme deity; otherwise local religious practices and traditions were usually respected.

Aztec political organization rested lightly on tributary towns, provided they were cooperative. In fact, it may be said that the Aztecs' policy of generous autonomy for subject provinces was a weakness in their political system. The subject peoples continued to be foreigners within the empire, which remained a conglomeration of tributaries with many different languages, customs, and religions. The provinces paid tribute under duress but were never assimilated into Aztec culture. Thus the empire lacked genuine unity and was honeycombed with discontent, a circumstance that would be fatal in the years ahead.

After the death of Nezahualcóyotl of Texcoco in 1472, the Triple Alliance had little significance, and Tenochtitlán gathered to itself almost all the power and most of the tribute. The emperor was elected from among the royal family by a select committee of about a hundred electors. The one chosen was considered to be the choice of the gods as well. Over the generations the emperor came to dictate appointment to offices that had previously been elective. He grew increasingly powerful, and the monarchy more absolute.

Aztec Art, Music, and Literature

The Aztecs borrowed much of their art from others. The Mixtecs exerted strong influence on Aztec gold and silver work, pottery, and pictographs. We have no examples of Aztec murals and little in the way of picture books. Aztec ceramic work was good but not superior. The Aztecs did excel, however, in stone sculpture. Although they lack the grace and loveliness of Olmec jade pieces, Aztec carvings are, nevertheless, striking. They are monumental in size and style and flawlessly executed. As Leopoldo Castedo has observed, "Aztec art was imbued with the dread, drama, and grandeur necessary to dazzle the subject peoples and convey the image of an omnipotent and implacable state."[4]

The artisans who made the gold and silver jewelry were also superb craftsmen. It is therefore lamentable that almost all of their work was either lost or destroyed during the Spanish Conquest, for the conquerors valued raw gold but all too often did

4. Ibid., p. 39.

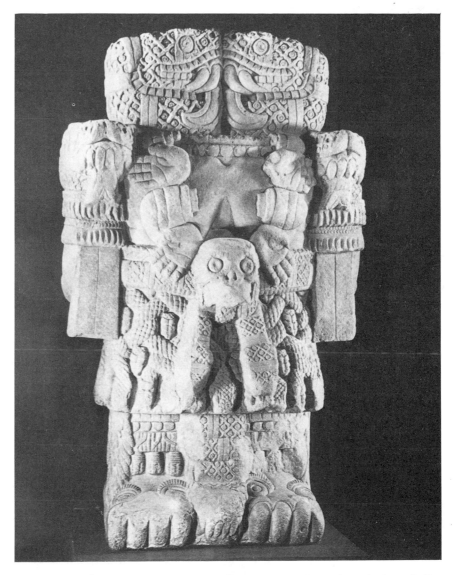

This fearsome image of the goddess Coatlicue, mother of Huitzilopochtli, stands over eight feet high.

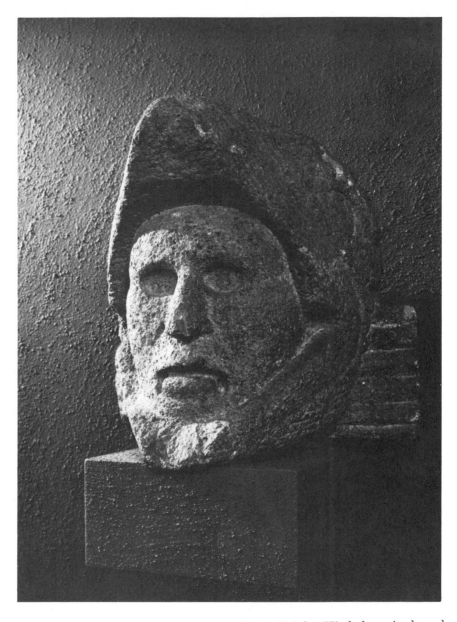

A realistic stone sculpture of an Aztec Eagle Knight. His helmet is shaped like an eagle's head; knights of the orders of the Jaguar and Coyote wore appropriate headgear and pelts.

not appreciate the fine workmanship. Equally impressive was the art of the lapidarists; from precious jadeite, turquoise, and other stones they fashioned fine jewelry and mosaics. Most unusual were the artists who worked with feathers. The Aztecs put great value on the long green plumes of the quetzal bird that lived in the highlands of Chiapas and Guatemala, but the feathers of many other birds, too, were woven into mosaics of wonderful patterns and colors. Only rare examples remain, the most spectacular being the great headdress of Moctezuma II. The contemporary German artist Albrecht Dürer was lavish in his praise of Aztec artisans: "In all my life I have never seen anything that rejoiced my heart so much; I have found an admirable art in them, and I have been astonished by the subtle spirit of the men of these strange countries."[5]

Aztec music was composed primarily for ceremonial purposes, and its range was consequently limited. Instruments consisted of flutes, whistles, rasps, rattles, trumpets, conch shells, and drums vital for providing rhythm. The music itself was mournful and no doubt would seem monotonous to our ears. Musicians were highly regarded because of their accompaniment in the religious rituals. Powerful lords were patrons to composers who created ballads recounting the nobles' military exploits. If they had pres-

Musicians played important roles in religious observances. From the Florentine Codex.

Careless musicians were sometimes punished by death.

5. Quoted in Jacques Soustelle, *The Daily Life of the Aztecs on the Eve of the Spanish Conquest*, trans. Patrick O'Brian (London, 1961), p. 68.

tige, musicians also bore great responsibilities. As no written form for recording music had developed, musicians had to memorize a very wide repertoire for the many ceremonies that often went on for hours. At the same time, as Robert Stevenson points out, "Imperfectly executed rituals were thought to offend rather than appease the gods, and therefore errors in the performance of the ritual music—such as missed drum beats—carried the death penalty."[6]

Neither in music nor in poetry was romantic love a popular theme. Aztec lyrics were often eloquent, moving, and sentimental, though for most modern tastes perhaps too concerned with flowers, jade, feathers, and rain. In a verse praising a goddess, for example, a poet sings:

> The yellow flower has opened,
> Our mother has opened like a flower.
> She came from our Place of Beginning . . .
> Butterfly of Obsidian. . . .[7]

Poets sometimes addressed themselves to the proper role of artists and appealed to the public at large to assume a responsible and dignified posture. Like poets the world over, they often waxed philosophical and examined the meaning of life:

> Truly do we live on earth?
> Not forever on earth; only a little while here.
> Although it be jade, it will be broken,
> Although it be gold, it is crushed,
> Although it be quetzal feather, it is torn asunder.
> Not forever on earth; only a little while here.[8]

The City of Tenochtitlán

Aztec architecture, like Aztec art, was essentially derivative. Buildings were basically elaborations of forms that went all the way back to Teotihuacán. But while many pre-Aztec structures survive in amazingly good condition, Tenochtitlán was thought to have been completely demolished by the Spaniards. However, excavations since 1978 have revealed important archaeological findings, including parts of the main temple intact. We do have, moreover, enough descriptions of Tenochtitlán from both native

6. Robert Stevenson, *Music in Mexico: A Historical Survey* (New York, 1971), p. 18.
7. Quoted in Frances Gillmor, *Flute of the Smoking Mirror: A Portrait of Nezahualcoyotl, Poet-King of the Aztecs* (Albuquerque, 1949), p. 23.
8. Quoted in Miguel León-Portilla, *Aztec Thought and Culture: A Study of the Ancient Nahuatl Mind*, trans. Jack Emory Davis (Norman, 1963), p. 7.

and Spanish contemporary accounts to appreciate what the city looked like.

By the time Moctezuma II was elevated to power in 1502, the island capital of Tenochtitlán was a most impressive city. How large it was we do not know, but in the cautious opinion of Ignacio Bernal, there were about eighty thousand residents. Miguel León-Portilla writes that "beyond question the Aztec capital contained a quarter of a million people."[9] Even with the conservative estimate, the Aztec capital was one of the largest cities in the world. Only four cities of Europe—Paris, Venice, Milan, and Naples—had populations of one hundred thousand or more at the time. Seville, the city from which Spanish ships sailed for Mexico, had a population in 1520 of around forty thousand; and by 1580, when it was the largest city in Spain, it had only slightly over a hundred thousand. The amazement of the Spanish conquerors at their first sight of Tenochtitlán is therefore understandable. Cortés wrote of "the magnificence, the strange and marvelous things of this great city," which itself was "so remarkable as not to be believed."[10] In the Valley of Mexico, an area of some three thousand square miles, there were about fifty different cities by the second decade of the sixteenth century. If we take into account "greater" Tenochtitlán, with its many satellite communities on the lake shores (of which Texcoco was perhaps as large as the capital itself), the area surely held one of the heaviest concentrations of population in the world at the time.

By the early sixteenth century the island was an area comprising about five square miles, densely settled, and occupying much of the present center of Mexico City. It was a metropolis swarming with activity. Some sixty thousand people gathered daily in its buzzing market places to barter and gossip. The core of the city, corresponding to the extensive plaza of today (the Zócalo), had a great double pyramid dedicated to Huitzilopochtli and Tláloc, along with the royal palaces and other large structures. Among the shocks to the conquering Spaniards was a giant rack, the *tzompantli*, on which many thousands of human skulls were displayed.

From that central precinct enclosing about 125 acres, the city extended out to the residences of the nobles, which were often of

9. Bernal, "Mexico-Tenochtitlan," p. 204; Miguel León-Portilla, ed., *The Broken Spears: The Aztec Account of the Conquest of Mexico*, trans. Lysander Kemp (Boston, 1972), p. xix.

10. Hernán Cortés, *Hernán Cortés: Letters from Mexico*, trans. and ed. A. R. Pagden, introd. J. H. Elliott (New York, 1971), pp. 101–02.

The center of Tenochtitlán, reconstructed by Ignacio Marquina from descriptions of Spanish conquerors and surviving Aztec monuments.

two stories and contained as many as fifty rooms and patios. Beyond were districts with the modest dwellings of the commoners. The city was interlaced with stone-edged canals, which served as thoroughfares for thousands of canoes carrying people and goods. Paralleling the canals were streets for pedestrians. The Aztecs loved flowers, which with trees and other plants, decorated many luxurious gardens. Aside from the royal botanical gardens, which displayed almost all species of plant life in the empire, there were also zoos, in which were represented practically all the animals and snakes of the country, as well as a large aviary full of all varieties of domestic birds. Large ponds were maintained for swans, ducks, and egrets. In special cages were Moctezuma's snakes, eagles, and jaguars, which consumed five hundred turkeys daily. Hundreds of people were kept busy in the maintenance of these gardens and zoos.

Five shallow lakes interconnected to form a network—two fresh water lakes in the south drained into the brackish water of Lake Texcoco. Three long causeways joined the island city to the shores: one stretched southward to Ixtapalapa, branching off with a road to Coyoacán; another causeway went west to Tlacopan, with an offshoot to Chapultepec; and a third made a connection to the north with Tepeyácac. These broad thoroughfares, twenty-five to thirty feet wide, were cut at intervals by drawbridges. Within the city itself many canals were spanned by stout bridges across which, according to Cortés, ten horsemen could ride abreast.[11]

Compared to other cities in the world at the time, Tenochtitlán was very clean. There was good drainage, and night soil and garbage were hauled away in barges. A crew of a thousand men swept and washed down public streets every day. Cleanliness was considered essential, and people bathed often, many once a day. Owing at least in part to good sanitation and clean air, Aztec society was healthy.

Moctezuma II

Moctezuma II reigned over a territory roughly the size of Italy. His domains included the modern states of Mexico, Morelos, Puebla, Hidalgo, most of Veracruz, much of Oaxaca and Guerrero, as well as the coasts of Chiapas. They contained thirty-eight "provinces," stretching from arid highlands to the sweltering tropics. If, as some authorities believe, all of Mexico had a population approaching 30 million,[12] it was more populous than any country in Europe. France, the largest, had about 20 million, and Spain, 10 at most.

With his immense authority, prestige, and luxurious style of life, Moctezuma II was the equal of any Oriental despot. Three thousand servants attended him in his huge palace. Each day he was presented with a choice of one hundred different dishes, although he ate sparingly, taking his meals behind a screen. For his pleasure he had an unlimited number of concubines, and he was entertained by the antics of dwarfs, jesters, tumblers, acrobats, musicians, and dancers. No one dared look him in the face or touch him, and it was forbidden to turn one's back on him. Moctezuma was indeed the epitome of royalty, held as semidivine, exalted far above any of the earliest Aztec rulers. Never-

11. Ibid., p. 103.
12. Sherburne F. Cook and Woodrow Borah, *The Indian Population of Central Mexico, 1531–1610* (Berkeley, 1960); Cook and Borah, *The Aboriginal Population of Central Mexico on the Eve of the Spanish Conquest* (Berkeley, 1963).

A ceramic foot juggler from Oaxaca, ca. A.D. 300.

Some 1200 years later, a similar foot juggler appeared in the Florentine Codex. Also shown are hunchbacks, a giant, and a dwarf, for whom the Indians had affection.

theless, he was an ultimately tragic figure, undone by historical forces with which he could not cope.

Moctezuma reigned with great authority and popularity for many years. His deep knowledge of Mexican history and his respect for tradition were factors in his successful rule and in the collapse of the Aztec state as well. Aside from his religious convictions, Moctezuma was superstitious and sensitive; he was also an amateur "wizard" who dabbled in astrology. He lived in the shadow of historical inevitability; sometime, he knew, the great Quetzalcóatl would return, as he had promised, to take back his rightful throne.

Just when Moctezuma learned of the presence of white men in the New World is not entirely clear. It is no doubt true that word of the Spaniards, who had been in the Caribbean for several years, drifted to the mainland. Perhaps he was not yet unduly concerned. Cuba, in fact, lay dangerously near—but it was not part of the Aztec world. Moctezuma was almost certainly informed by his agents that Spaniards had landed on the Yucatán Peninsula in 1517 and that others the following year were making their way up the Gulf coast. Indians reported seeing "towers or small mountains floating on the waves of the sea." Meanwhile, strange phenomena, construed by the emperor's priests as evil portents, had occurred. Lightning, unaccompanied by thunder, "like a blow from the sun," damaged a temple; a strange bird was found with "a mirror in its head," in which Moctezuma saw a host of foreign warriors. In 1517 a comet appeared "like a flaming ear of corn . . . it seemed to bleed fire, drop by drop, like a wound in the sky."[13] These and other unexplained signs heightened general anxiety. Then, in the spring of 1519 (the Aztec year Ce Acatl), the emperor was filled with apprehension when a courier arrived bearing ominous paintings—they depicted the encampment on Aztec shores of bearded white men with crosses.

Recommended for Further Study

Anawalt, Patricia Reiff. *Indian Clothing Before Cortés: Meso-American Costumes from the Codices.* Norman: University of Oklahoma Press, 1981.

13. León-Portilla, ed., *The Broken Spears*, pp. 13, 5, 6, 4.

Anton, Ferdinand. *Women in Precolumbian America.* New York: Abner Schram, 1973.

Bernal, Ignacio. "Mexico-Tenochtitlan." In *Cities of Destiny,* edited by Arnold Toynbee, pp. 194–209. New York: McGraw-Hill, 1968.

Bierhorst, John, trans. *Cantares Mexicanos. Songs of the Aztecs.* Stanford, Calif.: Stanford University Press, 1985.

Gibson, Charles. *The Aztecs under Spanish Rule.* Stanford, Calif.: Stanford University Press, 1964.

Gillmor, Frances. *Flute of the Smoking Mirror: A Portrait of Nezahualcoyotl, Poet-King of the Aztecs.* Albuquerque: University of New Mexico Press, 1949.

———. *The King Danced in the Market Place.* Tucson: University of Arizona Press, 1964.

Keen, Benjamin. *The Aztec Image in Western Thought.* New Brunswick, N.J.: Rutgers University Press, 1971.

León-Portilla, Miguel. *Aztec Thought and Culture: A Study of the Ancient Nahuatl Mind.* Translated by Jack Emory Davis. Norman: University of Oklahoma Press, 1963.

———. *Fifteen Poets of the Aztec World.* Norman: University of Oklahoma Press, 1992.

———. *The Mind of Ancient Mexico.* Norman: University of Oklahoma Press, 1963.

Offner, Jerome A. *Law and Politics in Aztec Texcoco.* Cambridge: Cambridge University Press, 1983.

Ortiz Montellano, Bernard R. *Aztec Medicine, Health and Nutrition.* New Brunswick, N.J.: Rutgers University Press, 1990.

———. "Counting Skulls: Comments on the Aztec Cannibalism Theory of Harner-Harris." *American Anthropologist* 85 (1983): 403–06.

Price, Barbara J. "Demystification, Enriddlement, and Aztec Cannibalism: A Materialist Rejoinder to Harner." *American Ethnologist* 5 (1978): 98–115.

Sejourné, Laurette. *Burning Water: Thought and Religion in Ancient Mexico.* New York: Grove Press, 1960.

Smith, Bradley. *Mexico: A History in Art.* Garden City, N.Y.: Doubleday, 1968.

Stevenson, Robert. *Music in Mexico: A Historical Survey.* New York: Crowell, 1971.

Westheim, Paul. *The Sculpture of Ancient Mexico.* Garden City, N.Y.: Anchor Books, 1963.

Zantwijk, Rudolf van. *The Aztec Arrangement: The Social History of Pre-Spanish Mexico.* Norman: University of Oklahoma Press, 1985.

Zorita, Alonso de. *Life and Labor in Ancient Mexico: The Brief and Summary Relation of the Lords of New Spain.* Translated, with an introduction, by Benjamin Keen. New Brunswick, N.J.: Rutgers University Press, 1962.

II THE SPANISH CONQUERORS

6

The Spanish Invasion

"Let us try for a moment to imagine," the late Ramón Iglesia wrote, "the astonishment of the inhabitants of a small island called Guanahaní one morning when they beheld three shapes out there in the water, three immense hulks, out of which issued several absurd beings who seemed human only in their eyes and movements, of light complexion, their faces covered with hair, and their bodies—if indeed they had bodies—covered with fabrics of diverse pattern and color."[1] As they had never conceived the existence of such people, it was natural enough that, in 1492, the natives of the Caribbean fancied Columbus and his Spaniards had descended from the sky. The white men, on the other hand, were aware that beings of different racial characteristics existed. Indeed, they had expected to find people of dark skins and black hair, and, thinking (or at least hoping) that they were in the East Indies, the Spaniards subsequently referred to the natives as Indians. In spite of the natural beauty of the islands and the naked innocence of their handsome natives, the discoverers' joy was restrained, for they found little sign of the precious metals, valuable spices, and other wealth they had sought, and no indication of the civilized and exotic kingdoms of the Orient they had anticipated.

Spanish Exploration and Settlement in the Caribbean

Later voyages to the New World (or the "Indies") dampened even the most optimistic spirits. Consequently the Caribbean

1. Ramón Iglesia, *Columbus, Cortés and Other Essays*, trans. and ed. Lesley B. Simpson (Berkeley, 1969), p. 8.

Islands attracted relatively few settlers, and even these became more disgruntled at each passing year, as hopes of finding either wealth or fame dwindled. Columbus, who was always happier sailing about than governing waspish colonists, let administrative matters slide, thus giving the Spanish crown a pretext for removing him as governor of Santo Domingo, as the New World colony was called, and revoking the generous terms earlier granted him. Ultimately, the great discoverer was sent back to the mother country in chains.

Royal officials then took charge, but the bickering continued. Nearby islands were explored, some were settled, and Indians were put to work washing the streams for gold, which provided good income for a few. Beyond that, and small profits from agriculture, there seemed little opportunity. By 1516 Spaniards had planted sugarcane in the islands with some success; but that enterprise rewarded only those with sufficient capital to finance the costly operation. As it slowly dawned on the Spaniards that they were not, in fact, on the rim of the Orient, they reasoned that they were at least close to it, and, if a strait through the land mass to the west could be found, they would soon be rich. With this vision dancing before them, several expeditions set forth to explore in various directions—up to the coast of Florida, to Central America, and down to South America.

The seat of royal government was on the island of Santo Domingo, but the larger island of Cuba held out more promise. Easily conquered in 1511, Cuba proved disappointing. But Spaniards remained in the islands, not only because they continued to hope that something exciting would turn up but also because they had little waiting for them back in Spain. At least in the Indies they had natives working their modest farms or, if they were lucky, mining for gold. However, one of the tragic consequences of the European occupation of the islands was a catastrophic loss of life among the Indians, partly because of fatigue and mistreatment but mostly because of their vulnerability to diseases to which they had no previous exposure or immunity. Epidemics of smallpox, measles, and other illnesses spread quickly among the natives, causing widespread death. With the great decline in the Indian population, a labor shortage ensued.

Governor Diego Velázquez of Cuba sent out an expedition in 1517 for the purpose of trading and finding other Indians to be enslaved. Under the command of Francisco Hernández de Córdoba, the party of three ships sailed west and touched the coast of Yucatán, thought at first to be an island. Further exploration

The chapel-de-fer, or kettle-hat, was a helmet popular with the Spanish infantry.

A halberd of the type used by the conquistadores.

An elaborate Spanish stirrup of the seventeenth century.

A warhorse of the sixteenth century was sometimes fitted with a chamfron, like the one shown here.

revealed the existence of cultures higher than those of the Caribbean, with people dressed in cotton fabric who tilled prosperous
fields and lived in stone houses. In their brief contact with the
natives the Spaniards understood that there was gold and silver
in the land, and they also saw the first signs of human sacrifices.
After a cautious initial reception, the Spaniards were attacked by
a large and very fierce army of warriors, and in the ensuing battle fifty of the Europeans were killed and almost all were
wounded. Accustomed to engagements with less bellicose Caribbean Indians, in which few Spaniards were killed, the invaders
had a rude awakening. Córdoba was badly wounded by ten arrows, and he returned to Cuba to report his findings. He later
died from his injuries, as did several more of his companions.

Despite the ferocity of the Yucatec warriors, the tantalizing
references to gold fired the Spaniards' cupidity, and Governor
Velázquez prepared to pursue the encouraging prospects. In 1518
he dispatched his nephew, Juan de Grijalva, with four ships and
two hundred eager men to investigate further. Making for Yucatán, they sailed up the Gulf side. At a place called Champotón
(Tabasco) they met the natives in a furious battle, which again
left most of the Spaniards nursing wounds. Now convinced that
Yucatán was not an island, Grijalva sailed up the coast to the
present state of Veracruz, stopping occasionally to trade European baubles for local goods. By the time they reached the area
of Pánuco, the Spaniards were discouraged, and, having been absent from Cuba for five months, they longed to go home. One of
the ships returned first, with some small gold objects and rumors
of Amazons. Of more interest, however, were the stories of a
wealthy lake kingdom to the interior dominated by the great
"Lord of Culhúa," by which title coastal Indians knew Moctezuma of the Aztecs. In Cuba this report was greeted with much
excitement, but when Grijalva finally arrived home, the governor, disgusted with his nephew's timorous actions, refused to
receive him. Grijalva lacked the daring and imagination for a
great enterprise and thereby let slip the opportunity that was
reserved for another. Sensing the potential for riches and power,
Velázquez sought a bolder captain to explore and conquer the
new land. Even before Grijalva returned to Cuba, Velázquez had
commissioned the thirty-four-year-old Fernando[2] Cortés to undertake this venture.

2. Cortés's first name is often shown as Hernán or Hernando, but he seems to have
   preferred Fernando.

Fernando Cortés

Cortés was a native of the arid Spanish province of Extremadura, the region from which so many of the prominent conquistadores came. Born in 1485 into an old, honorable family of slender means, the frail boy grew into a robust youth. At fourteen he was sent to the city of Salamanca to study grammar in a private home, in preparation for a career in law. But the youth was restless and often into mischief, finally choosing to seek his fortunes with the Spanish army at Naples. Subsequently he changed his mind, and, deciding there was more opportunity in the Spanish Indies, he prepared to sail with a large fleet. An amorous adventure frustrated his plans, however; he fell off a wall outside a bedroom and narrowly escaped death from a wrathful husband. Injured and ill, he missed the sailing. Later, when he did catch a ship to the New World, it was 1504, and Cortés was nineteen.

Benefiting from his acquaintance with the governor of Santo Domingo, Cortés received a job as notary and a grant of Indians to work for him. For five or six years his life was uneventful enough, aside from accompanying Diego Velázquez on an expedition to the interior of the island.

When Velázquez was sent to conquer Cuba in 1511, he asked Cortés to go along as clerk of the treasurer, and during the campaign the youthful Cortés demonstrated his abilities and resourcefulness. Velázquez, who subsequently became governor of the island, rewarded him with another grant of Indians, along with various positions of trust. Cortés settled in the first Spanish town in Cuba, Santiago de Baracoa, where he raised livestock. His Indians mined enough gold for him to enter into a trading partnership, and he looked forward to a promising career as a merchant. With an official position in local government, Cortés was a secure and respected member of the community. Had it not been for the indecision of the governor's nephew, Fernando Cortés would very likely have ended his days in obscurity.

As Cortés began recruiting men and acquiring ships and supplies for the expedition to Yucatán, Velázquez grew apprehensive about mounting expenses. Worse, the ambitious Cortés assumed pretentious airs, leading the governor to wonder if he could control the headstrong captain. When an agent of Velázquez sought to dissuade Cortés from accepting the command, Cortés quickly raised anchors in November 1518. In western

Cuba he gathered more supplies and was joined by many former companions of Grijalva. But a messenger from the governor ordered the expedition canceled; and, meanwhile, deputies of Velázquez were on their way to arrest Cortés.

Alerted to the danger, Cortés addressed his men, promised them riches and glory, and then prepared to sail immediately. At muster, he counted 550 men, perhaps a hundred of whom were sailors, along with several Cuban Indians and some blacks. The soldiers were divided into eleven companies, each with a captain, and put aboard eleven vessels. The flagship was only one hundred tons, and the other ships were even smaller. Sixteen scarce and expensive horses were put on board, as well as some small cannons. All of this had put Cortés heavily in debt, and there was no money to pay the men wages. But on February 18, 1519, they set sail as adventurers, to gamble on the potentially lucrative outcome.

The Initial Reception

After weathering stormy seas, the ships put in at the island of Cozumel, where friendly natives told them of two white men who lived in nearby Yucatán. Cortés made contact with one of them, Jerónimo de Aguilar, a survivor of a ship wrecked in 1511 en route from Panama to Santo Domingo. The other was thoroughly assimilated into Indian society, but Aguilar was overjoyed to be among his own again. His knowledge of the native language and local customs would be of great assistance to the Spaniards in the months ahead.

Later, at Potonchán (Tabasco), the local natives resisted Cortés's overtures for peace and attacked with abandon. After a bloody contest, Cortés took the city by force. In this and other fights the Spaniards suffered many wounded, but only two men were killed. The Indians, on the other hand, lost two hundred men and were convinced that the Spaniards were invincible. Little gold was found, but the natives said that people to the west had great amounts of it. After lecturing the Indians on their need for salvation through Christianity and describing the mag-

Fernando Cortés (1485–1547) dressed in the half armor used in battle. Full armor was not as heavy as one might think, but it did make the wearer very warm. Most Spaniards eventually adopted use of Indian layered-cotton protection.

Doña Marina, or Malinche, and other Indian girls are given to Cortés and his men in this romanticized version of a European artist.

nificence of the king of Spain, Cortés accepted a gift of twenty young maidens and continued up the Gulf coast.

Reaching San Juan de Ulúa, near the present city of Veracruz, the Spaniards met people who spoke a tongue foreign to Aguilar. However, one of Cortés's young maidens, baptized Marina, understood the language. Her role in the Conquest proved to be of great significance. Doña Marina, as she became known to her contemporaries (and Malinche to Mexicans, who consider her part in the Conquest as treasonous) became Cortés's interpreter and adviser. More than that, she was later his mistress and bore him a son. As a small child she had been given to merchants who sold her to people of the south, and consequently she knew not only her native Náhuatl but the Maya language as well. She communicated with the Indians, passed on the words in Maya to Aguilar, who then translated into Spanish for Cortés.

Realizing that the Indians would report to Moctezuma, Cortés had his men perform a mock battle to impress them. He then asked the local chief to send greetings to Moctezuma and to tell the Indian ruler that the Spaniards had a disease of the heart which could be cured only by gold. Tenochtitlán lay two hundred miles to the interior, but, by swift relay runners, reports of the Spaniards reached the Aztec capital in a day and a half. Pictures of the ships had been sent as soon as they were spotted, so the presence of Cortés was by this time no surprise to Moctezuma. The cautious emperor, fearful that Quetzalcóatl, or his emissaries, had returned to take the throne, now gave careful thought to his next move. For the moment, he sent word that he rejoiced in the coming of the strangers. He sent rich presents and promised to send more; however, he was unable to meet with Cortés because he was ill and could not make the long journey. Moreover, it was out of the question for Cortés to come to see him because the trip through rugged mountains and deserts was too rigorous. Beyond these hardships, the Spaniards would have to pass through dangerous enemy territories. In this fashion Moctezuma wished Cortés well, as if to dismiss him—all of which disheartened the Spanish captain not one bit. He replied by message that he would not think of missing the opportunity of greeting the great Lord of Culhúa after traveling across a great sea and suffering privations that were surely worse than the ones ahead. Anyway, he had an important message from his king and had no choice but to deliver it in person.

Meanwhile, Cortés was well aware of the tenuous legal position in which he found himself. Spaniards were not allowed to go off exploring on their own, but only with royal permission. The administration in Santo Domingo had authorized Governor Velázquez to send out an expedition, but Cortés had ignored the revocation of the governor's commission to him. He was, therefore, something of an outlaw, and dangerously close to treason. Consequently, he sought to clothe his actions with a veneer of legality, gambling that all would be forgiven in the event of a glorious conquest.

With that in mind, he founded a settlement called La Villa Rica de la Vera Cruz (today Veracruz), according to established ceremony, in the king's name, with the procedure duly noted by witnesses. Cortés appointed town councilmen and other appropriate municipal officials and resigned his leadership. The officials of Veracruz then proceeded to elect him captain and *justicia mayor* with authority in military matters, pending royal orders to the contrary.

In order to gain the loyalty and affection of his men, Cortés turned over to them all the supplies and equipment, which, he said, had put him seven thousand ducats in debt. He already had enemies among the troops, especially those adherents of Governor Velázquez, but by this magnanimous, if calculated, gesture he gained considerable goodwill. In keeping with the generosity of the moment, the men agreed that, after the king's share of 20 percent—the *quinto*—was deducted, their captain would receive one-fifth of the remaining spoils.

The Totonacs and a Mutiny Suppressed

Pushing on to the Totonac city of Cempoala, the Spaniards were enthusiastically greeted by citizens bearing flowers and fruit. The obese ruler, who had sent regrets that he was too heavy to travel to meet them, complained of the Aztec tyranny and gave Cortés a detailed description of Tenochtitlán. He suggested an alliance of the Spaniards with the victims of the oppressors.

Shortly thereafter an incident occurred that illustrates the guile of the Spanish captain in his psychological warfare with the perplexed Moctezuma. The appearance of five Aztec tribute collectors threw fear into the fat *cacique* (chief), who thought they would resent his hospitality to the Spaniards. These imperious agents of Moctezuma ignored the presence of the Spaniards, reproached the cacique for receiving the strangers, and demanded twenty Totonacs for sacrifice in Tenochtitlán. On the side, Cortés told the terrified chief to seize the tribute collectors. When the Totonac leader protested that such an act was sure to bring harsh retribution from Tenochtitlán, Cortés explained that he would protect the Cempoalans should any trouble arise, but that trouble was unlikely, for Moctezuma was, in fact, his friend. And so the Aztec officials were arrested, roughed up when they resisted, and bound, unaware that this treatment had been ordered by the Spaniard. That night, in secrecy, Cortés released two of the Aztecs, posing as their friend. He gave them a message of good wishes for their emperor and repeated his urgent request for a meeting.

In the morning, when the Cempoalans discovered the escape of the tribute collectors, they were frightened and so sure of Aztec vengeance that they decided to rebel against Tenochtitlán. Cortés agreed to stand by them and told them to send word to potential allies to be prepared. Cortés then directed other Indian towns to stop tribute payments to the Aztecs. When an Aztec garrison punished some Cempoalans, Cortés destroyed it and

The frontispiece illustration of Cortés's Second Letter to Charles V, printed in Seville in 1522.

then released the captives in a gesture intended to impress both the coastal Indians and Tenochtitlán.

His army strengthened by the arrival of a ship from Cuba bearing sixty Spaniards and nine horses, Cortés made plans to press inland. In order to maintain a coastal base, a fortress and houses were built at Veracruz, to be staffed by the ill, wounded, and older men. Cortés wrote the king, telling of his progress to date, assuring him of his devotion, and sending most of the treasure accumulated to that point. He added that he needed help, and he requested financial assistance. The town council wrote another letter to the king, asking that the election of Cortés be confirmed. A ship with the letters, treasure, and two delegates sailed for Spain in late July 1519.

Anticipating the dangers and hardships that lay ahead, some men, especially the followers of Velázquez, plotted mutiny. Their intention was to steal a ship and inform the governor of events so that he could seize the vessel dispatched to Spain. Cortés learned of the conspiracy, and, after a trial and confessions, he hanged two of the leaders and sentenced the pilot to have his feet cut off, while the others were given two hundred lashes. Minor participants, including a priest, were released unpunished.

The companions of Cortés were not soldiers but soldiers-of-fortune, and only firm leadership based on respect (and fear) could maintain discipline. As weaker Spanish captains discovered, such men were prone to mutiny under stressful conditions. Cortés was both intelligent and tactful, but his great authority stemmed most of all from his own fearlessness; he was in the front ranks of battle, and he shared with his men all the fatigues, privations, wounds, fevers, and narrow escapes from death and sacrifice. He was fearless in taking decisive action as well.

Now determined to drive to the highlands as soon as possible, Cortés arranged to give the weakhearted no alternative and the disloyal no opportunity to desert. Alleging the unseaworthiness of the ships, he instructed loyal pilots to strip the vessels and then scuttle them as quietly and quickly as possible. When the men, encamped inland at Cempoala, learned what had happened, they were shocked and angry. According to some versions, the men were told that one ship had been saved to take back to Cuba any who wished to go; then, taking careful note of those who indicated they would be on the vessel, Cortés had the ship sunk. His audacity brought the army close to mutiny, and some no doubt questioned his sanity; but by this bold stroke he cut off all means of retreat. There was now no question of the Spaniards' course—they would have to conquer the mighty Culhúa-Mexica or die in the attempt. So Cortés led his men into the heart of the Aztec empire, on one of the greatest epic adventures of all times.

The Tlaxcalans and Reports to Moctezuma

Moctezuma's depiction of the hardships before the Spaniards was only slightly exaggerated, for the march upcountry would take them some two hundred miles, on a rough and twisting path, from the steamy tropics to the chilling highlands, where they would find the Aztec capital at seventy-five hundred feet. Aside from the wild terrain, there was indeed danger from enemies—both those hostile to the Aztecs and those who acted under the orders of the wily emperor himself.

Leaving 150 men and two horses at Veracruz, Cortés returned to Cempoala with fresh assurances of friendship. He accepted some Indian nobles as hostages and a thousand carriers to bear supplies. The Spaniards departed the city in the middle of August with four hundred troops, the remaining horses, and three cannons. As they pushed inland they were well received by towns subject to Moctezuma, for the emperor had ordered them to be friendly. Cortés sent some of the Cempoalans ahead to make amicable contact with the Tlaxcalans, known to be dedicated enemies of the Aztecs. But the Tlaxcalans, aware of the communications between Cortés and Moctezuma, were suspicious. An advance party of Spaniards ran into a small band of Tlaxcalans, who closed with them and killed two horses. Although finally routed, these few warriors dramatically showed the ferocity and skill that, when they shifted sides, would give the Spaniards a crucial edge. For the moment, the skirmish was considered most unfortunate, for until that time no horse had been killed. The word now spread that the beasts were mortal, a loss of great psychological advantage for the invaders.

While Cortés was trying to win over the Tlaxcalans, noble envoys from Moctezuma arrived to reaffirm the emperor's friendship and willingness to pay a yearly tribute to the king of Spain, provided Cortés halted his ascent to the interior. Cortés thanked the envoys for their concern for his safety and urged them to observe how he would deal with the Tlaxcalans. Moctezuma remained fearful and perplexed as to the best way to treat with the strangers, for he was unsure of not only who but what they were. Hoping to appease the white men, who appeared to be some kind of invincible deities, the Aztec emperor ordered his agents to sacrifice captives whose blood the "gods" might wish to drink; but when the Spaniards reacted with revulsion, Moctezuma was reminded that Quetzalcóatl, too, abhorred human sacrifice.

The European animals with Cortés were terrifying to the natives. Indians could only equate horses with deer, but later descriptions graphically depicted creatures of a more fearful aspect, as beasts who snorted and bellowed and sweated heavily, whose muzzles spilled over with foam. Their running produced tremors, "as if stones were raining on the earth." Although Cortés seems to have utilized war dogs very little in battle, these animals, sometimes trained to kill Indians, accompanied the Spaniards. The very appearance of the swift greyhounds and huge mastiffs, which weighed as much as two hundred pounds, intimidated the natives, one of whom recorded that

> their dogs are enormous, with flat ears and long, dangling tongues. The color of their eyes is a burning yellow; their eyes flash fire and shoot off sparks. Their bellies are hollow, their flanks long and narrow. They are tireless and very powerful. They bound here and there, panting, with their tongues hanging out. And they are spotted, like an ocelot. . . . They raised their muzzles high; they lifted their muzzles to the wind. They raced on before with saliva dripping from their jaws.[3]

In order to frighten Moctezuma's messengers further, on one occasion Cortés tied them down and fired one of the guns, at which the Indians were deafened and fainted dead away.

Receiving descriptions of all these strange and unnerving things, the emperor ordered his magicians and warlocks to work their magic on the Spaniards, to send an evil wind their way. He called for more human sacrifices to the gods. And finally, when these strategies failed to halt the Spaniards' advance, he commanded his people to give the strangers whatever they desired. But Moctezuma was surrounded by warriors who counseled resistance, and the emperor had not ruled out force.

Seeing large numbers of Indians as they proceeded, the Spaniards themselves grew apprehensive about their situation. A potential mutiny was averted by a stirring speech from Cortés. Then came the cheering news that Xicoténcatl, the commander of the Tlaxcalan forces, had decided to deliver his people to the Spanish camp. He agreed to be an ally, after which he listened while Cortés scolded him for not accepting his initial offers of peace and chided him for attempts at deception. Cortés could never resist an opportunity to lecture.

The Cholula Massacre

Moctezuma, who had been kept abreast of these developments by his agents, now sent word requesting Cortés to travel to the city of Cholula to await his decision about a meeting. In fact, it seems

3. Miguel León-Portilla, ed., *The Broken Spears: The Aztec Account of the Conquest of Mexico,* trans. Lysander Kemp (Boston, 1972), pp. ix, 31, 41.

clear that he wanted the Spaniards away from the Tlaxcalans, who in turn warned Cortés of treachery. The lords of Cholula, at first reluctant to meet the Spanish captain, eventually appeared, pleading friendship and offering tribute. Cortés had their pledge interpreted and recorded by notaries and witnesses. His act was no mere formality, because if a people who had sworn fealty to the Spanish sovereign later rebelled, they could be dealt with as traitors. The inhabitants of the city turned out with great fanfare, showering food and flowers on the strangers and perfuming them with incense.

This pleasant interlude did not last long; shortly thereafter the Cholulans ignored their guests and brought no more provisions. Moctezuma had apparently determined to test at Cholula the belief of his militant advisers that the foreigners were simply men of flesh and blood. Secretly encamped in nearby ravines were thirty thousand warriors, and the Cholulans were to bottle up the Spaniards in the city.

Cortés's suspicions were confirmed by Cempoalans, who had noted fortifications and covered pits in the streets, evidently for the entrapment of horses. Then Doña Marina was informed by a friendly Cholulan woman of a plot. Summoned by a ruse to Cortés's quarters, nobles of the city, who had planned in such secrecy, were astonished when the Spanish captain angrily told them that he knew of their treachery. The nobles confessed, swearing that they acted under orders from Moctezuma. Cortés dispatched a message to the Aztec ambassadors, saying that he did not believe this story of the "lying" Cholulans, as he was sure that a great ruler like Moctezuma would never be party to such duplicity. Cortés then ordered the summary execution of some of the nobles as an object lesson.

The Spanish captain now moved to a preemptive strike; he gave a prearranged signal to his men, who were poised for the attack, and the guns raked the main plaza, cutting down the unsuspecting citizens. Cortés gave orders to spare women and children, but in the ensuing five-hour battle some six thousand Cholulan warriors were killed. Much of the ancient holy city was burned and then put to the sack by the Spaniards' Indian allies, who richly savored the defeat of their old enemies.

The massacre at Cholula was a turning point, for Moctezuma, stunned at the Spaniards' prescience, now despaired of stopping them, although more halfhearted attempts would be made. The tragedy of that day is the blackest mark against Cortés in the minds of most Mexicans, who believe that, without provocation,

The Cholula Massacre as depicted by a sixteenth-century Indian artist in
the Lienzo de Tlaxcala.

he planned the slaughter. As with so many other events of the
Conquest, it is difficult to ascertain the whole truth of the affair,
especially since there are few Aztec sources.

Into the Valley of Anáhuac

Cheered by the utter defeat of the first Aztec allies with whom he
fought, Cortés now summoned the ambassadors of Tenochtitlán
and sternly informed them that, while he had wished to enter
the imperial capital in peace, Moctezuma seemed determined to
have the Christians killed. Therefore, matters were on a footing
of war. Again the emissaries begged Cortés not to be angry but
to await another message. Tenochtitlán lay only about sixty
miles distant, but it took six days for word to come, along with

the usual gifts. The emperor denied any part of the Cholula conspiracy and, finally, invited Cortés to an audience. Pleased that he would not have to fight his way into the capital, the Spanish commander and his men made their way toward the Valley, observed by incredulous natives, one of whom later preserved the striking impression made by the aliens.

> They came in battle array, as conquerors, and the dust rose in whirlwinds on the roads, their spears glinted in the sun, and their pennons fluttered like bats. They made a loud clamor as they marched, for their coats of mail and their weapons clashed and rattled. Some of them were dressed in glistening iron from head to foot; they terrified everyone who saw them.[4]

The Spaniards climbed to the snowy pass between the spectacular volcanic peaks of Popocatépetl and Iztaccíhuatl. As they began the descent into the Valley, they saw laid out in the distance before them the grand prospect of the lake cities. In that breathless moment, viewing one of the most awe-inspiring sights man has ever seen, the soldiers had mixed emotions—a tense excitement from the drama of the occasion and all that it promised but also a chilling realization of the audacity of their scheme, the dimensions of which were now for the first time abundantly clear. Cortés went among the men, optimistically soothing their fears. But as they neared the heart of the Aztec empire none was

ROUTE OF CORTÉS

4. Ibid., p. 41.

more alive to the peril than the captain. He spread the rumor to impress the Indians that the Spaniards did not sleep at night or even remove their armor. The horses were kept saddled.

As the army moved toward the lake, an embassy of prominent lords, including the young Cacama, lord of Texcoco, approached to escort the Spaniards, expressing Moctezuma's regrets that he was unable to be there because of illness. The test of wills was not quite over; the lords insisted that Cortés give up, a suggestion that must have become tiresome to the Spanish leader by that point.

Cacama repeated that the Spaniards' way would be resisted and blocked, a threat that now rang hollow. Aside from the botched attempt at Cholula, there had been no serious military opposition on the part of the Aztecs. Since Moctezuma could quickly raise large armies in various parts of the empire, doubtless the Aztecs could have stopped the intruders on the beach, in the mountain passes, or other places suitable for ambush. But there had been the lingering fear that they were divine agents of Quetzalcóatl, a sentiment that Cortés did nothing to dispel. Had a large Aztec army confronted the Spaniards, Moctezuma would be held responsible; and therefore if the strangers were actually gods, as it appeared, the emperor would feel their wrath. Thus he resorted to deception, which could always be denied. Finally, however, the fatalistic emperor was demoralized and resigned to facing Cortés.

Indians of the Valley flocked to observe the entrance of the newcomers, who descended on Ixtapalapa, which anchored the longest causeway. From that beautiful city the Spaniards could look straight down the thoroughfare to where the red and white towers of Tenochtitlán rose out of the water and the torches of the temples shimmered on the lake. Proceeding down the causeway, the Spanish force of about four hundred, with their six thousand native allies, moved through throngs of the curious who lined the way with their canoes. At length the party crossed a drawbridge that gave access to the city, and there, under a canopy of green, gold, and silver, and attended by a splendid retinue, was the lord of the Aztec empire. Moctezuma leaned on the arms of two nephews. Clothed in gorgeous finery, the fifty-two-year-old emperor was of dignified mien, slender, of average height, with longish hair and a very sparse moustache and chin whiskers. As he walked forward, servants placed mantles on the ground so that the royal sandals did not touch the earth. Following him was a magnificent procession of two hundred courtiers.

For his part, Moctezuma must have been struck by the exotic appearance of the white captain, dressed in shiny armor and bright European fabrics and mounted on his war horse. As Cortés dismounted and strode forth to embrace Moctezuma, the nobles restrained him, signifying that the emperor's person was not to be touched. Instead, the leaders saluted each other, obeisance was made all around, and the two exchanged necklaces: the European piece of pearls and diamonds for the Aztec chain hung with several large golden shrimps. Then Moctezuma addressed the Spaniard, greeting him as Quetzalcóatl and welcoming him back to his throne. The "gods" were then domiciled in the palace of Axayácatl. It was November 8, 1519, and, by incredible good fortune, the Spaniards had made it safely into the stronghold of the Culhúa-Mexica.

Recommended for Further Study

Bancroft, Hubert H. *History of Mexico*. 6 vols. San Francisco: A. L. Bancroft, 1883.

Bishko, Charles Julian. "The Iberian Background of Latin American History: Recent Progress and Continuing Problems." *Hispanic American Historical Review* 36 (1956): 50–80.

Chaison, Joanne Danaher. "Mysterious Malinche: A Case of Mistaken Identity." *The Americas* 32 (1976): 514–23.

Collis, Maurice. *Cortés and Montezuma*. London: Faber and Faber, 1954.

Cortés, Hernán. *Hernán Cortés: Letters from Mexico*. Translated and edited by A. R. Pagden, with an introduction by J. H. Elliott. New York: Orion Press, 1971.

Davies, R. Trevor. *The Golden Century of Spain, 1501–1621*. New York: Harper & Row, 1961.

Díaz del Castillo, Bernal. *The True History of the Conquest of New Spain, 1517–1521*. Translated by A. P. Maudslay, with an introduction by Irving Leonard. New York: Farrar, Straus and Giroux, 1966.

Elliot, John H. *Imperial Spain, 1469–1716*. New York: St. Martin's Press, 1962.

Hassig, Ross. *Aztec Warfare: Imperial Expansion and Political Control*. Norman: University of Oklahoma Press, 1988.

Iglesia, Ramón. *Columbus, Cortés and Other Essays*. Translated and edited by Lesley B. Simpson. Berkeley: University of California Press, 1969.

Johnson, Harold R., ed. *From Reconquest to Empire: The Iberian Background to Latin American History*. New York: Knopf, 1970.

Kirkpatrick, F. A. *The Spanish Conquistadores*. New York: World, 1962.

León-Portilla, Miguel, ed. *The Broken Spears: The Aztec Account of the Conquest of Mexico*. Translated by Lysander Kemp. Boston: Beacon Press, 1972.

López de Gómara, Francisco. *Cortés: The Life of the Conqueror by His*

Secretary. Translated and edited by Lesley B. Simpson. Berkeley: University of California Press, 1964.

Lynch, John. *Spain Under the Habsburgs*. Vol. 1: *Empire and Absolutism, 1576–1598*. Vol. 2: *Spain and America, 1598–1700*. New York: Oxford University Press, 1964, 1969.

Merriman, Roger B. *The Rise of the Spanish Empire in the Old World and the New*. 4 vols. New York: Cooper Square Publishers, 1962.

Parry, John H. *The Age of Reconnaissance*. Cleveland: World, 1963.

Pike, Ruth. "Seville in the Sixteenth Century." *Hispanic American Historical Review* 41 (1961): 1–30.

7

The Fall of Tenochtitlán

The Spaniards spent several days wandering about the city, taking in the marvelous sights, much like any tourists in a foreign land. They admired the palaces with their cedar-lined chambers, the gardens, and the canals. Other scenes had quite the opposite effect: they were aghast at the great rack festooned with human skulls; and the priests, their long hair matted with dried blood, were repulsive to them. The visitors were properly fascinated by the zoo, as Bernal Díaz del Castillo noted, but, as for "the infernal noise when the lions and tigers roared, and the jackals and foxes howled, and the serpents hissed, it was horrible to listen to and it seemed like a hell."[1]

A Test of Wills

Moctezuma and his nobles visited their guests' quarters often to provide for all their needs. This attention and gracious hospitality notwithstanding, the peril of the situation was not lost on Cortés, who perceived with the greatest clarity that they were in fact trapped—if Moctezuma chose to make it so. Outside their luxurious palace the Spaniards were surrounded by a multitude of Indians who could rise on signal to ensnare them. The Spanish soldiers manifested their anxiety to Cortés, who now resolved on a bold and desperate course—he would seize as hostage Moctezuma himself.

1. Bernal Díaz del Castillo, *The True History of the Conquest of New Spain, 1517–1521*, trans. A. P. Maudslay, introd. Irving Leonard (New York, 1966), p. 213.

After the Tlaxcalan allies confirmed that the Aztecs were indeed planning to kill the Spaniards, Cortés found a convenient pretext: some of his men at the Spanish garrison at Veracruz had been killed, and Cortés accused Moctezuma of ordering their deaths and, worse, of preparing to massacre the Spaniards in Tenochtitlán. Despite the emperor's vehement denials, Cortés courteously but firmly told Moctezuma that he must remain in custody. The emperor would continue to rule his people and would be treated with the greatest respect. Meantime he was to counsel calm and patience among his people, because any outbreak of hostilities would result in his death.

This turn of events was inconceivable to the dignified lord of the Aztecs, who protested that his subjects would never suffer such an outrage, but he finally submitted. To check the rising anger among his people, Moctezuma announced that he was not a prisoner; rather, he resided with the strangers at his pleasure, because it was the will of the gods. Though kept under guard, Moctezuma was treated with kindness. His servants, women, and advisers were free to visit him, and he was allowed to leave his chambers to worship at the great temple. Cortés even gave him permission to go hunting with his own people, with the understanding that the Spanish guards would kill him if he attempted to bolt. The emperor, however, seemed strangely resigned to remaining with his captors. To a greater extent than previous rulers, he was an intellectual, like his grandfather, Nezahualcóyotl. He was a man of sentiment and reason, both of which Cortés played on with consummate skill. Woe to the Spaniards if they had arrived a few years earlier, during the reign of Ahuítzotl!

The general populace of Tenochtitlán abided by the ruler's wish for peace out of respect for his exalted rank, but some of the leaders did so only grudgingly. They were incensed at Cortés's demands that human sacrifice cease and pagan idols be smashed, to be replaced by crosses and images of the Virgin Mary.

Acts of Moctezuma attributed to pusillanimity may in fact have stemmed merely from his acceptance of a prophecy come true. If the gods had allowed this to happen, it was foolish, if not wrong, to resist. Other Aztecs, however, less devout and tradition bound, remained skeptical of the divine attributes of the strangers. The Spaniards remained about six months before the Aztecs reacted strongly. Outraged at the desecration of their religion, the priests roused the populace and joined the warriors in calling for an attack. Moctezuma advised Cortés, with the greatest urgency, to leave the city.

The Spanish captain agreed to depart whenever Moctezuma wished. The relieved ruler promised more gold and added that there was no great hurry in leaving. But even as the interpreter was translating the first words of the conversation, Cortés dispatched one of his men to alert the Spaniards to stand by. He told Moctezuma that, since his ships had been destroyed, he would need others to carry them away, and he requested Indian carpenters to help build them. At the same time, he instructed his own carpenters to stall for time and to stay alert. Cortés, of course, had no intention of departing.

However, this abrupt change in the state of affairs altered Cortés's plans to bring more men from the Caribbean in order to complete his take-over of Mexico and to introduce clergymen to effect the mass conversion of the Indians to Christianity. Under the ominous circumstances, the Spaniards nervously bided their time, planning and praying for a miracle. They did not get one, but a diversion of serious import did arise to break the tense atmosphere. Moctezuma asked to see Cortés, and the Spaniard, bearing in mind their recent meeting, feared the worst. Before leaving, he addressed his men, exhorting them to fight bravely, to commend themselves to God, and to die with dignity if this were to be the final act. But what Cortés learned from the emperor was news of a very different sort. The pleased ruler told Cortés that the Spaniards could leave immediately—a fleet of eleven ships, bearing nine hundred men, stood off the shore at Veracruz.

The Narváez Expedition

In Cuba, Diego Velázquez seethed with anger against Cortés and grew more bitter with news of his protégé's success. To Velázquez, Cortés's deeds represented a blatant act of rebellion. The governor's hand was strengthened, however, when the king, in ignorance of the Cortés venture, appointed Velázquez governor of whatever territories he could control in "Yucatán." Armed with this extended jurisdiction, Velázquez assembled a large force to pursue the rebel captain and arrest him. Under the command of Pánfilo de Narváez, the expedition included not only a very sizable complement of foot soldiers but also eighty horses.

Making port at Veracruz, Narváez ordered two soldiers and a priest to the garrison, now under the command of the capable Gonzalo de Sandoval, to demand submission. Sandoval arrested the three of them and sent them off·to Cortés. Narváez then landed his troops and proceeded instead to Cempoala, where the Totonacs, assuming the newcomers to be associates of Cortés, lavished gifts and provisions on them. Narváez insinuated himself into the good graces of the Cempoalans, convincing them that Cortés and his men were traitors and adding that he intended to behead Cortés and send his men back to Cuba. He confided similar tidings to the agents of Moctezuma, with the assurances that, after Cortés was taken, all Spaniards would leave the country and the emperor would again rule as before. Moctezuma, unknown to Cortés, responded with presents and encouragement to Narváez. But the emperor was no fool; in actuality, he was exploiting the quarrel between the two Spanish forces. For the first time since the strangers arrived, the hapless ruler found himself in a favorable position, and now he was playing both sides against the middle. With good fortune, the white men might kill each other off.

On first learning of the large Spanish expedition on the coast, Cortés had a sense of foreboding—it was an army roughly twice as large as his own. If they were friends, he would have the strength necessary to take Mexico, but if, as he suspected, they were from Velázquez, his prospects were in the most serious jeopardy. After learning of Narváez's intent, Cortés sent his agents with gifts and instructions to inquire if Narváez had a commission from the king. Cortés would obey any royal orders, but if there were none, then he considered himself the authority in the land. In any case, he suggested a peaceful meeting to work out some compromise. But Narváez, believing he held the whip hand with his superior forces, was not disposed to parley.

Cortés mustered his men and told them that Narváez and his men had dishonored them by insults and were trying to steal what they had won with their sweat and blood. The captain selected some volunteers to accompany him to Veracruz and asked Moctezuma to assure the safety of the Spaniards left behind. The emperor agreed, offering the use of Aztec warriors to Cortés. Leaving Pedro de Alvarado in command of about 140 men in the city, Cortés departed for the coast with the same number. In Cholula he was joined by 120 of his men who had been settling a town on the lower Gulf coast.

In a rapid march Cortés soon put his men on the outskirts of

A crossbow with windlass of the type used in the Conquest. Because of its devastating force, popes forbade its use against Christians; but it was used very effectively in wars against Moslems and natives of the New World.

A wheel-lock pistol of the sixteenth century. This one belonged to Charles V.

Cempoala, arriving under cover of darkness. He attacked suddenly, at midnight during a driving rainstorm, and in the confusion and darkness he gained the advantage. It appears that many of the newcomers were less than anxious to resist Cortés, and, in fact, some of the key people may well have been suborned. After a frenzied skirmish Narváez took a pike in the eye and surrendered.

The swift and decisive action of Cortés, which saw the ignominious rout of a much larger force, served to enhance his prestige among the Indians as well as with the men of Narváez. A diplomat of genius, Cortés now showed generosity to the defeated soldiers, most of whom he had known in Cuba. They were eager enough to join him when they were promised their share of the spoils. With his ranks now swelled and sanguine of the outcome, the captain was ready to seize the land. But as he set out for the return to Tenochtitlán, a battered messenger brought news of disaster—the Aztecs had risen up, and Alvarado and his companions were pinned down in their quarters.

The Spaniards Besieged and the Sad Night

The nobles of Tenochtitlán had received from Alvarado permission to celebrate their most important fiesta, that of Toxcatl, in honor of Huitzilopochtli. The Spaniard agreed to the singing and dancing, but there was to be no human sacrifice. There are conflicting versions of the tragedy that subsequently occurred. We assume, in any event, that the reduced Spanish garrison was edgy, especially since Narváez had sent provocative messages to the Aztecs, inciting them to rebel against the men of Cortés. Whatever the results of the confrontation at Veracruz, the Indians were presented with a tempting opportunity, as Cortés was absent and so few Spaniards were left in the city.

According to Alvarado, he was informed that the ceremonial dance to the war god was a prelude to an attack on the Spaniards, who were to be sacrificed. Therefore he determined to strike first. Others have maintained that he was moved by bloodlust, or that he simply overreacted to rumors without basis in fact. Whatever the truth, during the festivities the Spaniards blocked the four exits from the square, drew their swords, and rushed the celebrants. There followed a wild and bloody scene in which the Indians, caught unprepared and without escape, had little chance. In a short time some two hundred Aztec nobles fell under Spanish steel. After the Spaniards retreated to their quarters they were besieged by thousands of grief-stricken and enraged Indians.

Cortés, fearing the worst, made forced marches to the Valley in order to lift the siege. Approaching Tenochtitlán, he found a strangely silent city, showing little sign of activity. He fired a cannon and was heartened to hear a return boom. Later he learned that only the influence of Moctezuma had saved the defenders in the palace of Axayácatl. Oddly enough, the entrance of Cortés was unopposed. The Aztecs observing the return of Cortés saw a much larger force, consisting of about one thousand soldiers and one hundred cavalrymen. Counting those already in the city, Cortés now commanded an army about three times larger than his original force. Although he gained the palace without difficulty, it soon became clear that the Aztecs had simply allowed him to walk into a trap.

The Spaniards preferred fighting in wide open spaces where they could deploy their guns to advantage and charge their horses into enemy ranks. Confined in the city, hemmed in by buildings that afforded protection to the Indians, they were less effective. The Aztecs made repeated assaults on the Spanish position, finally resorting to what resembled suicide squads. The cannons put shot into them at close range, while the harquebuses, falconets, and crossbows took a frightful toll—and still they came. Cortés led a counterattack, but the swath he cut was immediately filled in. As fresh relays of Aztecs rushed the Spaniards, the defenders grew weary.

The Spaniards then began building three tall wooden barricades, mounted on rollers. With this protection they hoped to move forward with less risk, but before the vehicles were finished the enemy attacked with such recklessness that Cortés persuaded Moctezuma, who was still held hostage, to urge the Aztecs to desist. The ruler mounted the rooftop to draw attention and began to speak. In the confusion of battle not everyone saw him, and so it was apparently by accident that one of the stones thrown by the Aztecs struck him in the temple. He died three days later.

This version of his death is best documented, although some charge that Moctezuma was strangled or stabbed to death on orders from Cortés. Because he was irresolute in dealing with the Spaniards, refusing to rally his people in opposition—eventually, in fact, appearing to favor the white men—Moctezuma is viewed in Mexican histories as less than heroic. The ruler was not a coward (his bravery had been tested on the field of battle), but his true sentiments and motives remain enigmatic. In a crisis that called for a leader of visceral instincts, Mexico was ruled by a man of deliberation.

As the Indians resumed the offensive, the Spaniards put their mobile barricades to the test. The vehicles were soon smashed, and the soldiers beat a hasty retreat. Thereafter things went badly for the Christians, for while they could make offensive thrusts, they could not sustain a retreat from the city, surrounded as they were by tens of thousands of their adversaries. With food and powder almost depleted and his men badly mauled from the fighting, Cortés sought to make a truce. But the Aztecs, although suffering heavy casualties, rejected the offer with shrill hoots and insults.

Cortés, seeing the Spanish position as untenable and deteriorating, decided to make a break for it that night. The chosen avenue for escape was the Tacuba causeway, which, though said to have been two miles long, was the shortest of them. The Aztecs had removed the bridges spanning the gaps in the causeways, so Cortés ordered the construction of a portable bridge, which was to be carried by forty Tlaxcalan warriors. The treasure acquired earlier from Moctezuma was divided, with each man allowed to take what he wished for his share. Some, especially those who had come with Narváez, foolishly weighted themselves down with precious metals and jewelry, which later hampered their movements and contributed to their capture or death.

Sandoval, who had returned to Tenochtitlán with Cortés, was put in charge of the lead columns, while Alvarado was given command of the rear guard. Cortés elected to lead a flying squad of one hundred men, ready to shift to any weak point. At midnight they stole quietly out of the palace, the horses' hooves wrapped in cloth to muffle their movements. A heavy fog and light rain helped obscure the figures but made the footing treacherous. It was early in the morning of July 1, 1520, the *Noche Triste*, or Sad Night, as it has come down in history.

Moving carefully over the causeway the Spaniards were able to place their bridge over the first channel and cross. Then suddenly an old woman drawing water from a canal spotted them and cried out. Sentries sounded the alarm with blasts on their conch shells, and the Aztecs came pouring out of the darkness. Thousands of warriors fell on the escapees, and some Spaniards in the rear were cut off and seized. Other Indians flanked the causeway in their canoes and shot into the mass. The Aztecs emitted their customary loud whoops, which, taken with the

The Spanish retreat from the island city of Tenochtitlán was a great Aztec victory.

clang of metal, cries of the wounded, and the thrashings of horses, set up a din that made for utter chaos. The Spanish formations broke as each man tried to save himself.

With great effort the bridge was thrown across the second breach, and Cortés and four other horsemen galloped across, followed by a hundred scrambling foot soldiers. Under such strain the bridge collapsed, throwing into confusion and panic those who followed. Cortés and his cohorts raced for the mainland, forced to swim the remaining breaks in the causeway. Placing the hundred foot soldiers to hold the end of the avenue, Cortés and the other horsemen wheeled and spurred back to the melee. The unit in gravest danger was the rear guard, for it was taking the brunt of the Aztec charge. Alvarado, seeing his men overwhelmed, called to Cortés for help. Alvarado's mare had fallen under him, and he now stumbled over the masses of the dead choking the breaches and crossed on the bodies. As the enemy closed, Alvarado, who was a powerful athlete, sprinted toward the last open channel, placed the point of his lance, and, according to some contemporary accounts, made a tremendous vault that carried him over to safety. Some of his companions who attempted the same feat fell short and drowned in the dark waters.

In that terrifying night, the most drastic reversal of Spanish arms in the conquests of the New World, at least 450 of Cortés's men died[2] and more than four thousand of the steadfast Indian allies fell. Forty-six of the horses lay sprawled along the littered causeway. The survivors gained the mainland where, according to tradition, Fernando Cortés was so moved by the disaster that he sat under a great tree and wept.

The Spaniards Regroup

Because of their catastrophic defeat at Tenochtitlán, the Spaniards were uncertain of their reception from the various Indian groups that had previously sworn them allegiance. As the Spaniards neared Tlaxcalan territory, however, they were greeted by lords from Tlaxcala and Huejotzingo who offered consolation and warriors. Had it not been for these allies Cortés and his men would have been lost.

It required all of Cortés's force of personality and subtle blandishments to prevent mass defections and rebellion among his men. Cortés, who seems never to have wavered in his determination to retake Tenochtitlán, began to lay plans for the return. He conceived an ingenious plan for securing the island city: he would assault it by water as well as by land. To that end he set carpenters to work constructing launches in sections, which could be carried across the mountains by native porters and assembled on the lake shore. The vessels would be fitted for both sails and oars. Events proved this strategy to be an inspiration of tactical brilliance.

Following the victory in Tenochtitlán, the elated Aztecs raised to the throne a nephew of Moctezuma, Cuitláhuac, lord of Ixtapalapa. With the Aztecs now geared for total war and with no moderate voice at their court, the next confrontation with the Spaniards would be much different. Certain of the earlier advantages were now lost to the white men. The Indians knew that the strangers were not deities—they had slain them, sacrificed them to their gods, and even tasted of their flesh. Nor did the horses inspire the same terror; it was futile to attempt outrunning them, but they bled, too, and the Indians learned that they could be hamstrung. This time there would be no slick diplomacy on either side, no intrigue, no pleasant embassies pleading friendship and exchanging gifts. Now the mutual hatred was exposed, with each

2. Bernal Díaz del Castillo, who was present, wrote that on the Sad Night and in the next five days, during which the Aztecs pursued them, over 860 Spaniards died. Ibid., p. 321.

Cuauhtémoc (1502?–1525), the last Aztec emperor, as he appeared to a post-Conquest artist.

side bent on the destruction of the other. All things considered, it appeared that the Aztecs had gained the advantage.

But the Spaniards had a silent, deadly, and totally unexpected ally in the land: one of Narváez's men came to Mexico infected with smallpox, which spread quickly with devastating consequences to the Indians. Tens of thousands were carried off by the disease. It was, some Spaniards noted with satisfaction, only just, for the Indians had introduced them to syphilis.[3] The pox was contracted by Emperor Cuitláhuac within a short time, and when he succumbed, the lords chose the last Aztec ruler. He was the eighteen-year-old Cuauhtémoc, another nephew of Moctezuma. Cuauhtémoc has become a symbol of valor, the cultural hero of Indian Mexico. In the view of most Mexicans, he came to power two years too late.

The Final Assault

In late December 1520 the Spanish army crossed the mountains and re-entered the Valley of Anáhuac, opposed only by harassing feints of the Indians. Cortés made headquarters at Texcoco, where he found a calm reception. Waiting for the launches to be

3. Francisco López de Gómara, *Cortés: The Life of the Conqueror by His Secretary*, trans. and ed. Lesley B. Simpson (Berkeley, 1964), p. 205.

completed in Tlaxcala, Cortés set out to isolate the island city of Tenochtitlán by winning over the surrounding population with diplomacy or force. Both tactics were used with considerable success.

Sandoval proceeded to Tlaxcala to escort the launches. Sections of the thirteen vessels were carried over the mountains by eight thousand porters, while another two thousand bore provisions. The long procession, stretching out almost six miles, arrived at the Spanish camp at Texcoco after a four-day journey, without grave incident. By failing to attack the vulnerable column, the Aztecs lost the opportunity to destroy the cutting edge of the Spanish offense.

Ready at last to launch the invasion, Cortés reviewed his forces, now augmented by the arrival of additional adventurers from the Caribbean. He counted 900 Spaniards, of whom 86 had horses, 118 carried crossbows and harquebuses, and all were armed with swords and daggers. Some wielded pikes and halberds, most had shields, and many wore some form of protective armor. There were fifteen bronze cannons and three heavy guns of cast iron. Supporting the Spaniards were native legions numbering some hundred thousand warriors.

The small Spanish fleet was crucial to their strategy, for if the causeways could be commanded, all transportation and communication to the island could be cut off. Moreover, the Aztecs could be prevented from attacking the Spaniards from their canoes. Each launch had about a dozen men manning the oars, and other Spaniards aboard were armed with crossbows and additional weapons. Cortés chose to command the fleet in person. Those fighting on land were assigned to three commanders, each of whom was to secure a causeway, and on May 10, 1521, they moved to occupy their positions.

On the lake Cortés first overpowered a fortified rocky isle, at which smoke signals went up from various positions to alert Tenochtitlán. Five hundred Aztec canoes appeared before the Spanish vessels, but they stopped just short of harquebus range, as the Indians contented themselves with hurling insults at the Spaniards. Then, suddenly, a stiff breeze came up and caught the sails, and Cortés bore down on the canoes with such speed that many were swamped and crushed. Some Aztecs escaped to the city, but a large number were captured. The rout was important: it demonstrated that the canoes were no match for the launches, which gave the attackers control over the lake. Spanish boats penetrated canals on the edges of the city, after which the attack-

An Aztec Jaguar Knight dressed for battle, wearing a pelt and wielding an obsidian-edged war club.

A mounted Spaniard in full armor.

ers set fire to many houses. With the success of the operation on water, Alvarado and Cristóbal de Olid charged down the causeways to engage the defenders of the barricades and bridges.

The Spaniards' early optimism proved unjustified. Furious fighting continued for weeks, for although the attackers were able to penetrate sections of the city, they could not easily hold positions. They were assailed by warriors who rained arrows and stones on them from the flat rooftops while others engaged them in hand-to-hand combat. The advantages of horse and cannon were greatly reduced in the close street fighting. Cortés concluded, to his regret, that he must level the city. Accordingly, his men began the systematic destruction of the great temples and palaces that afforded his adversaries protection.

Early on, the aqueducts had been cut, and the launches swept the lake to prevent water, food, and reinforcements from reaching the besieged defenders. Still, in the face of heavy casualties, illness, and a lack of food and drinking water, the Aztecs held out, resigned to the warrior's death. Attempts to effect a truce failed. Finally, in a last concerted offensive, the Spaniards and their native allies overran the Aztec position. In the savage finale Cortés and Alvarado backed the survivors to the wall, and it was all over. Tenochtitlán fell on August 13, 1521.

Cuauhtémoc had escaped in a large canoe, but he was captured on the lake. He was taken to Cortés, who treated the ruler with courtesy. Cuauhtémoc then touched the dagger in Cortés's belt and spoke: "I have done everything in my power to defend myself and my people, and everything that it was my duty to do, to avoid the pass in which I now find myself. You may do with me whatever you wish, so kill me, for that will be best."[4]

When the tumult subsided and the dust settled, there remained a scene of desolation: the beautiful metropolis effectively smashed, the gardens flattened, and the canals filled with rubble. The destruction of one of history's grandest cities was accompanied by great heroism and suffering on both sides. Aside from their superior weapons and armor, the Spaniards derived great advantage from their horses, the spread of smallpox, and a favorable psychological atmosphere. They benefited, moreover, from their practical application of a strategy that ignored the ceremonial formalities inherent in Aztec warfare.

Brilliant as it was in certain respects, Aztec civilization thrived on militarism; therefore, the character of its fall was consistent with its rise. And it was poetically apt that its last great warrior-

4. Quoted in ibid., p. 292.

king was Cuauhtémoc, whose name translates "Falling Eagle" or, in another sense, "Setting Sun."

Recommended for Further Study

Cerwin, Herbert, *Bernal Díaz, Historian of the Conquest*. Norman: University of Oklahoma Press, 1963.

Chance, John K. *Conquest of the Sierra: Spaniards and Indians in Colonial Oaxaca*. Norman: University of Oklahoma Press, 1989.

Denhardt, Robert M. "The Equine Strategy of Cortés." *Hispanic American Historical Review* 18 (1938): 550–55.

———. "The Truth about Cortés's Horses." *Hispanic American Historical Review* 17 (1937): 525–32.

Gardiner, C. Harvey. *The Constant Captain: Gonzalo de Sandoval*. Carbondale: Southern Illinois University Press, 1961.

———. *Martin López, Conquistador Citizen of Mexico*. Lexington: University Press of Kentucky, 1958.

———. *Naval Power in the Conquest of Mexico*. Austin: University of Texas Press, 1956.

Gosner, Kevin. "Caciques and Conversion: Juan Atonal and the Struggle for Legitimacy in Post-Conquest Chiapas." *The Americas* 2 (1992): 115–30.

Graham, R. B. Cunninghame. *The Horses of the Conquest*. London: Heinemann, 1930.

Kelly, John E. *Pedro de Alvarado, Conquistador*. Princeton, N.J.: Princeton University Press, 1932.

MacNutt, F. A. *Fernando Cortés and the Conquest of Mexico, 1485–1547*. New York: Putnam, 1909.

Madariaga, Salvador. *Hernán Cortés, Conqueror of Mexico*. Chicago: Regnery, 1955.

Megged, Amos. "Accommodation and Resistance of Elites in Transition: The Case of Chiapa in Early Colonial Mesoamerica." *Hispanic American Historical Review* 3 (1991): 477–500.

Padden, Robert C. *The Hummingbird and the Hawk: Conquest and Sovereignty in the Valley of Mexico, 1503–1541*. New York: Harper & Row, 1970.

Prescott, William H. *History of the Conquest of Mexico*. New York: Bantam Books, 1967. There are many other editions.

Scholes, France V. "The Last Days of Gonzalo de Sandoval, Conquistador of New Spain." In *Homenaje a Don José María de la Peña y Cámara*, pp. 181–200. Madrid: Ediciones José Porrúa Turanzas, 1969.

Vigil, Ralph H. "A Reappraisal of the Expedition of Pánfilo de Narváez to Mexico in 1520." *Revista de Historia de América* 77–78 (1974): 101–25.

Wagner, Henry R. *The Rise of Fernando Cortés*. Los Angeles: Cortés Society, 1944.

White, Jon Manchip. *Cortés and the Downfall of the Aztec Empire*. New York: St. Martin's Press, 1971.

8

The Settlement of New Spain

The conquerors withdrew to nearby Coyoacán, leaving the Aztecs to remove their dead. The Spaniards decided to build a new city over the ruins of Tenochtitlán, and soon armies of native laborers under the direction of Spanish architects and artisans laid the foundations for the splendid city of Mexico. It would be the capital of New Spain, by which name the country would be officially known for the next three centuries.

The Encomienda System

The Conquest had been the result of a great effort by individual adventurers who received no pay for their work. Many had gone into debt in order to outfit themselves for the enterprise; all had suffered great hardships and had seen companions die horrible deaths; almost all had been wounded. Those who survived thanked God and prepared to enjoy the fruits of victory. But the treasure for which they had endured so much proved to be a pittance. Some of the survivors of the Noche Triste had escaped with a few valuable objects, but the bulk of the riches had been lost in the lake waters.[1] Of the spoils, a horseman received as his share only about a hundred gold pesos, one-fifth of the cost of a horse. Foot soldiers, who constituted the bulk of the army, received even less. As the mood of his companions grew more ugly,

1. In 1981, several feet underground in Mexico City a crude gold bar was found. Quite possibly it was dropped on the retreat.

Cortés relented and allowed the torture of Cuauhtémoc and other lords, hoping thereby to learn the location of any remaining hoard of riches. The royal feet of the nobles were oiled and held over fire. Despite their agonies, they gave no information, for there was no cache—or at least none has ever been found.

One of Cortés's first concerns was to secure the tribute rolls of the Aztec treasurer, which contained paintings identifying the subject towns along with the kinds and amounts of tribute paid to Tenochtitlán. There were 370 such towns, each having yielded to the Aztec emperor one-third of its production. Thus the Spanish captain acquired knowledge of the population, the geography, and the economy—not to mention the tribute that the conquerors could now enjoy. In order to calm his irate soldiers, Cortés agreed, with some misgivings, to distribute the Indian towns to them as rewards.

There was a precedent for this practice; in the Caribbean Islands, Spaniards had been granted native villages for their profit. As originally conceived, this system, the *encomienda*, was seen as the best solution for all concerned. The individual deserving Spaniard (the *encomendero*) received the tribute of the Indians, as well as their free labor, in return for which the natives were commended to the encomendero's care. He was to see to their conversion to Christianity, to ensure good order in the village, and in all ways to be responsible for their welfare. It was hoped that by this system the Indians would be more easily acculturated, better controlled, and protected. What happened in practice was quite another matter, as the system, subjected to every imaginable abuse, kept the Indians in a state of serfdom and led to all sorts of horrors. Indians were overworked, separated from their families, cheated, and physically maltreated. The encomienda in early decades was responsible for demeaning the native race and creating economic and social tragedies that persisted in one guise or another into modern times.

The tremendous loss of Indian lives, attributable at least in part to this system, was a grim warning against awarding encomiendas in other lands. Moreover, the Spanish crown wanted the tribute for itself and thus sought to maintain direct control over the Indians to retain them as royal vassals. The thought of the conquered multitudes being subject to the whims of the conquerors was unsettling to the sovereign. Yet the crown could not —or would not—compensate those who had won extensive territories and millions of people for Spain. And so the king grudg-

An early map of "Temixtitan" (Tenochtitlán). Probably drawn at the request of Cortés, it appeared in the Latin edition of his Second Letter,
printed in Nuremburg in 1524. In order to ingratiate himself, Cortés wrote
five long letters to the king in which he related the progress of the Conquest.

ingly allowed the awarding of encomiendas for New Spain.
Nonetheless, he was never at ease with the arrangement and
from the first sought the means to bring all Indian towns under
royal control. The struggle between the crown and the individuals who held encomiendas was a dominant theme for much of
the sixteenth century.

The Spread of Conquest

Even before the fall of Tenochtitlán, Cortés had sent small parties to explore the land's resources. They returned with informa-

tion on sources of gold and silver and reported on the location of natural ports and timber for the construction of ships. Once he had secured the Valley, Cortés lost no time in dispatching expeditions in all directions to bring under Spanish control other inhabitants in the country. He was impelled to do so for various reasons: to gather more information about the people and the land, to satisfy a consuming interest in the existence of a strait through the continent to Asia, and to dominate as much territory as possible before rivals staked their claims. His time was short, for the crown had ordered an agent to take over the government and to arrest him. By August 1521 Cristóbal de Tapia had arrived, but he was intimidated by partisans of Cortés and withdrew. The conqueror meanwhile sent the king word of his defeat of the Aztecs, after which Cortés was forgiven his insubordination.

During the course of the next several years Spanish forces under many different lieutenants overran Mexico, parts of Central America, and much of what is now the southwestern United States. And although the Conquest of the Mexica-Aztecs had taken a relatively short time, the Spaniards soon discovered that bringing under their sway the entire land was a vastly more difficult enterprise.

Highly centralized states strongly dependent on a dominant capital are vulnerable, tending to disintegrate quickly when the center falls. Hence the collapse of the imperial capital of Tenochtitlán was tantamount to the surrender of almost all towns under the city's control, and, therefore, much of central Mexico automatically fell to the invaders. There were many other areas of Mexico, however, that had remained outside the Aztec pale. Some threw in with the Spaniards early, and some came around as the Spaniards gained in reputation. But others, which had successfully resisted the Aztecs, rejected Spanish overlordship as well. While none could command forces comparable to those of the Aztecs, their more fragmented political structure made conquest difficult. Fighting the loosely organized tribes of Mexico presented the same frustrations and vexing problems that confront those dealing with guerrilla tactics in modern warfare.

Cortés was eager to plant settlements with a view to legitimizing his actions. In 1521 he sent Gonzalo de Sandoval to Coatzacoalcos (later called Puerto México but now known also by its Indian name) to settle that region and establish better communications with the islands. The same year Luis Marín departed for Oaxaca, where he encountered little success in his attempt to pacify the Zapotecs in hill country. He was more fortunate far-

A Lacandón Indian by an altar at Bonampak. Now almost extinct, the Lacandones resisted Christian domination with great tenacity and ferocity.

ther south in Chiapas, remaining until 1524 to establish a town; but in 1527, the Chiapanecos rebelled, and the territory had to be reconquered by Diego de Mazariegos.

The governor of Jamaica, Francisco de Garay, had earlier been granted a royal commission to govern the Pánuco region north of Veracruz on the Gulf coast. Hoping to prevent what they considered an incursion, Cortés and Alvarado used force and diplomacy to convince Garay to withdraw. Meanwhile Cristóbal de Olid, one of Cortés's closest friends and confidants, was sent to western Mexico in 1522. After a cordial reception in Michoacán, he explored the Pacific coast, but in Colima he was stiffly opposed and forced to pull back.

Aware that expeditions from Panama were pushing northward up into Central America, Cortés moved to seize control first. Rumors circulated of cities rivaling Tenochtitlán in size and wealth, and in late 1523 Alvarado was ordered into the old Maya territory of Guatemala. After some arduous campaigns, he drove into El Salvador and conquered that region as well. For Alvarado's brilliant, though sanguinary, accomplishments, a grateful Spanish king appointed him governor and captain general of the lands he had won.

Shortly after Alvarado's departure from Mexico, Olid set sail

PRINCIPAL EXPLORATIONS AND CONQUESTS IN THE SIXTEENTH CENTURY

The flamboyant Pedro de Alvarado (1485–1541), Cortés's lieutenant and the conqueror of Guatemala.

to secure Honduras, stopping by Cuba for provisions. At this point Olid threw off loyalty to his captain and made common cause with the enemy, Governor Velázquez. When Cortés learned that Honduras was to be taken in the name of Olid and Velázquez, he was furious. He dispatched a punitive expedition, then decided to go down himself. It was the most costly decision the conqueror ever made.

Departing Mexico with a party of Spaniards mostly mounted, along with many Indian allies, musicians, tumblers, acrobats, and some young Spanish noblemen, Cortés headed to the Gulf coast and then cut southward across unknown country. The journey took them through Tabasco, Campeche, and the base of Yucatán. Because they were not following native trade routes, they encountered few settlements and had to survive off the wilderness. Great numbers of the porters collapsed from exhaustion, and many of the horses perished also. Indians and Spaniards alike contracted fevers and dysentery, and all suffered from near

starvation. Though lacking the drama of the Aztec Conquest, the
Honduras march exceeded the earlier enterprise in sheer hard-
ship. For months the expedition cut its way through thick jun-
gles, waded in swamps, and crossed swollen rivers. Once, within
a distance of fifty miles, the Spaniards were forced to build fifty
bridges, one of which, by Cortés's account, required a thousand
trees. During this disastrous march a tragic episode occurred.
Cuauhtémoc and several other high Indian lords had been taken
along as hostages lest, in the absence of Cortés from Mexico, they
encourage a native rebellion. When they allegedly attempted to
foment an uprising among the Indians on the expedition, all, including Cuauhtémoc, were summarily tried and hanged.

At last Cortés and his men stumbled into Honduras, only to
find that all had been in vain, for the advance punitive party had
beheaded the rebel Olid and returned to Mexico. After spending
some time trying to establish a settlement in his name, the captain set about returning, this time wisely traveling by sea. The
nineteen-month venture was a remarkable achievement of exploration and endurance but a fiasco in all else.

Cortés Is Discredited

Before departing for Honduras, Cortés had entrusted the government to the hands of royal treasury officials, with Alonso de Estrada in charge. Estrada was an honorable judge, but he found it
difficult to govern the various factions that had formed, and he
finally lost control. Because the expedition to Honduras remained out of contact with civilization so long, the rumor spread
in Mexico that Cortés and the others had perished. Encouraged
by word of Cortés's death, various factions moved to dispossess
his followers of their encomiendas and other privileges, which
were then handed over to supporters of corrupt treasury officials.
It was a time of anarchy, as both Spaniards and Indians were
maltreated.

The usurping governors ordered funeral ceremonies for Cortés
and his men and then granted permission for the "widows" to
remarry. When one of the wives, Juana Ruiz de Marcilla, criticized the action and heaped scorn on the officials, she was given
one hundred lashes in public. Cortés later paid her great honors,
carrying her on his horse and addressing her as "Doña." Most
damaging for the captain (irreparably damaging, as it turned
out) were the accusations made against him in dispatches sent

to Spain, in which he was charged with having hidden Aztec treasure for himself, misusing crown funds, and cheating the royal treasury in other respects. The reports also cast doubt on his loyalty to the king. The dramatic news that Cortés was alive caused his men to rise up and seize the usurpers, who were thrown in cages and put on public display. Cortés's return to Mexico had a calming effect on political strife, but his reputation was not so easily restored.

The charges against the conqueror were never substantiated, but they planted seeds of suspicion, which were nourished by partisans of the treasury officials in Spain. Moreover, the allegations provided a convenient pretext for which the crown may well have been thankful. At precisely the time Cortés was campaigning against the Aztecs, Emperor Charles V, the king of Spain, faced a revolt of his nobles at home, and although he was able to prevail, he retained a distrust of the fractious Spanish nobility. Thus Charles viewed with some concern the concentration of so much prestige and power in the hands of a budding aristocracy in the New World, especially since these "nobles" were rough adventurers and far distant from his royal armies in Europe. Crown policy had been to ease explorers and conquerors from political power, but, for the sake of appearances, the crown sought pretexts to void earlier signed agreements. Hence, Columbus's maladministration of Española had given the crown an excuse to replace him. And now the accusations against Cortés would serve the same purpose.

Receiving word of the defeat of the Aztecs, the king had appointed the conqueror as governor and captain general of New Spain in 1522. As an administrator, Cortés demonstrated many attributes of a statesman and a responsible colonizer. In addition to moving energetically to explore the land and seek ports for further discoveries, he also began to develop the economy. He undertook the search for mines, introduced European plants and livestock, and promoted commerce. He issued intelligent ordinances for the good order of the colony, sought ecclesiastics and educators, promoted justice, and in most respects acted as an enlightened governor should. And while he probably commanded sufficient respect and fear among both Spaniards and Indians to seize the land as his own, the evidence is that he remained stoutly loyal to his sovereign. The king and his council could not, however, ignore the allegations made against the conqueror—after all, he had acted in a high-handed manner against Velázquez,

Charles V (1500–58), King of Spain and Holy Roman Emperor, reigned during the decades of the Spanish conquests of the New World.

Tapia, and Garay, and there were other disturbing incidents that left doubt as to his true character. His enemies had powerful support at court and gave advice prejudicial to Cortés. It would be best to suspend him, for the time being at least. Royal officials were sent to supplant Cortés's authority. Growing increasingly frustrated and disgusted, he resolved to lay his case before the king in person.

With a grand retinue of Indian nobles, exotic Mexican plants and animals, and rich gifts for Charles V, Cortés arrived in Spain in 1528. His entrance caused a great sensation, and he was received with considerable fanfare. Charles V, pleased with his gifts and charmed by the conqueror's gallant manner, was satisfied that most of the rumors of misconduct were false or exaggerated. He allowed Cortés to choose for his encomiendas twenty-two towns, and the captain proceeded to select some of the richest settlements in the land. He was granted twenty-three thousand Indians as his vassals, confirmed as captain general, and awarded the grand title of the marqués del Valle de Oaxaca.

Despite the king's generosity, however, Cortés was miffed; he had hoped to be made a duke. Moreover, although he was accorded wide privileges and powers within his private domains, he was not confirmed as governor of New Spain, and he took this slight as a special rebuke. Yet he might not have come off as well as he did had he not married (his first wife having died) the daughter of a count. She was also the niece of the duke of Béjar, whose influence on behalf of Cortés was helpful.

The Administration of New Spain

Prior to the settlement of Mexico there were few Spaniards in the Indies. The territories under Spanish control were small and required little attention from Spain. Ferdinand and Isabella appointed counselors for matters pertaining to the New World and turned their full attention to more pressing matters in Europe. In 1503, shortly before her death, Isabella created the Casa de Contratación, a house of trade to deal with affairs of the Indies, especially with regard to commerce, shipping, and emigration to the colonies. Juan Rodríguez de Fonseca, the bishop of Burgos, was given prime authority for making overseas policy.

The situation changed considerably, however, following the Conquest of Mexico, with its extensive lands and millions of people. Shortly thereafter Central America was penetrated, and early reports on Peru and other South American lands promised even more far-flung colonies. Affairs in the New World now clearly required a more broadly organized administration. Consequently, in 1524 Charles V created a supreme body called the Council of the Indies. This committee, composed of able, high-ranking Spaniards, would oversee all aspects of the colonies, both counseling the king and acting in his behalf.

Earlier, in 1511, there had been created in Santo Domingo a court of appeals so that matters of justice could be handled in the Indies instead of being referred to Spain. But the three judges of that body, called the *audiencia*, came to have broader duties. Traditionally, audiencias in Spain were courts of justice only, but in the New World they assumed executive and legislative functions as well. The judges (*oidores*) in Santo Domingo were the most powerful individuals in the Indies. With the lack of good government in New Spain, it was determined by the crown in 1527 that a similar court was needed in Mexico. Four experienced judges in Spain were appointed, but two died before taking office. The president of the audiencia was Nuño de Guzmán, a lawyer from a noble family with powerful connections.

Guzmán joined the two surviving judges in Mexico in early 1529. The rule of these three judges proved to be of the worst sort and a low point in the history of government in Spanish Mexico. As an adherent of Governor Velázquez of Cuba, Guzmán was a dedicated enemy of Cortés, and, with the conqueror absent in Spain, the audiencia moved against his followers. Once again their encomiendas were taken, and some were removed from offi-

Juan de Zumárraga (1468–1548), a Franciscan, was the first bishop and archbishop of Mexico.

cial positions. It was a time of graft, corruption, and injustice for Indians and Spaniards alike.

Meanwhile, a bishop, Juan de Zumárraga, had arrived in Mexico City. Although he bore the title "Protector of the Indians," the judges refused to recognize his authority and prevented the Indians from seeking help from him or any other clergyman. Angered by the chaos and iniquities engendered by the misrule, Zumárraga bravely preached a sermon condemning the oidores, which brought threats against his life. All correspondence critical of the government was intercepted before it reached Spain, until the bishop traveled to Veracruz and entrusted a letter to the crown to a faithful sailor who smuggled the message aboard a departing vessel. As it became clear to Guzmán that his days were numbered, and fearing imminent arrest by royal agents, he set off in late 1529 for the west of Mexico, hoping to regain the royal confidence by a spectacular conquest of new territories.

Guzmán invaded Michoacán with a large force of Spaniards and thousands of native auxiliaries. He cut a bloody path through the west, burning villages, murdering chiefs, enslaving the Indians, and abusing them in every manner. One of the most brutal incidents saw the Tarascan king dragged behind a horse until he was almost senseless and then burned alive. The soldiers pressed

north, lured by tales of a bountiful island ruled by attractive
amazons, tales fabricated by the natives to induce their tormentors to move on. Quite aside from his depredations, Guzmán explored and conquered a large area, all the way up to southern
Sonora. Altogether he founded five cities.

The extensive western region was isolated from central Mexico
and was later created as the separate administrative territory of
New Galicia, over which its conqueror was appointed governor.
But Guzmán's dark deeds caught up with him at length. After
his long odyssey, notable for its duration no less than its savagery,
Guzmán was ordered in 1533 to appear before a new audiencia to
answer charges. In 1538 he was sent to Spain, where he spent the
next two decades of his life as a virtual prisoner of the court.

While Guzmán was terrorizing the hinterlands of the west, the
southeast region of Yucatán, the areas first sighted in 1517 by
Spaniards from Cuba, remained outside Spanish control. Its conquest had been unsuccessfully attempted in 1527 by Francisco de
Montejo, an early companion of Cortés. The enterprise went
badly because of unfavorable terrain and a lack of local provisions, but mostly because of the indomitable spirit of the Maya.
In one lengthy battle they killed 150 Spaniards. Montejo, though
not without talent, was deficient as a leader of men, and he failed
to pacify the region of Yucatán and Tabasco. In 1536 he was
made governor of Honduras, only to be eased out of that position
by the redoubtable Pedro de Alvarado. After nine years of stalemate in Yucatán, the conquest was renewed in 1537, and Montejo's son and nephew, both of whom were also named Francisco,
brought most of the region under Spanish control by 1542, when
the city of Mérida was founded. In 1547 a serious insurrection
broke out, and many Spanish settlers were killed before calm was
restored. After two decades of conflict, the conquest of Yucatán
was finally effected, but at the cost of an estimated five hundred
Spanish lives.

After the fiasco of the first audiencia, the king and the Council
of the Indies were more circumspect in their choice of oidores.
They chose wisely in the appointment of Sebastián Ramírez de
Fuenleal, who had served as both president of the Audiencia of
Santo Domingo and bishop of that island. A man of highest integrity and proven abilities, he stood much in contrast to his
predecessor in Mexico. He was joined in Mexico City by fellow
judges of uniformly high quality, including Vasco de Quiroga,
who would distinguish himself later in other undertakings.
Within five years (1530–35) these learned magistrates wrought

significant changes in the troubled colony. Bringing to bear the full weight and authority of the crown and maintaining a busy schedule, they proceeded to correct many abuses. A semblance of good order was restored, and ordinances were passed to improve the conditions of the Indians.

Cortés, now more commonly known as "the Marqués," had meantime returned to the colony in mid-1530 to a grand reception by the populace, somewhat to the discomfiture of the judges of the audiencia. Sorely disappointed in being deprived of political power, he had to be satisfied with the limited title of captain general. Problems with the audiencia began when the oidores undertook to investigate the actual number of Cortés's tributaries; he probably had three times the twenty-three thousand he was allowed. To make matters worse, he was deprived of various properties and privileges. Cortés remained the most prestigious individual in New Spain, but in 1535 even that status was challenged with the arrival of a viceroy.

The king and Council of the Indies had decided by 1528 that New Spain needed a ruler who would personify the dignity and authority of the crown and offset the affection of the people for Cortés. Such a person would have to be a great nobleman, jealous of his honor and above staining his name with acts of avarice and injustice, one whose competence and loyalty to the king were beyond question. After all, he would literally be a "vice-king." Many—and no doubt Cortés himself—assumed that the conqueror of New Spain would be the obvious choice for the post of viceroy. But Cortés had neither the desirable lineage nor the administrative experience for the high honor. Furthermore the very qualities that brought him success as a conqueror—audacity, independence of thought, and imagination—were anathema to the centralized bureaucracy of an absolute monarch. And there were too many disturbing and unanswered questions about his past actions.

The first three noblemen offered the august appointment declined the honor. The fourth, Don Antonio de Mendoza, the count of Tendilla, accepted, and he proved to be an excellent choice. An able ambassador to Rome, Mendoza was scion of one of Spain's most distinguished families and related to the royal house itself. He received his commission as viceroy in 1530, but the press of personal affairs prevented his arrival in Mexico until 1535. The viceroy's charge was to observe all matters of consequence affecting the colony except judicial matters, which would continue as the province of the audiencia. He had special orders

Don Antonio de Mendoza (1492?–1552), served as first viceroy in New Spain, from 1535–50.

to increase crown revenues and to ensure good treatment of the Indians. He was also vice-patron of the Church and responsible for the defense of New Spain. Allowing the viceroy a good salary as well as perquisites that included a palace and a personal guard, the crown purposely sought to enhance the prestige of the office.

In Search of Fabled Cities

During the 1520s and 1530s many fantastic tales circulated about wondrous lands in the New World. Among the more intriguing was the so-called Northern Mystery, which embraced not only the persistent myth of the amazons but also stories of the Seven (Golden) Cities of Cíbola. Speculation about fabulously rich kingdoms in other parts of the New World was rife, and it is not strange that men were ready to believe them. Had not the first rumors of Tenochtitlán and the dazzling Inca empire (conquered in the early 1530s) appeared just as fanciful?

Pánfilo de Narváez, the one-eyed casualty of Veracruz, commanded a fleet to Florida in 1528, hoping to discover the fabled lands of Apalachee. After an overland expedition, Narváez failed to make contact with his supply ships, and he and his men tried to reach Mexico by sailing makeshift boats down the Gulf coast. Most of them perished, but a few made the Texas coastline. In the end only four survived: Alvar Núñez Cabeza de Vaca, two other

Spaniards, and Estéban, a black slave. For years they wandered among the Indians of the present-day Southwest of the United States, sometimes as slaves, sometimes as respected medicine men. In 1536, after many travails, they reached the northern Mexican outpost of Culiacán, where they were received with astonishment by their fellow countrymen.

Having spent so much time in the north, they were plied with questions about the Seven Cities, of which they had heard vaguely. That was enough to cause excitement, and prominent men scrambled for the privilege of undertaking the great search. The viceroy sensed an opportunity for an expedition that might overshadow the achievements of Cortés, and so of course he kept the rights for himself. But he took the precaution of sending an advance party, guided by Estéban and under the command of a Franciscan friar named Marcos de Niza. Pushing ahead of the main party, Estéban met an ironic end, for, having survived so long among the northern tribes, he apparently angered some Indians, who killed him.

Distraught by this news, Marcos de Niza proceeded with extreme caution. He seems to have viewed from a distance one of the Zuñi villages in New Mexico, which he later reported as being larger than Tenochtitlán. Moreover—so he said—local chiefs told him that the city he saw was the smallest of the seven. In kindness to the friar, it must be said that sometimes, toward sunset, the fading light in that part of the country casts a rosy glow, and there may have been pieces of reflective quartz stuck in the adobe walls of the two-story dwellings he saw from afar; and so it is possible that he imagined he saw something truly marvelous. In any case, the Spaniards in Mexico wanted to believe the existence of such cities, and preparations were eagerly made for the adventure. Those who had missed the earlier conquests would now have their chance.

Mendoza chose his friend, Francisco Vázquez de Coronado, the governor of New Galicia, to lead the well-equipped expedition. In 1540, 336 Spaniards, with hundreds of Indian allies and about a thousand horses and swine, moved out with high expectations. When they saw the mud village at the end of a grueling march they must have cursed Friar Marcos. Their anger abated somewhat, however, when Indians told them of "the Land of Quivira," some distance away but even more wonderful than the legendary cities of Cíbola. Their hopes raised, off they went.

The natives, aware that the Spaniards were interested primarily in gold, soon found that the best way to get rid of the unwel-

ROUTE OF CORONADO'S EXPEDITION, 1540–42

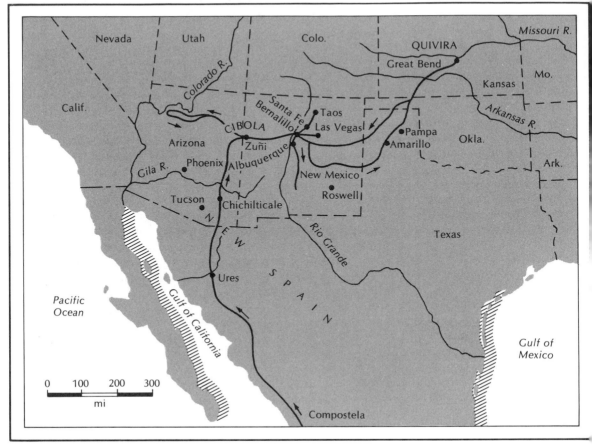

come intruders was to tell them that, while they had no wealth, there were abundant riches *más allá*—farther on. Because of such information the Spaniards wandered aimlessly for months, finally reaching the vicinity of Wichita, Kansas. Now greatly disheartened, having seen only squalid villages over a vast prairie, the miserable survivors dragged themselves back to Mexico. When they reached the capital in 1542 the viceroy, having not the slightest interest in their reports of the strange "shaggy cows" (buffaloes), refused to talk to his erstwhile friend Vázquez de Coronado. The captain had proved to be a less than ideal leader, but he was surely blameless for not discovering what was never there, in the land of más allá.

In 1542 a party commanded by Juan Rodríguez de Cabrillo sailed up along the beaches of California. The modern attractions of the area, however, had little appeal for the Spaniards, and they would not settle California for a very long time. That same year Mendoza dispatched Ruy López de Villalobos to the Philippines (named for prince Philip), but the expedition failed to return to Mexico.

The Vázquez de Coronado mission occasioned serious problems of another sort. When the expedition left western Mexico a good number of Spaniards who had settled New Galicia went along, leaving the frontier sparsely occupied by Christians and militarily weakened. Conscious of the situation, the Indians, who harbored resentments going back to the cruelty of Nuño de Guzmán, were roused by their priests to rebel. The ensuing Mixtón War (1540–41) was the most serious revolt prior to the struggle for Independence. The whole frontier was aflame. Natives attacked isolated Spanish ranches and then fortified themselves on well-stocked hilltops called *peñoles*, from which they could not be dislodged.

When the governor of New Galicia failed to subdue the rebels, he turned for assistance to Pedro de Alvarado, who had sailed up from Guatemala on his way to explore the Pacific. Courageous to a fault, Alvarado rashly ignored the advice to wait for reinforcements. A furious counterattack by the Indians produced a panicky Spanish retreat, during which a horse fell on Alvarado, crushing him. The great rebellion ended only after the viceroy himself took the field at the head of a strong army.

The Last Years of Cortés

Meanwhile Cortés, having been excluded from the search for the Northern Mystery and feeling insulted by his treatment from the viceroy and the audiencia, returned to Spain in 1540 to put his grievances once again before the king. Charles V was abroad, however, and crown representatives gave the Marqués a cool reception. The crisis of instability appeared to have been resolved in the colony, and with the royal bureaucracy entrenched and functioning well, government officials saw no need to humor the conqueror. Cortés volunteered his services for a Spanish expedition to Algeria in 1541, but his advice in military matters was ignored, and he became increasingly alienated. Beset by invidious rivals in Mexico and an indifferent sovereign in Spain, he spent his last years in frustration, then resignation. He was about to return to New Spain when, in 1547, he fell ill. Shortly thereafter, in his sixty-second year, he died in a village outside Seville. In 1556 his bones were deposited in Mexico, according to his wishes.

Though the last two decades of Cortés's life were fraught with disappointment, there is no greater example of rise to fame and fortune in the history of the New World. Through his diverse talents he gained immortality as one of the greatest military figures of the ages. He married into one of Spain's most noble families, was awarded a high title himself, and became one of the richest men in the Spanish empire. With all his defects (which were common to his time), Cortés was a captain who preferred diplomacy and persuasion to force. A disciplinarian who punished disloyalty with severity, he also, on many occasions, demonstrated compassion. He was the founder of Spanish civilization in Mexico and was clearly the most effective and capable person to establish the fledgling colony. But the defects remain. Three centuries after the Conquest of the Aztecs, when Mexico finally gained Independence from Spain, one of the first official acts of the new government called for the destruction of his bones. His remains were successfully hidden by the historian Lucas Alamán. Later in the nineteenth century his reputation was somewhat rehabilitated, but since the Revolution of 1910 his memory has been vilified. Revolutionary philosophy as conceived in the 1920s and 1930s was antiforeign and exalted native values. Thus, Cortés, the fair invader, the perpetrator of the Cholula massacre, the exterminator of Indian civilizations, the destroyer of Tenochtitlán, and the executioner of Cuauhtémoc, is viewed in Mexico in dark terms.

Stability under Viceroy Mendoza

Despite the reversals of the ill-fated Coronado expedition and the costly Mixtón War, by 1542 the colonial government was finally ready to achieve stability and order. There was good cause for optimism, for Mendoza was a firm and capable viceroy and the audiencia he worked with was responsible. Bishop Zumárraga was an energetic and positive complement to civil government. Yet there was brewing in Spain a reform movement that was destined to inflame passions once again. Bartolomé de Las Casas, a powerful Dominican friar and an indefatigable lobbyist on behalf of Indian liberties, had successfully convinced the crown to introduce legislation aimed at curtailing abuses of the natives, whose numbers had declined drastically. These New Laws of

1542–43 called for, among other things, the freedom of natives who had been unjustly enslaved and the easing of labor requirements. Most threatening from the standpoint of the Spanish conquerors, the laws eroded the encomienda system, for encomiendas awarded to conquerors and first settlers were to escheat to the crown on the death of the original encomendero. News of the provision caused a great outcry among the encomenderos, who remonstrated bitterly that they would have nothing to leave their children. Surely, they insisted, the king could not be so ungrateful to those who had won and settled lands larger than Spain itself.

The continuance of the encomienda system was regarded in Mexico, even by many royal officials, as vital to the maintenance of the colony's prosperity, for without it, it was feared, many Spaniards would leave. In fact, most ecclesiastics also favored its retention, seeing it as the best instrument for control of the Indians. Furthermore, tribute and labor helped support various charities, educational facilities, and religious institutions. The bishop himself held an encomienda. Many Spaniards agreed that natives under crown control were abused more by royal agents than by encomenderos. When an official investigator, Francisco Tello de Sandoval, was sent from Spain to help implement the New Laws, he found widespread opposition in the colony.

Tello de Sandoval and Viceroy Mendoza, assessing the situation and fearing a general revolt, exercised the prerogative of withholding the laws. Under the circumstances, they probably chose wisely: when the viceroy in Peru insisted on imposing the ordinances a serious insurrection ensued, which took his life and embroiled the colony in civil war for years. Finally giving way to the outraged encomenderos, the crown modified the laws in 1545 by removing the offending limitation to the encomiendas. For the moment, at least, the conquerors had won a victory.

Although the crown had retreated, it still intended to reform the encomienda system. In 1549 it ordered that encomenderos could no longer avail themselves of the free labor of their Indians but would have to be content with their tributes only. In the same year there was a flurry of excitement when a small group of Spaniards plotted to overthrow the government. But they were inept and persons of little consequence. They were tried, found guilty, and summarily hanged.

By 1550, as Mendoza's rule of nearly fifteen years came to a close, the colony was well implanted and thriving. In the crown's view Mendoza was the ideal administrator. His dreams of extending Spanish realms into rich areas (that did not exist) were unrealized, but his contributions in other respects were impressive. The part played by Mendoza was of crucial importance, because, as the first viceroy, he established patterns that would be followed by his successors. Although guilty of questionable profiteering and occasional lack of compassion, he was for the most part a wise, patient, and enlightened ruler. He left a flourishing economy and a capital that had already assumed the appearance of a beautiful city distinguished for its cultural life. He established order and stability; he founded schools, hospitals, and charitable foundations; he fostered religion and helped bring about a better measure of justice for all. Because of his government royal authority was firmly stamped on New Spain. The colony had survived the turbulent first three decades of its life.

Recommended for Further Study

Aiton, Arthur S. *Antonio de Mendoza, First Viceroy of New Spain*. Durham, N.C.: Duke University Press, 1927.

Bishop, Morris. *The Odyssey of Cabeza de Vaca*. New York: Century, 1933.

Blom, Frans. *The Conquest of Yucatan*. Boston: Houghton Mifflin, 1936.

Bolton, Herbert E. *Coronado: Knight of Pueblos and Plains*. Albuquerque: University of New Mexico Press, 1949.

Chamberlain, Robert S. *The Conquest and Colonization of Yucatán, 1517–1550*. Washington, D.C.: Carnegie Institute of Washington, 1948.

Chipman, Donald. *Nuño de Guzmán and Pánuco in New Spain, 1518–1533*. Glendale, Calif.: Clark, 1966.

Clendinnen, Inga. *Ambivalent Conquests: Maya and Spaniard in Yucatán, 1517–1570*. Cambridge: Cambridge University Press, 1987.

Hallenbeck, Cleve. *Alvar Núñez Cabeza de Vaca: The Journey and Route of the First European to Cross the Continent of North America, 1534–1536*. Glendale, Calif.: Clark, 1940.

Hirschberg, Julia. "Social Experiment in New Spain: A Prosopographical Study of the Early Settlement at Puebla de los Angeles, 1531–1534." *Hispanic American Historical Review* 59 (1979): 1–33.

Holmes, Maurice G. *From New Spain by Sea to the Californias, 1519–1668*. Glendale, Calif.: Clark, 1963.

Jones, Grant D. *Maya Resistance to Spanish Rule: Time and History on a Colonial Frontier*. Albuquerque: University of New Mexico Press, 1989.

Wagner, Henry R. *Spanish Voyages to the Northwest Coast of America in the Sixteenth Century*. San Francisco: California Historical Society, 1929.

Warren, J. Benedict. *The Conquest of Michoacán: The Spanish Domination of the Tarascan Kingdom in Western Mexico, 1521–1530*. Norman: University of Oklahoma Press, 1985.

III THE COLONY
OF NEW SPAIN

9

The Imperial System Entrenched

The Political Administration of New Spain

"Do little and do it slowly" had been Viceroy Mendoza's stated philosophy of administration. It was an attitude less than acceptable to reformers but consistent with royal wishes. The sixteenth-century viceroys, facing many crucial situations, were allowed considerable latitude, but their successors in the seventeenth century were reined in. Later kings and their councils increasingly gathered authority to themselves, discouraging the viceroys and audiencias from independence of thought and action.

Yet given the difficulty of communication and the time lapse between a request for instructions and the response from Spain, a certain amount of autonomy was implicit. Correspondence between colonial officials and the crown was necessarily slow, because for most of the colonial period ships sailed only once a year between Mexico and Spain. It was common for authorities in New Spain to wait many months, and even longer, for guidance. Consequently high officials often made important rulings on their own, pending royal approval. When a crown order seemed contrary to the best interests of the local situation, a viceroy sometimes noted, in all deference, *Obedezco pero no cumplo* (I obey but do not execute). The process of government was further bogged down by the endless detailed reports, requiring action, sent to Spain by officials, clergymen, and private subjects.

Colonial policy of the Hapsburgs (that is, up to the eighteenth century, when the new Bourbon dynasty instituted administrative reforms) was ponderous and inefficient. But sluggish as the

bureaucracy was, the crown concerned itself less with competence than with loyalty. The preoccupation with conformance
and fidelity manifested itself in the system of checks and bal-
ances. Officials were encouraged to comment on and criticize the
performance of others. The viceroy was the most powerful individual, but as the judges of the audiencia reported directly to the
king and the Council of the Indies and were often at odds with
the viceroy, they were a restraint on the viceroy's actions. Moreover, treasury officials and various other bureaucrats, as well as
clergymen, members of town councils, and private individuals,
contributed their complaints, and as a result, the crown was exposed to a wide spectrum of opinion on the operation of colonial
administration.

In order to ascertain the true state of affairs, the crown occasionally sent a royal inspector (*visitador*) to make an on-the-spot
investigation (*visita*). The crown visitador had great authority:
on arrival, he usually assumed rule of the colony for the tenure
of his inspection, which could take weeks or months. The visita
was sometimes undertaken in response to a specific set of charges
emanating from the colony, but in other instances it was more
routine in nature. In some instances the visitador traveled in-
cognito, taking officials by surprise, before adequate cover-ups
could be arranged. At other times the imminent arrival of the
inspector became known in time for precautionary measures on
the part of local officials.

Visitadores, usually men trained in the law, were responsible
for correcting abuses and instituting reforms. Moreover, their
charges included judging the performance of the viceroy and
other high functionaries. Such a judicial review, or trial, was
known as a (*juicio de*) *residencia*, so called because the official
being reviewed was required to remain in residence during the
trial. A residencia usually came at the end of an official's term of
office, although in the case of those who served for many years, a
review was sometimes taken periodically. Notice of an impending
review was made public, so that all within the official's jurisdiction with grievances could bring charges.

The admirable institutions of the visita and the residencia were
models that might well profit all governments. Unfortunately,
like so much in Spanish administration, there existed a wide
breach between theory and practice. Witnesses were sometimes
bribed or intimidated; perjury and obfuscation were common;
and judges were occasionally bought. Furthermore, despite the
long lists of allegations posted—and testimony that often con-

vincingly established the official's guilt—relatively few were punished in accordance with their crimes. Many of the higher functionaries were of the Spanish nobility, and the crown was reluctant to punish them with any severity.

Various restrictions were imposed on officials with a view to averting corruption. They were forbidden to hold encomiendas or to participate in commercial activities. They were to be circumspect in their social behavior and were to pick their company with care to avoid appearances of favoritism. In order to obviate conflicts of interest, they could not marry women from their jurisdictions without prior royal approval. In other ways, too, there were genuine attempts, at least on paper, to ensure honest government. Needless to say, the infractions were numerous, although certainly one finds many officials of integrity and humanity who died poor and were often unjustly treated for their honest attempts at good government.

Of the sixty-two viceroys who served in New Spain, almost all came from the high nobility and were born in Spain. Men born in the New World could attain this highest office (Mexico had three in the seventeenth century), but as sons of high nobles serving as viceroys themselves, they were not identified as locals. Most viceroys proved reasonably good rulers; a few were truly outstanding. The colony was fortunate that the first two viceroys, Mendoza (1535–50) and Luis de Velasco (1550–64), were wise

Luis de Velasco I (1511–64), the second viceroy of New Spain, served until his death. He continued the prudent policies established by his predecessor Mendoza.

administrators who set New Spain on firm footing. Mendoza was a superb politician who carefully played off troublesome factions to achieve order. Velasco abolished Indian slavery and in other ways was so instrumental in easing the sufferings of the natives that he is remembered as "the Father of the Indians." These first two viceroys served many years, but there was no specified term for a viceroy, and most remained in office for shorter periods. The quality of the viceroys declined in the seventeenth century, but the following century saw the emergence of some great talent in the office. Not surprisingly, the abilities of the viceroys rose and fell with the quality of Spanish monarchs.

It is more difficult to assess the character of the oidores of the audiencias. As the functions of the courts expanded, more judges were added. With the settlement of western lands, a new audiencia, that of Nueva Galicia, was created in 1548. It usually had four or five oidores, while the Audiencia of Mexico counted ten by late eighteenth century, plus other lawyers. Consequently, during the colonial era a great many judges served, and since so few have been studied in any detail, one cannot confidently offer judgments on them as a whole. One has the impression, however, that despite many individual cases of corruption, the majority of the oidores were dedicated servants of the crown.

The same cannot be said for the provincial officials. As new territories were colonized and towns founded, it became impossible to govern outlying provinces from the capital. Subdivisions of administration were, therefore, formalized, and many smaller administrative districts were created within the audiencia jurisdictions. Such districts were administered by officials known variously as *corregidores*, *alcaldes mayores*, or *gobernadores*, whose territories of jurisdiction were called *corregimientos*, *alcaldías mayores*, or *gobiernos*. There was little difference among the duties of these officials, and a brief discussion of the position of corregidor serves, in essence, to describe the others as well. Corregidores were responsible for the good order of their districts, but their judicial and legislative responsibilities were limited, as they were subject to higher authorities in all matters. In the early years of the system these positions often went to conquerors or their sons, or other early settlers, as a form of pension in lieu of encomiendas. As can be imagined, most appointees had little or no training for administrative posts, with the result that the office was held in low esteem and was rewarded with a correspondingly low salary. It came to be accepted that these provincial officials would supplement their salaries where they could—

which usually meant cheating the natives or other lower-class groups. Gradually more qualified individuals often lawyers, from Spain took over, yet corregidores continued to be notorious as the crown agents who most abused the trust placed in them.

Least enlightened were those with the designation of *corregidor de indios*, whose responsibility it was to administer Indian towns. The natives had been gathered into new villages to facilitate their conversion and acculturation, and the corregidor de indios was charged with the good order of those under his jurisdiction, in those towns paying tribute to the crown rather than to individual encomenderos. These Spanish supervisors, or their agents, collected the king's tributes in the "crown towns" and supposedly guaranteed justice. In fact, they were the greatest enemies of the Indians, defrauding them in a variety of ways, often in collusion with the native chiefs.

Distinct from the royal authorities were those in municipal government. Beginning with the founding of Veracruz in 1519 by Cortés, as Spanish towns were established a town council was immediately formed. In the earliest years Cortés simply appointed many local administrators, but it became customary for them to be elected annually. The municipal council, called the *cabildo* (or *ayuntamiento*), consisted of members known as *regidores*. These councilmen numbered anywhere from four or five in smaller communities up to fifteen in late colonial Mexico City. A council usually had two senior officials, called *alcaldes ordinarios*, who had some judicial powers and more importance than the regidores, who were simply councilors.

The cabildos were responsible for such purely local matters as defending the town, keeping the peace, controlling prices, allocating lots, cleaning streets, and seeing to drainage, water supplies, public food, and a multitude of other concerns. Generally speaking, the cabildos of the various towns represented the interests of the local colonists, which were frequently in conflict with the wishes of the crown. But, with a corregidor close at hand, the pervasive royal influence was felt.

Although in early decades there was something of a democratic character to the cabildos, the crown took away even that small concession to popular representation. When Philip II became king in 1556, he inherited heavy debts from his father, and one of the ways in which he attempted to raise funds was through the sale of offices. Positions in the cabildos were awarded to the highest bidders, even though consideration was supposed to be given to those with the best credentials. Such posts were cherished because of the distinction they offered in the community, not to mention the opportunities for making profits on the side. The result was that membership in the cabildos came under the control of certain families, who held proprietary interest in them for generations. Since the seats were often sold in perpetuity, they were passed on from father to son. By the late colonial period fifteen regidores in Mexico City owned their positions.

It has sometimes been suggested that the cabildos were fairly representative because they were composed, by and large, of criollos, or Mexican-born Spaniards. Criollos on the cabildos, however, were from the leading families who controlled local affairs, and their rulings reflected the interest of the colonial elite. In addition, because the seats were so often inherited, or purchased by incompetents, the cabildos were frequently staffed by those who gave poor leadership and bungling administration. Administration of Indian towns was modeled after that of the Spanish communities, with regidores almost always chosen from among the Indian aristocracy. In practice, very strong influence was exerted by local clergymen or Spanish officials, whose wills were executed by the Indian leaders.

Disturbances during the "Colonial Siesta"

By the middle of the sixteenth century the Spanish imperial system was established, and the bureaucracy took control with a firm grip and imposed a good measure of order. Still, it is somewhat misleading to conclude that for the next two and a half centuries little of consequence disturbed the colony. Inevitably, from time to time, there were serious challenges to the authorities of New Spain. And although the decades of the seventeenth century, in particular, were calm, they were hardly the "colonial siesta" so often portrayed. There was very considerable expansion of settled territories, and a number of disorders afflicted the land.

One of the most dramatic episodes occurred in the 1560s, when the simmering feud between the encomenderos and the crown boiled over. Charles V had yielded after the fiery reactions to the New Laws, and in 1555 he extended encomiendas to a "third life"—that is, to the grandsons of the conquerors as well as to the sons. But by the early 1560s, when Philip II reigned, most of the conquistadores were aged or dead. It seemed safe enough to move against their less belligerent sons.

In contrast to their fathers, the first generation of Mexican-born Spaniards, the criollos, inherited status and incomes that made their lives comfortable. They were on the whole an amiable group, much given to the pursuits of the idle class. Underneath their insouciance, however, they were troubled, because their privileged positions were by no means secure. When rumors reached them in 1562 that the encomiendas were not, after all, to pass on to their heirs, their emotions ran from outrage to despair. Without a powerful leader their cause seemed lost. They were, therefore, elated to learn that the son of Cortés, the second marqués del Valle, was returning to Mexico. Fresh from the court of Philip II, the worldly young criollo, himself the greatest of encomenderos, was their natural leader. Or at least so they thought.

Don Martín Cortés, the only legitimate son of the conqueror and his heir, is a curious figure in Mexican history. Born probably in Cuernavaca in 1532, he was taken as a young boy to the royal court, where he was treated with all the respect and consideration due a child of high nobility. He became one of the favorites of Prince Philip, who later included him in his entourage. When at length Martín Cortés wished to return to the land of his birth, King Philip II generously confirmed—with some modifications—the rights and privileges previously conceded to Fernando Cortés.

Rich, educated, and famous, Don Martín at thirty was ambitious and haughty but not without charm. Yet he had inherited few of his father's good qualities and so posed no apparent threat to the crown. His own estates secured in perpetuity,[1] Martín Cortés could have lived out his life in honor and splendor. Instead, his pretentious manner was offensive to many, including the good Viceroy Velasco. Don Martín had his own seal with a crown on it (though, in modesty, the seal was somewhat smaller than the king's); he was preceded by a lance page when he went out on horseback; and, not content with being a marqués, he styled himself a duke.

The resident leader of the young criollos in Mexico City had been Alonso de Avila, the wealthy son of a prominent conqueror. He and his companions, anticipating the eventual losses of their encomiendas, talked loosely of assassinating the oidores and other high officials, throwing off allegiance to the crown, and making Martín Cortés king of Mexico. They claimed 120 followers. Mar-

1. The only other perpetual encomiendas conceded by the crown were those belonging to two daughters of Moctezuma.

tín's role in all this is not entirely clear—he seems to have done little to discourage the plotters from putting a crown on his head without, however, having the audacity to pledge himself to the cause. His temporizing combined with the bumblings of Avila to abort the conspiracy.

In a series of fascinating intrigues the patient and scheming judges of the audiencia strengthened their case against the rebels, who appeared to have abandoned whatever plans they had. Then, in one of the most poignant scenes ever enacted in the colonial capital, the elegant and popular young Alonso de Avila knelt before the headsman's axe in horror and disbelief. His decapitation was followed by that of his brother. The heads of both were exhibited on pikes as grisly reminders of the penalty for treason against the king. The citizens of the capital, believing that the criollo brothers and their friends had been merely foolish, were stunned.

The chastened Martín Cortés escaped with his life, thanks to his high station, but the severity with which many others were punished shocked the community and intimidated the criollo encomenderos. The Avila affair was their last convincing show of force, and its tragic result signaled the end of Conquest society. The age of heroes was past, and the time of the lawyers had arrived. Spanish attitudes were about to change even more: the year Fernando Cortés died Cervantes was born, and this genius of Spanish letters would ridicule the conceits so common to those who conquered the New World. Most of the sons of the conquerors were now in middle age, and they confined future actions to litigation through proper channels. They fed on the accomplishments of their fathers, seeking consideration for former deeds. The time of rebellion was past—at least for the white man.

Disturbances of a different kind upset the capital in the seventeenth century. In 1624, as a result of bitter animosities, the viceroy and the religious orders arrayed against a coalition of the archbishop and the audiencia. The archbishop excommunicated the viceroy, who responded by ordering the prelate banished from Mexico. The lower classes, fiercely loyal to their spiritual leader, formed a rampaging mob that threatened the viceroy. Their demonstration ended in violence and in some seventy deaths. So bitter were the denunciations that the viceroy was recalled.

A second great disturbance occurred in 1692. A crisis brought on by severe food shortages, the result of crop failures, was exacerbated by the rumor that authorities had connived to corner the grain market to their profit. The resentment of the Indians and mestizos—persons of mixed Spanish and Indian blood—burst into destructive riots in which the viceregal palace was burned and looted. Other government buildings were destroyed, along with 280 shops and stalls, before the viceroy's troops finally restored order through harsh measures.

These extreme examples of the breakdown of law and order were relatively few, but the government of New Spain had to cope continuously with widespread crime in both city and countryside as well as other threats to security. It was ill equipped to do so because for many years there was nothing resembling a large, well-organized professional force to maintain peace.

Authorities also had to contend with various natural calamities over which they had little control. Very destructive were the many floods that plagued the capital in the colonial period. The dike whereby the Aztecs had controlled the lake waters was destroyed by the Spaniards and never replaced. From the middle of the sixteenth century on, the city was inundated at intervals, with very serious losses. Officials were equally helpless in dealing with such periodical disasters as earthquakes, pestilences, and crop failures, even though some minimal precautions were taken.

Expansion into Northern Mexico

While much of central and southern Mexico was under Spanish control by the middle of the sixteenth century, the wide expanses of the north remained unsettled by the white man. Interest in the northern frontiers had quickened, however, with the discovery of silver ore in the 1540s, setting off a rush into the region. Within a few years mining camps appeared in many locations, but bellicose Chichimec warriors made supplying the camps difficult and dangerous. The long distances between Spanish settlements and the isolated mining camps offered the Indians ample opportunity to strike the wagon trains. For half a century the indomitable northern tribes resisted the Spanish advance, and the fighting subsided only in the last decade of the sixteenth century when Viceroy Luis de Velasco II, with the help of brave clergymen, inaugurated a policy of conciliation. In return for annual supplies of cattle and clothing, many of the natives were persuaded to put down their arms.

Missionaries braved the dangers of the hinterlands, and in the

Luis de Velasco II (1539–1617), the son of Mexico's second viceroy, went on to serve twice in the same office himself. He was instrumental in making peace with the Chichimecs in the 1590s.

seventeenth century the Jesuits, in particular, pushed northward, all the way to Baja California and Arizona. Following their trails, other Spaniards began to settle the northwest. Francisco de Ibarra explored and settled the areas of Durango and Chihuahua, which were formed into a distinct region known as New Biscay. In the 1570s Luis de Carvajal was given a commission to pacify the northeast of the country. Finding little of mineral wealth, the settlers of that land enslaved the local Indians, who were sold as miners to north central Mexico. Carvajal founded the city of Monterrey and settled other towns in the new province, which was named New León.

In the 1590s the viceroy of New Spain sent out more expeditions to the far north earlier traversed by Vázquez de Coronado. Following the march of Juan de Oñate in 1598, an outpost was established and Franciscan friars began converting Indians at Taos and other pueblos. In 1609, two years after the English colonized Jamestown, the northern capital was planted at Santa Fe. Nevertheless, the extensive region of New Mexico remained sparsely populated; there were some friars, a few soldiers, and a scattering of miners, traders, and ranchers, along with various officials. The harsh land yielded little revenue and offered hardly more to the imperial system than Indian souls and a tenuous hold on the land in the face of French expansion.

Expeditions by sea continued to explore new lands for the Spanish empire. After earlier attempts to plant colonies in the Pacific had failed, the historic voyage in 1565 by Miguel López de Legazpi and the friar Andrés de Urdaneta led to settlement. Most important, Urdaneta discovered a satisfactory route back to the western hemisphere, sailing for the California coast and then turning southward to Mexico. Manila was founded, and shortly thereafter the fabulous trade between the Orient and New Spain began, with one ship a year—the Manila Galleon—making its way from the Philippine capital to Acapulco and back.

The Manila trade piqued new interest in the coast of Califor-

The Pacific port of Acapulco in a 1671 Dutch engraving.

nia, where the galleons first sighted the mainland of America. In
the 1590s Sebastián Vizcaíno explored the coastline with indifferent success. In 1602 another expedition under his command
produced a commendable chart of California waters, and Vizcaíno founded the port of Monterey. Like others before him,
he missed seeing the great bay of San Francisco. There was
still no compelling reason to make serious attempts at colonizing
California.

Rivals in the New World

A growing concern of Spanish authorities was the encroachment
of foreigners on the fringes of New Spain, both by land and sea.
A French force led by the Chevalier de La Salle journeyed southward from Canada in the 1680s into the region of Texas, where,
it was rumored, a settlement was planted. In response Spaniards
began to occupy Texas, and in 1698 a Spanish fort was established on the Gulf coast at Pensacola (Florida).

A more serious threat was posed by foreigners on the seas.
North European powers had never accepted the pope's division of
the New World, which gave most of it to Spain, and, especially
following the growth of Protestantism, they challenged Spain's
hegemony. Pirates, often with the blessings of their sovereigns,
aggressively attacked Spanish property. French interlopers were
cruising the eastern coastline of South America little more than
a decade after Columbus's first voyage. The ship sent by Cortés
carrying Aztec treasure to Charles V had been seized by French
corsairs when it was in sight of Iberian shores. Later the French
moved closer to the source, attacking Spanish ships in American
waters and looting ports. Along the Gulf coast, from Yucatán to
Tampico, French filibusters raided with little opposition. In
1561 they sacked the town of Campeche and a decade later
seized valuable treasures from a Franciscan convent in Yucatán.

Somewhat later the English, too, appeared off Mexican shores.
In 1567 John Hawkins sailed boldly into the port of Veracruz
under pretext of repairing his ships, but he actually planned to
sell his cargo of black slaves in defiance of laws that forbade
Spanish trade with foreigners. Hawkins was trapped by an in-
coming Spanish fleet bearing a new viceroy. Despite a gentleman's agreement for a truce, the viceroy brought his ships to
bear and peppered the English vessels, allowing only two of
Hawkins's nine ships to escape. The captured English corsairs

A Spanish shield of the seventeenth century.

were given sentences at labor, and later some were tried and burned by the Inquisition, not for piracy but for heresy. The defeat of Hawkins was a great feather in the viceroy's cap, but the Spaniards would pay dearly for it, for escaping on one of the English ships was Hawkins's cousin, Francis Drake. Before long *El Draque* took his vengeance, becoming the terror of the Spanish Indies, raiding with considerable success in both the Caribbean and the Pacific, and driving the Spaniards to distraction.

From the middle of the sixteenth century until the end of the eighteenth century English and French corsairs attacked the coasts of Yucatán and Campeche many times, though the rewards were often modest. Some of the small, isolated ports were so poorly defended that they could be taken by a handful of pirates. In Pacific waters both the English and Dutch were active, the most successful being Thomas Cavendish, who captured a richly laden Manila Galleon.

The most vicious attack, however, was not on sea but on land. In 1683, after laying careful plans, a Frenchman known as Lorenzillo led a force of about a thousand ruffians of mixed nationalities to the strongly fortified port of Veracruz and invested the city under cover of night. Over six thousand local citizens were rounded up, held inside the churches, and denied food and water for three days and nights. Many were horribly tortured, and most of the females, of all ages, were raped. The pirates carried off about a million dollars worth of loot.

By the end of the seventeenth century the viceroyalty of New Spain stretched out over a vast expanse of territory. It embraced all land on the mainland north of Panama, extending up to New Mexico, the islands of the Caribbean, and even the Philippines. Ostensibly all these far-flung regions were under the control of the viceroy; in actual practice, his authority was nominal, for the more remote areas were effectively beyond his reach. Central America, the islands of the Caribbean, and the Philippines had their own audiencias, which were for all intents and purposes autonomous.

Spain itself, after boasting the richest and most powerful empire in the world during the sixteenth century, began to decline in the early decades of the seventeenth century. But the Spanish empire remained intact and relatively prosperous, thanks to an administrative system that, despite its flaws, held the immense territories together.

Recommended for Further Study

Altman, Ida. "Spanish Society in Mexico City After the Conquest." *Hispanic American Historical Review* 71 (1993): 413–46.

Bannon, John F. *The Spanish Borderlands Frontier, 1513–1821.* New York: Holt, Rinehart and Winston, 1970.

Benítez, Fernando. *The Century after Cortés.* Translated by Joan Maclean. Chicago: University of Chicago Press, 1965.

Bolton, Herbert E. *Rim of Christendom: A Biography of Eusebio Francisco Kino, Pacific Coast Pioneer.* New York: Macmillan, 1936.

Borah, Woodrow. *Justice by Insurance: The General Indian Court and the Legal Aides of the Half-Real.* Berkeley: University of California Press, 1983.

———. "Representative Institutions in the Spanish Empire in the Sixteenth Century: The New World." *The Americas* 12 (1956): 246–57.

Burkhart, Louise M. *The Slippery Earth: Nahua-Christian Moral Dialogue in Sixteenth Century Mexico*. Tucson: University of Arizona Press, 1989.

Cline, S. L. *Colonial Culhuacan, 1580–1600: A Social History of an Aztec Town*. Albuquerque: University of New Mexico Press, 1986.

Farriss, Nancy M. *Maya Society under Colonial Rule. The Collective Enterprise of Survival*. Princeton, N.J.: Princeton University Press, 1984.

Fisher, Lillian Estelle. *Viceregal Administration in the Spanish American Colonies*. Berkeley: University of California Press, 1926.

Gerhard, Peter. *The North Frontier of New Spain*. Princeton, N.J.: Princeton University Press, 1982.

——. *Pirates on the West Coast of New Spain, 1575–1742*. Glendale, Calif.: Clark, 1960.

Gibson, Charles. *The Aztecs under Spanish Rule: A History of the Indians of the Valley of Mexico, 1519–1810*. Stanford, Calif.: Stanford University Press, 1964.

——. *Spain in America*. New York: Harper & Row, 1967.

Haring, Clarence H. *The Spanish Empire in America*. New York: Oxford University Press, 1947.

Haskett, Robert. *Indigenous Rulers: An Ethnohistory of Town Government in Colonial Cuernavaca*. Albuquerque: University of New Mexico Press, 1991.

Himmerich y Valencia, Robert. *The Encomenderos of New Spain, 1521–1555*. Austin: University of Texas Press, 1991.

Jones, Oakah L. *Nueva Vizcaya: Heartland of the Spanish Frontier*. Albuquerque: University of New Mexico Press, 1988.

Liss, Peggy Korn. *Mexico under Spain, 1521–1556: Society and Origins of Nationality*. Chicago: University of Chicago Press, 1975.

Mecham, J. Lloyd. *Francisco de Ibarra and Nueva Vizcaya*. Durham, N.C.: Duke University Press, 1927.

Naylor, Thomas H., and Charles W. Polzer, eds. *The Presidio and Militia on the Northern Frontier of New Spain: A Documentary History*. Vol. 1: *1570–1700*. Tucson: University of Arizona Press, 1986.

Parry, John H. *The Audiencia of New Galicia in the Sixteenth Century: A Study in Spanish Colonial Government*. Cambridge: Cambridge University Press, 1948.

Pike, Frederick B. "The Cabildo and Colonial Loyalty to Hapsburg Rulers." *Journal of Inter-American Studies* 2 (1960): 405–20.

Poole, Stafford. "The Church and the Repartimientos in the Light of the Third Mexican Council, 1585." *The Americas* 20 (1963): 3–36.

Powell, Philip W. *Mexico's Miguel Caldera: The Taming of America's First Frontier, 1548–1597*. Tucson: University of Arizona Press, 1977.

——. *Soldiers, Indians, and Silver*. Berkeley: University of California Press, 1952.

Sluiter, Engel. "The Fortification of Acapulco, 1615–1616." *Hispanic American Historical Review* 29 (1949): 69–80.

Vigil, Ralph H. *Alonso de Zorita, Royal Judge and Christian Humanist, 1512–1585*. Norman: University of Oklahoma Press, 1987.

10

The Colonial Economy

Spain's Economic Policies

Mexico, as the colony of New Spain, existed for the benefit of the mother country. At least that was the view of the Spanish crown's economic advisers. Like other European colonial powers, Spain subscribed to the economic philosophy of mercantilism, which held that the purpose of a colony was to make the mother country stronger and more self-sufficient. If a colony did not return such advantages to the mother country it could be more of a liability than an asset. There were other considerations, both religious and strategic, but profit was no doubt the primary consideration.

Spain's colonial economic policies were protectionist in the extreme, which meant that the economy in New Spain was very much restricted by limitations imposed by the imperial system. Thus the natural growth of industry and commerce was significantly impeded, because manufacturers and merchants in Spain were protected from the competition of those in the colony. In accord with the classic pattern, the Spanish Indies were to supply Spain with raw products, which could be made into finished goods in the mother country and sold back to the colonists at a profit. As a consequence, the character of the colonial economy in Mexico was essentially extractive.

In early years of the colony whites lived parasitically off many Indians and a few blacks, but the picture changed considerably after a time. The importance of the encomiendas in the overall economy of New Spain did not last long, for few of those who

168

came after the conquerors received grants of Indian villages. Within a short time the encomenderos formed but a small minority of the Spaniards in Mexico. At one time there were 934 encomenderos, but their numbers dropped to 537 by 1550, and in 1604 there were only about 50 left in central Mexico. Most of the encomienda towns escheated to the crown for lack of legitimate heirs, but some were confiscated for illegal activities. The system continued into the eighteenth century, but by then only a handful of villages remained in private hands.

In all events, even in the palmy decades of the sixteenth century the majority of the encomenderos had encomiendas that offered only modest incomes. It is true, however, that the more prominent conquerors had large numbers of tributaries, and such men were prosperous, especially if they diversified their interests. The wealthiest of all was Fernando Cortés, who had many rich towns. He held real estate and engaged in commercial transactions in New Spain as well as in other colonies; he raised blooded horses and other stock and experimented with the production of silk; and he had interests in mining, shipbuilding, sugar processing, and farming.

Meanwhile many more Spaniards poured into the colony, and, contrary to the view often held, most of them had to work. True, most had the preferred occupations in society; but as officials, clergymen, merchants, artisans, miners, ranchers, lawyers, physicians, teachers, sailors, or whatever, they were productive. While it was certainly advantageous to be white, a light complexion by no means guaranteed a life of ease. Indeed, some Spaniards of low socioeconomic status were reduced to menial labor and occasionally became beggars or brigands. Enterprising mestizos, on the other hand, might be more prosperous than the less energetic of lower-class Spaniards.

In spite of official attempts to encourage Spanish farmers and laborers to emigrate to America, almost none did. As a consequence, the necessary physical labor was performed by those of the colored classes. It has often been noted that the true wealth discovered by the Spaniards consisted of the millions of natives whose labor kept the colonies functioning. In the years following the Conquest a good number of Indians were slaves, either because they were already in that category in their own societies or because they were enslaved by Spaniards for continued resistance to Spanish authority. As chattel slaves, they were branded and became legally the property of their masters, who could buy and sell them. Slaves were often worked to the point of exhaustion and usually had short lives. Owing to the bitter protests of

Spaniards of conscience—most notably the Dominican friar Bartolomé de Las Casas—Indian slavery was finally abolished in the
1550s.

The percentage of Indians who were truly chattels was relatively small; those assigned to encomiendas constituted a far
greater number. In addition to the tribute owed to their encomenderos, Indians were also required to contribute labor under a
regulated system. When they could not provide the assessed tribute, they were allowed to work it off. Often the encomendero
rented the services of his Indians to merchants and others who
drove them mercilessly. In 1549 the labor obligation was abolished, and labor in lieu of tribute was forbidden. Without slaves
and forced labor, who was then to carry out the necessary tasks
of labor? The policy makers in Spain reasoned that if Indians
were paid a fair wage for their work, and if they were treated
humanely, they would volunteer. But few among the dwindling
number of Indians stepped forward to assume the burden.

Consequently the crown decreed a system of forced labor called
the *repartimiento*, or *cuatequil*. Under this system each adult
male Indian had to contribute about forty-five days of labor a
year, usually a week at a time at various intervals. Only a small
percentage of the men from any village were to be absent simultaneously, and the head of a family was to have time free to cultivate his own fields. Provisions stipulated that each laborer was
to be paid for his work and treated with consideration. In practice, however, Indians were forced to work twelve hours a day,
and they were frequently mistreated and cheated of their pay.
Numerous abuses of the system kept the natives in abject misery
until, finally, in the early seventeenth century the cuatequil was
abolished, except for mine labor.

There had been frequent labor shortages, especially following
the devastating epidemics, but now there was increased pressure—
at least insofar as cheap labor was concerned—for the decree
of abolition coincided with the lowest point of Indian population. Black slaves had been introduced, but they were expensive and it was not feasible to use them in labor with low profit
yield. As a result there was competition for Indian labor, and
wages rose somewhat. Employers now induced Indians to work
by offering them advances on their pay, which many were unable to resist. Enough money was advanced to the workers that
they could never hope to pay off the debt, and since they could
not legally leave their place of employment until accounts were
settled, such workers sometimes became debt *peones*, tied to their

A Spanish overseer directs Indian laborers on a sugar plantation in this painting by the modern muralist Diego Rivera (1886–1957).

Indian *tamemes* were the traditional bearers of cargo, transporting goods to all corners of the colony. From the Florentine Codex.

employers for life. Their debts were inherited by their sons, thus perpetuating the system.

The economy of Indian Mexico was transformed by the Conquest. The Spaniards introduced European crops, draft animals, and technology. In some respects the benefits were slow in coming, as in transportation. In pre-Hispanic times everything that had to be moved was transported on the backs of porters, called *tamemes*, and the Spaniards continued to employ them. Despite a legal limit of fifty pounds for each load, it was not uncommon for tamemes to be forced to carry twice that weight over mountain passes. Prominent Spaniards arriving at Veracruz were conveyed to the capital two hundred miles distant in sedan chairs (*icpallis*) carried by Indians. One even reads of the conquerors' dogs being carried by tamemes. So many carriers succumbed to fatigue that a royal decree ordered the increased use of mules and horses and the opening of roads for carts. But the sight of men bent under staggering loads remained familiar.

Mining

The lands of the Spanish Indies belonged to the Spanish sovereigns personally, but their subjects were allowed to exploit the land at the pleasure of the rulers. The royal quinto of American riches applied to Indian treasure, precious metals and jewels, and the sale of slaves, to cite a few examples. The crown was, therefore, no less anxious to promote the search for gold and silver than the most avaricious colonist. The search for precious minerals continued unabated and ultimately succeeded. It was silver, however, not gold, that provided the great wealth of colonial Mexico. By the early 1530s silver was being mined in various locations, but not until a quarter century after the fall of Tenochtitlán was a great strike made. Between 1546 and 1548 the fabulous silver deposits of Zacatecas were revealed, and within a few years more rich mines were found at Guanajuato, San Luis Potosí, Pachuca, and other sites.

The great wealth of the mines dramatically transformed the economy of the colony. Mining camps, some of which became the important cities we see today, sprouted in many locations in north central Mexico. By the early years of the seventeenth century Zacatecas had become the third largest city in the colony,

A panoramic view of a silver-mining operation.

surpassed only by the capital and Puebla. A few miners became very wealthy and lived in ostentation. Other entrepreneurs made their fortunes by supplying those who flocked to the mining camps seeking silver. Commerce was profitable for merchants who risked taking their goods over the dangerous trails, past the Chichimecs. Others established stores and provided diverse services for the miners. Equally prosperous were farmers who furnished the food that was so much in demand in the barren north. At first cattle and sheep were driven north in herds, but eventually ranchers saw the wisdom of establishing ranches in the vicinity of the mines, and this was the genesis of the great livestock spreads of northern Mexico.

For decades Indians constituted most of the mine labor force. They labored far underground in the dark, damp shafts, breathing the noxious airs; some were drowned by floods or killed in explosions. They hauled ore out of the mines by climbing up notched logs that served as crude ladders, carrying their heavy loads in the same blankets with which they covered themselves at night. Poor diets, fatigue, and the unhealthful conditions in the mines made the workers susceptible to disease and early death. Yet, because the pay was good, at least in later years, there seems to have been enough labor for the mines. The mines of Zacatecas, producing one-third of Mexico's silver, required some five thousand laborers at the height of production and suffered no serious labor shortage.

Spaniards embraced the theory of bullionism—that is, they believed that true wealth consisted of precious metals. So intent were they on stockpiling bullion that they neglected other important aspects of the economy, to both their own and their colonies' detriment. And the ambitious European policies of the Spanish crown simply absorbed the income. Fabulous as the production of American mines was, the total impact is usually exaggerated; Spain's income from her various European sources was greater than the silver of the Indies. Ruinous economic policies placed Spain in a precarious posture by the early seventeenth century, when mining production began to decline.

Agriculture and Ranching

Although mining was the most salient enterprise, agriculture remained the basic occupation in all parts of New Spain. It was, of course, absolutely essential for the sustenance of the colony, and

This graceful aqueduct at Querétaro was built between 1729 and 1739. With seventy-four arches, it is 85 feet high at one point, and carried water to the city over a distance of five miles.

most agricultural production was for domestic consumption. To the variety of foods native to the land the Spaniards introduced an assortment of plant life—citrus and other fruits, wheat, sugarcane, and many edibles to enrich the colonial diet. Early Spanish settlers were given, in addition to town lots for residences, small garden plots outside of town for their own needs, to be cultivated by Indian farmers. The natives had their own personal lands, held privately or in common, to provide food for themselves.

Colonists were allowed to grow what they wished as long as their production did not conflict with interests in Spain. Often they ended up having to pay inflated prices for imported necessities that could easily have been grown in Mexico. Wine and olive oil, for example, were not luxuries, but staples. They were considered essential to the traditional Spanish table, and wine was necessary for mass. Yet so great were the profits to producers and middlemen in Spain that the growing of vines and olive trees was forbidden in the colonies. As a supplemental beverage, beer was brewed in Mexico as early as 1544.

Export crops were an important part of royal income. Essential to the booming textile industry in Europe were good dyes, and Mexico produced one of the best with the native product called cochineal. This red dye was of considerable value and convenient for export because of its compact nature. It was extracted from tiny insects found in the nopal cactus, which was soon planted in extensive tracts. Another profitable dye was the blue extracted from the indigo plant. Cacao, from which chocolate was made, had long been a favorite food with the Indians, and eventually it caught the fancy of Europeans, providing yet another valuable export for Spain. Both vanilla and henequen were additional products of some importance. Finally, sugar was introduced into Mexico by Cortés in 1524, and soon there were many plantations and mills in the warmer climes of the colony. Even though Mexican exports of sugar were comparatively modest, they added to the diversity of New Spain's economy.

The deleterious effects of labor in both sugar and indigo processing were such that the crown finally attempted to prohibit use of native laborers, but not altogether successfully. Nevertheless, black slaves were used more extensively, and by the seventeenth century they supplied the main labor for the numerous sugar mills, some of which employed as many as two hundred of them.

At the same time, the Mexican ranching industry evolved. Many great livestock spreads developed in the north because of the availability of land that was almost useless for cultivation. Multiplying herds were branded and regulated. Travelers reported seeing herds of as many as 150,000 head, and in the region of Zacatecas over two million sheep grazed in summer pastures. Even though beef was inexpensive, colonists consumed much more of the costlier mutton. Sheep thrived better in the north than cattle, and their wool brought very good returns on investments.

Stockmen in the mother country had acquired extraordinary influence, and some of it was transferred to Mexico in a controlled manner through their guild, the Mesta. This organization regulated the yearly migrations of flocks and herds and allowed ranchers special grazing privileges. In the dry season animals migrated to better grass, and later, during the annual *rodeo*, they were rounded up and separated according to brands.

Large Mexican estates are usually associated with the vast haciendas of the north, but in central and southern Mexico there were important, though smaller, landholdings devoted to the growing of sugar, henequen, and other agricultural products. The conquerors were often rewarded with tracts of land consisting of twenty to a hundred acres, and many were able to add to their holdings. With fewer encomiendas available, land titles were granted. Thus the acquisition of large estates began in the second half of the sixteenth century. Individuals with the capital necessary for an enterprise appealing to royal interests were either given land outright or allowed to purchase it at a low price. It was understood that for the grazing of livestock large acreage was essential. Foraging cattle and sheep, especially in the semidesert regions of the north, spread out over large areas. One entrepreneur of the northern frontier began putting together parcels in 1583, and by his death, in 1618, the family estates stretched over 11,626,850 acres.[1] In many instances ranchers acquired land from Indians, either by purchase, fraud, or coercion. While it is traditional to assume that a large percentage of Indian lands were lost to the Spaniards, in fact, the natives retained a good many of their ancestral holdings. They did, however, often lose their water rights to encroaching Spanish towns and private haciendas. The colonial court dockets were crowded with disputes over water and the Indians were at a decided disadvantage in litigation with the Spaniards. Gradually the mechanisms for conflict resolution were defined and water disputes were generally resolved by some form of compromise in which neither party suffered irreparable damage.

Industry and Commerce

With industry so closely regulated to prevent competition with Spain, Mexico produced very little in the way of manufactured goods for export. Almost all luxury goods had to be imported from Spanish merchants, even though most were not Spanish in origin, for Spain had neglected her own domestic industries and commerce. Expensive fabrics were imported by Spain from northern Europe, while the production of fine cloth was forbidden to the colonies. Silk, for example, flourished for a while in Mexico, especially during the sixteenth century. But its production was discouraged following objections of Spanish silk merchants in the mother country and ultimately by the competition of inexpensive silk from China.

Still there were many products for everyday use coming out of small industries in Mexico. Coarse cloth, for instance, was manufactured in *obrajes*, the textile mills that existed in various loca-

1. See Charles H. Harris, III, *A Mexican Family Empire: The Latifundio of the Sánchez Navarro Family, 1765–1867* (Austin, 1975), p. 6.

tions. Since few could afford imported finery, local mills were numerous, more than eighty by 1571. In 1604 there were twenty-five obrajes in the capital alone. These "sweatshops" were notorious for the unconscionable manner in which the Indian workers were treated. They were placed behind locked doors and forced to work long hours, breathing the lint that caused respiratory problems. Often they were locked in the mill at night, and married workers were allowed to see their families only on Sundays.

The city of Puebla was (and is) famous for its excellent ceramic products. Pots and tiles are richly decorated and glazed in the styles known as *majolica* and *talavera*. *Above right*, a typical seventeenth-century Puebla bowl. *Above left*, Moorish influence is evident in this vase. *Right*, this flowerpot is of a Chinese type.

Other manufactured items were produced by the many artisans in the colony—the tailors, blacksmiths, cobblers, candlemakers, goldsmiths, and so on. There were guilds, or *gremios*, for each of these crafts. Well established by the late sixteenth century, the guilds fixed both the quality of goods and the prices of work. People of the colored classes were allowed to join the gremios, but only whites were allowed to attain the rank of master, which followed successful completion of examinations and the presentation of the "masterpiece" that demonstrated the applicant's skill. In a more positive sense, the gremios were protective of their members, making provisions for those who suffered accidents and illness as well as extending help to widows. They were also active in promoting religious celebrations and philanthropic undertakings for the community. Eventually there were about a hundred guilds in Mexico City. A professional merchants' guild, the Consulado, was established in the capital in 1592. Its function was to arbitrate commercial disputes, to protect the interests of merchants, to establish rules of business conduct, and to foster the interests of the community.

Commerce was closely supervised by the imperial system

Muleteers (*arrieros*) were a familiar sight on the roads of New Spain.

through the agency of the Casa de Contratación. This house of trade was located in Seville, which served as the official entrepôt for all traffic with the Indies. As in industry, tight controls were imposed on commerce in order to benefit the merchants in Spain. Everything and everyone going to or coming from the colonies passed through officials who checked all papers with care. Traders in the city of Seville sent to the colonies a wide variety of goods—expensive fabrics, hats, wax for candles, wine, liquors, vinegar, olive oil, paper, steel and iron implements, fruit preserves, and other items. The masses rarely enjoyed such luxuries, however, and had to rely on native products sold in open markets. The main plaza of Mexico City was crowded with shoppers who could make their selections among the 323 stalls that existed in 1686.

All products destined for the Spanish Indies were required to go on Spanish ships with Spanish crews, and, to facilitate the collection of duties, cargoes were channeled through the one official port of Veracruz. Because of pirates, after the 1560s ships sailing to and from the New World went in annual convoys with armed escort vessels. One of the big events in New Spain was the arrival of the fleet in the spring, at which time merchants purchased their supplies for the coming months. The prevalence of yellow fever and malaria discouraged any sizable permanent population in Veracruz, but when the fleet arrived tents bristled on the beach almost overnight, as great numbers of buyers came to negotiate in the colorful trade fair that ensued. In some years the cargos were taken to Mexico City rather than remaining in the pestilential airs of the port. Eventually the fair was relocated inland at the higher, more salubrious climate of Jalapa, which had the added advantage of being a safer depository for silver destined for Spain.

A similar, though smaller, scene was presented on the Pacific coast at Acapulco. Once a year the Manila Galleon arrived at the port city laden with rich luxuries of the Orient, including silks, jade, ivory, perfumes, incense, and other goods. Merchants who escaped the fevers of Acapulco returned to Mexico City to sell their wares locally or to those buying for the market in Spain.

The Results of Spain's Policies

In addition to its profits through mining and agricultural exports, the Spanish crown realized revenues through retention for

A piece-of-eight minted in Mexico in 1609. Such coins were used mainly for trading with Spain for manufactured goods or purchase of Oriental spices and silks carried by the Manila Galleon.

itself of monopolies on such items as mercury, gunpowder, salt, pulque, and, in the eighteenth century, tobacco. The crown's quinto was eventually reduced to a tenth, but it still constituted a substantial source of royal income. As the encomienda system withered away, more Indian villages came under the crown, to whom tribute was paid. The king's treasury also benefited from the sale of licenses, offices, and land, and from the various taxes paid by the colonists. Altogether there were about sixty different taxes, of which the most detested was the *alcabala*, a sales tax payable on almost everything sold. At first only 2 percent of the item's value, the alcabala went as high as 14 percent during Spain's wars of the eighteenth century. The *almojarifazgo* was a tax of 7.5 percent on all imports and exports, so the crown was paid twice for goods moving between Spain and its colonies, for a total income of 15 percent.

The economic policies of the Hapsburg kings, who ruled up to 1700, were ultimately counterproductive. Excessive and arbitrary control of internal colonial economies stifled incentive and the natural growth of industry and commerce. Moreover local conditions, such as underdeveloped transportation, rural banditry, and, especially in the north, the attacks of Chichimecs, inhibited the evolution of a strong and diversified economy. Equally restrictive were the limitations imposed by an unrealistic imperial supply system. Colonists had little choice but to purchase some imported products; yet the supply seldom met the demand. It was bad enough that ships were dispatched from Spain only once a year, but they sometimes arrived late and there were years when no ships arrived at all. High prices and the irregular supply of essential goods drove colonists to contraband sources.

The general depression of the seventeenth century saw the colonists of New Spain withdrawing more and more from the mother country, becoming more introspective and self-reliant. It was a bleak time, with the wealth, power, and glory of the Spanish empire a fading memory. In the following century, however, Spain and its colonies would have a dramatic resurgence under the more dynamic rule of the Bourbon monarchs.

Recommended for Further Study

Bakewell, Peter J. *Silver Mining and Society in Colonial Mexico: Zacatecas, 1546–1700.* Cambridge: Cambridge University Press, 1971.

Barrett, Elinore M. *The Mexican Colonial Copper Industry.* Albuquerque: University of New Mexico Press, 1987.

Barrett, Ward. *The Sugar Hacienda of the Marqueses del Valle.* Minneapolis: University of Minnesota Press, 1970.

Bishko, Charles J. "The Peninsular Background of Latin American Cattle Ranching." *Hispanic American Historical Reivew* 32 (1952): 491–515.

Borah, Woodrow. *Early Trade and Navigation between Mexico and Peru.* Berkeley: University of California Press, 1954.

———. *New Spain's Century of Depression.* Berkeley: University of California Press, 1951.

———. *Silk Raising in Colonial Mexico.* Berkeley: University of California Press, 1943.

Boyd-Bowman, Peter. "Spanish and European Textiles in Sixteenth Century Mexico." *The Americas* 29 (1973): 334–58.

Boyer, Richard. "Juan Vázquez, Muleteer of Seventeenth-Century Mexico." *The Americas* 37 (1981): 421–44.

———. "Mexico in the Seventeenth Century: Transition of a Colonial Society." *Hispanic American Historical Review* 57 (1977): 455–78.

Brockington, Lolita Gutiérrez. *The Leverage of Labor: Managing the Cortés Haciendas in Tehuantepec, 1588–1688.* Durham, N.C.: Duke University Press, 1989.

Chevalier, François. *Land and Society in Colonial Mexico: The Great Hacienda.* Berkeley: University of California Press, 1963.

Dusenberry, William. *The Mexican Mesta: The Administration of Ranching in Colonial Mexico.* Urbana: University of Illinois Press, 1963.

Frank, Andre Gunder. *Mexican Agriculture, 1521–1630. Transformation of the Mode of Production.* New York: Cambridge University Press, 1979.

Hassig, Ross. *Trade, Tribute, and Transportation: The Sixteenth-Century Political Economy of the Valley of Mexico.* Norman: University of Oklahoma Press, 1985.

Israel, J. I. "Mexico and the 'General Crisis' of the Seventeenth Century." *Past and Present* 63 (1974): 33–57.

Kicza, John E. *Colonial Entrepreneurs: Families and Business in Bourbon Mexico City.* Albuquerque: University of New Mexico Press, 1983.

Konrad, Herman W. *A Jesuit Hacienda in Colonial Mexico: Santa Lucia, 1576–1767.* Stanford, Calif.: Stanford University Press, 1980.

Ladd, Doris. *The Making of a Strike: Mexican Silver Workers' Struggles in Real del Monte, 1766-1775.* Lincoln: University of Nebraska Press, 1988.

Leiby, John S. *Colonial Bureaucrats and the Mexican Economy.* New York: Peter Lang, 1986.

Lockhart, James. "Encomienda and Hacienda: The Evolution of the Great Estate in the Spanish Indies." *Hispanic American Historical Review* 49 (1969): 411–29.

Meyer, Michael C. *Water in the Hispanic Southwest: A Social and Legal History, 1550–1850.* Tucson: University of Arizona Press, 1984.

Osborn, Wayne S. "Indian Land Retention in Colonial Metztitlán." *Hispanic American Historical Review* 53 (1973): 217–38.

Riley, G. Micheal. *Fernando Cortés and the Marquesado in Morelos: A Case Study in the Socioeconomic Development of Sixteenth Century Mexico.* Albuquerque: University of New Mexico Press, 1973.

Salvucci, Richard J. *Textiles and Capitalism in Mexico: An Economic History of the Obrajes, 1539–1840.* Princeton, N.J.: Princeton University Press, 1988.

Schurz, William L. *The Manila Galleon.* New York: Dutton, 1939.

Seeger, Martin L. "Media of Exchange in 16th Century New Spain and the Spanish Response." *The Americas* 35 (1978): 168–84.

Semo, Enrique. *The History of Capitalism in Mexico: Its Origins, 1521–1763.* Translated by Lidia Lozano. Austin: University of Texas Press, 1993.

Simpson, Lesley B. *The Encomienda in New Spain.* Berkeley: University of California Press, 1960.

Smith, Robert S. "Sales Taxes in New Spain, 1575–1770." *Hispanic American Historical Review* 28 (1948): 2–37.

Stein, Stanley J. "Bureaucracy and Business in the Spanish Empire, 1759–1804: Failure of a Bourbon Reform in Mexico and Peru." *Hispanic American Historical Review* 61 (1981): 2–28.

Super, John C. "Querétaro Obrajes: Industry and Society in Provincial Mexico." *Hispanic American Historical Review* 56 (1976): 197–216.

Taylor, William B. "Landed Society in New Spain: A View from the South." *Hispanic American Historical Review* 54 (1974): 387–413.

———. *Landlord and Peasant in Colonial Oaxaca.* Stanford, Calif.: Stanford University Press, 1972.

West, Robert C. *The Mining Community in Northern New Spain: The Parral Mining District.* Berkeley: University of California Press, 1949.

Young, Eric Van. *Hacienda and Market in 18th-Century Mexico. The Rural Economy of the Guadalajara Region, 1675–1820.* Berkeley: University of California Press, 1981.

11

The Colonial Church

A traveler in colonial Mexico approaching the outskirts of a town first saw in the distance a bell tower rising over all other structures. Before long he would hear the tolling of bells resounding over town and countryside. In the streets priests, friars, and nuns mingled prominently in the crowds. If the physical presence of the church was everywhere, in other ways, too, it was the most pervasive of colonial institutions, and none left its imprint more deeply on the culture.

Church Organization

Because of its expulsion of the Moslems in Spain and its discovery of the New World, the Spanish crown was granted extraordinary privileges by the papacy. In effect, through the royal patronage (*patronato real*) Spanish kings were heads of the Roman Catholic Church in their domains. While this conferred great power and prestige, it also imposed many responsibilities. And, significantly, it meant that the church became an arm of the state.

Church organization consisted of two distinct branches—the secular clergy and the regular clergy. The secular group was composed of priests who served under their bishops. The regulars were missionaries under the separate authority of the superiors of their various orders—the Franciscans, Dominicans, Augustinians, and others.

The Spanish conquerors were devout in their religious observances, confessing their sins and praying frequently, especially in times of danger. During the months of the Conquest five priests accompanied the Spaniards. Cortés demonstrated his pious fervor in his adamant insistence, even in threatening circumstances, that Indians cast down their idols, forbear human sacrifices, and abandon their old gods. His zeal more than once jeopardized the safety of the Spaniards, and he had to be restrained by his own priests.

Typical fortress-like construction is apparent in this sixteenth-century Dominican monastery at Tepoztlán, Morelos. There are some striking Renaissance details in this important structure.

As early as 1519 the crown created a bishopric for Cozumel and Yucatán, but later changed the location to Tlaxcala. In 1527 the Dominican Julian Garcés arrived in Tlaxcala to assume his duties as the first bishop in the land. That same year another bishopric was created for the city of Mexico, and the following year Juan de Zumárraga, a Franciscan friar, arrived as bishop. With the additional title "Protector of the Indians," Zumárraga not only established the form of the early secular church but also took an active part in alleviating the sufferings of the Indians, a policy that brought him into conflict with encomenderos and Spanish officials. A Christian humanist and wise administrator, Zumárraga was a stabilizing factor in the early years of the colony. He was elevated to archbishop of Mexico shortly before his death in 1548.

An event of considerable significance was said to have occurred in 1531. According to tradition, a newly converted Indian by the name of Juan Diego beheld a vision of the Virgin, who commanded him to have a temple built in her honor. Juan Diego's experience was seen as all the more miraculous because the Virgin was dark skinned, and so had a special meaning to the conquered peoples. Moreover, the apparition appeared on the hill of Tepeyac, just north of the capital, where Indians had always worshiped Tonantzin, mother of gods. A shrine was built to this Virgin of Guadalupe, and it is still of utmost importance to religious pilgrims as a symbol of cultural fusion.

As the Spaniards spread out over the land, new bishoprics were formed: seven were established in the sixteenth century, one in the seventeenth century, and two in the eighteenth. They were staffed by large numbers of priests who ministered to the needs of all segments of society.

The Religious Conquest

Meanwhile the important work of the regular orders had begun. In 1521 Cortés requested that missionaries be sent, and in 1523 three lay brothers arrived, the most remarkable of whom was Pedro de Gante. The following year twelve Franciscan friars landed at Veracruz and walked barefoot to the capital. One of them, lamed and tattered, was Father Toribio de Benavente, called affectionately by the Indians Motolinía, "the Poor Little One." He became one of the most renowned churchmen in Mexico's history. As monasteries were built to accommodate their ac-

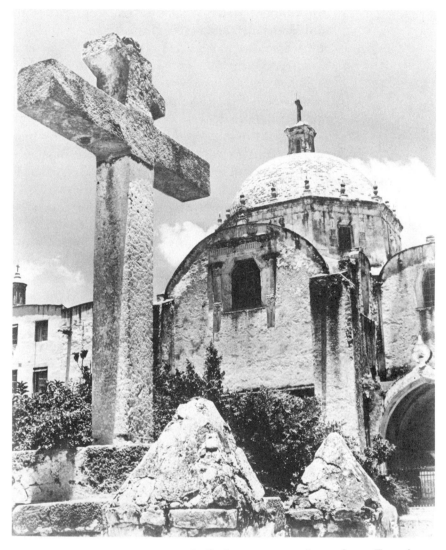

The cathedral at Cuernavaca, built in 1529, was formerly a Franciscan monastery. In later years, the structure was altered extensively.

tivities, other Franciscans traveled to the colony. They were the most numerous of the various orders and probably the most popular with Spaniards and Indians.

Friars of the Dominican Order arrived in 1525. Distinguished for their intellectual discipline, the Dominicans had long been powerful in Spain, where they were associated with the Inquisition. In the colonies the Dominicans promoted the reformation of Indian legislation. Among their numbers was the militant and influential Bartolomé de Las Casas, later bishop of Chiapas and the most celebrated churchman in the Americas. The Dominicans were particularly important in southern Mexico, where they frequently dominated affairs, both civil and religious.

The Augustinians reached Mexico in 1533 and proceeded to construct some of the finest monasteries in the land. All of these orders flourished early: by 1559 there were thirty Franciscan houses with 380 religious; 210 Dominicans labored out of forty houses; and there were 212 Augustinians with forty houses.[1] Other orders had convents as well, in addition to those for nuns. The fruit of their activity is astounding; Motolinía claimed (no doubt with considerable exaggeration) that as early as 1537 some nine million Indians had been baptized, four million of them by the Franciscans alone.

Founded years after the Conquest of Mexico, the Jesuits entered the land only in 1571, when other religious groups were well established. In their first years they occupied themselves with teaching the sons of Spaniards and soon won the reputation of being superior teachers. But they also taught Indian children, and within a few years they undertook the arduous task of converting natives on the northern frontiers. In the late seventeenth century a number of very able Jesuits, such as Fathers Eusebio Francisco Kino and Juan Manuel de Salvatierra, labored in isolation to take Christianity and Spanish civilization to Indians in Sonora, Arizona, and Baja California. Like other missionaries, they taught their converts animal husbandry, better agriculture, and crafts in order to induce them to lead a more settled way of life and to enhance their security.

Spaniards thought their nation favored by God because of their discovery of the New World. The great conquests of Mexico, Peru, and other rich areas were seen as divine intervention—the millions of new converts in America would make up for those Europeans lost to the Protestant movement. The first half century of Spanish occupation in Mexico witnessed the phenomenon referred to as the Religious Conquest. Those were decades when selfless men of the church worked with great devotion and energy against heavy odds. Their task was an unparalleled opportunity but also an awesome challenge. Friars set out to learn local languages to facilitate communication, and they had to overcome hostility that remained because of Spanish excesses. Moreover many of the Indians clung with tenacity to their tra-

1. José Miranda et al., *Historia de México* (Mexico, 1971), p. 293.

An anonymous Mexican artist of the early eighteenth century rendered this St. Michael.

ditional religion and to certain social habits abhorrent to the Christians. Missionaries were in a hurry to accomplish their objective, and as a result many converts were superficially instructed and only vaguely conversant with the Christian religion. Similarities between aspects of pagan ritual and Christianity facilitated conversion but also led to the mingling of the two in religious syncretism. Though the church sought to discourage all manifestations of pagan practices, it gradually learned to accommodate some of the minor rituals. The obstacles notwithstanding, missionaries had notable success in their conversion of the New World natives, probably the greatest missionizing achievement in history.

Religious Disputes and Anticlericalism

From the beginning, clergymen in Mexico became embroiled in bitter disputes. Ecclesiastics and encomenderos competed for control of the Indians. Friars and priests tried to protect the natives from abuses of Spaniards, while the latter resented the

The glazed tile façade of the baroque eighteenth-century church of Santa María Tonantzintla, Puebla.

Detail of San Francisco Acatepec. The tiles are green, yellow, and blue, bordered by red brick.

interference of the clergymen in the encomienda towns. Men of the church saw the colonists as examples of bad Christians who corrupted Indian morals in addition to mistreating them physically and exacting exorbitant tributes. The encomenderos, in turn, regarded many of the ecclesiastics as hypocrites who were guilty of the same crimes of which they accused others. Within the church itself there were other quarrels, usually of a jurisdictional nature. The various orders differed over the assignment of territories, and the secular priests resented the preemption of some of their traditional functions by the regulars. On occasion the disputes ended in violence.

There were, moreover, some acrimonious quarrels between ecclesiastical and civil authorities, involving not only lesser figures in the provinces but even archbishops and viceroys. One of the most notorious and scandalous episodes took place in the 1640s between the Jesuits and the bishop of Puebla, Juan de Palafox, who also held a number of high civil posts and served as viceroy. This contest involving the wealth and power of the Jesuits became a *cause célèbre* in which several important people were excommunicated and a Jesuit school was almost burned. For the moment the Jesuits were victorious and the powerful bishop withdrew. Eventually, however, the secular arm of the church gained the upper hand in Mexico, as the crown consciously strove to weaken the influence of the regular orders.

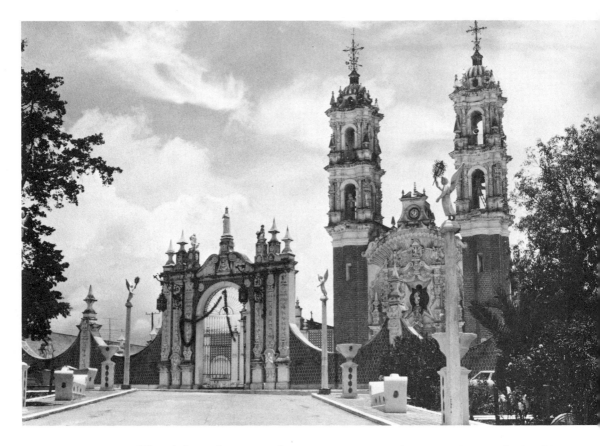

The eighteenth-century baroque Sanctuary of Nuestra Señora de Ocotlán, Tlaxcala. Its richly decorated interior is a prime example of the Churrigueresque.

Finally, some clergymen felt discriminated against because of the social circumstances of their birth. As in the civil bureaucracy, those born in Spain were much favored in the religious hierarchy, and most of the higher positions were denied those of Spanish blood born in Mexico. One authority estimates that "in Mexico during the entire colonial period only 32 of the 171 bishops and archbishops were Mexican."[2] Yet, by the seventeenth century the majority of Franciscans, Augustinians, and Dominicans were criollos.

While almost all Spaniards were practicing Catholics, anti-

2. Antonine Tibesar, O.F.M., quoted in Richard E. Greenleaf, *The Roman Catholic Church in Colonial Latin America* (New York, 1971), p. 6.

clerical sentiment abounded in the colony. Aside from their conflicts with clergymen over the control of Indians, Spaniards were often critical of the personal behavior of churchmen. On the whole, those of the orders were of a higher moral type than most parish priests. More dedicated and better educated than the secular clergy, the regulars usually led more commendable lives; however, the cloistered tradition of the Old World gave way in America to a more open style of living, which led a few somewhat astray. But the majority of the regulars were of high caliber, for which reason a number of them were selected for bishoprics and important civil positions, including that of viceroy.

Complaints were more widespread against the secular priests; owing to their lower standards, they were sometimes poorly educated and lacking in commitment. The church had, indeed, become something of a haven for large numbers who were less than devoted to their vows. Reports accused the priests of taking mistresses, imbibing to excess, gambling, soliciting in the confessional, and engaging in commerce. Others were charged with exacting excessively high fees for the sacraments and subjecting the Indians to harsh punishment. Again, while there is a measure of truth in the allegations, it would be distortion to ignore indications that the majority of priests observed their vows, lived modestly, and performed good works for their parishioners.

Juan de Palafox y Mendoza (1600–59) was bishop of Puebla and also served as viceroy. He was involved in serious political disputes.

The tiled domes of Iglesia del Carmen in Mexico City.

The collective burst of energy and accomplishments of the first half century gradually waned. By 1570 there was a slump in missionary activity, accompanied by a moral lassitude on the part of the clergy. The humility and simplicity evident in earlier decades yielded to a more material and increasingly profane mode of behavior that may be attributed to a decline in interest as the novelty of the crusading spirit wore thin and routine set in. Then, too, in a practical sense the challenge was less in terms of numbers, for the Indian population had declined drastically. But it is also true that during the reign of Philip II (1556–98) there was an official check on the vigorous debate concerning Indian policy, which became institutionalized and less flexible. Thus the reforming clergy were frustrated in their desires to ease the conditions of the native peoples and less inclined to aspire to the elevated goals of their predecessors. No subsequent period would see the equal of the extraordinary clergymen of the first fifty years, the phase of the so-called primitive church in New Spain.

The early ideal of a priest for every 2,000 Indians proved impractical, especially in provincial areas. There were by 1650 no more than 2,000 secular priests in the colony, of whom about a quarter resided in Mexico City. At that time the capital had roughly 1,000 nuns. There were about 800 friars in New Spain in 1559; their numbers grew to 1,500 in the 1580s and to about 3,000 by 1600, some 1,000 of whom were in Mexico City. J. I. Israel concludes that Puebla had around 1,400 ecclesiastical personnel by 1650, including 600 nuns. "In Valladolid, capital of Michoacan," he adds, "there were in 1654 . . . more ecclesiastical personnel than white laity." Altogether, including 350 to 400 Jesuits, there were perhaps 6,000 ordained priests in New Spain by the 1640s.[3]

The Inquisition

Religious affairs assumed a more somber cast in 1571 with the entrance of the Holy Office of the Inquisition. With its roots in the Middle Ages, the Inquisition was employed in Spain when Ferdinand and Isabella were striving to achieve political and cultural unity in the state. Under those "Catholic Kings" conformity was seen as essential, Christianity was equated with the very soul of Spain, and heresy was akin to treason. Jews were forced to convert or leave, and later on Protestants were forbidden in Spanish realms. The essential function of the Inquisition was to maintain the purity of the faith, to preserve religious orthodoxy; it would, however, come to assume a much broader charge, not without sinister aspects.

Although emigrants to the New World were screened with care, some heretics slipped by. Particularly suspect were *conversos*, or New Christians, that is, those of Jewish origins who had converted to Christianity, and the Inquisition was determined to root out "crypto-Jews" in New Spain. Some unfortunate Protestant corsairs were also tried for heresy. Moreover,

---

3. J. I. Israel, *Race, Class and Politics in Colonial Mexico, 1610–1670* (London, 1975), p. 48.

Pedro Moya de Contreras (?–1591) who arrived in the colony in 1571, established the formal Inquisition in Mexico, became archbishop, and was appointed viceroy in 1584.

many colonists, including clergymen and even persons in high official positions, were tried for purely moral offenses.

Indians were not tried for heresy by the Inquisition as they were considered childlike and irresponsible. In earlier years, however, bishops had exercised inquisitorial powers, and some natives had been brought before the court, usually for idolatry. The most notorious case involved Don Carlos of Texcoco, who was accused of idolatry, though his outspoken statements allegedly contained political and social overtones. Bishop Zumárraga found the noble guilty and, in 1539, had him burned at the stake. This and other examples of excessive zeal helped convince the crown that the conquered peoples should be allowed special consideration. Of 131 trials presided over by Zumárraga, only thirteen involved Indians. The prelate also tried twenty individuals for sorcery, of whom fifteen were women of various races.

The Inquisition also exercised control over printed matter that entered the colony, being concerned primarily with works that dealt with liberal, "dangerous" ideas, which, it was feared, would corrupt and lead astray the unsophisticated Indians as well as Spaniards. In fact, however, many prohibited writings, including those of the eighteenth-century French and English Enlightenment, found their way into the private libraries of educated people, among whom were a good number of clergymen.

The Inquisition in colonial Mexico was much less active than in Spain. Although it is often asserted that only about fifty prisoners were executed during the two and a half centuries of its existence in the colony, that figure is somewhat misleading. Deaths attributable to the Inquisition must include the many who died in prison of illness, neglect, torture, or suicide.

Those who paid the extreme penalty had been convicted, in most cases, of the serious crime of heresy, often compounded by "obstinacy"—that is, the refusal to recant. Prisoners sentenced to burning at the stake were often strangled first. Most of those

The Inquisition headquarters in Mexico City.

The frontispiece of a treatise against heresy printed in Spain in 1519. Much of colonial publishing dealt with religious subjects.

tried by the Inquisition were judged for lesser offenses, like adultery, bigamy, and blasphemy, and received sentences of floggings, fines, service in the galleys, or exile. Few who were arrested escaped without some punishment, for, as a saying went, "One can leave the Inquisition without being burned, but he will assuredly leave scorched." Those found guilty even of relatively minor crimes were made the objects of public shame and ridicule as an example to others. The solemnity of official proceedings notwithstanding, *autos de fé* assumed a carnival spirit for which elaborate preparations were made. People came from near and far to jeer the parade of those who carried candles and wore penitential garb with pointed hoods, as well as to regard the special ceremony reserved for those consigned to the stake. From the reviewing stand the viceroy, bishops, and other high dignitaries, with their ladies, viewed the macabre spectacle.

The first auto de fé in the colony took place in 1574. Sixty-three prisoners had been judged, of whom five were burned and most others flogged. Eight more autos occurred in the next twenty years. In 1528, long before the formal tribunal was established, two Spaniards died at the stake, accused of being crypto-Jews.[4] But perhaps the most sensational proceeding involving crypto-Jews concerned Don Luis de Carvajal, the colonizer and governor of Nuevo León, who was accused of harboring relatives who practiced Jewish rites. In an auto that included sixty-seven persons, some of his family were burned.

Always coercive in religious and moral affairs, the Inquisition became, in later times, less concerned with spiritual matters. As an instrumental of royal policy, it was utilized in the eighteenth century to check dissident political elements. Both of the liberal priests who led the struggle for Independence from Spain in the early nineteenth century were tried by the Inquisition before being turned over to secular authorities for execution. The tribunal persisted almost to the end of the colonial period and was not abolished until 1820.

The church touched the lives of those in New Spain from baptism to burial. Altogether some twelve thousand churches were built in the colony during the three centuries of Spanish rule. To the Spaniards the church was a link with the mother country, a familiar and comforting association that made them feel less alien in the New World. But perhaps it became even more im-

---

4. Richard E. Greenleaf, *The Mexican Inquisition of the Sixteenth Century* (Albuquerque, 1969), pp. 26, 169–71.

The seventeenth-century cathedral of Morelia, one of Mexico's most beautiful churches.

Carved wooden mask used in a dance celebrating the Christian victory over the Moors.

portant for the Indians, for religious services, soon an integral part of their lives, were a relief from drudgery. The Indians were entranced by the solemn ceremonies; the tolling of chimes and tinkling of bells, the incense, and the burning candles combined to inspire a sense of reverence and awe and to provide an interlude in an otherwise miserable existence. On the lighter side, the frequent religious festivals were usually holidays, offering an opportunity for celebration and relaxation. On a personal level, the Indians and impoverished mestizos considered men of the church to be about the only ones concerned with their welfare. All of these factors contributed to the essential conservatism and piety of the lower classes.

Recommended for Further Study

Adams, Eleanor. "The Franciscan Inquisition in Yucatán: French Seamen, 1560." *The Americas* 25 (1969): 331–59.
Braden, Charles. *Religious Aspects of the Conquest of Mexico.* Durham, N.C.: Duke University Press, 1930.

Chowning, Margaret. "The Consolidación de Vales Reales in the Bishopric
of Michoacán." *Hispanic American Historical Review* 3 (1989):
451–78.
Dunne, Peter M. *Pioneer Jesuits in Northern Mexico.* Berkeley: University
of California Press, 1944.
Farriss, Nancy. *Crown and Clergy in Colonial Mexico, 1759–1821.* London:
University of London Press, 1968.
Friede, Juan, and Benjamin Keen, eds. *Bartolomé de Las Casas in History:
Toward an Understanding of the Man and His Work.* De Kalb:
Northern Illinois University Press, 1971.
Greenleaf, Richard E. *The Mexican Inquisition of the Sixteenth Century.*
Albuquerque: University of New Mexico Press, 1969.
———. *Zumárraga and the Mexican Inquisition, 1536–1543.* Washington,
D.C.: Academy of American Franciscan History, 1961.
Hanke, Lewis. *Bartolomé de Las Casas: Bookman, Scholar, and Propagan-
dist.* Philadelphia: University of Pennsylvania Press, 1952.
Hordes, Stanley M. "The Inquisition as Economic and Political Agent:
The Campaign of the Mexican Holy Office Against the Crypto-Jews
in the Mid-Seventeenth Century." *The Americas* 39 (1982): 22–38.
Lamb, Ursula. "Religious Conflicts in the Conquest of Mexico." *Journal of
the History of Ideas* 17 (1956): 526–39.
Lavrin, Asunción. "The Role of the Nunneries in the Economy of New
Spain in the Eighteenth Century." *Hispanic American Historical
Review* 46 (1966): 371–93.
Liebman, Seymour. *The Jews in New Spain: Faith, Flame and the Inquisi-
tion.* Coral Gables: University of Miami Press, 1970.
Liss, Peggy Korn. "Jesuit Contributions to the Ideology of Spanish Empire
in Mexico." *The Americas* 29 (1973): 314–33, 449–70.
Morales, Francisco. *Ethnic and Social Background of the Franciscan Friars
in Seventeenth Century Mexico.* Washington, D.C.: Academy of
American Franciscan History, 1973.
Murray, Paul V. *The Catholic Church in Mexico: Historical Essays for the
General Reader.* Mexico: Editorial E.P.M., 1965.
Phelan, John L. *The Millennial Kingdom of the Franciscans in the New
World: A Study of the Writings of Gerónimo de Mendieta.* Berkeley:
University of California Press, 1956.
Poole, Stafford. *Pedro Moya de Contreras: Catholic Reform and Royal
Power in New Spain, 1571–1591.* Berkeley: University of California
Press, 1987.
Ricard, Robert. *The Spiritual Conquest of Mexico.* Berkeley: University of
California Press, 1966.
Riley, James D. "The Wealth of the Jesuits in Mexico, 1670–1767." *The
Americas* 33 (1976): 226–66.
Schwaller, John F. *The Church and Clergy in Sixteenth-Century Mexico.*
Albuquerque: University of New Mexico Press, 1987.
Sheridan, Thomas, Charles W. Polzer, Thomas Naylor, and Diana Hadley.
The Franciscan Missions of Northern Mexico. Spanish Borderland
Source Books, no. 20. New York: Garland, 1992.
Shiels, William E. *King and Church: The Rise and Fall of the Patronato
Real.* Chicago: Loyola University Press, 1961.

12

Colonial Society: Race and Social Status

Racial Groups

The conquistadores of Mexico were adventurers, not true colonists. They sought no religious haven, nor were they searching for fields to cultivate or shops to tend. Heirs of a military tradition, they responded to the allure of danger and the promise of wealth in the New World. Not for them the prosaic toil of the pioneer.

The married among them left their wives and children in Spain; thus the restraints of domesticity were absent, and few felt any moral qualms about their sexual behavior in the Indies. From the beginning Spaniards mixed freely with female natives, leaving offspring of a new ethnic type. Just as readily they consorted with black women, fathering more progeny of mixed blood. Later cohabitation of the mixed children themselves resulted in additional racial distinctions, so that within a couple of generations the ethnic pattern was quite diverse.

Society in New Spain was composed of three basic ethnic groups: Spanish, Indian, and African. Miscegenation, however, produced offspring of mixed bloods who were called *mestizos*. Commonly, a mestizo is considered to be of Spanish–Indian parentage, but it is helpful to distinguish the racial categories more precisely:

> *Euromestizos:* those of a Spanish–Indian mixture, with European (Spanish) ethnic and cultural characteristics predominating. Such persons in the early colony were often considered as *Spanish* and later as *criollo*.

203

Indomestizos: persons of a Spanish–Indian mixture, with Indian ethnic and cultural characteristics predominating. They formed the bulk of those termed *mestizo.*

Afromestizos: persons of mixed bloods in which a black strain was evident. If Spanish–black, the designation was *mulatto;* if black–Indian, the designation was *zambo.*

Because all of the above combined in further strains, racial and cultural traits often became hopelessly confused; a minimum of sixteen different ethnic types were identified during the colonial period. Generalizations about the different groups of colonial society can be misleading, however, because conditions did not remain static. Some of the nonwhite castes could not hold official positions in royal government or become clerics, carry arms, serve in the military, or dress like Spaniards, but such prohibitions were by no means always in force. Anyone who relies extensively on published Spanish legislation will have a distorted view of the reality of colonial life; not only did laws change frequently, but in many instances they were not enforced. Although a fairly rigid class system was defined in the sixteenth century, by the eighteenth century society was quite different in several respects. The most notable change was the greatly increased number of those of mixed bloods, who were diverse in character and socioeconomic circumstances. The majority of the colored castes were in a depressed state, but enough of them achieved a measure of prosperity and recognition for their abilities and accomplishments to make facile generalizations invalid.

The Spaniards

The elite of society in the post-Conquest colony was made up of the more than two thousand Spaniards in Mexico in 1521. As the conquerors and first settlers, they were undisputed lords of the land; yet many were oddly cast in this role, coming as they did from humble origins. Some did indeed spring from the *hidalgo* class in Spain, that is, from the lower rung of nobility. Men in easy circumstances, however, seldom leave the comfort and security of family, friends, and familiar surroundings for the dangers, hardships, and uncertainties of alien shores—unless of course they are drawn by some noble cause. While some of the conqueror-hidalgos came from good families, more often than not they had little material wealth. In Spain property was passed on intact from one generation to the next, and it was customary for the eldest sons to inherit all. Under this practice of primogeniture, younger sons, as well as daughters, were left with no inherited wealth. The options open to penniless youths of good family were limited because their pretensions to hidalgo status prevented them from taking employment deemed unworthy of their class. A career in law might enable one to find a place in the royal bureaucracy, but it required a university education. So the best career possibilities lay in the church or the army. Owing to the long history of warfare in Spain, by the High Middle Ages the warrior was a figure of assured social standing, associated with the nobility. And as Lyle N. McAlister writes, "The bearing of arms was honorable while productive occupations—agriculture, trade, manufacturing—were dishonorable. Quality and honor, moreover, came to be conceived of not as individual attributes which could be acquired but as deriving from lineage."[1] The New World presented a rare opportunity—one of dubious distinction for a career-minded hidalgo, perhaps, but holding out the potential of great material rewards for the adventurer. Furthermore, the Spanish Indies offered those of ignoble birth the opportunity to acquire "quality and honor." Soon many expected to be called "Don" as if it were a birthright.

The majority of the conquerors, in fact, came from the working class, and many of them had trades. Suddenly, tailors, carpenters, masons, cobblers, seamen, and the like found themselves part of the new post-Conquest aristocracy. History offers few comparable examples of such rapid upward social mobility. Aside from the true hidalgos, the conquerors were an unlikely lot of "nobles." Many were coarse in speech, unrefined in manner, half literate (if indeed they were lettered at all), ignorant of the social amenities, and altogether possessing few of the attributes associated with even the minor nobility.

The needs of these Spaniards were taken care of by Indian servants and laborers, and their time was free to enjoy the simple diversions available in the developing society. Even though most of them groused about their pinched circumstances, individual economic well-being varied so much as to render generalizations difficult. Some of them ended up isolated in remote provinces with very few Indians, while others were favored with large Indian towns near one of the main Spanish settlements. A few

1. Lyle N. McAlister, "Social Structure and Social Change in New Spain," *Hispanic American Historical Review*, 43 (1963): 350.

found official positions, either in local government or in the royal bureaucracy, both of which could open the way to profiteering. It is probably safe to say that all enhanced their pre-Conquest socioeconomic status.

The natural leader of this early society was Fernando Cortés, who wielded great power and authority. He had a house in Coyoacán, another large residence built on the site of Moctezuma's demolished palace in Mexico City, a palace in Cuernavaca, a house in Oaxaca, as well as other dwellings. With his many tributaries and powers Cortés resembled one of the great feudal lords of Europe.

The heyday of the conquerors was short lived. Soon the colony was invaded by a different type of Spaniard, educated and well connected in the mother country. Royal officials with legal training entered to look after the crown's interests, and private lawyers (despite Cortés's plea that they be excluded) arrived to involve themselves with the interminable lawsuits that arose. Cultured men of the church came to set a higher moral and intellectual tone. Most of these newcomers were of a more elevated social status than the conquerors, and they were favored at the royal court. Crown favorites who had never faced a Mexican warrior were awarded encomiendas and official sinecures, while some veterans of the Conquest were in need. The men of Cortés bitterly resented this turn of affairs, seeing the late arrivals as grasping, officious types who were taking what rightfully belonged to those who had won the land. At the same time the more refined newcomers from Spain ridiculed the pretensions of the "hidalgos" of the Indies, some of whom had been given high titles and coats of arms. This was the germ of the long conflict between those who felt a deep bond to the land of Mexico and those from Spain who served the king's interest and whose real attachment was to the mother country. The permanent settlers observed that most officials and many clergymen were only temporary residents, passing a few years in the colony en route to bigger and better things and therefore insensitive to local concerns about the future.

A number of the conquerors, dissatisfied with the spoils in Mexico, left for the conquests of Central America and Peru and other ventures. Following the restraints imposed on Cortés, the symbol of encomendero power, and the seating of royal control through the audiencia and viceroy, the first settlers were further hurt by the passage of the New Laws of 1542. Although important parts of the legislation were not implemented, the laws were symptomatic of the trend to erode the encomenderos' position. After the clumsy attempt to assert themselves during the Avila-Cortés conspiracy, encomenderos were reduced to despair.

With the phasing out of Conquest society, the remainder of the colonial period would be dominated in circles of influence by men sent from the Spanish peninsula—the *peninsulares*, or *gachupines*, as they were derisively called by those born in Mexico. The peninsulares held the best positions in government and in the church, and they had the most prestige in the community. They were seen as attractive suitors for the daughters of conquerors; the gachupín gained an encomienda in such a match and the daughter rose in social stature. It is estimated that during the three centuries of colonial rule between 250,000 and 300,000 Spaniards entered Mexico, but their numbers were never large at any one time.

The Criollos

The second level of colonial society was formed by those of Spanish blood born in Mexico. These criollos were by physical appearance indistinguishable from the peninsulares, but the mere fact of their New World birth was sufficient to prejudice their status. It was commonly held by those born in Europe that America's environment was somehow detrimental, that the climate was enervating and corrosive, and that the atmosphere produced beings who were physically, mentally, and morally inferior. Thus the criollos were viewed by the peninsulares as innately lazy, effete, irresponsible, and lacking in both vigor and intelligence. To these defects were joined all the social and cultural limitations of life in the colony. Such opinions formed a convenient pretext for the gachupines to justify their favored position; and, although for various reasons the characteristics ascribed to the criollos were not entirely erroneous, they had nothing to do with geography. Nor were the criollos themselves completely wrong in considering the peninsulares arrogant, hypocritical, and rapacious. Both views were, of course, overdrawn.

The criollos, despite their secondary rank, were in a relatively favorable position in the society of New Spain; merely by virtue of their light skins they were considered superior to the darker masses below them. They could rise to respectable levels in church organization and to lower- and middle-rank posts in the royal bureaucracy, and they were able to dominate the cabildos.

WHITE POPULATION OF NEW SPAIN

Year	Whites	Comments
1521	2,329	peninsulares
1529	8,000	peninsulares
1560	20,211	peninsulares and criollos
1570	57,000	peninsulares and criollos
1646	114,000–125,000	mostly criollos
1770	over 750,000	mostly criollos
1793	1,095,000	70,000 of these were peninsulares

In fact some criollos were successful in attaining the highest offices of both church and government, and eventually a number also held high military rank. Nevertheless, although criollos were legally eligible to all offices, there is no question that they suffered discrimination. Distance from the power centers in Spain and the less prestigious academic degrees of the colony prevented their having equal opportunity.

Therefore many criollos devoted themselves to ranching, agriculture, and mining, and some prospered. Commerce, which had been held in low esteem by the socially conscious in Spain, was undertaken without hesitation by criollos. Accordingly, there emerged a criollo aristocracy, based on wealth, that lived in comfort, educated its sons (sometimes sending them abroad), and acquired considerable prestige, especially in regions outside the capital. The powerful criollo *hacendados*, or owners of large ranches, and mining barons felt in no way inferior to the presumptuous gachupines of the petty bureaucracy. Gradually the criollos (very few of whom, after all, had ever seen Spain) became alienated from the mother country. Traditional ties were especially weak in provincial areas, which were remote from the ceremonial and emotional trappings of church and state that symbolized royal authority and evoked mother Spain.

The Mestizos

During the Conquest friendly caciques gave women to the Spaniards, and other native females either joined the conquerors by choice or were taken forcibly. These women cooked for their men, nursed their wounds, carried their belongings, and shared their beds. Informal unions of Spaniard and native spawned the new physical type of the mestizo. Many such liaisons were fleeting, but others ripened into long, comfortable arrangements. In the early, hopeful years the conquerors visualized advantageous marriages with Spanish girls. But when, as happened in most cases, circumstances prevented their returning to Spain in desirable style, they remained in Mexico, where their relative positions were sounder. Other Spaniards already had wives in Spain or in the Caribbean, and, although by law they were obligated to send for them, by one pretext or another many avoided doing so. In 1551, according to the bishop of Mexico, there were five hundred married Spaniards in his diocese whose wives languished outside the colony. Meantime most of these men took native concubines, and some even remarried, thereby risking trial for bigamy.

Crown and church wanted Spaniards married and settled down in order to give the colony stability, and for that reason they encouraged Spaniards to marry Indian girls, through whom Spanish culture would more readily be transmitted to the conquered people. Mixed marriages involving Spaniards usually meant Spanish men and Indian women, because Spanish women seldom married outside their caste, except for an occasional mestizo of some prominence. In particular, the crown encouraged Spaniards to marry daughters of the Indian nobility and often compensated those who did so with encomiendas and official posts. Some of the conquerors found the proposition attractive, and those who took as wives the daughters or nieces of Moctezuma or other native aristocrats usually found themselves in comfortable circumstances.

But in the immediate post-Conquest years most Spaniards rejected marriage with Indian women as socially unacceptable. The shortage of Spanish women in the colony, however, made it difficult for many to find suitable wives. Encomenderos felt particular pressure, as they were required to marry within three years or lose their grants of Indians. So as time passed, quite a few Spaniards married their Indian mistresses, often legitimizing their children.

At the fall of the Aztec confederation the 2,329 people in the company of Cortés included only seven Spanish women, and between 1520 and 1540 no more than 6 percent of Spanish immigrants to Mexico were female. The problems arising from the shortage of women were real, but they have been somewhat exaggerated. Most of the married conquerors eventually sent for their wives. And, before long, more Spanish women arrived, for many of the early settlers, officials, and ecclesiastics brought their unmarried sisters, nieces, and other female relatives with them. In addition, by 1540 there were a good number of mestizo girls of marriageable age. They may not have been the preferred, pure Spanish types, but many were recognized daughters of prosperous and socially prominent conquistadores. As such, they often brought substantial dowries and position, along with names of distinction in the colony. The child of a Spaniard and a mestizo woman was classified as a *castizo* and often passed as criollo. Thus by late sixteenth century there seem to have been almost enough females considered white to go around. Consequently, few Spaniards or criollos of any social standing were still marrying Indian women.

Financial considerations were important factors in marriage; a woman of property had a decided advantage, often to the exclusion of certain other qualities. A widow of an encomendero, for example, seldom remained unmarried very long. If she happened to be an Indian or mestizo she might well be more attractive to a poor Spaniard than a penniless Spanish girl. If an encomendero died leaving no son or widow to inherit his Indian villages, the encomienda passed to his eldest daughter. If single, she was required to marry within a year in order to keep the encomienda—or, if a minor, within one year of reaching legal age. Women in these circumstances seldom lacked for suitors.

Mestizos formed a large, discrete group in society, and it is impossible to draw easy conclusions on their status. To take a notable case, Don Martín Cortés was the son of the captain and Doña Marina. Technically he was a mestizo, but such was the standing of his parents that he was certainly considered to be a Spaniard and entitled to every honor—except of course the inheritance of the estate of the marqués del Valle, which went to his younger but legitimate criollo brother (who was also named Martín). Fernando Cortés took his mestizo son with him to Spain when the boy was only five. While still a young child, Martín was made a knight of the prestigious Order of Santiago and a page to the prince (later Philip II). He fought with distinction in Spanish armies in Algeria and Germany and later he fell in crown service battling the Moriscos in Granada. Pedro de Alvarado's mestizo daughter also had high social status; she married a cousin of the duke of Alburquerque, one of Spain's most powerful nobles. Many less prominent mestizos likewise married well and achieved highly respectable places in society.

The majority of the mestizos, however, were much worse off. A high percentage were illegitimate, especially during the sixteenth century, when the term *mestizo* was almost synonymous with *bastard*. Unrecognized by their fathers, most stayed with their Indian mothers and so became culturally more Indian than Spanish. The mestizos were, by and large, poor, uneducated, and in a distinctly inferior socioeconomic class. For every mestizo who gained a comfortable place in society, there were a hundred others who remained culturally adrift, living in miserable circumstances and scorned by the upper class. For most of the colonial period they were grouped socially with Indians, blacks, and mulattoes.

The Indians

Central Mexico alone (roughly equal to the size of France) may have had a pre-Conquest population perhaps as high as twenty-five million, and for many decades the Indians of Mexico vastly outnumbered all other racial groups in New Spain. Then their numbers were catastrophically reduced. Waves of devastating plagues swept over the land, and after a century of Spanish occupation, during which many died from overwork and maltreatment, there were only about one million natives left. From their lowest number around 1630 they began to increase slowly. By the end of the colonial period the Indians were still the largest ethnic group, but not by so vast a percentage.

As a conquered people the natives were humbled and exploited by the victors. With the achievements of the Maya unknown and the splendor of Tenochtitlán a receding memory, the Spaniards saw the Indians as an inferior people. There were some enlightened ecclesiastics and a few royal officials who pleaded the Indian cause; they appealed to Christian ethics, emphasized the natives' positive qualities, and pressed for humane treatment. All too many Spaniards, however, considered the Indians simply pagans, cannibals, and sodomites. Natives were frequently described as lazy, disposed to vices, devious, and backward. Their capacities became such a subject of dispute that in 1537 the pope was moved to issue a bull (*Sublimis Deus*) declaring that the natives were indeed men and capable of reason! But by insisting on the low character of the conquered peoples,

INDIAN POPULATION OF CENTRAL MEXICO

Year	Indians	Plague Years	Comments
1519	25,200,000		
		1520	smallpox
		1529	measles
1532	16,800,000		
		1545	matlazáhuatl (typhus?); Indian deaths est. 800,000
1548	6,300,000		
1568	2,650,000		
		1576	matlazáhuatl; Indian deaths est. 2,000,000
1580	1,900,000		
1595	1,375,000		
1605	1,075,000		
1625–50	1,000,000 (or less?)		lowest point of Indian population
		1737	matlazáhuatl
		1779–80	smallpox? almost 20 percent of Mexico City's population died
		1784	respiratory infection plus famine; Indian deaths est. 1,300,000
1793	2,500,000		
1810	3,676,281		

Sources: Figures to the year 1605 are based on the researches of Sherburne F. Cook and Woodrow Borah: *The Indian Population of Central Mexico, 1531–1610* (Berkeley, 1960), and *The Aboriginal Population of Central Mexico on the Eve of the Spanish Conquest* (Berkeley, 1963). Their counts, especially those prior to 1568, are considered much too high by some scholars.

self-serving Spaniards justified keeping them in bondage, in line with Aristotelian philosophy that some men were the "natural slaves" of those "superior" to them.

Legally Indians were considered as minors and wards of crown and church. Their care and supervision were commended to clergymen, corregidores, and encomenderos. The church is sometimes criticized for keeping its wards childlike, but the crown must share the blame. Yet, because of their tutelary status, the Indians were, at least in some respects, protected and given consideration. There is little reason to doubt the genuine concern of the crown and church for the Indians' welfare, and many laws were passed for their benefit. Lawyers eagerly encouraged Indians to file lawsuits, and a surprisingly large number were settled in the Indians' favor. Ultimately, however, the colony's

Pre-Columbian dress of Mexican women. Modern versions of the blouses (*uipilli*) and skirts (*cueitl*) are still worn today in some regions.

welfare depended upon the labor of the Indians, and so they were doomed to serve the interests of the Spaniards.

Despite the cruelty of certain pre-Conquest practices and the ferocity of native warriors, when the fighting ended most of the Indians proved to be gentle, pliable people. Those within the Spanish pale converted to Christianity and Spanish ways with surprising ease. The process was facilitated by the shortage of strong Indian leaders, for many nobles had died from battle wounds or disease. They were replaced by lackeys of the Spaniards, who imitated Spanish ways and frequently exploited their own people.

The extent to which Indians were integrated into the society of New Spain depended upon their proximity to Spanish population centers. Those in isolated regions had little contact with the white men, aside from their clergymen, an occasional provincial official, and perhaps the overseer of their encomendero. They lived in small villages, called *pueblos*, preserved their customs, cultivated their small plots of land, and never learned Spanish. They paid tribute to their encomenderos and took their turns at required labor but otherwise lived in a world set apart.

Interestingly enough, by the seventeenth century quite a large number of Indians had willingly left their ancestral villages and migrated to the cities to work in Spanish homes or shops and even volunteered to labor on estates of white men. It appears that European culture came to have some attractions for them. Indians as individuals had not been acquisitive, but as they became acculturated to Christian ways, the promise of possessions and a more varied life drew some from their native villages. Another reason for the migrations, however, was the steady erosion of agricultural lands, which made life in some farming regions difficult. But life with the Spaniards was not easy either, and Indians were all too often overworked and abused in various ways. Tied to the land, without hope of anything better, many lost initiative and in their despair often turned to alcohol.

The Blacks

During the Conquest there were half a dozen blacks with the Spanish forces. In the Caribbean an expanding sugar economy resulted in the importation of large numbers of African slaves, and eventually many were taken to Mexico. At first most slaves were personal servants imported by prominent men, who often had three or four in their household staffs. Less fortunate were those slaves assigned to hard labor, especially in the mines. Indian laborers, both slave and free, had never been satisfactory in regimented labor, and it was commonly thought that one black could do the work of four Indians. And as a consequence of the declining Indian population, 120,000 or more slaves entered Mexico between 1519 and 1650. But blacks were expensive, while natives cost little. Accordingly, slaves from Africa used for labor were put where they could produce returns justifying their high purchase price, and because of their value some care had to be shown for their health. They produced well in the mines, but the dank shafts made them ill. On the other hand, they were well able to withstand enervating labor in the humid, fever-ridden tropics. They were often trained for important skilled positions and sometimes put in charge of Indian workers as overseers in mining operations, small factories, and ranches. Other blacks be-

BLACK POPULATION OF NEW SPAIN

Year	Blacks	Blacks and/or Afromestizos	Comments
1521	6		
1553	20,000		Afromestizos uncounted
1560	17,312		Afromestizos uncounted
1570	18,535	1,465	perhaps 2,000 blacks or mulattoes were escaped slaves
1580	18,500	1,500	figures are probably low
1600		140,000	
1646	35,089		Afromestizos uncounted
1650		130,000	including 20,119 black and mulatto slaves
1793	6,000		Afromestizos uncounted
1810	10,000	624,461	

came accomplished artisans, bringing their masters good profits. It was not uncommon for the slave to be given a share of the profits, which eventually allowed him to purchase his freedom.

Mulattoes, offspring of the union of Spaniards and blacks, were often able to improve their circumstances, both because they were thoroughly Hispanicized and because their Spanish fathers could ease the way for them by making sure they were free. Otherwise the mulatto would inherit the status of his mother according to law and would be a slave if she were one. By late sixteenth century there were many free blacks and mulattoes. The number of mulattoes increased as time passed because black women were attractive to the Spaniards, and, although marriage between them was infrequent (and officially discouraged), they certainly commingled freely. Over the generations, however, the church discouraged the practice of concubinage by pressuring Spaniards to marry their mistresses, of whatever color. Under threat of being deprived of absolution, for example, twenty Spaniards married black and mulatto slaves and free women in Puebla between 1690 and 1695.[2]

Perhaps two hundred thousand Africans entered Mexico during the colonial period. It appears that by around 1560 there

2. Magnus Mörner, *Race Mixture in the History of Latin America* (Boston, 1967), p. 66.

were almost as many blacks as whites in New Spain. The number of pure blacks was never great, however, while the number of mulattoes increased greatly. By 1650 there were over 35,000 blacks and about 130,000 Afromestizos. There was always a shortage of black women (the usual ratio of slaves introduced being two males for every female), which led many black men to take Indian wives. When blacks mated with Indian women the racial type of the zambo evolved. Despite official attempts to prevent it, contact between blacks and Indians was frequent, particularly in household staffs, where there were often numerous servants of various ethnic strains under one roof.

From the early years of Spanish occupation black slaves in Mexico had frequently run away from their masters, sometimes joining Indians in isolated regions. As more slaves were imported, free blacks were seen as a threat to the colony. There were apprehensions that blacks would incite a general rebellion, and many instances of black resistance worried settlers. As early as 1537, for example, blacks in Mexico City were rumored to have a "king" who was enlisting Indians to help them overthrow white authority. The viceroy arrested the leaders and had them hanged and quartered. In the 1540s other conspiracies produced grave concern and talk of limiting the importation of slaves. Blacks were forbidden to carry arms; they were forced to observe a curfew; and no more than three could gather in public. Despite such precautions in the 1560s and 1570s there were several slave insurrections, particularly in the northern mining and ranching areas. Often in alliance with natives, free blacks attacked ranches and assaulted wagon trains. In response, runaway slaves (maroons, or *cimarrones*) were hunted down by bounty hunters and punished with floggings, or hanging if they had committed serious crimes. And in spite of a royal order in 1540 that forbade the punishing of slaves by cutting off "parts that one cannot in modesty name," castration was revived when rebellions continued. By 1570 it was believed that some two thousand maroons were living outside the law and committing crimes.

Around the beginning of the seventeenth century the threat of black resistance centered in the eastern region, especially near Veracruz. There an elderly slave named Yanga had held out in the mountains for thirty years. In 1609 the viceroy sent an army of six hundred men against Yanga, whose camp had eighty men and some women and children. The viceroy's soldiers were given some lessons in guerrilla maneuvers by Yanga, and, when the skirmishing finally ended in a standoff, the government agreed to treat with the black rebel. It was an extraordinary concession on the part of royal authority, and Yanga's struggle was surely one of the most successful instances of black resistance in the New World. He and his followers remained free by agreeing to cause no more trouble and to help track down other runaways. Not long afterward an independent black town, San Lorenzo de los Negros, was founded near modern Córdoba.

Through miscegenation, manumission, and the purchase of freedom by slaves themselves black slavery declined considerably over the generations. Although toward the end of the colonial period there were many Afromestizos, only around ten thousand could be considered blacks. Of those, perhaps only six thousand or so were slaves by 1800, mainly congregated in the environs of Veracruz and Acapulco.

Other Groups

It may be noted briefly that there were other distinct groups in colonial Mexico. Despite the ban on foreigners for much of the three centuries, a substantial number of Portuguese entered along with Italians, a few Frenchmen, Germans, Middle Europeans, Englishmen, and Greeks. Some were specialists, such as scientists, who were in New Spain with royal approval, but others sneaked in, usually by bribing officials. Officials were more concerned with religious orthodoxy than with nationality. Yet there were many, especially among the Portuguese, of Jewish origin in the colony. Finally, a large number of Orientals—Filipinos and Chinese for the most part—entered the country on the Manila galleons. One authority believes that in some decades of the seventeenth century as many as six thousand may have arrived.[3]

The diversity of race in Mexico was well advanced before the close of the sixteenth century. White remained the color of privilege, but the typical colonist came to be one of various shades of brown. In a true fusion of races, the modern Mexican emerged. He became what has been called *la raza cósmica*—the cosmic race.

3. J. I. Israel, *Race, Class and Politics in Colonial Mexico, 1610–1670* (London, 1975), p. 76.

Population Figures

Tenochtitlán had a population of perhaps 250,000 at the advent of the Spaniards, but the Christian city that arose on its ruins began with far fewer people. In 1560 Mexico City had about 8,000 Spaniards. By 1574 there were around 15,000 Spaniards, in addition to a large Indian population and significant numbers of blacks and mixed bloods. By 1800 Mexico City had approximately 137,000 souls; it was the largest city in the western hemisphere, but still had perhaps less than half the population boasted by the Aztec capital at the time of the Conquest.

Population figures for the colony as a whole are especially suspect because of the difficulty of counting people in so many isolated villages. An estimate of 1560 showed a total of 20,211 Spaniards (which no doubt included criollos), 16,147 black slaves, 2,445 mestizos, and 1,465 mulattoes. Excluding the Indians, who still constituted the vast majority of the people of New Spain, the other racial groups totaled 40,268. Of those, around 50 percent were white, 40 percent were black, 6 percent were mestizos, and 3.5 percent were mulattoes.[4] This count almost certainly minimizes the numbers of the castes: doubtless many of the "Spaniards" were technically castizos and mestizos, and a good share of the blacks were probably mulattoes and zambos. The 1793 census reflects the slow recovery of the Indian population, from its lowest point of 1 million around 1630 to 2.5 million. The same count shows a mestizo figure that is probably much too

GENERAL POPULATION OF NEW SPAIN

1793

Racial Category	Number	Percentage (rounded)
Indians	2,500,000	52
Europeans (peninsulares)	70,000	1
Criollos	1,025,000	21
Mestizos (various mixes)	1,231,000	25
Blacks	6,000	0.1
Total population		
	4,832,000	

Source: Based on Agustín Cue Cánovas, *Historia social y económica de México (1521–1854)* (Mexico, 1972), p. 134.

4. C. E. Marshall, "The Birth of the Mestizo in New Spain," *Hispanic American Historical Review* 19 (1939): 184.

low. At Independence, in 1821, almost exactly three hundred years after the Conquest, the total population of Mexico was around 7 million, of many varied racial strains.

Recommended for Further Study

Aguirre Beltrán, Gonzalo. "The Slave Trade in Mexico." *Hispanic American Historical Review* 24 (1944): 412–31.

Anderson, Arthur J. O., Frances Berdan, and James Lockhart, eds. *Beyond the Codices: The Nahua View of Colonial Mexico.* Berkeley: University of California Press, 1976.

Ashburn, P. M. *The Ranks of Death: A Medical History of the Conquest of America.* New York: Coward-McCann, 1947.

Bacigalupo, Marvyn Helen. *A Changing Perspective: Attitudes Toward Creole Society in New Spain (1521–1610).* London: Tamesis, 1981.

Borah, Woodrow. "Race and Class in Mexico." *Pacific Historical Review* 23 (1953): 331–42.

Caravaglia, Juan Carlos and Juan Carlos Grosso. "Mexican Elites of a Provincial Town: The Landowners of Tepeaca (1700–1870)." *Hispanic American Historical Review* 2 (1990): 255–94.

Carroll, Patrick J. *Blacks in Colonial Veracruz: Race, Ethnicity, and Regional Development.* Austin: University of Texas Press, 1991.

Chance, John K. *Race and Class in Colonial Oaxaca.* Stanford, Calif.: Stanford University Press, 1978.

Chandler, Dewitt S. *Social Assistance and Bureaucratic Politics: The Montepíos of Colonial Mexico, 1767–1821.* Albuquerque: University of New Mexico Press, 1991.

Cook, Sherburne F. "The Incidence and Significance of Disease among the Aztecs and Related Tribes." *Hispanic American Historical Review* 26 (1946): 320–25.

Cook, Sherburne F., and Woodrow Borah. *The Aboriginal Population of Central Mexico on the Eve of the Spanish Conquest.* Berkeley: University of California Press, 1963.

———. *The Indian Population of Central Mexico, 1531–1610.* Berkeley: University of California Press, 1960.

Cooper, Donald. *Epidemic Disease in Mexico City, 1761–1813.* Austin: University of Texas Press, 1965.

Crosby, Alfred W., Jr. *The Columbian Exchange: Biological and Cultural Consequences of 1492.* Westport, Conn.: Greenwood Press, 1973.

Davidson, David. "Negro Slave Control and Resistance in Colonial Mexico, 1519–1650." *Hispanic American Historical Review* 46 (1966): 235–53.

Dusenberry, William H. "Discriminatory Aspects of Legislation in Colonial Mexico." *Journal of Negro History* 33 (1948): 284–302.

Franco, Jean. *Plotting Women: Gender and Representation in Mexico.* New York: Columbia University Press, 1989.

Guthrie, Chester. "Riots in Seventeenth-Century Mexico." In *Greater America: Essays in Honor of Herbert Eugene Bolton,* edited by Adele Ogden and Engel Sluiter, pp. 243–58. Berkeley: University of California Press, 1945.

————. "Trade, Industry and Labor in Seventeenth-Century Mexico City." *Revista de Historia de América* 7 (1939): 103–34.

Hanke, Lewis U. *Aristotle and the American Indian: A Study in Race Prejudice in the Modern World.* Bloomington: Indiana University Press, 1970.

————. *The Spanish Struggle for Justice in the Conquest of America.* Philadelphia: University of Pennsylvania Press, 1949.

Hoberman, Louisa. "Bureaucracy and Disaster: Mexico City and the Flood of 1629." *Journal of Latin American Studies* 6 (1974): 211–30.

————. *Mexico's Merchant Elite, 1590–1660.* Durham, N.C.: Duke University Press, 1991.

Israel, J. I. *Race, Class and Politics in Colonial Mexico, 1610–1670.* London: Oxford University Press, 1975.

Keen, Benjamin. *The Aztec Image in Western Thought.* New Brunswick, N.J.: Rutgers University Press, 1971.

Lavrin, Asunción, and Edith Couturier. "Dowries and Wills: A View of Women's Socioeconomic Role in Colonial Guadalajara and Puebla, 1640–1790." *Hispanic American Historical Review* 59 (1979): 280–304.

Lavrin, Asunción, ed. *Sexuality and Marriage in Colonial Latin America.* Lincoln: University of Nebraska Press, 1989.

Love, Edgar F. "Legal Restrictions on Afro-Indian Relations in Colonial Mexico." *Journal of Negro History* 55 (1970): 131–39.

McAlister, Lyle N. "Social Structure and Social Change in New Spain." *Hispanic American Historical Review* 43 (1963): 349–70.

Marshall, C. E. "The Birth of the Mestizo in New Spain." *Hispanic American Historical Review* 19 (1939): 161–84.

Morales, Francisco. *Ethnic and Social Background of the Franciscan Friars in Seventeenth Century Mexico.* Washington, D.C.: Academy of American Franciscan History, 1973.

Mörner, Magnus. *Race Mixture in the History of Latin America.* Boston: Little, Brown, 1967.

Nunn, Charles F. *Foreign Immigrants in Early Bourbon Mexico, 1700–1760.* Cambridge: Cambridge University Press, 1979.

Palmer, Colin A. *Slaves of the White God: Blacks in Mexico.* Cambridge: Cambridge University Press, 1976.

Reff, Daniel. *Disease, Depopulation, and Cultural Change in Northwestern New Spain.* Salt Lake City: University of Utah Press, 1991.

Tutino, John. "Power, Class, and Family: Men and Women in the Mexican Elite, 1700–1810." *The Americas* 39 (1983): 359–82.

Zambardino, Rudolph. "Mexico's Population in the Sixteenth Century: Demographic Anomaly or Mathematical Illusions?" *Journal of Interdisciplinary History* 11 (1980): 1–27.

13

Culture and Daily Life in New Spain

Education

When Don Antonio de Mendoza arrived in Mexico fourteen years after the fall of Tenochtitlán, he was greeted by, among others, an Indian boy who recited in classic Latin. The amused viceroy soon learned that the energetic friars had already made a significant impact, Hispanicizing the natives through education. It was a plan devoutly encouraged by both crown and church, for quite aside from sentiments of altruism, there were practical considerations. The sincere desire to Christianize the conquered people was feasible only through their understanding Spanish; moreover, it hastened their assimilation of Spanish ways, which was essential to the goal of a more settled society.

In Spain a broad educational system was not seen as a responsibility of the state. Education was, rather, an individual concern, usually involving only those of the privileged class, while instruction itself was the province of the church. Only on the university level did the crown evince strong interest, primarily to prepare young men for careers in the bureaucracy. The church was equally concerned with higher education in order to instruct clergymen, who would in turn run the schools in the colonies, as in Spain. But in Mexico there developed the curious irony of at least a few well-educated Indians being held inferior by some illiterate Spaniards.

One is struck by the cultural vitality in the early years of a Conquest society that was in so many ways both turbulent and rustic. The impulse to refinement came from learned clergymen primarily because educated laymen were usually involved in

government, law, or other professional interests. Therefore the
debt owed to the intellectual and cultural attainments of the religious orders is immense.

The first prominent educator in Spanish Mexico was Pedro de
Gante, a Franciscan lay brother and illegitimate relative of
Charles V. By 1524 he was teaching Indian boys, and later he
founded the famous school of San José, where under his direction hundreds of native youths were given primary instruction
and adults were taught trades. While the children were drilled
in Latin, music, and other academic subjects, the elders became
the colony's masons, carpenters, blacksmiths, painters, and
sculptors. Their skills were put to good use by Gante, who
claimed to have supervised personally the building of one hundred chapels and churches.

The school of Santa Cruz de Tlatelolco was founded in 1536
by Viceroy Mendoza and Bishop Zumárraga. With such powerful patrons it became the outstanding Indian school and aimed at
the higher instruction for the sons of nobles, through whom it
was thought Spanish culture would more easily be passed on to
commoners. Aside from the fundamentals of reading and writing, courses were offered in Latin, rhetoric, logic, and philosophy, as well as music and native medicine. Taught by learned
humanists, the youths received excellent instruction, and they in
turn aided the friars in schools and church.

The most appealing figure in early education was Vasco de
Quiroga, whose practical approach to education was distinct. A

The Colegio de Santa Cruz de Tlatelolco.

Vasco de Quiroga (1470?–1565). A distinguished judge of the audiencia and later bishop of Michoacán, "Tata Vasco" successfully experimented with utopian Indian villages.

man of varied interests, Quiroga was a humanist, lawyer, and a judge in the second audiencia. But his fame rests on his personal crusade to benefit the conquered peoples. Using his own capital, the aging lawyer established his first hospital-school of Santa Fé in 1531–32, on the outskirts of Mexico City. Shortly thereafter he moved to Michoacán, near Lake Pátzcuaro in the area of the old kingdom of the Tarascans. There, in the region so troubled since the depredations of Núño de Guzmán, the benevolence of Quiroga inspired trust from the natives. Intrigued by Thomas More's *Utopia*, Quiroga attempted, with considerable success, to create an ideal society in the New World. He formed communities in which the Indians received training not only in religion but also in practical arts and crafts as well as in the rudiments of self-government. Each person worked six hours a day, sharing and contributing equally to the common welfare. Under Quiroga's tutelage the Indians became self-sufficient in agriculture and increased their prosperity through the preservation of traditional crafts. Appointed bishop of Michoacán in 1537, Quiroga continued to lead a productive life until past the age of ninety. With his death the utopian villages declined, but he had established some fine traditions that persisted, and descendants of his specialized artisans ply their crafts still.

There were various other Indian schools. The Jesuit San Gregorio Magno was started in 1586. Concern for abandoned or orphaned mestizos led to the opening in 1547 of the orphanage-school of San Juan de Letrán. But in the end the attempts to educate young Indians and mestizos, however congenial to the best interests of the young colony, were limited in scope. A small number of clergymen were involved, and, despite their intensive labors over the first half century, few of the natives learned to read and write. What had begun on such an auspicious note fell largely into neglect, as the cultural transition passed and apathy set in. After several decades of association with their conquerors, many of the Indians naturally absorbed the language and customs of the Spaniards, and the danger of large-scale rebellion seemed past. Now educating Indians and mestizos was perceived as not only unwarranted but socially undesirable.

The Franciscans are most identified with early education of Indians, and, similarly, the Jesuits and Augustinians were foremost in instructing criollos. Though many Spanish conquerors were uncultured, their sons inherited a social position that called for some measure of refinement. Consequently, there were primary schools, at least, in all Spanish communities of any size, and several advanced institutions in the colony. The most prestigious of such schools was the elite Jesuit Colegio de San Pedro y San Pablo, founded in 1576 and supported by profits from efficient Jesuit haciendas. Its graduates were equal, and sometimes superior, to those of the University of Mexico. An Augustinian institution, established a year earlier by the prominent intellectual Alonso de la Veracruz, also provided superior studies. There were in addition excellent seminaries where a high level of scholarship was maintained, perhaps the best being those of San Ildefonso and Tepotzotlán, both of which belonged to the Jesuits.

The most notable institution of learning was the Royal and Pontifical University of Mexico, created at the petition of Viceroy Mendoza and Bishop Zumárraga. The crown authorized it in 1551, and classes began in 1553, making it the first university to function in the New World. Founded with the aim of educating criollos for the clergy, the University was modeled on the Spanish University of Salamanca, with which it was supposed to be equal in rights and privileges. With an excellent faculty, it would produce many of New Spain's leading literary figures, scientists, lawyers, medical doctors, and theologians. During the colonial period the University granted around thirty thousand bachelors' degrees, and over one thousand masters' and doctorates. Late in the colonial period, in 1791, another university was founded in Guadalajara.

Girls were not completely ignored in the educational system, although, to be sure, they were given fewer opportunities. As early as 1534 women teachers arrived in Mexico and opened a school for girls, and soon nuns of various orders continued the tradition. Indian girls, under the tutelage of Gante, were taught mainly how to be good wives in the Spanish manner. In 1548 the Caridad school was established for orphaned *mestizas*, and in the late sixteenth century schools were founded for young criollo ladies.

Scholarship and Literature

Perhaps the most remarkable aspect of scholarship in the colony began not long after the Conquest with the diligent studies made by friars, among whom were a number of non-Spanish Europeans educated in France, Flanders, or other countries. Their inquiries into the nature of the native peoples and the land were truly phenomenal.

The Conquest itself was described by Cortés in his famous letters to the king, which have been translated into several languages and appear in many editions. A more popular account, however, remains the *Historia verdadera de la conquista de la Nueva España*, written by Bernal Díaz del Castillo, a footsoldier in Cortés's army. Díaz later moved to Guatemala, where he wrote his delightful, personalized account years after the events. He has left us a work that, with its simple prose and graphic descriptions, has become a classic of its kind.

Especially noteworthy are scholarly studies of the Indians: Motolinía's *Historia de los Indios*; the Spanish judge Alonso de Zorita's *Breve y sumaria relación de los señores de la Nueva España*; and the magisterial *Historia general de las cosas de la Nueva España* by Father Bernardino de Sahagún, a compendium of Aztec life that forms the basis for our knowledge of that people. Many other important works of the sixteenth century, including church histories, are eloquent testimony to the intellectual curiosity, industry, and painstaking scholarship of these early historians.

Although the scholarly studies of the sixteenth century were outstanding, valuable works were written in the seventeenth and eighteenth centuries as well. The most significant work is the

Carlos de Sigüenza y Góngora (1645–1700) was an eminent scholar of wide-ranging scientific and historical interests.

Historia antigua de México by the celebrated Jesuit Francisco Javier de Clavijero, a native-born Mexican considered to be the founder of modern Mexican historiography. Another erudite Jesuit was Francisco Javier Alegre, accomplished in many fields but best known for his history of the Jesuits in New Spain.

Like early anthropologists and ethnohistorians, clergymen preserved Indian histories, customs, and languages. They created dictionaries and grammars so that Indians could read and write in their own languages. Many of the friars became proficient in three or four native tongues. There were fewer scholars of note in other disciplines, although some excelled in studies of the flora, fauna, and medicines of Mexico. Occasionally research was sponsored by the crown: in 1571 the royal cosmographer was ordered to take a census, study eclipses, and undertake both a general and a natural history. The towering figure in scientific thought was Carlos de Sigüenza y Góngora, a criollo of universal renown during the seventeenth century. He studied to be a Jesuit at Tepotzotlán but was expelled for an infraction of the strict rules. Poet, historian, mathematician, astronomer, and antiquarian, he exemplifies the scientific curiosity in the colonial period.

Leaving aside chronicles of the Conquest, the literary achievements in New Spain began with the *Dialogues* of Cervantes de Salazar, who extolled the beauty of Mexico City and the quality of the university. The brightest literary light of all, however, and holding first place in the hearts of Mexicans, was a woman, *Sor* (Sister) Juana Inés de la Cruz (1651–95). Sor Juana grew from a child prodigy who amazed intellectuals at the viceregal court into a beautiful, graceful young woman with astonishing talents. An early exponent of women's rights, she lamented the disdain with which female efforts were greeted and the subordinate position of women generally. Her disenchantment was well expressed in one of her poems:

> Hombres necios que acusáis
> a la mujer sin razón,
> sin ver que sois la ocasión
> de lo mismo que culpáis;
>
> . . . .
>
> ¿Cuál mayor culpa ha tenido,
> en una pasión errada:
> la que cae de rogada
> o el que ruega de caído?
> ¿O cuál es más de culpar,
> aunque cualquiera mal haga:
> la que peca por la paga,
> o el que paga por pecar?[1]

At the age of eighteen she stunned her admirers by ignoring favorable prospects of marriage and her privileged position at court and entering a convent. She devoted the rest of her life to contemplation, intellectual exercises, and the writing of prose and lyric poetry that was surpassed in the Spanish-speaking world at the time perhaps only by Calderón de la Barca. This

1. Ah stupid men, unreasonable
   In blaming woman's nature,
   Oblivious that your acts incite
   The very faults you censure.

   . . . .

   Which has the greater sin when burned
   By the same lawless fever:
   She who is amorously deceived,
   Or he, the sly deceiver?
   Or which deserves the sterner blame,
   Though each will be a sinner:
   She who becomes a whore for pay,
   Or he who pays to win her?
   Translated by Robert Graves, in Joseph Sommers and Antonia Castañeda Shular, eds. *Chicano Literature: Text and Context* (Englewood Cliffs, N.J., 1972), pp. 10–11.

Colonial Mexico's greatest literary figure
was Sor Juana Inés de la Cruz (1651–
95). The portrait is by Miguel Cabrera.

nun-poetess, the first great poet in the New World, composed passionate, almost erotic, love poems of great beauty.

The eighteenth century, so full of conflicting ideologies and
intellectual ferment, did not produce creative writers comparable to those of the seventeenth century. Late in the colonial
period, however, Mexico had a major figure in José Joaquín Fernández de Lizardi. His satirical *El Periquillo Sarniento* (translated as *The Itching Parrot*) (1816), a picaresque depiction of
life in early nineteenth-century Mexico, is widely considered to
be the first true novel written in Spanish in Latin America.

Mexico City had a printing press by 1537–39. In the latter
year the first book was printed in the colony, a religious tract
written in both Náhuatl and Spanish by Bishop Zumárraga. Before the century was out, about 220 books had been produced in
the capital, although no other Mexican city had a press until a
century later. It is estimated that during the colonial period
some fifteen thousand books were printed in Mexico, among
them books in at least nine different Indian languages. In addition to many religious studies, there were dictionaries, gram-

mars, accounts of navigation, descriptions of natural phenomena like earthquakes, and works on medicine, methods of teaching reading, and simple arithmetic. In the second half of the sixteenth century at least twelve liturgical books containing music were published; in the same period only fourteen came out of presses in Spain.

Various obstacles were placed in the way of authors; permission for publication had to be obtained from both viceroy and bishop, and books treating American subjects required authorization from the Council of the Indies. Despite such impediments and the restrictions of the Inquisition, books were available in considerable variety, and there were some large and excellent private libraries in New Spain. When Vasco de Quiroga died in 1565, he had accumulated more than six hundred volumes, and in her convent Sor Juana was surrounded by four thousand of her own books. By the seventeenth century the College of Discalced Carmelites had twelve thousand volumes. Probably the finest library in the New World, however, at least by the eighteenth century, was the one originally started by Bishop Juan de Palafox y Mendoza in Puebla.

The literate public without means, however, had limited reading material, for there were no public libraries and, until late in the colonial period, no newspapers. Communication within the colony was, for the general populace, mainly rumor, gossip, and the information brought by travelers. In early times official announcements were made in the public square by a town crier, following the ringing of church bells, drum beats, or the blast of trumpets. Eventually broadsides were tacked up in public places. The curious were drawn to such places no more by official pronouncements than by the graffiti that showed up mysteriously. These *pasquines* were a way of venting displeasure with government or scoring personal enemies. Usually in rhyme, they were witty, sarcastic, and frequently risqué. No one was safe from these lettered shafts, and the more prominent the victim the sweeter the vengeance. Although illegal, they could no more be prevented than the scrawls that decorate our public walls today.

News from Spain and other parts of Europe came with the annual fleet, at which time enterprising printers published sheets with the "latest" information. For domestic events of high interest, such as a pirate attack in Campeche or a destructive earthquake in Oaxaca, a special sheet might be run off. Sigüenza y Góngora published a periodical, *Mercurio Volante*, beginning in

1693. It was not until 1805, however, that a daily newspaper—
the *Diario de México*—was offered to the public.

Music

Spanish musicians had entertained Cortés and his men during
the Conquest, and as life in the colony became more sedate, others performed more formally in the viceregal court and before
bishops and wealthy, cultured ladies and gentlemen of various
occupations. The clergymen, aside from using music in solemn
religious ceremonies, also staged plays written in prose in which
music had a place. The performers were often Indians.

Music had been important to the Aztecs, especially for ritual
ceremonies, and musicians had very respectable status in the
Indian community. Spanish clergymen soon found that the Indians' love of music was an expedient through which the natives
could be attracted to Christianity. Hearing the mass sung, neo-
phytes came to identify the Spaniards' religion with music. Natives were also pleased to perform, not only because of the enjoyment and the prestige involved but also because performers
were, at least part of the time, exempt from paying tribute. By
1576 there were about ten thousand Indians singing services.

In the beginning, Indians sang to the accompaniment of native flutes, but organs were later introduced from Spain. Before
long the variety of European instruments arrived, and local musicians became familiar with sackbuts, clarinets, rebecs, viols,
bassoons, lutes, guitars, cornets, and so forth. Indians quickly
learned to make such instruments, including even the great organs. Native artists also reproduced choirbooks, complete with
illuminated letters. In addition, Spanish masters encouraged Indians to compose music, which they did with considerable skill.

The church discouraged some Indian music identified with
paganism. Clergymen were horrified by the "obscene motions
and lewd gestures" of native dances, in which "the ultimate intricacies of the conjugal act" were pantomimed. To complicate
matters, uninhibited dancing found new life with the introduction by black slaves of dances, such as the *porto rico*, from the
Caribbean. And clerical admonitions notwithstanding, the
dances continued to be popular, especially in rural areas where
it was almost impossible to impose control. In the eighteenth
century the Inquisition protested the *jarabe gatuno*, "so indecent,
lewd, and disgraceful, and provocative, that words cannot en-

compass the evil of it. The verses and the accompanying actions, movements, and gestures, shoot the poison of lust directly into the eyes, ears, and senses."[2]

Yet the church did not discourage many forms of frivolous amusement, including some of the popular songs. Enjoying sensational popularity was the *villancico*. Originally a type of traditional Spanish Christmas carol usually sung in church, the villancico developed in Mexico as a popular song for festive occasions. While this lighter form was officially frowned upon during the sixteenth century, in the seventeenth century it emerged, like the contemporary baroque taste in art, as an exuberant display of lightheartedness. Felicitous lyrics celebrated not only saints' days but also the rites of spring and the emotions of profane love in startlingly modern form. There was at least a flirtation with a higher form of secular composition in the early eighteenth century when Manuel Zumaya wrote the New World's first opera, *La Parténope*, which was staged in 1711.

Architecture

The highest form of creative expression in colonial Mexico was achieved in architecture. Naturally enough, Spaniards tried to create buildings in the colony similar to those in Spain, and in the early years an essentially medieval style predominated. It was, nevertheless, modified in Mexico: churches assumed a fortresslike appearance because of the threats of Indian attacks; dangers of earthquakes called for buildings with very thick walls, often supported by great flying buttresses; and the humid tropics required provision for better ventilation. Moreover, architecture in Mexico took on a distinctively local character because building materials in the colony offered more color. In wide use was the red, porous *tezontle* pumice, the local whitish limestone, and a green stone found in Oaxaca. As the bright Puebla (*poblano*) style emerged, polychrome tiles came to be used extensively and in some cases dominated the façades of buildings. Indian influence crept in as native craftsmen insinuated their motifs in carvings and paintings. And because even the large churches could not accommodate the great crowds of Indian wor-

2. Robert Stevenson, *Music in Mexico: A Historical Survey* (New York, 1971), p. 184. The section in this chapter on music and dances is based to great extent on this excellent book.

The church and convent of San Agustín, Hidalgo.

shipers, broad courtyards, or "open-air chapels," were a familiar sight.

The first decades of architecture in Mexico saw a *mestizaje* of styles, in which features of the romanesque, Gothic, and *mudéjar* (Moorish) merged. By the middle of the century, however, they yielded to the influence of the Spanish Renaissance which, because its intricate plasterwork resembled the art of silversmiths, was called plateresque. In line with the general philosophic outlook of their order, Franciscan churches had a simplicity that contrasted with the massive, richly ornate Augustinian piles. The secular clergy, feeling fewer stylistic restraints, indulged a taste for even more elaborate architecture.

The great cathedrals stand out by virtue of sheer bulk, but those of Mexico City and Puebla, designed by the same architect and competing in excellence, are especially noteworthy structures. Begun in 1563, the cathedral of Mexico City occupied teams of craftsmen for a century and even then was not completed until the late colonial period. That of Puebla, considered by many to be the finer of the two, was laid out around 1575 and dedicated in 1649. Vasco de Quiroga's plan for a cathedral in Michoacán to match the dimensions of St. Peter's was obviously never realized.

Civil architecture fared less well over the centuries. We know that splendid buildings arose—palaces of the viceroy and bishops, offices of the audiencia and ayuntamiento, and various other

Cathedral of Mexico

A water tower at Teoloyucan, with its flared buttresses, one of the many remaining monuments to colonial artisans.

government structures. But some were destroyed, and the original forms of others were altered by later constructions. It is sad,
too, that the Renaissance mansions of the conquerors have almost
all disappeared, although we gain some appreciation of their
elegance from the residence of Francisco de Montejo in Mérida
and the modified palace of Cortés in Cuernavaca.

In the seventeenth century a style more distinctively Mexican
emerged. The moderate expression of the Spanish baroque gave
way in the colony to what is often referred to as "ultra" baroque
—that is, a style dominated by a profusion of decorative effects.
The trend began in Puebla, where one sees the best examples of
the form. In the eighteenth century the love of ornamentation
was carried to the ultimate in the Churrigueresque (for José
Churriguera, a Spanish architect). Surfaces were encrusted with
decoration, and façades and altarpieces were stifled with riotous
detail. It was, in a way, the glorious celebration of the optimism
and prosperity of criollo society; and, although too busy for some
tastes, it nevertheless produced some of the finest examples of

religious architecture and is held by many to be the highest form of the builder's art in colonial Mexico.

Such excesses inevitably exhaust the senses, and it is not surprising, therefore, that the next phase of architecture was a reaction. The severe, formal, neoclassic was a sober turn. Reflecting the stern realities of late colonial life, it was cold and devoid of the color and fantasy that have generally characterized Mexican art from the marvelous Maya façades to the brilliant murals of the twentieth century.

Sculpture and Painting

Sculpture was, to great extent, an adjunct to architecture. Sculptors, many of whom were Indians and mestizos, rendered in stone and plaster the incredibly complex designs of ceilings and façades, and they carved wooden altarpieces, images of saints, and other adornments that contributed to the grandeur of the art of New Spain. Most of these artists remain anonymous, but one prominent sculptor deserves mention. Manuel Tolsá, a Spaniard, created the admirable equestrian statue of Charles IV that is affectionately known as "the Caballito." Prominently on display in Mexico City today, it is regarded as one of the finest works of its kind in the world.

Second-story façade of the sixteenth-century residence of Francisco de Montejo in Mérida, Yucatán.

The first European painter in Mexico was a companion of Cortés who painted his captain at prayer. With the construction of churches and monasteries, frescoes were painted by friars and Indians trained in Gante's school. Good examples of these early efforts have been preserved at Acolman, Cuernavaca, and Acto-pan. Also to the first decades belong the post-Conquest códices, painted, with official encouragement, by Indian artists in the pre-Hispanic style. The códices that survive have not only inval-uable historical importance but genuine artistic qualities as well. For the most part, however, native painters lost the traditions of their primitive, though charming, style as they were pressed into studios for training in the realism of the Spanish school.

Painting advanced in quality with the arrival in 1566 of the Flemish master Simón Pereyns. He gathered around him a tal-ented group of criollo artists who painted canvases in the Span-ish manner. By the seventeenth century, when Spain enjoyed a splendid period of art, their successors imitated Francisco de Zur-barán, José Ribera, Bartolomé Murillo, and other prominent Spanish artists. The seventeenth century saw the epitome of co-lonial painting. Whereas most of the earliest artists were associ-ated with religious art, more opportunities now opened for the studio artist who prospered through rich patrons. The prominent and wealthy adorned their residences with paintings, and por-traits were in great demand. One may weigh the skills of those portraitists in the paintings of the viceroys, most of whom stare down from the walls with grim and baleful countenance. Al-though the colony had many good and popular artists, it cannot be said that their work was comparable to the best being done in Europe. Yet by the eighteenth century such painters pros-pered, satisfying the egos of the silver barons and others who sought to be preserved for posterity.

As part of the "progressive" trend in Spain, the Art Academy of San Carlos was dedicated in Mexico City in 1785, and aca-demic training was introduced to give equal opportunity to as-piring artists of all races. The stiff formal approach gave impulse to a controlled, less Mexican, school of art, consonant with the neoclassic in architecture.

Daily Life

The poverty, ugliness, injustices, and the general misery of the lower classes notwithstanding, colonial life was not a scene of unrelieved tragedy. It was indeed close to that for most of the Indians throughout the sixteenth century, but thereafter conditions eased somewhat. And while the daily routine of peasants in the provinces was mostly drudgery, urban life was more exciting.

Visitors to Mexico City who recorded their impressions usually commented on its fine buildings and broad, straight avenues. In the seventeenth century, travelers asserted that everything one could desire was available, including abundant supplies of foods that were both delicious and inexpensive. Daily more than one thousand boats and three thousand mules carried in provisions from outlying provinces. Foreigners remarked on the excellence of the city's construction, with its plazas, fountains, and sidewalks. An Englishman living in Mexico City in 1625 estimated that the capital had fifteen thousand coaches, some of which were trimmed with gold, silver, and Chinese silk.[3]

Color, of which Mexicans have always been almost excessively fond, was what struck the foreigner's eye. Color was everywhere, from the flower gardens and blossoming trees, to the textured hues of walls, to the kaleidoscope of the great open markets where bright exotic fruits and vegetables vied with polychrome tiles and pottery, brilliant native textiles, and jewelry. There was an astonishing variety of goods available in the marketplace, where thousands of people gathered to bargain and exchange gossip. A motley population thronged the streets, their rich skin tones adding to the mosaic of color. Dark habits of the ecclesiastics heightened the bright sashes of university students and the dress of criollo dandies who paraded in plumed, scarlet taffeta hats, ruffled laces, and velvet capes. A dignified worthy clothed in severe ebony might be accompanied by black slaves attired in blue or yellow breeches, with white silk stockings.

Both men and women wore jewels in the street, and it was not uncommon to see hatbands set with pearls and diamonds. Occasionally the procession of the viceroy or archbishop with his retinues passed, causing a mild sensation. Women, who were just as fashion conscious as men, flaunted exquisite cloths of the Orient and the richest textiles of Europe. Wealthy ladies frequently observed modesty by making their way through the streets in veiled palanquins, sedan chairs borne by slaves. But other females enjoyed the approval (or jealousy) provoked by scanty dress. Visitors were especially taken by beautiful mulatto women wearing expensive silks and sparkling gems, despite sumptuary

3. Irving A. Leonard, *Baroque Times in Old Mexico: Seventeenth-Century Persons, Places, and Practices* (Ann Arbor, 1971), pp. 73, 76.

laws that were passed from time to time to prevent them from dressing like whites. Women of various classes applied rouge and eye makeup.

Beneath all the finery and cosmetics, however, were people who aged quickly and who enjoyed fewer of the beauty aids available to serve the vanities of our times. In close conversation with a colonist one would become aware of a strong musty odor, a smile marred by missing or rotting teeth, and a face scarred

Glazed pottery was introduced to Mexico from Talavera de la Reina, Spain, in the sixteenth century. In the first half of the seventeenth century, about forty potters were registered in the city of Puebla. The informality of design and execution in Mexican ceramics make them appealing today, but in colonial times Puebla pottery was mainly used by the poor; the rich preferred their tables set with silver and Chinese porcelain. Examples are shown below and on the facing page.

Late seventeenth-century ceramic fountain from Puebla suggesting Chinese influence.

A Puebla vase decorated in Oriental style, late seventeenth century.

Flower pot of the style commonly used in the halls and patios of colonial houses.

Tiles from Puebla were commonly used on building façades.

and pitted. At least on social occasions some were considerate: a strong perfume might disguise the infrequency of bathing, and offensive breath could be tamed by chewing cloves or licorice.

Among the more pathetic elements of society were the many vagabonds who swarmed into the colony. They lounged around city streets, living by their wits and making a general nuisance of themselves in both urban and provincial areas. These *picaros*, so charmingly presented in literature, were in fact parasites infecting the society of New Spain, much to the dismay of the authorities and the general public. They were seen as a disruptive element, unsettling to the colony, and potentially dangerous.

Some of these beggars (later called *léperos*) were lads in their early teens who made their way to the Spanish Indies, where they picked up vices and venereal diseases. Much of their time was spent molesting Indian girls and spoiling for adventure, and they often ended up as petty criminals. Moreover the colony produced its own domestic vagabonds, of all racial groups. Many were syphilitic wretches, dressed in filthy rags, who hung about public places where they displayed open sores, grotesque tumors, and maimed limbs. Some were blind (or pretended to be) and joined other indigents outside churches to collect alms. Modest attempts were made to provide care for them and the church regularly dispensed food and small sums of money. In the countryside vagabonds often lived illegally in Indian villages, forcing villagers to support them and sometimes seizing their women. As early as 1560 there were three to four thousand of these parasites in New Spain without visible means of support.

All of these social types, elegant and rustic, were part of daily scenes in streets that were alternately muddy or dusty, depending on the season. Cursing mule drivers prodded their braying beasts along, stirring up clouds of dust or making quagmires, while other herders pushed swine, sheep, or turkeys through the crowds. Peddlers hawked their wares, Indian servant girls carried jugs of water from the public fountains, and tamemes bent under the loads that almost obscured them. Eventually some streets had cobblestones, but gutters remained like open sewers, strewn with garbage and an occasional dead dog. If color delighted the eye, stench assailed the nostril. But such aromas and unsanitary conditions were, after all, not much different from those in other parts of the world at the time. The filth did pose a serious health problem, however, and the government moved to keep the capital cleaner. The pigs that ran loose in the streets and scavenged for food were relied upon less fully after an ordinance of 1598 provided for twelve teams of two Indians, with mule carts, to collect refuse from city streets every day. Public buildings, including storehouses and jails, were to be cleaned every four months. There was little improvement in sanitary conditions throughout the colonial period, however, and swine, mongrel dogs, and vultures continued to be counted on to help keep streets clean.

A wide assortment of diversion was offered in the cities of New Spain, especially in the capital. At the center of social life was the viceregal court, although bishops and wealthy laymen often rivaled the court in extravagant entertainment. For the cultured elite there were the latest plays, music, and literature from Spain and clever conversation in the salons. Some recitals and performances were private, but a great many were for the general public. Dancing was popular with all, from the formal balls of the wealthy to the more spontaneous, often earthy, dances of the lower classes. Bullfighting, introduced shortly after the Conquest, found wide favor with all segments of society. An archbishop in early seventeenth century was such an *aficionado* that he had his own private bullring on the grounds of the archiepiscopal palace. The more intellectual enjoyed chess, and cards were played by all classes. Gambling was a vice to which almost everyone was addicted, as wagers were made at dice, cards, horse races, cockfighting, or any contest available for betting purposes. Such diversions were indulged in mainly by men, but new arrivals to the colony were shocked to see criollo ladies of presumed high social standing dealing cards with males. For the aristocrats there were jousting and other games played on horseback, and they rode to the hunt with their greyhounds and falcons.

Leisure time was abundant for most; colonists enjoyed many holidays, with eighty-five religious festivals annually. Individuals celebrated their saints' days, and towns had their special saints to be honored as well. These and other holy days were enjoyed to the fullest. Solemn religious rites, processions, and sometimes penance were followed by fireworks, feasting, singing, dancing, and no small amount of drinking—which in turn often led to fighting. Gentlemen might settle accounts of honor with a duel; the lower classes would more likely find satisfaction informally and im-

The picturesque Alameda Park in the center of Mexico City was first laid out in 1593 during the rule of Viceroy Luis de Velasco. Now much enlarged, it is still the scene of promenades under the tall trees and along the pathways past fountains and bright flower gardens.

mediately with knives or machetes. A favorite—and healthier—diversion at parties (during which daughters were watched by hawk-eyed chaperones) was the throwing of eggshells filled with confetti or of hollow wax balls containing perfumed water. All of this was conducted with great merriment and a consuming interest in sweet-meats and the opposite sex.

Other events demanded celebration. The birth of a royal child, a royal marriage, the coronation of a new king, the arrival of a new viceroy or archbishop, or a great victory over one of Spain's enemies, all called for displays and merrymaking. The most glorious of spectacles were the *mascaradas*, often planned far in advance and summoning the most creative talents to assure sensational (and sometimes bizarre) effects. The essential part of the show was the grand parade. It might lead off with Indian chiefs decked out in traditional native garb, followed by dignitaries of the church in their rich vestments, high royal officials mounted on superb horses with silver trappings, and faculty members of the university in their gaudy robes. There were also decorated floats, clowns, acrobats, jugglers, and musicians. Some individuals were masked (from which the ceremonies took their names), wearing costumes representing mythical or historical figures, while others personified Pride, Greed, Lust, or perhaps one of the virtues.

Sometimes the mascarada was sponsored, at great cost, by a wealthy individual and other times by the state, but the aim of the organizers was always to surpass previous extravaganzas. No expense or labor was spared—even to the extent of importing camels and ostriches for the parade, to the great delight of the spectators.

A cherished ritual of the elite youth was the daily *paseo*, in which the young men gathered around five o'clock in Mexico City's Alameda Park. These popinjays arrived in fancy carriages or perhaps mounted on blooded horses and were attended by black slaves suitably dressed to display their young masters' elegance. Young ladies arrived in much the same fashion, for the same purpose. The congregation indulged in what passed as witty repartee and strolled around the park, flirting with the opposite sex all the while. It was harmless enough, except when excesses of bravado led to drawn swords.

The impression should not be left that colonial society witnessed a continual round of parties and sport. The foregoing observations of colonists at play pertain mostly to large centers like Mexico City and Puebla. Smaller towns had similar amusements, but they were on a scale less grand and carried off with less flair. Occasions such as saints' days in small communities called for celebrations that were simple but lively, and the custom of the paseo—which has persisted into modern times—saw the gathering of young people of more humble aspect in village plazas. Local celebrations might consist of little more than a mass followed by fireworks and drinking to stupefaction.

Life in the colony also had its grim aspects. Throughout most of the colonial period streets were dark at night, with no provisions for lighting. Thus assaults were not unusual, and few went out late at night without arms and companions. Thievery was widespread, and so were crimes of passion. Rural brigandage was a plague to all. In the sixteenth century there were almost no inns, and Indian villages were required to furnish food and lodging for travelers. Later on, crude facilities for those on the road were maintained.

A common sight was that of criminals hanged by the roadside and left as a warning to others. Death by hanging was decreed for many crimes, and for especially serious offenses, such as treason, the body of the culprit was drawn and quartered, with the head and limbs prominently and gruesomely displayed. Mutilation of limbs, the severing of a hand or foot, the crushing of a foot in a diabolical device known as "the boot," and other tortures were employed on occasion. Floggings of one or two hundred lashes were not uncommon. Those of high social position, however, were usually spared humiliating and cruel punishment, escaping with fines or sometimes jail sentences. Nobles found guilty of treason, however, could not avoid the severest penalty, but they were given the preferred death of decapitation, for hanging was considered too undignified for one of high rank.

The plagues that so devastated the Indian population by no means left Spaniards untouched, even though they had better resistance. One of the most virulent of the diseases was *matlazáhuatl*. Known in Mexico apparently before the advent of the white man, the malady, similar to typhus, was thought by the Indians to have been caused by comets, volcanic eruptions, or earthquakes. Smallpox continued to be a great killer, and when it struck Mexico City in 1779–80, nearly 20 percent of the capital's population perished. Toward the end of the colonial period an extensive vaccination program succeeded in checking the spread of smallpox. But life expectancy for the colonists was half that of ours today.

When Spaniards landed at the port of Veracruz their first thought was to get out of the fever-ridden town and up into higher altitudes where the climate was more salubrious. The same unhealthful conditions prevailed at the Pacific port of Acapulco. Both ports were populated in the majority by blacks and mulattoes. Colonists suffered from intestinal parasites and all sorts of digestive disorders, from leprosy, kidney stones, rheumatism, gout and a variety of other complaints that were only vaguely diagnosed. There was little to relieve suffering, although bleeding and purging were widely used as standard cures for many complaints.[1]

Bishop Zumárraga established a hospital in the capital for

1. See Michael C. Meyer, "Health and Medical Practice on the Northern Frontier of New Spain, 1550–1821," *Locus* 2 (1993): 111–30.

those ailing from venereal diseases. Later an asylum for the insane was opened. At first there were hospital facilities for Spaniards only, but a royal order of 1553 made provision for a hospital for ill and indigent Indians. By 1580 Mexico City had six hospitals—four for Spaniards, one for Indians, and another for blacks and mestizos. Facilities were minimal, and these hospitals were actually what we might today call rest homes. Nuns operated seven convents that served as convalescent retreats, as did an equal number of monasteries.

Medical practitioners, identified as surgeons, were usually barbers as well and no doubt more skilled in the latter practice. Details of surgical operations may be left to the imagination— the doctors probably killed as many patients as they saved. They were, however, skillful in performing Caesarean sections. Medical doctors often had their own bags of tricks, with favorite cures of dubious merit. Spaniards sometimes resorted to Indian healers, who were apparently just as effective, if not more so.

At least some attempts were made by the crown to impose controls over the qualifications of doctors; after 1535 those practicing medicine were supposed to have been examined by university specialists. A professorship of surgery and anatomy was established at the University in 1621, and a medical board was formed a quarter century later. Medical inspectors were sent to the colony from time to time to improve medical practices, especially with regard to better training for surgeons and druggists. By 1790 there were fifty-one medical doctors in Mexico, along with 221 "surgeons and barbers," most of whom resided in the capital or other large centers. Despite modest attempts of authorities to improve medical services, the state of the profession advanced very little throughout the eighteenth century. People in Mexico learned to be familiar with death, to dwell upon it, and sometimes to make light of it; they were fatalistic and anxious to make their peace with God.

Far from being the vulgar backwater one might have supposed, New Spain had a vibrant and diverse cultural life, especially in the larger cities. From early years erudite clergymen introduced a strong tradition of scholarship, and refined Spanish immigrants spread their cultivated tastes. The cultural milieu was advanced with strong support from the viceroys and bishops. In summary, the society of New Spain during its first two centuries was a culture embodying the best and the worst of its times, more complex than colonial life in English colonies in America but more rustic than the European model it imitated.

By 1700 it had a uniquely Mexican character, with customs and traditions so firmly impressed on society that the patterns are still evident today.

Recommended for Further Study

Baird, Joseph H. *The Churches of Mexico, 1530–1810.* Berkeley: University of California Press, 1962.

Castedo, Leopoldo. *A History of Latin American Art and Architecture from Precolumbian Times to the Present.* New York: Praeger, 1969.

Charlot, Jean. *Mexican Art and the Academy of San Carlos, 1785–1915.* Austin: University of Texas Press, 1962.

Deeds, Susan M. "Rural Work in Nueva Vizcaya: Forms of Labor Coercion on the Periphery." *Hispanic American Historical Review* 3 (1989): 425–50.

Estrada, Dorothy T. de. "The 'Escuelas Pias' of Mexico City, 1786–1820." *The Americas 31* (1974): 51–71.

Fernández, Justino. *Mexican Art.* London: Spring Books, 1965.

Gage, Thomas. *Thomas Gage's Travels in the New World.* Edited by J. Eric S. Thompson. Norman: University of Oklahoma Press, 1969.

Gibson, Charles. "Writings on Colonial Mexico." *Hispanic American Historical Review* 55 (1975): 287–323.

Haskett, Robert S. " 'Our Suffering With the Taxco Tribute': Involuntary Mine Labor and Indigenous Society in Central New Spain." *Hispanic American Historical Review* 3 (1991): 447–76.

Jacobsen, Jerome V. *Educational Foundations of the Jesuits in Sixteenth-Century New Spain.* Berkeley: University of California Press, 1938.

Keleman, Pál. *Art of the Americas: Ancient and Hispanic.* New York: Crowell, 1969.

Kubler, George. *Mexican Architecture of the Sixteenth Century.* 2 vols. New Haven, Conn.: Yale University Press, 1948.

Lanning, John Tate. *Academic Culture in the Spanish Colonies.* London: Oxford University Press, 1940.

Leonard, Irving. *Baroque Times in Old Mexico: Seventeenth-Century Persons, Places, and Practices.* Ann Arbor: University of Michigan Press, 1971.

———. *Books of the Brave.* Cambridge, Mass.: Harvard University Press, 1949.

———. *Don Carlos de Sigüenza y Góngora, A Mexican Savant of the Seventeenth Century.* University of California Publications in History, vol. 18. Berkeley: University of California Press, 1929.

Lipsett-Rivera, Sonya. "Indigenous Communities and Water Rights in Colonial Puebla: Patterns of Resistance." *The Americas* 4 (1992): 445–62.

McAndrews, John. *The Open-Air Churches of Sixteenth-Century Mexico.* Cambridge, Mass.: Harvard University Press, 1965.

Martin, Cheryl E. *Rural Society in Colonial Morelos.* Albuquerque: University of New Mexico Press, 1985.

Mathes, Michael. *The Americas' First Academic Library, Santa Cruz de Tlatelolco*. Sacramento: California State Library, 1985.

Mathes, Valerie. "Enrico Martínez of New Spain." *The Americas* 33 (1976): 62–77.

Meyer, Michael C. "Health and Medical Practice on the Northern Frontier of New Spain, 1550–1821," *Locus* 2 (1993): 111–30.

Mullen, Robert J. *Dominican Architecture in Sixteenth Century Oaxaca*. Tempe: Arizona State University's Center for Latin American Studies, 1975.

Ouweneel, Arij. "Growth, Stagnation, and Migration: An Explorative Analysis of the Tributario Series of Anáhuac (1720–1800)." *Hispanic American Historical Review* 3 (1991): 531–78.

Paz, Octavio. *Sor Juana. Or, The Traps of Faith*. Translated by Margaret Sayers Peden. Cambridge, Mass.: Harvard University Press, 1988.

Robertson, Donald. *Mexican Manuscript Painting of the Early Colonial Period: The Metropolitan Schools*. New Haven, Conn.: Yale University Press, 1959.

Rojas, Pedro. *The Art and Architecture of Mexico*. Translated by J. M. Cohen. Feltham, Eng.: Hamlyn, 1968.

Ronan, Charles E., S.J. *Francisco Javier Clavijero: His Life and Works*. Chicago: Loyola University Press, 1977.

Schurz, William L. *This New World: The Civilization of Latin America*. New York: Dutton, 1964.

Seed, Patricia. *To Love, Honor and Obey in Colonial Mexico. Conflicts over Marriage Choice, 1574–1821*. Stanford, Calif.: Stanford University Press, 1988.

Simpson, Lesley B. *Many Mexicos*. Berkeley: University of California Press, 1959.

Smith, Bradley. *Mexico: A History in Art*. Garden City, N.Y.: Doubleday, 1968.

Stevenson, Robert. *Music in Mexico: A Historical Survey*. New York: Crowell, 1971.

Taylor, William B. *Drinking, Homicide and Rebellion in Colonial Mexican Villages*. Stanford, Calif.: Stanford University Press, 1979.

Thompson, Angela. "To Save the Children: Smallpox Inoculation, Vaccination, and Public Health in Guanajuato, Mexico, 1797–1840." *The Americas* 4 (1993): 431–56.

Toussaint, Manuel. *Colonial Art in Mexico*. Translated and edited by Elizabeth W. Weismann. Austin: University of Texas Press, 1967.

Warren, Fintan B. *Vasco de Quiroga and His Pueblo Hospitals of Santa Fé*. Publications of the Academy of American Franciscan History, vol. 10. Washington, D.C.: Academy of American Franciscan History, 1963.

Weismann, Elizabeth W. "The History of Art in Latin America, 1500–1800: Some Trends and Challenges in the Last Decade." *Latin American Research Review* 10 (1975): 7–50.

IV REFORM AND REACTION: THE MOVE TO INDEPENDENCE

14

The Bourbons Restructure New Spain

Early Bourbon Reforms

The nadir of Spain's fortunes by the late seventeenth century was nowhere better exemplified than in the person of the king himself. Inheriting the throne in 1665 at age four, Charles II was feeble in mind as well as body and was even in maturity clearly incompetent to rule. This wretched king, called in all kindness *El Hechizado*, "the Bewitched," sought desperately in off moments to hang himself with his bedclothes. His retainers, in dubious service to the nation, put a stop to that. He was, after all, the monarch; and so his idiosyncrasies were accommodated by an indulgent people. While exorcists tried to drive out his devil, advisers made policy of sorts.

Charles was the last of the Spanish Hapsburgs, and there was justifiable concern over the matter of succession. Despite two marriages, the king did not sire an heir. Who, then, would rule the Spanish empire after his anticipated early demise? While Spaniards weighed their fate with apprehension, others in Europe schemed to exploit the situation. Then, as now, there was considerable intermarriage among the various royal families of Europe, and relatives floated their pretensions to the Spanish throne. In the end the Austrian and French factions emerged as the two strongest claimants, and their diplomats maneuvered for years. To the exasperation of almost all concerned, Charles II refused to die. Finally, as his days grew short, he named as his successor Philip of Anjou, a grandson of Louis XIV of France. Charles joined his ancestors in 1700, and a new dynasty, the line of Spanish Bourbons, began with the rule of Philip V (1701–46).

Charles II (1661–1700). The death of this unfortunate king, the last
Spanish Hapsburg, precipitated the War of the Spanish Succession.

The Austrian party and their allies contested Philip's crowning during the long War of the Spanish Succession (1701–13), but the final outcome saw the Bourbons established in Spain.

Philip inherited a ruined Spain, a country wracked by foreign wars and internal revolts. The economy was in shambles, and the demoralized Spaniards lived in an age of cynicism, their proud intellectual and cultural tradition now barren. The new king was beset by further strains on revenues and manpower because of the war, but he approached the country's problems with vigor and intelligence. He applied many of the administrative policies that other Bourbons had used in France, and his centralization of authority proved effective. An immediate concern was the strengthening of the military forces. The Spanish infantry, invincible throughout the sixteenth century, had lost its incentive; the seventeenth century witnessed the spectacle of Spanish troops running from battle, and by the early years of the eighteenth century the army numbered only about twenty thousand soldiers. The nation that in 1588 had launched the great Spanish Armada now had a puny naval force of only twenty ships. Philip undertook a program of rehabilitation with some success.

Equally shattered at the time of Philip's coronation was the internal economy. Its treasury empty, its industry and agriculture deteriorated, Spain was beholden to foreigners. Trade with the colonies was to great extent in the hands of non-Spanish merchants who enjoyed extraordinary concessions from the Spanish crown. So dependent was the nation on others that two-thirds of the American silver went directly to foreign ports. The early Hapsburg bullionists must have rolled in their graves.

As his government began to bring some order to Spain, Philip also looked to his colonies with an eye to improving their economies for the financial benefit of the empire and as compensation for Spain's territorial losses in Europe. In 1702 a royal decree allowed two ships a year, instead of one, to sail from Manila to Acapulco. The antiquated trading system was further improved in 1717 when the official port for the New World trade was formally changed from Seville to Cádiz, which had better facilities. This was an important break in the monopoly of vested interests. Then, in 1740 the fleet system, which had operated so inefficiently for two centuries, was suspended. The threat of piracy having subsided, there seemed little point in restricting both merchants and consumers. In case of war, however, privateers could freely attack Spanish shipping, and, in fact, the fleets were revived later, sailing off and on until their final abolition in

1789. Although these colonial economic reforms were modest enough, along with other changes they were indicative of the Bourbon commitment to modernization.

Revival of the Colonial Economy

In the second half of the century momentous change took place. Following the relatively calm reign of Ferdinand VI (1746–59), Spain had a dramatic resurgence under one of its greatest sovereigns, Charles III (1759–88). A devotee of the Enlightenment philosophies then current in Europe, Charles not only introduced important reforms within Spain but also moved to restructure the colonies. To that end, in 1765 he dispatched to New Spain José de Gálvez with the powers of visitor general. Gálvez energetically undertook a long tour of the colony, and over the next five years he compiled important information on which he based sweeping economic and political reforms. He had two overriding concerns: the economy of New Spain and the defense of the colony's frontiers.

Not the least of New Spain's economic woes stemmed from the monopolies held by merchants and guilds of the two official ports of Veracruz and Acapulco. Their privileges were prejudicial to competition and kept prices unnaturally high; consequently, the economy was sluggish. In the 1760s Charles relieved this stifling situation by opening other official ports in Campeche and Yucatán, and before the end of the century additional ports in Mexico were given similar rights of trade. About the same time a different royal decree permitted New Spain to trade with other Spanish colonies. In 1764–65 the monopoly of Cádiz was broken when certain other ports in Spain were allowed to trade freely with the colonies. Finally, in 1790 the Casa de Contratación, having tightly controlled shipping and commerce for 287 years, was abolished. The crown also stimulated the economy by lowering some taxes, revising offensive customs duties, making quicksilver more easily available for miners, and organizing a miner's guild.

The cause of most rejoicing was the dramatic recovery of silver mining, and, except for a slight dip in the 1760s, production rose consistently throughout the century. The silver boom was partially attributable to more realistic royal policies but resulted from improved technology and the discovery of rich new mines as well. From slightly more than 3.25 million pesos in 1700, silver production rose to over 13.5 million by 1750, and by 1804 it had reached the substantial figure of 27 million pesos. Mexico alone produced about as much silver as the rest of the world. Between 1690 and 1822 Mexico minted over 1.5 billion pesos in silver and some 60 million in gold.

By the late colonial period there were about three thousand mines in the colony, although most had been abandoned and many of those being worked were small operations. In 1774 thirty-five sizable mining camps existed, of which only a few produced most of the silver. Mines could be worked with increased efficiency because of more scientific refining techniques and better drainage facilities. Modernized technology also permitted deeper mine shafts, and that of the great Valenciana (Guanajuato) reached into the earth some two thousand feet, deeper than any other mine in the world.

Important as precious metals were, however, the general production of the colony increased considerably in other ways, too. Always very profitable, cochineal dye was the second most valuable export during the eighteenth century. It was produced primarily in Oaxaca, where as many as thirty thousand Indians were employed in the industry. Another important commodity was sugar; by 1774 the town of Córdoba (Veracruz) alone had more than fifty sugar mills, employing mostly black slaves. Toward the close of the century the colony produced around twenty-five thousand tons of sugar annually, of which some two-thirds were exported. The city of Puebla was a manufacturing center of note, specializing in both textiles and ceramics. It sent more than a million pounds of cloth a year to the capital and in 1793 had forty-six shops producing pottery and glass. Native cotton had been cultivated over the centuries, and in 1803 Mexico exported more cotton to Europe than did the United States. A very lucrative crop by the late eighteenth century was tobacco; Mexico City and Querétaro each had factories employing about seven thousand workers. Among the many other export commodities were hemp, cacao, vanilla, and hides. Few manufactured goods were exported from the colony; 93 percent of exports consisted of silver, cochineal, and various agricultural products.

By the second half of the eighteenth century New Spain had become by far the most prosperous of Spain's holdings. Around 1800 the port of Veracruz had a trade in excess of thirty million pesos annually. By 1810 New Spain contributed three-fourths of the profits from all the Spanish American colonies. Nevertheless, the domestic economy had become more important than the export economy. More workers were employed in the production of goods for Mexican consumption—in agriculture, ranching, minor industry, and local commerce—than in export commodities.

Through its various taxes, duties, and monopolies the crown profited enormously from the improved colonial economy, as the following chart shows:

CROWN INCOME FROM NEW SPAIN, 1786–1789

Source	Value in Pesos (round figures)
Tobacco monopoly	16,000,000
Sales tax (alcabala)	15,500,000
One-tenth of precious metals	9,000,000
Coinage	6,000,000
Pulque monopoly	3,500,000
Indian tributes	3,500,000
Customs duties (almojarifazgo)	3,000,000
Total	56,500,000

Source: José Miranda et al., Historia de México (Mexico, 1971), p. 263.

What strikes one immediately is that, notwithstanding the considerable value of precious metals to the crown, royal income from the tobacco monopoly and sales tax was over three times as great. Of the revenues raised in the colony, part went to subsidize the administrative costs of New Spain, another portion contributed to the support of less prosperous colonies, and the remainder found its way to the royal treasury in Spain.

The state of the colony's overall economy toward the end of the colonial period, before fighting interrupted production, can be seen from the following estimates:

VALUE OF NEW SPAIN'S ANNUAL PRODUCTION, ca. 1810

Source	Value in Pesos	Percentage
Agriculture	106,285,000	56
Manufactures	55,386,000	29
Mining	28,451,000	15

Source: David A. Brading, Miners and Merchants in Bourbon Mexico, 1763–1810 (Cambridge, 1971), p. 18.

Reform of Colonial Administration

International rivalries among colonial powers in the eighteenth century led to wars that were fought in various theaters, including the New World. The power of Great Britain and its expanding colonies in North America was perceived in Madrid as a threat to the Spanish Indies, and not without reason. Thus, in 1762, during the Seven Years' War, Charles III authorized a professional standing army for New Spain. The troops were few in number, but the addition of various militia groups brought the armed forces in 1810 up to roughly thirty-three thousand, of whom no more than a third were regular soldiers.

During his inspection tour José de Gálvez became acutely conscious of the defenseless northern borders. Spanish settlement had pushed northward slowly during the seventeenth century, for, although the church generally had lost much of its early vigor, Jesuit and Franciscan missionaries on the frontiers continued in their selfless labors. In the late seventeenth century Fathers Kino and Salvatierra, both Jesuits, worked among the Indians of Baja California, Sonora, and Arizona. About the same time Fray Antonio Olivares and other missionaries began to establish missions in Texas, which was formally settled in 1718. The later and more famous Franciscan friar, Junípero Serra, was founding missions in California by 1769. These and other missionaries were followed by a few soldiers, ranchers, and miners, but the northern lands remained very sparsely settled and vulnerable to encroachments by other powers. Even though the French threat was no longer a reality, British expansion presented a menace, as did the appearance of Russian ships in California waters.

One result of the increasing international tensions was that viceroys and other high officials appointed in the last decades of the colonial period were often men with military training and experience. But even they were too far removed from the distant north to render effective defense of the frontiers. Therefore Gálvez planned an independent military government. After he returned to Spain and was appointed to the powerful post of minister of the Indies, he created, in 1776, the position of commandant general of the Interior Provinces. The new territorial organization of the commandancy general embraced the Interior Provinces of the present north Mexican states as well as Texas, greater New Mexico, and California. The commandant general oversaw the military and political administration of this large area, and he was independent of the viceroy, reporting directly to the king.

Operating out of Chihuahua City, he was responsible for establishing frontier forts (*presidios*) and patrolling the wilderness. While the foreign threats did not materialize in any important way, the Indian tribes who resisted fiercely Spanish expansion presented a real and continuing problem on the frontier.

The flaccid and corrupt bureaucracy of the colony also came under the careful scrutiny of Gálvez. He contemplated a drastic reorganization, even advocating the abolition of the viceregal position. He had to settle for less, but he did effect some profound changes for New Spain's administration at the provincial level. Since the first decades of settlement alcaldes mayores and corregidores had been notorious as the worst tormentors of the Indians. Their inadequate salaries had always encouraged extralegal commercial activities, and by the early eighteenth century these officials received no salaries at all. Instead they were expected to engage in business ventures. In effect, they were petty merchants who lived by purchasing the products and labor of the natives with cheap trinkets and forcing them to buy, at inflated prices, goods that they neither needed nor wanted.

Gálvez proposed that such officials be replaced by others called *intendants*. Intendants had served well in France and were subsequently utilized by the Bourbons in Spain. But Gálvez, who had enjoyed a cordial relationship with Viceroy Carlos Francisco de Croix, found that the succeeding viceroy, Antonio María de Bucareli, strongly opposed the substitution of intendants in the colony. So efficient and prosperous was Bucareli's rule that the crown deferred implementation of the reform for years. Finally, in 1786 Charles III agreed to the appointment of twelve intendants (of whom only one was a criollo) to replace some two hundred alcaldes mayores and corregidores in Mexico.

Implicit in the reforms decreed by the Bourbons was centralization and the imposition of unity, order, and efficiency. And paramount to the reorganization was the firm and effective management of crown revenues. The intendants sent to New Spain were charged with the control of royal monopolies, the collection of taxes, and overseeing the whole range of treasury interests in the colony, including suppression of smuggling. More than that, however, they had broad responsibilities to improve general administration in their districts, called intendancies, including such matters as justice, public facilities, and defense. Appointed from Spain, they were well paid, earning more even than the audiencia judges, and they were for the most part experienced, educated, and capable administrators. They enjoyed considerable

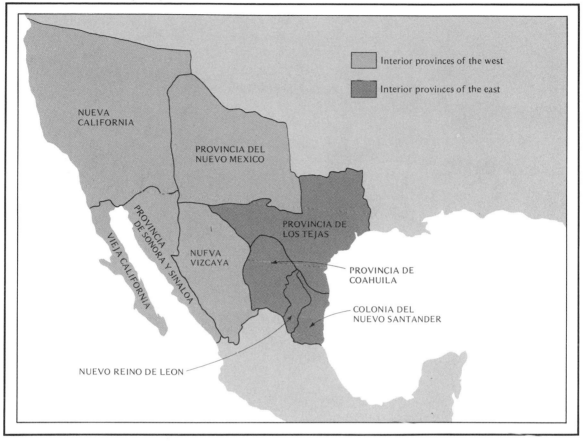

prestige and had ample authority in their large districts. It was not unnatural, therefore, that the creation of the new offices engendered the resentment of both the oidores and the viceroys, many of whom saw their own authority vitiated as a consequence.

The Effects of Bourbon Reforms

A confluence of factors brought about significant change in the colony of New Spain by the time of the death of Charles III in 1788. Still, change is not necessarily progress, and the ultimate effects of the Bourbon reforms must be viewed in the light of recent findings. On the whole, the economic reforms had a positive effect on the colony. One must not, however, exaggerate the

Carlos Francisco de Croix (1730–?) was viceroy from 1766–71. Born in France, of Flemish extraction, Croix served with distinction in New Spain.

Antonio María de Bucareli (1717–79), the 46th viceroy, served from 1771 until his death. He was a popular ruler, renowned for his integrity.

benefits. It is true that wealth was somewhat redistributed as a result of the broken monopolies of Mexico City merchants and the Consulado interests. But the crown gave itself, at the same time, certain monopolies that inevitably hurt other groups. The king's exclusive control over tobacco, for instance, took great sums of money out of private hands and displaced a large number of individuals involved in its production and marketing. But the monopoly was an important part of the imperial policy of restructuring, since these new crown revenues went to the support of the professional army. The pulque monopoly also put local merchants out of business, while the surtax imposed on this drink of the plebeian class outraged the populace.

And one must not attach too much significance to the so-called free trade policies that emerged under the Bourbons. Despite the undeniable improvement of the Mexican economy, new strictures in the form of taxes were imposed. Moreover there was a flood of peninsulares to the colony, and they were the ones who all too often profited from the rejuvenated business climate. The redistribution of wealth to great extent merely created a new group of wealthy gachupín aristocrats. The essence of mercantilism survived; the Bourbons had simply made it more efficient. Mexico's economy was increasingly manipulated for the benefit of the mother country. Dependency of the colonists on the mother country remained a fundamental tenet of the imperial system.

Political reforms were equally mixed blessings. Although intendants were capable, they were not able to administer their extensive intendancies alone and, of necessity, appointed subdelegates for various districts. These agents were ill paid, poorly qualified, and corrupt, and, in effect, they tended to recreate the old system under a different guise. What had been envisioned as a more centralized, tighter colonial administration became in the end an expanded bureaucracy, in which the number of highly paid officials quadrupled. Furthermore almost all the intendants were Spaniards, and they replaced many criollos who were persons of importance in their localities and who had come to regard the positions as criollo sinecures. The result was increased resentment on the part of criollos against the peninsulares.

The commandancy general brought slightly better administration to the borderlands without, however, effecting any significant change. Increased military organization of the northern provinces may have discouraged foreign intrusions, but on reflection, the point is academic: French ambitions were blunted in the 1760s, and within two decades the British were out of the borderlands. By the late century the British threat was real, but it was more likely to come from the Gulf coast. The meager resources of the fledgling United States would not be sufficient to support a westward advance for decades, despite some blustering to the contrary. As it was, the commandant general had his hands full trying to cope with Comanches and Apaches. Power, like wealth, was redistributed, creating new vested interest groups. As the prerogatives of the viceroys and audiencia judges were diminished, the intendants, military men, and tax collectors assumed considerable influence.

In summary, it is fair to say that under the Bourbons much had improved. Spain under Charles III had made a remarkable recovery, to some extent because of intelligent reforms but also because of fluctuating international fortunes that for the moment favored it. Spain was once again a world power, and Mexico was the incidental beneficiary. As we have seen, however, the colonists paid a price for increased prosperity and improved administration. What appeared in the 1780s to have been promising for the future of the Spanish empire faded rather quickly. Charles III was succeeded by a son lacking in wisdom; political affairs on the European continent would ultimately engulf Spain;

The Mining College (Colegio de Minería), designed by Manuel Tolsá, was constructed at great cost between 1797 and 1813. One of Mexico's handsomest colonial buildings, it has 238 rooms, 13 stairways, 11 fountains, and 7 courtyards. Its grandeur is an indication of the importance of silver mining in the late Spanish period.

and these and other events would foster a growing disenchantment among the colonists in New Spain. For it has historically been true that the rising expectations of an aroused populace are not easily checked. Once conventions were relaxed in economic and political spheres, it was natural for colonists to hope for a shift in social attitudes. But the royal intent was to benefit Spain, not the colonists, and tradition-bound monarchs of the eighteenth century saw no plausible benefits in social reform. Quite to the contrary: the year following the death of Charles III the French masses rose up in the name of social justice, beheaded their king, and went on the rampage. The shudder that passed through the royal courts of Europe was felt in Madrid as well.

Recommended for Further Study

Archer, Christon I. *The Army in Bourbon Mexico, 1760–1810.* Albuquerque: University of New Mexico Press, 1977.

Arnold, Linda. *Bureaucracy and Bureaucrats in Mexico City, 1742–1835.* Tucson: University of Arizona Press, 1988.

Bobb, Bernard. *The Viceregency of Antonio María Bucareli in New Spain:* Austin: University of Texas Press, 1962.

Brading, David A. *Miners and Merchants in Bourbon Mexico, 1763–1810.* Cambridge: Cambridge University Press, 1971.

Brinckerhoff, Sidney B., and Pierce A. Chamberlain. *Spanish Military Weapons in Colonial America: 1700–1821.* Harrisburg, Pa.: Stackpole Books, 1972.

Burkholder, Mark A. "The Council of the Indies in the Late Eighteenth Century: A New Perspective." *Hispanic American Historical Review* 56 (1976): 404–42.

DePalo, William A., Jr. "The Establishment of the Nueva Vizcaya Militia during the Administration of Teodoro de Croix: 1776–1783." *New Mexico Historical Review* 48 (1973): 223–49.

Fisher, Lillian Estelle. *The Intendant System in Spanish America.* Berkeley: University of California Press, 1929.

Garner, Richard L., and Spiro E. Stefanou. *Economic Growth and Change in Bourbon Mexico.* Gainesville: University Press of Florida, 1992.

Greenleaf, Richard E. "The Mexican Inquisition and the Masonic Movement: 1751–1820." *New Mexico Historical Review* 41 (1969): 93–177.

———. "The Nueva Vizcaya Frontier, 1787–1789." *Journal of the West* 8 (1969): 56–66.

Greenow, Linda. *Credit and Socioeconomic Change in Colonial Mexico: Loans and Mortgages in Guadalajara, 1720–1820.* Boulder, Colo.: Westview Press, 1983.

Hamnett, Brian R. *Politics and Trade in Southern Mexico, 1750–1821.* Cambridge: Cambridge University Press, 1971.

Howe, Walter. *The Mining Guild of New Spain and Its Tribunal General, 1770–1821.* Cambridge, Mass.: Harvard University Press, 1949.

Kuethe, Allan J., and Lowell Blaisdell. "French Influence and the Origins of the Bourbon Colonial Reorganization." *Hispanic American Historical Review* 3 (1991): 579–607.

Lipsett-Rivera, Sonya. "Puebla's Eighteenth Century Agrarian Decline: A New Perspective." *Hispanic American Historical Review* 3 (1990): 463–82.

McAlister, Lyle N. *The "Fuero Militar" in New Spain, 1764–1800.* Gainesville: University of Florida Press, 1967.

———. "The Reorganization of the Army of New Spain, 1763–1766." *Hispanic American Historical Review* 48 (1973): 223–49.

Ouweneel, Arij, and Catrien C. J. H. Bijleveld. "The Economic Cycle in Bourbon Central Mexico: A Critique of the *Recaudación del diezmo líquido en pesos*" 3 (1989): 479–530.

Priestley, Herbert I. *José de Gálvez, Visitor General of New Spain, 1765–1771.* Berkeley: University of California Press, 1916.

Thomas, Alfred B. *Teodoro de Croix and the Northern Frontier of New Spain, 1776–1783.* Norman: University of Oklahoma Press, 1941.

Thomson, Guy C. P. *Puebla de los Angeles: Industry and Society in a Mexican City, 1700–1850.* Boulder, Colo.: Westview Press, 1989.

15

Society and Stress
in the Late Colonial Period

The Wealthy

In 1704 the royal treasurer in Mexico City gave a party for the viceroy that lasted several days and cost twenty thousand pesos. Among those in attendance, we may be sure, was a young lady of the capital whose dowry amounted to the incredible sum of six hundred thousand pesos. Affairs of this kind were part of the colonial social scene even before the later economic boom, for despite the general recession of the previous several decades, the small aristocracy of New Spain had maintained itself in luxury. Over the next few decades their numbers would increase significantly, as would their assets.

The poor did not get any poorer, but the rich certainly got richer. A disproportionate number of the wealthiest were peninsulares who had made good in America, but there were many prosperous criollos as well. Great fortunes were made in mining, such as those of the counts of Valenciana, Regla, and Bassoco. Regla's staggering wealth (the greatest fortune in the colony) is difficult to assess, but in the late eighteenth century Valenciana sometimes took a net profit of more than a million pesos annually, quite aside from his millions tied up in land and various other interests. Bassoco, elevated to count only in 1811 after a gift to the government of two hundred thousand pesos, accumulated assets worth some three million pesos.

These mining barons, along with some wealthy ranchers and merchants, frequently made generous gifts to the crown, which in gratitude conferred on the donors cherished titles of nobility— usually that of *conde*, less often that of *marqués*. Some prominent

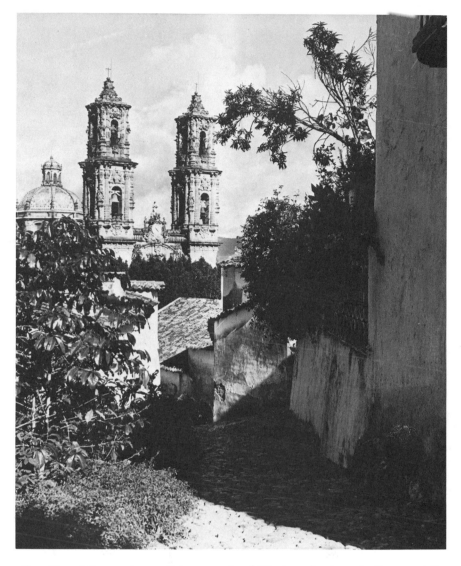

Considered the most complete example of Mexican baroque is the exquisite church of Santa Prisca in Taxco. Built between 1751 and 1759, its cost was underwritten by the mining baron Don José de la Borda.

men had to be content with knighthood in one of the prestigious military orders. During the eighteenth century about fifty titles of nobility were granted to residents of New Spain, most of them after 1750.

But while these dignities appealed to the vanity of the recipients, many of the rich were philanthropic for less fatuous reasons. They contributed large sums of money to religious organiza-

This magnificent colonial residence, rising four stories, is a good example of the extravagant architectural style known as Churrigueresque. Built in the eighteenth century for the Count of San Mateo de Valparaíso, it was later used as a palace by Emperor Agustín I (Iturbide). Subsequently it served as a hotel and today it is beautifully maintained by a bank.

tions, funded charities, and financed the construction of schools, hospitals, and lovely churches. They also financed festivals and cultural events for the enjoyment of the community. In times of pestilence the rich often paid for medicines, and when famine struck they distributed large supplies of grain and other foods. Unfortunately these gestures were often little more than tokens, for some catastrophes were overwhelming. In 1784, for example, some three hundred thousand people in Mexico perished from starvation or illness induced by undernourishment. Thousands more died from a respiratory infection.

Among the most powerful men of Mexico were the rich hacendados in the north. As missionaries, miners, and soldiers penetrated the frontier, the Indians were gradually pushed back and the land came into the possession of wealthy and influential ranchers. Much of the region consisted of desert and could be acquired at low cost; in 1731 the marqués de Aguayo purchased 222,000 acres from the crown for a paltry 250 pesos. Within four decades his family controlled over fourteen and a half million acres, some of which were patrolled by the marqués's private

A rural scene of an hacendado and his foreman.

A spirited mount and fine clothing typify this scene of rural landowners in the early nineteenth century. The Mexicans' equestrian skill and love of fine horses have long been known.

cavalry to protect the livestock from marauding Indians. By the
late colonial period the northern haciendas, sprawling and isolated, were like private fiefdoms. Yet the stereotype of the hacienda as an operation little concerned with profit and efficiency,
a self-sufficient enterprise maintained primarily for the status
inherent in the ownership of vast expanses of land, does not always survive examination. A study of the huge holdings of the
Sánchez Navarro family, for example, shows the owners to have
been capitalists who diversified their interests. Aside from running sheep, cattle, and horses, they were also involved in mining,
agriculture, and commerce. They were hard-working men who
were by no means cut off from the outside world, although their
latifundio, eventually covering an area almost as large as the
country of Portugal, was the largest ranch in Spanish America.[1]

The colony's increased prosperity was reflected not only in
ornate religious edifices but also in the many impressive public
buildings. In Mexico City today one can still see enough of those
surviving to appreciate the grandeur of the capital in the late
colonial era. There also remain about thirty of the magnificent
mansions belonging to the wealthy of that period, some preserved
either by the government or commercial firms. The spectacular
House of Tiles, covered on the exterior and the interior with tiles
said to have been brought expressly from China, is a modern
landmark. Once the residence of the conde del Valle de Orizaba,
it is today a restaurant. The stately townhouse of the counts of
San Mateo de Valparaíso (also known as the Palace of Iturbide)
has been restored by a bank, while the large residence of the
counts of Santiago de Calimaya is now the interesting Museum of
the City of Mexico.

The colony, and especially the capital, benefited from the
improvements made by one of the greatest viceroys, the second
count of Revillagigedo (1789–94). Among his many intelligent
innovations was the lighting of streets, which lowered the rate of
crimes and accidents. He also paved the streets and authorized
the first public transportation system, and when that added to
the crowded traffic in the capital, he set speed limits, restricted
parking, and issued laws against shrill whistling and shouting
imprecations at pedestrians and riders. He is remembered also
for having ordered an important census and for improving the
postal service. Sad to say, there were few public servants of his
wisdom and vision.

1. See Charles H. Harris III, *A Mexican Family Empire: The Latifundio of the
Sánchez Navarro Family, 1765–1867* (Austin, 1975).

This imposing residence, built in 1528, had been altered by the counts of Santiago de Calimaya by 1779. Today it is the Museum of the City of Mexico.

The Casa de Alfeñique ("Sugar-candy House"), an eighteenth-century showplace in Puebla, a city of many colonial treasures.

In rural territories, where Indians predominated, society had changed relatively little. Many of the natives in remote areas, and particularly in southern Mexico, had scarcely been acculturated into Spanish society, and to great extent they lived much as they had in pre-Hispanic times. Those who lived closer to Spanish centers, however, naturally took on many of the characteristics of the white society. As a result of generations of miscegenation, the mestizo population had increased enormously. By the late eighteenth century more than four-fifths of the population were nonwhite, most of them constituting the lower class. There existed a small, indistinct group that could be termed middle class, but perhaps the designation lower-upper class would be more accurate, for the people were considerably above the poverty level of the masses. Around 1810 a population in excess of six million included more than three and a half million Indians. Over a million were considered criollos, and only 15,000 were peninsulares. The remainder were mestizos of various mixes.

The aristocracy of the eighteenth century differed from its counterpart of the two preceding centuries primarily in the matter of style rather than attitude. Later aristocrats were wealthier and more cultured. Some had studied and traveled in Europe. They adopted continental fashions, the women appearing on festive occasions in expensive gowns and elaborate coiffures, the men in knee breeches, tricorn hats, and, on formal occasions, powdered wigs. To some extent Mexican high society had, like that of Spain, become "Frenchified" through tastes acquired with the Bourbon accession. Also in imitation of European styles were the fancy dress balls and salons in which the elite discoursed on

The second count of Revillagigedo (Juan Vicente de Güemes-Pacheco y Padilla) (1740–99). Viceroy from 1789–94, he is considered to have been one of the most outstanding rulers of New Spain.

A portrait of an aristocratic lady by Miguel Cabrera (1695–1768). A Zapotec Indian, Cabrera was New Spain's most successful and most prolific painter.

the new philosophies emanating from France and England and conversed about art, literature, music, and, inevitably, the economy and politics. Poetry was read (sometimes, mercilessly, the reader's own efforts), and scientific papers were presented. All this was spiced with gossip and expressions of horror at the vulgarities of the masses.

Criollo Discontent

The proliferation of wars during the eighteenth century, far from the shores of Mexico, occasioned little more than casual notice, enlivened perhaps by the personal account of a Spanish veteran. But interest increased with the successful revolt of the English colonists to the north and the outbreak of the French Revolution. Later came news of the astounding success of black slaves who overthrew their French masters in Haiti and declared their independence. Informed criollos could hardly fail to observe that in both revolts in the hemisphere, colonial populations smaller than Mexico's had thrown over imperial powers greater than Spain. But criollos also recognized that their own society was far more heterogeneous than either the United States or Haiti.

The opulent extreme of the rich was in glaring contrast to the majority, who lived in poverty. The lot of the colored castes had improved somewhat over the centuries. They were less abused physically and were usually paid for their labor. The encomiendas, long in decline, had finally been abolished in the eighteenth century, so the Indians were no longer subject to the abuses of

A typical scene along a provincial road.

that institution. But wages were niggardly, allowing only the
barest necessities, and many were tied to the evils of peonage.
There was little recourse for peones, who lacked the security
and financial resources to risk a change in employment. Indians still bore the humiliating obligation of paying tribute to
the crown, and they were forbidden to wear European clothing
under pain of a hundred lashes and a month in jail. By the end of
the colonial era there were few black slaves, but free blacks and
mulattoes shared the indignities of the lowest classes. Illiterate,
inhibited, and conditioned to their fate, the colored masses were
generally ignorant of, and little affected by, imperial political
and economic decisions. But they nursed a deep resentment
against all whites, Spanish or criollo.

In the stratified society of New Spain there was little cohesion
among the various groups. The lower classes were dispersed, the
majority of them living and working in the provinces and having almost no communication outside their immediate acquaint-
ances. Lacking organization and leadership, their occasional attempts to improve their conditions by violence were conceived in
desperation and ended in tragedy. When time came for a political
revolution, the impetus came not from any spontaneous uprising
of the masses but rather from the actions of criollo conspirators.
Criollo grievances combined with a succession of disruptive ex-
ternal circumstances to sever the colonial tie.

Criollos had from the beginning been forced into a secondary
position by those born in Spain. The peninsulares, or gachupines,
had always enjoyed special privileges and occupied the favored
positions in church and state. There was a certain logic in this,
for the peninsulares receiving high office were usually well educated and had more administrative experience and polish than
the criollos. Beyond that, an official with strong ties to the mother
country was likely to be more loyal to the interests of Spain. Few
criollos, on the other hand, had ever seen Spain, and by birth,
education, cultural milieu, property, and familial relationships
they naturally identified strongly with the colony. As officials,
they might succumb to the temptation of favoring their countrymen, perhaps at the expense of royal interests.

Still, the policy that apportioned relatively few good bureaucratic posts to criollos has perhaps been given more emphasis
than it deserves. Criollos were not blind to the realities, and they
did not aspire to the office of viceroy or archbishop. They did
hope, however, that more of the important positions would go to

the most competent among the Mexican-born. In the eighteenth century the Bourbons appointed some criollos to high office, and others were able to purchase posts put up for bidding. A few even served as judges in the audiencias as well as in other powerful positions. By 1769 at least eight of the twelve members of the Audiencia of Mexico were criollos. They were even more successful in obtaining rank in the church. This promising state of affairs came under some change during the reign of Charles III, who agreed with Gálvez that the colonists' participation in government should be restricted. As a result the number of criollos in the audiencia of the capital had declined by 1780 to only four of sixteen, and later there were even fewer. Criollos were, however, able to secure rank in the military; by the close of the eighteenth century of a total of 361 officers in the regular regiments 227 were criollos, and in the militia they held 338 commissions of 624 officer positions.[2]

The distinctions they perceived between the gachupines and themselves were increasingly galling to the criollos. Although no more than 10 percent of the former were legitimate hidalgos, all Spaniards in Mexico assumed nobility and expected to be addressed as "Don." The peninsulares, no matter how lacking in education and culture, considered themselves superior to all and disparaged the capacities of the criollos. These arrogant gachupines were greatly outnumbered, but they formed a small, tight circle, both in business and social affairs; only occasionally did they marry into criollo aristocracies. Far from accepting the stigma of congenital inferiority that Spaniards had placed on them, however, the criollos asserted their self-worth more vocally in the eighteenth century. They envied the privileges of the peninsulares and resented their pretentious manner, and they insisted that the demonstrable achievements of the Mexican-born were equal to those of the Spaniards. The criollos did not consider themselves Spaniards living in the Indies but rather as a distinct people. There was reason for pride in their land; foreign travelers had affirmed that Mexico City compared favorably with Spanish cities, even Madrid. Colonists extolled the unique charm of Mexico, a country with its own flavor and a society with its own character, more exotic and colorful than Spain.

One immediately noticeable difference was in the language, now losing its Castilian lisp and enriched by Indian words and

2. David A. Brading, *Miners and Merchants in Bourbon Mexico, 1763–1810* (Cambridge, 1971), pp. 40–42.

diminutives. The Mexican diet was distinctive; the architecture of Spain had been modified; customs and dress had acquired their own traits. The Mexican ambience had colored the literature, art, and music. The people, the landscape, the flora, and the fauna were all peculiar to Mexico. What was originally Spanish had been altered, and while the Spaniards showed disdain at the corruption of Spanish culture, the native-born began to celebrate their mexicanidad. Shunning the socially tainted designation of *criollo*, they considered themselves *americanos*.

Yet tradition takes a firm hold. Emotional ties to Spanish history and traditions, the felt personal relationship to the monarchy, the devotion to the Spanish church—all these bound tightly. Criollo discontent led at first not to a criticism of the crown so much as to a more profound consideration of the historical past in Mexico itself. In spite of the alert agents of the Inquisition, inflammatory literature from Europe circulated in the colony, provoking reflection on Spanish institutions. In guarded conversation—and ultimately in audacious published tracts—references were made to "the barbarity of Conquest" and "three centuries of slavery." The inequities and absurdities of colonial policies were satirized in popular verse and song.

In spite of the grumbling, serious consideration of rebellion against Spain was entertained by only the most radical of colonists. There were complaints about the imposition of new taxes, and the general tightening of administration pinched here and there. Colonists were displeased with the ubiquitous officials of the swollen bureaucracy, and some resented attempts to press them into the militia. But while some criollos had been hurt by royal economic policies, others had prospered, and, all things considered, the colonists were better off than ever before. Certainly conditions had been more ripe for rebellion in 1700 than in 1800.

What the criollos really wanted was to be on an equal footing with the peninsulares, or, better yet, somehow to replace them altogether. Aristocrats by virtue of complexion, the criollos wanted to maintain the class system. Their attitudes toward the lower masses were no less haughty than the peninsulares' opinion of the criollos. In no way did the criollos advocate social equality for those below them. As the visiting German scientist Alexander von Humboldt observed in the late colonial period, "In America, the skin, more or less white, is what dictates the class that an individual occupies in society. A white, even if he rides barefoot on horseback, considers himself a member of the nobility of the country."[3] Rebellion evoked the specters of anarchy and race war, in which the colored masses, who made little distinction between gachupín and criollo, might rise against all white persons.

Clerical Discontent

The provincial conservatism of the colonists was offended by the conscious crown policy of diminishing the traditional power, wealth, and prestige of the church. Long favored by Hapsburg monarchs, the religious establishment came under a cloud during the Bourbon period and was subjected to rigorous examination by Charles III. Above all, it was the Jesuits who stuck in the monarch's craw. The Society of Jesus had distinguished itself in various ways, especially in educating and missionizing, but it had also grown very powerful and wealthy. The king, wary of papal ascendancy, saw the Jesuits' allegiance to the pope as detrimental to the interests of Spain. Moreover, like other rulers of his time, he suspected the order of political intrigue and of spreading dangerous ideas.

In 1766 the Jesuits were accused of fomenting a riot against Spain's prime minister. The following year, without warning, they were suddenly expelled from all Spanish kingdoms. Sealed orders were opened throughout the Spanish empire on the same day in 1767, ordering the expulsion of the Jesuits forthwith and decreeing the confiscation of their properties. Colonists were stunned by this bold move of the crown. Initial shock gave way to outrage that exploded into violent demonstrations, especially by Indians, in half a dozen communities.

New Spain was notably affected by the expulsion. Of 678 Jesuits who left, some 400 were Mexican-born; of the 243 missionary houses, 114 had belonged to the Society of Jesus. The Jesuits had maintained the best schools in the colony, with twenty-three colleges and many seminaries that housed the most distinguished faculties. Their graduates, especially those of San Ildefonso, were some of the most prominent men in Mexico, including audiencia judges. Some of the Jesuit schools were turned over to the Franciscans, but the Franciscans were not prepared to carry on in the same way, nor could they sufficiently fill in the Jesuit missionary fields.

The crown charged the church with "excessive wealth," which

3. Quoted in Magnus Mörner, *Race Mixture in the History of Latin America* (Boston, 1967), pp. 55–56.

was, in fact, extensive, consisting of considerable urban real estate as well as latifundio. Beyond that, crown economic counselors emphasized that ecclesiastical properties were not being used to their potential, thus obstructing government efforts to stimulate the economy. Ironically, the Jesuit holdings had been among the best managed estates in the empire. In Mexico there were about eighty Jesuit estates worth some ten million pesos.

The steady pressure against the church continued to be a matter of concern to many in New Spain, not least among them the ecclesiastics themselves. In particular the lower echelon of parish priests became alienated, and they communicated their growing disillusionment with crown policies to their flocks. Exacerbating the already tender sensibilities of clergymen, in 1804 the crown decreed the Act of Consolidation, according to which assets of the church's charitable funds were sequestered. The huge sum involved was 44.5 million pesos, henceforth used to pay for Spain's misadventures in Europe rather than for the needy in Mexico. The church, formerly a major source of credit in the colony, was forced to call in notes and mortgages, thereby reducing some criollos to financial ruin. The disastrous Act crippled the activities of the church and embittered more priests, friars, and people throughout Mexico.

Conspiracies in New Spain and Confusion in Spain

It is sometimes the impression that there was comparatively little resistance to Spanish domination in Mexico until the outbreak of insurgency in 1810. This is erroneous; in fact, there were more than a hundred conspiracies and rebellions during the colonial period.[4] Some posed serious threats to Spain's hegemony, while others were trivial affairs. At least in a few there was mention of independence, but such movements were considered aberrations and slightly insane by the general populace. Most of the disturbances found their origins in local grievances and lacked broad support. However, some of the Indian rebellions found numerous ardent followers—with violent and bloody consequences.[5] From the northern province of New Mexico, where the Pueblo Revolt of 1680 drove out the Spaniards, to the southernmost province of

4. These are listed in Agustín Cue Cánovas, *Historia social y económica de México (1521–1854)* (Mexico, 1972), pp. 183–87.
5. Roberto Mario Salmón, *Indian Revolts in Northern New Spain: A Synthesis of Resistance (1680–1786)* (Lanham, Md., 1991).

Chiapas, where the 1712 revolt of the Tzeltal Maya shook the colonial system, the native peoples resisted.[6]

In 1794, the popular Viceroy Revillagigedo was replaced by the vain, corrupt marqués de Branciforte. His appointment aroused anger, which was ventilated in September in wall posters appearing in the capital. The messages acclaimed the ideals of the French Revolution, and rumors of a plot spread throughout the city. A conspiracy had, in fact, formed, with plans to seize the government, release eight hundred prisoners from jail, free the Indians from the tribute obligations, and liberate Mexico. The plotters, including a priest, were taken into custody, but the trials were delayed for years and in the end the prisoners were incarcerated in exile. Curiously enough, these intriguers were not criollos but peninsulares.

Hardly had their cases been disposed of when, in 1799, an ill-conceived conspiracy of criollos was discovered in Mexico City. Their plan was so naive that their cache of arms consisted only of machetes, and their plot became known, therefore, as the Machete Conspiracy. The plotters were arrested quietly to avoid a sensation. After languishing in prison, some died, but others were eventually released, escaping execution because of official fears that the affair would create criollo martyrs. The leniency toward rebels, including some Indian conspirators in 1801, suggests the crown's concern with the festering discontent in New Spain. Ironically, royal forbearance served only to underscore Spain's impotence. The weak response did little to discourage further plots.

Ultimately the deterioration of Spain's position in Europe brought on a crisis. At the death of his father in 1788, Charles IV had become king, and he quickly lent weight to the commonplace that great men seldom beget sons of their equal. He was inept and had little apparent interest in ruling the empire. His subjects grew weary of him and impatiently awaited the succession of Prince Ferdinand. The queen (no prize herself, if we trust the brush of Goya) also tired of him and found solace in the intimate company of a handsome provincial guardsman named Manuel de Godoy. The clever, ambitious Godoy maneuvered himself at the age of twenty-five into the rank of prime minister. He then proceeded to make a series of unwise alliances, which finally encouraged the invasion of Spain in 1808 by the troops of Napoleon

---

6. See Kevin Gosner, *Soldiers of the Virgin: The Moral Economy of a Colonial Maya Rebellion* (Tucson, 1992).

María Luisa of Parma, the queen of Spain, at age fourteen married her cousin, who became Charles IV.

Bonaparte. When Madrid fell to the French army, Charles IV and his son became prisoners, and shortly thereafter the king abdicated in favor of the prince. But the new Ferdinand VII was a king without a throne. Napoleon appointed his own brother Joseph to rule over Spain, while much of the country resisted. Some Spanish patriots formed a government in exile in the fortified city of Cádiz.

When news of the king's capture and the occupation of Spain by the French reached New Spain there was confusion as to who was to rule the colony. Joseph Bonaparte as sovereign was unthinkable, but what was the logical alternative? Although a few saw the situation as a golden opportunity to gain independence, the majority of the colonists advocated the formation of a caretaker government to run affairs in the name of Ferdinand VII until such time as the king was released. The viceroy seemed the obvious person to assume rule in Mexico, but the audiencia insisted on sharing power. Eventually, in cities throughout the Spanish American colonies, the cabildos asserted their own claims. They argued that historically, when a legitimate ruler was lacking, provisional bodies, or *juntas*, formed to manage local affairs. Following such a bold proclamation, several members of the Cabildo of Mexico City were arrested.

Viceroy José de Iturrigaray had shrewdly assessed the developments: if he played his cards right he might see a Mexican crown on his head. He decided that the criollos had the best prospects, and he played to their interests by allowing them to form a junta. A group of peninsulares now made their move, viewing Iturrigaray's actions as both stupid and treasonous. On the evening of September 15, 1808, a small band of Spaniards forcibly removed the viceroy from his palace and packed him off to Veracruz to await passage to Spain, where he was later imprisoned. The peninsulares also arrested half a dozen prominent criollo leaders. Replacing Iturrigaray was Pedro Garibay, a senile field marshal in his eightieth year who had to contend with various militant factions.

The instability of government in 1809 only added to the anxieties arising from a threatening economic picture. Insufficient rain fell that summer, and the resulting shortage of corn caused prices in some areas to inflate to four times their normal level. The consequences were far-reaching, affecting, for example, mining production, since there was too little food for draft animals, and workers had to be laid off. Interrupted commerce with the occupied mother country further dislocated the Mexican economy. Taken altogether, it was a time of confusion and stress, with all segments of society growing restless.

Among the more sophisticated criollos in Mexico City the mood remained conservative. They might espouse the principles of the French Revolution, but rebellion against the crown was a painful thought, especially amid reminders of rich Spanish traditions. Attitudes in the provinces were somewhat different. More isolated from ritual and pomp, more independent, and more

The great central plaza of Mexico City, popularly known as the Zócalo. It is bordered by the cathedral, the viceregal (now the national) palace, the cabildo quarters, and other public buildings.

closely identified with the land, the criollos in smaller communities had a more fully developed sense of the *patria chica*—their own little world—where they wanted to run their own affairs. They were incensed by the thought of Joseph Bonaparte planning their destinies. Their surge of nationalism was triggered not so much by French philosophy as by French guns. Less worldly than criollos of the capital, less meticulous, and less pensive about the multiple consequences, the provincial criollos assumed a bolder stance. In many communities small groups had been meeting, sometimes under the guise of "literary clubs," to discuss what was to be done. Royal officials were cognizant of such gatherings, suspecting, correctly, that they were conspiratorial in nature. One plot, which included clergymen, military officers, and Indian groups, was exposed in Vallodolid in 1809. Although the principals were imprisoned for a while, most were in the vanguard of the insurrection that was to follow shortly.

In 1810 the important cities of southern Spain fell to French troops, compromising without question the sovereignty of the nation. The colonists were bewildered and apprehensive. In that same year it also came to the attention of royal authorities in Mexico City that a conspiracy had formed in Querétaro. Its ringleaders included an aging, dissident priest named Hidalgo. Once again troops were dispatched to deal with yet another provincial incident.

Recommended for Further Study

Anna, Timothy. "The Last Viceroys of New Spain and Peru: An Appraisal." *American Historical Review* 81 (1976): 38–65.

Arrom, Silvia Marina. *The Women of Mexico City, 1790–1857.* Stanford, Calif.: Stanford University Press, 1985.

Brading, David A. "Government and Elite in Late Colonial Mexico." *Hispanic American Historical Review* 53 (1973): 389–414.

———. *Haciendas and Ranchos in the Mexican Bajio: León, 1700–1860.* Cambridge: Cambridge University Press, 1978.

Cook, Sherburne F. "The Smallpox Epidemic of 1797 in Mexico." *Bulletin of the History of Medicine* 8 (1940): 937–69.

Cooper, Donald B. *Epidemic Disease in Mexico City, 1761–1813.* Austin: University of Texas Press, 1965.

Cortés, José. *Views from the Apache Frontier: Report on the Northern Provinces of New Spain.* Edited by Elizabeth A. H. John. Norman: University of Oklahoma Press, 1989.

Couturier, Edith R. "The Philanthropic Activities of Pedro Romero de Terreros: First Count of Regla (1753–1781)." *The Americas* 32 (1975): 13–30.

Gosner, Kevin. *Soldiers of the Virgin. The Moral Economy of a Colonial Maya Rebellion.* Tucson: University of Arizona Press, 1992.

Griffen, William B. *The Apaches at War and Peace: The Janos Presidio, 1750–1858.* Albuquerque: University of New Mexico Press, 1988.

Hamnet, Brian R. *Roots of Insurgency, Mexican Regions, 1750–1824.* Cambridge: Cambridge University Press, 1985.

Humboldt, Alexander von. *Political Essay on the Kingdom of New Spain.* Edited, with an introduction, by Mary Maples Dunn. New York: Knopf, 1972.

Ladd, Doris M. *The Mexican Nobility at Independence, 1780–1826.* Austin: University of Texas Press, 1976.

Lafaye, Jacques. *Quetzalcóatl and Guadalupe: The Formation of Mexican National Consciousness, 1531–1813.* Translated by Benjamin Keen, with an introduction by Octavio Paz. Chicago: University of Chicago Press, 1976.

Lafaye, Jacques, and James Lockhart. "A Scholarly Debate: The Origins of Modern Mexico—Indigenistas vs. Hispanistas." *The Americas* 3 (1992): 315–30.

Lavrin, Asunción. "The Execution of the Law of Consolidation in New Spain: Economic Gains and Results." *Hispanic American Historical Review* 53 (1973): 27–49.

Lindley, Richard B. *Haciendas and Economic Development: Guadalajara, Mexico, at Independence.* Austin: University of Texas Press, 1983.

MacLachlan, Colin M. *Criminal Justice in Eighteenth Century Mexico: A Study of the Tribunal of the Acordada.* Berkeley: University of California Press, 1974.

Mörner, Magnus, ed. *The Expulsion of the Jesuits from Latin America.* New York: Knopf, 1965.

Motten, Clement. *Mexican Silver and the Enlightenment.* Philadelphia: University of Pennsylvania Press, 1950.

Probert, Alan. "The Real del Monte Partido Riots: 1766." *Journal of the West* 12 (1973): 85–125.

Rodríguez O., Jaime E., ed. *Patterns of Contention in Mexican History.* Wilmington, Del.: Scholarly Resources, Inc., 1972.

Scardaville, Michael C. "Alcohol Abuse and Tavern Reform in Late Colonial Mexico City." *Hispanic American Historical Review* 60 (1980): 643–71.

Schmitt, Karl M. "The Clergy and the Independence of New Spain." *Hispanic American Historical Review* 34 (1954): 289–312.

Stein, Stanley J., and Barbara H. Stein. *The Colonial Heritage of Latin America: Essays on Economic Dependence in Perspective.* New York: Oxford University Press, 1970.

Tambs, Lewis A. "The Inquisition in Eighteenth Century Mexico." *The Americas* 22 (1965): 167–81.

Tutino, John. *From Insurrection to Revolution in Mexico: Social Bases of Agrarian Violence, 1750–1940.* Princeton, N.J.: Princeton University Press, 1986.

Whitaker, Arthur P. "The Elhuyar Mining Missions and the Enlightenment." *Hispanic American Historical Review* 31 (1951): 557–85.

Wolf, Eric. "The Mexican Bajío in the Eighteenth Century." *Middle American Research Institute Publications* 17 (1969): 85–113.

Young, Eric Van. "Urban Market and Hinterland: Guadalajara and Its Region in the Eighteenth Century." *Hispanic American Historical Review* 59 (1979): 593–635.

Zeitlin, Judith Francis. "Ranchers and Indians on the Southern Isthmus of Tehuantepec: Economic Change and Indigenous Survival in Colonial Mexico." *Hispanic American Historical Review* 1 (1989): 23–60.

16

The Wars for Independence

Hidalgo and Early Success

Born in 1753 of moderately well-to-do criollo stock, Miguel Hidalgo y Costilla spent his first twelve years on the Hacienda de San Diego Corralejo in Guanajuato, where his father served the owner as *mayordomo* (resident manager). Encouraged by his father, the boy moved with his older brother, José Joaquín, to Valladolid (today Morelia) and matriculated at the Jesuit College of San Francisco Javier. The brothers had been at their studies only two years when shocking news reached the city: King Charles III of Spain had banished the Jesuits from New Spain and all Spanish possessions in the New World. Left without teachers, the boys had to interrupt their schooling, but within a year they had enrolled in the diocesan College of San Nicolás Obispo, also in Valladolid, and one of the nineteen colleges and seminaries in Mexico that prepared students for degrees eventually to be awarded by the Royal and Pontifical University in Mexico City. Young Miguel Hidalgo steeped himself in rhetoric, Latin, and Thomistic theology, and, in the tradition of generations of Mexican priests before him, found time to study Indian languages. His bachelor's degree was awarded by the University of Mexico in 1774, and he immediately began preparations for the priesthood. The bishop celebrated his sacrament of ordination in the fall of 1778.

Enthusiastic and self-assured, the twenty-eight-year-old priest returned to Valladolid to teach at the College of San Nicolás Obispo, where he eventually became rector. But he was scarcely exemplary from the church's point of view. Before the turn of the century the Holy Office of the Inquisition had been apprised, by rumor and fact, of a curate whose orthodoxy was suspect, who questioned priestly celibacy, who read books proscribed by the *Index Expurgatorius*, who indulged in gambling and enjoyed dancing, who challenged the infallibility of the Most Holy Father in Rome, who doubted the veracity of the virgin birth, who dared to suggest that fornication out of wedlock was not a sin, who referred to the Spanish king as a tyrant, and who—alas!— kept María Manuela Herrera as a mistress and procuress. Hidalgo was hailed before the Inquisition in 1800, but nothing could be proved. The testimony was carefully filed, however, to be used later.

Hidalgo's future fortunes and misfortunes were cast when, in 1803, he accepted the curacy of the small parish of Dolores. Devoting only minimal time to the spiritual needs of his parishioners, Father Hidalgo concerned himself primarily with improving their economic potential. He introduced new industries in Dolores: tile making, tanning, carpentry, wool weaving, beekeeping, silk growing, and wine making. He preferred to spend his spare time reading and engaging his fellow criollos in informal debate rather than listening to the confessions of his Indian charges. A few years after his arrival in Dolores, Hidalgo's path crossed that of Ignacio Allende, a thirty-five-year-old firebrand who was a captain in the Queen's Cavalry Regiment in nearby Guanajuato. Allende took the priest into his confidence and introduced him to a coterie of friends: Juan de Aldama, also a military man; Miguel Domínguez, a former corregidor of Querétaro, and his wife, Doña Josefa Ortiz de Domínguez, remembered in Mexican history as *La Corregidora*; Epigmenio González, a grocer; Marino Galván, a postal clerk; and a few others.

The group had organized a "literary club," but the members were less interested in disputing the latest tour de force of Goethe, Schiller, Wordsworth, or Chateaubriand than in plotting the separation of the New Spain from the old. As converts were attracted and the plans matured, a date was set for the uprising—December 8, 1810. Although the conspirators were all admonished to hold their tongues, Marino Galván, the postal clerk, leaked the news to his superior who, in turn, informed the audiencia in Mexico City. The forewarned Spanish authorities moved on September 13, when they searched the house of Epigmenio González in Querétaro, found bountiful arms and ammunition, and ordered the arrest of the panic-stricken owner. The events of the next few days are known to every Mexican schoolchild, for they

Miguel Hidalgo y Costilla (1753–1811). One of the most renowned individuals in nineteenth-century Mexican history, Father Hidalgo provided the initial spark for the Independence movement.

are repeated every September 16 amidst a wide array of Independence Day celebrations.

Doña Josefa entrusted Ignacio Pérez with the task of carrying the news of the arrest to Ignacio Allende in San Miguel. Not finding him at home, the messenger relayed the news to Juan de Aldama, who immediately set out to inform Father Hidalgo in Dolores. When, about two o'clock on the morning of September 16, he arrived at the priest's house, Aldama found Allende there also. The three realized that orders for their own arrest had probably been issued and decided to strike out for Independence at once. Hidalgo rang the church bells summoning his parishioners to mass earlier than usual that morning. Assembled at the little church in Dolores the Indians and mestizos, including a group of prisoners already released from the local jail, were harangued about matters of this world, not the next. The exact words of this most famous of all Mexican speeches are not known, or, rather, they are reproduced in almost as many variations as there are historians to reproduce them. But the essential spirit of the message is this:

> My children: a new dispensation comes to us today. Will you receive it? Will you free yourselves? Will you recover the lands stolen three hundred years ago from your forefathers by the hated Spaniards? We must act at once. . . . Will you not defend your

religion and your rights as true patriots? Long live our Lady of
Guadalupe! Death to bad government! Death to the gachupines!

The immediate response to the *Grito de Dolores* was enthusiastic. With Hidalgo at their head, the motley band of poorly armed
Indians and mestizos struck out for San Miguel, picking up hundreds of recruits along the way. When they stopped for a rest
about noon at the hamlet of Atotonilco, Hidalgo entered the local
church and emerged carrying a banner of the Virgin de Guadalupe—the dark-skinned lady who had appeared to Juan Diego almost three centuries before. The priest adopted this Virgin as the
emblem of his crusade, but for reasons less religious than political. How better appeal to the Indian population who would make
up the rank and file of his revolutionary army? What better contrast to the Spanish gold-brocaded Virgin de los Remedios than
the humbly robed Indian Virgin de Guadalupe?

By dusk Hidalgo's band had taken San Miguel without difficulty, for the local militia joined the rebels. The day's dramatic
events should have ended with the imprisonment of the local
Spanish populace, but as night fell the unpredicted happened.
The Indians were not ready to rest on their laurels and bed down
for the night. If it were true that the Spaniards were to blame for
everything that had befallen the aboriginal population of Mexico since the arrival of Cortés in 1519, then it was time that they
be held accountable. Hidalgo's army became a mob. Bent on destruction, they moved through the streets with their clubs, slings,
machetes, bows and arrows, lances, and occasional firearms, and
they pillaged in blind despair. Hidalgo could not reason with
them, and only Ignacio Allende, racing through the streets on
horseback and warning prompt retribution, was able to contain
the passions of the crowd. By morning chaos had begun to sub-
side, but the problem would prove monotonously recurrent during the next few months. From San Miguel the rebels moved on
Celaya, and after taking the town the mob again subjected the
gachupín population to pillage. But Celaya was merely a re-
hearsal for a major encounter at Guanajuato, where the rebel
army would be seriously opposed for the first time.

Hidalgo asked the intendant of Guanajuato, Juan Antonio de
Riaño, to surrender the city, and he offered full protection to the
Spanish citizenry in return. But the news from San Miguel and
Celaya had already reached Guanajuato, and Riaño knew that
Hidalgo could give no such assurance. He felt it better to make a
stand and congregated the Spanish population in the Alhóndiga

de Granaditas, the public granary. Although his people were greatly outnumbered, he believed they could hold out until reinforcements from Mexico City arrived.

Shortly before noon on September 28 Hidalgo began his approach to Guanajuato. He was joined by hundreds of workers from the surrounding silver mines. As the first wave of Indian foot soldiers rushed the improvised fortress, Riaño gave the order to open fire. Hundreds of Indians were cut down by the intendant's artillery. Before the second assault began, Riaño led a group of soldiers outside the wall to position them strategically. Just as he was about to re-enter the granary through the huge wooden gate, he took a musket ball on the side of the head and fell dead on the spot. But it would not have mattered at any rate. The attackers gathered up a bunch of soft pine torches used in the mines and laid them at the foot of the wooden gate. They set fire to them, and, as the gate was consumed, a few Indians charged through into the central patio. They were quickly followed by hundreds, perhaps even a thousand. Within the hour most of the gachupines were dead. They were stripped, and their naked bodies dragged unceremoniously through the streets to the nearby cemetery of Belén, where they were buried in makeshift graves. It was then time for the looting.

An eyewitness to the events of that day was eighteen-year-old Lucas Alamán, later one of Mexico's most renowned conservative statesmen and historians. In his multivolume history of Mexico he recollected:

> This pillage was more merciless than would have been expected of a foreign army. The miserable scene of that sad night was lighted by torches. All that could be heard was the pounding by which doors were opened and the ferocious howls of the rabble when the doors gave way. They dashed in in triumph to rob commercial products, furniture, everyday clothing, and all manner of things. The women fled terrorized to the houses of neighbors, climbing along the roof tops without yet knowing if that afternoon they had lost a father or husband at the granary. . . . The plaza and the streets were littered with broken pieces of furniture and other things robbed from the stores, of liquor spilled after the masses had drunk themselves into a stupor.[1]

It took a day and a half to restore order. The casualty figures were tremendous: over five hundred Spaniards and two thousand Indians killed. Hidalgo and Allende now felt strong enough to

1. Lucas Alamán, *Historia de México* (Mexico, 1942), 1: 403–04.

split their army into two striking forces, and within a month they had captured Zacatecas, San Luis Potosí, and Valladolid. By late October Hidalgo had an army of about eighty thousand marching on Mexico City. The anticipated battle took place on October 30 at the Monte de las Cruces, and there Hidalgo proved that sheer numbers could overcome a small, well-equipped, and disciplined professional army. The Spaniards were forced to retreat back into the city, and as Hidalgo camped on the hills overlooking the capital, he pondered what to do next.

A decisive strike at the capital might have ended the Wars for Independence after only a month and a half of fighting. But Hidalgo had taken heavy losses at Las Cruces, he was short on ammunition, and he was uneasy about turning his mob loose on Mexico City—they would have devastated the capital. Over Allende's objections he therefore decided to order a retreat rather than follow up his victory; as a consequence the Wars for Independence would drag on for eleven more years.

Moving northwest toward Guadalajara many of the rebel troops, their greatest opportunity denied, began to desert. At the same time Spanish forces under General Félix Calleja started to regroup. Guadalajara fell to the insurgents unopposed, but in January 1811 the royalist troops from the south caught up with the rebels and engaged them at the Puente de Calderón on the Río Lerma. Again Hidalgo and Allende had the numerical superiority, but General Calleja conducted his operations superbly and, in addition, was aided by a battlefield accident. A Spanish artillery shot hit a rebel ammunition wagon, and the resulting explosion caused a grass fire in the midst of Hidalgo's army. Panic ensued, and thousands of rebels broke rank and fled. The retreat turned into a rout. Hidalgo, Allende, and a number of other leaders recognized the futility of trying to regroup their forces and so moved northward, hoping to obtain relief in Coahuila and Texas. But their days were numbered. In March 1811, near the scorched desert town of Monclova (Coahuila), they were ambushed by a Spanish detachment that had been forewarned they were going to pass that way. Captured by Governor Manuel Salcedo of Texas, the rebels were marched in chains to Chihuahua, where Allende and the other nonclerical leaders were immediately executed as traitors. Hidalgo, because he was a priest, was subjected to an arduous trial conducted under the auspices of the Holy Office of the Inquisition. Finding him guilty of heresy and treason, the court defrocked him and turned him over to the secular arm for execution. At dawn on July 31 the firing

José María Morelos (1765–1815). With Hidalgo's execution in 1811, Morelos assumed the leadership of the Independence movement. Although a strong supporter of Hidalgo, he had very different ideas about how to wage a war and how to constitute a new nation.

squad did its job. Hidalgo's corpse was decapitated, and his head, fastened to a pole, was displayed on the charred wall of the granary in Guanajuato as an object lesson to potential rebels.

Morelos and the Decline of Rebel Fortunes

With the death of Hidalgo the rebel leadership was assumed by another parish priest, José María Morelos y Pavón, a mestizo. But by this time sympathy for the cause of Independence had waned considerably. Many wealthy criollos had become alarmed at the radical twist the revolution seemed to be taking. The mob attacks on aristocratic property made some apprehensive and others openly hostile. Shut off for centuries from the decision-making positions in both church and state and obliged to compete for minor posts, the criollos favored the elimination of their Spanish rivals (and realized that Independence was the way to do it) but not at the expense of being swept up in some kind of social revolution. They recognized that to the downtrodden Indians and mestizos their white skin, if not their social position, was indistinguishable from that of the gachupines.

When the mantle of insurgent leadership fell on Morelos he knew full well that he could not count on criollo support. Unlike his predecessor, he trained a small but effective army that relied primarily on guerrilla tactics to keep the enemy off guard. Dividing his attention almost equally between military and political matters, he devised a strategy that called for the encirclement of Mexico City. By the spring of 1813 the circle was completed, and the capital was isolated from both coasts. Morelos then called for a congress to meet in Chilpancingo (Guerrero) to discuss plans for the nation once the Spaniards were driven out.

Some of the conservative criollos were still unsure of the direction in which Morelos wished to move, but his speech to the delegates at Chilpancingo cleared the air. If the Conquest of Mexico by Cortés represented a negation of Indian values by the Spanish, the Wars for Independence represented a negation of Spanish values by the Indians. Morelos invoked the names of the ancient emperors, Moctezuma and Cuauhtémoc, and implored the delegates to avenge the shameful disgrace of the last three centuries. The chains that enslaved the native population in Tenochtitlán in 1521 would be broken in Chilpancingo in 1813.

The congress formally declared independence and agreed upon a series of principles that should be incorporated into a new constitution: sovereignty should reside in the people and male suffrage should be universal; slavery and all caste systems should be abolished; government monopolies should be abolished and replaced by a 5 percent income tax; all judicial torture should be abolished. The nineteenth-century liberalism of the delegates was tempered only by their insistence that Roman Catholicism should be made the official religion of the new state.

But while the delegates at Chilpancingo engaged in political debate, General Calleja and his Spanish army assumed a new military offensive. In six months' time the Spaniards broke the circle around Mexico City and captured Valladolid, Oaxaca, Cuernavaca, Cuautla, Taxco, and even Chilpancingo itself. The delegates hurriedly packed their bags and moved to the more secure environs of Apatzingán, where they promulgated the constitution they had already largely agreed upon. But what the Constitution promised Mexicans on paper the viceroy's army denied them on the field of battle. Morelos became more of a fugitive than the commander of an organized rebel force. And in the fall of 1815 he was captured by an enemy detachment and escorted to Mexico City, where he was tried for treason and, like Hidalgo before him, shorn of his religious vestments and executed by a firing squad.

For the next five years the Independence movement consisted of little more than sporadic guerrilla fighting. A number of independent bands, inadequately supplied and without any meaning-

TERRITORY UNDER INSURGENT CONTROL, 1811–13

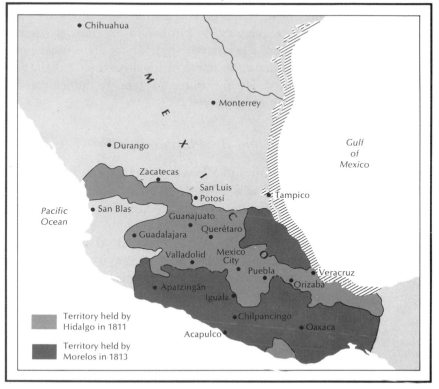

ful coordination, operated in isolated mountain pockets and the heavy foliaged areas of the coast. But the Spanish army was unprepared to conduct an effective counterinsurgency campaign, and the rebel's lack of organization proved to be a strength. Not even the viceroy's newly introduced "flying brigades" (*cuerpos volantes*) could match the mobility of guerrillas conducting hit-and-run warfare. While never able to capture major cities, or to turn back the viceregal army, the two most effective Independence leaders, Guadalupe Victoria (with two thousand ragged troops in the mountains of Puebla and Veracruz) and Vicente Guerrero (with a thousand men in Oaxaca), seemed themselves invulnerable to defeat. While guerrilla bands of 200 or 300 insurgents proliferated and began dominating more and more of the countryside, the chore of the counterinsurgency army became impossible. Lack of military success took its toll as the viceroy's troops became increasingly despondent and demoralized; defections followed defections. Nevertheless, in 1819 the Spanish viceroy in Mexico City, Juan Ruiz de Apodaca, reported to the Spanish king, Ferdinand VII, that the situation was so well under control that he anticipated no further need for reinforcements. To hasten the final victory he published an *indulto* (pardon) for all those who would lay down their arms. The most generous interpretation that can be made of his assessment is that he was badly misinformed. His position had steadily deteriorated while that of the enemy had improved.

Iturbide and the Plan de Iguala

King Ferdinand VII was not concerned only with events in Mexico. He found himself facing insurrection in Central America, the Caribbean, and South America as well. In order to quell all of these movements he assembled a powerful fighting force for service in the New World. While the troops underwent the final preparations, Colonel Rafael Riego proclaimed himself in revolt against his sovereign and was promptly seconded by thousands of troops. The Spanish insurgents demanded that Ferdinand swear allegiance to the Spanish Constitution of 1812, a liberal document that affirmed the sovereignty of the people, contained several mildly anticlerical provisions, and enunciated a liberal bill of rights. When the conservative criollos in New Spain learned that King Ferdinand had yielded to Riego's demands and accepted the Constitution, many for the first time decided to cast their lot with the revolution for Independence. Ironically, a conservative colony would thus gain independence from a temporarily liberal mother country.

Of the numerous defections from the cause of Spain to that of an independent Mexico the most significant was that of Agustín de Iturbide. Born in Valladolid of conservative Spanish parents in 1783, Iturbide early displayed an interest in pursuing a military career. He entered the army at the age of fourteen and soon received a royal commission as a lieutenant in the infantry regiment of Valladolid. When Father Hidalgo issued his Grito de Dolores in 1810, Lieutenant Iturbide decided to support the crown in its fight against the rabble that followed the banner of Guadalupe. For almost a decade he fought against the insurgents and on several occasions distinguished himself in the zeal with which he persecuted the enemy.

In the fall of 1820 Viceroy Apodaca invited Iturbide, by then a colonel, to discuss plans for a new offensive against Vicente Guerrero. Iturbide was placed in charge of twenty-five hundred men and left Mexico City for the south in late November. After a few indecisive skirmishes he asked Guerrero to a meeting during which he proposed to make peace—not war. Iturbide's price for the treason he was contemplating was to dictate the terms of Independence. But Guerrero was not easily convinced of either Iturbide's sincerity or his ideas for an independent Mexico. A series of conferences had to be held before the guerrilla warrior and the new convert could issue, on February 24, 1821, their *Plan de Iguala*.[2] Unlike the United States Declaration of Independence, which berated the mother country in a tirade of denunciations, the Plan de Iguala had an entirely different orientation and appeal. In order to attract conservative support it praised the Spanish endeavor in the New World and held out Spain as the most Catholic, holy, heroic, and magnanimous of nations. But after three hundred years of tutelage it was time for Mexico to strike out on its own. The plan contained twenty-three articles but only three major guarantees: first, the independent Mexican nation would be organized as a constitutional monarchy, and the crown would be offered to King Ferdinand or some other appropriate European prince; second, the Roman Catholic religion would be given a monopoly on the spiritual life of the country and its clergymen would retain all the rights and privileges they currently enjoyed; and, third, criollos and peninsulares would be treated equally in the new state. In order to uphold the promises a new army, the *Ejército de las Tres Garantías* (the Army of the Three Guarantees) would be placed directly under Iturbide's command.

In the Plan de Iguala Iturbide played his cards with consummate skill. The proposal was imaginative, even brilliant, in its conception. Mexicans were weary of a decade of war, and many of stout heart had given up hope. The liberal Constitution of Apatzingán had failed to attract sufficient support, and it was clear that to succeed the movement needed help from the conservatives. With liberalism temporarily manifesting itself in the mother country, the timing was perfect. In seeking to reconcile the interests of opposing factions, the plan changed the nature of the fight for Independence. Instead of urging death to the gachupines, Iturbide curried their favor. He recognized and capitalized upon the fact that both liberals, who favored the establishment of a republic, and conservatives, who preferred an absolute monarchy, could compromise on this plan as it held out the best hope for Independence, something that both groups wanted most.

2. In Mexican history revolutionary movements are almost always preceded by a plan that outlines the principles to be embraced and seeks to widen the base of support.

Within several weeks the broadly based plan began to yield its first dividends as converts began to arrive. Military contingents throughout the country joined the Army of the Three Guarantees; priests urged cooperation from the pulpits; Masonic groups pledged support; and thousands of drifters again took up the cause. But, most important, the community of Spaniards, some fifty thousand strong, found in the Plan de Iguala the promise of a good future in a newly independent Mexico; as a result they, too, pledged support. When Guanajuato, Puebla, Durango, Oaxaca, Querétaro, and Zacatecas all fell to the insurgents, Viceroy Apodaca tendered his resignation. The Spanish crown, however, was unprepared to accept the inevitability of a rebel victory and appointed a replacement, Juan de O'Donojú, as Captain–General of New Spain. O'Donojú quickly perceived that Apodaca had assessed the situation correctly. New Spain was irrevocably lost, and there was little to be gained by not recognizing the fact. At the town of Córdoba, Iturbide and O'Donojú affixed their signatures to a treaty that, for the most part, accepted the terms of the Plan de Iguala. The highest-ranking Spanish official in New Spain had thus recognized Mexican Independence. But Iturbide, thinking of the future, incorporated into the Treaty of Córdoba one important modification. If no suitable European monarch could be persuaded to accept the Mexican crown, a Mexican congress could choose a New World emperor instead. The commander of the Army of the Three Guarantees had begun to feather his own nest.

The Effects of the Wars for Independence

Iturbide's triumphal entry into Mexico City in September of 1821 marked the end of eleven years of war. The *Gaceta Imperial de México* proclaimed theatrically that not even Rome in its days of grandeur had ever witnessed such an exultant spectacle. Upon receiving gold keys to the city the commander-in-chief explained that they would be used to lock the doors of irreligion, disunion, and despotism and to open the doors of general happiness. But the first door Iturbide opened in Mexico City was that of the great cathedral on the central plaza. Cementing his future relationship with the archbishop, he received communion and listened to a Te Deum offered in his honor.

From the campaigns, Mexico acquired not only its share of heroes and traitors but also a legacy of political violence and economic devastation. The wars exerted an incalculable influence on Mexico's future. The army had converted the dream of Independence into reality and was by no means ready to step aside and allow civilians to control the nation's destiny. For a full century the Mexican military would be very much involved in the political processes of government and would bargain with opposing factions for a greater and greater share of the nation's wealth. The military clique would constitute a ready instrument for unscrupulous politicians to use for their own purposes. More important yet, the basic issues separating different segments of society had not been resolved. Competing groups had cooperated long enough to achieve a common end, but, once Independence was achieved, the alliance called together by the Plan de Iguala proved very transitory. For some the revolution was simply anticolonial in nature and therefore it was over; others wanted its momentum to be carried into the arena of political and economic reform. The internal struggles between liberals and conservatives, between republicans and monarchists, between federalists and centralists, and between anticlericals and proponents of clerical privilege would consume the energies of the neophyte nation for much longer than the most pessimistic political analyst would have dared to predict.

But in 1821 only few Mexicans could have had premonitions of the drama that was about to unfold. The large majority of the population had not been affected directly by the wars, and the illiterate masses most assuredly did not know that a change, important at least for those on the threshold of power, had taken place. The nineteenth century would vindicate the general apathy of the rural Mexican, for his life would change little, if at all. The fate of the Mexican Indian continued to rest totally in the hands of others, as it had for the last three hundred years. His privations went unnoticed. He could take little solace in the fact that the politically articulate groups in Mexico City that completely overlooked his interests demonstrated precious little ability to govern even themselves.

Recommended for Further Study

Almaraz, Felix D. "Governor Antonio Martínez and Mexican Independence in Texas." *Permian Historical Annual* 15 (1975): 44–55.
———. *Tragic Cavalier: Governor Manuel Salcedo of Texas, 1808–1813.* Austin: University of Texas Press, 1971.
Anna, Timothy E. *The Fall of Royal Government in Mexico City.* Lincoln: University of Nebraska Press, 1978.
Archer, Christon I. "La Causa Buena": The Counterinsurgency Army of New Spain and the Ten Years War" in *The Independence of New*

Spain and the Creation of the New Nation, edited by Jaime Rodríguez, pp. 85–108. Los Angeles: UCLA Latin American Center, 1989.

Benson, Nettie Lee. "The Contested Mexican Election of 1812." *Hispanic American Historical Review* 26 (1946): 336–50.

———, ed. *Mexico and the Spanish Cortes, 1810–1822*. Austin: University of Texas Press, 1966.

Fisher, Lillian Estelle. *The Background of the Revolution for Mexican Independence*. Gainesville: University of Florida Press, 1966.

Gronet, Richard W. "The United States and the Invasion of Texas, 1810–1814." *The Americas* 25 (1969): 281–306.

Hamill, Hugh M. "Caudillism and Independence: A Symbiosis?" In *The Independence of Mexico and the Creation of the New Nation*, edited by Jaime E. Rodríguez O., pp. 163–74. Los Angeles: UCLA Latin American Center, 1989.

———. *The Hidalgo Revolt: Prelude to Mexican Independence*. Gainesville: University of Florida Press, 1966.

———. "Royalist Propaganda and 'La Porción Humilde del Pueblo' During Mexican Independence." *The Americas* 36 (1980): 423–44.

Hamnett, Brian R. "Royalist Counterinsurgency and the Continuity of Rebellion: Guanajuato and Michoacán, 1813–20." *Hispanic American Historical Review* 62 (1982): 19–48.

Lieberman, Mark. *Hidalgo: Mexican Revolutionary*. New York: Praeger, 1970.

Lombardi, John V. *The Political Ideology of Fray Servando Teresa de Mier, Propagandist for Independence*. Cuernavaca: Centro Intercultural de Documentación, 1968.

Robertson, William S. *Iturbide of Mexico*. Durham, N.C.: Duke University Press, 1952.

Rodríguez O., Jaime E. "From Royal Subject to Republican Citizen: The Role of the Autonomists in the Independence of Mexico." In *The Independence of Mexico and the Creation of the New Nation*, edited by Jaime E. Rodríguez O., pp. 19–43. Los Angeles: UCLA Latin American Center, 1989.

Rydjord, John. *Foreign Interest in the Independence of New Spain*. Durham, N.C.: Duke University Press, 1935.

TePaske, John Jay. "The Financial Disintegration of the Royal Government of Mexico during the Epoch of Independence." In *The Independence of Mexico and the Creation of the New Nation*, edited by Jaime E. Rodríguez O., pp. 63–84. Los Angeles: UCLA Latin American Center, 1989.

Timmons, Wilbert H. "Los Guadalupes: A Secret Society of the Mexican Revolution for Independence." *Hispanic American Historical Review* 30 (1950): 453–79.

———. *Morelos: Priest, Soldier, Statesman of Mexico*. El Paso: Texas Western College Press, 1963.

Woodward, Margaret L. "The Spanish Army and the Loss of America, 1810–1824." *Hispanic American Historical Review* 48 (1968): 586–606.

17

The First Mexican Empire

Pomp and Circumstance

In the best of circumstances nation building is a precarious business, but how does one create a nation out of a newly independent state when the economy is in shambles and the political atmosphere is pervaded by acrimony and mistrust? The question obsessed many Latin American leaders in the nineteenth century once parental authority had been successfully challenged. Iturbide did not have all of the answers, but he felt that he had one reliable formula. Identify the head of government with the state, subsume the two into one, and by some miraculous metamorphosis a nation will emerge. But the crucial element in the process, he believed, was to identify a dynamic, resourceful, and charismatic leader. Not worried about overstepping the bounds of modesty, he could identify only one Mexican possessed of all these redeeming prerequisites.

Joel Poinsett, an American who would later become the first United States minister to Mexico, met Iturbide in the fall of 1822 and recorded his impressions.

> I will not repeat the tales I hear daily of the character and conduct of this man. . . . He is accused of having been the most cruel and blood-thirsty persecutor of the Patriots, and never to have spared a prisoner. . . . in a society not remarkable for strict morals, he was distinguished for his immorality. . . . To judge from Iturbide's public papers, I do not think him a man of talents. He is prompt, bold and decisive, and not scrupulous about the means he employs to obtain his ends.[1]

1. Joel R. Poinsett, *Notes on Mexico Made in the Autumn of 1822, Accompanied by an Historical Sketch of the Revolution* (New York, 1969), pp. 68–69.

As provided by the Plan de Iguala, Iturbide named a provisional junta to govern the country. This junta, completely dominated by conservative criollo interests, in turn named him to serve as its presiding officer. The first order of business was to select a five-man regency to exercise executive functions until an emperor could be designated. The junta chose Iturbide as one of the five. But the presidency of the junta and membership on the regency was deemed an insufficient tribute to the leader of the Independence movement, so the group awarded him a new military title, *Generalísimo de Tierra y Mar*, and, to go along with it, a salary of 120,000 pesos annually.

While the junta, the regency, and Iturbide threw flowers in each other's path, an independent Congress, also dominated by conservatives, debated Mexico's future. Although a small group of recalcitrants tried to muster sympathy for a republic, Iturbide's conservative cohorts controlled the organizational proceedings. While they beat back all attempts at republicanism they began to waver on a series of economic and military issues. When the Congress, though divided, decided to cut back on the size of the Army of the Three Guarantees and decreed that no member of the regency could simultaneously hold military office, Iturbide realized that his ranks were being thinned and that time was no longer on his side. If he failed to act decisively the crown he wanted so desperately might be denied him.

On the evening of May 18 the Generalísimo staged a dramatic demonstration in his own behalf. Troops were ordered out of the barracks and into the streets. Firing muskets and rockets into the air and shouting "Viva Agustín I, Emperor of Mexico!" they enticed other soldiers to join them. As the frenzy grew in the downtown business district, thousands of civilians accompanied the mob on its way to Iturbide's residence. Once there, the multitudes demanded that their favorite declare himself emperor at once. Iturbide told friends who were in his home at the time that he wanted to go out on his balcony and turn them down. But he later wrote:

> If I restrained myself from appearing before them for that purpose, it was solely in compliance with the counsel of a friend who happened at the moment to be with me. "They will consider it an insult," he scarcely had time to say to me, "and the people know no restraint when they are irritated. You must make this fresh sacrifice to the public good: the country is in danger; remain a moment longer undecided, and you will hear their acclamations

turned into death shouts." I felt it necessary to resign myself to circumstances.[2]

With good reason historians have concluded that Iturbide's reluctance was feigned, that his submission to the inevitable was not so stoic, and that the sergeant orchestrating the event had acted under his explicit instructions. The following morning Iturbide appeared personally before the Congress, and, with his mob in the galleries shouting, the intimidated body named him constitutional emperor of Mexico. He demonstrated no concern that a legal quorum was missing. In his oath of office he swore before God and the Holy Evangels to uphold and defend the Roman Catholic religion at the exclusion of all others and to enforce all laws and decrees promulgated by the Congress that chose him.

With the throne thus occupied, the Congress set to work, not on the conspicuous demands of the Mexican nation, but on defining proper etiquette and protocol in an obvious attempt to emulate the greatest imperial regime the world had ever known. It would not only appropriate for the emperor all of the prerogatives of the Spanish nobility but would add to them. In June the Congress refined the organizational structure of the monarchy, declaring it to be hereditary. The heir was Iturbide's eldest son, Señor Don Agustín, who was designated "Prince Imperial," while the other sons and daughters of the emperor were to be Mexican princes and princesses. Iturbide's father would carry the title "Prince of the Union" and his sister, Doña Nicolasa, "Princess of Iturbide." May 19, the day of Iturbide's proclamation, was declared a national holiday, as were his birthday and the birthdays of his children. Defining the accouterments of regality took months and at times prompted the most ludicrous debate, such as that concerning whether the motto appearing below Iturbide's bust on the new metal coinage should be in Latin or Spanish. The Congress opted for *Augustinus Dei Providentia* on one side and *Mexici Primus Imperator Constitutionalis* on the other.

The greatest preparations of all were made for the official coronation ceremonies in July. Although several liberal deputies argued that kissing of the hand and bending of the knee were repugnant to the dignity of free peoples, their voices were lost to the monarchist majority. The efforts were all based on a French

2. Quoted in William Spence Robertson, *Rise of the Spanish-American Republics as Told in the Lives of Their Liberators* (New York, 1961), p. 130.

model, and the Congress hired a French baroness who had designed the costumes for Napoleon Bonaparte some twenty-two years before. Serious thought was given to ordering a national fast for the three days prior to the ceremonies, but the idea was finally dismissed as impractical to enforce outside of prisons and convents. The Congress did, however, authorize a new Mexican order, the Knights of Guadalupe, to participate in the coronation. As the day of the coronation approached, jewelry was borrowed, thrones were erected, banners and flags were hung from church towers, and teams of peasants were engaged to scour the streets. The citizenry of the capital were being prepared for the most pretentious spectacle ever to occur in Mexico City.

At 8:00 A.M. on Sunday, July 21, 1822, amidst the din of artillery salvos and the clamor of several military bands, the imperial cortège worked its way along a carpeted and flower-strewn path to the provisional palace, and the royal family was escorted to the central cathedral by an honor guard recently designated by the Congress. At the door the emperor and empress were met by two bishops who blessed them with holy water and led them to the two thrones placed on the altar. When the lesser dignitaries, including the diplomatic corps, were seated according to the complicated body of protocol, the bishop of Guadalajara celebrated high mass and consecrated the emperor and empress with sacred oil. With tremendous solemnity the president of the Congress placed the crown on Iturbide's head and he, in turn, placed a slightly smaller one on the head of the empress. The bishop then intoned *Vivat Imperator in aeternum*. It was time for the bishop of Puebla to participate, and his contribution, ending the ceremony, was a long eloquent speech eulogizing the new emperor.

While the outer trappings of the empire were pretentious to the absurd, they were not entirely without purpose and meaning. Iturbide's understanding of Mexico's past, while by no means profound, was acute enough. He realized that the entire governmental system of the colonial period had been predicated upon loyalty to the king and the crown. Even provincial and local officials decreed and implemented ordinances in the king's name. Independence obviously undercut the personal loyalty that sealed Mexican society together, but the emperor wanted to capitalize upon the time-tested tradition. He wanted to reap advantages from the fact that Mexico was not immune to the forces of history. While he became emperor in name, in fact he became a *caudillo*, a military leader with a personal following. The Con-

Agustín de Iturbide (1783–1824). Changing allegiance from the Spanish to the insurgent cause, Iturbide successfully concluded the fight for Independence and had himself named emperor of Mexico.

gress had given him the legal base he considered vital; the ostentation that engulfed his person helped to reinforce the mystique of his indispensability and to blur the distinctions between the man and the office. The words *Augustus Dei Providentia Mexici Primus Imperator Constitutionalis*, even if they were not understood, sounded enough like the unintelligible locutions of the Sunday mass to inspire awe in the large unsophisticated portion of the citizenry. Iturbide worked hard to identify the new state with his own person and, for a while, seemed to be succeeding.

Problems Facing the New Empire

The empire was huge. Embracing much of the old viceroyalty of New Spain, it stretched in the north to California and the present-day Southwest of the United States and to the south included all of Central America with the exception of Panama. Long subject to what they considered the autocratic rule of Guatemala, many Central Americans favored union with the Mexican empire, but when rebellious elements in Honduras, El Salvador, and Costa

Rica demurred, Iturbide sent in an army of six hundred men to ensure adhesion. That was sufficient.

A more serious problem occurred with the neighbor to the north. The new regime quite naturally wished to secure the official recognition of the United States. The cultivation of harmonious relations was deemed vital to the security of Mexico's northern provinces (the United States had already exhibited expansionist tendencies) and could lead to extensive commercial ties. In addition, the boundary between the two countries had never been properly defined and needed to be drawn. Most of all the Mexican monarch hoped for a loan of $10 million to help his new government meet its obligations. But President James Monroe's explicit purpose in extending diplomatic recognition to the newly independent Latin American states was to promote the establishment of free republican governments. When the Mexican Congress named Iturbide emperor, Monroe was discouraged and ventured the opinion that the monarchy could not last long.

Iturbide took the lead when he dispatched Manuel Zozaya as minister to Washington. Reception of the Mexican would, in effect, recognize the Mexican regime. With mixed emotions the United States president urged the Congress to authorize recognition in December of 1822. To reject Zozaya would impair relations with Mexico from the beginning, and business interests in the United States wanted to cultivate trade relations. In January 1823 Monroe appointed Joel Poinsett as minister to Mexico even though Poinsett had expressed serious reservations about the Mexican regime. Iturbide, through no concerted effort of his own, had won a minor diplomatic victory.

But all was not well in Mexico City. The showy imperial façade rested on vulnerable socioeconomic foundations. Mexico's eleven years of war had cost more than most governmental officials, the emperor not excepted, were willing to admit. Most serious of all was the perilous state of the Mexican economy.

Mexico's colonial economy was overwhelmingly dependent upon the gold and silver mines in the central part of the country. But it was in precisely this area that the Wars for Independence had exacted their highest toll. During the years of internecine strife mine workers left their jobs to join the fight, mine owners and operators were killed, machinery was damaged, and many of the mines were flooded. Without sufficient bullion reaching the mints, coinage was curtailed. Over $26 million was minted in 1809; in 1821, less than $6 million. Without operation of the mines, unemployment was rampant in the mining centers, and the situation was aggravated by the mustering out that began shortly after the military campaigns ended.

The impact of the wars on Mexico's agricultural output was similar. Both Spanish troops and insurgents destroyed fields, commandeered crops, and killed off cattle and sheep that might have been of benefit to the enemy. Many an hacendado was killed, and those who escaped could likely have seen their haciendas in flames if, during their flight, they had time to glance over their shoulders. Mexico was a rural country at the time of Independence, but thousands in Mexico City (population 155,-000), Puebla (population 60,000), Guadalajara (population 50,-000), and other cities suffered as the price of agricultural products rose steadily in 1822.

The average citizen in the city felt the impact of the economic decline, and the government did too. In an attempt to make the cause of Independence even more popular, the Congress lowered many old taxes, such as those on pulque and tobacco, and eliminated others altogether. But commerce and the revenues to be derived therefrom stagnated as trade with Spain ended and free trade with new areas was slow to take up the slack.

To ensure loyalty soldiers and bureaucrats had to be paid and officers promoted, but the depleted revenues could not begin to cover the extravagant expenses of the imperial regime. Month after month expenses exceeded income. Virtually nobody was willing to invest in the shaky economy or loan money to the government. Available capital was largely in the hands of the Spaniards, and most of them began to depart soon after Independence. The few moneylenders around proposed interest rates that were nothing short of exorbitant. In response to the growing crisis the Congress decreed a forced loan on ecclesiastical properties, but this measure was no more than a temporary expedient. Several issues of paper currency, not backed by hard reserves and not trusted by anyone, caused more problems than they solved, and, as the wheels of the economy ground into ominous stagnation, Mexicans became more and more critical of their new regime.

Criticism was leveled at the emperor from many quarters: from disgruntled veterans who found no employment, from deputies in the Congress who really never accommodated themselves to the concept of monarchy, and from a number of courageous journalists who exposed the burlesque aspects of Mexico's empire. Sensitive to criticism, in the summer the emperor suppressed several liberal newspapers that espoused republican ideals and even one conservative one that favored monarchy but argued that the throne should be offered to a European prince. With the newspaper suppressions a group of liberals in the Congress, led by Fray Servando Teresa de Mier, an accomplished orator, and Carlos María de Bustamante, began to conspire. Through a government spy who infiltrated congressional circles Iturbide was able to secure an accurate list of his leading enemies and, on August 20, 1822, had them all arrested. The Congress protested, and even some of Iturbide's staunchest supporters in the legislative body defended their arrested colleagues. The opposing positions were irreconcilable, and the debates in the fall were heated; their substance was less significant than the fact that they demonstrated a steadily growing majority against the emperor and the imperial concept itself. Even Guadalupe Victoria, Iturbide's erstwhile ally, denounced him as a tyrant with all the fiery eloquence he could command. On October 31 Iturbide became the first Mexican chief executive to dissolve the legislative branch of government. The precedent, once established, would be repeated many times before the nineteenth century ran its course.

The reaction in both Mexico City and the provinces was resolute. The antimonarchists found their ranks swelling, and a specific plot crystalized in Veracruz. The self-acclaimed leader was Iturbide's commander in the port city, Antonio López de Santa Anna. Although it is possible that Santa Anna had been schooled in the virtues of republicanism by Carlos María de Bustamante, whom he had met and befriended a few years before, his decision to lead a revolt against the monarchy seems to have had a more fundamental root. As commander of Veracruz, Santa Anna had been assigned the task of driving the last remaining Spanish troops from San Juan de Ulloa, the harbor fortress they still held. But Iturbide believed that Santa Anna was not pursuing the enemy forcefully enough and was even considering turning Veracruz over to them. As a result he ordered Santa Anna to Mexico City where he could be closely observed. But Santa Anna would countenance no such move. On December 1, 1822, at the head of some four hundred troops, he rode through the streets of Veracruz proclaiming a republic. A few days later he formally launched his revolt under the Plan de Veracruz. Within a month Vicente Guerrero, Nicolás Bravo, and Guadalupe Victoria had joined the movement, enhancing its prestige. Iturbide recognized the seriousness of the problem; it was one thing for deputies in the Congress to attack the regime with words and quite another for army officers to attack it with arms and ammunition.

Placing José Antonio Echáverri, the captain general of Veracruz, in charge of the imperial campaigns, Iturbide felt that he
had little to fear. Echáverri and Santa Anna had been at each
other's throats for months over the most expeditious means for
driving the Spaniards out of San Juan de Ulloa. But Echáverri
decided to give the emperor a little of his own medicine. Much
as Iturbide had made common cause with Vicente Guerrero
when dispatched to engage him, Echáverri joined Santa Anna.
On February 1, 1823, Echáverri and thirty-three cohorts proclaimed the *Plan de Casa Mata*. Santa Anna, not having encountered much military success in recent months, and realizing
that the Plan de Casa Mata was not inconsistent with his own
Plan de Veracruz, accepted the new plan. Two antiimperial
movements now became one.

One military contingent after another swore allegiance to the
Plan de Casa Mata. One province after another fell to the insurgents, and they began marching on Mexico City. They did not
have to take the capital by force, however. Realizing that his experiment with monarchy had ended in failure, Iturbide abdicated his throne in the middle of February 1823, some ten
months after coming to office, and accepted a generous pension
that would have enabled him to live comfortably. In his resignation address he stated he did not desire to have his name become
a pretext for civil war. Then with his family he made his plans
to go into European exile. The rebel army marched into Mexico
City unopposed.

An Assessment

The first Mexican empire had been a dismal failure. In conception it had merely substituted a new criollo oligarchy for the old
gachupín oligarchy and indeed had satisfied many Mexicans
hostile to the innovations of nineteenth-century liberalism. The
royal household, with all of its gaudy trappings, underscored
that very little had changed since New Spain won control of its
own destiny. The diplomatic initiatives, the loan from the United
States, and an equitable settlement of the boundary had languished.

With the advantage of historical hindsight, the revolt, fought
under the banner of the Plan de Casa Mata, is laden with irony.
The entire antimonarchy fight was made in the name of the Con-

gress, which Iturbide had emasculated from the day it accepted his oath of office. One would have thought that at best legislative supremacy, and at worst legislative equality, would have been the political dictum of the nineteenth century. In fact, just the opposite was true. Executive dominance and legislative subservience may have been bequeathed to Mexico during the three centuries of colonial tutelage, but they were sufficiently enforced during the empire never to be successfully challenged again. Few practical lessons in nation building derived from the empire. Administrative and legislative experience was still in short supply. The Mexican elite did not yet consider the fact that successful leadership in the Wars for Independence was by no means synonymous with statesmanship. In the period following the empire Mexico would once again turn to military heroes who had emerged from the campaigns with more than life-sized stature.

But in at least one respect the collapse of the empire marked the beginning of a new day. It brought to power for the first time the criollo middle class, which had early supported the Independence movement only to be outflanked by the conservatives after the Riego revolt in Spain. These criollos were not social revolutionaries in any sense. While on occasions they attacked intrenched interests, their objectives were political, not social. In all innocence they seemed to believe that the docility of the lower classes had no bounds and that the poor would endure their privations forever.

As Mexico prepared to embark upon its second experiment as an independent nation, only one major question had been answered. The monarchists had been so thoroughly discredited that virtually nobody, at least for a while, harbored serious notions about reviving the concept. Iturbide's wasteful pomp had converted more monarchists to republicans than could have been persuaded by a team of skillful rhetoricians. Mexico would be organized as a republic; the nature of that republic would now be the issue at stake. It would provoke violent debate, near anarchy, and finally civil war.

Recommended for Further Study

Anna, Timothy E. "The Iturbide Interregnum." In *The Independence of Mexico and the Creation of the New Nation*, edited by Jaime E. Rodríguez O., pp. 185–200. Los Angeles: UCLA Latin American Center, 1989.

————. *The Mexican Empire of Iturbide.* Lincoln: University of Nebraska Press, 1990.

Beezley, William H. "Caudillismo: An Interpretive Note." *Journal of Inter-American Studies* 11 (1969): 345–52.

Benson, Nettie Lee. "The Plan of Casa Mata." *Hispanic American Historical Review* 25 (1945): 45–56.

————, and Charles R. Berry. "The Central American Delegation to the First Constituent Congress of Mexico, 1822–1823." *Hispanic American Historical Review* 49 (1969): 679–702.

Cotner, Thomas E. *The Military and Political Career of José Joaquín de Herrera, 1792–1854.* Austin: Institute of Latin American Studies, 1949.

Harrison, Horace V. "The Republican Conspiracy against Agustín de Iturbide." In *Essays in Mexican History,* edited by Thomas E. Cotner and Carlos E. Castañeda, pp. 142–65. Austin: Institute of Latin American Studies, 1958.

Kenyon, Gordon. "Mexican Influence in Central America, 1821–1823." *Hispanic American Historical Review* 41 (1961): 175–205.

Lewis, William Francis, III. "Xavier Mina and Fray Servando Mier: Romantic Liberals of the Nineteenth Century." *New Mexico Historical Review* 44 (1969): 119–36.

Lombardi, John V. *The Political Ideology of Fray Servando Teresa de Mier, Propagandist for Independence.* Cuernavaca: Centro Intercultural de Documentación, 1968.

McElhannon, Joseph Carl. "Relations between Imperial Mexico and the United States." In *Essays in Mexican History,* edited by Thomas E. Cotner and Carlos E. Castañeda, pp. 127–41. Austin: Institute of Latin American Studies, 1958.

Poinsett, Joel R. *Notes on Mexico Made in the Autumn of 1822, Accompanied by an Historical Sketch of the Revolution.* New York: Praeger, 1969.

Robertson, William S. *Iturbide of Mexico.* Durham, N.C.: Duke University Press, 1952.

Tenenbaum, Barbara. "Taxation and Tyranny: Public Finances during the Iturbide Regime." In *The Independence of Mexico and the Creation of the New Nation,* edited by Jaime E. Rodríguez O., pp. 201–14. Los Angeles: UCLA Latin American Center, 1989.

Villoro, Luis. "The Ideological Currents of the Epoch of Independence." In *Major Trends in Mexican Philosophy,* edited by Mario de la Cueva et al., pp. 185–219. Notre Dame, Ind.: University of Notre Dame Press, 1966.

V THE TRIALS
OF NATIONHOOD, 1824-55

18

The Early Mexican Republic, 1824-33

The Constitution of 1824

With the collapse of the empire, a three-man junta governed Mexico provisionally. All three—Nicolás Bravo, Guadalupe Victoria, and Pedro Celestino Negrete—were military men. The precedent of miscasting soldiers as statesmen was now well established. The first order of business was to call elections for delegates to a constitutional congress that would be charged with framing the new charter. The constituent body met for the first time on November 27, 1823, and before the week was out the lines of combat had been drawn. The focus narrowed to a question that on the surface seemed simple enough: should the new republic be federalist or centralist?

Although there were some exceptions to the general alignment of forces, the centralists found their strength among the clergy, the hacendados, and the army officers, while the federalist firebrands drew support from those liberal criollos and mestizos who considered themselves intellectual heirs of the French and American revolutions and students of the United States Constitution and the liberal Spanish document of 1812. The chief spokesmen for the federalists were Miguel Ramos Arizpe from Coahuila and Valentín Gómez Farías from Zacatecas. The centralist cause was championed by Fray Servando Teresa de Mier and Carlos María de Bustamante. When Ramos Arizpe presented the body with a working paper modeled very closely after the Constitution of the United States, Fray Servando, an iconoclast who once questioned the authenticity of the Virgin of Guadalupe, responded with an eloquent speech. He observed that the experience of the northern neighbor had been entirely different from that of Mexico, and, while a federal system might well be suited to the needs of the United States, it could not work in Mexico for it would weaken the country just when strength from union was required. Speaking of the thirteen colonies to the north, Fray Servando argued:

> They were already separate and independent one from another. They federalized themselves in union against the oppression of England; to federalize ourselves, now united, is to divide ourselves and to bring upon us the very evils they sought to remedy with their federation. They had already lived under a constitution that, when the name of the king was scratched out, brought forth a republic. We buckled for three hundred years under the weight of an absolute monarch, scarcely moving a step toward the study of freedom. We are like children barely out of diapers or like slaves who have just unshackled their chains. . . . We might say that nature itself has decreed our centralization.[1]

Fray Servando was not speaking for rhetorical effect. But his arguments, although having much to commend them, failed to persuade. Ramos Arizpe and his federalist cohorts also drew upon the irrefutable lessons of history but interpreted them quite differently. Centralism they equated with despotism. As examples they pointed to the three hundred years of colonial rule, which were centralistic and despotic, and the ten months of monarchy, which were also centralistic and despotic. They preferred the dispersion of powers inherent in the federal structure and argued that such a system was more in harmony with Mexico's recently won liberties. A would-be dictator could be thwarted in his nefarious attempts to subject the people only if the states and localities enjoyed a respectable measure of independent power. Arizpe's plea appealed more to emotion than to rigorous logic, but nevertheless he carried the day. It was simply too irresistible for some to attribute the tremendous progress recorded by the United States since its independence to its federal form of government.

Under the Constitution of 1824 the Estados Unidos Mexicanos were organized as a federal republic composed of nineteen states and four territories. In the separation-of-powers clause delineating governmental authority into the executive, legislative, and judicial branches, the philosophical influence of Montesquieu

1. Quoted in *Antología del pensamiento social y político de América Latina* (Washington, D.C., 1964), pp. 242–43.

THE MEXICAN REPUBLIC IN 1824

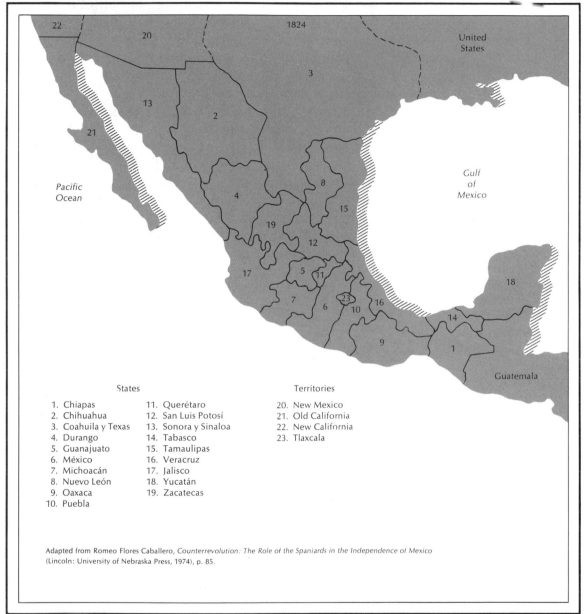

States

1. Chiapas
2. Chihuahua
3. Coahuila y Texas
4. Durango
5. Guanajuato
6. México
7. Michoacán
8. Nuevo León
9. Oaxaca
10. Puebla
11. Querétaro
12. San Luis Potosí
13. Sonora y Sinaloa
14. Tabasco
15. Tamaulipas
16. Veracruz
17. Jalisco
18. Yucatán
19. Zacatecas

Territories

20. New Mexico
21. Old California
22. New California
23. Tlaxcala

Adapted from Romeo Flores Caballero, *Counterrevolution: The Role of the Spaniards in the Independence of Mexico* (Lincoln: University of Nebraska Press, 1974), p. 85.

and the practical influence of the United States Constitution of 1787 are both patent. The legislature was made bicameral, the upper house designated as the Senate and the lower house as the Chamber of Deputies. Each state was represented by two senators and one deputy for every eighty thousand inhabitants. In at least one respect the federal system established in 1824 went beyond its United States model and gave the states even greater power than those to the north: both the president and the vice-president were to be elected not by popular vote or an electoral college but by the state legislatures, for a term of four years.

While the federalists thus won on the major points of governmental organization, in an important sense they gave up as much as they gained. The centralists regrouped and scored at least three victories of their own. First and foremost, the Catholic Church retained its three-hundred-year monopoly on Mexico's spiritual life. Many Mexican conservatives still held that religious toleration was somehow incompatible with public morality. In addition, the president of the country was given extraordinary powers in times of emergency, powers that could convert him into a dictator while at the same time investing him with the sanction of law. The word *emergency* in the nineteenth century came to be interpreted rather loosely. Finally, the Constitution guaranteed members of the clergy and the military their special *fueros*. This time-worn Spanish institution exempted clergymen and military personnel from having to stand trial in civil courts, even if they were charged with the violation of civil law.

The Victoria Presidency

In Mexico's first presidential election the state legislatures chose as president Guadalupe Victoria and as vice-president Nicolás Bravo. The new president, a man of goodwill, was honest and unassuming. He always had time to meet the public and had proven his courage on the battlefield, but he was not a particularly talented individual. In a mood of compromise he invited several conservatives to serve in the cabinet. They accepted, not for purposes of reconciliation but to secure a power base within the government. The president sought to be impartial, but his attempts at fairness degenerated into indecision. Those in whom he placed trust took advantage of him. The problems that beset him were immense. Woefully unprepared by education or tem-

Guadalupe Victoria (1785–1843). Mexico's first president, Victoria found his term disrupted by the internal chaos that came to dominate the country's political life in the first half of the nineteenth century.

perament, he was not only unable to kindle popular imagination but proved unequal to the task.[2]

The debates of the empire and over the nature of the new republic had bequeathed an intensely political atmosphere, pervaded by mistrust, self-righteousness, rancor, and despair. Those in high office, including the president himself, found a constant friend a rare thing. While exaggerated jealousies magnified trifles, basic ideological cleavages emerged as well and began to manifest themselves in a unique manner. Both of the major political factions identified themselves and their efforts with a branch of freemasonry. The federalists attached themselves to the York Rite Masons (*Yorquinos*) and the centralists to the Scottish Rite (*Escoseses*). Masonic meetings, of course, were held in secret, and, because the lodges were inviolable, all manner of cabal could be plotted behind closed doors with little fear of exposure.

One of the more unfortunate incidents to occur during the Victoria presidency was the execution of the former emperor,

2. Recent scholarship has suggested it is not unlikely that a series of physical impairments gradually took their toll and left Victoria mentally unfit for the high office he held. See Elmer W. Flaccus, "Guadalupe Victoria: His Personality as a Cause of His Failure," *The Americas* 23 (1967): 297–311.

Agustín de Iturbide. Taking up residence first in Italy and later in England, the exiled monarch heard rumors that the restored Spanish king, Ferdinand VII, backed by the Holy Alliance, was about to undertake a reconquest of Mexico. Early in 1824 he offered his services to the republican government. He had defeated the Spanish army once and was prepared to do battle again in the name of Mexican Independence. Congress turned down his good offer and, in fact, passed legislation stipulating that should he dare return to Mexico he would be considered a traitor and, as such, would face immediate execution. Impatient and imprudent as ever, Iturbide did not wait for an answer. On May 11, 1824, he left England with his family and retainers for the New World. Disembarking at Soto la Marina, north of Tampico, he was soon recognized by the local military commander. The Tamaulipas state legislature met in hurried session and decreed that it must enforce the order of treason handed down by the national Congress the month before. On July 19, 1824, standing before a firing squad at the small town of Padilla, Iturbide could not resist making one final rambling and emotional speech protesting his innocence to his executioners: "Mexicans! Even in this act of my death I recommend to you love of our fatherland and observance of our holy religion. . . . I die for having come to assist you, and I die happy because I die among you. I die with honor, not as a traitor."[3]

The execution of Iturbide was really incidental to the Victoria presidency. The administration scored high marks in foreign policy. Not only was Mexico's Independence formally recognized by most of Europe, but several treaties of amity and commerce were concluded as well. A treaty with the United States pledged both countries to accept the Sabine River as the eastern boundary of Texas, thus ostensibly settling the boundary question. But President Victoria found representatives of foreign nations to be more reasonable than his opponents at home and international problems more soluble than domestic imbroglios.

The Victoria administration was unable to do much about the new nation's steadily worsening financial situation. For years prior to Independence the criollos had argued that the weakness of Mexico's economy was a result of poor management by the gachupines. But now in power themselves, the criollos could do no better. Not concerned that a large standing army could be a menace to civil liberties, to any hope of future civilian govern-

3. Quoted in Lucas Alamán, *Historia de México* (Mexico, 1942), 5: 736–37.

ments, and to a healthy economy, the president kept over fifty thousand men under arms at all times. The new government assumed all national debts from the late colonial period and the monarchy (over 76 million pesos) and sought to support itself by means of import taxes, sales taxes, and new government monopolies. The import duties were largely circumvented by rampant smuggling; the sales taxes were largely avoided by failure to report transactions; and the monopolies, after collection expenses, brought in little cash. Not only were the revenues insufficient to pay installments on the debt, but they were unequal to the day-to-day costs of government. Yet the deficit was less significant than the fact that the entire fiscal structure was unsound. Loans from England were deemed to be the salvation and small amounts were received. These minor infusions of foreign capital were insufficient to stimulate the economy but did mark the first step of Mexican economic dependency.

While efforts to heal the breach between rival factions foundered, the political and economic pressures merged in 1827 and expressed themselves in an armed revolt against President Victoria. The leader of the insurrection was none other than Vice-President Nicolás Bravo, who drew upon the Scottish Rite lodges for support. The Yorquinos rallied around the president, and ultimately the revolt was suppressed by Generals Santa Anna and Guerrero. But the precedent of the military coup had been set.

Domestic Turmoil and a Spanish Invasion

Passions had not yet subsided when the new presidential elections were held in September of 1828. The liberal candidate, Vicente Guerrero, an uneducated hero of the wars, was opposed by conservative Manuel Gómez Pedraza, an accomplished scholar who had served in the Victoria cabinet as secretary of war. The election results showed that Gómez Pedraza carried ten of the nineteen state legislatures, but the liberals, feeling no obligation to pay homage to the Constitution, charged that he had used his influence with the army to intimidate the legislators. Rather than turn the government over to their enemies, the liberals opted instead for revolution. Once again they found their champion in Antonio López de Santa Anna, but on this occasion the odds were strongly against him. Through persuasion and deception he gradually won others over to the liberal cause. When

Juan Alvarez rose up in Acapulco and Lorenzo de Zavala in the environs of Mexico City, the government army had to disperse its forces and the rebels made such headway that the president-elect, already disgusted with partisan abuse, announced that he was giving up the fight. As a result the defeated candidate, Vicente Guerrero, became president and Anastasio Bustamante, a compromise conservative, vice-president. Santa Anna, for his efforts, was awarded a division generalship, the highest military rank in the country.

The second president of Mexico was much more active and decisive than the first. He was not the least troubled that he alienated various segments of the population in pursuit of goals he considered worthwhile. The most progressive measure he undertook was the abolition of slavery. The bill, signed in September 1829, was accepted without protest except in Texas, where the institution of slavery had actually been encouraged by previous Mexican legislation.

Scarcely comfortable in the presidential chair, the new president received word that Spain, which had not yet recognized Mexico's independence, was indeed planning a reconquest of Mexico. The Spanish timing seemed to be excellent. The same day that the Congress named Guerrero president it decreed the enforcement of a law, passed under the previous administration, expelling almost all remaining Spaniards from Mexico. The country was rent with factionalism and considerably weakened. Just as the first Spanish conquest in 1519 had been served admirably by internal dissension, maybe the second, three hundred and ten years later, could profit as well.

The Spanish expedition of some three thousand troops left Havana, Cuba (one of the few remaining Spanish possessions in the New World), in July 1829 under the command of General Isidro Barradas. Landing on the coast of Tamaulipas at the height of summer, the Spaniards were exhausted and demoralized by intense heat, yellow fever, and an acute scarcity of water. To their amazement, however, they found that Tampico had been evacuated in anticipation of a much larger expedition, and they took the forfeited prize.

President Guerrero decided to place government operations in the hands of the man who had ostensibly saved the nation several times, the new division general, Antonio López de Santa Anna. On August 21 Santa Anna attacked Tampico but was repulsed by Barradas's well-intrenched forces. But the Spaniards had not established any sure line of supply, and Santa Anna opted for a long siege, which, he reasoned, would take its toll. As inadequate provisions and yellow fever taxed Spanish resistance, General Barradas decided to surrender. By October most of the Spanish troops were on their way home. The attempted reconquest was Spain's last Mexican hurrah. It touched off a series of reprisals against the few remaining Spaniards in the country, and they began leaving hurriedly. The exodus of these middle-class Spanish merchants further weakened Mexico's economy.

Santa Anna had saved Mexico again. By 1830 there were few in the country who could rival his popularity. Honorific but unremunerative titles began to flow in from all corners of the republic: *Vencedor de Tampico* (Victor of Tampico) and *Salvador del País* (Savior of the Country). And the national Congress authorized a medal inscribed "At Tampico he defeated Spanish arrogance" and officially named him *Benemérito de la Patria* (Benefactor of the Fatherland). Undoubtedly, he could have taken advantage of his position immediately if he had wanted to. But he was not quite ready.

The Federalist–Centralist Struggle Continues

With the Spanish threat removed, the Mexican liberals and conservatives now returned to anathematizing one another. When President Guerrero refused to relinquish the extraordinary powers Congress gave him to cope with the threat, Vice-President Bustamante posed as the champion of constitutionalism. For the second time in Mexico's brief republican history a conservative vice-president led an armed revolt against a liberal president. But where Nicolás Bravo had failed, Bustamante, largely because of his influence with the army, succeeded.

With Bustamante in the presidential office, the conservatives were back in power for the first time since the overthrow of the empire. But their promises would be so totally unredeemed as to imply that promises were made only for the pleasure of breaking them. All along the conservatives had been substituting catchy syllogisms for penetrating analyses of Mexico's problems, and when they found themselves in power they did not know what to do. Although they cut back on the size of the army and renegotiated the English loan, Bustamante was no more able to bring about stability and progress than had his liberal predecessors. And he compounded his shortcomings by giving his fellow Mexicans their first real lessons in military dictatorship.

Repressions taken against the Yorquinos were grossly intemperate. Freedom of the press was suppressed as only those presses upholding the government were allowed to roll. The federal legislature and the judiciary were badgered into acquiescence. Political corruption, not unknown in Mexico's past, reached new heights. But the incident that occasioned the greatest public outrage was the capture and execution of the former president, Vicente Guerrero. After his ouster by the Bustamante army, Guerrero gradually made his way to Acapulco, where he accepted passage on the *Colombo*, a ship flying the Italian flag. But Captain Picaluga, a Genoese citizen, had already made a trip to Mexico City and for $50,000 had agreed to sell Guerrero to the government. As soon as the former president boarded the *Colombo*, he was bound hand and foot and turned over to federal authorities. He was subsequently tried, convicted of treason, and on January 14, 1831, executed.

The execution had a sobering effect as Mexicans began to tally up. Of the five outstanding leaders of the Wars for Independence, four—Miguel Hidalgo, José María Morelos, Agustín de Iturbide, and now Vicente Guerrero—had died before the firing squad. Only Guadalupe Victoria escaped this fate. The word *traitor* had come to be used too easily and the charge invariably carried the supreme penalty. As a nation, Mexico was unsure of itself. It had drifted and vacillated since Independence. National, state, and local governments were plagued by civil disorder and insolvency. The state was still little more than an abstraction, and the criollo leadership had not served it well. The social structure had not changed in any meaningful way. Abolishing the caste system scarcely abolished poverty. Emancipating the slaves did not eliminate malnutrition and illiteracy. It seemed time for a change of direction, and there was one Mexican now ready to seize the opportunity. Santa Anna marshaled his forces once again, overthrew the Bustamante government, and returned to Veracruz to revel in his latest victory and await the outcome of the 1833 presidential elections.

Recommended for Further Study

Arrom, Silvia M. "Popular Politics in Mexico City: The Parián Riot, 1828." *Hispanic American Historical Review* 68 (1988): 245–68.

Benson, Nettie Lee. "Servando Teresa de Mier, Federalist." *Hispanic American Historical Review* 28 (1948): 514–25.

Callcott, Wilfrid H. *Church and State in Mexico, 1822–1857.* Durham, N.C.: Duke University Press, 1926.

Campbell, Randolf. "Henry Clay and the Poinsett Pledge Controversy of 1826." *The Americas* 28 (1972): 429–40.

Cline, Howard F. "The Aurora Yucateca and the Spirit of Enterprise in Yucatán, 1821–1847." *Hispanic American Historical Review* 27 (1947): 30–60.

Costeloe, Michael P. "Guadalupe Victoria and a Personal Loan from the Church in Independent Mexico." *The Americas* 25 (1969): 223–46.

Flaccus, Elmer W. "Guadalupe Victoria: His Personality as a Cause of His Failure." *The Americas* 23 (1967): 297–311.

Flores Caballero, Romeo. *Counterrevolution: The Role of the Spaniards in the Independence of Mexico.* Lincoln: University of Nebraska Press, 1974.

Gardiner, C. Harvey. "The Role of Guadalupe Victoria in Mexican Foreign Relations." *Revista de Historia de América* 26 (1948): 379–92.

Gilmore, N. Ray. "Henry George Ward, British Publicist for Mexican Mines." *Pacific Historical Review* 32 (1963): 35–47.

Green, Stanley. *The Mexican Republic: The First Decade, 1823–1832.* Pittsburgh: University of Pittsburgh Press, 1987.

Hale, Charles A. *Mexican Liberalism in the Age of Mora, 1821–1853.* New Haven, Conn.: Yale University Press, 1968.

Hutchinson, C. Alan. "The Mexican Government and the Mission Indians of Upper California, 1821–1835." *The Americas* 21 (1965): 335–62.

Lamar, Quinton Curtis. "A Diplomatic Disaster: The Mexican Mission of Anthony Butler, 1829–1834." *The Americas* 45 (1988): 1–18.

Macune, Charles W. "The Impact of Federalism on Mexican Church–State Relations, 1824–1835: The Case of the State of Mexico." *The Americas* 40 (1984): 177–90.

McKenzie-Johnstone, Henry. *Mission to Mexico: A Tale of British Diplomacy in the 1820s.* New York: St. Martin's Press, 1992.

Rippy, J. Fred. *Joel R. Poinsett, Versatile American.* Durham, N.C.: Duke University Press, 1935.

Rodríguez O., Jaime. "The Conflict Between Church and State in Early Republican Mexico." *New World* 2 (1987): 93–112.

Sims, Harold Dana. *The Expulsion of Mexico's Spaniards, 1821–1836.* Pittsburgh: University of Pittsburgh Press, 1990.

Weber, David J. *The Mexican Frontier, 1821–1846: The American Southwest Under Mexico.* Albuquerque: University of New Mexico Press, 1982.

Winn, Wilkins B. "The Efforts of the United States to Secure Religious Liberty in a Commercial Treaty with Mexico, 1825–1831." *The Americas* 28 (1972): 311–32.

19

Santa Anna
and the Centralized State

Santa Anna is the first of three towering Mexican political figures who would leave a preponderant imprint on their country's nineteenth-century historical experience. His contributions, corrosive perhaps, were quite at variance with those of his successors, Benito Juárez and Porfirio Díaz, but they were no less pronounced for he, too, was an event-making man. His intelligence, resolution, and temperament, his sins and ambitions, charted the course Mexico was to follow from the early 1830s to the middle 1850s. Mexican history from 1833 to 1855 constantly teetered between simple chaos and unmitigated anarchy. Victories were only slightly less barren than defeats. The country needed an "Era of Good Feelings" like that to the north but instead entered a phase of intense mutual recrimination. Nobody seemed willing to admit that some measure of compromise was essential to the system of government that had been inaugurated in 1824. Between May 1833 and August 1855 the presidency changed hands thirty-six times, the average term being about seven and a half months. Santa Anna occupied the presidential chair on eleven different occasions, and his whim was Mexico's imperative. Even when he was out of office he was a powerful force to be reckoned with and a constant danger to the incumbent regime and to anyone aspiring to the succession.

Santa Anna: The Expediency of Political Principles

Antonio López de Santa Anna Pérez de Lebrón was born on February 21, 1794. His schooling in Veracruz left much to be desired, but the criollo youth showed no real flair for books anyway. Shortly after his sixteenth birthday he joined the army and within a year received his baptism of fire in a small engagement against a band of pro-Hidalgo rebels. For the next decade the young royalist cavalry officer staunchly supported the crown's efforts in New Spain and not only won special commendation for his heroics but also, for a short time, became an aide-de-camp to Viceroy Apodaca in Mexico City. But in 1821 Santa Anna, like many of his criollo comrades, followed Iturbide's lead and switched allegiance; in the process they sealed Spain's fate.

The highlights of Santa Anna's career in the period immediately following Independence have already been touched upon. In 1823, under the banner of the Plan de Casa Mata, he led the republican forces against the empire and contributed in no small way to the overthrow of Iturbide. When Mexico's first vice-president, conservative Nicolás Bravo, proclaimed a revolt against President Victoria, Santa Anna took the lead in suppressing the movement and, following the next presidential election, saw to it that the defeated liberal candidate, Vicente Guerrero, was installed in office. In 1829, when Spain tried to bring its former colony back into the fold, it was Santa Anna again who defeated the Spanish forces at Tampico to save the infant republic and, in 1832, when the Bustamante dictatorship became intolerable, he overthrew it. On the surface, at least, his entire career seemed to constitute an unbroken chain of victories in the defense of Mexican liberalism. As the accolades mounted, Santa Anna fell victim to the greatest temptation of the wartime hero. He would change the field of battle from the military to the political front.

When the state legislatures cast their presidential votes in 1833, no one was surprised at the outcome. Santa Anna won by the largest majority in Mexican history. The vice-presidency went to Valentín Gómez Farías, a man of intellectual distinction and a politician whose liberal credentials were impeccable. Because both the new president and the new vice-president had upheld the cause of liberalism for years, Mexico seemed not to have to fear still another revolt of a vice-president against a president because of ideological disputation.

Santa Anna had coveted the presidency for a decade, but once he achieved the goal he quickly wearied of the daily routine, long hours, and general tedium of presidential business. The excitement was in getting there, not being there. For the first time in his career he could not devote himself to the strenuous life, flitting around the country on his white charger and making or unmaking presidents. Moreover, as the champion of liberalism, he was expected to embark upon a series of far-reaching reforms long called for by his liberal cohorts. Such reforms were bound to prompt controversy, divide the society once again, and erode his tremendous popularity. Santa Anna's response was unique but not entirely out of character. He decided to return to his magnificent estate, Manga de Clavo, in Veracruz, leaving the office in the hands of Vice-President Gómez Farías. The presidency was, it seemed, a toy to be cast aside when he tired of playing the game.

The vice-president, in good nineteenth-century liberal fashion, immediately began to sponsor a number of reforms aimed at two intrenched institutions: the army and the church. The military reforms were modest. To curtail the inordinate influence of the army, the Gómez Farías administration reduced the size of the military and legislated the abolition of the military fueros; army officers would now have to stand trial in civil courts. The clerical reforms were much more wide-ranging, as the liberals maintained that the Mexican clergy, if not having outlived its usefulness, was contributing less to the spiritual needs of the community than ever before. The initial step was a hesitant one, designed perhaps to test the wind. Clergymen throughout the country were advised that they should limit their directives and admonitions from the pulpit to matters of religion. Emboldened by the lack of a forceful rejoinder, the Congress, under the prodding of Gómez Farías and his liberal theoreticians José María Luis Mora and Lorenzo de Zavala, then voted to secularize education. One of the first steps taken in the name of educational progress was to close down the University of Mexico because its faculty was made up primarily of priests. In addition, all future clerical appointments in the republic would be made by the government rather than by the papacy. But the anticlerical reforms were just beginning. Within the month the government struck out at the church where it really hurt—the ecclesiastical treasury. The mandatory payment of the tithe was declared illegal. The individual was asked to search his own conscience and respond as he would. In addition, in the name of individual freedom (a concept much in vogue with nineteenth-century liberals) the Congress enacted legislation permitting nuns, priests, and lay brothers, who had taken oaths to spend their entire lives as brides and servants of Christ, to forswear their vows. And in one final measure the Franciscan missions in California were secularized and their funds and property sequestered.

General Antonio López de Santa Anna (1794–1876). The dominant figure of the first half of the nineteenth century, Santa Anna actually served in the presidency on eleven different occasions. A master politician, nobody understood Mexico's political dynamics better.

The response from the vested interests was almost predictable. To the rallying cry of *Religión y Fueros* the church, the army, and other conservative groupings banded together and called for the overthrow of the government. The conservatives scouted the country for a figure to protect their prerogatives and lead them to victory and turned to the maker and unmaker of presidents par excellence—Antonio López de Santa Anna. Again thirsting for public acclaim the retired president jumped at the new opportunity for action and agreed to lead the movement against his former vice-president, Gómez Farías. Not embarrassed by lack of consistency, the embattled champion of all liberal causes since 1821 suddenly began denouncing anticlerical atheists, York Rite Masons, naive federalists, subversive anarchists, Jacobins, Gómez Farías, and his liberal cohorts. The insurrection, although hampered by a cholera epidemic among the troops, succeeded, and within a short time Santa Anna made his second sortie into the presidency and rescinded most of the Gómez Farías reforms.

The new Santa Anna regime was openly conservative, Catholic, and centralist. The president's response to the perplexities of making a more perfect union was to abolish the federalist Constitution of 1824 and replace it with one more to his liking. The new charter, consisting of seven main parts, is remembered in Mexico's constitutional evolution as the *Siete Leyes*, or the Constitution of 1836. In a feature designed to ensure centralist organization, the states of the old federal republic were transformed into military departments governed by political bosses hand-picked by the president himself. The presidential term was extended from four years to eight, but no president under the Constitution was to serve so long. The right to hold high political office was extended only to those with a high annual income ($1,500 to be eligible for election to the Chamber of Deputies, $2,500 for the Senate, and $4,000 for the presidency). The financial qualifications for voting and officeholding gave the Siete Leyes an aristocratic flavor that obviously pleased the regime's conservative backers.

Foreign Affairs and Finances

Santa Anna's decision to abolish the federal republic and to replace it with a centralist state precipitated a series of interrelated events that were to dominate his life and his country for the next twelve years. The switch to centralism was well received by some, as the concept of federalism had already lost much of its magic appeal, but liberal politicians in many parts of Mexico were dismayed, and several led revolts against him. The most serious opposition by far came from the northern province of Texas, which, in turn, provoked a disastrous war with the United States. These matters are of such importance as to be treated separately.

Even leaving the Texas issue temporarily aside, foreign relations during the age of Santa Anna were troubled, for in 1838 Mexico became involved in a war with France. The conflict was deeply rooted in the internal chaos that had marked Mexican political life since Independence. During the unremitting series of revolts and counterrevolts, the property of foreign nationals was often damaged. Foreign governments then submitted claims in behalf of their own citizens. Among the numerous French claims were those of a French pastry cook whose delicacies were appropriated and consumed by a group of hungry Mexican soldiers in 1828. In ridicule of the event that followed, Mexican journalists immediately dubbed the episode the Pastry War.

Conflicting property evaluations, rapid changes in the Mexican government, and the always near-bankrupt state of the Mexican treasury prevented resolution of the French claims for years. In early 1838 the French king, Louis Philippe, demanded payment of $600,000. Because a favorable reply was not immediately forthcoming, in March a French fleet appeared off the coast of Veracruz, and the French minister, Baron Deffaudis, issued an ultimatum demanding payment of the claims by April 15, a series of assurances for French citizens residing in Mexico, and a few trading concessions. The Mexican government replied that it could not countenance any demands made with the French squadron anchored menacingly in Mexican waters. The deadline arrived and passed, whereupon France broke diplomatic relations and announced a blockade of Veracruz. When King Louis Philippe decided to increase the size of the French fleet to twenty-six vessels and over four thousand men, the Mexicans decided that it was time to negotiate. In October they agreed to pay the $600,000 but, to their surprise, found that the matter could no longer be resolved so easily. The French minister calculated that the blockade had cost his government about $200,000; the total bill was now $800,000. On this point the Mexican government could not yield. A thousand men were dispatched to reinforce the twelve hundred stationed at the venerable, moss-mottled fortress of San Juan de Ulloa in the harbor of Veracruz.

The French initiated their bombardment on the afternoon of November 27, rending a portion of the fortress walls, exploding supplies of ammunition inside, and forcing the Mexican troops to abandon their first line of defense. As night fell the Mexican commander opted to give up the fortress as indefensible. With Mexico's invincible Gibraltar abandoned, Veracruz seemed at the mercy of the French. As an incensed Mexican citizenry bemoaned incompetence and intimated treason, it was time for Santa Anna, temporarily out of the presidency, to exert himself once again. Proclaiming that God and justice were on the side of Mexico and that honor demanded he take up the challenge, he offered his services to the fatherland. They were accepted immediately as the Mexican Congress declared war on France.

Santa Anna arrived at Veracruz on December 4; the following morning some three thousand French troops made a landing. In the street fighting that ensued Santa Anna led his troops personally and drove the French back toward the coast. In one of the assaults the Mexican commander had his horse shot out from under him and, in the process, was severely wounded in the left leg. A few days later it was amputated below the knee. The French, however, had been driven back to their ships and, rather than prolong the venture, they agreed to accept the $600,000 as earlier offered by the Mexican government.

INCOME AND EXPENDITURES, 1839–46

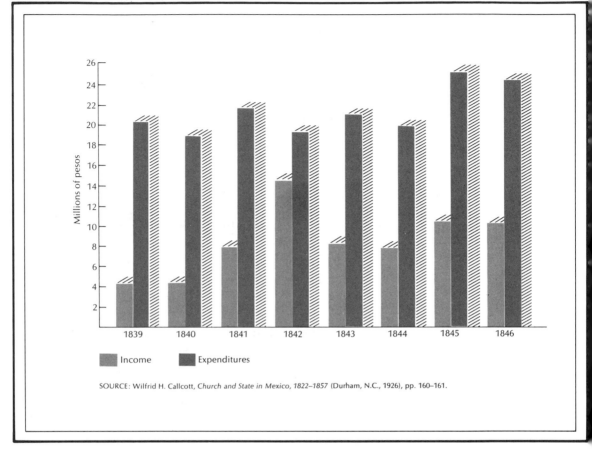

SOURCE: Wilfrid H. Callcott, *Church and State in Mexico, 1822–1857* (Durham, N.C., 1926), pp. 160–161.

The Mexicans could take some heart from having defeated the legions of King Louis Philippe, but there was little time for rejoicing. The liberal-conservative struggle continued unabated. Larger and larger armies (a standing army of ninety thousand by 1855) and a huge civilian bureaucracy drained the treasury, while industry and commerce stagnated. Successive governments tried every imaginable expedient to replenish the coffers. Old currencies were recalled and new ones issued; forced loans were made on businesses and on nunneries and other ecclesiastical corporations; voluntary loans were obtained from private money lenders called *agiotistas*; properties were confiscated; new taxes were levied on carriages, coach wheels, all internal trade, and even on dogs, pulque shops, and the gutters of houses; old taxes on real estate and imports were raised; lucrative mining concessions were sold to the British. In addition, the government declared a head tax of one and one-half pesos annually on all males between the ages of sixteen and sixty. But while Santa Anna raised more money than his predecessors, he also spent more. The average government deficit between 1839 and 1846 was 12.7 million pesos annually.

The Legacy of Santa Anna

It is fair to ask if Santa Anna was the cause of Mexico's problems or if Mexico was the cause of Santa Anna's problems. Our reading of the record suggests the first alternative more nearly approximates the truth.[1] He presided over a brazenly corrupt regime. Bribery was the calling card of those seeking concessions. Santa Anna quickly became a millionaire as he accumulated riches with the greed of poverty remembered. His landholdings in 1845 totaled some 483,000 acres, and over forty thousand head of cattle bore the ALSA brand. Because local officials studied well the lessons of their superiors, graft and corruption soon penetrated all levels of government. Contraband was rampant, indeed, was encouraged by venal port officials.

Even allowing for the exaggerations of his critics, one must conclude that Santa Anna's lust for power and quest for glory knew no bounds. Until the middle of the nineteenth century, Mexican presidents had been called simply "His Excellency." But because Santa Anna felt that too many reprobates had already held that title, he had his official designation changed to "His Most Serene Highness." He arranged for gala balls and banquets to be staged in his honor. When a sumptuous new theater was constructed in Mexico City at a cost of 350,000 pesos, it was named the Gran Teatro de Santa Anna. His busts and statues adorned public parks and streets. The presidential home in Tacubaya became a palace, and its newly imported furniture, rugs, and tapestries from Europe and the Near East would have made even Iturbide comfortable.

Salvos of artillery fire and twenty-one-gun salutes preceded the dictator and announced his presence everywhere he went. Congress declared that the small presidential bodyguard was insufficient for a man of his stature and authorized a new guard of twelve hundred men, styled the Lancers of the Supreme Power.

1. For a different opinion, see Donald Fithian Stevens, *Origins of Instability in Early Republican Mexico* (Durham, N.C.: Duke University Press, 1990).

Santa Anna's saint's day became a national holiday; while all private and public business came to a screeching halt, friends and favor seekers brought him gifts, totaling several tens of thousands of pesos on a good year. Favorite journalists grasped the occasions to lavish eulogistic editorials, while sycophants in the government delivered orations in honor of His Most Serene Highness. When Santa Anna made awards to others he signed them with an ostentatious display of titles. In 1853 one certificate of merit presented to José Angel Benavides was signed by "Santa Anna, Savior of the Fatherland, General of Division, Knight of the Great Cross of the Royal and Distinguished Spanish Order of Charles III, President of the Mexican Republic, Grand Master of the National and Distinguished Order of Guadalupe."[2]

But the most bizarre episode of all occurred in the fall of 1842. Santa Anna ordered the disinterment of his amputated leg from its quiet repose on his hacienda of Manga de Clavo. The mummified member was transported to Mexico City and, after an impressive procession through the streets of the capital in which the presidential bodyguard, the army, and the cadets from the Chapultepec Military Academy all participated, it was taken to the cemetery of Santa Fe where it was placed in a specially designed urn and set atop a huge stone pillar. The ceremony was typically Santanesque. Conducted at the site of the shrine, it was attended by the entire cabinet, the diplomatic corps, and the Congress. The speeches, songs, and poems offered in Santa Anna's honor paled all previous efforts at sanctification as the leg shattered by the French cannonball was now being offered to the fatherland.

The Santa Anna dictatorship exacted a heavy price. The only immutable law of the period was that the liberals and conservatives would never agree or compromise on matters of substance. A series of governments concerned more with show than with development, officials pilfering the treasury with impunity, political factions rife with internal dissension, an economy mired in its own inertia, all militated against progress. Time after time the country ignited in conflagration. Santa Anna himself must bear much of the responsibility. Often clever but never wise, he set an example of dishonesty, deception, and complete failure to adhere to any set of principles. All of his loyalties were mercurial, and the tone he established for the age proved contagious.

2. Quoted in Oakah L. Jones, Jr., *Santa Anna* (New York, 1968), p. 125.

An 1845 lithograph depicting a one-legged Santa Anna standing on a Manga de Clavo built on extortions of various kinds.

He was always able to muster sufficient military support to seize the moment but never sufficient political support to seize the hour. The intelligentsia cried out for constructive leadership but did not receive it. By the middle of the nineteenth century some of the obligations of Mexican nationhood had been defined, but precious few had been implemented. The political atmosphere was still charged with mistrust. Revolts and counterrevolts were accepted as inevitable concomitants of the social order. Some material improvements had been recorded, at least in the larger cities. The textile industry had developed rapidly during the 1840s and 1850s but the retrogressions in the political and economic orders were more noteworthy. Roads were in disrepair, mines were still abandoned, fertile agricultural fields lay vacant, industrialization was but a vague hope for the future, foreign trade was notable only for its absence, and the national debt was growing.

But by far the greatest misfortune of the age of Santa Anna has not yet been discussed. The loss of Texas and the war with the United States contributed more to Mexico's impoverishment, its apparent sterility, its xenophobia, its lack of self-esteem, and its general demoralization than any other event of the nineteenth century. These episodes warrant separate consideration.

Recommended for Further Study

Callcott, Wilfrid H. *Church and State in Mexico, 1822–1857*. Durham, N.C.: Duke University Press, 1926.

———. *Santa Anna: The Story of an Enigma Who Once Was Mexico*. Norman: University of Oklahoma Press, 1936.

Costeloe, Michael P. *Church and State in Independent Mexico: A Study of the Patronage Debate, 1821–1857*. London: Royal Historical Society, 1978.

———. "Federalism to Centralism in Mexico: The Conservative Case for Change, 1834–1835." *The Americas* 45 (1988): 173–86.

———. "The Triangular Revolt in Mexico and the Fall of Anastasio Bustamante, August–October, 1841." *Journal of Latin American Studies* 20 (1988): 337–60.

Harris, Charles H., III. *The Sánchez-Navarros: A Socio-Economic Study of a Coahuilan Latifundio, 1846–1853*. Chicago: Loyola University Press, 1964.

Jones, Oakah L., Jr. *Santa Anna*. New York: Twayne, 1968.

Lavrin, Asunción. "Mexican Nunneries from 1835 to 1860: Their Administrative Policies and Relations with the State." *The Americas* 28 (1972): 288–310.

Mayo, John. "Consuls and Silver Contraband on Mexico's West Coast in the Era of Santa Anna." *Journal of Latin American Studies* 19 (1987): 389–411.

Randall, Robert W. *Real del Monte: A British Mining Venture in Mexico*. Austin: University of Texas Press, 1972.

Robertson, William S. "French Intervention in Mexico in 1838." *Hispanic American Historical Review* 24 (1944): 222–52.

Samponaro, Frank N. "Santa Anna and the Abortive Anti-Federalist Revolt of 1833 in Mexico." *The Americas* 40 (1983): 95–108.

Sanders, Frank J. "José María Gutiérrez Estrada: Monarchist Pamphleteer." *The Americas* 27 (1970): 56–74.

Santa Anna, Antonio López de. *The Eagle: The Autobiography of Santa Anna*. Edited by Ann Fears Crawford, and translated by Sam Guyler and Jaime Platón. Austin: Pemberton Press, 1967.

Stevens, Donald Fithian. *Origins of Instability in Early Republican Mexico*. Durham, N.C.: Duke University Press, 1991.

Tenenbaum, Barbara. *The Politics of Penury: Debts and Taxes in Mexico, 1821–1856*. Albuquerque: University of New Mexico Press, 1986.

Walker, David W. "Business as Usual: The Empresa del Tabaco in Mexico, 1837–44." *Hispanic American Historical Review* 64 (1984): 707–36.

20

The Loss of Texas
and the War with the United States

Discontent in Texas

Throughout the colonial period Texas was one of the northern
provinces of New Spain. It was sparsely populated, and the Franciscan missionaries who penetrated the area found the Indian
population intractable. At the beginning of the eighteenth century the Texas territory had fewer than three thousand sedentary colonists and, a hundred years later, only seven thousand.
Because the Spanish crown wanted to populate and colonize the
territory, in 1821, just prior to the winning of Mexican Independence, the commandant general in Monterrey granted Moses
Austin, an American pioneer, permission to settle some three
hundred Catholic families in Texas. Austin died and Mexico became independent before the project could be initiated, but Austin's son, Stephen F. Austin, took up the idea, had the concession
confirmed by the new Mexican government, and began the colonization at once. Under the terms of the new concession Stephen
Austin was authorized to bring in as many as three hundred families the first year provided that they were of good moral character, would profess the Roman Catholic religion, and agreed to
abide by Mexican law. No maximum was set on future immigration into Texas, and, in fact, other concessionaires were awarded
similar grants.

The influx of Americans into Texas was tremendous. The land
was practically free—only ten cents an acre as opposed to $1.25
an acre for inferior land in the United States. Each male colonist
over twenty-one years of age was allowed to purchase 640 acres
for himself, 320 acres for his wife, 160 acres for each child and,

significantly, an additional 80 acres for each slave that he brought with him. As a further enticement the colonists were given a seven-year exemption from the payment of Mexican taxes. By 1827 there were 12,000 United States citizens living in Texas, outnumbering the Mexican population by some 5,000. By 1835 the immigrant population had reached 30,000, while the Mexican population had barely passed 7,800.

The Mexican government originally believed that immigrants from the United States could be integrated into the Mexican community and passed a number of laws to foster this integration. In addition to the requirement that the colonists be Roman Catholic, all official transactions were to be concluded in the Spanish language, no foreigners would be allowed to settle within sixty miles of the national boundary, and foreigners who married Mexican citizens could be eligible for extra land. All governmental efforts to encourage peaceful integration failed, however, as tensions rose between the Mexicans, always more and more in the minority, and the immigrants. The colonists who came were not, by and large, Roman Catholics, although they knew how to make the proper declaration if asked. Very few bothered to learn Spanish. In addition, the political traditions of the two groups were far from kindred. Political, religious, and cultural conflict did not take long to surface.

One major grievance of the Texans was that the province was appended politically to the state of Coahuila, which had nine times its population. Although Texas was represented in the state legislature with one, then two, and finally three representatives (out of a total of twelve), they were easily outvoted by the Coahuilans on issues they considered crucial. In addition, all appellate courts were located far away in Saltillo, and the time and expense involved in carrying out an appeal completely discouraged the use of the judicial machinery.

But the Mexicans had serious grievances as well. A number of filibustering expeditions from the United States prompted genuine fear that the United States government was bent on securing the Texas territory for itself. The most serious of these forays saw James Long, a Tennesseean, invade Texas with a private army, capture Nacogdoches, declare Texas independent, name himself president, and affirm that Texas really belonged to the United States. Although Long's army was subsequently defeated by the Mexicans, clamor in the U.S. Congress and in the American press for changing the boundary or for acquiring much or all of

Texas through a new treaty or by stealth excited apprehensions in Mexico City.

As Mexican politicians began to realize that their problems in Texas were getting out of hand, they plotted a remedial course of action. The first important piece of legislation designed to prevent a further weakening of Mexican control was President Guerrero's emancipation proclamation of 1829. Because slavery was not important anywhere else in the republic, the measure was clearly directed at Texas. Although manumission was not immediately enforced, it was hoped that the decree itself would make Mexico less attractive to colonists from the U.S. South and would thus arrest future immigration. More important was the colonization law of April 6, 1830, which explicitly forbade all future immigration into Texas from the United States and called for the strengthening of Mexican garrisons, the improvement of economic ties between Texas and the remainder of Mexico by the establishment of a new coastal trade, and the encouragement of increased Mexican colonization. If the colonists already there could not be displaced, an intensive Mexican colonization could at least hope to re-establish the population balance.

None of the plans curtailed the growing antagonism between the two groups of colonists, for the Texans considered them not accommodative but sternly repressive. The last straw, as far as the Texans were concerned, was receipt of the news from Mexico City that Santa Anna had arbitrarily annulled the federal Constitution of 1824. The centralist tendencies of the new regime meant that, instead of having a greater voice in the management of local affairs, the Texans were to have no voice at all. As the Texas leaders began to debate their future course of action, they were urged to separate themselves not only by United States expansionists, who argued theatrically that the Texans should detach themselves from the yoke of dictatorship, but also by a number of Mexican liberals opposed to everything Santa Anna stood for. Among the latter, the most active was Lorenzo de Zavala, a leader of the Constitutional Congress of 1823–24, a founder of the York Rite lodges, and most recently a Mexican minister to France. When Santa Anna took all governmental powers into his own hands, Zavala advised the Texans that the dictator had forfeited all claims to obedience. The Texans needed little prompting, however; they had decided on independence and subsequently chose David Burnet as president of the Lone Star Republic and Zavala as vice-president.

The War for Texas Independence

It was time for Santa Anna to take the field again, and with no false modesty he later explained his decision in his memoirs.

> I, as chief executive of the government, zealous in the fulfillment of my duties to my country, declared that I would maintain the territorial integrity whatever the cost. This would make it necessary to initiate a tedious campaign under a capable leader immediately. . . . Stimulated by . . . courageous feelings I took command of the campaign myself, preferring the uncertainties of war to the easy and much coveted life of the palace.[1]

In the winter of 1835 Santa Anna moved north at the head of some six thousand troops. But because of innumerable difficulties during the long trek it was not until early March of 1836 that he reached the outskirts of San Antonio de Béxar (today San Antonio) and found that the Texans, under the command of William Barrett Travis, had taken refuge in the old Franciscan mission of the Alamo. Among them were such Texas luminaries as Davy Crockett and Jim Bowie. The essentials of what happened on March 6 are known to every schoolchild both north and south of the Rio Grande (called the Río Bravo in Mexico), though the distortions of nationalism have taken their toll on the history in both countries.

For several days prior to March 6, 1836, Santa Anna had laid siege to the Alamo. The high, stout walls seemed impregnable, and the defenders were not about to surrender to the greatly superior Mexican force. On the late afternoon of March 5 the Texans might have heard a bugle, but most assuredly they did not recognize the sounds coming over the walls as the *degüello*, a battle call used since the time of the Spanish wars against the Moors to signal that the engagement to follow was to be to the death, with no quarter to be shown the enemy. The order had come directly from Santa Anna, and he planned to enforce it.

The next morning the Mexican commander threw waves of soldiers against the adobe fortress. In the face of heavy artillery the Mexicans attacked bravely. Hundreds were cut down, but after the first hour the numerical superiority of the attackers began to tell. Several breaches were opened in the wall, and the fighting continued inside. The defenders also comported them-

---

1. Antonio López de Santa Anna, *The Eagle: The Autobiography of Santa Anna*, ed. Ann Fears Crawford, trans. Sam Guyler and Jaime Platón (Austin, 1967), pp. 49–50.

selves with great heroism. They were killed to the last man, including five who were executed as prisoners after the fighting had ended. The high toll on both sides did nothing to diminish resolve—to the contrary, it underscored that a peaceful settlement was impossible.

While the battle of the Alamo is famous in the military annals and folklore of the Texas Revolution, a much more significant episode took place several weeks later. General José Urrea engaged a force of Texans under the command of Colonel James W. Fannin at the small town of Goliad. Surrounded and outnumbered, Fannin surrendered in the belief that he and his men would be afforded the recognized rights of prisoners of war. Realizing that the tenor of the war had been set at the Alamo, General Urrea wrote to Santa Anna urging clemency for Fannin and the other prisoners. Urrea then moved on to another engagement and left the Texas prisoners in the charge of Lieutenant Colonel Nicolás de la Portilla. Using the national law of piracy as his authority, Santa Anna sent his reply to Portilla on March 23.

> I am informed that there have been sent to you by General Urrea, two hundred and thirty-four prisoners . . . as the supreme government has ordered that all foreigners taken with arms in their hands, making war upon the nation shall be treated as pirates, I have been surprised that the circular of the said supreme government has not been fully complied with in this particular. I therefore order, that you should give immediate effect to the said ordinance. . . . I trust that, in reply to this, you will inform me that public vengeance has been satisfied by the punishment of such detestable delinquents.[2]

Santa Anna had his figures slightly wrong. There were 365 prisoners. Nicolás de la Portilla found himself in the position of many a military commander from the Peloponnesian War to Vietnam. His military duty conflicted directly with his moral principles, but he was of insufficient moral fiber to reject the illegal order. In his diary he recorded his two terrible days.

> March 26. At seven in the evening I received orders from General Santa Anna by special messenger, instructing me to execute at once all prisoners taken by force of arms agreeable to the general orders on the subject. . . . At eight o'clock, on the same night, I received a communication from Gen. Urrea by special messenger in which among other things he says, "Treat the prisoners well,

2. Quoted in Wilfrid H. Callcott, *Santa Anna: The Story of an Enigma Who Once Was Mexico* (Norman, 1936), pp. 132–33.

especially Fannin." . . . What a cruel contrast in these opposite instructions! I spent a restless night.

March 27. At daybreak I decided to carry out the orders of the general-in-chief because I considered them superior. I assembled the whole garrison and ordered the prisoners, who were still sleeping, to be awakened. There were [365]. . . . The prisoners were divided into three groups and each was placed in charge of an adequate guard. . . . I gave instructions to these officers to carry out the orders of the supreme government and the general-in-chief. This was immediately done.[3]

The month following the battles of the Alamo and Goliad was one of reorganization for the Texas army. Although Santa Anna could take heart from the early military campaigns, and although he had Sam Houston and the Texans on the run, his victories proved to be costly ones. The excesses committed by his troops in both engagements, but especially the execution of the prisoners at Goliad, crystalized opposition to Mexico in the United States. Supplies and men began to pour into Texas, and by the third week in April Houston felt strong enough to make a stand. He chose his own ground and, in the middle of the afternoon on April 21, caught Santa Anna's troops off guard near the San Jacinto River. Within half an hour the Mexican army was routed, and Santa Anna himself fled for safety. Two days later he was captured by one of Houston's patrols.

The Lone Star Republic

As a prisoner Santa Anna signed two treaties, one public and one private, with Texas President David Burnet. In the public treaty he agreed that he would not again take up arms against the movement for Texas independence nor would he try to persuade his fellow Mexicans to do so. All hostilities between Mexico and Texas were to cease immediately, and the Mexican army would be withdrawn across the Rio Grande. Prisoners of war in equal numbers would be exchanged. From the Mexican point of view, the secret agreement, later made public, was much more controversial. In return for his own release and transportation to Veracruz, Santa Anna agreed to prepare the Mexican cabinet to receive a peace mission from Texas so that the independence of the Lone Star Republic could be formally recognized.

3. Quoted in Carlos E. Castañeda, ed. and trans., *The Mexican Side of the Texas Revolution* (Dallas, 1928), p. 236n.

Santa Anna as a prisoner of Sam Houston. The Mexican victory at the Alamo was offset by Santa Anna's defeat and capture following the battle of San Jacinto.

When he returned to Mexico, Santa Anna must have been shocked at the reactions his treaties had prompted. While the great masses were apathetic, the intellectual community, the liberals, and many ardent nationalists rejected them as the grossest blasphemy. His sensitivities dazed, Santa Anna was on the defensive, and from his seclusion at Manga de Clavo he offered the best excuses he could. He did nothing in the name of the nation, he argued. The promises he made as an individual, to secure his release, were not binding on the government. Where was the treason? he asked. The legislature responded by enacting a law stipulating that any agreement reached by a Mexican president while held prisoner should be considered null and void. No peace commission from Texas was to be received, and no recognition would be extended.

Texas remained independent as the Lone Star Republic from 1836 to 1845. On the surface it would appear preposterous that without the direct support of the United States, Texas should have been able to retain this independent status in face of greatly superior Mexican resources and manpower. But Mexico was so racked with internal convulsions during these nine years that it was unable to bring Texas back into the fold. The Texas issue, in fact, served to magnify political tensions in Mexico. The ultimate fate of Texas, however, would be decided not on the battlefields of northern Mexico but on the desk tops of Washington, D.C.

The United States recognized the independence of Texas in March of 1837. Although there was a good deal of sympathy for immediate annexation in both Texas and the United States Congress, calmer heads prevailed for eight years. Not only did many congressmen believe that annexation would provoke war with Mexico, but the matter became inexorably entangled in the slavery issue. If Texas entered the Union it would come in as a slave state, and, as a result, annexation was generally opposed by the North. In 1844, however, James K. Polk won the presidency on a platform that included annexation. After the election, but prior to Polk's inauguration, President John Tyler had an annexation measure introduced as a joint resolution of Congress. It passed both houses in early 1845. The stage was set for a major conflict, and Mexico was clearly being swept into the vortex of war.

The Prelude to War

As soon as the joint resolution annexing Texas passed the U.S. Congress, the Mexican minister in Washington lodged a formal protest and asked for his passport. Within a month his counterpart in Mexico City had received his passport as well. As diplomatic relations were ruptured, both countries began preparing for war. The Mexican government sought to negotiate a new loan, the proceeds of which would be directed into the war effort, if, indeed, the conflict occurred. It also authorized the formation of a new voluntary civilian militia to reinforce regular army units. President Polk ordered army troops into the border region and dispatched naval vessels to the Mexican coast. But, not particularly relishing the thought of being branded a warmonger, at the same time he made one belated effort to settle the dispute through negotiation. He asked the Mexican president, José Joaquín Herrera, to receive a special envoy in Mexico City, and Herrera agreed to receive John Slidell.

The specific issue Slidell was asked to negotiate was a boundary dispute in Texas. Throughout the entire colonial period the western boundary of Texas had been the Nueces River. When Moses Austin had received his grant to settle in Texas the western boundary of Texas was still the Nueces River; so, too, when Stephen Austin's contract was reaffirmed. But in spite of thousands of Spanish colonial documents, Mexican documents, and all reliable maps, in December of 1836 the Congress of the Republic of Texas claimed the Rio Grande as the western boundary. The Texans based their claim on two flimsy grounds. During the period of Texas colonization the Mexican government had allowed some United States immigrants to settle in the territory between the Nueces and the Rio Grande. It was all Mexico, so it really did not matter. Second, and even more important for the Texas argument, when Santa Anna agreed to withdraw his troops following his stunning defeat at San Jacinto, he ordered them back across the Rio Grande, tacit admission, so the Texans cried, that the western boundary was indeed the Rio Grande. At stake were not merely the 150 miles between the Nueces and the Rio Grande where they entered the Gulf of Mexico. The Rio Grande meandered aimlessly not north, but northwest, and the Texans claimed it to its source. Thousands and thousands of square miles of territory, indeed, half of New Mexico and Colorado, fell within the claim. When Texas entered the Union as the twenty-eighth state, the Polk administration decided to support the Texan pretensions. Albuquerque, Santa Fe, and Taos belonged to the United States as well as San Antonio, Nacogdoches, and Galveston.

But the American president wanted still more. Slidell also carried secret instructions to secure California and the rest of New Mexico. Five million dollars was deemed a fair price for the New Mexico territory and twenty-five million, or even more, for California. But diplomatic secrets had a way of leaking out, even in the middle of the nineteenth century. The Mexican press, learning the true nature of the Slidell mission, was understandably indignant. Appealing to Mexican nationalism, newspapers, circulars, and broadsides threatened rebellion if President Herrera negotiated with the ignominious Yankee pirates. The Herrera administration, like most of the caretaker governments during the age of Santa Anna, was not very secure, and the president promptly informed President Polk that he had nothing to discuss with John Slidell.

Not even in the face of a potentially calamitous war with the

U.S.-TEXAS BORDER DISPUTE

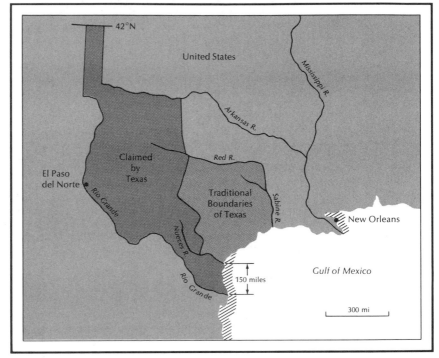

United States could the Mexicans lay aside their internal differences and present a united front. While Mexico's antagonist in the White House plotted his next course of action, General Mariano Paredes, dispatched north to reinforce Mexican troops along the border, decided to use his army on his own president instead. He overthrew the government and was himself installed in the highest office. What an inviting picture northern Mexico presented to the expansionists of the United States!

When Slidell returned to Washington, President Polk held a special cabinet meeting to weigh war feeling. Influential voices cautioned against precipitate action, but the president had already made up his mind. In his diary for May 9, 1846, he noted the following:

> I stated to the Cabinet that up to this time, as we knew, we had heard of no open act of aggression by the Mexican army, but that the danger was imminent that such acts would be committed. I said that in my opinion we had ample cause of war, and that it

was impossible that we could stand in *status quo*, or that I could remain silent much longer.[4]

Secretary of the Navy George Bancroft and Secretary of State James Buchanan would not vote for a declaration of war unless the United States was attacked by Mexico. By a strange quirk of history, hostilities began that very day. Polk had already ordered General Zachary Taylor into the disputed territory between the Nueces and the Rio Grande. The Mexican commander ordered him to withdraw, but instead Taylor penetrated all the way to the Rio Grande. While the cabinet was meeting, a skirmish broke out between Taylor's dragoons and General Mariano Arista's cavalry. On the evening of May 9 Taylor reported to Washington that sixteen of his men had been killed or wounded. Polk now had the perfect excuse. He went before the Congress and delivered a war message that bore little resemblance to the truth. The message was remarkable for its distortion and provocative to the absurd.

> We have tried every effort at reconciliation. The cup of forbearance had been exhausted even before the recent information from the frontier of the Del Norte. But now, after reiterated menaces, Mexico has passed the boundary of the United States, has invaded our territory, and shed American blood on American soil. She has proclaimed that hostilities exist, and that the two nations are now at war.[5]

With a provision limiting debate to two hours, the declaration of war was stampeded through Congress. How different things looked from Mexico City: not only had the Americans taken Texas, but they had changed the traditional boundary to double its size! When the Mexicans sought to defend themselves against the additional encroachment, the Yankees cried that Mexico had invaded the United States! But there was little time for contemplation of moral issues, and the Mexican nation was as divided as ever. President Paredes declared that the centralist Constitution was of no use, but years later Justo Sierra, Mexico's leading educator, philosopher, and historian of the late nineteenth century, noted wryly that "what was actually of no use was the army,

---

4. James K. Polk, *Polk: The Diary of a President, 1845–1849*, ed. Allan Nevins (New York, 1968), p. 81.
5. Quoted in Armin Rappaport, ed., *The War with Mexico: Why Did It Happen?* (New York, 1964), p. 6.

debased into an instrument of cynical ambitions."[6] Yet it was this army that would have to defend the nation against the invasion everyone knew was on its way. The army seemed less concerned with the war in the north than with politics in the south. It took out time to overthrow President Paredes and invite Santa Anna back from his most recent exile. The general who had fought the Spanish in 1829, the Texans in 1836, and the French in 1838 would lead his fellow countrymen against the Americans in 1846.

The Course of the War

Because President Polk, in spite of a good deal of opposition, was able to move more decisively than the ephemeral governments in Mexico City, Mexico from the outset was on the defensive. The American strategy called for a three-pronged offensive. The Army of the West would occupy New Mexico and California; the Army of the Center would be sent into northern Mexico; and the Army of Occupation would carry the battle to Mexico City. General Stephen W. Kearny, commanding the Army of the West, got under way first. Leaving Ft. Leavenworth, Kansas, with some fifteen hundred men in June of 1846, he began the nine-hundred-mile trek toward Santa Fe. Governor Manuel Armijo, not a favorite in the Mexican history textbooks, either accepted a bribe or was afraid to make a stand. He ordered his three thousand troops to evacuate the town shortly before the Americans arrived on August 19. New Mexico had fallen without the firing of a single shot.

Kearny then divided his Army of the West into three. One contingent, under Colonel Sterling Price, continued the occupation of Santa Fe; a second, under Alexander Doniphan, was dispatched directly south to Chihuahua; Kearny himself led the third west to California. California was almost a repeat of New Mexico. By the time Kearny arrived it was already in American hands, having fallen to Naval Commodore John D. Sloat and Colonel John C. Frémont with little opposition. Doniphan, on the other hand, had to engage the enemy in Chihuahua. The major battle, fought on the Sacramento River on the outskirts of Chihuahua City, was an artillery duel. The Mexican artillery pieces

6. Justo Sierra, *The Political Evolution of the Mexican People*, trans. Charles Ramsdell (Austin, 1969), p. 235.

UNITED STATES INVASION, 1846–48

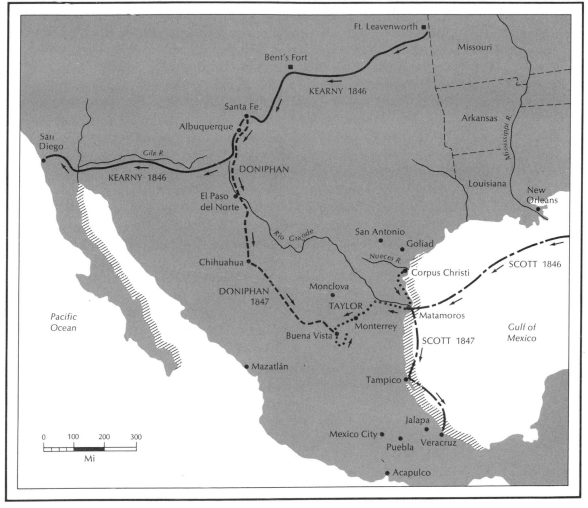

were grossly inadequate, and the supply of powder was not reliable either. Doniphan won the battle, and by February 1847 Chihuahua was under American control. Chihuahuenses were treated to the spectacle of American troops bathing in public fountains, cutting down boulevard shade trees for firewood, and singing "Yankee Doodle" in the Plaza de la Constitución.

The successes of Zachary Taylor's Army of the Center were not so easily won. Taylor's force, some six thousand strong, moved on Monterrey in August 1846. By September they were in sight of the city but were blocked off by the seven thousand Mexicans under General Pedro de Ampudia guarding the entrance. Three days of fierce battle were recorded in the middle of the month. Heavy losses were sustained on both sides before Ampudia sent up the white flag and surrendered the city. By this time Santa Anna had raised an army of about twenty thousand men and was training them in San Luis Potosí. The hard march to Saltillo was disastrous. Insufficient food and water supplies and an unusually harsh winter not only weakened the men but prompted thousands of desertions along the way. Preliminary fighting on February 21 saw Santa Anna force Taylor to pull in his perimeters. The following morning Santa Anna brazenly demanded that Taylor surrender. His messenger informed the American commander that twenty thousand seasoned troops (an exaggeration) were poised to cut his army to pieces. "Tell Santa Anna to go to Hell," Taylor barked to an aide, but the message actually sent observed proper military niceties and read, "In reply to your note of this date summoning me to surrender my forces at discretion, I beg leave to say that I decline acceding to your request."[7]

The battle of Buena Vista began in earnest later in the day. Santa Anna's assaults on Taylor's well-fortified positions did a good deal of damage, but all were repulsed. Evening found a stalemate. Santa Anna could have attacked again the following morning but instead decided to gather up a few war trophies— a few flags and three cannons—and carry them back to Mexico City as proof of his smashing victory. Northeast Mexico was lost to the invaders.

The major United States offensive, however, was waged by General Winfield Scott's Army of Occupation. Mexico's losses in the north and the constant bickering in the capital had not predisposed its leaders to abandon the fight. The United States therefore resolved to carry the battle to Mexico's heartland and to the capital itself. Making his amphibious landing on March 9, 1847, slightly to the south of the harbor of Veracruz, General Scott and his ten thousand men were not opposed as they established their beachhead. Veracruz, for centuries an object of foreign invasion and attack, was a walled city currently garrisoned by four thousand troops. The fortress of San Juan de Ulloa, in the harbor, held an additional twelve hundred. Unlike the French nine years earlier, Scott decided to avoid the fortress altogether. By ordering his troops to surround the city and attack from the rear, he not only neutralized the fortress but also cut off

7. Quoted in Charles L. Dufour, *The Mexican War: A Compact History* (New York, 1968), p. 172.

The U.S. Navy's bombardment of Veracruz resulted in extremely high civilian casualties.

the city's source of land supplies and all avenues of exit. Militarily sound, but morally questionable, the plan of attack called for a heavy mortar bombardment of the city; coincidentally it meant that hundreds of innocent civilians with no possibility of escape would be sacrificed to the apparent exigencies of war.

For the next forty-eight hours Scott devastated the city and refused all implorations of foreign consuls to allow women, children, and other noncombatants to evacuate. He would countenance no manner of truce not accompanied by unconditional surrender. Another day of intense fighting with heavy bombardment ensued.

With military and medical supplies diminished, hundreds of civilian corpses building up in the streets, fires gutting buildings, hospitals destroyed, and the frightening specter of a yellow-fever epidemic mounting, Veracruz surrendered on March 27. A total of sixty-seven hundred shells had been lobbed into the beleaguered city. The Eagle and Serpent came down the flagpole and the Stars and Stripes were hoisted up. Sixty-seven Americans had been killed or wounded, while the toll of Mexican dead within the city was between one thousand and fifteen hundred. Civilian casualties outnumbered military casualties almost two to one.

Santa Anna had reached Mexico City when news of the loss of
Veracruz arrived. He set out to block General Scott's expected
advance on the capital. The opposing forces met in the middle of
April at the mountain pass of Cerro Gordo, some twenty miles
east of Jalapa. Santa Anna had selected a seemingly excellent
position. He could command the entire road as the Americans approached. But Scott's reconnoitering scouts had noted the possibility of bypassing the entrenched Mexicans on the left flank.
While a small advance force feigned an attack along the road,
the bulk of the Americans skirted the left flank and attacked
from the rear. In the confusion that followed, the Mexican defenders broke and fled, and Santa Anna himself barely escaped
capture. He wanted to make one more stand, at Puebla, but the
citizenry there not only declined his offer of defense but informed him that they would not cooperate. Scott took the city
unopposed.

As Scott rested in Puebla the citizens of Mexico City began
bracing themselves for the imminent attack. The destruction of
Veracruz was well known, and apprehension set in. But not even
in the light of this crisis did the politicos in Mexico City join
forces. The war proved as divisive as the internal struggles that
had preceded it. The states would not provide money and men
for a national government they distrusted. The city council in
the capital originally pledged the support of all municipal employees in the work of constructing fortifications but then withdrew the pledge, arguing to the federal government that there
was no way to defend Mexico City. The government simply
placed the Federal District under martial law and began con-
scripting a civilian work force to help in the defense preparations. Santa Anna argued with his leading generals and with the
national Congress. He condemned the legislature for not giving
him the support he needed and they, in turn, chastised him for
his obvious failures on the military front.

As might be expected, the battles for control of Mexico City
were the most monumental of the war. The major preliminary
engagements were fought in the districts of Contreras and Churubusco on the outskirts, and in both cases the Americans proved
superior in leadership, armament, and tactics. At Churubusco,
however, the Mexicans had their finest hour. Fighting bravely,
they refused to yield ground to the larger and better-equipped
fighting force. The issue was finally resolved by intense hand-to-
hand combat in which the Mexicans were at last worn down.
On August 20, with the doors to the city ajar if not open, Scott

asked for a surrender. Santa Anna agreed to negotiate and used the respite to shore up his defenses within the city itself. When the armistice expired without positive result, Santa Anna was in a position to do battle again.

On the morning of September 7, Scott's cavalry charged Mexican positions at Molina del Rey, and the infantry moved in behind. It was the bloodiest single encounter of the war, as the Mexicans suffered over two thousand casualties and the Americans over seven hundred. When the position fell there was only one fortified position left in the city—Chapultepec Castle. Located at the crest of a two-hundred-foot hill and surrounded by a thick stone wall, the castle was defended by some one thousand troops and the cadets of the Military Academy. After a furious artillery barrage failed to dislodge the defenders, Scott ordered that the castle be stormed on the morning of September 13. The Mexican land mines failed to explode, and the attackers were able to breach the walls with pickaxes and crowbars. The scaling ladders arrived, and the Americans poured over the top and initiated the bitter hand-to-hand combat. Reputedly the last defenders were the cadets—the *Niños Héroes*—and many died rather than surrender. The battle of Chapultepec ended the war, and the United States government prepared to negotiate a tough peace.

The Treaty of Guadalupe Hidalgo and the Aftermath of War

After a series of difficult negotiations, the treaty ending the war was signed on February 2, 1848, at the village of Guadalupe Hidalgo, just outside of Mexico City. The treaty confirmed United States title to Texas and ceded the huge California and New Mexico territories as well. In return Mexico was to retain everything south of the Rio Grande. The United States agreed to make a cash payment of $15,000,000 to the Mexican government and to assume $3,250,000 in claims that United States citizens had against that government. For a total of $18,250,000—less than one year's budget—Mexico's territory was reduced by half.

When the United States signed the Treaty of Guadalupe Hidalgo it did more than annex half of Mexico. The war and its treaty left a legacy of hostility that would not be easily overcome. While many Mexican intellectuals had not been hesitant to praise the United States, its culture and institutions, prior to

1846, such commendations were increasingly infrequent in the second half of the nineteenth century. Mexicans had to be fatalistic about the year 1848, which Mexican positivist Justo Sierra lamented was proof of Darwin's theory of the survival of the fittest. From the middle of the sixteenth century, Mexican expeditions had been seeking the Gran Quivira in the north, and finally it was found, at Sutter's Fort, but a few months too late. The gold of California would not make Mexican fortunes or pay its share of Mexico's industrial revolution.

The war reinforced the worst stereotypes that each country held about the other, and these stereotypes in turn contributed to the development of deep-seated prejudices. United States historians rationalized, justified, and even commended the decision to wage the war as well as the prosecution of it. On grounds ranging from regenerating a backward people to fulfilling a preordained destiny, they went so far as to use this war of aggression for the purpose of instilling historical pride in generations of American children. Mexican historians, too, stereotyped and distorted. Not content with an understandably vigorous condemnation of the United States government, they pinned responsibility on the American people and the congenital defects of their Anglo-Saxon heritage.

It is almost axiomatic that wars nurture the development of xenophobia, especially on the part of the country that is dismembered. This particular war yielded its own particular variety—a virulent, almost pathological, Yankeephobia. The fears and hatred of the United States ran deep and were disseminated and popularized in the traditional Mexican *corrido*, the folk song of the common people. And the Yankeephobia was given additional respectability by the intellectual community's tirades against Yankee imperialism. But the war had at least one positive effect as well; it contributed to the development of a genuine nationalism in Mexico for the first time. This was a small consolation, perhaps, but not insignificant in a country still trying to become a nation. The Niños Héroes came to symbolize all that was best in the Mexican people, especially the young cadet Juan Escutia who reputedly wrapped himself in the Mexican flag and threw himself over the battlements rather than surrender to the enemy. Every September 13 pilgrimages are made to the monument erected in honor of the boy cadets at the entrance to Chapultepec Park.

The treaty signed at Guadalupe Hidalgo left a stunned and despondent Mexico, but the national humiliation brought no more unity than had the war itself. Local revolts kept the national government constantly on the defensive. Governors and presidents passed offices on to one another as though they were personal patrimony. In 1853 the Santanistas rallied for what turned out to be the last hurrah. With the $15 million from the United States already spent, President Santa Anna, not yet humbled by the defeats of his armies, decided that the treasury (and his own office) could be saved only by selling some more of Mexico to the United States. The United States wanted the Mesilla Valley (today southern New Mexico and Arizona) as it offered the best location for building a railroad to newly acquired California. Santa Anna agreed to sell and negotiated what is known in United States history as the Gadsden Purchase. For $10 million he alienated thirty thousand square miles of territory, but, more important, he alienated the liberal opposition so thoroughly that they would be rid of him for the eleventh and last time. The revolution the liberals proclaimed, the Revolution of Ayutla, was a new kind of movement, one in which for the first time ideology was clearly more important than personalities. It would usher in a new breed of Mexican politician who would try to set the country on a new course.

Recommended for Further Study

Bacarisse, Charles A. "The Union of Coahuila and Texas." *Southwestern Historical Quarterly* 61 (1958): 341–49.

Barker, Eugene C. *Mexico and Texas, 1821–1835.* Dallas: Turner, 1928.

Berge, Dennis E. "A Mexican Dilemma: The Mexico City Ayuntamiento and the Question of Loyalty, 1846–1848." *Hispanic American Historical Review* 50 (1970): 229–56.

Caruso, Brooke A. *The Mexican Spy Company: United States Covert Operations in Mexico, 1845–1848.* Jefferson, N.C.: McFarland & Company, 1991.

Castañeda, Carlos E. "Relations of General Scott with Santa Anna." *Hispanic American Historical Review* 29 (1949): 455–73.

Costeloe, Michael P. "Church–State Financial Negotiations in Mexico during the American War, 1846–1847." *Revista de Historia de América* 60 (1965): 91–124.

Graebner, Norman A. "The Mexican War: A Study in Causation." *Pacific Historical Review* 49 (1980): 405–26.

Griswold del Castillo, Richard. *The Treaty of Guadalupe Hidalgo: A Legacy of Conflict.* Norman: University of Oklahoma Press, 1990.

Hale, Charles A. "The War with the United States and the Crisis in Mexican Thought." *The Americas* 14 (1957): 153–73.

Hutchinson, C. Alan. "Valentín Gómez Farías and the Movement for the Return of General Santa Anna to Mexico in 1846." In *Essays in Mexican History*, edited by Thomas E. Cotner and Carlos E. Castañeda, pp. 169–91. Austin: Institute of Latin American Studies, 1958.

Jones, Oakah L., Jr. *Santa Anna*. New York: Twayne, 1968.

Lack, Paul D. *The Texas Revolutionary Experience: A Political and Social History, 1835–1836*. College Station: Texas A & M University Press, 1992.

McWhiney, Grady, and Sue McWhiney, eds. *To Mexico with Taylor and Scott, 1845–1847*. Waltham, Mass.: Blaisdell, 1969.

Miller, Howard. "Stephen F. Austin and the Anglo-Texan Response to the Religious Establishment in Mexico, 1821–1836." *Southwestern Historical Quarterly* 91 (1988): 283–316.

Pletcher, David M. *The Diplomacy of Annexation: Texas, Oregon and the Mexican War*. Columbia: University of Missouri Press, 1973.

Richmond, Douglas, ed. *Essays on the Mexican War*. College Station: Texas A & M University Press, 1986.

Robinson, Cecil, ed. *The View from Chapultepec: Mexican Writers on the Mexican-American War*. Tucson: University of Arizona Press, 1979.

Ruiz, Ramón Eduardo, ed. *The Mexican War: Was It Manifest Destiny?* New York: Holt, Rinehart and Winston, 1963.

Santa Anna, Antonio López de. *The Eagle: The Autobiography of Santa Anna*. Edited by Ann Fears Crawford, and translated by Sam Guyler and Jaime Platón. Austin: Pemberton Press, 1967.

Santoni, Pedro. "A Fear of the People: The Civic Militia of Mexico in 1845." *Hispanic American Historical Review* 68 (1988): 269–88.

Singletary, Otis. *The Mexican War*. Chicago: University of Chicago Press, 1960.

Smith, George W., and Charles Judah, eds. *Chronicles of the Gringos: The U.S. Army in the Mexican War, 1846–1848*. Albuquerque: University of New Mexico Press, 1968.

Smith, Justin H. *The War with Mexico*. 2 vols. Gloucester, Mass.: Peter Smith, 1963.

Tyler, Daniel. "Gringo Views of Governor Manuel Armijo." *New Mexico Historical Review* 45 (1970): 23–36.

Tyler, Ronnie C. "The Mexican War: A Lithographic Record." *Southwestern Historical Quarterly* 77 (1973): 85–110.

Vásquez, Josefina. "The Texas Question in Mexican Politics, 1836–1845." *Southwestern Historical Quarterly* 89 (1986): 309–44.

21

Society and Culture in the First Half of the Nineteenth Century

It is ironic, yet understandable, that historians seeking to understand how a people lived often rely upon the accounts of foreign travelers. That which is commonplace to a local inhabitant is often colorful or unique to a foreigner. The young Frenchman Alexis de Tocqueville related to the citizens of the United States much that they did not know about themselves, and a series of perceptive visitors to Mexico during the first half of the nineteenth century did the same for its people. While their analyses often reflected their own prejudices, their commentaries are invaluable. One has only to disregard their chauvinism and naïvely antiseptic view of the world to read these accounts with pleasure and profit.

Population

The Mexican Wars for Independence, although small in comparison with other world conflicts, nevertheless took their toll. Accurate casualty figures do not exist, but reliable estimates suggest that a half a million deaths, or about one-twelfth of Mexico's population, is not an exaggeration. The battles left tens of thousands of orphans, widows, cripples, and infirm. The dislocations occasioned by war were not quickly overcome. Impending engagements caused civilians to flee, shopkeepers to close their doors, mothers to pull their children out of school, and those who could afford it to hoard supplies. Many who left a town or city did not return, and families were permanently separated. Sev-

MEXICAN POPULATION GROWTH, 1800–50

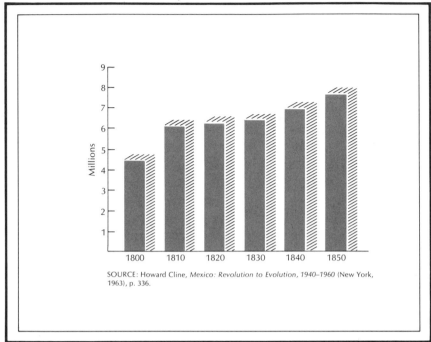

SOURCE: Howard Cline, *Mexico: Revolution to Evolution, 1940–1960* (New York, 1963), p. 336.

eral years after the wars ended visitors to Veracruz reported desolate, grass-grown streets and a generally ruinous appearance. Mexico's rate of population growth, which was rapid prior to 1810, leveled off dramatically for the next twenty years.

Although recovery was slow, change in the prevailing social structure was even slower. As one reads the accounts of travelers from the late colonial period and compares them to accounts in the nineteenth century, he is struck by how little conditions actually changed. To be sure, the gachupines were eliminated at the top of the social structure, but the criollos simply stepped into the vacuum. The population grew from 4.5 million in 1800 to over 7.5 million fifty years later, but the social categories of that population remained amazingly static.

Indian Pueblos

Mexico was a rural country in the first half of the nineteenth century. The Indians, making up over a third of the population, lived for the most part in thousands of tiny villages, socially and economically isolated from the remainder of the country. Although these pueblos varied physically from one climate to another, they presented a uniform cultural pattern. Pueblos were the most tradition-bound unit in Mexican society. Each maintained a system of internal government that had changed very little since the early colonial period. With the exception of an occasional parish priest, a white or mestizo rarely lived in the village. In south and central Mexico the huts were made of split reeds covered with thatched roofs. In the north adobe was more common, but in both cases dogs, pigs, and chickens shared the quarters with the family. In 1850 Carl Sartorius, a German natural scientist traveling in Mexico, drew a composite interior from the many Indian dwellings he had seen.

> Inside the hut, upon a floor of earth just as nature formed it, burns day and night the sacred fire of the domestic hearth. Near it, stands the *metate* and *metapile*, a flat and cylindrical stone for crushing the maize, and the earthen pots and dishes, a large water pitcher, a drinking cup and a dipper of gourdshell constitute the whole wealth of the Indian's cottage, a few rude carvings, representing the saints, the decoration. Neither table nor benches cumber the room within, mats of rushes or palm leaves answer for both seat and table. They serve as beds too for their rest at night, and for their final rest in the grave.[1]

Only the larger Indian towns had churches; practically none had schools. Spanish was unknown except to the select few. Medical care, as it existed, was entrusted to the questionable hands of the local *curandero*. The Indian agriculturalist lived outside the monetary economy. His own garden provided his daily needs—corn, beans, chile, and, occasionally, in some areas, squash and a few other vegetables and fruits. The craftsman sometimes had money pass through his hands as he could sell his wares at a neighboring market. But he was scarcely better off than the farmer in the next hut because, if his money did not vanish in momentary extravagance, he was easy prey to the unscrupulous gambler, pulque vendor, or highwayman as he returned to the pueblo.

The woman in the Indian village was much more than a housekeeper. Even when kept pregnant, she often worked in the field and shared in the physical labor as well as performed all the expected domestic functions. Foreign travelers frequently commented on the heavy loads of firewood the Indian women

---

1. Carl Sartorius, *Mexico about 1850* (Stuttgart, 1961), p. 69.

carried to the hut. Because daily life was difficult, the Indian woman was an integral part of the whole apparatus of survival; nevertheless, rural society was highly patriarchal and the male was the dominant, authoritarian figure in the household as well as in the community. The woman by tradition was expected to be faithful, reverential, and completely obedient in the entire conjugal relationship, and she seldom broke out of this mold, at least in public. She enjoyed a reputation of frugality and from the village tradition, for practical as well as metaphorical considerations, a phrase was born: *Donde las mujeres comen, las hormigas lloran* (Where women eat, the ants cry).

Rural Towns

The larger rural towns of from a thousand to perhaps thirty-five hundred housed primarily mestizos and Indians who had accommodated themselves to the Hispanic way of life. Spanish was the language of the street and the home. Market day, sometimes weekly and sometimes biweekly, attracted Indians by the hundreds from the surrounding pueblos and provided a festive air. The plaza would be filled with vendors trafficking in cloth, clothing, pottery, cutlery, trinkets, earthenware, and blankets, and with Indian women bent over charcoal fires preparing food for passersby. The day's work finished, the evening hours would be given over to gambling, cards, dancing, and perhaps wagering at the local cockfight. The towns generally had one or two *pulquerías* where hours could be idled away sipping the fermented juice of the century plant, the maguey. For those who found the local shop too depressing or the stench too unbearable, itinerant vendors with full jars on their heads made house calls. Invariably, the church was the most prominent architectural structure in the town. Adorned with a respectable number of saints and a few paintings, the gilded altar stood out in crass contrast to the impoverished surroundings.

If life in the rural towns was somewhat easier than in the Indian pueblo, it still left much to be desired. The streets were dirt, causing dust in the dry season and awful quagmires during the rains. The schools, in those few towns that had them, were equipped with the crudest of facilities, and the teachers were often only slightly more literate than those who sat at their feet. The one-story houses were constructed of adobe or stone and usually left unpainted. Travelers found no hotels, inns, or public

The village of Chalco, southeast of Mexico City, looked much as it had during the colonial period until the railroad passed through during the second half of the nineteenth century.

restaurants; they were generally put up for the night in the town hall or in the house of a relatively affluent resident who took pity on them. Joel Poinsett, a man who enjoyed his comforts, was not impressed with the facilities he found in a small Veracruz town as he was working his way to Mexico City in 1822.

> We supped on our cold provisions, and stretched ourselves out on the landlady's bed, which did not prove a bed of rest. It consisted only of canes laid lengthways, and covered with a blanket. This, and even the smell of raw meat, might have been endured, but we were visited by such swarms of fleas, sancudos, and musquitos [*sic*] that we rejoiced when we saw the light of day beaming through the cane enclosure that constituted the walls of the hut.[2]

The poor males in the towns had one concern that did not trouble those in the Indian village: like their counterparts in the larger cities, they were subject to the dreaded *leva*. A system of forced conscription directed at the uneducated masses (the Indi-

2. Joel R. Poinsett, *Notes on Mexico Made in the Autumn of 1822, Accompanied by an Historical Sketch of the Revolution* (New York, 1969), pp. 23–24.

ans in the villages were generally excluded simply because they did not speak Spanish), the leva was used by local commanders to fill their military quotas. Troublemakers, vagabonds, and prisoners were taken first, but as the demands of the Wars for Independence, and then the civil wars, continued in the first half of the nineteenth century, tens of thousands of illiterate males were picked up off the streets and pressed into long periods of service without even being allowed to return home to say good-by to wives, children, and parents.

Both in the Indian village and the small rural town there was little conception of the larger Mexico. Those loyalties that existed were to the locality—to the patria chica. Contact with the outside world was limited to the occasional traveler passing through or to a body of soldiers on horseback. Mexico was an abstraction not easily fathomed, and even neighbors in the next village were not really trusted.

Provincial Cities

One had to visit the larger provincial cities, generally the state capitals, to find any evidence whatsoever of culture, wealth, and sense of nationalism. Ranging in population from seven or eight thousand to seventy-one thousand (Puebla in 1852), these cities were well laid out in the classic Spanish pattern. The main streets, paved and well lighted, led into the central plaza surrounded on four sides by the main cathedral, the state or municipal office buildings, and several rows of good shops, generally under a stone arcade. In addition to an impressive selection of native products from many parts of the country, the shops also stocked foreign merchandise; the sizable merchant class thrived. The dreary, repetitive life of the smaller towns was averted by a bullring, a theater, traveling sideshows with tightrope walkers and jugglers, decent book stores, and a wide array of public and religious festivals. Unlike in the pueblo or the rural town, many criollo faces could be picked out of the crowd, and, in fact, if one wandered from the grisly slums to the better residential areas, the complexions of the property owners lightened appreciably. A few provincial aristocrats led lives of primitive plenty, but they were exceptions even among the criollo population. The schools were not bad, but they were only for the wealthy. In 1842, for example, there were only about thirteen hundred

A nineteenth-century woodcut depicting the central plaza of Mérida, Yucatán, about 1850.

schools in all of Mexico. Total enrollment was barely sixty thousand, or less than 1 percent of the population. Only about one-third of the schools were free.

Most of the state capitals grew rapidly in the first half of the nineteenth century. Aguascalientes doubled in population, and Mérida tripled. Veracruz and Guanajuato were almost alone in declining, the former because of constant warfare and heavy bombardments from naval vessels in the harbor and troops on the shore, and the latter because of the generally depressed character of the surrounding mines. By mid-century Puebla and Guadalajara were competing for second place on the nation's population rosters, with Puebla holding a slight lead.

Mexico City: The Rich and the Poor

Mexico City was a world unto itself, where all of the richest and many of the poorest in the country seemed to congregate. It was the focal point of the entire nation and exerted an influence on the country quite out of proportion to its size or its political

POPULATION OF SELECTED CITIES, 1794–1859

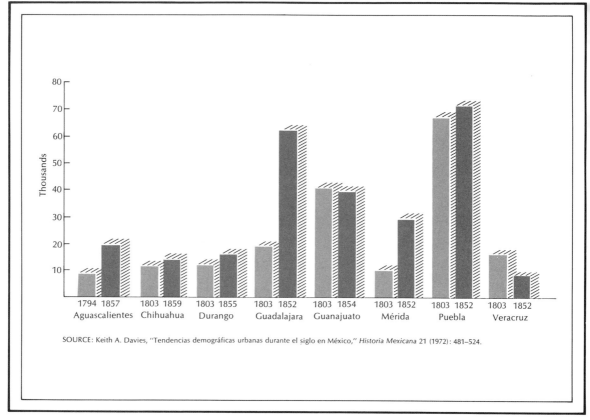

SOURCE: Keith A. Davies, "Tendencias demográficas urbanas durante el siglo en México," *Historia Mexicana* 21 (1972): 481–524.

prominence as the national capital. From a population of 137,000 at the turn of the century, it grew to 160,000 at the time of Independence and to 170,000 by 1852. Its wide, clean streets (better lighted than those in New York or Philadelphia) were crowded with expensive imported carriages, a status symbol among the rich. The main cathedral on the central plaza, the zócalo, could certainly rival any in Europe. The very bustle of the city set it apart from any other place in the republic. Street urchins hawked newspapers and pamphlets, scribes sitting on the sidewalks penned out messages for the illiterate, gentlemen on horseback paraded their finest mounts, and foreign artists gathered on park benches to sketch Chapultepec Castle or the snow-covered volcanoes of Popocatépetl and Iztaccíhuatl. In addition to numerous primary and secondary schools (again reserved largely for the affluent), Mexico City housed the venerable University, a school of mines, the Art Academy of San Carlos, a well-endowed botanical garden, libraries, museums, and a surprising number of public parks. By the middle of the century a thriving opera was an integral part of the city's cultural life. The literacy rate, for both men and women, rose modestly during the first half of the nineteenth century.

The Mexico City aristocracy, like their counterparts throughout the world, enjoyed their amenities and were conspicuous in their display of wealth. Many of the homes were truly luxurious. For security and privacy they were generally enclosed by high walls. Interior walls boasted fine imported tapestries. Aristocratic women, whether attending the theater, the opera, or even a high mass, displayed the immodest clothes designed by their favorite French *modiste*, and the men, while not outdoing their wives in fanciful dress, prided themselves on their ability to duplicate the latest fashions from Paris or London. The accumulation of wealth was greatly facilitated by the consistent intermarriage of *la gente decente*.

Describing a ball she attended in 1840, the wife of the Spanish minister to Mexico City noted the female costume.

> One, for example, would have a scarlet satin petticoat, and over it a pink satin robe, trimmed with scarlet ribbons to match. Another, a short rich blue satin dress, beneath which appeared a handsome purple satin petticoat. . . . All had diamonds and

The urban aristocracy, secular and religious, looked good and lived well in spite of the political chaos that engulfed Mexico in the twenty-five years following Independence.

pearls . . . I did not see one without earrings, necklace, and broach.[3]

The poorest of the poor Indian population was concentrated in the Mexico City districts of Santiago Tlatelolco and San Juan Teochtitlán, but they spilled over into other areas of the capital. When the upper class filed out of the theater or left the opera they could not fail to see the *léperos*. Described variously in the literature as beggars, vagabonds, panhandlers, riffraff, and outcasts, thousands of them could be seen in the streets of Mexico City every day. Although there were undoubtedly some fakers and reprobates among them, most were genuinely wretched physical specimens: children with bloated bellies, men and women crippled by war or accident or suffering serious genetic deformities, and those of all ages and both sexes in constant drunken stupors. Not unknown in the colonial period, the léperos became institutionally endemic in the first half of the nineteenth century. No foreign traveler to Mexico City failed to notice them. In 1822, for example, Joel Poinsett recorded:

> In front of the churches and in the neighborhood of them we saw an unusual number of beggars, and they openly exposed their disgusting sores and deformities to excite our compassion. I observed one among them wrapped in a large white sheet, who, as soon as he perceived that he had attracted my attention, advanced towards me, and unfolding his covering, disclosed his person perfectly naked and covered from head to heel with ulcers. . . . No city in Italy contains so many miserable beggars, and no town in the world so many blind.[4]

Life for the urban poor who worked rather than begged offered few material rewards. Domestic service, though remuneration was small, was highly sought by both sexes because it generally offered a clean room in which to sleep and food enough to sustain one well. In the streets the most visible employee was the *cargador*, a direct descendant of the tameme of the colonial period and nothing more than a human beast of burden. In the cities, and between the cities, the sight described by Edward Tayloe, Joel Poinsett's private secretary, was common.

> There are no carts or drays for the transportation of goods, so that everything is carried upon the backs of these poor creatures, who are enabled to carry a load of 300 lbs. by means of a leather band

3. Fanny Calderón de la Barca, *Life in Mexico: The Letters of Fanny Calderón de la Barca*, ed. Howard T. Fisher and Marion Hall Fisher (Garden City, N.Y., 1970), pp. 132–33.
4. Poinsett, *Notes on Mexico*, p. 73.

The cargadores, a legacy of the colonial tamemes, carried everything on their backs.

or strap, the cargador leaning forward at an angle of about 45°, the burden resting on the back supported by this strap. With so heavy a load they travel great distances, moving in a brisk walk or trot.[5]

But the cargador carrying supplies into the city or delivering on his back an imported French piano had little to complain about in comparison to his counterpart who was taken from the city to work in the mines. Employed to bring the ore out of the deep shafts and paid by the pound, the cargadores often carried extremely heavy loads on their backs as they worked their way up ladders. Accidents were frequent; the widows might sometimes be given a small share of the last load.

The Indians and mestizos, whether they lived in a small village or in Mexico City, constituted Mexico's labor force: farmers, servants, day laborers, cargadores, vendors, military recruits, craftsmen, and errand boys. Women worked as domestic servants, spinners in the textile mills, food preparers, waitresses, and as vendors on the streets and in the marketplaces. And much as in the colonial period, the labor force enjoyed no real rights that the white population felt obliged to respect. If accused of a crime, the word of the employer was generally taken and the worker had no recourse. Held in filthy prisons, often without

5. Edward Thornton Tayloe, *Mexico, 1825–1828: The Journal and Correspondence of Edward Thornton Tayloe*, ed. C. Harvey Gardiner (Chapel Hill, 1959), pp. 50–51.

formal charges, the father who stole a loaf of bread was confined in the same common cell with the convicted murderer, the young boy with the hardened criminal, and the pregnant prostitute with the mentally insane. If Mexican politicians in the first half of the nineteenth century did little to change the fabric of society, if they were strangers in their own land, it was not because the intelligentsia failed to urge a new course of action. And it was this very talented group of Mexican writers, musicians, artists, and scholars that made Mexico City so different from the remainder of the republic.

Intellectuals and Artists

The prime literary current in Mexico, as in all of Latin America, in the period following Independence was romanticism. Intensely concerned with freedom and individualism, the Mexican romantics, in both prose and poetry, set out to explore the meaning of their newly won independence and to foster a distinctive culture. They turned their backs on Spain and sought to define a new form of national artistic expression. But to understand and convey the nascent nationalism they had to understand their Mexico, and thus they began writing with great emotion and sentimentality about the aboriginal heritage, the physical environment, the wars of Conquest, and, of course, the recent movement for Independence.

In 1836 the young novelists, poets, and dramatists began meeting in the newly formed Academia de San Juan de Letrán, and for the next twenty years the academy midwifed the birth of Mexican national literature. Of the early romantic coterie who met there regularly, only two left indelible impressions on the romantic movement itself: Fernando Calderón (1809–49) and Ignacio Rodríguez Galván (1816–42). Calderón, a sometime soldier and liberal politician, experimented with lyric poetry, then turned to drama, both comedy and tragedy. His amusing satirical plays, some with veiled criticism of the Santa Anna dictatorship, were performed on the leading stages of Mexico in the 1840s and 1850s and earned him his place among Latin American romantic dramatists. Rodríguez Galván was a better poet than Calderón but less successful as a dramatist. Self-taught and constantly poverty stricken, he penned patriotic verse and described the Mexican landscape, but, most important, lamented the Spanish injustices against the Indian populations. In the process he won his position as Mexico's foremost lyrical poet of the first half of the nineteenth century. His *Profecía de Guatimoc* (1839) has been called the masterpiece of Mexican romanticism. The passion, the sentimentality, and the anti-Spanish, pro-Indian orientation are exemplified in the following verse:

> Nada perdona el bárbaro europeo.
> Todo lo rompe, y tala, y aniquila
> Con brazo furibundo.
> Es su placer en fúnebres desiertos
> La ciudades trocar (¡Hazaña honrosa!).
> Ve el sueño con desdén, si no reposa
> Sobre insepultos muertos.[6]

Mexican music, like its literature, rejected its Spanish parentage in the early post-Independence years. Nowhere is this more graphically illustrated than in the decision of José Mariano Elízaga (1786–1842), Mexico' most famous composer of the second quarter of the nineteenth century, to drop the title "Don" (signifying the Spanish gentleman) from his name. Once the Spanish army was driven back across the Atlantic, the composer informed the Mexican populace that henceforth he preferred to be called simply Citizen Elízaga.

By sheer chance Elízaga, during the Wars for Independence, was the piano tutor to Anna María Huarte, who subsequently married Agustín de Iturbide. With the defeat of the Spanish and the establishment of the empire, Iturbide brought him to Mexico City and underwrote the preparation of Elízaga's theoretical treatise, *Elementos de música*. But Elízaga is remembered less as a musical theoretician than for his original compositions and great organizing skills. His compositions were all designed for use in the churches, but the liturgy was much too radical for the conservative, Spanish-thinking hierarchy. As a result his masses and lamentations were never performed within the walls of the church. But Citizen Elízaga did encounter success in an important ancillary venture. In 1824 he founded Mexico's first philharmonic society, and the following year this group initiated

6.   The barbarous European forgives nothing.
   He breaks and he destroys and he annihilates
   With a frenzied aim.
      He takes pleasure in converting cities
   Into desert wastes (Honorable, indeed!).
   He views sleep with contempt if he cannot rest
   On unburied bodies.
   Quoted in John Lloyd Read, *The Mexican Historical Novel, 1826–1910* (New York, 1939), p. 59.

Mexico's first national conservatory, the Academia de Música.

The Mexican artistic community strove for a type of new nationalistic expression as well. Scarcely had the new republican government of Guadalupe Victoria been established when Pedro Patiño Ixtolinque, the general director of the Art Academy of San Carlos and Mexico's most famous sculptor, set to work on a monument honoring Father Morelos. An early American visitor to the academy was impressed with its facilities but, displaying a common anti-Catholic bias, also found fault: "Connected with this academy is a disgusting sort of work shop, where gods and saints are manufactured in wood and stone for the churches in town and country."[7]

Both in painting and the plastic arts the rejection of Spain and many things Spanish was abundantly evident, much more in the choice of theme, however, than in esthetic innovation. If the emulation of Spanish technique bordered on the abject, the selection of subject matter showed the budding of a Mexican consciousness. Although the young republic housed a few artists of unusual talent, the three decades following Independence were not particularly distinguished years for Mexican art. Within the century, however, the experimentation with native Mexican themes would pay dividends.

Of all the great Mexican historians of the post-Independence years only one—Lucas Alamán (1792–1853)—did not allow an anti-Spanish bias to vitiate his historical scholarship, but he was no less partisan than his ideological foes. A criollo aristocrat, a convinced monarchist, and a firsthand witness to the excesses committed by Hidalgo's Indian army in Guanajuato, he came to the defense of the Spanish officials and, by logical extension, of the Spanish crown. His five-volume *Historia de México* (1849–52) indicates clearly that he considered Cortés the conveyer of civilization and religion and the founder of the Mexican nation. Spain's imperial system in the New World was benevolent and progressive. The Wars for Independence, according to Alamán, had to be viewed in two stages. The early stage, that of Father Hidalgo, he censured as insane attack on property and civilization itself. But the conservative conclusion of the Independence movement by Iturbide could be rationalized. The mother country, defying all true Hispanic values, had turned disturbingly liberal with King Ferdinand's acceptance of the Constitution of 1812. The leadership of the Independence movement in the colo-

7. Tayloe, *Mexico, 1825–1828*, p. 58.

nies was actually defending traditionally Hispanic values but had to sever political ties to do so.

But Lucas Alamán stands almost alone in the historiography of the 1830s and 1840s. His contemporaries, Carlos María de Bustamante, Lorenzo de Zavala, and José María Luis Mora, viewed history quite differently. While they could not agree among themselves on many of the intricacies of the Wars for Independence, they all viewed the movement as a struggle against three centuries of Spanish tyranny. The Black Legend, stressing the avarice, inhumanity, and bigotry of the Spaniards, is not difficult to spot. The Independence movement was a repudiation of Spain, and the three histories mirroring this repudiation contributed in their own way to the cultural disavowal of the Hispanic part of the Mexican spirit. This pervasive anti-Hispanism was strongly reinforced by Spain's attempted reconquest in 1829.

The greatest weakness of Mexico's post-Independence culture was its essentially negative quality. The new nationalism was defined primarily in terms of what it was not—it was not Spanish. Mexico, the linguistic purist insisted, should be written not with the Spanish *j* but with an *x*, considered more Indian. The cultural nationalism expressed dissatisfaction with the past and, by extension, with much of the present but did not spell out precisely the direction in which Mexico ought to move. It was sufficient for the time being to propose that an anti-Hispanic intellectual emancipation should follow the political emancipation begun by Hidalgo. The more positive approach in defining the cultural essence of the new nationality would have to wait another generation of Mexican intellectuals and artists.

Recommended for Further Study

Arrom, Silvia Marina. *The Women of Mexico City*. Stanford, Calif.: Stanford University Press, 1985.

Berlandier, Jean Louis. *Journal to Mexico During the Years 1826 to 1834*. 2 vols. Austin: Texas State Historical Association, 1980.

Brushwood, John S. *Mexico in its Novel: A Nation's Search for Identity*. Austin: University of Texas Press, 1966.

Calderón de la Barca, Fanny. *Life in Mexico: The Letters of Fanny Calderón de la Barca*. Edited by Howard T. Fisher and Marion Hall Fisher. Garden City, N.Y.: Doubleday, 1970.

Caponigri, A. Robert, trans. *Major Trends in Mexican Philosophy*. Notre Dame, Ind.: University of Notre Dame Press, 1966.

Fernández, Justino. *Mexican Art*. London: Spring Books, 1965.

Ferry, Gabriel. *Vagabond Life in Mexico*. New York: Harper and Brothers, 1856.

Gilmore, N. Ray. "The Condition of the Poor in Mexico, 1834." *Hispanic American Historical Review* 37 (1957): 213–26.

Green, Stanley C. *The Mexican Republic: The First Decade, 1823–1832*. Pittsburgh: University of Pittsburgh Press, 1987.

Hale, Charles A. *Mexican Liberalism in the Age of Mora, 1821–1853*. New Haven, Conn.: Yale University Press, 1968.

Lyon, G. F. *Journal of a Residence and Tour in the Republic of Mexico in the Year 1826*. 2 vols. Port Washington, N.Y.: Kennikat Press, 1971.

Olivera, Ruth R., and Liliane Crete. *Life in Mexico Under Santa Anna, 1822–1855*. Norman: University of Oklahoma Press, 1991.

Poinsett, Joel R. *Notes on Mexico Made in the Autumn of 1822, Accompanied by an Historical Sketch of the Revolution*. New York: Praeger, 1969.

Rosaldo, Renato. "The Legacy of Literature and Art." In *Six Faces of Mexico*, edited by Russell C. Ewing, pp. 245–310. Tucson: University of Arizona Press, 1966.

Sartorius, Carl. *Mexico about 1850*. Stuttgart: F. A. Brockhaus Komm, 1961.

Shaw, Frederick J. "The Artisan in Mexico City (1824–1853)." In *Labor and Laborers through Mexican History*, edited by Elsa Cecilia Frost, Michael C. Meyer, and Josefina Zoraida Vásquez, pp. 399–418. Mexico City and Tucson: El Colegio de México and University of Arizona Press, 1979.

Stevenson, Robert. *Music in Mexico: A Historical Survey*. New York: Crowell, 1971.

Tayloe, Edward Thornton. *Mexico, 1825–1828: The Journal and Correspondence of Edward Thornton Tayloe*. Edited by C. Harvey Gardiner. Chapel Hill: University of North Carolina Press, 1959.

Ward, Henry G. *Mexico in 1827*. 2 vols. London: Colburn, 1828.

VI LIBERALS AND CONSERVATIVES SEARCH FOR SOMETHING BETTER, 1855-76

22

From Ayutla to the Reform

The Revolution of Ayutla

The Revolution of Ayutla, the armed movement that ousted Santa Anna from power in 1855, brought together some of the most original and creative minds in Mexico. Far from being ivory tower scholars, they were a group of writers and intellectuals who syncretized their own creative work with a spirit of public service, a sense of social consciousness, and a profound desire to see Mexico emerge at last from its long night of political shame. Humiliated by the war with the United States, they sought to re-evaluate the Mexican national conscience and redefine national goals. Secularly oriented and antimilitarist, they deeply mistrusted the church hierarchy and had little use for the ambitious, self-serving Mexican army.

Melchor Ocampo was introduced to the works of Voltaire, Rousseau, and Balzac while a student in Mexico, but when he traveled to Europe Pierre Proudhon caught his fancy. He translated many of the Frenchman's works into Spanish, and his editions were subsequently published in Mexico City. Returning to Mexico in 1842, Ocampo practiced law, began farming scientifically, cataloged flora and fauna, studied Indian languages, and collected one of the best private libraries in Mexico. He also made the decision to enter politics. In the 1840s and 1850s he served as governor of Michoacán and as a congressman in the national legislature. Shortly after the war with the United States he won acclaim when he became involved in a virtual death struggle with the clergy of Michoacán. The issue—the refusal of a local curate to bury the body of a penniless peón because the widow could not pay the sacramental fees—became a *cause célèbre* and was used effectively by Ocampo to demonstrate the ineptitude and decadence of the ecclesiastical effort.

Santos Degollado, another law professor in Morelia, shared Ocampo's interest in French philosophy and natural history. He followed Ocampo in the governorship of Michoacán for a term and, like his predecessor, spoke out against corruption in both church and state. In a short time he found himself in serious difficulties with the Santanistas in the Mexican capital. He took refuge in neighboring Jalisco and patiently bided his time.

Guillermo Prieto, the son of a Mexico City baker, received a scanty education but had a natural talent for writing. After serving as editor of the progovernment *Diario Oficial* for several years, disillusionment set in, and he moved to the camp of the opposition. In his new post as chief editor of *El Siglo xix* he experimented with new poetic forms and attacked Santa Anna. He was arrested on a number of occasions, only to be released when the Santanistas were thrown out of office temporarily. When the caudillo returned for the last time in April 1853, Prieto was sent back to his jail cell. Although he did not play an active role in the rebellion that would force Santa Anna from office two years later, he had, through his writings and personal example, popularized the cause.

But the real leader of the young, socially motivated intellectuals, and the personification of Mexican history in the two decades following mid-century, was Benito Juárez, a Zapotec Indian from the state of Oaxaca. Born on March 21, 1806, in the mountain village of San Pablo Guelatao, Juárez was orphaned at the age of three and raised by an uncle. Only a handful of the 150 villagers knew any Spanish, and Juárez had learned but a few words when, at the age of twelve, he left the adobe hut in the Zapotec village and walked forty-one miles to the state capital. An older sister working as a cook in Oaxaca City found employment for the boy in the home of a Franciscan lay brother who was a part-time bookbinder. In return for daily chores in the house and helping in the bindery, the Franciscan paid Juárez's tuition so that the boy could begin his schooling. At his benefactor's insistence he entered the seminary in Oaxaca but quickly realized that the priesthood was not his calling. He opted instead for the law and worked his way through law school.

The lawyer's certificate Juárez was awarded in 1831 not only sanctioned his judicial competence but, in effect, constituted his passport to politics. The year he was graduated he entered political life as an alderman in the Oaxaca City Council and subsequently served in the state legislature. But he did not abandon his career as a barrister and defended, without fee, groups of poor villagers challenging the exorbitant rates charged by the clergy for the sacraments or protesting the arbitrary dictates of the local hacendado class. Not notably successful in his legal campaign to make the lives of the poor easier, Juárez slowly began to realize that only structural alteration of the system could effect the changes he envisioned, and his liberalism strengthened.

When war broke out between Mexico and the United States, Juárez, a delegate in the national Congress in Mexico City, was recalled to his home state to serve a term as provisional governor. Later the defeated and disgraced Santa Anna sought refuge in Oaxaca, but Governor Juárez let him know he was not welcome there. While Santa Anna would never forgive him this indiscretion, the Oaxaqueños did, and in 1848 they elected Juárez to a full term as constitutional governor.

The Juárez governorship was far from revolutionary, but he did give the state a genuine lesson in energetic, honest, and sound management. Not only did he preside over the construction of fifty new rural schools and encourage female attendance, but he also sought to open the state up to world trade by rehabilitating the abandoned Pacific port of Huatulco (today Puerto Angel). Even more amazing for mid-nineteenth-century Mexico he cut back markedly on the huge state bureaucracy and was able to accomplish his material advances while making regular payments on the state debt. It was the kind of performance that was worthy of emulation on a broad scale.

Not long after Juárez completed his term as governor the Santanistas made their final entrance into Mexico City. Although Juárez had done little as governor to excite conservative passions, he was arrested by order of Santa Anna—the dictator certainly remembered Juárez's refusal to grant him asylum following the war. In addition, Melchor Ocampo's fiery public exchange with Santa Anna's clerical allies made this last regime hypersensitive to the liberal threat. After being kept in prison for several months, Juárez was escorted to Veracruz and subsequently placed aboard an English vessel bound for Havana and New Orleans. When he arrived in the Louisiana city he found that other Mexicans of his ilk had already taken refuge there. José María Mata and Ponciano Arriaga were active members of a revolutionary clique that was led by Melchor Ocampo. Juárez joined the exiles in plotting to overthrow the dictatorship when they decided to cast their lot with an old guerrilla chieftain, Juan Alvarez, then leading an antigovernment rebellion in the state of Guerrero. Early in 1854 they offered their support to Alvarez and sent him a statement of principles. A few months later Alvarez's lieutenants, Florencio Villareal and Ignacio Comonfort, published the *Plan de Ayutla*, which closely paralleled the statement of principles provided by exiles. After setting forth a long list of grievances against Santa Anna, the plan called for the convocation of a liberal junta to designate an interim president to replace the dictator.

The Revolution of Ayutla rapidly gained strength. In Jalisco, Santos Degollado gathered a formidable rebel army around him. In Nuevo León, Santiago Vidaurri and in Guanajuato, Manuel Doblado pronounced against the dictatorship and joined the Ayutla movement. The exiles in New Orleans helped with arms and ammunition, and in the early summer of 1855 they sent Juárez to Acapulco to join Alvarez as a political aide.

The Revolution of Ayutla enjoyed a wider base of support than most previous antigovernment movements. Santa Anna's indecisive attempts to ease up on his dictatorship dissuaded none of the enemy. The rebellions throughout the country were, at best, loosely coordinated but effective nevertheless. By August 1855 Santa Anna, his reputation tarnished and his popularity at its lowest ebb, recognized the futility of continuing the fight. He tendered his resignation and went into exile for the last time.

The Reform Laws

The government established in Mexico was composed primarily of luminaries of the Ayutla Revolution. Juan Alvarez became provisional president; Ignacio Comonfort, secretary of war; Melchor Ocampo, secretary of the treasury; Miguel Lerdo de Tejada, secretary of development; and Benito Juárez, secretary of justice. The provisional presidency of Alvarez marks the beginning of a period in Mexican history remembered as the Reform. For the first time since the Gómez Farías administration in 1833 the liberals set themselves in earnest to the task of destroying the sustaining structures of the conservative state.

The first significant piece of legislation to emerge from the Reform bore the name of the secretary of justice. *Ley Juárez*

Ignacio Comonfort (1812–63). A bureaucrat of minor importance for most of his life, Comonfort was thrust into the presidency in 1855 and found himself caught in the endless liberal-conservative struggle.

abolished the military and ecclesiastical fueros, the special dispensations exempting soldiers and clerics from having to stand trial in civil courts. Ley Juárez did not, as is sometimes contended, abolish all military and ecclesiastical courts; rather, it placed stringent restrictions on their jurisdictions. The ecclesiastical and military courts were now competent to sit only on cases involving the alleged transgression of canon or military law. If, on the other hand, a cleric or a soldier were charged with a violation of civil or criminal law, he would be required, like everyone else, to stand trial in a state or federal court.

The acrimony occasioned by Ley Juárez should not have come as a surprise. Mexico's entire historical experience belied the notion of a homogeneous and harmonious society. The church, with understandable emotion but scant logic, cried out that religion had again been attacked in Mexico. Conservatives throughout the country searched through attics and pulled out dusty old banners proclaiming *Religión y Fueros*. But, most important, the furor generated by the new law proved schismatic within the ranks of the newly victorious revolutionaries of Ayutla, and it did not take long to recognize that the movement itself represented disparate, if not contradictory, interests. The moderates (*moderados*) favored backing down, while the more staunchly liberals (*puros*) refused. Before the month was out President Alvarez and most of the cabinet had resigned. The presidency devolved on Ignacio Comonfort, who was more of a compromiser than a firebrand.

In June of 1856 President Comonfort's secretary of the treasury, Miguel Lerdo de Tejada, drafted an important new law that the radicals hoped would weaken the church and the moderates hoped would increase national revenues. *Ley Lerdo* prohibited ecclesiastical and civil institutions from owning or administering real property not directly used in day-to-day operations. The Roman Catholic Church could retain its church buildings, monasteries, and seminaries and local and state units of government their meeting halls, jails, and schools, but both had to divest themselves of other urban and rural property. The massive holdings the church had gradually acquired through the centuries were to be put up for sale at public auction.

Ley Lerdo indicates that neither the puros nor the moderados of the nineteenth century were thinking in terms of social revolution. The properties were not to be distributed to the landless peón but were to be sold. Only the wealthy or at least those in a position secure enough to obtain credit were able to buy. Even if an occasional peón could have obtained financing to purchase a small plot, threats of ecclesiastical penalty from the local priest were enough to dissuade him from pursuing the idea. The radicals were still making simple anticlericalism synonymous with progress, and the moderates were concerning themselves with administrative and economic reform. In practice, the enforcement of Ley Lerdo worked to the detriment of the rural masses. One of the civil corporations forced to sell its property was the *ejido*, the communal landholding of the Indian village. While the extent to which Indian communities lost their traditional lands has not been adequately studied, many were forced to turn over their properties for sale at the various auctions.[1] In the first six months property worth over $23 million had been adjudicated, $20 million of which had belonged to the church.

The reformers were not yet finished. In January 1857 President Comonfort signed into law a statute taking the powers of registry out of the hands of the church and giving them to the state. All births, marriages, adoptions, and deaths were henceforth to be registered by civil functionaries. At the same time cemeteries were taken out of church jurisdiction and placed under the control of a Department of Hygiene. Still another blow

1. Many of the generalizations about the Reform Laws have been brought into question in a provocative article by Charles R. Berry, "The Fiction and Fact of the Reform: The Case of the Central District of Oaxaca," *The Americas* 26 (1970): 277–90. Because we do not have comparable studies for other areas, however, we do not know whether the case of Oaxaca's central district is unique or whether the generalizations themselves are invalid.

at the church was struck a few months later. *Ley Iglesias* prohibited the church from charging high fees for administering the sacraments. The poor were to receive their sacramental blessings at no charge, and those who could afford to pay were to be charged modestly.

The Constitution of 1857

The internal tensions provoked by the Reform Laws were in full evidence when, as provided by the Plan de Ayutla, delegates met to draft a new constitution. Because the conservatives had opposed the Revolution of Ayutla, they were largely unrepresented in the constitutional assembly. The debates would be between moderados and puros.

The federal Constitution of 1857 in many ways was modeled after its ancestor of 1824. The major difference in political structure was provided by an article setting up a unicameral national legislature. For purposes of economy and efficiency the framers of the document believed that a single house was sufficient, but the main reason for switching from two houses to one was neither of these. Mexico's experience since the time of Independence, like that of most of Latin America, demonstrated the perils of executive dominance and legislative subservience. It would be better, many believed, to have one strong house, instead of two weak ones, as a bulwark to dictatorship. But Mexican history showed as well that a strong national government was mandatory if the country were to escape the perils of exaggerated regionalism. The Reform liberals were not nearly so federalist as some have believed. As recent scholarship has demonstrated, on a number of key issues they took powers away from the states and gave them to the government of the nation.[2]

The Constitution of 1857 represented much more of a liberal victory than its federal predecessor of 1824. Most of the liberal legislation of the Reform, including Ley Juárez, Ley Lerdo, and Ley Iglesias, was actually incorporated into the Constitution, and, in addition, Mexico was given its first genuine bill of inalienable rights. The first thirty-four articles of the document spelled out in detail equality before the law and freedom of speech, of the press, of petition, of assembly, of the mails, and of education. They further abolished slavery, other compulsory

2. Richard N. Sinkin, "The Mexican Constitutional Congress, 1856–1857: A Statistical Analysis," *Hispanic American Historical Review* 53 (1973): 1–26.

service, and all titles of nobility and guaranteed the rights to carry arms and to have bail and of *habeas corpus*.

The articles that prompted the most heated debate were, of course, those which in some way touched upon the religious issue. While the Constitution contained no article specifying freedom of religion, it did not establish Roman Catholicism as the state church and thus provided for the exercise of other cults. Church defenders had their opportunity to express their views on several articles of the bill of rights. Freedom of education, they argued, conflicted with Christ's directives to the priesthood to "go and teach all nations"; freedom from compulsory service suggested that nuns and priests could renounce their vows; and freedom of the press could invite all manner of attack against the church. The inclusion of Ley Juárez and Ley Lerdo brought the church defenders to their feet again, but they met with defeat after defeat. When the question of religious liberty itself reached the floor the moderates and the few conservatives allied to hand the puros their only major setback. Emotional attacks against Protestantism garnered some votes, eloquent rhetoric won others, while precise Jesuitical logic convinced still more. The sophistry of the argumentation could be, at one and the same time, technically correct and banefully absurd, as in the argument that religious toleration would nullify the abolition of slavery and allow thousands of Muhammadan immigrants to enter the Mexican republic with their concubines! Others warned that freedom of religion would lead to the disintegration of the family and eventually provoke rebellion and anarchy. The puros were gradually worn down. In the end a vote on religious freedom was never taken, as a majority of the delegates voted to remove the article from debate.

Did the church believe that its defenders had done a sufficient job? Most assuredly not. The Mexican hierarchy issued decree after decree in an attempt to nullify the new Constitution. Those Catholics who took advantage of Ley Lerdo by purchasing church property were threatened with excommunication as were those who swore allegiance to the objectionable articles of the Constitution. Bishop Clemente de Jesús Munguía of Michoacán and Archbishop Lázaro de la Garza of Mexico City specified that the faithful could not accept, among other articles, those which provided for freedom of education, freedom of speech, freedom of the press, freedom of assembly, and, of course, Ley Juárez and Ley Lerdo. Pope Pius IX lent the support of the Holy See when, in an extraordinary statement, he declared:

> The Chamber of Deputies, among the many insults it has heaped upon our Most Holy Religion . . . has proposed a new constitution containing many articles, not a few of which conflict with Divine Religion itself. . . . For the purpose of more easily corrupting manners and propagating the detestable pest of indifferentism and tearing souls away from our Most Holy Religion, it allows the free exercise of all cults and admits the right of pronouncing in public every kind of thought and opinion. . . . And so that the Faithful who reside there may know, and the Catholic world may understand, that We energetically reprove everything the Mexican government has done against the Catholic Religion . . . We arise our Pontifical voice in apostolic liberty . . . *to condemn, to reprove, and declare null and void the said decrees and everything else that the civil authority has done in scorn of ecclesiastical authority and of this Holy See.*[3]

Although many of the charges were palpably untrue, the strong reaction of the church created a real quandary for Mexicans. If they did not swear allegiance to the Constitution they would be considered traitors to the state, and if they did they would be heretics in the eyes of the church. The quandary was not merely theoretical, however. Civil servants who refused to take the oath of allegiance to the Constitution lost their jobs; soldiers who took it were not treated in Catholic hospitals; if they died they did not receive the last rites nor were they buried in the proper ground. Priests who offered the sacraments to communicants who had not forsworn the Constitution were suspended. By pitting brother against brother and father against son, the Reform Laws and the Constitution divided Mexican society into two hostile and completely uncompromising camps. As tensions mounted Mexicans realized that they were beyond pragmatic compromise and began girding themselves for yet another civil war.

The War of the Reform

The War of the Reform, the civil conflict that engulfed Mexico from 1858 to 1861, was in many ways the culmination of the ideological disputations, the shuffling of constitutions, the church-state controversies, and the minor civil wars that had shattered the peace periodically since Independence. Mexicans had not yet defined the kind of society they wanted to the satisfaction of one

3. Quoted in Lesley Byrd Simpson, *Many Mexicos* (Berkeley, 1952), pp. 244–45.

another, and the intense passions of the age precluded the possibility of a rapprochement without still another resort to arms. The war began, as most Mexican wars, with a new plan, this time the *Plan de Tacubaya*, proclaimed by conservative general Félix Zuloaga. Emboldened by promises of clerical and military support, Zuloaga promptly dissolved the Congress and arrested Benito Juárez, the chief liberal spokesman within the Comonfort government. Juárez had recently been elected chief justice of the Mexican Supreme Court, a position that, according to the new Constitution, made him next in line for the presidency should a vacancy occur in the top office. President Comonfort believed in compromise but proved himself unequal to the task of blending the diverse views. As he vacillated, liberals in the provinces announced their support of the Constitution and the Reform Laws it embodied. Finding himself caught between the two extremes and not really sure who were his friends and who his enemies, the president resigned. When the army declared Zuloaga as the new president, Juárez managed to escape north to Querétaro, where his liberal cohorts proclaimed him president. With two presidents, two governments, and two uncompromising ideologies, Mexico plunged headlong into the most passionate and horrifying civil war to date.

The opposing sides in the three-year war defy the simple classification historians have traditionally given. It was not Indians versus whites and the country versus the cities. While it is true that the clergy and the army generally supported the Zuloaga government in Mexico City, the Indian masses were found in both camps. Some Indian communities, convinced correctly that their ejido lands had been taken away by the liberals under Ley Lerdo, were persuaded that their future rested with the conservatives. Led by Indian caciques such as Tomás Mejía of Querétaro, they gave the conservatives an important source of strength scarcely counted on. But the conservatives' principal leadership came from the army generals such as Miguel Miramón and Leonardo Márquez. And the liberals certainly were not without Indian support of their own, as many leaders convinced their people that their interests would best be served by casting their lot with their fellow Indian, Benito Juárez. These chieftains placed themselves and their followers under the orders of liberal commanders Santos Degollado, Santiago Vidaurri, and Manuel Doblado.

The liberals eventually succeeded in establishing their capital in Veracruz, where they could control the customs receipts and obtain military supplies from the outside world. From there Juárez and his government issued manifestos damning the enemy, enticing support, seeking the recognition of foreign governments, and outlining military strategy. At the same time in Mexico City the Zuloaga administration declared the Reform Laws null and void, swore allegiance to the Holy See, took communion in public, and planned military campaigns.

For the first two years of the war the liberals had a hard time holding their own. The conservative army, better trained, equipped, and led, won most of the major engagements and held the most populous states of central Mexico. But when, in the early spring of 1859, General Miramón attempted to dislodge the liberals from Veracruz, he was beaten back. The fighting throughout the republic was vicious, and noncombatants were subjected to wanton depredation by overzealous commanders of both armies. The conservatives shot captured prisoners in the name of holy religion, and the liberals did the same in defense of freedom and democratic government. In a particularly intemperate incident after a battle for the control of Mexico City, General Márquez, flushed with victory, ordered the execution of all doctors and medical aides who had treated wounded liberal soldiers. For this daring bit of bravado he won himself the sobriquet *El Tigre de Tacubaya*. But the liberals were far from guiltless themselves. Churches were desecrated with childish enthusiasm. Priests who refused the sacraments to the liberal rank and file were placed summarily before firing squads.

The intensity of the military campaigns manifested itself in the political arena as well. The Juárez government issued a series of decrees from Veracruz that made the earlier Reform Laws seem innocuous by comparison. The liberals who had felt shortchanged by the Constitution would now be satisfied. Births and marriages were made civil ceremonies, all cemeteries were secularized, monastic orders were outlawed, no new nuns could be admitted to the nunneries, all church properties and assets were nationalized, the number of official religious holidays was curtailed, religious processions in the streets were severely limited, and, most important, church and state were separated. The reforms tried to rivet together a society in which the church would be indisputably subordinate to the state.

By 1860 the tide of the battle had turned in favor of the liberals. Juárez found two excellent field commanders in Ignacio Zaragoza and Jesús González Ortega, while the enemy unwittingly aided the liberal cause by bickering among themselves. In

August, Zaragoza and González Ortega combined their forces at Silao to hand General Miramón his first serious defeat. Within the next two months Oaxaca fell to the rebels, and Zaragoza gave General Márquez a stunning setback at Guadalajara. With the conservatives disheartened from the series of reverses, the final battle occurred three days before Christmas when González Ortega crushed Miramón's army of eight thousand at the little town of San Miguel Calpulalpan. The newly victorious army, some twenty-five-thousand strong, entered Mexico City to a tumultuous welcome on New Year's Day. Juárez arrived ten days later.

Recommended for Further Study

Bazant, Jan. *Alienation of Church Wealth in Mexico: Social and Economic Aspects of the Liberal Revolution, 1856–1857.* Cambridge: Cambridge University Press, 1971.

Berbusse, Edward J. "The Origins of the McLane-Ocampo Treaty of 1859." *The Americas* 14 (1958): 223–46.

Berry, Charles R. *The Reform in Oaxaca, 1856–1876: A Microhistory of the Liberal Revolution.* Lincoln: University of Nebraska Press, 1981.

Brading, D. A. "Liberal Patriotism and the Mexican Reforma." *Journal of Latin American Studies* 20 (1988): 27–48.

Broussard, Ray F. "Vidaurri, Juárez and Comonfort's Return from Exile." *Hispanic American Historical Review* 49 (1969): 268–80.

Cadenhead, Ivie E., Jr. *Jesús González Ortega and Mexican National Politics.* Fort Worth: Texas Christian University Press, 1972.

Johnson, Richard A. *The Mexican Revolution of Ayutla.* Rock Island, Ill.: Augustana College Library, 1939.

Knapp, Frank A., Jr. "Parliamentary Government and the Mexican Constitution of 1857: A Forgotten Phase of Mexican Political History." *Hispanic American Historical Review* 33 (1953): 65–87.

Knowlton, Robert J. *Church Property and the Mexican Reform, 1856–1910.* DeKalb: Northern Illinois University Press, 1976.

Olliff, Donathan C. *Reforma Mexico and the United States: A Search for Alternatives to Annexation, 1854–1861.* University: University of Alabama Press, 1983.

Powell, T. G. "Priests and Peasants in Central Mexico: Social Conflict during La Reforma." *Hispanic American Historical Review* 57 (1977): 296–313.

Roeder, Ralph. *Juárez and His Mexico.* 2 vols. New York: Viking Press, 1947.

Scholes, Walter V. *Mexican Politics during the Juárez Regime, 1855–1872.* Columbia: University of Missouri Press, 1957.

Sinkin, Richard N. *The Mexican Reform, 1855–1876: A Study in Liberal Nation Building.* Austin: Institute of Latin American Studies, 1979.

23

The French Intervention

With the War of the Reform finally over, Mexico desperately needed a period of uninterrupted peace. Juárez and the liberals needed time for reflection and for the convalescence of their war-torn country. The desolation left in the wake of the civil conflict showed on the landscape dotted with burned haciendas and mills, potted roads, unrepaired bridges, neglected fields, and sacked villages. But, more important, it was epitomized in the minds and bodies of tens of thousands of exhausted, crippled, and aggrieved Mexicans. Soldiers slowly drifted back to their villages to find no work. Bandits continued to infest the highways. Frustration set in quickly. Only the national government could be expected to smooth the transition, but the tired nation was to have no relief. The liberal victory in 1861 proved to be but a brief respite from the ravages of war. The armies would soon begin marching again, but on this occasion one would wear foreign uniforms.

Discontent

Among the numerous legacies bequeathed by the war there emerged a pronounced mistrust within the victorious liberal party. Although Juárez won the presidential elections held in March 1861, the liberals were badly split on many issues, especially on what type of punishment should be meted out to their erstwhile enemies. Some favored harsh retribution, but the president opted instead for a more conciliatory policy. Only a few

Benito Juárez (1806–72). The presidential terms of Mexico's most note-worthy politician of the mid-nineteenth century were disrupted by civil wars and foreign interventions.

bishops and leading conservative generals were not included in his sweeping amnesty declaration. The moderate stance he assumed presaged difficulties with radicals in the new Congress, men such as Francisco Zarco, Sebastián Lerdo de Tejada, Ignacio Altamirano, and Ignacio Ramírez. They could see little sense in treating the conservatives with kid gloves. Allied with the corrupt and exploitative clergy, had not these same conservatives been responsible for the holocaust from which Mexico had just emerged? Should not they be made to pay for their sins?

But President Juárez was not easily swayed, and he continued to be magnanimous in his use of the presidential power of commutation of sentences. Benito Juárez believed in the chastening impact of open debate. He considered opposition in an open forum a healthy political development in Mexico, and he would not muzzle the barbed criticism in the Congress. But congressional bickering in his own party, coupled with pressure from the opposition, prompted several cabinet resignations and kept the administration in a constant state of turmoil. On one occasion a congressional vote taken to demand Juárez's resignation lost by a single vote.

Troubled Finances and Foreign Intervention

In the final analysis, however, it was economic rather than political difficulties that precipitated the next war. Juárez inherited a bankrupt treasury and an army, a corps of civil servants, and a police force that had not been paid. The income from the sale of church property had been considerably less than expected because during the desperate days in Veracruz much of it had been sold at a fraction of its true worth. Commerce was stagnant, and most of the customs receipts were already pledged. The nation's transportation system was woefully inadequate, as merchandise was still being conveyed by pack mules, oxen, and human cargadores. Transportation was slow, costly, and inefficient.

In the spring of 1861 the monthly treasury deficit amounted to $400,000, and there was practically no currency in circulation. Worst of all, Mexico's European creditors began clamoring for the repayment of debts, some half a century old. Fully sensitive to the dangers his action might portend, Juárez declared a two-year moratorium on the payment of Mexico's foreign debt. Although he took care to stress that his action was not a repudiation, but simply a suspension in time of stress, the outcry in Europe was predictably anguished.

The large majority of the English, French, and Spanish claims were quite legitimate, for foreign citizens had suffered outrages and losses of life and property. Foreign legations had been destroyed and foreign silver shipments had been stolen on the roads from the mines to the ports.

On October 31, 1861, representatives of Queen Isabella II of Spain, Queen Victoria of Great Britain, and Emperor Napoleon III of France affixed their signatures to the Convention of London. The three nations agreed upon a joint occupation of the

Mexican coasts to collect their claims. The specific plan they envisioned was to occupy the customshouse at Veracruz and apply all customs receipts on the debt. Article II of the Convention pledged: "The high contracting parties bind themselves not to seek for themselves, in the employment of coercive measures foreseen by the present convention, any acquisition of territory, or any peculiar advantage, and not to . . . impair the right of the Mexican nation to choose and freely to constitute the form of its own government."[1]

England and Spain were apparently sincere in their pledge not to seek special advantage in Mexico, but France had other plans. The enigmatic Louis Napoleon Bonaparte, nephew of Napoleon I, won the presidency of the French republic in 1848 but craved for the imperial status of his famous uncle. Ever since 1852, when a French plebiscite approved the title and dignity that he desired, Emperor Napoleon III had embarked upon an aggressive foreign policy. In the name of the Second French Empire he reinforced earlier claims to Algeria, established a protectorate in Indochina, landed troops in Lebanon, founded French colonies on the west coast of Africa, and helped to defeat Russia in the Crimean War. But, most important, the emperor dreamed of planting the Tricouleur in the New World and of reincarnating France's lost empire in America. By coming to the rescue of the church in Mexico he could also hope to curry favor with the strong Catholic element in France. The Mexican imbroglio seemed to present him with a perfect opportunity.

The Spanish troops actually landed in Veracruz first. In December 1861 some six thousand Spaniards disembarked in the port. Seven hundred British marines and two thousand French troops arrived early the next month. The commissioners of the three nations initiated a series of conferences during the course of which it became obvious that the French harbored notions of conquest. Acrimonious notes were exchanged between the three governments, and the queens of Spain and Great Britain decided to order their respective troops home.

The French Occupation

Within a month after the Spanish and British withdrawal the French army, reinforced with an additional forty-five hundred

---

1. The Spanish text of the Convention is reproduced in Ernesto de la Torre Villar et al., eds., *Historia documental de México* (Mexico, 1964), 2: 314–15.

Porfirio Díaz as a young man. Later to serve as president of Mexico for a third of a century, Díaz was catapulted to national fame because of his role in the victory over the French on May 5, 1862.

troops, began to march inland on its war of occupation. The French minister in Mexico City informed the invading commander, General Charles Latrille, that the French would be welcomed with open arms in Puebla and that the local clergy would not only shower them with magnolia blooms but would offer a special Te Deum in their honor. But Puebla, although conservative and proclerical, was not to be such an easy prize. President Juárez had assigned the defense of the city to General Ignacio Zaragoza. Encountering unexpected opposition on the morning of May 5, 1862, Latrille attacked recklessly, and within two hours the French had expended half of their ammunition. The French troops, many weakened by the affliction that sometimes smites the foreign visitor to the Mexican countryside, did not acquit themselves well. General Zaragoza, on the other hand, managed his troops with rare aplomb. The decisive maneuver of the day was carried out by young Brigadier General Porfirio Díaz, commanding the Second Brigade. Late in the afternoon Díaz repelled a determined French assault on Zaragoza's right flank. The dejected invaders, many veterans from more glorious days in Crimea, retreated to lick their wounds in Orizaba. May 5 —*Cinco de Mayo*—would be added to the national calendar of holidays in honor of the Mexican victory.

Not all Mexicans rejoiced at the news of the French defeat. Many conservative monarchists and just as many church officials not only succored the recuperating French army but openly exhorted other Mexicans to lend assistance. President Juárez was furious that priests were using their pulpits to urge their communicants to collaborate with the enemy against his godless government. On August 30, 1862, he issued the following presidential decree:

> In use of the broad powers with which I have been invested, I have found it proper to declare that
>
> Article 1: Priests of any cult who, abusing their ministry, excite hate or disrespect for our laws, our government, or its rights, will be punished by three years' imprisonment or deportation.
>
> Article 2: Because of the present crisis all cathedral chapters are suppressed, except for that of Guadalajara because of its patriotic behavior. . . .
>
> Article 3: Priests of all cults are forbidden from wearing their vestments or any other distinguishing garment outside of the churches. . . . All violators will be punished with fines of ten to one hundred pesos or imprisonment from fifteen to sixty days.[2]

Upon hearing of the disaster at Puebla, Napoleon, with a sizable reservoir of manpower to draw upon, ordered some thirty thousand reinforcements. It took fully a year before the French army was prepared to march again. Once more they encountered their heaviest resistance at Puebla, but on this occasion the result would be quite different. On the untimely death of General Zaragoza, Juárez had placed General Jesús González Ortega in charge; the new commander immediately began constructing a series of fortifications around the city. In the middle of March the French encircled Puebla and launched a heavy bombardment. The mortars and artillery pounded away for days. Only when the walls surrounding the city had been reduced to rubble did the French infantry attack, but they were beaten back by the Mexican defenders. The siege that ensued lasted almost two months. Juárez's plans to resupply and reinforce the city were unsuccessful, for the invaders were able to interdict and repel the supply trains sent out from Mexico City. With the civilian and military population of Puebla finally reduced to nourishing themselves on rodents, pets, and leaves, González Ortega agreed to turn the city over to the French.

2. Quoted in Ernesto de la Torre Villar, *La intervención francesa y el triunfo de la república* (Mexico, 1968), 2: 159.

President Juárez realized that the fall of Puebla opened the doors to Mexico City, but he initially resolved to make a final stand in the capital. Only after consulting with his leading military advisers did he admit that the lack of troops available to him made the defense of Mexico City impossible. On May 31, his decision to evacuate Mexico City well known, he received a strong vote of confidence and a grant of extraordinary powers from the Congress. He answered by assuring the Congress that the evacuation of the capital was not tantamount to abandoning the fight. "Adversity," he exhorted the deputies, "discourages none but contemptible peoples."[3] As Juárez, his cabinet, and what was left of his army withdrew for San Luis Potosí, the French army entered the Mexican capital unopposed. The Te Deum that had been promised in Puebla over a year before was now offered in the great cathedral in Mexico City.

The New Government

Much of Mexico's conservative leadership was less concerned with their country's recent loss of sovereignty than with how the conservatives might profit from the demise of Benito Juárez and his liberal government. It did not take them long to learn. On June 16, 1863, the French commander selected a provisional government consisting of thirty-five Notables. The conservative orientation of the group was clearly manifest when it selected its executive triumvirate: General Juan Almonte, a disgruntled Santanista who had already met secretly with Napoleon in Paris to peddle monarchist schemes; General Mariano Salas, who had previously served the conservatives as provisional president of the republic during the era of Santa Anna; and Pelagio Antonio de Labastida, the bishop of Puebla and archbishop-elect of Mexico, who had been exiled to Europe by Ignacio Comonfort for opposing the Reform Laws.

Napoleon III had already made up his mind about the future of Mexico. Having conferred with numerous conservative Mexican émigrés, he had decided that if a monarchy was good for France, it would be good for Mexico as well. The French emperor and his conservative Mexican allies agreed that the Austrian archduke, Ferdinand Maximilian of Hapsburg, would be a perfect emperor. Napoleon had discussed the possibility with Maximilian even before the Convention of London. In October

3. Quoted in Charles Allen Smart, *Viva Juárez!* (London, 1964), p. 276.

1863 a delegation of Mexican conservatives visited Maximilian at Miramar, his magnificent palace on a promontory overlooking the Adriatic near Trieste. The Mexicans, led by José Miguel Gutiérrez Estrada, a monarchist for many years, and Father Francisco Javier Miranda, leader of the arch-conservatives, offered Maximilian the crown on behalf of the Assembly of Notables. Maximilian accepted only on the condition that his emperorship be approved by the Mexican people themselves. As strange as his stipulation must have sounded to the conservative monarchists, they agreed to indulge Maximilian in this folly. The plebiscite, held under the auspices of the French army and among the illiterate and indifferent masses, was a farce; when Maximilian was informed that the Mexican people had voted overwhelmingly in his favor, he accepted the throne.

Before leaving for Mexico, Maximilian entered into an agreement with his benefactor, Napoleon III. The Convention of Miramar pledged the new Mexican emperor to pay all expenses incurred by the French troops during their fight for control of the country. Maximilian also agreed to pay the salaries of the French troops, twenty thousand of whom were to remain in Mexico until the end of 1867, and to assume responsibility for payment of all the claims. In return Napoleon gave Maximilian full command over the French expeditionary force in Mexico. The new emperor, by signing the Convention of Miramar, had tripled Mexico's foreign debt before even setting foot on Mexican soil. But Maximilian was eager to begin a new life in a new world. He had his wife Charlotte hire a Spanish tutor; after the first lesson she had mastered a few salutations and had learned that her name henceforth, would be Carlota.

The Arrival of the Monarchs

Ferdinand Maximilian Joseph and Marie Charlotte Amélie Léopoldine arrived in Veracruz aboard the Austrian frigate *Novara* at the end of May 1864. He was thirty-two years old and she only twenty-four when they set out to mount the imperial throne. The most distinguished blood of Europe ran through their veins. He was descendant from the Josephs, Leopolds, and Francis of Austrian Hapsburg fame and ultimately from Charles V, and she from Queen Louise of Orléans, Louis Philippe, and the French Bourbons. They were products of European education at its best, schooled in the etiquette of court life, and accustomed to the niceties, proprieties, and extravagances of Viennese aristocratic society; their first glimpse of Mexico came as a shock.

Veracruz was not fondly remembered by visitors in the 1860s. Though carefully laid out, it was a dirty, depressing, and disease-ridden town of fewer than ten thousand where the flies never slept. In the hot, sultry temperature, the surrounding swamplands festered with mosquitoes carrying malaria and yellow fever. Hardly a visitor failed to note the horrible *zopilotes*, the black birds that hovered over the entire town. They constituted, in effect, the only garbage collection system in the port.

The welcome the emperor and empress received in Veracruz was as cold as the weather was hot. Traditionally liberal, the Veracruzanos refused to come out of their whitewashed adobe houses to greet their new monarchs. The dignitary scheduled to meet the couple, General Juan Almonte, arrived late. By the time the small royal party, accompanied by a few minor French officials and conservative leaders dispatched from Mexico City, reached the railroad station to begin the tedious journey, Carlota was in tears. As the train wound its way toward Mexico City, the weather cooled and the scenery improved. But the railroad tracks ended at the little pueblo of Totalco, and the royal party made the rest of the trip by stage. Maximilian had brought his own ornate carriage from Vienna, and, while it would catch many eyes on the good streets of Mexico City, it was scarcely designed for the atrocious tracks that passed for roads in the mountains of rural Mexico. After several breakdowns the imperial party wisely moved from the carriage to the stage for the remainder of the journey The carriage would be saved for the triumphal entry into the capital. Cordially received in Córdoba, Orizaba, and Puebla, the cavalcade finally reached Mexico City on June 12. On their way into the city they stopped to hear mass at the Basílica de Guadalupe. Maximilian had been advised that it would be wise for the blond Austrian to pay his obeisance early to the brown virgin. Not only was the appeal to the Indian masses obvious, but the clergy was pleased as well. Eleven Mexican prelates released a pastoral letter proclaiming that the days of godless radicalism were over.

Because the national palace was deemed unsuitable, the royal family established their magnificent imperial court at Chapultepec Castle, built originally for the Spanish viceroys at the end of the eighteenth century. Maximilian's salary was set at $1,500,000 annually, with an additional $200,000 for Carlota. But unlike Agustín I, Mexico's first emperor, Maximilian made

A mass was celebrated for Maximilian and Carlota when they reached Mexico City after the difficult journey from Veracruz.

himself accessible to the people. Once a week he opened the palace to his subjects, and in many small ways he tried hard for acceptance. To acquaint himself with Mexico's problems he toured the provinces and, on occasion, even donned the regional costume and ate the local food. Upon his return he shocked his conservative friends by suggesting that many priests he had met could profit from some basic lessons in Christian charity.

Believing that magnanimity would serve him well and win him converts, Maximilian declared a free press and proclaimed a general amnesty for all political prisoners serving terms of less than ten years. When aides suggested to him that a marble arch should be built and dedicated to Empress Carlota, he demurred and countered with the suggestion that a new monument honor Mexican Independence.

The emperor was pleased with the first few months of his reign, especially when diplomatic recognition began to come in from Europe. And before he fully realized that his conservative backers had placed him in a completely untenable position, he was also pleased with his new life. In the summer he wrote his younger brother an enthusiastic letter.

I found the country far better than I expected . . . and the people far more advanced than supposed at home. Our reception was cordial and sincere, free from all pretence and from that nauseating official servility which one very often finds in Europe on such occasions. The country is very beautiful, tropically luxuriant in the coast lands. . . . The so-called entertainments of Europe, such as evening receptions, the gossip of teaparties, etc., etc., of hideous memories, are quite unknown here, and we shall take good care not to introduce them. The Mexicans only enjoyment is to ride about his beautiful country on his fine horse and go to the theatre frequently; I too naturally treat myself to the latter.[4]

Internal Divisions and External Interference

But Maximilian's position was scarcely as idyllic as he imagined. His first serious problem, strangely enough, came from his conservative supporters rather than from the liberals who had been driven out of Mexico City to make room for him. The conservatives, led by Juan Almonte, naturally expected that the emperor would immediately set about to suspend the Reform Laws and return the church properties seized by Benito Juárez. Archbishop Labastida called upon Maximilian early to remind him of the need for the prompt restitution of church lands. When a papal nuncio arrived from Rome with credentials from the pope and a list of demands, the conservatives believed that the church question would be promptly settled to their complete satisfaction. But Maximilian refused to entertain seriously the pontiff's exactions. The emperor was a Mason and, in many respects, fancied himself a liberal and certainly not in the mold of the Hapsburg champions of the Counter Reformation. He would countenance no demands from Rome. Hoping to attract some liberal support to his government he not only refused to return church lands, re-establish Roman Catholicism to the exclusion of all other creeds, and decree education a church monopoly, but, when he found himself in a financial squeeze similar to that of his republican predecessors, he even levied several forced loans against the church. If conservative enthusiasm was dampened by Maximilian's church policy, his allies were aghast when he named José Fernando Ramírez, a moderate liberal, as secretary of foreign relations.

The liberals could well understand sectarian quarrels and

4. Quoted in Egon Corti, *Maximilian and Charlotte of Mexico* (New York, 1928), 2: 431–32.

were not impressed; few of them were persuaded that Maximilian's mildly anticlerical posture and winks at liberalism should occasion a change of attitude on their part. A monarchy, supported by foreign arms and headed by a foreigner, had been established in Mexico, and it was their duty as honorable citizens to overthrow it. Maximilian's position was not unlike that of Ignacio Comonfort a few years before. By attempting to find a middle ground between the liberals and the conservatives, he succeeded only in alienating both.

When Juárez withdrew from Mexico City before the French onslaught, he established his government first in San Luis Potosí and then in Chihuahua. But French troops sent out by Marshal François Bazaine pushed him and his small loyal army north until it found refuge only in El Paso del Norte (today Ciudad Juárez) on the United States border. But the French hold on the country was tenuous as the Juaristas quickly taught the Europeans the meaning of guerrilla warfare. While the French invariably won the few battles that were fought, they could not completely pacify the country, nor could they hold onto territory once the troops moved on.

In late 1864 and early 1865 the empire was at its strongest. Bazaine defeated Porfirio Díaz in Oaxaca and temporarily secured that pivotal southern state. In October of 1865 Maximilian's French advisers informed him, incorrectly, that Juárez had finally given up the fight and had fled the country, seeking refuge in the United States. Believing that the country was almost completely pacified and desiring to avoid a relapse into civil war, the emperor was importuned to issue a controversial and extremely significant decree. The death penalty was made mandatory for all captured Juaristas still bearing arms, to be carried out without appeal within twenty-four hours of capture. The October decree was implemented a few days after it was issued when two republican generals were captured by the French army and put to death. Maximilian had been given and had followed bad advice. In signing the decree he had also signed his own death warrant. Juárez had not abandoned the country and repeatedly promised his supporters that he had no intention of giving up the fight. He realized, however, that he needed substantial help and was gradually convinced by his cabinet and advisers that it could come only from north of the Rio Grande.

The government of Abraham Lincoln had been more than casually interested in France's Mexican venture from the outset. In 1823 President Monroe had intoned his famous doctrine declaring that the American continents were henceforth not to be considered as subjects for future colonization by European powers; any attempt to do so would be viewed as an unfriendly act toward the United States. In the years subsequent to its promulgation the Monroe Doctrine was disregarded incessantly by various countries in western Europe but never so blatantly as in 1862 and 1863 when the French army overran central Mexico, overthrew the Juárez government, and placed Maximilian on the Mexican throne. But Napoleon III had chosen his time well; six months prior to the signing of the Convention of London the shots fired at Fort Sumter had initiated the Civil War in the United States. Convulsed with difficulties far more serious than ever before, the government in Washington was able to do little but look askance and issue a few mild protests. The Union hardly wanted to push France into an alliance with the Confederacy. When it came time to consider recognition of the Mexican empire, however, the Lincoln administration refused. Juárez's government in exile was considered by Washington to be the legitimate representative of the Mexican people.

As the fortunes of the North improved and those of the Confederacy declined, Juárez embarked upon an all-out campaign to secure assistance from the United States. He was encouraged when in April of 1864 the House of Representatives passed a resolution declaring that the Congress of the United States was not an indifferent spectator to the deplorable events transpiring in Mexico and that it was not U.S. policy to view with inaction the establishment of monarchical governments, backed by European powers, on the ruins of republican ones. Juárez charged the head of the Mexican legation in Washington, Matías Romero, a young but forceful diplomat, with the task of securing some implementation of the resolution; at approximately the same time he dispatched an entire team of secret agents to the United States to secure financial and military aid and to begin recruiting American soldiers of fortune. Romero, who had been partially responsible for securing the earlier House resolution, opened discussions with representatives of the Lincoln administration. Progress was slow, and before any firm resolution could be reached, Lincoln was assassinated and Romero was forced to open a new round of negotiations with the government of Andrew Johnson.

The end of the Civil War brought about a major change in United States policy. The North had over nine hundred thousand men under arms when Lee surrendered to Grant at Appomattox, a formidable fighting force as the South had discovered. No longer fearful of offending the French, Secretary of State William Seward began applying pressure to Napoleon III. At the same time the government in Washington, prompted by Romero, closed its eyes to violations of neutrality legislation and allowed Juarista agents to purchase arms and ammunition in California for shipment to west coast Mexican ports under republican control. If an occasional zealous official tried to obstruct the shipments, Romero would use his considerable influence with Secretary Seward or General Grant to put the offending official in his proper place. Within a matter of a few months some thirty thousand muskets reached the Juaristas from the Baton Rouge arsenal alone. Juárez's agents were also allowed to pass back and forth across the international line without hindrance from customs officials or border patrols. Some three thousand Union veterans, attracted by good pay and a promised land bonus, joined the Juarista army. With the diplomatic atmosphere heating up, with the military potential of Juárez's army considerably bolstered, and with a new threat to French security in Europe in the form of Otto von Bismarck, Napoleon made his belated decision to begin withdrawing his foreign legion in November 1866.

The gradual withdrawal of the French troops in late 1866 and early 1867 left Maximilian in an impossible position. He sent a series of envoys to Paris to convince Napoleon that he should honor the commitment he had made in the Convention of Miramar. When the envoys reported that the French emperor would not admit the error of his ways, Maximilian toyed with the idea of abdicating his throne. Carlota, however, appealed to his sense of Hapsburg dignity and convinced him that he must stay on. She would travel to Europe herself and appeal directly to Napoleon for a countermand of his withdrawal order. But Napoleon was no less obdurate with her than he had been with the previous emissaries. She thereupon traveled to Rome for an audience with Pope Pius IX. While she pleaded with the pope to use his influence with Napoleon, he wondered why Maximilian had taken no steps to restore the church lands in Mexico. Carlota's impassioned plea was rejected, and she soon lost her mind.

The Republican Victory and the Aftermath

Spurred on by the fortuitous combination of events in Europe and America and recognizing that the underpinnings of the empire were collapsing, Juárez and his republican army assumed the offensive in the spring of 1866. General Luis Terrazas captured Chihuahua City while General Mariano Escobedo shattered a strong French column between Matamoros and Monterrey. During the summer the republicans recaptured Saltillo, Monterrey, Tampico, Guaymas, and Durango, and by the end of the year they added Guadalajara and Oaxaca to the list of reoccupied territories. With the French army pulling out of Mexico, the treasury empty, and Carlota sick in Europe, Maximilian, perhaps thinking that he could plead French deception to the world, for a second time planned to abandon his thankless task and abdicate. But again his pride overshadowed his reason, and he decided to make one last stand.

Mexico's second empire collapsed in the colonial city of Querétaro while the last installment of French troops were marching toward Veracruz for their European embarkation. Maximilian decided to take command of a few thousand Mexican imperial troops but quickly found himself surrounded by a republican army four times as strong. Hostilities commenced on February 19, 1867. Although prolongation of the inevitable made little sense, the imperial defenders inside the walls of the city held off the attackers for almost a hundred days. By the second week in May, with the aqueduct carrying the city's water supply cut and food and ammunition in short supply, the situation was desperate. Although careful plans had been laid for the emperor's escape, he preferred the solemn dignity of surrender. Maximilian turned over his sword to General Escobedo on May 15.

Juárez immediately decided Maximilian's fate; the emperor would be tried by court-martial, and the state would request the death penalty. In spite of a rain of pleas for clemency from European monarchs, New World presidents, and delegations of tearful, supplicating women, Juárez remained adamant. Thirteen accusations were leveled against Maximilian, including violation of Mexico's sovereignty, but the most important was that he had signed the infamous decree of October 1865 resulting in the death of innumerable Mexican citizens. The chief defense attorneys, Mariano Riva Palacio and Rafael Martínez de la Torre, were brilliant advocates; they ardently denied the competence of the court to sit on the case and argued that the leniency shown to Jefferson Davis in the United States after the Civil War should serve as a precedent. The verdict, however, was based more on political considerations than on legal ones. After the War of the Reform Juárez had been magnanimous in his use of executive

A contemporary woodcut depicting the execution of Maximilian on the Hill of the Bells outside Querétaro.

clemency, and he now believed that Mexico had paid a terrible price as a result. He wanted to demonstrate to the world that Mexico's existence as an independent nation would not be left to chance or to the goodwill of foreign heads of state. Three members of the six-man court voted guilty, with banishment from Mexico for life. The other three voted guilty, with the death penalty. The tie-breaking decision fell to the president of the court, Lieutenant Colonel Platón Sánchez. Fully cognizant of Juárez's wishes, he voted for the death penalty. The final appeal to President Juárez was automatic, as was his response: "The petition for clemency, and all other requests for lenience, having been carefully examined, as the gravity of this case demands, the Honorable President of the republic makes known: that he cannot honor them as the most serious considerations of justice and the need to assure public peace require that he reject them."[5]

On the morning of June 19, after having received the last sacrament, Maximilian was led by his executioners to the Hill of the Bells on the outskirts of Querétaro. There he was shot

5. Quoted in Vicente Riva Palacio, *México a través de los siglos* (Mexico [1940?]), vol. 5, pt. 2, p. 855.

along with several Mexican conservative officers who had been tried with him. As tragic and senseless as the event might have appeared from the calm of abroad, fifty thousand Mexicans had just as surely lost their lives fighting the French.

The price of the French Intervention, however, cannot be assessed solely in terms of the lives lost. The attempt to tamper with Mexico's sovereignty had ended in dismal failure, and, as a result, Mexican nationalism and self-esteem began to grow perceptibly for the first time. The United States had helped in a small way but it had been Mexicans who drove out the French. The republican victory was, at least in part, a vindication of the Constitution of 1857 and the principles it had espoused. The clerical party had been defeated, and although the country had not seen the last of its major church-state struggles, the church and its defenders in the future would seek goals much more modest than the establishment of a theocracy. The conservatives were discredited, at least for the time, because liberalism in the popular mind became identified with moral authority and independence from foreign aggression.

On the other hand, the Intervention and the empire, in spite of Maximilian's best efforts, had left Mexican commerce, industry, and agriculture in a quagmire. Education had suffered immeasurably, and the treasury was still empty. The years without a single, central authority reinforced tendencies toward localism and blunted the nationalism that the victory began to abet. Thousands of armed men roamed the countryside. In short, the dramatic events of the years 1861 to 1867 contributed markedly to Mexico's lack of political stability and economic growth in the nineteenth century.

Recommended for Further Study

Anderson, William Marshall. *An American in Maximilian's Mexico, 1865–1866: Diaries of William Marshall Anderson.* Edited by Ramón Eduardo Ruiz. San Marino, Calif.: Huntington Library, 1959.

Barker, Nancy Nichols. *The French Experience in Mexico, 1821–1861: A History of Constant Misunderstanding.* Chapel Hill: University of North Carolina Press, 1979.

Blasio, José Luis. *Maximilian, Emperor of Mexico: Memoirs of His Private Secretary.* Translated by Robert Hammond Murray. New Haven, Conn.: Yale University Press, 1934.

Blumberg, Arnold. "The Italian Diplomacy of the Mexican Empire, 1864–1867." *Hispanic American Historical Review* 51 (1971): 497–509.

Cadenhead, Ivie E., Jr. "González Ortega and the Presidency of Mexico." *Hispanic American Historical Review* 32 (1952): 331–46.

———. *Jesús González Ortega and Mexican National Politics*. Fort Worth: Texas Christian University Press, 1972.

Corti, Egon. *Maximilian and Charlotte of Mexico*. 2 vols. New York: Knopf, 1928.

Dabbs, Jack A. *The French Army in Mexico, 1861–1867*. The Hague: Mouton, 1962.

Delaney, Robert W. "Matamoros, Port for Texas during the Civil War." *Southwestern Historical Quarterly* 58 (1955): 473–87.

Egan, Clifford L. "The United States and the Spanish Intervention in Mexico, 1861–1862." *Revista de Historia de América* 63–64 (1967): 1–12.

Goldwert, Marvin. "Matías Romero and Congressional Opposition to Seward's Policy toward the French Intervention in Mexico." *The Americas* 22 (1965): 22–40.

Gordon, Leonard. "Lincoln and Juárez: A Brief Reassessment of Their Relationship." *Hispanic American Historical Review* 48 (1968): 75–80.

Hanna, Alfred Jackson, and Kathryn Hanna. *Napoleon III and Mexico*. Chapel Hill: University of North Carolina Press, 1971.

Miller, Robert R. "Matías Romero: Mexican Minister to the United States during the Juárez–Maximilian Era." *Hispanic American Historical Review* 45 (1965): 228–45.

———. "Plácido Vega: A Mexican Secret Agent in the United States, 1864–1866." *The Americas* 19 (1962): 137–48.

Robertson, William S. "The Tripartite Treaty of London." *Hispanic American Historical Review* 20 (1940): 167–89.

Roeder, Ralph. *Juárez and His Mexico*. 2 vols. New York: Viking Press, 1947.

Schoonover, Thomas D. *Dollars over Dominion: The Triumph of Liberalism in Mexican–United States Relations, 1861–1867*. Baton Rouge: Louisiana State University Press, 1978.

———. *Mexican Lobby: Matías Romero in Washington, 1861–1867*. Lexington: University Press of Kentucky, 1986.

Sheridan, Philip J. "The Committee of Mexican Bondholders and European Intervention in 1861." *Mid-America* 42 (1960): 18–29.

Smart, Charles Allen. *Viva Juárez!* London: Eyre and Spottiswoode, 1964.

Tyler, R. Curtis. "Santiago Vidaurri and the Confederacy." *The Americas* 26 (1969): 66–76.

———. *Santiago Vidaurri and the Southern Confederacy*. Austin: Texas State Historical Association, 1973.

Weber, Frank G. "Bismarck's Man in Mexico: Anton von Magnus and the End of Maximilian's Empire." *Hispanic American Historical Review* 46 (1966): 53–65.

24

The Restored Republic, 1867-76: Nascent Modernization

Modern Mexican history begins with the liberal victory of 1867.[1] In a very real sense the republic became a nation. Concerned with the growth of political democracy in Mexico, Juárez and his republican cohorts would try for a decade to consolidate their victory by implementing the letter and spirit of the Constitution of 1857 and, at the same time, by setting Mexico on the path of modernization. The sailing was far from smooth, but the political process did show definite signs of maturation. The scars from the recent wars of the Reform and the Intervention were deep, and, while the conservatives endeavored to eliminate the distinctions between victors and vanquished, the liberals set out to inaugurate a new era of peace and material progress. They both had to overcome the deeply engrained suspicion that differences of opinion, ideology, and practical politics should inevitably be settled by force rather than by reason. And while all antagonisms did not dissipate during the Restoration, bellicosity became at least less of a reflex action. But, more important, this nine-year period established the guidelines for the profound changes that would occur in Mexico during the last quarter of the nineteenth century.

Juárez's Third Term

In marked contrast to Maximilian's entrance into Mexico City in his ornate European carriage in 1864, Juárez entered the capital

1. Daniel Cosío Villegas, ed. *Historia moderna de México*, 9 vols. (Mexico, 1955–72). The first three volumes treat the restored republic.

403

on July 15, 1867, in a stark black coach. Cheers welled up from
the thousands who lined the streets. His reception was triumphant, as it well should have been, but although Juárez enjoyed
the display of camaraderie and goodwill, he recognized that it
was no time to rest on past laurels. He immediately called for
presidential elections, announcing himself as a candidate for a
third term. Under the circumstances, few knowledgeable politicians believed that a third term was excessive. Most of the first
two had been spent on the run with virtually no chance of implementing a progressive program. While preparing himself for
the elections, the president undertook an important political reform. In order to manifest the primacy of civilian over military
rule, he reduced the size of the Mexican army from sixty thousand to twenty thousand men.

In October Juárez won the presidential election and late in the
year was sworn into office for a third term. In one respect he was
faced with a situation not unlike that which he had encountered
in 1861 when he returned to office following the liberal victory
in the War of the Reform. The administration had to enunciate
a policy toward the conservatives who had supported the French-
imposed monarchy. During the fight against the empire, the decrees issued from the Juarista headquarters concerning French
sympathizers had been harsh indeed. The no-nonsense policy
was reaffirmed in Querétaro with the trial and execution of Maximilian. But by late 1867 few liberals were still crying for re-
venge, and it seemed time to adopt a more conciliatory policy.
In a gesture of goodwill Juárez set free many political prisoners
and reduced the sentences of others.

Economic and Educational Reforms

The new administration wisely directed its energies into two
main fields: a revamping of the economy and a restructuring of
the educational foundations of the country. Juárez named Matías
Romero, who had served his exiled government so effectively in
Washington, as secretary of the treasury. Romero formulated a
plan for economic development that called for the improvement
of transportation facilities and the fuller exploitation of natural
resources through the attraction of foreign capital. He believed
that Mexico's economic future rested largely on the revitalization
of the mining industry rather than upon industrialization. The
key to increased mineral production was a major revision of

Mexico's tax and tariff structure. Despite much congressional opposition, through hard work and thrift Secretary Romero succeeded in bringing some order out of the economic chaos by 1872, but the dividends he expected in the form of substantial capital investment would not be noticeable for several years.

While tariff and tax revision were important, other factors still discouraged the potential investor. Mexico had an image to live down. Political instability, minor rebellions, the presence of private armies and groups of bandits for whom lawlessness had become a way of life, all dissuaded foreign capitalists seeking lucrative investment fields. Travel on Mexico's roads and shipment of merchandise were precarious. One of the answers was found in a relatively new concept of public security. Prior to the French Intervention, Benito Juárez had authorized the establishment of a rural police force, the *rurales*, modeled in some ways on the Spanish *guardia civil*. But jurisdiction over the security guard was divided between two government departments: War and Interior. The overlapping and often confusing jurisdictions undermined the effectiveness of the organization, and it did not amount to much. After the overthrow of the empire, however, Juárez's Congress authorized an increased budget for the rurales, and, in 1869, placed them under the sole jurisdiction of the Department of Interior. With more adequate funds and with the organizational problem resolved, the rurales began to play a major peace-keeping role. Patrolling the roads, assisting the army, guarding special shipments of bullion and merchandise, and policing local elections, they contributed toward stabilization of life in the countryside.

Without question the most important economic development to occur during the early years of the Restoration was the completion of the Mexico City–Veracruz railroad. The enterprise had begun in 1837, and short segments of a couple of kilometers had been completed periodically since that time. But in 1860, when the United States had over 30,000 miles of track in operation, Mexico had barely 150 miles. The stage between Mexico City and Guadalajara (a distance of some 425 miles) often took more than a week even if it was not mired in the mud or assaulted by bandits. To be sure, construction in the rugged terrain between the Mexican capital and Veracruz on the Gulf was an engineering nightmare, for the roadbed had to rise from sea level to over nine thousand feet and had to be built across huge canyons and precipices. But railroad technology was clearly ahead of Mexico's determination to see the project through.

Spanning the Metlac Ravine was an engineering achievement of major proportions.

During the period of the empire the concession rights were held by the Imperial Mexican Railway Company, a corporation registered in London. The British engineers who worked for Maximilian made considerable progress in laying portions of the roadbed, but by 1866 the company was almost bankrupt and all work stopped. Upon the restoration of the republic Juárez articulated his profound concern for completion of the line. He exempted the company from the forfeiture legislation that applied to all who had supported Maximilian on the condition that construction be resumed. Realizing that the company was broke, Juárez also agreed to pay it an annual subsidy of 560,000 pesos for twenty-five years. The agreement reached by the government and the company produced considerable bombast in the Mexican

Congress. Among the leading stockholders was Antonio Escandón, a conservative who had been a member of the Mexican delegation that visited Miramar in October 1863. Cries of governmental favoritism to traitors were heard in the Congress, but Juárez believed that the railroad was more important than partisan politics and went ahead with his plans.

In an attempt to soothe passions the company was renamed the Ferrocarril Mexicano (Mexican Railroad Company). The British engineers did a fantastic job of construction, digging endless tunnels and breaching the Barranca de Metlac, a chasm 900 feet across and 375 feet deep. Gradually all the gaps were closed, the rails tied to one another, and the job finished on December 20, 1872. The line was officially inaugurated on January 1 of the following year. Archbishop Pelagio Antonio de Labastida formally blessed the new project at the Buenaventura station in Mexico City, signifying a reduction in tensions between church and state. Church endorsement of a liberal government enterprise a decade before would have been unthinkable. The successful completion of the railroad whetted the appetite, encouraging others to begin thinking of the desirability, indeed the necessity, of constructing other major lines.

Education, too, began to move in a new direction with the restoration of the republic. In the fall of 1867 Juárez appointed a five-man commission to reorganize the entire educational structure of the country. The committee was headed by Gabino Barreda, a medical doctor who had studied in France and become a devotee of the positivist philosophy of Auguste Comte. While positivism would not become the official state doctrine in Mexico for another fifteen years, its roots most definitely can be found in Barreda's educational values. The curriculum recommended by the committee and adopted by the Congress in late 1867 placed heavy emphasis on arithmetic, the rudiments of physics and chemistry, and practical mechanics in the primary schools, and further emphasis on mathematics and the natural sciences in the secondary schools. The arts and the humanities, while not entirely ignored, were subordinated to an understanding of the physical world.

More important to Juárez than the curriculum itself was the fact that primary education in Mexico was made free and obligatory for the first time. All towns with a population of over five hundred were to have one school for boys and one for girls. Two more schools were to be built for every additional two thousand

FERROCARRIL MEXICANO, COMPLETED IN DECEMBER 1872

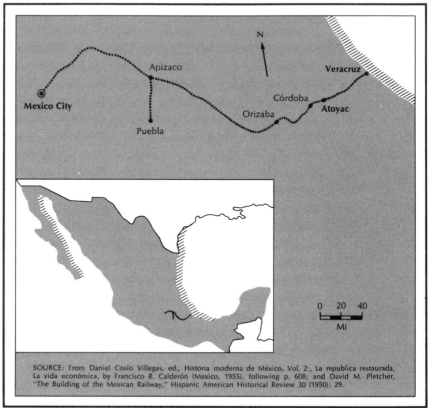

SOURCE: From Daniel Cosío Villegas, ed., Historia moderna de México, Vol. 2:, La republica restaurada, La vida económica, by Francisco R. Calderón (Mexico, 1955), following p. 608; and David M. Pletcher, "The Building of the Mexican Railway," Hispanic American Historical Review 30 (1950): 29.

inhabitants. But, as had been the case in Mexico since the arrival of the Spaniards in 1519, theory and practice, the law and the reality, seldom merged. Universal primary education remained but a liberal dream.

Juárez and his secretary of foreign relations, Sebastián Lerdo de Tejada, took special care to cultivate friendly diplomatic relations with Mexico's neighbors and with the powers of Europe, most of which had recognized the empire of Maximilian. In his first address to the Congress in 1867 the president acknowledged the sympathy and support the United States had given him during the recent unpleasantness. The relationship between the two countries was further cemented when William Seward visited Mexico in 1869, and the two countries agreed to lay claims, accumulated since the Treaty of Guadalupe Hidalgo, before a mixed claims commission. Gradually relations with Europe were renewed as well.

Division among the Liberals and the Death of Juárez

Juárez's third term was his best, and in the presidential elections of 1871 he decided, against the advice of many friends, to seek a fourth. The onetime pillar of constitutional liberalism had become prey to the nineteenth-century Latin American political myth of indispensability; he had allowed his very human desire for power and accomplishment to impugn his earlier ideals. His popularity had been ebbing for at least a year. The election of 1871 was one of the most hotly contested of the nineteenth century as two former supporters ran against him: Porfirio Díaz, who had won his military laurels in the wars against the French; and Sebastián Lerdo de Tejada, the brother of the author of Ley Lerdo. The election thus occasioned a three-way split in the undisciplined liberal party—Juaristas, Porfiristas, and Lerdistas. Juárez still enjoyed a wide base of popular support and, in addition, had most of the federal bureaucracy working in his behalf. Lerdo counted on the strong backing of the professional classes and many of the socially prominent and wealthy, while Díaz was supported by some of the military outcasts from the conservative party and a vast entourage of disappointed office seekers.

A caricature by Santiago Hernández of Juárez and his opposition. Entitled "Little Fingers," it illustrates how the opposition whittled away at Juárez's power.

Both the Lerdistas and the Porfiristas attacked the concept of constant re-election as a violation of the republican principles Juárez had always espoused.

When the ballots were counted after the June election, none of the three candidates received the requisite majority of the votes. The choice, according to the Constitution of 1857, thus fell upon the Congress. The Juaristas had done well in the congressional elections and dominated that body when it convened in the early fall. After a number of bitter credentials fights the new delegates were seated, and when the important vote was taken, Juárez was elected. Of the two defeated candidates, Díaz accepted the decision with less grace. On November 8, 1871, he proclaimed himself in revolt against the Juárez regime.

The *Plan de la Noria* proclaimed that indefinite re-election of the chief executive repudiated the principles of the Revolution of Ayutla and endangered the country's national institutions. It was necessary to overthrow those who considered national office to be their personal prerogative. No officeholder who exercised national jurisdiction of any kind in the year preceding presidential elections should be eligible to run for that high position. Those who accept the plan, Díaz proclaimed, "will fight for the cause of the people and the people will be the only victors. The Constitution of 1857 will be our banner and less government and more liberty our program."[2] But Díaz's fellow citizens were not yet ready for another armed insurrection, and Díaz was disappointed at the lack of interest his plan generated. While a few local caciques declared for the movement, Díaz had not struck a responsive chord. The army he put in the field was quickly defeated by the federals.

The revolt of La Noria was in complete disarray when, on July 19, 1872, Juárez suffered a coronary seizure and died in office. Sebastián Lerdo de Tejada, the chief justice of the Supreme Court, became acting president and scheduled new elections for October. Lerdo enjoyed a reputation for keen intelligence, great administrative ability, and unquestionable republican sympathies. In public speeches and debates he often attained forensic perfection. He decided to run against Porfirio Díaz in the elections and defeated him easily. Since Díaz's revolution against Juárez had been predicated almost entirely on the principle of no-re-election, the caudillo from Oaxaca accepted the outcome.

2. Quoted in Ernesto de la Torre Villar et al., eds., *Historia documental de México* (Mexico, 1964), 2: 361.

Pilgrimages were made to Juárez's Tomb in Mexico City long after his death in 1872.

Lerdo's Presidency

President Lerdo believed that the foundation of Mexico's future progress rested heavily on the establishment of peace. The material progress he envisioned was impossible without order, and order was impossible without firm executive control. The national government had to curb disruptive localism and weaken the army. Mexican liberalism was undergoing a significant change. It was becoming increasingly elitist and was no longer antithetical to centralism and dictatorship. When political disputes occurred in the states, Lerdo did not hesitate to intervene with federal forces.

Lerdo wisely retained many Juaristas in his government and, in seeking his goals, followed the same general policies that had been formulated by his famous predecessor. He used the rurales to patrol and protect the Mexico City–Veracruz railroad. To foster communications development he let railroad contracts for the construction of a new line north from Mexico City to the United States border. A company made up of both Mexican and British investors—the Central Railroad of Mexico—obtained the concession. A United States concern, headed by Emile la Sere of New Orleans, received promise of a subsidy of 12,500 pesos for each mile of track it laid down across the Isthmus of Tehuantepec. And, finally, the government encouraged feeder lines to connect with the recently completed Ferrocarril Mexicano and negotiated other contracts for the construction of telegraph lines. Lerdo's goal—to connect all of the state capitals to Mexico City by telegraph—was not reached, but he did add over sixteen hundred miles of telegraph line.

In the field of education Lerdo surpassed the efforts of his predecessor. Augmented federal and local funds resulted in a sharp increase in school construction but only a gradual increase in school enrollment. Between 1870 and 1874 the number of schools in Mexico almost doubled, but even in the latter year the 349,000 students represented only one out of nineteen school-age children. And years of tradition had established another pattern that was difficult to break; of these only 77,000 were female.

School construction grew much more rapidly than enrollment, and many school seats remained empty: availability of classroom space was not the answer. An available school seat did not mean that a competent teacher would be found or that a poor father would sacrifice the meager supplement to the family income that

SCHOOLS AND STUDENT ENROLLMENT 1844–74

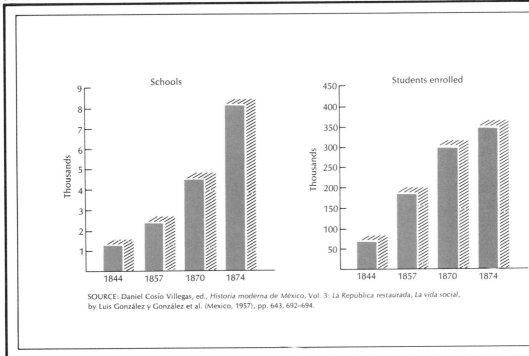

SOURCE: Daniel Cosío Villegas, ed., *Historia moderna de México*, Vol. 3: *La República restaurada, La vida social*, by Luis González y González et al. (Mexico, 1957), pp. 643, 692–694.

three or four small children working in the fields, shining shoes, or selling newspapers might provide.

The Lerdo administration made progress in other areas. The government added France to the list of European countries with which diplomatic relations had been restored. Secretary of the Treasury Romero continued his work on tariff revision and was able to codify his efforts. Lerdo also broke ground on one important political reform. The unicameral national legislature provided by the Constitution of 1857 had been under attack for years. The president proposed that a second house be added, and the legislative branch responded to the request in 1875. A Senate was added to the Chamber of Deputies, bringing the legislature back to the formula that had been first tested in 1824. Lerdo wanted the second, more elite body because he believed that it could be useful to him in his centralization efforts.

Lerdo's administration turned out to be one of the better ones that Mexico had yet experienced. But as any man of action, he could not emerge from the Mexican presidency unscathed. The

enemies mounted, the press assailed him mercilessly, and prominent politicians of both parties spoke out strongly against him.
The rumors were vicious. He had at one time studied for the
priesthood and was even charged with making up for lost time
as a celibate. When Lerdo announced that he was planning to
seek re-election in 1876, Porfirio Díaz perceived that history was
finally on his side. In March of 1876, five years after his unsuccessful attempt to overthrow Benito Juárez under the Plan de la
Noria, Díaz was ready to try again. He issued the *Plan de Tuxtepec*, charging that Lerdo had repeatedly violated the sovereignty
of the states and the municipalities, sacrificed Mexico's best interests in negotiating the railroad contracts, reduced the right of
suffrage to a farce, and squandered public funds. But, most important, the plan established no-re-election of the president and
the governors of the states as the supreme law of the land. Effective suffrage and no-re-election were to be the guiding principles
of the Mexican political process.

The Revolution of Tuxtepec was decided in one decisive battle
as soldiers in a score of states flocked to the new banner. The
opposing forces met on November 16 at Tecoac in the state of
Tlaxcala; Díaz, reinforced by cohort Manuel González, carried
the day. Recognizing that the path to Mexico City was wide
open, the president, with little disposition to carry on, abandoned
the struggle and made his way to Acapulco where a steamer was
waiting to carry him to the United States. Porfirio Díaz occupied Mexico City on November 21, 1876; he would control the
country, directly or indirectly, for the next third of a century.

**The restored republic has never received the kind of attention
it deserves in the survey literature of Mexican history. One general synthesis classifies it as part of a more general period of
"marking time."[3] It was almost anything but that. Careful examination of the Restoration period reveals it to be a critical
transition between the demise of the empire and the establishment of the Díaz dictatorship. For the first time in Mexican history the administrations in power seemed more to pull the country
together than to drive it apart. All of the major changes generally attributed to Díaz and his successive cabinets in the last
quarter of the nineteenth century and first decade of the twentieth are firmly rooted in the years 1867 to 1876: tax and tariff
reform; increased public security, especially in the rural areas;**

3. Charles C. Cumberland, *Mexico: The Struggle for Modernity* (New York, 1968),
   pp. 141–89.

recognition of the need to attract foreign capital; the improvement of transportation and communication facilities; the cultivation of better relations abroad; a slightly less antagonistic relationship between church and state; and increased centralism disguised as federalism. Juárez and Lerdo, especially the former, laid the foundations, and Porfirio Díaz would construct the edifice. But modern Mexico did begin in 1867. Díaz's subsequent accomplishments were possible because his two predecessors in the presidential chair had paved the way.

Recommended for Further Study

Acuña, Rodolfo F. *Sonoran Strongman: Ignacio Pesqueira and His Times.* Tucson: University of Arizona Press, 1974.

Bazant, Jan. *Alienation of Church Wealth in Mexico: Social and Economic Aspects of the Liberal Revolution, 1856–1875.* Cambridge: Cambridge University Press, 1971.

Berbusse, Edward J. "General Rosecrans' Forthright Diplomacy with Juárez's Mexico, 1868–1869." *The Americas* 36 (1980): 499–514.

Falcone, Frank. "Benito Juárez Versus the Díaz Brothers: Politics in Oaxaca, 1867–1871." *The Americas* 34 (1977): 630–51.

Glick, Edward B. *Straddling the Isthmus of Tehuantepec.* Gainesville: University of Florida Press, 1959.

Knapp, Frank A. *The Life of Sebastián Lerdo de Tejada: A Study of Influence and Obscurity.* Austin: University of Texas Press, 1951.

Pletcher, David M. "The Building of the Mexican Railway." *Hispanic American Historical Review* 30 (1950): 26–62.

———. "General William S. Rosecrans and the Mexican Transcontinental Railroad Project." *Mississippi Valley Historical Review* 38 (1952): 657–78.

Scholes, Walter V. *Mexican Politics during the Juárez Regime, 1855–1872.* Columbia: University of Missouri Press, 1957.

Sinkin, Richard N. *The Mexican Reform, 1855–1876: A Study in Liberal Nation Building.* Austin: Institute of Latin American Studies, 1979.

Smart, Charles Allen. *Viva Juárez!* London: Eyre and Spottiswoode, 1964.

Steward, Luther N., Jr. "Spanish Journalism in Mexico, 1867–1879." *Hispanic American Historical Review* 45 (1965): 422–33.

Vanderwood, Paul. "Genesis of the Rurales: Mexico's Early Struggle for Public Security." *Hispanic American Historical Review* 50 (1970): 323–44.

Weeks, Charles A. *The Juárez Myth in Mexico.* University: University of Alabama Press, 1987.

25

Society and Culture in the Middle of the Nineteenth Century

Rural Life

Mexico was still overwhelmingly rural in the 1850s, 1860s, and 1870s, and life for the average citizen changed very little. Those who resided in the Indian pueblo or the mestizo village lived much like their parents or their grandparents. In terms of earning power, standard of living, diet, life expectancy, and education, the life of the rural Mexican during the empire and the restored republic closely mirrored that which two earlier generations of independent Mexicans had experienced. In almost every important respect he remained outside of the mainstream of national society, and his life was one of privation.

The gap separating brown and white Mexico, poor and rich Mexico, was not bridged in the middle of the century. It might even have grown more pronounced. The dichotomy of Mexican worlds in 1865 was described by Francisco Pimentel.

> The white is the proprietor; the Indian the worker. The white is rich; the Indian poor and miserable. The descendants of the Spaniards have within their reach all of the knowledge of the century and all of the scientific discoveries; the Indian is completely unaware of it. The white dresses like a Parisian fashion plate and uses the richest of fabrics; the Indian runs around almost naked. The white lives in the cities in magnificent houses; the Indian is isolated in the country, his house a miserable hut. They are two different peoples in the same land; but worse, to a degree they are enemies.[1]

1. Quoted in Daniel Cosío Villegas, ed., *Historia moderna de México*, vol. 3: *La república restaurada, La vida social*, by Luis González y González et al. (Mexico, 1957), p. 151.

416

Foreign travelers to Mexico found the main roads slightly better than they would have a generation earlier, but most others were still an abomination. They were all very dangerous because of the bandits who continued to infest the highways. Scarcely a visitor to the country failed to note this institutionalized ill. The wife of Prince Salm-Salm, one of Maximilian's confidants, described the anxieties of passengers of the stagecoach from Veracruz to Mexico City as follows:

> It occurs very frequently that the diligence is attacked and plundered by robbers, and many horrible adventures of that kind are recorded, furnishing the passengers not very reassuring matter for conversation, and keeping them in a continual excitement. . . . The coachman does not even attempt to escape or resist; it is his policy to remain neutral, for if he acted otherwise it would not only be in vain, but cost him his life—a bullet from behind some bush would end his career on the next journey. . . . Though the escort now and then furnished by the authorities is mostly absent when needed, it sometimes happens that they are at hand, and to escape such danger the robbers are compelled to act without any ceremony. Whilst one of them takes care of the team, two others, cocked pistol in hand, invite the passengers to descend and to undress, as it is well known that they generally try to conceal their valuables in their clothes. The terror and confusion created by such an order may be imagined, especially if there are ladies amongst the passengers.[2]

Overnight lodging in the larger towns, while generally not elegant, had improved since the early post-Independence years. But villages and Indian pueblos remained unchanged. William Marshall Anderson, a United States citizen who visited Mexico during the empire, found in one southern village "no shelter or place to rest but a miserable grass covered shanty, no bigger or better than my sheep pen." As he moved north the architecture changed but not the amenities. "Unplastered stone walls and a dirt floor constitute the comfort and elegance of our accommodation.[3]

By the 1850s and 1860s rural Mexicans were certainly long accustomed to the indignities of an army marching through their village or, if they were unfortunate, stopping for food or supplies. But the Intervention and Restoration periods added several new

2. Princess Felix Salm-Salm, *Ten Years of My Life* (London, 1876), 1: 183–85.
3. William Marshall Anderson, *An American in Maximilian's Mexico, 1865–1866: The Diaries of William Marshall Anderson,* ed. Ramón Eduardo Ruiz (San Marino, Cal., 1959), pp. 15, 80.

Saltillo, the capital of Coahuila, hardly grew at all in the 1860s and 1870s, but it was one of the more charming provincial capitals of the north.

ingredients. The French troops comported themselves even worse than their American predecessors of 1846–48. They treated the Mexican peasants with utmost disdain and were far from polite in their solicitation of female indulgence. Common sense defies that the generation of blue-eyed, light-skinned babies born in Mexico in the 1860s were all the product of French debauchery, but the not-too-subtle physiognomic changes in those villages hosting a French garrison, or having one nearby, suggest that to the victor belong the spoils.

The social consequences of war did not end with the expulsion of the French. When President Juárez cut back on the size of the Mexican army, tens of thousands of former soldiers were left jobless and hundreds of miles from home. Not a few of them formed bands, and, with a horse, gun, and tattered uniform still bearing military insignia, many took out their frustrations on rural villages or hacienda complexes. The newspapers of the period were filled with stories of brigandage and plunder. Lawlessness became a social cancer reaching epidemic proportions.

Population and Social Problems

As might be expected during a period of foreign war and domestic turmoil, the population of Mexico grew very slowly during the middle of the nineteenth century. Some of the state capitals even lost inhabitants, and northern Mexico still supported only a scanty population. From a figure of 7,860,000 in 1856, the census counters could find only 8,743,000 Mexicans in 1874. The slow rate of growth cannot be attributed to a low birth rate. To the contrary, the birth rate was high, but war casualties and a very high infant mortality rate kept the population down.

Policy makers during both the empire and the restored republic wished to open up new lands, and some even spoke of the need to encourage the development of a new class of independent farmers. Because of the slow rate of population growth, however, European immigration was deemed to be the answer. In spite of Mexico's one sad experience with foreign immigrants in Texas, laws were put on the books in the 1850s and 1860s to encourage immigration from Europe. But religious intolerance, political instability, and much administrative mismanagement all mitigated against a successful program. When the liberals consoli-

POPULATION OF SELECTED CITIES, 1849–78

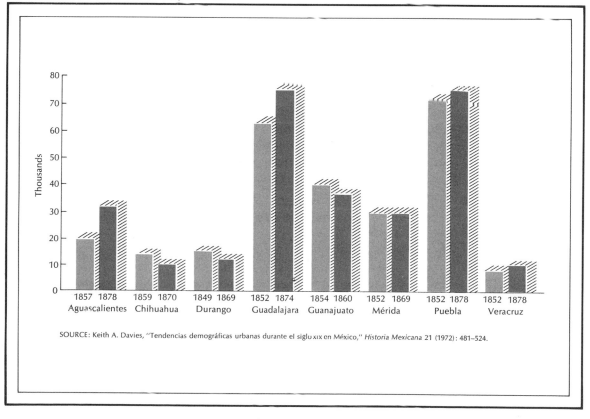

SOURCE: Keith A. Davies, "Tendencias demográficas urbanas durante el siglo xix en México," *Historia Mexicana* 21 (1972): 481–524.

The turbulence of the French Intervention and the Restoration made it inevitable that soldiers would be found congregating in Mexico City.

dated their victory after the expulsion of the French, they believed that the basic problems were resolved and that part of the flow of immigrants to Argentina, Chile, Brazil, and the United States would be diverted to Mexico. But their project met with no more success than had earlier ones. Mexico had not yet lived down its reputation, and the three thousand immigrants from western Europe, the United States, and China who began to arrive annually during the Restoration did not even offset the emigration of Mexicans to the United States. In 1876 only about twenty-five thousand people in Mexico were foreign-born, and they almost all resided in the larger cities.

Mexico City's population grew to two hundred thousand during the Restoration, and in the process the city experienced increased social problems. Prostitution had long been accepted as a necessary evil in Mexico, but when the women of the street began openly soliciting clients at the entrance to the main cathedral and the hundreds of smaller churches, a public uproar followed. Those who called for a crackdown pointed to the burgeoning rate of venereal disease and the perversion of the young and innocent. The defenders argued somewhat theatrically that the institution had to be retained as a safeguard of the chastity of honorable women who would be deflowered on the street if the virile *machos* of the capital had no such release. A sensible compromise was reached. The women of pleasure were pushed into well-defined red-light zones so as not to offend the casual passerby and were made subject to periodic medical inspection to arrest the rate of venereal disease.

The Roman Catholic Church had always made alms giving a virtue, and by the middle of the nineteenth century mendicancy was as institutionalized as prostitution. While léperos could be found in all of the larger towns and cities, they congregated by the thousands in Mexico City. Men and women with one hand extended—cripples, the blind, alcoholics, even abandoned children—were found everywhere in the capital. If unsuccessful on the streets or in the churches, they moved from door to door in both residential and business zones. Government attempts to curb mendicancy included the establishment of new charitable institutions and hospitals for the poor, but such efforts, as well intentioned as they might have been, accomplished little.

The Three Classes

The lot of the urban working class at mid-century was in some ways even worse than that of the beggars. Workers could not count on private charity, church support, government aid, or welfare institutions. Job security was nonexistent, the worker being completely subject to the whims of his employer. While the industrial revolution had scarcely touched Mexico, the capital did have its share of factories producing textiles, soap, cigarettes, flour, and alcoholic beverages. The thousands working in these small industries enjoyed but few protective laws. Legislation regulating child labor, safety precautions, and other working conditions was scant, and those laws on the books were seldom enforced. Slightly better off were people who worked for themselves, the tens of thousands of street vendors each with a distinctive call hawking tortillas, sweet bread, fruit, flowers, water, ice, candy, pottery, straw baskets, tamales, pulque, roasted corn, milk, ice cream, rosaries, crucifixes, pictures of the Virgin of Guadalupe, and an endless variety of other goods. But their diet was grossly deficient and their life expectancy short; they were all illiterate and lived in shacks on the outskirts of Mexico City.

One of the best jobs the illiterate city dweller could hope for was domestic service. As a generation earlier, the maids, gardeners, doorkeepers, valets, stable masters, chambermaids, and nanas did relatively well. They received up to fourteen or fifteen pesos a month without food, or three or four with. But they were at least assured a clean room in which to live and, in spite of long hours, tolerable working conditions in one of the nicer residential districts of the capital.

The still tiny middle class—composed of shopkeepers, merchants, small independent entrepreneurs, professional men, government officials, and other white-collar workers—lived comfortably but without amenities. The houses (often rooms above their stores) were small but adequately furnished with locally made products. Tiles or straw mats covered the floor; rugs were unusual. Because of a grossly inadequate water supply system, very few smaller homes had private baths. Public bathing facilities were scarce and inconvenient enough that neither daily nor weekly bathing was common; the trade in cheap perfumes and colognes was good.

The palatial residences of the wealthy families were mainly in the district of Tacubaya, at the western end of the city. It was a genuine showplace, described by an English visitor in the 1860s as a district where "all the men with heavy purses build villas and country houses, to which they retire in the summer months. . . . It is really a very pretty place. . . ."[4]

The façades of the houses were often decorated by students or professors from the Art Academy of San Carlos. Elegant patios, marble staircases, carved doors, crystal chandeliers, gold candelabra, imported pianos and carpets, rosewood furniture, and old Spanish paintings were staple items in every aristocratic home. Most also had private chapels with the patron saints of the family's members represented. The real marks of distinction, however, were the resplendent private baths, decorated with imported French fixtures. Many of these aristocratic homes required twenty or twenty-five servants to keep them going. Some of the affluent required fewer but hired more in unabashed ostentation.

Women who visited Mexico in the 1860s and 1870s often commented upon the general ignorance of the ladies of the genteel aristocracy they found there. Princess Salm-Salm dwelled upon the subject in her memoirs, but the best description comes from Countess Paula Kollonitz, a lady-in-waiting to Empress Carlota.

> I never saw any book in the hand of a lady, except her prayer book. . . . They write letters, for the most part, with an unpractised hand. Their ignorance is complete; they have not the smallest idea of geography and history. Europe to them consists of

4. J. F. Elton, *With the French in Mexico* (London, 1867), pp. 37–38.

Growing from a squalid Indian community to the most fashionable suburb of Mexico City, by 1850 Tacubaya often housed Mexican presidents, cabinet ministers, bishops, and all of the wealthiest residents of the capital, both Mexican and foreign. At mid-century its population stood at 5,000, but vacationers swelled the count to 6,500 during the summer months.

Spain, from whence they sprang; Rome, where the Pope rules; and Paris, from whence come their clothes. They have no conception of other countries or other nations, and they could not comprehend that French was not our native tongue.[5]

One wonders just how much the ladies of Europe knew about Mexico, Argentina, or Chile, much less Honduras, Ecuador, or Bolivia, but the point should not be lost. Women, even aristocratic women, had received short shrift in the educational system, and the results were patent.

Social Amusements and Cultural Achievements

Everyday diversion was one of the few activities that could easily cut across class lines. Members of the lower, middle, and upper strata could be seen enjoying the promenades around the Alameda, the great central park in the downtown business district, which was equipped with hydrogen gas lamps in 1873. Everyone enjoyed the free concerts staged in the bandstands of the public parks, and all partook of secular or religious fiestas. Public fairs

5. Countess Paula Kollonitz, *The Court of Mexico* (London, 1868), pp. 160–61.

and touring circuses from Europe or the United States also attracted all elements of society, as did games of dice played on
outdoor tables. But the greatest social leveler of all was the bullfight, a spectacle where the cabinet minister could converse with
his shoeshine boy and the aristocrat from Tacubaya could debate
the awarding of ears and tails with his gardener.

The bullfight was introduced in Mexico in the early sixteenth
century and quickly became a cultural institution. The main
ring used in Mexico City in the middle of the century was the
Plaza del Paseo Nuevo. Built in 1851 at a cost of almost a hundred thousand pesos, it seated ten thousand and was filled each
time a fight was held. To be sure, the more affluent sat in the
shade and the masses in the sun, the rich drank cognac and the
poor pulque, but they all saw the same show. Toreros Bernardo
Gaviño, Pablo Mendoza, and Ignacio Gadea were the rage of the
era. But not all of the performances were good, and after one
particularly bad fight in 1867, during which several horses were
killed and blood filled the ring, the press began a concerted campaign for abolition of the sport. Emphasizing the brutality of the
spectacle, the opponents succeeded in having the Congress pass
legislation outlawing bullfighting in the Federal District over
which it had jurisdiction. But the owners of the bullrings, the
raisers of fighting stock, the performers, and the thousands of
fans argued for reconsideration. The law remained on the books
for twenty years, but, meanwhile, ingenuity accomplished what
congressional lobbying could not. In 1874 a new ring was dedicated in Tlalnepantla, just outside the Federal District but not so
far as to deter the avid aficionados of Mexico City. The placards
announcing the Sunday spectacles were plastered all over the
walls of the capital.

If popular culture reached virtually everyone, "high culture"
was obviously not directed to the illiterate masses. Yet in many
ways the arts of the mid-nineteenth century were socially aware
and embodied much more than the rejection of the Spanish past
that had typified creative endeavors in the first three decades
after Independence. The social awareness of the 1850s, 1860s,
and 1870s did not generally manifest itself as a series of pleas
for the impoverished masses. Rather it called for the establishment of a new, stronger, secular, more developed, and progressive Mexico. It began to inculcate pride in the concept of mexicanidad and to show what patriotism could mean. Further, it
tried to overcome the damage that had been done to Mexico's
self-image.

A Sunday bullfight at the Plaza de Toros de San Pablo, near Mexico City.

In literature the romantic novel was not superseded but did assume a distinctly new flavor. The new novel, while no less moralistic than the old, was more instructive. To a generation that had witnessed many civil wars and two foreign wars, the cultural orientation was historical, and the historical novel lent itself perfectly to the goals of the new intelligentsia. Armies, and especially foreign ones, marching through poor native villages, raping and looting on their way, provided an abundance of subject matter for historical novelists like Juan A. Mateos, Ireneo Paz, and Vicente Riva Palacio. These writers evoked compassion in the reader not because the Indians and mestizos were poor and subject to abuse but because they were Mexican and subject to abuse.

The literary giant of the period was Ignacio Manuel Altamirano (1834–95). Born to Indian parents in Tixtla, Guerrero, he went to school first in the pueblo and later in Mexico City, but his education was interrupted by the wars of the Reform and the French Intervention. In 1861 he had been elected to the Congress, where he voiced radical opinions. After the expulsion of the French he edited several literary journals and then turned his attention to the novel, a literary form he believed should be didactic. In 1869 and 1871 he published two widely acclaimed short novels, *Clemencia* and *La Navidad en las montañas* (translated as *Christmas in the Mountains*). Set in Guadalajara during the French Intervention, *Clemencia* propounded the ideal of patriotism through the characterization of an officer in the republican army. The social content of *La Navidad en las montañas*, however, is still more apparent. In it the author attacked forced conscription (the leva), urged the development of a new educational system, and denounced the clergy for its failure to meet the real needs of the Mexican community.

The period of Maximilian's empire could have been a productive one for Mexican music and art. The Hapsburg emperor had polished and refined cultural interests and lent his personal support and that of his office to the fine arts. He even underwrote the production costs of an opera by Melesio Morales, Mexico's foremost mid-century composer. But not even the fine arts could escape the intense partiality of the age. The old Art Academy of San Carlos, subsequently changed to the National Academy, was redesignated the Imperial Academy by Maximilian. Dedicated Juarista liberals in the academy could not serve Maximilian in good conscience, and many resigned their posts. When the French were expelled, the academy was reorganized again, this time as the National School of Fine Arts, and many of those artists who had painted for the French found it expedient to step down.

Mexican art in the 1850s, 1860s, and 1870s was dominated by two figures of primary importance: Pelegrín Clavé (1810–80) and Juan Cordero (1824–84). Clavé, a Spaniard by birth, taught at the academy for almost twenty years. He was a portrait painter of the first class; his most famous work was a portrait of Benito Juárez, which today hangs in the Chapultepec Museum. Cordero, almost a generation younger than Clavé, studied in Italy. When he returned to Mexico he keenly resented that Clavé, a Spaniard, should have been named director of the academy. Out of his deep sense of mexicanidad, something he shared with the other young intellectuals of the age, he rejected the assistant directorship of the academy. Cordero was Mexico's first great muralist, and in the late 1850s he began decorating church domes with oils and temperas. But as the anticlericalism of the Reform converted him, he turned his attention to the walls of public buildings instead.

Cordero, much like the historical novelists of the period, was comfortable with historical and philosophical themes that taught a message. In 1874 he completed a mural in the main staircase of the National Preparatory School entitled *Triumph and Study*

Gabino Barreda (1818–81). Barreda, who founded the National Preparatory School in 1867, also introduced Mexico to the positivism of Auguste Comte and in the process provided the philosophical underpinnings for Mexican *cientificismo*. In good positivist fashion, the curriculum he introduced at the school subordinated the arts to the sciences.

over Ignorance and Sloth. It depicted Mexican progress in terms of science, industry, and commerce. This trilogy, he believed, would destroy ignorance and greed. The new muses, Electra and Vaporosa, did not toy with harps but rather with a magnetic compass and an apparatus that converted water into steam. A locomotive pulling heavy freight cars depicted the benefits of science. It is not surprising that the positivist creed is clearly present in this work; it was commissioned by Gabino Barreda, the director of the National Preparatory School.

The music of social awareness also followed on the heels of the collapse of Maximilian's empire. Aniceto Ortega's two most famous marches, both completed in 1867, celebrated the defeat of the invader. They were appropriately entitled *Marcha Zaragoza* and *Marcha Republicana*.

Nowhere is the mid-century culture of a new Mexico better illustrated than in the field of philosophy, and seldom can the beginning of a philosophical movement be so accurately pinpointed as Mexican positivism. On September 16, 1867, in an Independence Day celebration in Guanajuato, Gabino Barreda delivered an eloquent speech subsequently known as the "Civic Oration." As a student of Auguste Comte, Barreda had read and observed widely. He interpreted Mexican history as a struggle between a negative spirit (represented most recently by the alliance of the conservative and the French) and a positivist spirit (embodied by the liberal republican forces). The combative phase of the struggle had ended with the execution of Maximilian, and the country was now prepared to embark upon the constructive phase. Barreda was optimistic. Mexico's material regeneration could be achieved through the most prudent application of scientific knowledge and the scientific method. He ended his speech by coining a new slogan for the new Mexico: "Liberty, Order, and Progress." Within a short time, however, Mexican liberals would sense that Liberty was not an equal partner in the positivist trinity. It would be sacrificed, almost meticulously, to Order and Progress. The liberal party would split asunder over the positivist issue, and the moderates, who placed their faith in Order and Progress, would gain the upper hand.

Recommended for Further Study

Altamirano, Ignacio Manuel. *Christmas in the Mountains*. Translated by Harvey L. Johnson. Gainesville: University of Florida Press, 1961.

Brushwood, John S. *Mexico in Its Novel: A Nation's Search for Identity*. Austin: University of Texas Press, 1966.

Elton, J. F. *With the French in Mexico*. London: Chapman and Hall, 1867.

Hale, Charles A. *The Transformation of Liberalism in Late Nineteenth-Century Mexico*. Princeton, N.J.: Princeton University Press, 1989.

Kollonitz, Countess Paula, *The Court of Mexico*. London: Saunders, Otley, and Company, 1868.

Raat, William D. "Leopoldo Zea and Mexican Positivism: A Reappraisal." *Hispanic American Historical Review* 48 (1968): 1–18.

Read, John Lloyd. *The Mexican Historical Novel, 1826–1910*. New York: Instituto de las Españas, 1939.

Rosaldo, Renato. "The Legacy of Literature and Art." In *Six Faces of Mexico*, edited by Russell C. Ewing, pp. 245–310. Tucson: University of Arizona Press, 1966.

Salm-Salm, Princess Felix. *Ten Years of My Life*. 2 vols. London: Richard Bentley & Son, 1876.

Stevenson, Robert. *Music in Mexico: A Historical Survey*. New York: Thomas Y. Crowell, 1971.

Wilson, Robert A. *Mexico: Its Peasants and Its Priests*. New York: Harper and Brothers, 1856.

Zea, Leopoldo. *The Latin American Mind*. Norman: University of Oklahoma Press, 1963.

———. *Positivism in Mexico*. Translated by Josephine H. Schulte. Austin: University of Texas Press, 1974.

VII THE MODERNIZATION
OF MEXICO, 1876-1910

26

The Making of the Porfiriato

Porfirio Díaz controlled the destiny of the Mexican nation for a third of a century. These were interesting and vital years in the entire western world. Innovation characterized the era—in technology, political and economic systems, social values, and artistic expression. Otto von Bismarck transformed the German states into a nation. William Gladstone introduced England to a new kind of liberalism. The leading powers of Europe partitioned Africa unto themselves. The United States emerged as a world power, and Spain lost Cuba, Puerto Rico, and the Philippines—the last remnants of its once-glorious empire. Russia experienced a revolution that, though abortive, presaged things to come in 1917. Émile Zola and Anatole France came heroically to the defense of Captain Dreyfus, and Pope Leo XIII enunciated *Rerum Novarum*, proclaiming that employees should be treated more as men than as tools. Thomas Hardy and Thomas Mann revolutionized the world of fiction, while Renoir and Monet did the same for art. But even in a world of profound change, Porfirio Díaz's Mexico must be considered remarkable.

Mexico in 1876

When Díaz assumed control of Mexico in 1876 the country was hopelessly backward. It had scarcely been touched by the scientific, technological, and industrial revolutions or the material conquests of the nineteenth century. The benefits and comforts of civilization, as they were found in Mexico, were confined to a handful of the larger cities. While much of western Europe and the United States had been transformed in the last fifty years, Mexico had languished, less out of inertia than because of the intermittent chaos and resultant exhaustion. In the fifty-five years since Independence the presidency had actually changed hands seventy-five times. For every constitutional president there had been four interim, provisional, or irregular presidents. Continuity of policy had been clearly impossible.

Although Presidents Juárez and Lerdo during the Restoration had pointed Mexico in a new direction and had given some indication of what had to be done and how it could be accomplished, they themselves had not been in office long enough, or continuously enough, to see their plans fully implemented. In 1876 Díaz inherited an empty treasury, a long list of foreign debts, and a huge bureaucratic corps whose salaries were in arrears. Mexico's credit rating abroad was abominable, and its politics had become somewhat of a joke in Europe. The value of Mexican imports consistently exceeded the value of exports, presenting a serious balance-of-payments problem. It was virtually impossible to secure sorely needed infusions of foreign capital, and the Mexican affluent, knowing the precarious nature of the political process, would not invest their own resources to any large degree. Because of graft, ineptitude, and mismanagement the public services were poorly run. The mail, if it arrived at all, came inexcusably late.

Mining had never really recovered from the chaotic and dour days of the Wars for Independence. Only a few of the proven mines had been drained and retimbered. Those mines in operation in 1876 were, for the most part, exploited in a haphazard fashion. Extraction and smelting techniques were dated and inefficient. The patio process of the sixteenth century was still the most common method of extracting silver from silver ore. Quite often the cost of production from the mine to the silver bar was over 25 percent of the final value. Some of the marginal mines had been operated at a loss for years, and no coordinated efforts at new geological exploration had been undertaken.

The economic situation of agriculture was much the same. Many implements still in use dated from the early colonial period. The most modern reapers and threshers and newly developed chemical fertilizers were still oddities. Even metal hammers and nails were luxuries. Practically nothing had been done to improve the breeding of stock animals.

When Díaz came to the presidency the iron horse had just

started to compete with the oxcart, the mule train, and the coach. Telegraph construction had barely begun. The dock facilities on both coasts were in sad disrepair, and many of the most important harbors were silted with sand. Veracruz was so unsafe for shipping that some favored abandoning it altogether. The rurales had not yet been able to contain banditry; rural violence consistently demonstrated contempt for law and authority. A tremendously high infant mortality rate testified to the lack of modern sanitation and health facilities even as the last quarter of the nineteenth century began. Yellow fever plagued the tropical areas of the Gulf coast, particularly in the immediate environs of Veracruz.

Mexico City had a special health problem. Situated in a broad valley, it was surrounded by mountains and a series of lakes, almost all of which were at a higher elevation than the city. Heavy rains invariably brought flooding. In addition to extensive property damage (floods often caused adobe walls to crumble), the waters then stagnated in low-lying areas for weeks and months. Disease, reaching epidemic proportions, frequently followed on the heels of a serious flood. Projects to provide an adequate drainage system for the city had been proposed since the seventeenth century. The height of the surrounding mountains, however, thwarted proposals for a foolproof system of drainage canals and dikes, and the projects initiated from time to time were never fully successful.

Order and Progress under Díaz

If Mexico were to emerge from its doldrums, if progress were to displace stagnation, Díaz believed it would be necessary first to change Mexico's image drastically and to remove the stigma popularly associated with Mexican politics. Only if the potential investors from the United States and Europe were convinced that stability was supplanting turbulence, that firmness was replacing irresolution and chaos, and that the political process was maturing could they be expected to offer their dollars and pounds sterling, for profit, in the chore of national development and modernization. The task, then, as Díaz perceived it, was first to establish the rule of law; from it incalculable benefits would accrue. He was fully prepared to accept the positivist dictum of Order and Progress, in that order.

Díaz's liberal credentials and personal integrity were impeccable. Born to a family of modest means in the city of Oaxaca in 1830, he studied first for the priesthood and then for the law. But the boy was not cut out to do well in the classroom, and politics got under his skin before he finished his law degree. There were only two avenues open to political prominence in nineteenth-century Mexico—the law and the army—and Díaz chose the latter. Joining the Oaxaca National Guard in 1856, he fought under the liberal banner during the War of the Reform. With the liberal victory promotions came with startling rapidity, and by the time of his history-making defeat of the French in Puebla on May 5, 1862, he was a thirty-two-year-old brigadier general. During the period of the empire he won additional military fame championing the cause of liberal republicanism as a guerrilla fighter against the French army. Not even his abortive revolt of La Noria against Benito Juárez or his successful revolt of Tuxtepec against Lerdo de Tejada tarnished his liberal reputation. Both were fought in defense of the liberal principle of no-re-election and against liberal apostates who had prostituted it.

During his first term, which lasted until 1880, Díaz was faced with a number of insurrections. Agrarian rebellions protesting seizure of village lands flared in many states, but not all the revolts were of an agrarian nature. Some, such as the rebellion of General Manuel Márquez de León in Sinaloa, were prompted by Díaz's failure, after he came to office, to reward former supporters adequately; others, such as that of General Diego Álvarez in Guerrero, ignited when the local populace objected to presidential appointments in the state. But the most serious were a number of revolts launched along the United States border in support of exiled president Lerdo de Tejada. These military movements not only threatened the success of Díaz's pacification program but also damaged his efforts to cultivate more friendly relations with his northern neighbor. But Díaz was not hesitant in meeting force with force. Rebel leaders who were not shot down on the field of battle were disposed of shortly after their capture. Characteristic of Díaz's attitude toward those who would disrupt the national peace was his reaction to a revolt in Veracruz during his first year in office. When Governor Luis Mier y Terán asked for instructions concerning captured rebels in that state, Díaz reportedly telegraphed him, *Mátalos en caliente* (Kill them on the spot). Such lessons were not lost on potential revolutionaries elsewhere. Mexico was not as tranquil in the post-1880 period as often portrayed. The claim of the government that a blond woman in a short skirt could walk unmolested from the

United States to the Guatemalan border is sheer nonsense. Yet the peace was not shattered as often or as violently as in the past. Over eight hundred corpsmen had been added to the rurales to curb brigandage. Order was gradually coming, and progress would accompany it.

Within a couple of years of his assumption of the presidency Díaz had been recognized by most of western Europe and Latin America, but the United States held out pending the satisfactory resolution of several outstanding problems. The mixed claims commission established under Presidents Juárez and Grant had labored for almost seven years with little to show for its efforts. Many United States congressmen, feeling pressure from their constituents, were restless. But a breakthrough in the negotiations finally occurred in late 1876. Díaz agreed to the terms set forth by a special umpire. Mexico would pay almost $4,000,000 in claims, in annual installments of $300,000. The first payment was met in January 1877 and augured well for future United States–Mexican relations, but the Hayes administration had one further grievance. Groups of Mexican bandits and Indians occasionally crossed the border, attacked settlements in the United States, and drove herds of cattle back into Mexico. The Mexican government, in the name of national sovereignty, refused to grant permission to United States forces to cross over into Mexico in pursuit. In the summer of 1877 border depredations brought the two nations almost to the brink of war. Díaz was at his best at this crucial juncture. While he would not permit American troops to enter Mexican territory, he did dispatch additional troops of his own to the border region to prevent further encroachments. Tensions gradually subsided, and President Hayes was slowly convinced that the Díaz administration meant to establish order and meet its foreign obligations. In an extremely significant step he authorized recognition of the Díaz regime in the spring of 1877.

During his first administration Díaz also began to put Mexico's economic house in order. As a symbolic gesture he reduced his own salary and then ordered similar reductions for other government employees. Thousands of useless bureaucrats were eliminated from the rolls altogether. In addition, the administration attacked a problem endemic since the colonial period—smuggling. To prevent the annual loss of hundreds of thousands of dollars in import and export duties along the United States border and in Mexico's leading ports, Díaz announced a new, tough government policy. Private individuals caught trying to circumvent the payment of duties would be subject to five years' imprisonment; government employees would be subject to ten years' for the same crime; and commercial establishments trafficking in smuggled goods would receive no government contracts. To stimulate additional commerce with the United States three new Mexican consulates were opened along the border, at Rio Grande City, Laredo, and Eagle Pass. But the economic reforms, though well intentioned, were insufficient to provide a surplus in the treasury.

As Díaz's first term drew to a close, several of the states urged that the no-re-election law be amended so that Díaz could be eligible to serve another term. But Díaz preferred the law as it was; it provided that neither the president nor the state governors were eligible for immediate re-election but could serve again after the lapse of an intervening term. The Revolution of Tuxtepec, built on the foundations of no-re-election, was still too recent to attempt a change; he dutifully retired from office. The peaceful passage of power from one president to another was no common occurrence in nineteenth-century Mexico. By voluntarily stepping aside Díaz could give further substance to the growing conviction abroad that Mexico had begun to mature politically. As the term ended, Díaz threw his support behind forty-seven-year-old Manuel González, an imposing military man who had rendered yeoman service in the fight against Lerdo and who was currently serving as secretary of war. González won the election with a large majority.

The González Presidency

The González presidency was controversial. The new president wanted to follow the patterns established by Díaz and, in fact, even brought his predecessor into the government for a short time as head of the Department of Development. Revenues increased, but so did expenditures as the administration plunged headlong into further development. Modernization was expensive. Railroad construction continued, but the companies required large subsidies from the government—as high as $9,500 for each kilometer of track laid. The government also fostered new steamship lines and established the first cable service in the country. But González had overextended his regime and found himself without sufficient funds to meet government obligations; rather than neglect foreign debts or railroad subsidies, he stopped the salaries of many government officials. The outcry was predictable, but its intensity was not.

Stories of graft and corruption began filling the press, and political pamphlets denouncing the regime circulated on the streets of Mexico City. If one believed the enemies of the regime, not since the days of Santa Anna had Mexico witnessed such debauchery in high government places. The president and his cabinet were charged with negotiating illegal contracts and receiving rebates, selling government properties to administration favorites for practically nothing, and stealing from the treasury at a fantastic rate. The president's personal life also came under vicious attack as he was accused of a wide array of sexual improprieties. The public turned against him.

The charges were either fabrications or gross exaggerations. It could be fairly argued that the bureaucracy's talent for peculation outstripped its administrative qualifications, but that González consented or personally benefited has never been documented. The suggestion that Díaz fabricated the stories to discredit González is more fanciful and cynical than accurate; the best recent scholarship suggests forcefully that Manuel González was not a puppet of Porfirio Díaz.[1] González called his own shots and, in fact, must be given credit for encouraging the developmental process that had begun timidly with the restoration of the republic. But perhaps the most important lesson to be drawn is that the attacks against the president, as intense as they were, did not occasion any serious armed insurrection. The vituperations certainly could have tarnished Mexico's changing image, but when elections, rather than a new revolutionary plan, followed, many were convinced that the country had finally turned the corner.

The Return of Díaz

Díaz used his four years out of office to relax and to build a new political machine. He served for a brief time in the González cabinet and for slightly over a year in the governorship of his native state of Oaxaca. His first wife, Delfina Ortega, had died in 1880, and the following year he married Carmen Romero Rubio, the daughter of Manuel Romero Rubio, a Lerdista statesman and cabinet member. She was eighteen; Díaz had just celebrated his

1. Donald M. Coerver, *The Porfirian Interregnum: The Presidency of Manuel González of Mexico, 1880–1884*. (Fort Worth: Texas Christian University Press, 1979.)

fifty-first birthday. They traveled to the United States on their honeymoon as Mexico's representatives to the New Orleans World's Fair; newspapermen often mistook her for his daughter. But the well-bred, sensitive, and perfectly-prepared-to-be-a-first-lady Señora Díaz began to educate her husband in the social graces. She performed her task admirably, and within a couple of years Díaz was much more the polished gentleman than the crude warrior who had catapulted himself into the presidency in 1876.

All knowledgeable Mexican politicians realized that Díaz would run for the presidency again in 1884, and most knew that he would win. Liberals and conservatives, and various factions thereof, began to gather around him in the year prior to the elections. He wisely held out vague promises to all but made very few definite commitments. In September Díaz swept to victory. From this time forward he would not feel the need to step out of office after completing each term and would remain in the presidency continually until 1911. The conditions that greeted him in 1884 were a far cry from those of 1876. He not only was ready to transform the face of the nation, but had a definite plan of action.

Recommended for Further Study

Beals, Carleton. *Porfirio Díaz: Dictator of Mexico*. Philadelphia: Lippincott, 1932.

Coatsworth, John. "Railroads, Landholding, and Agrarian Protest in the Early Porfiriato." *Hispanic American Historical Review* 54 (1974): 48–71.

Coerver, Donald M. *The Porfirian Interregnum: The Presidency of Manuel González of Mexico, 1880–1884*. Fort Worth: Texas Christian University Press, 1979.

Cosío Villegas, Daniel. *The United States versus Porfirio Díaz*. Lincoln: University of Nebraska Press, 1963.

Creelman, James. *Díaz: Master of Mexico*. New York: Appleton, 1916.

García Cubas, Antonio. *The Republic of Mexico in 1876*. Mexico: La Enseñanza Printing Office, 1876.

Gregg, Robert D. *The Influence of Border Troubles on Relations between the United States and Mexico, 1876–1910*. New York: De Capo Press, 1970.

Hannay, David. *Díaz*. Port Washington, N.Y.: Kennikat Press, 1970.

27

The Process of Modernization

*Economic Reform and the
Improvement of Mexico's Image*

As Porfirio Díaz consolidated his political position and stabilized the country, Mexico entered a period of sustained economic growth the likes of which it had never before experienced. In the process, Mexico entered the modern age. Steam, water, and electric power began to replace animal and human muscle. A number of new hydraulic- and hydroelectric-generating stations were built as the modernization process tied itself to the new machines it supported. The telephone arrived amid amazement and wonder in the 1880s. The Department of Communications and Public Works supervised and coordinated the installation of the wireless telegraph and submarine cables. A hundred miles of electric tramway connected the heart of Mexico City to the suburbs.

A major breakthrough in health and sanitation occurred when Díaz hired the British firm of S. Pearson and Son, Ltd., to bring modern technology to the drainage problem of Mexico City. For 16 million pesos the English engineers and contractors, with the experience of the Blackwell Tunnel under the Thames and the East River Tunnel in New York behind them, successfully completed a thirty-mile canal and a six-mile tunnel that relieved the Mexican capital of the threat of constant flooding and resultant property damage and disease. At approximately the same time the face of the country was scoured to bolster the country's own self-respect and its image abroad. A public building spree

439

changed the contours of boulevards, parks, and public buildings. Monuments and statues were dedicated to the world's leading statesmen, intellectuals, and military figures. A new penitentiary costing 2.5 million pesos opened in 1900, and a 3-million-peso post office in 1907. A new asylum for the insane, a new municipal palace, and a new Department of Foreign Relations were dedicated prior to the centennial celebrations of 1910. The white marble National Theater, however, missed the centennial target date, and the heavy structure began to sink into the spongy subsoil of Mexico City before it could be finished. Each time a new project was completed, it was formally dedicated in an elaborate and well-planned ceremony to which foreign diplomats, dignitaries, and businessmen received special presidential invitations. Their impressions of Mexico, relayed to colleagues back home, would help effect the change of image.

Mexico's own adaptation of positivism provided the philosophical underpinning of the regime, and the scientific method had great appeal in a prescientific society. The *científicos*, as those who followed in the footsteps of Gabino Barreda came to be known, were not all orthodox Comteans. Some blended Comte with John Stuart Mill, and others added a large dose of Herbert Spencer. A few of the científicos called for modest programs ushering the Indian masses into a rapidly modernizing world, but many were paternalistic toward the Indian at best and elitist at worst, believing that Mexico's future lay solely with the criollo class. Some felt that they might eventually be willing to share political and economic power with the aboriginal population, but, they contended, the time was not yet at hand. According to Justo Sierra, a científico spokesman, Mexico had to pass through a period of "administrative power" (a euphemism for dictatorship) before it could attain nationhood. Then the time would be ripe to discuss the broadening of the participatory base.

The president and his científico advisers realized first of all that a series of structural reforms were needed to place Mexico's economic house in order, and they were fortunate to find an economic genius in their midst. José Ives Limantour, soon renowned in European financial circles, was the son of a French émigré. A man of many talents, he was a scholar, an accomplished jurist, and a dedicated linguist. But he rejected the life of studious solitude for public service. First as subsecretary and then secretary of the treasury, he applied the best positivist thought of the day to the reorganization of the country's finances, which offered a fertile field for his talents. For Limantour, Mexico's future was

José Limantour (1854–1935). An advocate of positivism, Limantour, as secretary of the treasury, brought order and reason to Porfirian finances.

fully dependent upon its economic regeneration. To be sure, Matías Romero, during the Restoration, had begun work on a revision of the tariff, but much remained to be done. Gradually, during the 1880s and 1890s Secretary Limantour lowered or eliminated the duties on many imports and permitted special tariff exemptions for economically depressed areas of the country. He also negotiated a series of loans at favorable rates of interest and, most important for the economic well-being of the country, shifted Mexico from the silver to the gold standard.

As significant as any of the individual reforms was Limantour's decision to overhaul the nation's administrative machinery so that the reforms could be properly implemented. While it would be foolhardy to suggest that all graft and corruption were eliminated, Limantour did improve the situation markedly, at least at the lower echelons of government. The tariff laws were enforced; useless bureaucrats, or those who were derelict in the performance of duty, were eliminated; and at least some dishonest officials were fined, arrested, and removed from office. The dividends were startling. In 1890 the last installment of the debt to the United States, growing out of the mixed claims settlement, was paid, and four years later Mexico had not only balanced its budget for the first time in history but actually showed that revenues were running slightly ahead of expenditures. When Díaz left office in 1911 the treasury had about 70 million pesos in cash reserves.

The image abroad did change. As Limantour applied his skills to the reorganization of the treasury and Mexico met its foreign obligations on a regular basis, diplomatic relations were opened with all of Europe, and new treaties of friendship, commerce, and navigation were signed with Great Britain, France, Norway, Ecuador, and Japan. For the first time Mexico began to participate actively in international conferences. The country ceased to be the butt of jokes. To the contrary, foreign heads of state were lavish in their praise of the Díaz regime. By the late 1880s and early 1890s Díaz had begun to receive medals and decorations from foreign governments.

The Railroad Boom

Díaz was fully prepared to take advantage of the good economic indicators and the new reputation he had so assiduously cultivated. His government embarked upon a multifaceted program to attract foreign capital into the transportation and mining sectors of the economy. The most dramatic improvement in transportation was the rapid growth of the railroads, the only solution to Mexico's mountainous and broken terrain. During Díaz's first term the federal government began to subsidize the Mexican states in their effort to construct new lines, but the program proved to be something less than a smashing success. Not only did the states drag their heels, but many of the short lines completed were shoddily constructed and constituted more of a danger than a boon to travel. By the 1880s it was obvious that foreign investment and technology were better equipped to do the job.

The Mexican Central Railroad Company, backed by a group of Boston investors, received the concession to construct the major line north from Mexico City to El Paso, Texas. Work began from both terminal points, and the 1,224-mile project was completed in an amazingly short four-year period. The Central was soon flanked by two other new lines to its east and west. In 1888 the Mexican National Railroad Company, originally chartered under the laws of Colorado but subsequently purchased by a group of French and English entrepreneurs, successfully completed a new narrow-gauge line between Mexico City and Laredo, Texas, a distance of eight hundred miles and the shortest route from the

Porfirio Díaz (1830–1915). As soldier, rebel, statesman, and president, Díaz dominated his country as no previous figure in the nineteenth century.

Mexican capital to the United States border. Shortly after the turn of the century it was converted to standard gauge. Finally the Sonora Railroad Company, headed by Thomas Nickerson, built the line between Guaymas, on the Pacific Ocean, and Nogales, Arizona. By 1890 the total trackage of these three major companies approached two thousand miles.

Efforts to connect the country from east to west did not proceed so smoothly. The old Lerdo de Tejada concession to Emile la Sere to build the line across the Isthmus of Tehuantepec eventually passed into the hands of Chandos S. Stanhope. Stanhope completed a line across the Isthmus in 1894, but the construction work and terminal facilities were grossly inadequate. Díaz was forced to grant a new concession to S. Pearson and Son, Ltd., the famous British concern. Sir Weetman Dickinson Pearson (later raised to the peerage as Lord Cowdray) drove an especially hard bargain, and when finally completed the line proved to be one of the most costly in Mexican history. In 1907 the trains were running regularly between Puerto México on the Gulf coast and Salina Cruz on the Pacific, but many wondered if the price was worth it after all. The Panama Canal was already under con-

The arrival of the daily train triggered a burst of activity in hundreds of Mexican towns. This station scene was captured by American photographer Sumner W. Matteson in the station of Amecameca in 1907.

struction, and the Tehuantepec Railroad would soon be rendered obsolete.

Numerous lesser lines were undertaken in the 1880s and 1890s. A line in the south connected Mexico City with Guatemala, and short feeder lines connected most of the state capitals with the major trunks running between Mexico City and the United States border. By the end of the Díaz regime railroads interlaced the entire country; from about four hundred miles of track in 1876, Mexico in 1911 could boast fifteen thousand. Approximately 80 percent of the capital outlay came from the United States. In 1908, however, under the constant prodding of Limantour, the Díaz government purchased the controlling interest in the major lines.

Not all of the lines were laid in the most desirable areas, and not all were of first-rate quality. Yet they contributed in no small way to the tremendous economic transformation of the country.

As the cities were linked to the outlying areas, raw materials could be shipped to industries and finished goods distributed to a greatly expanded domestic market. As products could be quickly transported to population centers and the leading ports, new agricultural lands, specializing in commercial agriculture, were opened, and land values increased.[1] Mexico's textile industry, for example, relied primarily upon imported cotton at the beginning of the Díaz period, but with the opening of new lands in the north, near the railroad lines, cotton production by 1910 not only doubled but made the country almost self-sufficient. When the railroad arrived in Morelos the sugar planters began importing new machinery and setting up new mills to expand production. The larger market for locally produced products drove the costs down and, at least theoretically, widened the base of consumer use. Communities isolated by geography and centuries of tradition were gradually brought into greater contact with one another, and, as a result, the phenomenon of patria chica was challenged seriously for the first time.

The Revival of Mining

The railroads were a means to many ends, and not least among these was the revival of Mexico's potentially wealthy mining industry. The railroads, of course, offered the only practical and economical means of transporting massive shipments of ore. But, equally important, the Díaz-controlled legislature passed a new mining code in 1884. In order to appeal to the foreign investor the code made no mention of traditional Hispanic jurisprudence reserving ownership of the subsoil for the nation. Further, the proprietor of the surface was explicitly granted ownership of all bituminous and other mineral fuels. Several years after the mining code was enacted, the mining tax laws were revised, exempting certain minerals altogether and lowering the tax rates on others. United States and European investors recognized that the potential profits were great and entered Mexico in increasing

1. Arthur P. Schmidt, Jr., "The Railroad and the Economy of Puebla and Veracruz, 1877–1911: A Look at Agriculture," paper presented at the Fifty-first Annual Conference of the Southwest Social Science Association, March 22, 1973. A recent analysis of some fifty-five agrarian protests during the early Porfiriato indicates that over ninety percent occurred at a distance of less than forty kilometers from a new or projected railroad line. See John Coatsworth, "Railroads, Landholding, and Agrarian Protest in the Early Porfiriato," *Hispanic American Historical Review* 54 (1974): 55–57.

PRODUCTION OF SILVER AND GOLD IN MEXICO, 1877–1908

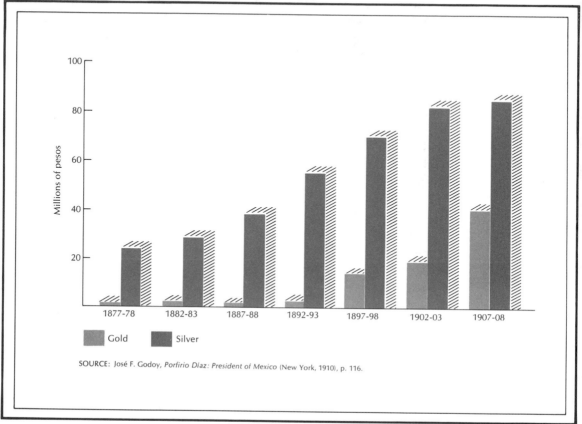

SOURCE: José F. Godoy, *Porfirio Díaz: President of Mexico* (New York, 1910), p. 116.

numbers in the 1880s and 1890s. The new miners introduced modern machinery and new processes of extracting the metal from the ore. Before the century was out they were responsible for radical transformation of the entire industry.

Between 1880 and 1890 three large mining developments were initiated by foreigners in Mexico: Sierra Mojada in Coahuila; Batopilas in Chihuahua; and El Boleo in Santa Rosalía, Baja California. Within a few years the Sierra Mojada region was yielding a thousand tons of silver and lead per week, and Batopilas had made a fortune for its owners. El Boleo, under French and German ownership, proved to be one of the richest copper mining areas in North America.

The introduction of the cyanide process, which made it profitable to extract metal from ores containing only a few ounces of metal to the ton, revolutionized the mining of gold and silver. Largely because of new explorations and the adoption of modern mining techniques, the value of gold production rose from about 1.5 million pesos in 1877 to over 40 million pesos in 1908. Silver production followed a similar pattern. From a production of 24.8 million pesos in 1877, over 85 million pesos worth of silver was being mined in 1908.

Some of the foreign investment came in the form of huge conglomerates. The Guggenheim interests, for example, spread out over much of Mexico and entered numerous interrelated mining activities. They owned the American Smelting and Refining Company, based in Monterrey but with large plants in Chihuahua, Durango, and San Luis Potosí as well. The Aguascalientes Metal Company, the Guggenheim Exploration Com-

Colonel William Greene's town of Cananea, Sonora, was the hub of Mexico's copper production and a symbol of the foreign domination of the country's natural resources.

pany, and the Mexican Exploration Company were either partially or totally owned and controlled by Daniel Guggenheim and his six brothers. In addition, the Guggenheims acquired many already proven mines, such as the Tecolote silver mines and the Esperanza gold mine, as well as new mines in Durango, Chihuahua, Coahuila, and Zacatecas. By 1902 Guggenheim investments in northern Mexico totaled some $12 million.

Other foreign investors came to Mexico with practically nothing and built multi-million-dollar businesses. Perhaps the best example is Colonel William Greene, the copper king of Sonora. In 1898 Greene obtained an option on a Sonora copper mine for forty-seven thousand pesos from the widow of Ignacio Pesqueira, a former governor of the state. Greene sold stocks for his mining venture on Wall Street, and within a few years his Cananea Consolidated Copper Company was one of the largest copper companies in the world, operating eight large smelting furnaces and employing thirty-five hundred men. With some of the profits Greene became a lumber factor and a rancher as well; one of his ranches grazed some forty thousand head of cattle.

Oil Fields and Other Industrial Enterprises

American and British investors engaged in a spirited competition for the exploitation of Mexico's oil. The first wells were sunk in areas where surface seepages clearly indicated the presence of petroleum reserves, but after the turn of the century systematic geological exploration began in earnest. The American interests were led by Edward L. Doheny, an American who had successfully developed oil fields in California; he now purchased over six hundred thousand acres of potentially rich oil lands around Tampico and Tuxpan. Within a short time his Mexican Petroleum Company brought forth Mexico's first commercially feasible gusher, El Ebano.

The British answer to Doheny was Sir Weetman Dickinson Pearson, who had worked on the drainage of Mexico City, the modernization of the Veracruz harbor, the reconstruction of the Tehuantepec Railroad, and the building of the terminal facilities at Puerto México and Salina Cruz. Enjoying cordial relations with Díaz, Pearson in 1901 secured an option on oil lands in the vicinity of San Cristóbal (today San Cristobal de las Casas, or Las Casas) on the Isthmus. But the Isthmian fields proved disappointing, and within a few years the regime granted Pearson drilling concessions in Veracruz, San Luis Potosí, Tamaulipas, and Tabasco. Progress came slowly at first to Pearson's El Aguila Company, but a dramatic hit brought forth the Potrero del Llano, Number 4, a gusher that, when successfully capped, produced more than a hundred million barrels in eight years. To cement the most friendly possible relations with the regime, Pearson appointed the dictator's son, Porfirio Díaz, Jr., to the board of directors of El Aguila. Doheny's Mexican Petroleum Company and Pearson's El Aguila Company dominated the petroleum industry in the early twentieth century and within a few years made Mexico one of the largest petroleum producers in the world.

It would be an exaggeration to suggest that Mexico experienced a profound industrial revolution during the Díaz years, but the industrial process did make itself felt. In 1902 the industrial census listed fifty-five hundred manufacturing industries. The volume of manufactured goods doubled during the Porfiriato. The process began in Monterrey, Nuevo León, where, in addition to the huge Guggenheim interests, other American, French, German, and British investors backed industrial enterprises. Attracted by excellent transportation facilities and by the progressive policies of Governor Bernardo Reyes, which included tax exemptions for industries, foreign and domestic capital was directed into Mexico's first important steel firm, the Compañía Fundidora de Fierro y Acero de Monterrey. Within a few years the company was producing pig iron, steel rails, beams, and bars, and by 1911 it was making over sixty thousand tons of steel annually. Monterrey was soon dubbed the Pittsburgh of Mexico.

In 1890 José Schneider, a Mexican of German extraction, founded the Cervecería Cuauhtémoc, which quickly became the largest and most important brewery in the country. Among its products was Carta Blanca, the number-one selling beer in Mexico. Its initial production capacity of ten thousand barrels and five thousand bottles of beer a day outstripped the available supply of bottles, so the company soon entered the glass business as well. By 1900 it was also producing other kinds of glassware, bottle caps, and packing cartons for both local use and national consumption.

Other industrial concerns based in Monterrey constructed new cement, textile, cigarette, cigar, soap, brick, and furniture factories, as well as flour mills and a large bottled-water plant. Capital investment in the city grew steadily throughout the Díaz regime but most dramatically during the first decade of the new century, when it rose from under 30 million to over 55 million pesos. Smaller fledgling textile and paper mills, cement factories, leather works, soap, shoe, explosives, and tile manufacturers, and a host of lesser firms located themselves in other areas of the country, but by 1910 Monterrey was without question the industrial capital of Mexico.

The improvement of harbor and dock facilities during the Porfiriato opened Mexico up to world commerce on a grander scale than ever before. Millions of pesos spent on Veracruz transformed it in a decade from a port many urged abandoning to one of prime importance. In 1876 Tampico, located at the mouth of the Panuco River, was inaccessible to ships drawing over nine feet. Díaz invited in United States engineers, and, when the harbor was properly dredged and the dock facilities modernized, the port began welcoming ships drawing as much as twenty-five feet. The city of Tampico grew rapidly as a business and commercial center and challenged Veracruz in volume handled. Similar improvements were made in the harbors of Mazatlán, Manzanillo, Puerto México, and Salina Cruz. By the turn of the century the number of serviceable ports had increased to ten on the Gulf coast and fourteen on the Pacific side. Partially because of the improvements in port facilities, and partially because of Limantour's reforms in the tariff structure, Mexico's foreign trade (exports and imports) increased from about 50 million pesos in 1876 to about 488 million pesos in 1910.

Although many of the trappings of traditional society were still to be found, the Mexico of the first decade of the twentieth century was a far cry from that of 1876. Improved public services and modern transportation and communication facilities opened the country to new ideas and challenged the concept of patria chica. The railroads began to drive some human carriers off the road, thus undoing, for the first time, the cargador system descended from the tamemes of the colonial period. The economy boomed, and dynamism permeated the atmosphere. Technology in general and mechanization in particular made tremendous strides. Foreign travelers for the first time marveled more than they criticized, for peace and growth allowed them the luxury of contemplating the many natural beauties Mexico had to offer. Mexico's foreign credit rating was firmly established throughout the world. But perhaps the most important product of the modernization process was that Mexicans, especially urban Mexicans, began to view themselves differently. Self-confidence replaced the embarrassment occasioned by the dec-

GROWTH OF FOREIGN TRADE, 1877–1910

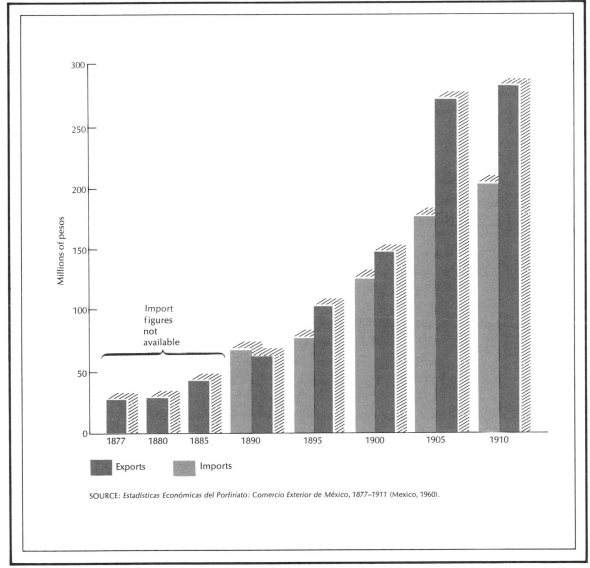

SOURCE: *Estadísticas Económicas del Porfiriato: Comercio Exterior de México, 1877–1911* (Mexico, 1960).

ades of internecine strife. For a third of a century there were no major civil wars, no major liberal-conservative struggles, and no major church-state controversies. Mexico was assuming its rightful position in the twentieth-century world. Very few yet questioned the costs the transformation had exacted because the material dividends seemed so self-evident. But the price paid was great, and the rapid modernization contained seeds of self-destruction.

Recommended for Further Study

Beato, Guillermo and Domenico Síndico. "The Beginning of Industrialization in Northeast Mexico." *The Americas* 39 (1983): 499–518.

Benjamin, Thomas and William McNellie, eds. *Other Mexicos: Essays on Regional Mexican History, 1876–1911*. Albuquerque: University of New Mexico Press, 1984.

Bernstein, Marvin D. *The Mexican Mining Industry, 1890–1950: A Study of the Interaction of Politics, Economics, and Technology*. Albany: State University of New York Press, 1964.

Coatsworth, John. "Railroads, Landholding, and Agrarian Protest in the Early Porfiriato." *Hispanic American Historical Review* 54 (1974): 48–71.

Davis, Thomas B. "Porfirio Diaz in the Opinion of His North American Contemporaries." *Revista de Historia de América* 63–64 (1967): 79–116.

Hibeno, Barbara. "Cervecería Cuauhtémoc: A Case Study of Technological and Industrial Development." *Mexican Studies* 8 (1992): 123–43.

Juárez, José Roberto. "The Use of Counter-Oaths in the Archdiocese of Guadalajara, Mexico, 1876–1911." *Journal of Church and State* 12 (1970): 79–87.

Kroeber, Clifton B. *Man, Land and Water: Mexico's Farmland Irrigation Policies, 1885–1911*. Berkeley: University of California Press, 1984.

Meyers, William K. "Politics, Vested Rights, and Economic Growth in Porfirian Mexico." *Hispanic American Historical Review* 57 (1977): 425–54.

Pletcher, David M. *Rails, Mines, and Progress: Seven American Promoters in Mexico, 1867–1911*. Ithaca: Cornell University Press, 1958.

Powell, T. G. "Mexican Intellectuals and the Indian Question, 1876–1911." *Hispanic American Historical Review* 48 (1968): 19–36.

Raat, William D. "Leopoldo Zea and Mexican Positivism: A Reappraisal." *Hispanic American Historical Review* 48 (1968): 1–18.

Randall, Robert W. "Mexico's Pre-Revolutionary Reckoning with Railroads." *The Americas* 42 (1985): 1–28.

Tinker Salas, Miguel. "Sonora: The Making of a Border Society, 1880–1910." *Journal of the Southwest* 34 (1992): 429–56.

Tischendorf, Alfred. *Great Britain and Mexico in the Era of Porfirio Díaz*. Durham, N.C.: Duke University Press, 1961.

Topik, Steven C. "The Emergence of Finance Capital in Mexico." In *Five Centuries of Mexican History*, edited by Virginia Gudea and Jaime E. Rodríguez, Vol. II, pp. 227–42. Mexico City and Irvine: Instituto Mora and University of California Irvine, 1992.

Wasserman, Mark. *Capitalists, Caciques and Revolution: The Native Elite and Foreign Enterprises in Chihuahua Mexico, 1854–1911*. Chapel Hill: University of North Carolina Press, 1984.

Wells, Allen. "All in the Family: Railroads and Henequen in Porfirian Yucatán," *Hispanic American Historical Review* 72 (1992): 159–209.

———. *Yucatan's Gilded Age: Haciendas, Henequen and International Harvester*. Albuquerque: University of New Mexico Press, 1985.

28

The Costs of Modernization

Dictatorship by Force

Modernization came to Mexico during the Díaz regime not simply as the result of positivist theory and careful economic planning. The peace that made it all possible was in part attributable to brute force. Díaz maintained himself in power from 1876 to 1911 by a combination of adroit political maneuvering, intimidation, and, whenever necessary, callous use of the federal army and the rurales. He was the consummate bully.

Throughout the thirty-four years the dictator maintained the sham of democracy. Elections were held periodically at the local, state, and national levels, but they were invariably manipulated in favor of those candidates who held official favor. The press throughout the epoch was tightly censored; journalists who dared to oppose the regime on any substantive matter found themselves in jail or exile, while recalcitrant editors found their newspapers closed down. Filomeno Mata, the editor of the *Diario del Hogar*, suffered imprisonment over thirty times for his anti-re-electionist campaigns. While a few persistent critics were killed, the large majority of the journalists were bludgeoned into submission and ceased to constitute a problem.

The dictator played off political opponents against one another, or bought them off. Potentially ambitious generals or regimental commanders were shifted regularly from one military zone to another to assure that they would be unable to cultivate a power base. State governors were invited to assume the same position in other states or to become congressmen, cabinet secretaries, or diplomats to remove their influence at home. Not even members of the Díaz family were immune. When the dictator's nephew, Félix Díaz, decided to run for the governorship of Oaxaca against Don Porfirio's wishes, he shortly found himself on a ship bound for Chile, where he was given a diplomatic post and allowed to cool off. Most influential Mexicans cooperated with the regime and were rewarded with political favors and lucrative economic concessions. Díaz himself never accumulated a personal fortune, but many of his civilian and military supporters in high positions had ample opportunity for graft. The científico advisers, for example, always seemed to know in advance the route of a new boulevard or railroad line, the property could thus be bought up at a low price and sold back to the government for a profit.

When Díaz needed to use force it was provided by the army and the rurales. He recognized the need for professionalizing the army, and, although he did not invite foreign military missions into the country, he did send military observers to West Point and to the French officer's school at St. Cyr. The recently reorganized Colegio Militar de Chapultepec provided formal instruction for the officer corps and made use of the most current European training manuals. By the turn of the century about half of the active officers (but very few of the generals) were graduates of the Chapultepec academy. The cadets, resplendent in snappy uniforms, were highlighted at the frequent military parades during which Díaz took the opportunity to display the latest armament obtained from France or Germany.

The rurales, Díaz's praetorian guard, also constituted an important enforcement tool for the *Pax Porfiriana*. The dictator strengthened the corps considerably, not simply to curtail brigandage in the rural areas but to serve as a counterpoise to the army itself. By the end of the regime the strength of the rurales had been increased to over twenty-seven hundred men. While the force was not large, it was used to good advantage by the dictator. In addition to its original patrolling functions, Díaz had rural corpsmen guard ore shipments from the mines, support local police forces, escort prisoners, enforce unpopular court decisions, and guard public payrolls and buildings. Recent scholarship has demonstrated that the rurales were neither as harsh nor as efficient as generally thought. While Díaz did not, as commonly understood, deliberately induct known bandits into the corps, neither did he try to set straight their image for cruelty

To reinforce the desired image, the rurales were always featured during military parades. Sumner Matteson photographed this salute to President Díaz on May 5, 1907.

and excess.[1] The myth served his purposes well, for the rurales were feared by brigands, marauders, political opponents, and recalcitrant villagers. When trouble flared it was often more prudent to send in the nearest corps than to allow a distinguished federal general the chance to enhance his reputation.

Díaz used the military not only to force compliance with the dictates of Mexico City but to administer the country as well. By the mid-1880s it was not unusual for military officers, most often generals of unquestionable loyalty, to dominate the state governorships and to be well represented among the three

1. Paul Vanderwood, "Mexico: The Porfirian Rurales," paper presented at Thirty-eighth Annual Meeting of the Southern Historical Association, November 17, 1972.

The federal artillery corps, well trained and well equipped, was the pride of the Díaz army.

hundred *jefes políticos* (local political bosses). In 1900, although relative peace had already been achieved, Díaz was still spending almost one-fourth of the total budget on the military establishment. He believed it was worth it because the modernization process was so intertwined with his concept of enforced peace. The relationship has been summarized by one scholar of Mexican militarism as follows: "The Díaz system was self-reinforcing. The military provided the order necessary for economic development, and economic development provided the revenues necessary to keep the military loyal. Economic growth also built a modern communications network, which made it far easier for the army to stamp out disorders in the outlying areas."[2]

Díaz's científico advisers have been labeled racist for their conscientious denigration of the Indian population. But the generalization has certain flaws, for it presupposes a monolithic philosophical framework within the científico community.[3] José

2. Edwin Lieuwen, *Mexican Militarism: The Political Rise and Fall of the Revolutionary Army* (Albuquerque, 1968), p. 3.
3. The revisionist position is cogently argued in William D. Raat, "Los intelectuales, el positivismo y la cuestión indígena," *Historia Mexicana* 20 (1971): 412–27; and in Raat, "Ideas and Society in Don Porfirio's Mexico," *The Americas* 30 (1973): 32–53.

Limantour was less a follower of Comte than of Darwin. He adapted notions of natural selection and survival of the fittest to Mexican reality as he understood it and emerged from his introspection calling for an aristocratic elite to reorder society. Little or no help could be expected from the Indian population. Francisco Bulnes, a prolific historian and apologist for científico rule, was more openly racist. Five million (white) Argentines, he argued, were worth more than fourteen million Mexicans. The Mexican Indian was sullenly intractable and hopelessly inferior, not because of innate corruption of his genes but because his grossly deficient diet sapped his mental, moral, and physical vitality. He responded more to the logic of force than to the art of persuasion. Less biologically oriented was Justo Sierra, the most famous científico of them all. Cofounder of the conservative newspaper, *La Libertad*, author of *Evolución política del pueblo mexicano*, secretary of education during part of the Porfiriato, and first rector of the national university, Sierra argued forcefully that social and cultural forces, not biological ones, had shaped the Indian's inferior position. And unlike Limantour and Bulnes, Sierra asserted the Indian's educability.

In the political sense the científicos may have had a point. Perhaps Mexico was not yet ready for democracy, and perhaps it was too early to broaden the participatory base. But their impassioned defense of the need for "administrative power" implied at best self-deception and at worst blatant hypocrisy. If they truly believed that the Indian masses could be prepared for a more active role in the political life of the Mexican nation, the logical place to begin the preparation process was an educational system that reached the people. But the schools built during the Porfiriato, even when the Department of Education was in Justo Sierra's hands, were almost all located in the cities where the criollos lived, not in the rural areas where they might serve the Indian and mestizo population. At the end of the Porfiriato Mexico still had two million Indians not speaking Spanish: They had been left aside.

The Hacendados

Mexico was still overwhelmingly a rural country when the twentieth century arrived, and the rural peasantry bore most of the costs of modernization. The payment was exacted in fear of the rurales, intimidation by local hacendados, constant badgering by jefes políticos and municipal officials, exploitation by foreign entrepreneurs, and, most important, seizure of private and communal lands by government-supported land sharks.

Life in rural Mexico had been dominated by the hacienda complex since the colonial period, but the abuses of the system were exacerbated markedly during the Díaz regime as railroad construction pushed land values up. The problem of exaggerated land concentration was directly attributable to a new land law enacted in 1883. This law, designed to encourage foreign colonization of rural Mexico, authorized land companies to survey public lands for the purpose of subdivision and settlement. For their efforts the companies received up to one-third of the land surveyed and the privilege of purchasing the remaining two-thirds at bargain prices. If the private owners or traditional ejidos could not prove ownership through legal title, their land was considered public and subject to denunciation by the companies.

The process that ensued was predictable. Very few rural Mexicans could prove legal title. All they knew for sure was that they had lived and worked the same plot for their entire lives, and their parents and grandparents had done the same. Their boundary line ran from a certain tree to a certain stream to the crest of a hill. The few who could produce documents, some dating back to the colonial period, were convinced by the speculators and their lawyers that the papers had not been properly signed, or notarized, or stamped, or registered. But not even those communal ejidos that could produce titles of indisputable legality were immune. The Constitution of 1857 with its Reform Laws was once again applied to the detriment of the ejidos, and with greater vigor than ever before.

Within five years after the land law became operative, land companies had obtained possession of over 68 million acres of rural land and by 1894 one-fifth of the total land mass of Mexico. Not yet completely satisfied, the companies received a favorable modification of the law in 1894, and by the early twentieth century most of the villages in rural Mexico had lost their ejidos and some 134 million acres of the best land had passed into the hands of a few hundred fantastically wealthy families. Over one-half of all rural Mexicans lived and worked on the haciendas by 1910.

The Mexican census of 1910 listed 8,245 haciendas in the republic, but a few wealthy individuals, often tied together by a marriage network of family elites, owned ten, fifteen, or even twenty of them. Though varied in size, haciendas of forty or fifty thousand acres were not at all uncommon. Fifteen of the richest

Mexican hacendados owned haciendas totaling more than three hundred thousand acres each. The state of Chihuahua affords a classic example of how the hacienda system operated and brought wealth and prestige to one extended family. Throughout the Díaz regime the fortunes of that north central Mexican state were guided by the Terrazas-Creel clan. Don Luis Terrazas, the founder of the dynasty, had served as governor prior to the French Intervention and fought with Juárez against the French in the 1860s. His land acquisitions began shortly thereafter, when he obtained the estate of Don Pablo Martínez del Río, a French sympathizer. In the 1870s, 1880s, and 1890s, in and out of the gubernatorial chair, he acquired additional haciendas, profiting immensely from the land laws of the Díaz government. By the early twentieth century Terrazas owned some fifty haciendas and smaller ranches totaling a fantastic seven million acres. Don Luis was the largest hacendado in Mexico and perhaps in all of Latin America; his holdings were eight times the size of the legendary King Ranch in Texas. He owned 500,000 head of cattle, 225,000 sheep, 25,000 horses, 5,000 mules, and some of the best fighting bulls in the western hemisphere. Encinillas, northwest of Chihuahua City, was the largest of his haciendas, extending to some 1,300,000 acres and employing some 2,000 peones. San Miguel de Babícora was over 850,000 acres, while San Luis and Hormigas were over 700,000 acres each.

But the wealth and power of the Terrazas family cannot be judged in terms of landholding and its related activities alone. Don Luis also owned textile mills, granaries, railroads, telephone companies, candle factories, sugar mills, meat packing plants, and several Chihuahua mines. Each of his twelve children was married with the care characteristic of Renaissance nobility. Daughter Angela Terrazas married her first cousin, Enrique Creel, the son of an American consul in Chihuahua and a man of wealth, erudition, and prestige. Enrique Creel also served several times in the state governorship and, in addition, was Mexico's secretary of foreign relations in 1910–11. Creel's own haciendas totaled more than 1,700,000 acres. He was also one of the founders and directors of the Banco Minero de Chihuahua, which gradually absorbed many of the other banks in the state. He was a partner, furthermore, in many of his father-in-law's enterprises and directed or owned iron and steel mills, breweries, granaries, and a coal company. Other daughters and sons also married well. The sons, as to be expected, became hacendados and entrepreneurs. Sons Alberto and Juan each had haciendas totaling over

600,000 acres, and son-in-law Federico Sisniega held some 260,-
000 acres and was a director of the Banco Nacional de Chihuahua. To strengthen the already strong Terrazas-Creel ties, son
Alberto married his niece, Emilia Creel, the daughter of his sister Angela and Enrique Creel. Son Federico Terrazas married
into the Falomir family and daughter Adela into the Muñoz
family, two of the other most wealthy and prestigious families in
the state.

It is virtually impossible to calculate the extent of either the
fortune or the power wielded by the Terrazas-Creel clan. Luis
Terrazas himself probably did not know how much he owned.
He surely did know, however, that the value of rural land in Chihuahua rose from about $.30 per acre in 1879 to about $9.88 per
acre in 1908. Had he been able to liquidate only his personal,
nonurban landholdings on the eve of the Mexican Revolution, he
would have carried over $69 million to the bank.

One can be certain that little of major importance occurred in
Chihuahua without the approval of patriarch Don Luis Terrazas.
During the Díaz regime members of the extended family sat for
a total of sixty-six terms in the state legislature and twenty-two
terms in the national legislature. Because residency requirements
were loosely defined, Enrique Creel and Juan Terrazas became
national senators from other Mexican states. Municipal and regional officialdom bore either the Terrazas-Creel names or their
stamp of approval. The immense power was built upon a foundation of land, and the state of Chihuahua was a microcosm of
what was happening throughout the Mexican republic.

The state of Morelos was dominated not by one extended family but rather by a handful of powerful sugar families: the García Pimentels, the Amors, the Torre y Miers, and a few others.
To fund the purchase of expensive new machinery these families
had to increase production and so began expanding into new
lands. As no public lands were available, they completely encircled small ranches and even villages, thereby choking off all
infusions of economic lifeblood. Some towns stagnated, while
others vanished from the map altogether. The town fathers of
Cuautla could not even find sufficient land for a new cemetery
and were reduced to burying children in a neighboring village.

The Peones

The millions of rural Mexicans who found themselves in dying
villages or subsisting as peones on the nation's haciendas were

worse off financially than their rural ancestors a century before. The average daily wage for an agricultural worker remained almost steady throughout the nineteenth century—about thirty-five centavos. But in the same hundred-year period the price of corn and chile more than doubled, and beans cost six times more in 1910 than in 1800. In terms of purchasing power correlated with the price of corn or cheap cloth, the Mexican peón during the Díaz regime was twelve times poorer than the United States farm laborer.

Working conditions varied considerably from region to region and even from hacienda to hacienda, but they were generally poor. Peones often availed themselves of the talents of a scribe to spell out their gamut of complaints. While it was not uncommon for the peón to be allotted a couple of furrows to plant a little corn and chile and on occasion he might receive a small ration of food from the hacienda, he worked from sunrise to sunset, often seven days a week, raising crops or tending cattle. Sometimes he was allowed to cut firewood free; on other occasions he paid for the right. The scant wages he received most often were not paid in currency but in certificates or metal discs redeemable only at the local *tienda de raya*, an all-purpose company store located on the hacienda complex. Credit was extended liberally, but the prices, set by the hacendado or the mayordomo were invariably several times higher than those in a nearby village. For the hacendado the situation was perfect. The taxes on his land were negligible; his labor was, in effect, free, for all the wages that went out came back to him through the tienda de raya with a handsome profit. The peón found himself in a state of perpetual debt, and by law he was bound to remain on the hacienda so long as he owed a single centavo. Debts were not eradicated at the time of death but passed on to the children. Should an occasional obdurate peón escape, there was scarcely any place for him to go. Many states had laws making it illegal to hire an indebted peón.

The bookkeeping procedures in the tienda de raya always seemed to work to the disadvantage of the illiterate peón. Goods charged against his account were more expensive than they would have been had he been able to pay cash. And other items were often debited to his account. Charges for a marriage ceremony or a funeral often exceeded the monthly wage. Fines for real or imagined crimes on the hacienda were added; forced contributions for fiestas and interest on previous debts were tallied. And, in the most ignominious charge of all, some hacendados

For a couple of centavos the rural, illiterate Mexicans could hire a scribe to scratch out a few lines to a relative or friend.

even added a monthly fee for the privilege of shopping at the tienda de raya.

Stories of corporal punishment of the peón (petty theft could bring two hundred lashes) and sexual violation of the young women on the haciendas are commonplace, but they are virtually impossible to prove or disprove. It is certain that conditions on the henequen haciendas of Yucatán were the worst in the republic. Because many of the peones in Yucatán were deportees from other parts of Mexico (some were recalcitrant Yaqui Indians from Sonora, and others were convicted criminals), they were forced to work in chains, and flogging was not uncommon. There is little evidence, however, that this type of physical maltreatment was widespread throughout Mexico. Surely the peón and his family were everywhere subject to the personal whims of the hacendado or the mayordomo, but hacienda records and correspondence to local, state, and even national officials reveal that complaints, while frequent, rarely contained charges of physical abuse. More common are complaints of intolerable working conditions, violence in the peón community itself, and dishonest record keeping in the tienda de raya—and always the sense of poverty, powerlessness, and hopelessness. During especially busy times like planting or harvesting, the permanent work force was augmented by temporary workers, often from surrounding villages. New arrivals, frequently earning a slightly higher wage than the resident peones seemed to break the socioeconomic equilibrium, and violence between the two groups of workers was a constant threat.

The dichotomies of nineteenth-century Mexican life, especially those of wealth and poverty, are almost all to be found on the hacienda. The main hacienda house was sumptuous, externally and internally. But the hacendado would seldom spend more than a few months a year there. Most often he had other haciendas to attend, inevitably businesses to manage in the cities, and then he had to visit his children in their fine European or United States boarding schools. The hacienda provided, in addition to its income, a summer vacation home, a change of pace, and social status. The hacendado's teen-age children, remarkable for their conspicuous consumption, used trips to the hacienda to impress their friends. The extended families could be comfortably accommo-

In 1907, photographer Sumner Matteson was surprised to find burros, horses, mules, and people sharing quarters in this pulque hacienda, where the stench of animals was rivaled only by the stench of fermenting pulque.

dated, and young boys, donned in charro costume and mounted on carefully bred and well-groomed horses, could fancy themselves country squires. Birthdays, saints' days, and feast days were reason enough to move the family from the state capital to the hacienda for an outing, and on special occasions, like an eighteenth birthday or a wedding, entire train cars could be reserved to carry guests, musicians, local dignitaries, and domestics.

The contrast between the hacendado and those who worked the hacienda and made it live is so stark as to be absurd. Because all "justice" on the hacienda was administered by the mayordomo, the peón had no genuine judicial rights or legal recourse. If a mayordomo overreacted in punishment of some real or imagined offense, he was accountable to nobody. Within a mile of the grand hacienda house were miserable, one-room, floorless, windowless adobe shacks. Water had to be carried in daily, often from long distances. The individual plots allotted to the peón were worked often after sunset, when the important work of the day had been completed. Twice a day a few minutes would be set aside to consume some tortillas wrapped around beans and chile, washed down with a few gulps of black coffee or pulque. Protein in the form of meat, fish, or fowl, even on the cattle haciendas, was a luxury reserved for a few special occasions during the year. Infant mortality on many haciendas exceeded 25 percent.

Diversion in the form of a local fiesta might occur once a year. An amateur bullfight could be staged in the hacienda corral, and resident aficionados would try their hand with a half-grown fighting bull that somehow looked bigger as it got closer. The peones, fortified with pulque or mescal, who found momentary escape entertaining their friends often paid dearly for their bravado, but a broken arm or a punctured thigh was a small matter when one had nothing to look forward to but the drab existence and appalling squalor of the next twelve months.

Porfirio Díaz had developed his country at the expense of his countrymen. He hermetically sealed himself off from the stark realities of Mexican masses. The great material benefits of the age of modernization in no way filtered down to the people. They were still an amorphous mass destitute of hope. Their lives were not in the least changed because the new National Theater was built in Mexico City or because José Limantour was able to borrow money in London or Paris at 4 percent. In fact, for them the cost of modernization had been too great.

Recommended for Further Study

Anderson, Rodney D. *Outcasts in Their Own Land: Mexican Industrial Workers, 1906–1911*. DeKalb: Northern Illinois University Press, 1976.

Beals, Carleton. *Porfirio Díaz: Dictator of Mexico*. Philadelphia: Lippincott, 1932.

Beezley, William H. "Opportunity in Porfirian Mexico." *North Dakota Quarterly* 40 (1972): 30–40.

Flandrau, Charles M. *Viva Mexico*. Urbana: University of Illinois Press, 1964.

Hu-Dehart, Evelyn. *Yaqui Resistance and Survival: The Struggle for Land and Autonomy, 1821–1910*. Madison: University of Wisconsin Press, 1984.

Joseph, Gilbert, and Allen Wells. "Summer of Discontent: Economic Rivalry Among Elite Factions During the Late Porfiriato in Yucatán." *Journal of Latin American Studies* 18 (1986): 255–82.

Katz, Friedrich. "Labor Conditions on Haciendas in Porfirian Mexico: Some Trends and Tendencies." *Hispanic American Historical Review* 54 (1974): 1–47.

Kitchens, John W. "Some Considerations on the Rurales of Porfirian Mexico." *Journal of Inter-American Studies* 9 (1967): 441–55.

Raat, William D. "Agustín Aragón and Mexico's Religion of Humanity." *Journal of Inter-American Studies* 11 (1969): 441–57.

———. "Ideas and Society in Don Porfirio's Mexico." *The Americas* 30 (1973): 32–53.

Ruiz, Ramón. *The People of Sonora and the Yankee Capitalists*. Tucson: University of Arizona Press, 1988.

Sandels, Robert. "Silvestre Terrazas and the Old Regime in Chihuahua." *The Americas* (1971): 192–205.

Schmitt, Karl M. "The Díaz Conciliation Policy on State and Local Levels, 1876–1911." *Hispanic American Historical Review* 40 (1960): 513–32.

Stabb, Martin S. "Indigenism and Racism in Mexican Thought, 1857–1911." *Journal of Inter-American Studies* 1 (1959): 405–23.

Vanderwood, Paul. *Disorder and Progress: Bandits, Police and Mexican Development*. Rev. ed. Wilmington, Del.: Scholarly Resources, 1992.

Walker, David W. "Homegrown Revolution: The Hacienda Santa Catalina del Alamo y Anexas and Agrarian Protest in Eastern Durango, Mexico, 1897–1913." *Hispanic American Historical Review* 72 (1992): 239–73.

———. "Porfirian Labor Politics: Working Class Organizations in Mexico City and Porfirio Díaz." *The Americas* 37 (1981): 257–90.

Wasserman, Mark. "The Social Origins of the 1910 Revolution in Chihuahua." *Latin American Research Review* 15 (1980): 15–38.

Wells, Allen. "Family Elites in a Boom-and-Bust Economy: The Molinas and Peóns of Porfirian Yucatán." *Hispanic American Historical Review* 62 (1982): 224–53.

Womack, John, Jr. *Zapata and the Mexican Revolution*. New York: Knopf, 1968.

29

Society and Culture during the Porfiriato

The changes in Mexican society and culture during the Porfiriato were every bit as profound as those in the political and economic realms. Most noteworthy perhaps was the fact that Mexicans began to view themselves differently. Self-esteem replaced the sense of shame that had characterized the introspective diagnoses of the past. For the first time Mexico had shown her potential and had begun to catch up with a rapidly changing world. Optimism had replaced pessimism, and xenophilia at least challenged xenophobia.

Population

The stability of the Porfiriato resulted in Mexico's first period of prolonged population growth. In the absence of war and its social dislocations and with modest gains recorded in health and sanitation, the population grew from 8,743,000 in 1874 to 15,160,000 in 1910. From 1810 to 1874 the average annual population growth had been about 43,000, but during the Díaz era population increased at an average of 180,000 per year. Mexico City and the state capitals grew even more rapidly than the population at large, increasing some 88.5 percent during the epoch. From a population of 200,000 in 1874, Mexico City in 1910 was the home of 471,066 Mexicans.

Railroad development, mining activities, and port improvements caused a number of tiny villages to burgeon into towns and cities. Torreón, at the intersection of the Mexican Central

POPULATION OF SELECTED MEXICAN CITIES DURING THE PORFIRIATO

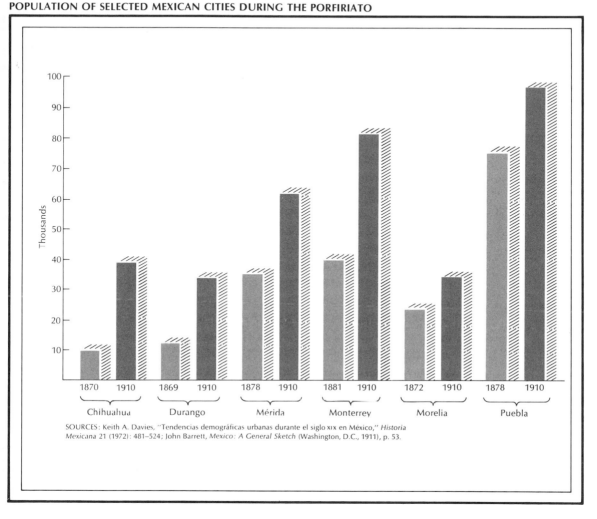

SOURCES: Keith A. Davies, "Tendencias demográficas urbanas durante el siglo xix en México," *Historia Mexicana* 21 (1972): 481–524; John Barrett, *Mexico: A General Sketch* (Washington, D.C., 1911), p. 53.

Railroad and the International Railroad (running from Eagle Pass, Texas, to Durango), jumped from fewer than 2,000 inhabitants in 1876 to over 43,000 in 1910; Sabinas, Coahuila, from 788 to 14,555; and Nuevo Laredo from 1,283 to almost 9,000. The two port terminuses of the Tehuantepec Railroad recorded similar gains. Puerto México had only 267 inhabitants in 1884 but reached 6,616 by 1910, while Salina Cruz grew from 738 in 1900 to almost 6,000 ten years later. Colonel Greene's copper town of Cananea hardly existed at the beginning of the Porfiriato. From a population of about 100 in 1876, it catapulted to almost 15,000 in 1910.

Urban Improvements

The rapid growth of towns and cities throughout the republic was accompanied by an obvious dynamism in society. The sleepy Mexico that caught the visitor's eyes earlier in the century had awakened from its slumber. Travelers were astonished by the amount of construction going on everywhere. By 1910 all the state capitals had electricity, and most had tramways. Weekly newspapers became dailies, potable water systems and sewage systems were extended, hospitals were constructed, and new hotels sprang up to cater to the greatly increasing tourist trade. Even small, out-of-the-way towns improved their facilities. Whereas travelers during the first fifty years after Independence were often horrified at Mexico's hotels and inns, tourists late in the Díaz regime were pleasantly surprised.

On occasion growth got out of hand. When Mexico City held its Independence Day celebrations in September 1882, the forty thousand tourists who descended on the capital simply could not all be accommodated. But the lesson was not lost. In 1910, during the more elaborate centennial celebrations, there were rooms for everyone.

The transportation system in the capital was excellent, with first-, second-, and third-class streetcars and cabs carrying passengers throughout the city. The streetcars were sometimes put to strange uses. One caught the eye of an Irish visitor during the late Porfiriato.

> A curious feature of the streets is the electric tramway hearse. Frequently one sees a funeral consisting of a number of cars on the rails; first comes an open one like a long low truck with a black catafalque covering, under which reposes the coffin and the wreaths; the next may be another piled up with wreaths and crosses, and then follows car after car with the mourners. This of course stops all the tramway traffic for the time being.[1]

But to many the most dramatic change was in the field of law and order. Scarcely a traveler in the late nineteenth century failed to comment upon the relative absence of obvious crime and political upheaval. Most were astute enough to realize that payment for law and order was exacted in fear of the army, rurales, and local law-enforcement agencies; they considered the result worth the price. Perhaps once Mexico had passed through the difficult transition from a law-breaking to a law-respecting society, the intimidating atmosphere could be relaxed.

1. Mary Barton, *Impressions of Mexico with Brush and Pen* (London, 1911), pp. 45–46.

The changing face of urban Mexico was accompanied by a not-too-subtle modification of the value structure. Porfirio Díaz recoiled at English and United States suggestions that the time-honored tradition of the Mexican bullfight was nothing more than a cruel and barbarous spectacle. It was the epitome of a clash of values. The phenomenon has been perfectly captured by historian William Beezley, who wrote that while most Mexicans saw "the ballet of cape and animal," foreigners "saw only blood and sand." Díaz ultimately placed a higher premium on international respect than on preserving this part of Mexico's Hispanic heritage and, although he later reversed himself, during his first administration prohibited bullfighting in the Federal District, Zacatecas, and Veracruz, areas where tourists would be most likely to witness the Sunday event. An American import soon offered itself as a substitute. Abner Doubleday's baseball made its Mexican debut in the 1880s and had caught on beyond anyone's expectations by the turn of the century. Not a few Mexican traditionalists lamented the exchange of the bat, the ball, and the baggy pants for the cape, the sword, and the suit of lights.[2]

Social Classes

The Porfiriato also witnessed some improvement in the lot of women as a select few began to enter professions hitherto regarded as the sole preserve of men. The medical school in Mexico City graduated its first woman doctor in 1887, and by the turn of the century others had followed. In the 1890s and early 1900s women began to make significant inroads into dentistry, law, pharmacy, higher education, and journalism. A new commercial school for women was inaugurated in 1903, and shortly thereafter its classes were filled. But Mexico was not yet quite ready for an active feminist movement designed to challenge in depth the traditional roles of the sexes. The prerogatives of the males were not to be questioned. The Admiradoras de Juárez, a militant feminist organization founded in 1904 by Laura Torres, was attacked by Justo Sierra as a refuge for old and ugly women whose only recourse was to try to become men. His advice to the women was to leave politics and law to the opposite sex and to concentrate instead on creating a better social atmosphere in

2. These themes are developed in William H. Beezley, *Judas at the Jockey Club and Other Episodes of Porfirian Mexico* (Lincoln, 1987), pp. 13–25.

which Mexicans could live more happily. In spite of Sierra, however, many talented Mexican women no longer felt the need to confine themselves exclusively to the home.

Of course, not everything changed from 1876 to 1910. There was certainly more crime and alcoholism than the foreign visitors saw in the tourist zones of the cities. The léperos and cargadores continued to attract their attention. Although most visitors were not aware of the working conditions in the factories throughout the republic, the plight of the urban laborer had changed little, but there were many more of them. A few employers initiated modest reform early in the twentieth century. The Cervecería Cuauhtémoc in Monterrey, a Mexican-owned and Mexican-managed enterprise, was the first major industrial concern to adopt the nine-hour day. Few other Mexican industries, however, and practically none owned by foreigners, followed suit. Even at the end of the Porfiriato the workweek for the large majority of urban laborers was seven days and the workday eleven or even twelve hours. Pensions were almost unknown, as was compensation for accidents suffered on the job.

The diet of the lower classes—day laborers, rank-and-file soldiers, beggars, domestics, street vendors, and the unemployed—remained monotonous and constantly inadequate. Corn, beans, chile, and pulque still constituted the staples; meat was almost totally absent. The grossly deficient diet and unsanitary living conditions made the masses susceptible to a wide array of debilitating diseases, and the large majority passed their entire lives without a single visit to a qualified doctor. Life expectancy remained constant—about thirty years. Infant mortality remained unacceptably high, averaging 30 percent for most of the Porfiriato. A Protestant missionary in Díaz's Mexico recalled his impressions.

> I used to ask, "How many of you, fathers and mothers, have children in heaven?" Usually all hands would promptly go up, while the replies came, *"Tengo cinco." "Tengo ocho."* . . . Deplorable ignorance as to proper sanitary conditions in the home and the care of children is responsible for a large proportion of this death harvest among the little ones. Children's diseases, as measles and scarlet fever, carry multitudes away.[3]

The lower-class barrios of Mexico City—La Merced, La Palma, and Nonoalco—were so bad that some suggested they be burned

3. Alden Buell Case, *Thirty Years with the Mexicans: In Peace and Revolution* (New York, 1917), pp. 61–62.

Modernization occurred at the expense of the poor, in both urban and rural settings.

to the ground. There was no indoor plumbing in these districts, and only one public bathhouse per fifteen thousand people. Garbage collection was sporadic at best. Only the completion of Mexico City's drainage canal registered a positive impact on the lower-class neighborhoods, as the masses at least were able to escape the ravages of seasonal flooding.

Consumption of pulque and other alcoholic beverages among the lower classes did not increase during the Porfiriato, but the public and private outcry against alcohol did. Because alcoholism was unempirically linked to robberies, sex crimes, child abandonment, and mendicancy, temperance societies sprang up throughout the country. The Catholic press initiated a journalistic campaign, and state and local governments enacted legislation to curtail the use of alcoholic beverages. But limiting the

Life for the peón on the hacienda was bad; living in a city slum was even worse. But nowhere was it more difficult than in the mines.

hours of pulquerías and restricting new openings seemed to do little good, so the establishments were made as uncomfortable as possible. To discourage the patron from squandering away too much time and money, pulquerías were to have no windows, no chairs, no music, and, most important, no women. But profuse legislation did not accomplish its goal. Both alcoholism and toxemia from the high bacterial content of the pulque were widespread as the nineteenth century gave way to the twentieth.

The most dramatic change in the social structure was the expansion of the middle class. The earning power of skilled artisans, government bureaucrats, scribes, clergymen, low-ranking army officers, and professional men had increased. They demonstrated no class solidarity, but their lives were perceptibly different from the lower classes whence they had sprung. The booming economy made it possible for many a small businessman and neighborhood merchant to move his family from the drab room above the store or from his parents' residence into a larger and more comfortable apartment or house. The extension of water and sewage facilities provided many the luxury of indoor plumbing for the first time in their lives. The middle-class diet included meat and soup several times a week.

With middle-class status, creating the proper impression became important. It was not unusual for the monthly wage or monthly profit to be idled away on a single night of entertainment for friends. While the middle-class wife was beginning to break out of the home, she generally resigned herself to her husband's marital infidelity and to having but a small voice in the family's decision-making process. Seemingly possessed of infinite patience, she found some solace in the church and endured her submissive role with remarkable stoicism.

Middle-class children were taught to make class distinctions based upon outward appearances. If a well-dressed person appeared at the door they were expected to report to their parents *Allí está un señor*, but if the caller was dressed poorly the proper announcement was *Allí está un hombre*.[4] Although only recently sprung from the lower class themselves, many members of the middle class could be callous in their appreciation of the problems of the downtrodden.

While the poor continued to live in misery and a new, small middle class emerged in the cities, the rich became more convinced than ever that upon the pillar of private property civilization itself was braced. The pinnacle of social acceptance during the Porfiriato was to be invited, for a monthly dues of seven hundred pesos, to enjoy the amenities of the Jockey Club in Mexico City. The club was located in the Casa de Azulejos, the most opulent mansion in the capital. One could enjoy a sumptuous dinner there, spend an hour at the baccarat table, and hope to see cabinet ministers, governors, military zone commanders, or perhaps even Don Porfirio and Doña Carmen themselves.

The true measure of aristocratic success was to see how French one could become in taste and manners. The advantages of a French education and a French governess for aristocratic children were beyond debate. Beautiful Spanish colonial furniture was stored away, and modern French furniture adorned the houses. When Mexican composer Gustavo E. Campa wrote an opera based on the life of Nezahualcoyótl, "the Poet King of Texcoco," he entitled it not *El Rey Poeta* but *Le Roi Pòete* and prepared the libretto in French. Membership in the Sociedad Filarmónica y Dramática Francesa assured one of brushing el-

4. Jesús Silva Herzog, *Una vida en la vida de México* (Mexico, 1972), p. 9.

José Guadalupe Posada (1852–1913), México's most famous printmaker, parodies a fashionable lady during the Porfiriato.

bows with the most Frenchified members of Mexican society at a concert or a ball and might even garner one an invitation to attend one of the famous soirées at the Lyre Gauloise. The Paseo de la Reforma was redecorated to look like the Champs Elysées, while architectural design aped *fin-de-siècle* Paris. When Mexican millionaire Antonio Escandón donated a statue of Columbus to adorn the fashionable avenue, he commissioned the Parisian sculptor Charles Cordier to do the work. Having no notion of the revolution that would soon engulf Mexico, the aristocracy blissfully celebrated Bastille Day, July 14, with almost as much enthusiasm as their own Independence Day.

French cuisine reigned supreme in the capital. The best and most expensive restaurants were the Fonda de Recamier and the Maison Doreé. Between the Consommé Brunoise Royale and the Tournedos au Cèpes, one could sip imported French wine and listen to the orchestra play "Bon Aimée," "Amoureuse," "Rendez-vous," or some other tune everyone knew to be *à la mode*. For the athletic there was also membership in the French Polo Club and for the more sedate a season ticket to the French comic opera to partake of such quickly forgettable productions as *Les cloches de*

Corneville or *La Fille de madame Angot*. Those who had pretensions to both music and athletics adopted the cancan, a French import that took Mexico by storm in the 1880s.

Cultural and Intellectual Life

Literary expression during the Porfiriato found nineteenth-century romanticism yielding first to realism and almost simultaneously to modernism. The realists of the period, unlike their romantic predecessors, were not interested in instruction or moralizing. Hoping that the enforced stability of the Porfiriato would encourage the development of the arts, they early made their peace with the regime. Not a socially conscious group, the realists viewed the poor not as oppressed but rather as lazy and shiftless. On occasion a crusader emerged from the realist ranks, such as Arcadio Zentella who decried the evils of the hacienda system in his novel *Perico* (1885). But Zentella was the exception.

More typical was José López Portillo y Rojas (1850–1923), perhaps Mexico's best realist novelist of the nineteenth century. Born to a prominent Guadalajara family, he studied law and traveled widely in Europe, imbibing the French spirit, before dedicating himself to literature. In his novel *Nieves* (1887) López Portillo did recognize that an occasional hacendado might brutalize a peón, but he found no fault with the system that conditioned the relationship or anything reprehensible in a society that tolerated it. His solution was a simplistic one. It was all a matter of volition. The poor of Mexico simply had no desire to improve themselves. "Our workers will come out of their abject condition," he wrote in *Nieves*, "when they aspire to eat well, to dress decently, and to acquire the comforts of life."[5]

The realistic period in Mexican literature was briefly prolific but not very distinguished. Much more important were the modernists of the Porfiriato. Culturally mature, stylistically innovative, and concerned with refinements in the language and a new kind of imagery, the modernists stood in favor of a symbolic revolt not against Porfirian society but against nineteenth-century culture. While the modernists generally also turned their backs on political, economic, and social problems as they sought refuge in the world of imagination, they succeeded in transforming Mexican literature into an art. Modernist literature was elitist—

5. José López Portillo y Rojas, *Cuentos completos*, vol. 1: *Nieves, El primer amor* (Guadalajara, 1952), p. 41.

it was designed for the upper class—but without question it was literature of vitality, perception, and grace. Just as Limantour's balancing of the budget had yielded economic confidence, just as Díaz's quelling of rebellion had yielded political confidence, the modernist movement brought forth genuine cultural confidence.

The best and most versatile of the modernist fiction writers was Amado Nervo (1870–1919). After studying briefly for the priesthood, Nervo left the seminary and became a journalist in Mazatlán. At the turn of the century he moved to Paris—for Mexicans a cultural mecca—where he met the founder of the Latin American modernist movement, the Nicaraguan poet Rubén Darío. Before his literary career had ended, Nervo had to his credit more than thirty volumes—novels, poetry, short stories, plays, essays, and criticism.

The theme of Nervo's first novel, *El bachiller* (1895), was sensational and even horrifying. A young priest, tempted by physical love, castrates himself to avoid seduction. But the theme was developed with such skill and grace that few took umbrage or reproved the licentious plot. If Mexicans really wanted to be wordly they had to understand that the French were not offended by Gustav Flaubert's even more salacious *Madame Bovary*. In much of his work Nervo showed himself a perceptive amateur psychologist. His insight into the motivations of the protagonists he created and his appreciation of the conflicts between the material and the spiritual captivated his readers. Like most of his contemporaries, he was not interested in analyzing broad social problems but rather in probing personal problems of both a psychological and a philosophical nature.

Mexican artists during the Porfiriato, unlike their literary colleagues, did not make their peace with the regime. The Art Academy of San Carlos continued to dominate the artistic community, but it was poorly supported by the government. The future giants of Mexican art—Diego Rivera and José Clemente Orozco—were students at the academy and began perfecting the techniques that would win them world acclaim two decades hence. While heavy emphasis was placed upon copying European models, a few of the students began to break with tradition and experiment with Mexican themes.

Díaz and his científico advisers, in art as in so many other areas, continued to show preference for all things foreign. To celebrate the centennial of Mexico's Independence, the government constructed a new building to house a Spanish art display and provided a subvention of thirty-five thousand pesos for the

Spanish show. When the Mexican artists at the academy protested that they wanted to put on a national art show to coincide with the celebrations, they were forced to limp along with their old building and a paltry three thousand pesos to realize their efforts. Those who saw the Mexican exhibition probably understood why the regime chose not to support it. It was youthful, exuberant, and iconoclastic in both technique and theme. Gerardo Murillo, who changed his name to Dr. Atl, a Náhuatl word meaning *water*, had experimented with wax, resin, and oil in several scandalous bacchanals, while other young artists developed Indianist themes. Many of Mexico's most promising artists exhibited there for the first time and seemed to take special pride in their bold departures from staid European models. Slums and brothels decorated canvases, and somber Indian faces depicted the stark reality of Mexican life. This was not the impression of the stable, conservative, white, progressive Mexico that Díaz wanted portrayed.

The Porfiriato also distinguished itself as a productive period in Mexican historical scholarship. The best of the historians put polemic behind them and moved into the archives for painstaking research. Manuel Orozco y Berra and Luis González Obregón interested themselves primarily in the colonial period and produced seminal works on the society and culture of New Spain. Perhaps the greatest historian of the epoch was Joaquín García Icazbalceta (1825–94), who collected and edited several monumental series of colonial documents and prepared a bibliography of the sixteenth century—*Bibliografía mexicana del siglo xvi*—listing and annotating all of the books published in Mexico between 1539 and 1600. But his most distinguished work was a four-volume biography of the first bishop and archbishop of Mexico, Fray Juan de Zumárraga.

Of those historians not concerned with the colonial period, one name stands out far above the rest. Justo Sierra (1848–1912) set himself to the task of attempting a new interpretive synthesis of Mexican history. The result would occupy a unique niche in Mexican historiography. *Mexico: Su evolución social* was published at the turn of the century and shows Sierra as an eclectic. Though the book was written during the period of positivist domination of Mexican intellectual thought, one can still detect the impact of historical romanticism on the author. Unlike the historians who preceded him, Sierra, from a new perspective, could view Mexican history with optimism. The chaotic and unseemly events of the early nineteenth century were, for him, necessary steps in the progress of mankind. Criticism of past Mexican politicians and institutions was abundant but never indulged. Sierra's analysis of his contemporary Mexico was especially brilliant: even Díaz did not emerge completely unscathed. Sierra trod a path between a tolerably mild censure and the apologia that Díaz undoubtedly would have preferred. While Sierra could not overlook the authoritarianism of the regime, on balance he found it worthwhile. For Justo Sierra the Díaz regime, much like the early nineteenth century, was simply a step in Mexico's evolutionary process. It, too, had to yield to something else. And in the best nineteenth-century liberal tradition, the ultimate goal was not a more equitable distribution of wealth but rather liberty.

Mexico's cultural and intellectual life flourished from 1876 to 1910. When it did not come into direct conflict with the goals of the dictatorship, it received encouragement and even direct support. The novelist could concern himself with refining the language, the artist with painting a landscape, and the historian with probing Mexico's colonial heritage, all with little to fear. But artistic and intellectual expression that ran contrary to the all-important image so assiduously cultivated by the regime did not fare so well. Freedom of expression existed for those who accepted the dictatorship for what it was and who, because of personal interests, rejected the sound instinct that makes the independent intellectual suspicious of government. Only they could continue to pursue their individual tasks.

During the three and one-half decades of peace and economic growth a younger generation of liberal intellectuals gradually emerged. As they began to test the cultural atmosphere with matters of honest concern, and as they began to expose some of the obvious shortcomings of the regime, they encountered no benevolent patronage or passive resignation. The more passionate and direct their indictments, the more likely they were to experience harsh retribution. In spite of harassment, intimidation, and incarceration, these young intellectuals were not easily dissuaded from their goals and contributed in no small way to the outbreak of revolutionary activity in Mexico in 1910.

Recommended for Further Study

Arnold, Channing, and Frederick J. Tabor Frost. *The American Egypt: A Record of Travel in Yucatán.* New York: Doubleday, Page & Company, 1909.

Barton, Mary. *Impressions of Mexico with Brush and Pen*. London: Methuen, 1911.

Beezley, William H. *Judas at the Jockey Club and Other Episodes of Porfirian Mexico*. Lincoln: University of Nebraska Press, 1987.

Bishop, W. H. *Old Mexico and Her Lost Provinces*. New York: Harper and Brothers, 1883.

Brushwood, John S. *Mexico in Its Novel: A Nation's Search for Identity*. Austin: University of Texas Press, 1966.

Case, Alden Buell. *Thirty Years with the Mexicans: In Peace and Revolution*. New York: Fleming H. Revell, 1917.

Charlot, Jean. *The Mexican Mural Renaissance, 1920–1925*. New Haven, Conn.: Yale University Press, 1967.

Díaz, María Elena. "The Satiric Penny Press for Workers in Mexico, 1900–1910: A Case Study in the Politicisation of Popular Culture." *Journal of Latin American Studies* 22 (1990): 497–526.

French, William E. "Prostitutes and Guardian Angels: Women, Work, and the Family in Porfirian Mexico." *Hispanic American Historical Review* 72 (1992): 529–53.

Gillpatrick, Wallace. *The Man Who Likes Mexico*. New York: Century, 1912.

Hale, Charles A. *The Transformation of Liberalism in Late Nineteenth-Century Mexico*. Princeton, N.J.: Princeton University Press, 1989.

McCarty, J. Hendrickson. *Two Thousand Miles through the Heart of Mexico*. New York: Phillips & Hunt, 1888.

Ober, Frederick A. *Travels in Mexico and Life among the Mexicans*. Boston: Estes and Lauriat, 1884.

Raat, William D. "Ideas and Society in Don Porfirio's Mexico." *The Americas* 30 (1973): 32–53.

Sierra, Justo. *The Political Evolution of the Mexican People*. Translated by Charles Ramsdell. Austin: University of Texas Press, 1969.

Tyler, Ron, ed. *Posada's Mexico*. Washington, D.C.: Library of Congress, 1979.

VIII THE REVOLUTION: THE MILITARY PHASE, 1910-20

30

The Liberal Indictment

The Liberal Leadership

The opening of the twentieth century found Mexico a far different place than it had been only twenty-five years earlier. It would be sheer folly to gainsay the tremendous material benefits that had accrued in the industrial, commercial, and mining fields. But there is no Ciudad Porfirio Díaz in Mexico today, no public school or street bears his name, and it is hard to find a public statue or monument erected in his honor. Porfirian capitalism shunned the masses; the economic surplus generated by the dynamic economy had been appropriated by the few. Fifty years earlier nobody would have batted an eye, but new ideological currents had swept through the western world in the second half of the nineteenth century and had begun to lay bare the social malaise of the old regimes. A system that perpetuated itself for the sake of order and economic progress, and atrophied in the process, became less and less palatable to an increasing number of young, socially aware Mexicans.

When a handful of astute observers began to balance the progress against the costs, they at first manifested greater interest in political abuse than in social stagnation. The federal Constitution of 1857, with its theoretical guarantees, had been violated incessantly. Elections at all levels of government were a farce. The administration of justice in rural Mexico was a euphemism for the capricious whims of the local jefe político. Freedom of the press did not exist, and the restrictions of the Reform limiting the participatory role of the clergy were not enforced. To those who were concerned with the longevity of the regime, Don Porfirio became "Don Perpetuo," while those more concerned with the brutality dubbed him "Porfiriopoxtli."

The intelligentsia as a class did not abandon the regime with the advent of the twentieth century. The científicos continued to be loyal apologists for the dictatorship, as it well behooved them. They had convinced themselves that to attack the Díaz system was to attack the foundation of civilization itself. But a younger generation of intellectual activists, embracing a new faith and unwilling to be intimidated by the arrogance of the científicos, began to question the effete dictatorship.

One of the first to speak out for reform was Wistano Luis Orozco, a jurist from Guadalajara. Unlike the majority of liberal malcontents, he was concerned with social, not political, issues. As early as 1895 he had written a volume criticizing the Díaz land laws and the land companies that profited from them. He conjectured that "the large accumulation of land in a single hand causes the ruin and degradation of peoples."[1] The regime was shirking its responsibilities in the rural areas. To reverse the ever increasing trend, he argued that the government should break up and sell all public lands and begin buying up some of the huge haciendas for the same purpose. But Orozco was not propagandizing for revolution. He believed the reforms he envisioned could be effected from within the administration.

In San Luis Potosí, Camilo Arriaga, a mining engineer by profession, rejected the positivist doctrine he had learned in the schools and by the turn of the century counted himself in the small anti-Díaz camp. A typical nineteenth-century liberal, Arriaga moved into the opposition fold because of Díaz's *modus vivendi* with the Roman Catholic Church. In late 1900 he called for the organization of liberal clubs throughout Mexico and summoned a national liberal convention to meet in San Luis Potosí early the next year. The response was better than expected, and fifty delegates attended. Although the resolutions adopted were narrowly conceived and primarily anticlerical, the malcontents had been brought together for the first time. Emboldened by one another, they would gradually broaden the base of their antigovernment attack.

The least timid members of the liberal movement in the early twentieth century were the Flores Magón brothers—Jesús, Ri-

---

1. Quoted in Arnaldo Córdova, *La ideología de la Revolución Mexicana: Formación del nuevo régimen* (Mexico, 1973), p. 115.

cardo, and Enrique. In August of 1900 the brothers began publication of *Regeneración*, a Mexico City weekly. Not yet ready to preach the injustice of private land ownership, through its columns they supported the nascent liberal movement in San Luis Potosí and decried the excesses of Porfirismo. While their early pamphleteering might have brought the regime into some disrepute, their activities were not yet seditious.

For attacking a local jefe político in Oaxaca in the columns of *Regeneración*, the brothers were arrested in the late spring of 1901 and confined to Belén prison for a year. Their arrest served to invigorate the liberal movement as freedom of the press and suppression of the jefes políticos became new causes the liberals could add to their militant anticlericalism. Through his own intemperate action in arresting the brothers, Díaz himself had contributed to converting the narrowly based anticlerical movement into an anti-Díaz movement. By the time the Flores Magón brothers were released Camilo Arriaga had been arrested, as had other leaders of the liberal cause. The brothers renewed their attacks, this time in the columns of *El Hijo de Ahuizote*; six months later they were in prison once again. A release and a third brief arrest convinced them of the futility of trying to conduct their campaign from Mexican soil; in January 1904, broke and disheartened, they crossed over into the United States to attack the Díaz regime from exile.

From San Antonio, Texas, the Flores Magón brothers and Arriaga, who joined them shortly, began soliciting funds from liberals to reinstitute *Regeneración*. Former subscribers and liberal clubs throughout Mexico made small contributions, and an unexpected benefactor was found in Francisco I. Madero, son of a wealthy Coahuila hacendado. The first issue of the newly revived tabloid came off the press in the fall of 1904. The *Regeneración* published from San Antonio was much more militant and belligerent; attacks against Díaz were more categorical and vicious and the remedies more radical. In one editorial Enrique lashed out as follows:

> Forever—for as long as Mexico can remember—today's slavery will be identified with the name of the devil that made it all possible. His name is Porfirio Díaz, and his bestiality is being carried out in Mexico. . . . The jefes políticos do not send thieves and other criminals to jail—rather they sell them as slaves. . . . You may say that Díaz does not benefit directly from this human commerce. . . . But what about the governors of Veracruz, Oaxaca,

Cartoon from *El Hijo de Ahuizote* entitled "The Governors Praying for Díaz Support."

Hidalgo, and other states and their cronies who do benefit? Who appointed these governors? Porfirio Díaz. . . . But the day of liberation is coming. Prepare yourselves my fellow citizens.[2]

San Antonio proved to be a little too close to the Mexican border for comfort. Díaz dispatched a would-be assassin to the Texas city to end once and for all his problem with the Flores Magón brothers. The assassination attempt failed, but the liberals in exile decided it would be wiser to move deeper into the heartland of the United States where agents of the Díaz dictatorship could not so easily blend into the local populace and where local law enforcement agencies, with their deeply engrained anti-Mexican prejudices, might not be so vigilant. The exiles chose St. Louis, Missouri, and in 1905 not only again began publishing *Regeneración* but also organized a revolutionary junta for the expressed purpose of overthrowing the Díaz dictatorship. But the local St. Louis authorities were no more friendly than those in San Antonio; they arrested the Flores Magón brothers, charging them with violating United States neutrality laws. A friendly campaign waged in their behalf by the St. Louis press, however, hastened their release.

2. Quoted in Samuel Kaplan, *Peleamos contra la injusticia: La epopeya de los hermanos Flores Magón* (Mexico, 1960), 1: 162–65.

In the summer of 1906 the junta in St. Louis published its Liberal Plan. Part of it was a simple rehash of nineteenth-century liberal concerns. It called for freedom of speech, freedom of the press, suppression of the jefes políticos, the complete secularization of education, and the nationalization of all church property. But the Liberal Plan of 1906 added a series of new concepts manifesting graphically that a new age of liberalism had finally dawned. Socially oriented measures included the abolition of the death penalty (except for treason), educational reform in favor of the poor, and prison reform emphasizing rehabilitation rather than punishment. More revolutionary yet was the call for a nationwide eight-hour workday and a six-day workweek, the abolition of the tienda de raya, the payment of all workers in legal tender, and the prohibition of child labor. The rural areas of Mexico were not overlooked as they had been so often in the past. All uncultivated lands were to be taken over by the state and redistributed to those who would work them. To enable the small farmer to take advantage of the new law, an agricultural credit bank would be established to provide low-interest loans. And, finally, special emphasis would be placed on restoring the ejido lands seized illegally from the Indian communities.

Treatment of the Mexican Liberal party. A cut by José Guadalupe Posada.

The discontent over the political abuses of the Díaz dictator-ship had been gradually transmuted into a new gospel of social reform. For the first time in Mexican history an articulate and organized minority, albeit a small one, had displayed genuine concern for the plight of the masses. Mexico had received its first application of classical capitalism late, and, as a result, the social-ist, anarchist, and syndicalist strictures of that system had also been late in making their appearance. While the Mexican exile community produced no social prophets of the stature of Karl Marx, Louis Blanc, or Mikhail Bakunin, the liberal leaders in exile had immersed themselves in European social thought and had begun to apply the lessons to Mexican reality as they under-stood it. In the thousands of copies of *Regeneración* smuggled into Mexico monthly, the Flores Magón brothers and their liberal compatriots in exile exposed the regime as intellectually impov-erished and socially bankrupt and so contributed immeasurably to the growth of the anti-Díaz movement.[3] They received their first promising news from the fatherland in the summer of 1906. It came from Cananea, Sonora.

Labor Unrest

On June 1, 1906, the Mexican workers at Colonel William Greene's Cananea Consolidated Copper Company went out on strike. The liberal junta had not planned the strike, but young socialist activists in Cananea—Manuel Diéguez, Estéban Calde-rón, and Francisco Ibarra—had been in correspondence with the exiles, had formed an affiliate liberal club in Cananea, and had agitated the workers, distributing copies of *Regeneración*.

The grievances of the miners at Cananea were manifold. Mex-icans were paid less than their United States counterparts for performing the same jobs. Qualified Mexican laborers were con-signed to undesirable posts, while the technical and managerial positions were staffed entirely by United States personnel. The workers elected a delegation, including Diéguez and Calderón, to negotiate these matters, and salary and hours, with the man-

3. A differing interpretation on the influence of the Flores Magón brothers on the nascent labor movement is found in Rodney D. Anderson, "Mexican Workers and the Politics of Revolution, 1906–1911," *Hispanic American Historical Review* 54 (1974): 94–113. Examining letters, flyers, petitions, and workers' newspapers, Anderson concludes that the impact of the Mexican liberals on the workers' move-ment has been overstated.

Mothers, wives, sisters, and daughters supported the miners' demands by demonstrating in Cananea.

agement. When Colonel Greene refused to arbitrate, the activists decided to stop all company operations.

The violence began in the company lumberyard. Disgruntled but unarmed workers attempted to force their way through a locked gate, and the resident manager ordered high-pressure water hoses to be turned on them. When the gate finally buckled and the workers swarmed into the yard, they were greeted with several volleys of rifle fire. During the chaos of the next hour several dozen Mexicans and two United States managers were slain. The remaining workers retired, leaving the lumberyard in flames. The atmosphere was explosive as the workers marched into Cananea, robbed two pawnshops of guns and ammunition, and exchanged fire with American residents. Colonel Greene informed Governor Rafael Izábal of the danger and telephoned friends across the border in Arizona to raise a volunteer force in his behalf. When the governor was apprised that the rurales could not arrive until late the next day, he gave permission for 275 Arizona Rangers to cross the border to patrol the streets of Cananea. To veil the violation of Mexico's neutrality, Izábal did not allow the Rangers to enter the country as a force. They crossed over individually and were subsequently sworn in as Mexican volunteers.

The situation in Cananea was still tense when the American force arrived, together with Governor Izábal. While no major military engagements ensued, the Rangers and the workers did exchange fire on several occasions, and deaths resulted on both sides. Late in the day a detachment of rurales arrived under the command of Colonel Emilio Kosterlitzky. "Justice" was quick for those workers Kosterlitzky considered ringleaders: they were rounded up, escorted out of town, and hanged from trees. The strike was broken, and the workers, threatened with induction into the army, returned to their jobs.

The Mexican workers at Cananea were not Molly Maguires, yet their fate was the same. But the strike did serve a purpose. It focused attention on the Díaz policy of protecting foreigners at the expense of Mexicans. United States troops had been allowed to cross into Mexican territory and kill Mexicans to guard the interests of an American mining magnate. More important yet, for the first time the masses had been organized for a show of strength.

The discontent of the miners at Cananea proved not to be an isolated phenomenon. Even as the strike in Sonora was being suppressed, liberal leaders among the textile workers in Veracruz organized the Gran Círculo de Obreros Libres and began seeking affiliate clubs in neighboring states. The last six months of 1906, with the echos of Cananea still fresh, witnessed the most intense labor conflict of the entire Porfiriato, but Díaz treated the disturbances as a political rather than a social problem. Late in the year textile strikes supported by the Gran Círculo occurred in Puebla, Orizaba, and Tlaxcala, but the major showdown was postponed until January 1907.

Working conditions in the Río Blanco textile mills were nothing short of horrible. The common workday was twelve hours, the wages were grossly inadequate, and, on top of everything else, the workers were required to pay for the normal depreciation of the machinery they used. Children of eight and nine years of age performed physically demanding work. All publications distributed among the workers had to be approved by management officials, and all strikes were illegal. Workers whose affiliation with the Gran Círculo became known were subject to immediate dismissal. The abuses seemed so patent that the workers agreed to lay their complaints directly before President Díaz for his arbitration. The dictator agreed to hear the complaints, but when he issued his decision he supported the textile owners on almost every count. On Sunday, January 6, the workers held a mass meeting and decided to strike the following day.

The trouble set in at the grocery counter of the tienda de raya. Several of the wives of the striking workers were refused credit for food. Insults led to pushing and shoving, then fisticuffs, and finally shooting. The enraged strikers put the tienda de raya to flame, and the local jefe político ordered in the rurales and the federal troops. When the troops arrived they fired point-blank into the crowd and killed several women and children along with numerous workers. The crowd dispersed, but when some of the workers returned later to collect the bodies of the dead they were again assaulted by the troops and even more were killed. The exact number of worker deaths at Río Blanco is impossible to calculate because the censored press gave no detailed account, but contemporary observers, including the nearby United States consuls, placed the figure at over one hundred.

The government reaction to the textile strike at Río Blanco was the grossest evidence of mass suppression yet. It was easy—too easy—to blame labor unrest entirely on liberal agitators in the United States without questioning seriously whether the grievances had any basis in fact. The regime showed itself no more willing to face up to the country's social maladies in 1907 than it had been in 1876. Again law and order was assured at the expense of personal liberty and social justice.[4]

Heightened Political Activity

In spite of the liberal indictment and in spite of the suppression of the nascent labor movement, most Mexican politicians believed that a revolution could be avoided and that change could be effected through the political process. The moderates were encouraged when in early 1908 the dictator granted an interview to the United States journalist James Creelman. Full of self-assurance, Díaz defended his governing philosophy to Creelman and then let loose a bombshell.

> No matter what my friends and supporters say, I retire when my presidential term of office ends, and I shall not serve again. I shall be eighty years old then. I have waited patiently for the day when

4. The labor crisis is carefully analyzed in Rodney D. Anderson, "Díaz y la crisis laboral de 1906," *Historia Mexicana* 19 (1970): 513–35.

the people of the Mexican Republic should be prepared to choose and change their government at every election without danger of armed revolution and without injury to the national credit or interference with the national progress. I believe that day has come. I welcome an opposition party in the Mexican Republic.[5]

Díaz's surprise announcement that he did not plan to seek reelection in the upcoming presidential elections of 1910 ushered in a rash of political activity and intellectual ferment. Shortly after this interview the Mexican literati went to work. The Yucatecan sociologist Andrés Molina Enríquez, a positivist but not a Porfirista, published an important volume entitled *Los grandes problemas nacionales* (translated as *The Great National Problems*). A brilliant analysis of contemporary Mexican society, the work called for a penetrating program of reform, especially in the rural areas. Molina Enríquez knew that agrarian discontent had already manifested itself in sporadic outbreaks of violence, and he feared that if positive steps were not taken the movement might fall into radical or anarchist hands.[6]

A still more influential book, *La sucesión presidencial en 1910* (translated as *The Presidential Succession in 1910*), came from the pen of Francisco I. Madero. Unlike Molina Enríquez, Madero held that Mexico's problems were primarily political in nature. The greatest danger to Mexico, as Madero perceived it, was continued military dictatorship with its concomitant absolutism. Although Madero himself did not believe that Díaz was going to step down voluntarily, he urged Mexicans to take the dictator at his word and to begin forming an opposition party, an anti-re-electionist party dedicated to the principles of effective suffrage and no-re-election. He was convinced that the desired change could be effected through the ballot box. *La sucesión presidencial en 1910* cannot compare to Molina Enríquez's *Los grandes problemas nacionales* in its scholarship, originality, or social significance. Yet it proved to be much more important historically as, together with the Creelman interview, it set into motion the political forces that would ultimately lead to the conflagration in the fall of 1910.

The political activity of 1909 and 1910 was quite unlike anything Mexico had known since the Revolution of Tuxtepec. Within the administration itself various factions began to vie for

5. Quoted in Frederick Starr, *Mexico and the United States* (Chicago, 1914), p. 253.
6. For a perceptive discussion of early agrarianism, see John M. Hart, "Agrarian Precursors of the Mexican Revolution: The Development of an Ideology," *The Americas* 29 (1972): 131–50.

the mantle of succession. The followers of General Bernardo Reyes, the capable and energetic former governor of Nuevo León and secretary of war, pushed their hero as a logical successor to Díaz. If Díaz should change his mind and run for office again, then Reyes should at least be placed on the official ticket as the vice-presidential candidate. However, the científicos within the administration, led by José Limantour, had a different candidate and opposed the steadily growing Reyista cause. At the national convention of the official party they urged another term for Porfirio Díaz and declared their belief that Ramón Corral, a former governor of Sonora and currently vice-president, should be retained for the number two position on the ticket. Without qualms the president and vice-president accepted the mandate.

The Reyista movement counted on a good deal of support from the army and from a number of active political clubs, but Reyes himself never agreed to offer himself as a candidate—for either president or vice-president. Some accused the general from Nuevo León of cowardice, but he always considered himself a loyal Porfirista. He had his disagreements with the regime but believed that reform could be effected from the inside. He wanted to avoid an open split within official circles at a time when pressure from without was beginning to build up noticeably. Díaz himself, however, was willing to take no chances. To test the general's loyalty he asked him to undertake a military study mission in Europe. Reyes's acceptance of the contrived assignment in November 1909 was tantamount to political exile.

Madero and the Anti-Re-electionist Cause

The political opposition to Díaz in the 1910 presidential elections would come, at any rate, from outside the official party, as Francisco I. Madero dedicated himself to the Anti-Re-electionist cause. Born in Coahuila in 1873 to a family of wealth and prestige, young Madero received the best education that money could provide. The family had garnered a fortune in mining, land speculation, cattle, and banking; Madero's father was happy to send his teen-age son to Paris and then to Berkeley, California, for proper grooming. Upon his return to Coahuila, Madero was placed in charge of some of the family haciendas and quickly developed an unusual interest in the welfare of the peones who worked them. He not only observed the gross social inequities firsthand but took time to ponder the pathetic written complaints

that crossed his desk daily. Stories of physical abuse at the hands
of the mayordomos were not as frequent as tales of poverty that
left children without shelter or food, of sickness without the possibility of medical care, of military conscription as a means of
punishment, and of incarceration without the formalities of law.[7]
He did what he could on the family properties, but he realized
fully that the Madero haciendas were simply a microcosm of
rural Mexico.

Shortly after the turn of the century, as liberals throughout the
country were increasingly manifesting their discomfort, Madero
entered politics on a small scale. Throwing his support behind
antiadministration politicians in Coahuila, he tasted defeat in
1904 and 1905 when Díaz intervened to assure the election in the
state of his own favorites. The problem was thus, from Madero's
point of view, primarily political—nothing could change until
democratic processes had a chance to work their miraculous
cures. Though Madero had initially contributed to the cause of
the Flores Magón brothers, he became estranged from them as
they grew more radical. In the spring of 1908 he set to work on
his manuscript, *La sucesión presidencial en 1910*. The publication of the book early the next year launched not only the Anti-
Re-electionist movement but also Madero's political career.

To foment anti-re-electionism and to test the political winds,
Madero toured Mexico in the last half of 1909. During the summer and early fall he made public appearances in Orizaba, Veracruz, Progreso, Mérida, Campeche, Tampico, Monterrey, and
Torreón. If the receptions were not always as enthusiastic as he
would have liked, he did leave each city with assurances that an
active group of liberals would be working there in his behalf.
And although he did not realize it at the time, he was also building a revolutionary network to which he would later appeal. The
winter months were no less hectic as Madero, his close confidants,
and his wife continued their political tours to Querétaro, Guadalajara, Manzanillo, Mazatlán, and into the northern states of
Sonora and Chihuahua. Gaining confidence and stature along
the way, Madero offered himself as an energetic, capable, and
articulate young leader in stark contrast to a tiring and decrepit
regime—not a member of Díaz's cabinet was under sixty; many
of the state governors were in their seventies. Especially well re-

7. The nature of the complaints that crossed Madero's desk are described in Michael
   C. Meyer, "Habla por ti mismo Juan: Una propuesta para un método alternativo
   de investigación," *Historia Mexicana* 22 (1973): 396–408.

ceived in Chihuahua, Madero held several meetings with Abraham González, an ardent foe of the dictatorship and president of the Centro Anti-Re-eleccionista Benito Juárez. After Madero's departure, González polled the various clubs in the state and decided to nominate Madero for the presidency at the upcoming Anti-Re-electionist convention in Mexico City.

The convention met in April 1910 with broad geographical representation. The 120 delegates in attendance, following the lead of Abraham González and his Chihuahua colleagues, officially nominated Madero for the presidency. The following afternoon the vice-presidential nomination was given to Dr. Francisco Vásquez Gómez, a distinguished physician but a lukewarm liberal at best.

The philosophy of the Anti-Re-electionist party came out gradually during the campaign that carried the candidate to twenty-two of the twenty-seven Mexican states. Madero simply expanded upon the ideas contained in his book. Political reform, predicated upon free and honest elections, was basic to the entire program. Social benefits might then accrue, but democracy was the one imperative. During a campaign speech in San Luis Potosí, Madero was interrupted by a question voiced from the audience asking why he did not break up his own haciendas. Madero's answer epitomized his philosophy. The Mexican people, he responded, did not want bread; they wanted liberty.

The campaign ended abruptly in Monterrey. A huge group of admirers broke through a police barricade to attend a demonstration in front of Madero's house. Madero shared the speakers' platform with cohort Roque Estrada, who criticized the police for trying to hamper the rally. The following day the police tried to arrest Estrada, but Madero detained them, allowing his companion to escape. Madero himself was then arrested for abetting a fugitive from justice. In reality his only crime had been to dare to oppose Díaz in the 1910 presidential elections.

Election day, June 21, 1910, found Madero in prison in San Luis Potosí and thousands of his Anti-Re-electionist colleagues in jails throughout the republic. Nobody was surprised when the government announced that Díaz and Ramón Corral had been overwhelmingly re-elected for still another term. The Madero family was able to arrange for Madero's release on bail with the proviso that he confine himself to the city of San Luis Potosí. He did remain in the city for several months, but in early October, when the rigor of his confinement was relaxed, he boarded a northbound train in disguise and escaped to the United States.

The Last Hurrah

Soon after the election Díaz began preparations for his final extravaganza. In September he would celebrate his eightieth birthday and Mexico the hundredth anniversary of its Declaration of Independence. The entire month was given over to pageants, celebration, and commemoration. A soaring column capped by a gold angel was unveiled on the Paseo de la Reforma in honor of the Independence movement. An equally impressive monument to the Niños Héroes was dedicated at the entrance to Chapultepec Park. Distinguished guests from abroad had their expenses paid to partake of the festivities. Gala balls were held in their honor, and imported French champagne flowed like water. Flags were displayed everywhere, banquets followed banquets, parades crowded the streets, fireworks lit up the night skies, and *mariachis* (folk musicians) strolled the downtown avenues. Foreign governments took part as well. The American colony, thinking of no better way of commemorating the heroic deeds of Father Hidalgo, sent Díaz and the Mexican people a statue of George Washington, and the Italians—not to be outdone—sent one of Giuseppe Garibaldi. In a rare display of *entente cordiale* the Third French Republic returned the keys to the city of Mexico that had been ingloriously sequestered by the army of Napoleon III a half-century before. King Alfonso XIII demonstrated the lasting confraternity of the Spanish people by returning the uniforms of José María Morelos.

The centennial celebrations epitomized everything that was right and everything that was wrong with the Díaz regime. Beggars were pushed off of the streets of the capital city for the duration so that the guests would receive the proper impressions of a prosperous Mexico. The cost of the celebrations exceeded the entire educational budget for the year 1910. Mexico was at last enjoying its place in the international sun—respect was no longer lacking. But while the champagne was flowing for a few, tens of thousands were suffering from malnutrition. While guests were treated to young female companions, Indian women in Yucatán were dying in childbirth. While European waiters served at the banquets, urban Mexicans were unemployed. While letters of congratulation arrived on time, 85 percent of the population was still illiterate. While visitors rode in shiny new motorcars on well-paved streets in the center of the city, mud and filth engulfed the workers' barrios in the suburbs. In September 1910

Mexico appeared to many to be enjoying its finest hour. But with social reform still alien to the Porfirian mentality, the peace would soon prove to be fragile and the showy façade would collapse with it.

Recommended for Further Study

Axelrod, Bernard. "St. Louis and the Mexican Revolutionaries, 1905–1906." *Bulletin of the Missouri Historical Society* 28 (1972): 94–108.

Brown, Lyle C. *The Mexican Liberals and Their Struggle against the Díaz Dictatorship, 1900–1906*. Mexico: Mexico City College Press, 1956.

Cadenhead, Ivie E., Jr. "The American Socialists and the Mexican Revolution of 1910." *Southwestern Social Science Quarterly* 43 (1962): 103–17.

Cockcroft, James D. *Intellectual Precursors of the Mexican Revolution, 1900–1913*. Austin: University of Texas Press, 1968.

Creelman, James. *Díaz: Master of Mexico*. New York: Appleton, 1916.

Cumberland, Charles C. *Mexican Revolution: Genesis under Madero*. Austin: University of Texas Press, 1952.

———. "Precursors of the Mexican Revolution of 1910." *Hispanic American Historical Review* 22 (1942): 344–56.

Hart, John M. "Agrarian Precursors of the Mexican Revolution: The Development of an Ideology." *The Americas* 29 (1972): 131–50.

———. *Revolutionary Mexico: The Coming and Process of the Mexican Revolution*. Berkeley: University of California Press, 1987.

Knight, Alan. *The Mexican Revolution*. Vol. 1: *Porfirians, Liberals and Peasants*. New York: Cambridge University Press, 1986.

Raat, William D. "The Diplomacy of Suppression: *Los Revoltosos*, Mexico and the United States, 1906–1911." *Hispanic American Historical Review* 56 (1976): 529–50.

Ross, Stanley R. *Francisco I. Madero, Apostle of Mexican Democracy*. New York: Columbia University Press, 1955.

Sherman, John W. "Revolution on Trial: The 1909 Tombstone Proceedings Against Ricardo Flores Magón, Antonio Villarreal and Librado Rivera." *The Journal of Arizona History* 32 (1991): 173–94.

Smith, Cornelius C. *Emilio Kosterlitzky: Eagle of Sonora and the Southwest Border*. Glendale, Calif.: Clark, 1970.

Turner, John Kenneth. *Barbarous Mexico*. Austin: University of Texas Press, 1969.

31

The Overthrow of Díaz

The Plan de San Luis Potosí

For years Francisco Madero had resisted the prodding of liberals who exhorted that Díaz must be overthrown by force. But when he escaped from San Luis Potosí and made his way north to the sanctuary of the United States border, he realized that the time had come at last. He had tried to unseat the dictator by constitutional means, but force had been used against him and his followers. He was finally ready to expose the inadequacies of enforced peace, and now he would call his fellow Mexicans to arms in the task of national redemption.

In the middle of October 1910, as supporters gathered around him in San Antonio, Texas, he began drafting a revolutionary plan. To avoid any possible international complications with the United States, he dated the plan October 5, the last day he had been in San Luis Potosí, and, in fact, called it the *Plan de San Luis Potosí*. He made his appeal emotionally.

> Peoples, in their constant efforts for the triumph of the ideals of liberty and justice, find it necessary at certain historical moments to make the greatest sacrifices. Our beloved fatherland has reached one of those moments. A tyranny that we Mexicans have not been accustomed to suffer since we won our independence oppresses us in such a manner that it has become intolerable. In exchange for that tyranny we are offered peace, but it is a peace full of shame for the Mexican nation, because it is based not on law but on force; because its goal is not the enrichment and prosperity of the country, but the enrichment of a small group. . . .
>
> But this violent and illegal system can no longer exist. I know

Aquiles Serdán and his family in Puebla. A cut by Fernando Castro Pacheco.

very well that if the people have designated me as their candidate for the presidency it is not because they have had an opportunity to discover in me the talents of a statesman or a ruler, but the vigor of a patriot ready to sacrifice himself, if necessary, to obtain liberty and to help the people free themselves from the odious tyranny that oppresses them. . . .

I declare the last election illegal and accordingly the republic, being without rulers, I assume the provisional presidency of the republic until the people designate their rulers pursuant to the law. . . .

I have designated Sunday, the 20th day of next November, for all the towns in the republic to rise in arms after 6 o'clock P.M.[1]

The Plan de San Luis Potosí, like *La sucesión presidencial en 1910* before it, demonstrates amply that Madero's concerns were primarily political. The few references to Mexico's social maladies were vague and ill conceived. Yet the boldness of the statement and the self-confidence it reflected struck a responsive chord. Once having received copies of the plan, the leaders who

1. The text of the plan can be found in Isidro Fabela, ed., *Documentos históricos de la revolución mexicana* (Mexico, 1960–73), 6: 69–76.

had previously worked for the Anti-Re-electionist party began preparing themselves for November 20.

The revolution actually began two days prematurely in the town of Puebla. There the local liberal leader, Aquiles Serdán, had stored arms and ammunition in his home. An informant notified the police, and the fight was on. Serdán and his family became the first martyrs of the new cause. Madero himself crossed over into Mexico on the evening of November 19, but, when his expected rebel army failed to rendezvous, he crossed back into the United States without firing a shot. The self-designated provisional president had no real assurance that anyone in Mexico would respond to his urgent call, but he would not be despondent for long. The masses immediately rallied to the cry of *¡Viva la Revolución!*

The Rise of Rebel Armies and the Resignation of Díaz

Names that are remembered more in local corridos than in history texts took up arms everywhere on the stipulated day. But nowhere did the sparks fly as in Chihuahua. Town after town responded on November 20 and 21. Toribio Ortega marched on Cuchillo Parado, Gaspar Durán on Calabacillas, José de la Luz Blanco on Santo Tomás, Guadalupe Gardea on Chuviscar, Feliciano Díaz on Témores, Cástulo Herrera on Temósachic, Guillermo Baca on Hidalgo del Parral, Pancho Villa on San Andrés, and Pascual Orozco on San Isidro and Miñaca.

The rebel armies were not armies, but neither were they merely peasant mobs. There were peones, to be sure, but in addition servants, shopkeepers, mechanics, beggars, miners, federal army deserters, lawyers, United States soldiers of fortune, young and old, bandits and idealists, students and teachers, engineers and day laborers, the bored and the overworked, the aggrieved and the adventuresome, all constituted the rank and file. Some were attracted by commitment to the cause and some by the promise of spoils; some joined impulsively and others with careful forethought. Some preferred Flores Magón radicalism and some Madero liberalism; many had heard of neither. Even among the politically astute some viewed the November movement as a fight against hacendados, others decided to offer their lives to oppose local jefes políticos, while still others saw the Revolution as a chance to recapture Mexico from the foreign capitalists. But they all had one thought in common: Díaz was the

The Mexican guerrilla at the beginning of the Revolution would soon be immortalized in legend and song.

symbol of all Mexico's ills, and they were convinced that almost any change would be a change for the better. Thus they were willing to strap cartridge belts on their chests, find, buy, or steal rifles somewhere, and become *guerrilleros*. Indifferently armed, without uniforms, with no notion of military discipline, the disparate rebel bands lived off the land and attacked local authorities and small federal outposts in tiny pueblos. Sometimes they were successful, and sometimes they were driven off to fall upon a still weaker prey. It did not take them long to realize that they enjoyed a dormant but fortuitous asset—the cooperation of much of rural Mexico. Madero's communications network began to inform him that his recent efforts had not been in vain.

The Díaz regime was by no means prepared to lay down and roll over. Unwilling to admit to himself that his system had grown obsolescent, Díaz determined to hold on. With more frenzy than care, army units and corps of rurales were dispatched on scattered missions in Mexico's ten military zones, and slowly they began to curtail the spread of the rebellion. Only in Chihuahua did the rebel movement continue to grow. The military leadership there had devolved upon Pascual Orozco, Jr., a tall, gaunt mule skinner whose business had suffered because he did not enjoy the favor of the Terrazas-Creel machine. When Orozco was contacted by Abraham González, the leader of the Anti-Re-electionists in the state, he had already been reading copies of *Regeneración* and did not have to be convinced that he should begin recruitment in Guerrero District and be ready to move on November 20. González supplied some modest funds and a few weapons. By the scheduled day Orozco had attracted about forty men to the cause. During the next two weeks, striking rapidly from the almost inaccessible *sierras* of western Chihuahua, he garnered four victories. Pancho Villa, José de la Luz Blanco, Cástulo Herrera, and other local leaders placed themselves under his command, and the Orozco army increased by twentyfold.

The new year opened well as on January 2, 1911, the Chihuahua rebels ambushed and almost totally destroyed a large federal convoy sent to pursue them. Now cocksure, Orozco stripped the dead soldiers of their uniforms, wrapped up the articles of clothing, and sent them to Don Porfirio with a graphically descriptive taunt: *Ahí te van las hojas; mándame más tamales* (Here are the wrappers; send me some more tamales).

In February Madero decided to cross over into Mexico for the second time and, although he had no special military talent, to assume military as well as political command. The next month he personally led an attack on Casas Grandes but, without Orozco's troops to support him, suffered the most punishing defeat of the entire northern campaign. The federal army not only routed the attackers but captured sixteen wagons of supplies and ammunition and three hundred horses. Madero realized that he had better leave the day-to-day fighting to Orozco, Villa, and the other guerrilla leaders who had already proved themselves on the field of battle.

Soon the insurrection began to bear fruit in Sonora, Coahuila, Sinaloa, Veracruz, Zacatecas, Puebla, Guerrero, and Morelos. In Baja California the Flores Magón brothers and their followers had the government on the run. Picking their own ground and their own time of battle, the small rebel contingents throughout the country kept the federals constantly off balance. The sparks were flying everywhere at the same time, and the vulnerabilities of the federal army became more acute. The military bureaucracy was inflexible, the government campaigns uncoordinated, the communications network tenuous, and the supply system inadequate. The rebels, on the other hand, moved in smaller units, lived off the land, and generally enjoyed the sympathy and cooperation of the local populace. They found it easier to smuggle in ammunition from the United States than federal commanders did to requisition it from Mexico City.

In the late spring of 1911 Orozco and Villa convinced Madero that the northern rebels should expend all their energy on capturing Ciudad Juárez, the border city across the Rio Grande from El Paso, Texas. By early May the most seasoned rebel troops had congregated on the outskirts of the city and were ready to attack. Suddenly, however, Madero changed his mind. Fearing that stray rebel shells might fall on El Paso and thus occasion United States intervention, he ordered a retreat. In direct violation of his commander's order, Orozco ordered the attack. Although the advantage of manpower and firepower lay with the rebels, the federal defense of the city, entrusted to General Juan Navarro, was stubborn. Thousands of El Paso residents climbed to their rooftops to watch the proceedings and cheer on their favorites. May 8 and 9 were indecisive, as most of the rebel assaults were blunted. But on the morning of May 10 the tide turned against the defenders of the city. Low on ammunition and completely encircled by the enemy, General Navarro decided to surrender and in the early afternoon hoisted a white flag over the federal barracks.

Madero did not know whether to be grateful, angry, or embarrassed. Against his order Orozco had handed him an important city, an official port of entry from the United States, and a provisional capital. When a few days later the provisional president named his cabinet, Orozco's name was curiously absent. The showdown took place on May 13 during a meeting of the new provisional government. Revolvers in hand to emphasize their point, Orozco and Villa burst into the room with a series of demands: General Navarro, who had executed captured rebel prisoners, must be tried as a war criminal; a new cabinet must be named from among those who had participated in the fighting; and Orozco's troops must be given their back pay. After a few tense moments cooler heads prevailed. Orozco and Villa were gradually convinced that Navarro could not receive a fair trial in the heated atmosphere following the battle for control of the city. Madero alone, by virtue of his position as provisional president, had the right to designate the cabinet. Only on their third demand were Orozco and Villa successful, as Madero wrote out a check to pay the troops lest they mutiny.

But the affair had significance that no one present could have foreseen. Though only five months old, the revolutionary coalition was already falling apart. The military's challenge to the civilian leadership would be repeated regularly for the next chaotic decade. But more important yet, the affair portended an age of bitter factionalism that exacerbated personal rivalries, turned Mexican against Mexican, extended the war, exacted a tremendously high toll of life, and increased the pain and anguish for hundreds of thousands.

The immediate results of the capture of Ciudad Juárez were less ominous. Rebels throughout the country took heart and redoubled their efforts. Tehuacán, Durango, Hermosillo, Cananea, Torreón, and Cuautla fell into revolutionary hands. Business fell victim to the trauma of uncertainty, and merchants bemoaned the lack of trade. The press became increasingly outspoken in criticism of the dictator and the sycophants who surrounded him, and the hour was too late to charge journalists again with seditious libel. Federal troops, who had not acquitted themselves too badly to this point, began deserting to the revolution *en masse*. Díaz slowly realized that an age was ending, and he agreed to dispatch a team of negotiators to treat with Madero and his staff. The Treaty of Ciudad Juárez provided that Díaz and

The battle of Ciudad Juárez (May 1911) proved to be the decisive engagement for control of the north.

The revolutionary leadership following the capture of Ciudad Juárez. The coalition would soon fall apart.

Vice-President Corral would resign before the month was out. Francisco León de la Barra, the secretary of foreign relations and an experienced diplomat, would assume the interim presidency until new elections could be held. The dictator did not wait until the end of the month. He signed his resignation and submitted it to the Congress on May 25.

A longtime United States resident in Mexico City described the mood as word of Díaz's resignation reached the public.

> Within an hour the news had traveled to the furthest corner of the capital and the peones who had been quiet all day now mustered into line. There was management in this, not accident, not spontaneous movement; yet all was joy. By eight o'clock that night a monster parade wound through the capital streets. . . . Cheers for Madero rent the heavens. The revolution had won.[2]

Díaz had indeed been overthrown, but the Revolution had scarcely triumphed. It had barely yet begun. The conviviality and jubilee of the next few days soon gave way to acrimonious debate as Mexicans began to ask themselves, what, exactly, they had won. Their answers, of course, were predicated upon what had motivated them to join the movement at the outset. As the dictator sailed away into European exile the one bond that had held them together vanished from sight. An old age had ended without a new age beginning.

2. Edward I. Bell, *The Political Shame of Mexico* (New York, 1914), pp. 82–83.

The Interim Presidency and Division within the Rebel Ranks

The interim presidency of León de la Barra (May to November 1911) turned out to be a crucial period. Madero's radical supporters, including the Flores Magón brothers, were unhappy enough with the choice of the interim president, but they were even more displeased when the provisional cabinet named by León de la Barra included a majority of Porfiristas. Emiliano Zapata in Morelos adopted a cautious wait-and-see attitude. Orozco in Chihuahua was still bristling from his recent encounter with Madero following the battle of Ciudad Juárez.

Unaware that the rumblings within his ranks were serious, in early June, Madero left the north for Mexico City. His seven-hundred-mile journey by train was truly triumphant, as thousands of enthusiastic admirers greeted him at large and small stations along the way. His reception in the capital was no less spectacular, as recorded by Edith O'Shaughnessy, the wife of the United States chargé d'affaires in the Mexico City embassy.

> There was a great noise of *vivas*, mingling with shouts of all kinds, tramping of feet, and blowing of motor horns. I could just get a glimpse of a pale, dark-bearded man bowing to the right and left. I kept repeating to myself: *"Qui l'a fait roi? qui l'a couronné?— la victoire."* . . . There were three days of continual plaudits and adoration, such as only the Roman emperors knew. . . . People came from far and near, in all sorts of conveyances or on foot, just to see him, to hear his voice, even to touch his garments for help and healing. . . .[3]

Among those there to greet Madero and talk to him was the most famous revolutionary of all—Emiliano Zapata. Like Orozco in the north, Zapata had never been a peón. His family had passed on a little land to him, and he supplemented his modest income as a muleteer, a horse trainer, and a stable master. Elected in 1909 to local office by the villagers of Anenecuilco, Morelos, he was regularly exposed to the full array of tragedies that had beset rural Mexico during the late Díaz regime. More concerned with local land problems than with the national movement to unseat the dictator, he did not call his villagers to support the Plan de San Luis Potosí on November 20, 1910. But within a few months he had linked the future of his own people

3. Edith O'Shaughnessy, *Diplomatic Days* (New York, 1917), p. 53.

Emiliano Zapata (1879–1919). Although Zapata played only a minor role in the fight again Díaz, his stature as a revolutionary grew steadily until his assassination in 1919.

with that of the Maderista cause and began recruiting an insurgent army. When appropriate, he made his appeal to local inhabitants in Náhuatl rather than in Spanish. A teen-age girl in Milpa Alta remembered when the Zapatistas first rode into the village.

> When he entered the village all of his men wore white clothes: white shirts, white pants, and *huaraches*. All of these men spoke Náhuatl, almost as we spoke it. Señor Zapata also spoke it, and as a result when those men came into Milpa Alta everyone understood them. . . . Señor Zapata went to the front of his men and spoke to all of the people of Milpa Alta.
>
> Notlac ximomanaca! Nehuatl onacoc; oncuan on ica tepoztli ihuan nochantlaca niquinhuicatz. Ipampa in Totazin Díaz aihmo ticnequi yehuatl techixotiz. Ticnequi occe altepetl achi cuali. Ilhuan totlac ximomanaca ipampa amo nechpactia tlen tetlaxtlahuia. Amo conehui ica tlacualo ica netzotzomatiloz. Noihqui nicnequi nochtlacatl quipiaz itlal: oncuan on quitocaz

ihuan quipixcaz tlaoli, yetzintli ihuan occequi xinachtli. Tlen
nanquitoa? Namehuan totlac namomanazque?[4]

Zapata's military contributions to the overthrow of the Díaz
dictatorship were not great, but he had scored a couple of victories over the federal forces by the time Díaz submitted his
resignation in May 1911. With the new day now supposedly
arrived, Zapata wanted to talk to Madero about the one matter
that concerned him most—the land problem in Morelos. To Zapata the overthrow of Díaz had genuine meaning only if land
were immediately restored to the pueblos. The encounter between the two men was dramatic. Zapata, with a large sombrero
on his head and his carbine in his hand, gestured to the gold
watch Madero sported on his vest and then made his point.

> Look, Señor Madero, if I, taking advantage of being armed,
> steal your watch and keep it, and then we meet again sometime
> and you are armed, wouldn't you have the right to demand that
> I return it?
> Of course, General, and you would also have the right to ask
> that I pay you for the use I had of it.
> Well, this is exactly what has happened to us in Morelos where
> some of the hacendados have forcibly taken over the village lands.
> My soldiers, the armed peasants, demand that I tell you respect-
> fully that they want their lands returned immediately.[5]

With characteristic caution Madero would make no immediate
commitment. He urged faith and patience, and to quiet Zapata's
qualms he agreed to visit Morelos within a week to assess the situation firsthand. The visit turned out badly. Madero insisted that
Zapata demobilize his army as a prerequisite to reducing tensions in the state. Zapata detected something absurd in the request. The revolutionaries had won; yet while the federal army
remained intact, the victorious rebels were asked to disband. To
show good faith the southern rebel reluctantly agreed, even
though in doing so he was undermining his own bargaining posi-

4. "Join me. I rose up. I rose up in arms and I bring my countrymen. We no longer
   wish that our Father Díaz watch over us. We want a much better president. Rise
   up with us because we don't like what the rich men pay us. It is not enough for
   us to eat and dress ourselves. I also want for everyone to have his piece of land so
   that he can plant and harvest corn, beans, and other crops. What do you say? Are
   you going to join us?"
   The Spanish and Náhuatl texts are found in Fernando Horcasitas, *De Porfirio
   Díaz a Zapata: Memoria Náhuatl de Milpa Alta* (Mexico, 1968), p. 105.
5. Quoted in Gildardo Magaña, *Emiliano Zapata y el agrarismo en México* (Mexico,
   1934–52), 1: 160.

tion. But when interim President León de la Barra determined that the mustering out of the Zapatista troops was not proceeding with all good speed, he decided to send federal troops into the state to enforce the demobilization order. Madero was furious when he learned that federal General Victoriano Huerta had exchanged fire with a band of Zapatistas north of Cuernavaca. He pleaded with the interim president to withdraw the troops, but the tenuous peace had already been shattered and, with it, Zapata's faith in Madero. By August the state of Morelos was again in angry revolt, and Madero, perhaps through no fault of his own, could add Zapata's name to his growing list of enemies.

When the campaign for the 1911 presidential elections got under way, the political atmosphere was already tense. Madero's party met in Mexico City in August and gave him the nomination by acclamation. But the vice-presidential nomination divided the convention. Madero decided to dump his 1910 running mate, Francisco Vásquez Gómez, in favor of a Yucatecan lawyer and journalist, José María Pino Suárez. The convention gave Madero his choice, but Vásquez Gómez and his followers would never reconcile themselves to their sudden political demise.

The opposition candidate around whom many of the old regime could rally, albeit without enthusiasm, was General Bernardo Reyes. Reyes returned from his European study mission in June and within a month had made up his mind to run against Madero for the presidency. By early fall the election was in full swing and the debate heated. In September a group of Madero's supporters, without their leader's knowledge or approval, physically attacked Reyes at a Mexico City rally. The Reyista party protested vigorously and petitioned the Congress to postpone the elections because of the unfair treatment afforded their candidate. But the Congress turned down the request, and Reyes, perhaps realizing that his campaign stood little chance of victory anyway, withdrew from the race and went into a self-imposed exile in San Antonio, Texas. Another powerful enemy was on the list.

The election was held without further incident on October 1, 1911. Only minor candidates opposed Madero, and he swept to an overwhelming victory. With relief interim President León de la Barra turned over the office on November 6. Madero's faith in democracy would soon be put to the test, and, while his faith would remain unshaken, democracy would fall victim to the rancor and passion of the day.

Recommended for Further Study

Beezley, William H. *Insurgent Governor: Abraham González and the Mexican Revolution in Chihuahua.* Lincoln: University of Nebraska Press, 1973.

Bell, Edward I. *The Political Shame of Mexico.* New York: McBride, Nast, 1914.

Berbusse, Edward J. "Neutrality Diplomacy of the United States and Mexico, 1910–1911." *The Americas* 12 (1956): 265–83.

Blaisdell, Lowell L. *The Desert Revolution: Baja California, 1911.* Madison: University of Wisconsin Press, 1962.

Cumberland, Charles C. *Mexican Revolution: Genesis under Madero.* Austin: University of Texas Press, 1952.

Grieb, Kenneth J. "Standard Oil and the Financing of the Mexican Revolution." *California Historical Society Quarterly* 49 (1971): 59–71.

Guzmán, Martín Luis. *Memoirs of Pancho Villa.* Translated by Virginia H. Taylor. Austin: University of Texas Press, 1965.

Henderson, Peter V. N. "Mexican Rebels in the Borderlands, 1910–1912." *Red River Valley Historical Review* 2 (1975): 207–19.

Johnson, William Weber. *Heroic Mexico: The Violent Emergence of a Modern Nation.* Garden City, N.Y.: Doubleday, 1968.

McNeely, John H. "Origins of the Zapata Revolt in Morelos." *Hispanic American Historical Review* 46 (1966): 153–69.

Meyer, Michael C. *Huerta: A Political Portrait.* Lincoln: University of Nebraska Press, 1972.

———. *Mexican Rebel: Pascual Orozco and the Mexican Revolution, 1910–1915.* Lincoln: University of Nebraska Press, 1967.

Ross, Stanley R. *Francisco I. Madero, Apostle of Mexican Democracy.* New York: Columbia University Press, 1955.

Taylor, Lawrence D. "The Great Adventure: Mercenaries in the Mexican Revolution, 1910–1915." *The Americas* 43 (1986): 25–46.

Womack, John, Jr. *Zapata and the Mexican Revolution.* New York: Knopf, 1968.

32

Madero and the Failure of Democracy

In late May of 1911, on his way to Veracruz and ultimate exile, Porfirio Díaz reputedly told Victoriano Huerta, the commander of his military escort, "Madero has unleashed a tiger. Now let's see if he can control it." The remark, both prophetic and reflective of Díaz's keen perception of his fellow countrymen, augured ominous consequences. For the next decade Mexico would be torn apart, and the catharsis would be slow in coming. There would be little time to repair the devastation of war or to refashion the contours of society.

Disappointing Reforms

Bursting with optimistic idealism, Madero approached his presidential challenge with all the fresh enthusiasm of the novice. Mexico was embarking upon a democratic era, and democracy, Madero contended, would be equal to the task. But Madero the president, unlike Madero the revolutionary, found himself quickly besieged with demands from all sides. Only when established in the presidential office did he begin to realize fully that the Revolution had profoundly different meanings to different groups of Mexicans. The spurious alliance began to break up irretrievably. Of the disparate elements he had previously counted in his ranks, those of nineteenth-century liberal persuasion, interested in political reform and the growth of democracy, supported him with unabashed devotion. But both the aristocratic elite he displaced and the social revolutionaries he embraced

Francisco I. Madero (1873–1913). President of Mexico in the crucial period following the overthrow of Díaz, Madero had a faith in democracy that proved ill suited to the political realities of the day.

were increasingly displeased with the modest steps he undertook. The press began to assail him mercilessly, but, in the best democratic tradition, he gave it full rein and stoically accepted the barbed criticism and cruel satires.

It was only natural that Madero should be more responsive to the prodding of his former supporters. Although he could defy anyone to show him where he had ever promised sweeping reform, he did, nevertheless, embark upon a meager and imperfect program to restructure the prevailing social order. Though unwilling to accede to Zapata's urgent demand that land be immediately restored to the villages, the president appointed a National Agrarian Commission, under the chairmanship of his conservative cousin Rafael Hernández, to study the land question. Hernández urged that the government begin purchasing a few private estates for subdivision and sale to the small farmer. But only 10 million pesos were allocated to the project, and the hacendados demanded such high prices for the land that even this modest plan was soon abandoned in favor of restoring some of the ejido lands that had been seized illegally during the late Porfiriato. The burden of proof, however, fell on the villages, and few village leaders were able to cope with the bewildering legal arguments thrown in their faces by the hacendados' lawyers. A handful of cases were settled in favor of the villages, but progress on the agrarian question was meager.

The story was much the same in the field of labor reform. Late in 1912 the Congress authorized the formation of a Department of Labor but placed it, too, under the jurisdiction of conservative Hernández, a man whose quixotic faith in the law of supply and demand was never shaken. The budget for the Department of Labor was a paltry forty-six thousand pesos. After a convention with government officials in Mexico City, a group of textile factory owners promised to initiate a ten-hour day, but in practice the working schedules did not change.

Perhaps the greatest benefit accruing to labor during the Madero presidency was that labor organizers no longer felt so intimidated as they had in the past. Encouraged by the possibilities of revolutionary change, a group of radicals under the leadership of Juan Francisco Moncaleano, a Spanish anarchist, founded the Casa del Obrero Mundial. Not properly a union, the Casa served as a place where labor leaders could meet, exchange views, and, through their official newspaper *Luz*, disseminate propaganda favorable to the cause. But the government, caught between business interests and labor demands, was jittery. Madero feared labor strikes, and, although no labor massacres on the scale of Cananea and Río Blanco were recorded, government troops and local police authorities were used to disperse striking workers on a number of occasions. Hernández interpreted the strikes as inspired by agitators rather than resulting from intolerable conditions and finally had Moncaleano expelled from the country. But the strikes continued, and labor unrest began to disrupt the Mexican economy, growing shaky once again. The gains by labor as a result of these strikes were negligible.[1]

In the field of education the social reformers were again disap-

1. Ramón Eduardo Ruiz, "Madero's Administration and Mexican Labor," in *Contemporary Mexico*, ed. James W. Wilkie, Michael C. Meyer and Edna Monzón de Wilkie (Berkeley, 1976), pp. 187–203.

pointed. Although Madero had promised to broaden the educational base during the presidential campaign, the annual budget for 1911 to 1912 allocated only 7.8 percent for educational programs, as opposed to 7.2 percent during the last year of the Porfiriato. The new president did manage to build some fifty new schools and to initiate a modest program of school lunches for the underprivileged. But his education program is really more notable for what it did not do. No dramatic increase in expenditures was requested, nor was any project for revising the científico curriculum advanced.

In sum, the liberals of the twentieth-century stripe felt swindled by Madero as the administration failed at both the national and state levels. As the disappointed asked themselves why the president did not do more, some most assuredly must have realized that he believed that reform should proceed at a slow and gradual pace so as not to disrupt the fragile economy. But another factor was involved as well. Madero's hands were tied and his energies diverted by a series of revolts that broke out against him before he even had a chance to make himself comfortable in the presidential chair. The Revolution's lack of ideological cohesion had begun to exact a terrible toll and in the process imperiled the administration itself.

Revolts against the New Government

Emiliano Zapata was the first to pronounce against the new regime. In November 1911 the Zapatistas promulgated their famous *Plan de Ayala*. The general principles were those of Zapata himself, but the development and articulation were the work of Otilio Montaño, a schoolteacher from Ayala. After withdrawing recognition of Madero and recognizing Chihuahuan Pascual Orozco as titular head of the rebellion, the plan spelled out its program of agrarian reform.

> The lands, woods, and water that the landlords, científicos, or bosses have usurped . . . will be immediately restored to the villages or citizens who hold the corresponding titles to them. . . . The usurpers who believe they have a right to those properties may present their claims to special courts that will be established on the triumph of the Revolution. Because the great majority of Mexicans own nothing more than the land they walk on, and are unable to improve their social condition in any way . . . because lands, woods, and water are monopolized in a few hands . . . one-third of these properties will be expropriated, with prior in-

demnification, so that the villages and citizens of Mexico may obtain ejidos, townsites, and fields.[2]

The armed conflict began immediately and quickly spread from Morelos to the neighboring states of Guerrero, Tlaxcala, Puebla, Mexico, and even into the Federal District. When Madero's federal commanders were unable to contain the spread of the rebellion, they were replaced by others who promised to conduct a more vigorous campaign. But the Zapatista army continued to grow, and Madero was unable to thwart it. By early 1912 Zapata had disrupted railroad and telegraph service and taken over a number of towns; he had repeatedly defeated the federals and had the government on the run.

At approximately the same time General Bernardo Reyes launched a second movement in the north. In some ways Madero was more concerned with the Reyistas than with the Zapatistas. He feared that General Reyes still enjoyed a wide base of support among the army. Reyes crossed over into Mexico from the United States in the middle of December 1911 but found few Mexicans willing to rally to his banner. Unlike Zapata, Reyes was associated in the public mind with the old regime, and the northern Mexicans were not prepared to embrace his movement, even if many believed that Reyes had been treated unfairly in the recent presidential elections. Realizing that his sluggish revolution was not garnering sufficient support, on Christmas Day Reyes surrendered to a detachment of rurales. The commander of Mexico's third military zone, General Jerónimo Treviño, sent him first to prison in Monterrey and then had him transferred to the Prisión Militar de Santiago Tlaltelolco in Mexico City to await trial for treason.

At the end of the year a third revolt broke out against Madero in Chihuahua. Emilio Vásquez Gómez, believing that he and his brother Francisco had been unfairly treated in the last elections, launched his movement calling for Madero's ouster from office. At the end of January Madero was shocked to learn that the Vasquistas had captured Ciudad Juárez. The president knew full well the significance of this border city—he had seen his own revolt triumph there. Realizing the popularity that Pascual Orozco enjoyed in the north, Madero commissioned the Chihuahua commander to take charge of the government campaigns. For the rank and file of the Vásquez Gómez army Orozco—not Madero

2. The entire plan is quoted in Jesús Silva Herzog, *Breve historia de la Revolución mexicana* (Mexico, 1962), 1: 240–46.

—had been responsible for the overthrow of Díaz. Orozco had re-
cruited the troops and led them in battle. He was the symbol of
Chihuahua manhood and living proof that a poor, indifferently
educated northerner could humble a professional army trained
in the big city. The Vasquistas did not want to fight Orozco, so
they agreed to meet with him. In the simple, folksy idiom of the
north, Orozco made an impassioned speech calling for national
unity in an hour of crisis, and he persuaded the rebel army to lay
down arms without firing another shot.

But a few months later the most serious antigovernment movement broke out in the north. Its leader was the same man who
had just called for national unity and saved Madero from the
Vasquista offensive—Pascual Orozco. The Orozco rebellion was
complex. While it combined nineteenth- and twentieth-century
liberalism, it enjoyed the conservative financial support of the
Terrazas clique in Chihuahua, who believed they could control
the movement once it triumphed.

The *Plan Orozquista*, dated March 25, 1912, was the most com-
prehensive call for reform yet voiced from Mexican soil. It caus-
tically attacked Madero for failing to abide by his own principles
as set forth to the Mexican nation in the Plan de San Luis Potosí.
Government corruption was still in evidence at the state and local levels, and nepotism and favoritism were more exaggerated
in 1912 than they had been at any time during the Porfiriato.
Not only had Madero's cousin, Rafael Hernández, been awarded
the critical cabinet position of secretary of development, but his
uncle, Ernesto Madero, had been made secretary of the treasury;
a relative by marriage, José González Salas, was secretary of war;
brother Gustavo Madero and four other members of the family
were in the Congress; brother Raul Madero was given a series of
government-supported military assignments; another relative
was on the Supreme Court, two were in the postal service, and
yet another was an undersecretary in the cabinet. Government
army uniforms came from cotton cloth manufactured in Madero
mills, while ammunition was purchased from cousin José Aguilar's munitions plant in Monterrey.

The Plan Orozquista, however, was more concerned with social
than political reform. Drawing its inspiration from the Liberal
Plan of 1906, it called for a ten-hour workday, restrictions on
child labor, improved working conditions, higher wages, and
the immediate suppression of the tiendas de raya. Anticipating
the surge of economic nationalism that would sweep over Mexico
in the next two decades, it called for the immediate nationaliza-

tion of the railroads and the utilization of Mexican nationals in their operation. Agrarian reform also figured prominently. Persons who had resided on their land for twenty years were to be given title to it, while all lands illegally seized from the peasantry were to be returned. All lands owned by the government were to be distributed, and, most important, land owned by the hacendados, but not regularly cultivated, would be expropriated.

With alarming speed Orozco amassed a large army—some eight thousand strong—and began marching south to Mexico City. Capturing federally held towns along the way the rebels prepared themselves for a major showdown. The anticipated battle occurred at Rellano, close to the Chihuahua-Durango border. Madero's secretary of war, José González Salas, opted to command the government forces personally, and the army career officer was humiliated by Orozco's untrained rebels. As the federals retreated in disarray, González Salas, fearful of public rebuke, committed suicide. With panic growing in Mexico City, Madero named Victoriano Huerta to head a new government offensive. Huerta planned his campaigns with much deliberation, and by late May 1912 felt strong enough to meet the rebels face to face. By sheer chance the artillery duel once again occurred on the fields of Rellano, but on this occasion the results were different. Not only was Huerta a better field commander than his predecessor, but the Orozquistas were handicapped by lack of ammunition. Huerta pushed them back to the north and in the process temporarily saved the teetering Madero government.

Madero had no time for rejoicing, for his woes were not yet over. In early October 1912 a fifth serious rebellion broke out against him. This time it was Félix Díaz, the nephew of Don Porfirio, who called an army together in Veracruz. The Felicista movement was clearly counterrevolutionary in orientation and comprised many disgruntled supporters of the former dictator. Félix Díaz appealed to the army and suggested that Madero had trampled on its honor by passing over many competent career officers and placing self-made revolutionary generals in charge of key garrisons. The troops stationed in Veracruz came to Díaz's support, but his appeal to other army units throughout the republic went unheeded. Late in October loyal army troops isolated the rebels in Veracruz and forced their surrender. A hastily conceived court-martial found Díaz guilty of treason and sentenced him to death. But Madero reviewed the sentence and, believing his enemies to be pitied rather than executed, commuted it to imprisonment. Díaz was taken under arms to the capital and

A federal machine gun nest awaits the rebel advance.

placed in the Federal District penitentiary. Madero's generosity was in no way reciprocated. Within two months Félix Díaz in one Mexico City prison had established contact with Bernardo Reyes in another, and the two were plotting to overthrow the government. This sixth rebellion would succeed, and Madero would lose not only his office but, a victim of his own ideals, his life as well.

The Overthrow of Madero

Planned for several months, the military coup that began in Mexico City on February 9, 1913, drastically altered the course of the Mexican Revolution. The capital had thus far been spared the ravages of the war that had engulfed much of the nation since November 1910. Now Mexico City residents would be given practical instruction in the full destructive significance of civil war. Early in the morning of February 9, General Manuel Mondragón, supported by several artillery regiments and military cadets, released Bernardo Reyes and Félix Díaz from their respective prisons and marched on the National Palace. Reyes, sporting a fancy military uniform and mounted on a white horse, led the charge and was felled by one of the first machine gun blasts. The rebel leadership then devolved on Félix Díaz. When loyal government troops repulsed the assault on the National Palace, Díaz led his troops westward across the city and installed his army in the Ciudadela, an old and well-fortified army arsenal. Madero, disregarding the advice of several confidants, named General Victoriano Huerta to command his troops. It proved to be a momentous decision.

For the next ten days—the *Decena Trágica*—Mexico City became a labyrinth of barricades, improvised fortifications, and trenches. Artillery fire exchanged between the rebels in the Ciudadela and the government troops in the National Palace destroyed buildings and set fires. As commercial establishments were forced to close their doors for the duration, consumer goods became scarce and people panicked. Downtown streets were strewn with burning cars, runaway horses, and abandoned artillery pieces. Live electric wires dangled precariously from their poles. Looters broke store windows and carried off wares with complete impunity. On one occasion an artillery barrage opened a breach in the wall of the Belén prison and hundreds of inmates scurried through the opening to freedom. A few surveyed the chaos outside and decided to remain.

With neither side able to gain a clear military advantage, civilian casualties mounted into the thousands and bodies began to bloat in the streets. Foreign residents sought the sanctuary of embassies, but not all made it in time. Most traffic came to a halt as only ambulances, military vehicles, and diplomatic automobiles, identified by special flags, moved on the streets. On February 17, after nine days of constant fighting, Madero summoned Huerta and asked when the fighting could be expected to cease. Huerta assured him that peace would be restored to the beleaguered city the following day. The residents of the capital were awakened early on the morning of February 18 by the sounds of artillery and machine gun fire, just as they had been for the previous nine days. But in the afternoon the clamor of war stopped. Huerta had decided to change sides. He withdrew recognition of the federal government and dispatched General Aureliano Blanquet to the National Palace to arrest the president. Blanquet encountered Madero in one of the patios and, with revolver in hand, proclaimed, "You are my prisoner, Mr. President." Madero retorted, "You are a traitor." But Blanquet simply re-affirmed, "You are my prisoner."[3] Within a half hour Vice-President Pino Suárez, Madero's brother Gustavo, and most of the cabinet had been arrested as well.

The agreement according to which Huerta joined the rebels is known as the Pact of the Embassy because the final negotiations were conducted under the aegis of the American ambassador in Mexico City, Henry Lane Wilson. A typical diplomat of the age of dollar diplomacy, Wilson saw his role as protector of United States business interests. Throughout the Madero presidency he had meddled shamelessly in Mexico's internal affairs, and during the Decena Trágica he played an active part in charting the course of events. On one occasion, in concert with the British, German, and Spanish ministers, he even demanded Madero's resignation, alleging as his reason the tremendous damage to foreign property in Mexico City. After being rebuffed by the Mexican president, Wilson changed his tactics and worked actively to bring Huerta and Díaz to an accord. On the evening of February 18 the two generals met with Wilson at the American embassy and hammered out the pact that was made public the following day.

> In the city of Mexico, at nine-thirty in the evening on February 18, 1913, Generals Félix Díaz and Victoriano Huerta met in conference. . . . General Huerta stated that because of the unbearable situation created by the government of Mr. Madero, he had, in order to prevent the further shedding of blood and to safeguard national unity, placed the said Madero, several members of his cabinet, and various other persons under arrest. . . . General Díaz stated that his only reason for raising the standard of revolt was a desire on his part to protect the national welfare, and in that light he was ready to make any sacrifice that would prove beneficial to the country. . . . From this time forward the former chief executive is not to be recognized. The elements represented by Generals Díaz and Huerta are united in opposing all efforts to restore him to power. . . . Generals Díaz and Huerta will do all in their power to enable the latter to assume . . . the provisional presidency.[4]

Wishing to cloak his assumption of power in some semblance of legality, Huerta first secured the official resignations of Madero and Pino Suárez and then convened a special evening ses-

---

3. Quoted in Michael C. Meyer, *Huerta: A Political Portrait* (Lincoln, 1972), p. 57.
4. The Pact of the Embassy has been translated and included in its entirety in ibid., pp. 235–36.

sion of the Congress. The resignations were accepted by the legislative body with only five dissenting votes, and the presidency legally passed to the next in line, Secretary of Foreign Relations Pedro Lascuráin. Sworn into office at 10:24 P.M., Lascuráin immediately appointed General Huerta as secretary of interior and at 11:20 P.M. submitted his own resignation. The Constitution of 1857 provided that in the absence of a president, a vice-president, and a secretary of foreign relations, the office passed to the secretary of interior. Huerta, clad in a formal black tuxedo, was sworn into office shortly before midnight. Madero-style democracy had ended in derision as Mexico had its third president in one day.

The political charade perpetrated before the Congress was not the greatest indignity Mexicans were called upon to suffer in February 1913. On the evening of February 21, Francisco Madero and José María Pino Suárez were transferred from the National Palace, where they had been held prisoners since the day of their arrest, to the Federal District penitentiary. The capital city newspapers the following day blared an improbable tale. A group of Madero's supporters attacked the convoy escorting the prisoners, attempted to free them, and during the ensuing melee both the former president and vice-president were killed.

Virtually no one believed this official version, but few Mexicans knew what really happened. Madero and Pino Suárez had been taken to the penitentiary under the guard of Francisco Cárdenas, a major in the rurales. When the convoy reached the prison, Cárdenas ordered the captives out of the cars and, by prearranged signal, the spotlights high on the wall were turned off. The hapless men were then shot point-blank. Perhaps Victoriano Huerta ordered the assassinations, or perhaps it was Félix Díaz, or even Aureliano Blanquet. The nature of the available evidence simply precludes positive determination. But what cannot be doubted is that the senseless murders of Madero and Pino Suárez set the tone of the Revolution for at least the next five years.

Recommended for Further Study

Beezley, William H. *Insurgent Governor: Abraham González and the Mexican Revolution in Chihuahua.* Lincoln: University of Nebraska Press, 1973.

Blaisdell, Lowell L. "Henry Lane Wilson and the Overthrow of Madero." *Southwestern Social Science Quarterly* 43 (1962): 126–35.

Calvert, Peter. *The Mexican Revolution, 1910–1914: The Diplomacy of the*

Anglo-American Conflict. Cambridge: Cambridge University Press, 1968.

Cumberland, Charles C. *Mexican Revolution: Genesis under Madero*. Austin: University of Texas Press, 1952.

Harris, Charles H., and Louis R. Sadler. "The Underside of the Mexican Revolution: El Paso, 1912." *The Americas* 39 (1982): 69–84.

———. "The 1911 Reyes Conspiracy: The Texas Side." *Southwestern Historical Quarterly* 82 (1980): 325–48.

Henderson, Peter V. N. *Félix Díaz, The Porfirians and the Mexican Revolution*. Lincoln: University of Nebraska Press, 1981.

Knudson, Jerry W. "The Press and the Mexican Revolution of 1910." *Journalism Quarterly* 46 (1969): 760–66.

LaFrance, David G. "Failure of Reform: The Maderistas in Puebla, 1911–1913." *New World* 1 (1986): 44–64.

McNeely, John H. "Origins of the Zapata Revolt in Morelos." *Hispanic American Historical Review* 46 (1966): 153–69.

Meyer, Michael C. *Huerta: A Political Portrait*. Lincoln: University of Nebraska Press, 1972.

———. *Mexican Rebel: Pascual Orozco and the Mexican Revolution, 1910–1915*. Lincoln: University of Nebraska Press, 1967.

Niemeyer, Victor. "Frustrated Invasion: The Revolutionary Attempt of General Bernardo Reyes from San Antonio in 1911." *Southwestern Historical Quarterly* 67 (1963–64): 213–25.

Ross, Stanley R. *Francisco I. Madero, Apostle of Mexican Democracy*. New York: Columbia University Press, 1955.

Turner, Frederick C. "Anti-Americanism in Mexico, 1910–1913." *Hispanic American Historical Review* 47 (1967): 502–18.

Wilson, Henry Lane. *Diplomatic Episodes in Mexico, Belgium and Chile*. Garden City, N.Y.: Doubleday, Page, 1927.

Wolfskill, George, and Douglas W. Richmond, eds. *Essays on the Mexican Revolution: Revisionist Views of the Leaders*. Austin: University of Texas Press, 1979.

Womack, John, Jr. *Zapata and the Mexican Revolution*. New York: Knopf, 1968.

33

Huerta
and the Failure of Dictatorship

Huerta

Victoriano Huerta was born of a Huichol Indian mother and a mestizo father in a small Jalisco village. Attending a poor local school run by the parish priest, he learned to read and write and showed some natural talent for science and mathematics. As a teenager he was taken on as an aide by General Donato Guerra, a career officer who had fought against the French. Guerra used his influence in Mexico City to have Huerta accepted at the National Military Academy. In spite of his mediocre educational background, he did well as a cadet and received his commission in 1876 as a second lieutenant assigned to the army corps of engineers.

Huerta's prerevolutionary career coincided almost exactly with the Díaz dictatorship, and he became an effective agent of Don Porfirio's system of enforced peace. During the thirty-four-year Porfiriato Huerta fought in the north against the Yaqui, in the south against the Maya, and in the central part of the country against other Mexicans unhappy with the autocratic regime. Encountering much success on the field of battle, he rose rapidly in the ranks and by the turn of the century had been awarded his brigadier-general stars. National prominence and some notoriety engulfed him for the first time in the summer of 1911 when interim President León de la Barra dispatched him to Morelos to enforce the demobilization of the Zapatista troops. His relationship with Madero was never good again.

When Bernardo Reyes and Félix Díaz planned the military

coup of February 1913, their emissaries approached Huerta and solicited his support. He refused the invitation, however, not out of loyalty to the Madero administration but rather because he wanted the leadership for himself. When Bernardo Reyes was killed during the first major encounter, the situation changed. Huerta dallied for a week and, having determined that he would be able to control Félix Díaz, made his decision to change sides. Sworn into the presidential office a few days later, Huerta was sure he had made the proper choice.

Within a few days federal generals and state governors began to pledge support of the new regime. A group of talented statesmen and intellectuals accepted cabinet portfolios. Sanitation workers started to scour the bloodstained streets of the capital and to attack a ten-day backlog of garbage. Red Cross units tried to identify hundreds of decaying corpses, and electricians repaired wires dangling dangerously from their poles.

Rebellion and Militarization

The first genuinely ominous sign came from the northeast where Coahuila Governor Venustiano Carranza, an ardent Madero supporter, announced his decision not to recognize the new regime. Carranza issued a circular telegram to other state governors exhorting them to follow his good example. Within a few weeks he found support in Chihuahua and Sonora. Pancho Villa assumed military leadership of the anti-Huerta movement in Chihuahua, while Alvaro Obregón, a man of considerable military talent, took charge of the antigovernment operations in neighboring Sonora. The alliance of the northern revolutionaries, and their formal pronouncement of defection, was sealed in late March when representatives from the three states affixed their signatures to the *Plan de Guadalupe*. After withdrawing recognition of the Huerta government, the plan named Venustiano Carranza as "First Chief" of the Constitutionalist Army and provided that he, or someone designated by him, would occupy the interim presidency upon Huerta's defeat. An exclusively political document, the plan embodied no program of social reform.

In southern Mexico Huerta encountered an implacable enemy of a different sort. Emiliano Zapata angrily rejected Huerta's invitation to pledge support of the government. In fact, the southern rebel arrested and subsequently executed the federal peace commissioners sent to garner his allegiance. Zapata, unlike the

Modern technology is brought to warfare. In one of the first military uses of aircraft, Huerta employed 80-horsepower planes similar to these in reconnaissance and bombing raids against the Villistas in the north.

Constitutionalists in the north, did not denounce Huerta for having overthrown Madero. While he found treason in Huerta's sudden shift of sides during the Decena Trágica, he declared himself in rebellion because he saw no hope that the federal government under Huerta would begin to restore the village lands in Morelos. Not trusting the Constitutionalist dedication to agrarian reform either, Zapata never allied himself with the anti-Huerta movement in the north. But by forcing the government to divert some of its war effort from the north to the south, Zapata placed additional military pressure on the new regime.

Facing rebellion in the north and in Morelos, Huerta's first priority was pacification. With a federal army numbering about fifty thousand, the president announced brazenly to the Congress that he would re-establish peace, "cost what it may." But pacification proved elusive on the field of battle. In March and April the Constitutionalists scored impressive victories in Sonora and Chihuahua, while in the south Emiliano Zapata had done the same. The psychology of the civil war changed drastically in May when First Chief Carranza, in a singularly intemperate decree, announced that federal soldiers who fell into rebel hands would be executed summarily. The Constitutionalists thus declared that they intended to give no quarter, and by the summer of 1913 Huerta had concluded that pacification would come only if he militarized Mexico to the teeth.

Factories and stores not related to the war effort were required to close on Sundays so that civilian employees could be given military training. Railroads left civilian passengers and freight standing in the stations so that military personnel and hardware could be shipped to where it was needed. The National Arms Factory, the National Artillery Workshops, and the National

Powder Factory received new equipment to increase their productive capacities. Military decorations were passed out in wholesale lot to the president's cronies, and new military awards were authorized to compensate favorites or to win over those of doubtful loyalty. Most important, the president decreed constant increases in the size of the federal army—from 50,000 to 100,000 to 200,000 and finally to a quarter of a million, or about twelve times the number of troops available to Porfirio Díaz when the Revolution broke out.

When small pay increases failed to attract enlistees in large numbers, Huerta fell back on a time-honored tradition—the leva, a system of forced conscription directed exclusively at the indigent masses. Tens of thousands of illiterate men were picked up off the streets of the barrios in the large cities and from the surrounding countryside and sent into the field. The crowds emerging from a bullfight or staggering out of a cantina closing its doors for the night were favorite targets, as were criminals in jail for minor offenses. But the effects of the leva were disastrous. The quality of the federal army declined steadily. The lack of adequate training meant no *esprit de corps*, no discipline, and tremendously high desertion rates. In the fall of 1913 it was not unheard of for entire units of new recruits to turn themselves and their equipment over to the enemy without firing a single shot.

The toll of the civil war in 1913 and 1914 was tremendous. The military presence was obvious everywhere. The population of a village could double or triple overnight as a large unit moved in to camp. Because there was no advance notice, a week's stay could deplete stores of food, supplies, and other basic necessities, thus aggravating the obscenities of war. When the troops withdrew, villages were often on the verge of starvation. The receipts a local merchant might receive as the troops emptied his store were scarcely worth the paper they were hastily scrawled on.

With his military position deteriorating, Huerta became increasingly impetuous, egotistical, and dictatorial. Cabinet secretaries could not work with him for very long, and turnovers followed one another in rapid succession. Recognizing the potential value of a controlled press, Huerta initiated an extensive policy of censorship. Editors who adopted hostile attitudes were removed from their positions, sent into exile, or jailed. A vast network of secret agents and spies reported on the activities of real and potential enemies, and by the fall of 1913 the jail cells in

Mexico City and many of the state capitals were crowded with political prisoners.

Without question the most reprehensible facet of the Huerta dictatorship was its unbridled use of political assassination. After the senseless slaying of Madero and Pino Suárez, Maderista Governor Abraham González was the next to be killed. Army officers, congressmen, professional men, and even petty bureaucrats who manifested their discontent were sacrificed to the ill-conceived exigencies of the day. The most celebrated case of all was that of Senator Belisario Domínguez from Chiapas, an outspoken critic of the regime. In late September 1913, against the good counsel of friends in the Senate, Domínguez asked for the floor to read a prepared statement.

> Peace, cost what it may, Mr. Victoriano Huerta had said. Fellow Senators, have you studied the terrible meaning of those words . . . ? The national assembly has the duty of deposing Mr. Victoriano Huerta from the presidency. He is the one against whom our brothers in the north protest with so much reason. . . . You will tell me, gentlemen, that the attempt is dangerous; for Mr. Victoriano Huerta is a bloody and ferocious soldier who assassinates without hesitation anyone who is an obstacle to his wishes; this does not matter, gentlemen! The country exacts from you the fulfillment of a duty, even with risk, indeed the assurance, that you are to lose your lives.[1]

Two weeks later Belisario Domínguez was dead from an assassin's bullet. The morally outraged Senate passed a resolution requesting full information from the president and resolving to remain in permanent session until the case be closed. Two days later Huerta responded by dissolving both houses of the legislature and arresting the majority of the congressmen.

Economic Problems and Foreign Relations

The war Huerta was fighting against the Constitutionalists in the north and the Zapatistas in the south was costly, and the regime had inherited an empty treasury. By relying on the leva to fill the ranks of the federal army, Huerta depleted the work force in both the cities and the countryside. With no pickers, cotton rotted in the fields, coffee beans fell off the trees, and sugarcane remained unharvested on the large plantations. Mines closed

1. Quoted in Michael C. Meyer, *Huerta: A Political Portrait* (Lincoln, 1972), pp. 137–38.

Together with several other kinds of scrip, this 20-peso note from Chihuahua state was used by the Constitutionalists in late 1913 and early 1914.

operations; cattlemen in the north lost thousands of head to the
rebels; and fruit growers, realizing their perishable products
were extremely vulnerable to transportation delays, cut back
production. As food and manufactured goods became scarce, a
black market began to flourish in the larger cities, and the entire
economic structure of the country was severely tested.

The first government expedient was to issue paper money
without adequate hard reserves to back it up. The new paper issue depreciated almost as soon as it rolled off the press. Not to be
outdone, the Constitutionalists and the Zapatistas issued their
own currency, as did a number of states and large mining and
industrial concerns. Late in 1913 there were at least twenty-five
different kinds of paper currency in circulation, and nobody was
able to ascertain accurately the fluctuating exchange rates. Coun-
terfeiters, of course, had a field day, while bankers and tax collectors were driven almost to insanity.

In addition to his military and economic problems, Huerta
faced one other dilemma as well. The United States not only
refused to recognize his regime but adopted a frankly hostile
attitude toward him. Woodrow Wilson came to the United States
presidency almost simultaneously with Victoriano Huerta's rise
to power. While the American ambassador to Mexico, Henry
Lane Wilson, urged recognition, President Wilson and his newly
appointed secretary of state, William Jennings Bryan, both with
an abiding faith in the concept of the democratic state, refused.
To the White House, Huerta, who came to power by forcefully
ejecting the previous regime, was a symbol of all that was wrong

with Latin America. Unprepared by temperament or training to understand the complexities of the Mexican Revolution, President Wilson decided to apply his own standards of political ethics to the situation. The moral judgment, as abstractly admirable as it was diplomatically impractical, once made proved unshakable.

Demonstrating little faith in the reports received from Ambassador Wilson, the president and the secretary of state decided to dispatch special agents to Mexico to report on the nature of the growing conflict. The first chosen for the special assignment was William Bayard Hale. Speaking no Spanish, Hale relied heavily on the United States business community for his information, but he managed interviews with several high-level Mexican officials as well. As his reports to the White House began, he noted that the businessmen in Mexico favored early recognition of the regime, but, sensing what the American president wanted to hear, he indicated that he himself did not. Appealing to President Wilson's sense of moral rectitude, Hale characterized Huerta as "an ape-like man, of almost pure Indian blood. He may be said to subsist on alcohol. Drunk or only half drunk (he is never sober) he never loses a certain shrewdness."[2] The American president was impressed with Hale's findings; he would not have written the report any differently, he claimed, had he gone to Mexico City himself. By summer Ambassador Wilson had been recalled and the White House had another special emissary in Mexico—John Lind, a former governor of Minnesota and a longtime friend of Secretary Bryan.

If there was ever any hope for a reconciliation between the United States and Mexico in the late summer and fall of 1913, Lind's reports to Washington eliminated it. Speaking no more Spanish than Hale and being even less conversant with Mexican politics, his dispatches were haughty, bellicose, inaccurate, and often laden with anti-Catholic and anti-Indian slurs. His characterization of the Mexican cabinet ("a worse pack of wolves never infested any community") reveals more about Lind than about Huerta's advisers. Given President Wilson's insistence that Huerta had to go, there were only two genuine avenues open: Wilson could intervene militarily in Mexico, or he could intervene indirectly by channeling United States aid to the Constitutionalists in the north. He chose the second alternative first, and, when that did not work, he opted for military intervention.

2. Quoted in Larry D. Hill, *Emissaries to a Revolution: Woodrow Wilson's Executive Agents in Mexico* (Baton Rouge, 1973), p. 31.

Domestic Reforms

Amazingly, in spite of the military, economic, and diplomatic pressures the regime faced, Huerta and his advisers found some time for domestic programs. The enemies of the dictatorship labeled them counterrevolutionary, an attempt to reincarnate the age of Díaz. But examination of the regime's social programs reveals that they were anything but that. While Porfirio Díaz had never allocated over 7.2 percent of his budget for education, and Madero had raised the percentage slightly to 7.8 percent, Huerta projected a 9.9 percent allocation for educational services. The funds were still inadequate, but Huerta did manage the construction of 131 new rural schools with seats for some ten thousand new students. Secretary of Education Nemesio García Naranjo, impressed with Henri Bergson's philosophical assault on positivism, decided to initiate a new curriculum at the National Preparatory School. Breaking sharply with the positivist tradition of Gabino Barreda, García Naranjo made more room for the study of literature, history, and philosophy. He did not abandon the sciences but argued persuasively that the other branches of learning should not be sacrificed to them. By creating a reasonable balance between the arts and the sciences, the secretary struck an important first blow at the científico philosophy of education.

The anticientífico posture of the regime manifested itself in Indian policy as well. Administration spokesman Jorge Vera Estañol was an early champion of *indigenismo*. National unity, he argued, was impossible when millions of Indians were estranged from the rest of the population by language, customs, diet, and life expectancy. The rural education program was well intended but was not sufficiently expansive to bring the Indian into the mainstream of national life. Huerta's secretary of interior, Aureliano Urrutia, a full-blooded Indian, began dispatching teams of government consultants into the pueblos to organize community projects that could make small but meaningful changes in the patterns of daily life. But again the program was so small as to make scarcely a dent in the prevailing structure.

It is in the matter of agrarian reform that the Huerta dictatorship has been most widely misrepresented. The regime initiated its program modestly by distributing free seed to anyone who asked for it and by expanding the activities of the agricultural school in Mexico City. Of greater practical significance Huerta authorized the restoration of seventy-eight ejidos to the Yaqui and Mayo Indians of Sonora. In the late spring of 1913 the president upgraded Madero's National Agrarian Commission to a cabinet department and instructed Eduardo Tamariz, Mexico's secretary of agriculture, to begin studying the problem of land redistribution. Tamariz could find nothing in the Constitution of 1857 that even faintly authorized the expropriation of land, so he had to devise another scheme. He found his solution in the taxation provisions of the Constitution. If taxes were increased on the large haciendas, the land would be less valuable for speculative purposes and hacendados would have to consider sale. Congressional authorization was not forthcoming, but Huerta went ahead on his own and decreed an increase in land taxes.

In the areas of labor, church policy, and foreign relations the Huerta regime also departed drastically from the models of the Porfiriato. The programs the administration sponsored did not add up to a social revolution. The reforms bore little demonstrable relationship to one another, no attempt at syncretization was made, and social mobility for the masses did not, as a result, increase. But the regime was no counterrevolution; it was in many ways, more farsighted than that of Madero. Huerta and his advisers allowed themselves to be tossed around by the winds of twentieth-century change and harbored no notions of pegging themselves to a Porfirian status quo. While it is true that Huerta's abuse of political power can justifiably be likened to Don Porfirio's authoritarianism, nevertheless, in the larger social sense both Huerta and his advisers recognized that the days of Díaz were gone forever.

United States Intervention and the Fall of Huerta

By the spring of 1914 Huerta was losing his wars on both the military and the economic fronts. But the final blow was precipitated by his steadily deteriorating relationship with the White House. Early in 1914 President Wilson beefed up the American fleet stationed off Mexican waters. In April a seemingly insignificant event augured the most serious United States–Mexican dispute since the war of the middle of the nineteenth century. Captain Ralph T. Earle of the USS *Dolphin*, stationed off the coast of Tampico, ordered a small landing party to go ashore to secure some badly needed gasoline. Tampico was still in government hands, but the Constitutionalists had attacked several days before and the federal forces were awaiting a more concerted assault. The United States sailors wandered into a restricted dock area and were arrested on the spot.

Within an hour orders came for the sailors' release, accompanied by an official apology. But Rear Admiral Henry T. Mayo, commander of the naval forces off Tampico, considered the apology insufficient and demanded something more elaborate. Since the boat carrying the sailors to shore allegedly flew the American flag, Mayo demanded, among other things, that the Mexican government hoist the American flag at some prominent place on shore and present a twenty-one gun salute to it. President Wilson considered the demands reasonable and prepared himself to make the incident a *casus belli* should Huerta not publicly recant in exactly the manner prescribed. Huerta's secretary of foreign relations insisted that the small landing craft had not carried the flag but agreed to the salute on the condition that the United States return the salute to the Mexican flag. The White House considered the rejoinder impertinent, for both President Wilson and Secretary of State Bryan realized that a United States salute to the Mexican flag could be considered tantamount to recognizing the Huerta regime.

With neither side knowing exactly what to do next, the stalemate was broken when the United States consul in Veracruz wired Washington that a German ship, the *Ypiranga*, was scheduled to arrive in that port on April 21 with a large shipment of arms for Huerta. President Wilson gave immediate orders for a naval occupation of Veracruz. The marines took the city but Mexican casualties mounted into the hundreds, including many noncombatants of both sexes. The public outcry in Mexico City was understandably indignant. Congressmen denounced the United States, and mobs looted American-owned businesses, tore down the statue of George Washington, and threatened tourists. Mexican newspapers urged retaliation against the "Pigs of Yanquilandia." In Monterrey the United States flag was ripped from the consulate and burned on the spot. But the Stars and Stripes, which had precipitated the furor in the first place, was subjected to even greater indignities in the capital. Tied to the tail of a donkey, it was used to sweep clean the streets of the central plaza.

President Wilson's attempt to rid Mexico of a dictator and himself of a self-made enemy almost backfired. Venustiano Carranza and the majority of his Constitutionalists, the supposed beneficiaries of the Veracruz intervention, expressed their strong disapproval of the blatant violation of Mexican sovereignty. Huerta,

U.S. Navy "bluejackets" engage Mexican defenders at Veracruz in April 1914.

however, was unable to capitalize upon their displeasure, and his call for all Mexicans to lay aside internal differences and present a united front went unheeded. Even the initial indignation expressed in Mexico City soon dissipated as the United States troops, in spite of rumors to the contrary, did not march on Mexico City as they had in 1847.

As Huerta called in his troops to make a show of force against the Americans, the Constitutionalists in the north and the Zapatistas in the south quickly moved into the military vacuums. By the early summer, with Pancho Villa's capture of Zacatecas, Huerta's military position had become completely untenable. The continued occupation of Veracruz meant that revenues from the customhouse were stopped before they reached the federal treasury. Recognizing that the diplomatic, economic, and military pressures had all conspired to his disadvantage, Huerta made his decision to resign on July 8, 1914. In his statement of resignation he placed the prime responsibility for what had happened to Mexico on the Puritan who resided in the White House.

It is true that Woodrow Wilson was in large measure responsible for Huerta's overthrow. He had meddled shamelessly in Mexico's internal affairs and, without the semblance of a threat to United States security, had shed innocent Mexican blood to effectuate the foreign policy objectives he deemed opportune. But Wilson cannot be held accountable for the larger calamity that had struck the Mexican nation. Not all Mexico's domestic ills were orphans of United States bullets. Mexicans had not yet agreed on the meaning of their Revolution. Francisco Madero's well-meaning but ineffectual experiment with democracy had failed when he had urged caution and moderation on the burning social issues of the day. But Huerta's dictatorship failed as well. While he was not unwilling to give the social reformers the chance to institute change, many Mexicans could no longer bring themselves to accommodate another brutal dictatorship that exalted order at the expense of liberty. The number of options still open were gradually being reduced, but the better day had not yet dawned.

Recommended for Further Study

Blaisdell, Lowell L. "Henry Lane Wilson and the Overthrow of Madero." *Southwestern Social Science Quarterly* 43 (1962): 126–35.

Calvert, Peter. *The Mexican Revolution, 1910–1914: The Diplomacy of the Anglo-American Conflict.* Cambridge: Cambridge University Press, 1968.

Cumberland, Charles C. *Mexican Revolution: The Constitutionalist Years.* Austin: University of Texas Press, 1972.

Grieb, Kenneth J. *The United States and Huerta.* Lincoln: University of Nebraska Press, 1969.

Hart, John M. "The Urban Working Class and the Mexican Revolution: The Case of the Casa del Obrero Mundial." *Hispanic American Historical Review* 58 (1978): 1–20.

Hill, Larry D. *Emissaries to a Revolution: Woodrow Wilson's Executive Agents in Mexico.* Baton Rouge: Louisiana State University Press, 1973.

Knight, Alan. *The Mexican Revolution.* Vol. 2: *Counter Revolution and Reconstruction.* New York: Cambridge University Press, 1986.

Meyer, Michael C. "The Arms of the *Ypiranga*." *Hispanic American Historical Review* 50 (1970): 543–56.

————. *Huerta: A Political Portrait.* Lincoln: University of Nebraska Press, 1972.

————. "The Militarization of Mexico, 1913–1914." *The Americas* 27 (1971): 293–306.

Quirk, Robert E. *An Affair of Honor: Woodrow Wilson and the Occupation of Veracruz.* New York: Norton, 1967.

Vanderwood, Paul J. "The Picture Postcard as Historical Evidence: Veracruz: 1914." *The Americas* 45 (1988): 201–26.

Wilson, Henry Lane. *Diplomatic Episodes in Mexico, Belgium and Chile.* Garden City, N.Y.: Doubleday, Page, 1927.

34

The Illusory Quest for a Better Way

The Convention of Aguascalientes and Near Anarchy

The years following Victoriano Huerta's ouster are the most chaotic in Mexican revolutionary history as the quarrels among erstwhile allies began. In 1914 First Chief Venustiano Carranza allowed that a convention should be held to determine, among other questions, who should be the provisional president of Mexico until such time as national elections could be scheduled. A proper choice, he believed, could finally put an end to the fragmentation that had characterized the Revolution almost from the beginning. The town of Aguascalientes, in neutral territory, was selected to host the convention, and invitations were extended to all the important revolutionary factions, the number of delegates being apportioned according to how many troops had been deployed in the recent anti-Huerta campaigns.

The military delegates, in a wide array of uniforms and most carrying rifles with full cartridge belts, began to arrive in Aguascalientes in early October. At one of the early sessions Alvaro Obregón, the First Chief's official spokesman, presented the Convention with a Mexican flag inscribed with the words, "Military Convention of Aguascalientes." Each of the delegates then went to the podium, placed his signature on the flag, and swore allegiance to the Convention, some offering a few garrulous remarks. The impressive display of confraternity was not destined to last for long, however. When the Zapatista delegation arrived, a few days late, its leader Paulino Martínez, asked to speak. In a deliberate affront to Carranza and Obregón he recognized Villa and Zapata as the genuine leaders of the Revolution. Manifesting the typical Zapatista aversion to gradualism, he argued that "effective suffrage and no-re-election" had no meaning for the vast majority of Mexicans. The Revolution had been fought for land and liberty. The speech presaged a serious schism in the Convention between Villistas and Zapatistas on the one hand and Carrancistas and Obregonistas on the other. The debates were not sectarian squabbles; rather they reflected fundamental differences of opinion on the direction the Revolution should take.

Martínez was followed to the rostrum by the vice-chairman of the Zapatista delegation, Antonio Díaz Soto y Gama. A thirty-year-old socialist and a polished orator, he delineated future lines of combat.

> I come here not to attack anyone but to evoke patriotism and to stimulate shame. I come to excite the honor of all of the delegates to this assembly. . . . Perhaps it is necessary to invoke respectable symbols [gesturing to the Convention flag], but I fear that the essence of patriotism does not lie in the symbols, which are, after all, quite similar to the farces of the church. . . . I believe that our word of honor is more valuable than all of the signatures stamped on this flag. In the last analysis this flag represents nothing more than the triumph of the clerical reaction championed by Iturbide. I will never sign this flag. . . . That which we called Independence was not independence for the Indian, but independence for the criollo, for the heirs of the conquerors who continue infamously to abuse and cheat the oppressed Indian.[1]

Soto y Gama's speech was continuously interrupted from the floor both by those who cheered him and by those who were livid at his ridicule of Mexican history and defamation of the flag. Not yet ready to embrace the chastening influence of open debate, some of the delegates even pointed pistols in his direction. The acrimony occasioned by the impassioned speech was not easily abated, and as the Convention set to work on naming a provisional president the underlying issue was whether the Revolution was going to follow the politically oriented plans of San Luis Potosí and Guadalupe or the agrarian Plan de Ayala.

When, against Carranza's wishes, the Convention chose Eulalio Gutiérrez as provisional president of Mexico, the First Chief, haughty as ever, disavowed the action and, from Mexico City, ordered his followers to withdraw. Some, including Alvaro Obregón, obeyed, while others made common cause with the Zapatistas and Villistas. As Villa's troops marched on the capital to install Gutiérrez in the presidency, it was obvious to all that

1. Quoted in Isidro Fabela, ed., *Documentos históricos de la revolución mexicana* (Mexico, 1960–73), 23: 181–82.

Mexico was on the verge of still another civil war. Carranza believed it was better not to make a stand in Mexico City and withdrew his Constitutionalist government to Veracruz. The United States government had agreed to pull out its troops just in time for Carranza to make the Gulf port his provisional capital.

Multiple Civil Wars

In early December 1914 Carranza's two principal antagonists, Pancho Villa, "the Centaur of the North," and Emiliano Zapata, "the Attila of the South," staged a dramatic meeting at Xochimilco on the outskirts of Mexico City. While their followers had knotted the bonds of intellectual camaraderie at the Convention, the two leaders had never before met. The historian Robert Quirk has recreated the encounter from eyewitness accounts.

> Villa and Zapata were a study in contrasts. Villa was tall and robust, weighing at least 180 pounds, with a florid complexion. He wore a tropical helmet after the English style. . . . He was clad in a heavy, brown woolen sweater, which was loosely woven, with a large roll collar . . . khaki military trousers, army leggings and heavy riding boots. Zapata, in his physiognomy, was much more the Indian of the two. His skin was very dark, and in comparison with Villa's his face was thin with high cheek bones. He wore an immense sombrero, which at times hid his eyes. . . .
>
> The conference began haltingly . . . both were men of action and verbal intercourse left them uneasy. . . . But then the conversation touched on Venustiano Carranza and suddenly, like tinder, burst aflame. They poured out in a torrent of volubility their mutual hatred for the First Chief. Villa pronounced his opinion of the middle class revolutionaries who followed Carranza: "Those are men who have always slept on soft pillows. How could they ever be friends of the people, who have spent their whole lives in nothing but suffering?" Zapata concurred: "On the contrary, they have always been the scourge of the people. . . . Those *cabrones!* As soon as they see a little chance, well, they want to take advantage of it and line their own pockets! Well, to hell with them!"[2]

But while Villa and Zapata could agree enthusiastically about their profound disdain for Carranza, their alliance was short lived. After a brief visit to Mexico City Zapata returned to Morelos and Villa turned north. Although each had promised to support the military engagements of the other, cooperation

2. Robert E. Quirk, *The Mexican Revolution, 1914–1915: The Convention of Aguascalientes* (New York, 1963), pp. 135–38.

Pancho Villa (left) and Emiliano Zapata (right) meet in Mexico City. The camaraderie was more apparent than real.

against Carranza was noticeable only by its absence. The early months of 1915 saw the Mexican Revolution degenerating into unmitigated anarchy. Civil wars ravaged many states. At times the Constitutionalists seemed to gain the upper hand only to be set back by internal bickering, badly planned campaigns, or the defection of important contingents. Civilian casualties mounted as atrocities were committed on all sides.

With his own Conventionist coalition falling apart as well, provisional President Gutiérrez abandoned Mexico City and Obregón took the capital unopposed. But nothing was thereby settled. Gutiérrez, still claiming to be president, established a new government in Nuevo León; Carranza, claiming national executive control as first chief, continued to govern from Veracruz; the Zapatistas supported Roque González Garza as president; while Pancho Villa, pretending to speak for the entire nation, ruled from Chihuahua. None of the governments recognized the paper money, coinage, or legal contracts of the others.

The muddied political waters were cleared somewhat in the

most famous military engagement of the Revolution—the battle of Celaya—in April of 1915. While Pancho Villa prepared to put his slightly tarnished record of military victories on the line, Alvaro Obregón had immersed himself in the battle reports from war-torn Europe. He had learned, among other things, that one of the best ways to blunt a concerted cavalry charge was to encircle carefully laid out defensive positions with rolls of barbed wire. In early April, when Villa attacked with a force estimated at twenty-five thousand men, Obregón was ready. He had planned his defenses with consummate skill, and, when Villa launched a furious cavalry charge, Obregón's well-placed artillery and machine guns began cutting the attackers to pieces. Villa was forced to retreat, but in the middle of the month tried again to dislodge Obregón's forces. The second Villista offensive was even less successful than the first; in fact, it was a disaster. Bent upon victory even at exorbitant costs, Villa threw his cavalry against the barbed-wire entrenchments only to see wave after wave massacred. When it all ended, thousands of bodies were strewn across the fields of Celaya and impaled on the barbed wire. Obregón's official report listed over 4,000 Villistas dead, 5,000 wounded, and 6,000 taken prisoner. He calculated his own losses at only 138 dead and 227 wounded.

The battle of Celaya did not immediately destroy Villa's capacity to make war, but it did presage his ultimate defeat. By the summer and fall of 1915 First Chief Carranza was clearly gaining the upper hand as both the Villistas in the north and the Zapatistas in the south found themselves increasingly isolated and without national support. In the White House President Wilson decided to throw the official support of the United States behind the Constitutionalists. He extended diplomatic recognition to the Carranza regime in October. Pancho Villa, who had courted the United States for years and who had not even criticized the invasion at Veracruz, was incensed. Determined not to turn the other cheek, he began to take his vengeance on private United States civilians.

The first serious incident occurred at Santa Isabel (today General Trías), Chihuahua. The strange scenario began on January 9, 1916, at El Paso, Texas, where a group of United States mining engineers and technicians from the Cusi Mining Company boarded a train for Mexico. Assured of a safe conduct and Mexican government protection, they set out to reopen the Cusihuiriachic mine. At the hamlet of Santa Isabel the train was stopped

Pancho Villa (1878–1923). Never an "armchair general," Villa often led his troops into battle.

by a barrier laid across the tracks. A band of Villistas boarded the car carrying the Americans, dragged them off, and murdered fifteen of them on the spot.

But an even more outrageous incident occurred exactly two months later. Early in the morning of March 9, 1916, Villa dispatched 485 men across the border from Palomas, Chihuahua, and attacked the dreary, sun-baked adobe town of Columbus, New Mexico. One of the first shots stopped the large clock in the railroad station at 4:11 A.M. For the next two hours the Villistas terrorized the town's four hundred inhabitants. Shouting *¡Viva Villa!* and *¡Muerte a los Gringos!* they shot and burned and looted. Troopers from the Thirteenth Cavalry succeeded in driving them off by daybreak, but eighteen Americans had been killed, many were wounded, and the town was burned beyond recognition.

The clamor for United States intervention was immediate and predictable. Senator Albert Bacon Fall of New Mexico called for a half-million men to occupy all of Mexico. President Wilson was not willing to go that far, but he did agree to dispatch a small punitive expedition under the command of General John J. Pershing, an army man who years before had chased the Apache chief, Geronimo, through the same northern Mexican desert. It took a week for Pershing to organize his expedition, and that was more than enough time for Villa to cover his tracks. Approximately six thousand United States army troops wandered hot and thirsty through the rough terrain in a futile effort to locate their prey. Little if any help could be expected from the rural Mexican, and as the Americans entered small pueblos they were often greeted with shouts of ¡Viva Mexico, Viva Villa! As the expedition cut south into Mexico, First Chief Carranza began to get nervous and ordered Pershing to withdraw. Not yet ready to admit defeat, Pershing engaged a group of Carrancista troops ordered to forestall his southward thrust. When hostilities began he received orders to withdraw gradually to the north, but the expedition was not pulled out of Mexico until January 1917. By

General Pershing's cavalry expedition into northern Mexico may have hardened his troops for the upcoming war in Europe, but his effort to capture Pancho Villa was in vain.

that time the United States had spent $130 million in its unsuccessful attempt to catch and punish the Columbus raiders.

The Constitution of 1917

The failure of the Pershing punitive expedition notwithstanding, Villa got progressively weaker and Carranza gradually consolidated his position in Mexico City. The First Chief's advisers convinced him that the time had come to give some institutional basis to the Revolution that had engulfed the nation for almost six years. In an attempt to legitimize the Revolution he reluctantly agreed to convoke a congress to meet in Querétaro for the purpose of drawing up a new constitution. Remembering how he had lost control of the Convention of Aguascalientes, he vowed not to repeat the error in Querétaro. No individual or group who had opposed the Constitutionalist movement would be eligible to participate; thus no Huertistas, Villistas, or Zapatistas were included among the delegates when the first session convened in November 1916. But First Chief Carranza quickly learned what he should have already known; the Constitutionalists themselves were scarcely in ideologic agreement.

The delegates at Querétaro represented a new breed of Mexican politician and, in a sense, constituted a new social elite. Unlike the Convention of Aguascalientes, military men constituted only 30 percent of the delegates. Over half had university educations and professional titles. The large majority were young and middle class; because they had been denied meaningful participation during the Porfiriato, many were politically ambitious.[3]

With every intention of controlling the proceedings, Carranza submitted to the Querétaro Congress a draft of a new constitution he himself approved. It showed him to be a liberal in the best nineteenth-century tradition. His draft differed little from the Constitution of 1857, although it contained a series of sections strengthening executive control. It occasioned an inevitable split in the Congress between those moderates who supported Carranza and the radicals (called Jacobins by their opponents) who desired something more likely to harbinger rapid social reform.

The debates in Querétaro, focusing on everything from temper-

3. The social background of the delegates and their votes on a number of key issues have been analyzed statistically in Peter H. Smith, "La política dentro de la Revolución: El congreso constituyente de 1916–1917," *Historia Mexicana* 22 (1973): 363–95.

ance to prison reform, were acrimonious. After the first few votes had been taken, it was clear that the radicals held the majority. Led by thirty-two-year-old Francisco Múgica, they succeeded in pushing through a number of anticlerical provisions and three extremely significant articles that came to embody the fundamental orientation the Revolution was to assume in the 1920s and 1930s.

The anticlericalism of the Congress was even more intense than it had been during the height of the liberal-conservative struggle during the nineteenth century. All of the old arguments were heard, but, in addition, the church was now seen to be blocking the path of the social revolution. Article after article limited the powers of the church. Marriage was declared a civil ceremony; religious organizations would enjoy no special legal status, and, as a result, priests were considered ordinary citizens; public worship outside the confines of the church was banned; state legislatures could determine the maximum number of priests to be allowed within state boundaries; all priests in Mexico had to be native born; clergymen were prohibited from forming political parties; priests had to register with civil authorities; and new church buildings had to be approved by the government. The anticlerical tenor of the Querétaro Congress also surfaced in one of the three most important articles.

The drafting of Article 3 was assigned to Múgica's committee on education, and his proposal touched off passionate exchanges on the floor of the Congress. Few took umbrage at the principle that primary education should be free and obligatory in the Mexican republic, but Múgica and his radical cohorts had one additional criterion to add. Education should be secular. The lessons of history convinced Múgica that the clergy had sacrificed all claim to obedience.

> I am an enemy of the clergy because I consider it the most baneful and perverse enemy of our country. . . . What ideas can the clergy bring to the soul of the Mexican masses, or to the middle class, or to the wealthy? Only the most absurd ideas—tremendous hate for democratic institutions, the deepest hate for the principles of equity, equality and fraternity. . . . Are we going to turn over to the clergy the formation of our future? . . . Fellow deputies, what morality can the clergy transmit as learning to our children? We have ample testimony: only the most corrupting and terrible morality.[4]

4. Quoted in *Diario de los debates del Congreso Constituyente, 1916–1917* (Mexico, 1960), p. 642.

The responses of Félix Palavicini and other Carranza supporters in the Congress were just as terse, personal, and caustic. But when the final vote was taken, Francisco Múgica's Article 3 passed by a margin of almost two to one. With the radicals' dominance well established, two other major issues were resolved in their favor. And if the debates on education reminded many of the anticlerical rhetoric of the Reform, the ensuing disputation on land and labor left no doubt that a new age of liberalism had dawned.

Article 27 addressed itself to Mexico's endemic land problem and can be considered a direct outgrowth of Díaz's alienation of Mexico's subsoil rights and his policy of allowing the land companies to appropriate the old communal lands. While the Zapatistas were not present in Querétaro, the issue that had made them a potent force had to be squarely faced. Article 27 required that lands seized illegally from the peasantry during the Porfiriato be restored and provision be made for those communities that could not prove legal title. Equally as important, the private ownership of land was no longer considered to be an absolute right but rather something of a privilege. If land did not serve a useful social function, it could be appropriated by the state: "The nation shall at all times have the right to impose on private property such limitations as the public interest may demand, as well as the right to regulate the utilization of natural resources . . . in order to conserve them and to ensure a more equitable distribution of public wealth." A special section of Article 27 deeply disturbed foreign nationals who owned property in Mexico.

> Only Mexicans by birth or naturalization have the right to acquire ownership of lands, waters, . . . or to obtain concessions for the exploitation of mines or waters. The state may grant the same right to foreigners, provided that they agree before the Department of Foreign Relations to consider themselves as nationals in respect to such property, and bind themselves not to invoke the protection of their governments.[5]

The last, precedent-breaking article treated the labor question and sought to provide a reasonable balance between labor and management. Article 123 provided for an eight-hour workday, a six-day workweek, a minimum wage, and equal pay for equal work regardless of sex or nationality. Most important, it gave

5. Ibid.

both labor and capital the right to organize for the defense of their respective interests and allowed that the workers had the right to bargain collectively and go on strike.

The Constitution of 1917 was not nearly as radical as many contemporary observers found it, but it did coagulate into a repudiation of nineteenth-century laissez-faire liberalism. Although ideologically indebted to the Liberal Plan of 1906, the Plan Orozquista, and the Plan de Ayala, it was more reformist than revolutionary. Carranza accepted it with great reluctance. It bore scant resemblance to the draft he had proposed, but he had set the requirements for delegates himself and, more important, wanted to become constitutional president after having served as First Chief for four years.

The Carranza Presidency

Carranza handily won the special elections that were held in March 1917 and took the oath of office on May 1. Not only was the country far from pacified, but the economy was in a state of acute distress. The banking structure had been shattered, in part because of the general chaos but also as a direct result of the worthless paper money that had inundated the commercial markets. Mining suffered enormous losses, with gold production declining some 80 percent between 1910 and 1916 and silver and copper production falling off 65 percent during the same period. Industrial production fell off as well, and wages were depressed. The communication and transportation networks in which Díaz had taken so much pride were in shambles. Agricultural shortages pushed food prices up, and the inflation took a terrible toll on poor urbanites trying to live on a monetary economy.

Carranza quickly let it be known that, although he had accepted the Constitution of 1917, he had no idea of enforcing it. Confusing change in government with change in society, he believed the Revolution to be over. In fact, it had scarcely begun. Still prompted by the inviolability of private property, under Article 27 Carranza distributed only 450,000 acres of land, a paltry sum when one considers that many hacendados had more than this and Luis Terrazas alone owned in excess of seven million acres. In addition, the land Carranza did distribute had been taken away from his political enemies. This was neither the spirit nor the intent of Article 27.

The record of the administration on labor was no better. Even before the new Constitution was enacted, Carranza's labor policy was known. In the fall of 1915, when workers in Veracruz struck protesting payment of wages in worthless paper currency, Carranza used his army to put down the strike. A year later, when railroad workers declared a strike, Carranza found it treasonous and arrested the leaders. Mexican labor leaders, hoping for a better day with the adoption of Article 123, were disappointed as well. On a few occasions innocuous concessions were granted to labor, but the labor movement did not have an advocate in the presidential chair.

Though without his blessings or support, an event did occur during Carranza's presidency that was a landmark in the Mexican labor movement. In 1918 the labor leader Luis Morones founded Mexico's first nationwide union, the Confederación Regional Obrera Mexicana (CROM). The gains made by the labor movement in the next two years were marginal, but the establishment of the confederation did lay the foundation for future progress.

There can be no doubt that Carranza's presidency was complicated by World War I. The eventual entrance of the United States into the European conflagration was a foregone conclusion, and the Mexican government was anxious that it be sooner rather than later. Perhaps Washington would then be too concerned with trans-Atlantic matters to intervene again in Mexican affairs. But Mexico's own position had to be carefully defined. Many Latin American nations were prepared to follow the lead of the United States and break diplomatic relations with Germany. Should not Mexico also align itself with its Western Hemisphere counterparts? While many prominent Mexicans urged this course of action, others argued with understandable passion that, unlike France, England, and the United States, Germany had never landed troops on Mexican soil; Germany had not stolen half of the national territory or presumed to dictate how Mexico should manage its own affairs.

As Carranza himself weighed the alternatives, he received a strange proposal from the German foreign secretary, Arthur Zimmermann. In return for a formal alliance with Germany, on the successful conclusion of the war Mexico would receive back the lands it had lost to the United States in the middle of the nineteenth century. However tempting the offer sounded, Carranza had to turn it down. Germany, he realized, was much too

Venustiano Carranza (1859–1920). The First Chief of the Constitutionalist Army assumed the presidency in 1917 but, in spite of revolutionary rhetoric, moved slowly on the issues of social reform.

bogged down in Europe to come to Mexico's assistance in a war with the United States. The best course for Mexico to follow, Carranza determined, was to maintain strict neutrality during the war.

Although the European conflict was disquieting to Mexico and resulted in some economic dislocation, the slow pace of the reform program cannot properly be attributed to it. Carranza did not want to accelerate the pace of the Revolution. Of all the disillusioned groups of revolutionaries in Mexico, the Zapatistas were most dismayed. The president sent thousands of federal troops into Morelos under trusted General Pablo González. Conducting a very competent campaign, González took a number of Zapatista towns, but the guerrilla chieftain himself eluded capture. The fighting in Morelos was relentless—perhaps the most terrible of the entire Revolution. Thousands of innocent civilians were charged with succoring Zapatistas and executed. Entire towns were burned, crops methodically destroyed, and cattle stolen. The Zapatistas responded in kind and on one occasion blew up a Mexico City–Cuernavaca train, killing some four hundred passengers, mostly civilians.

In March of 1919 Zapata directed an open letter to Carranza. It was a passionate statement but one that helps to explain why Zapata had fought every Mexican head of state for a full decade.

It was not written to the president whom he did not recognize, nor to the politician whom he did not trust, but to Citizen Carranza.

> As the citizen I am, as a man with a right to think and speak aloud, as a peasant fully aware of the needs of the humble people, as a revolutionary and a leader of great numbers, . . . I address myself to you Citizen Carranza. . . . From the time your mind first generated the idea of revolution . . . and you conceived the idea of naming yourself Chief . . . you turned the struggle to your own advantage and that of your friends who helped you rise and then shared the booty—riches, honors, businesses, banquets, sumptuous feasts, bacchanals, orgies. . . .
>
> It never occurred to you that the Revolution was fought for the benefit of the great masses, for the legions of the oppressed whom you motivated by your harangues. It was a magnificent pretext and a brilliant recourse for you to oppress and deceive. . . .
>
> In the agrarian matter you have given or rented our haciendas to your favorites. The old landholdings . . . have been taken over by new landlords . . . and the people mocked in their hopes.
>
> EMILIANO ZAPATA[6]

Carranza was not about to retire in the face of polemical thunder. He had one more plan for ending his problem with Zapata. The president discussed with General Pablo González a daring plot to deceive Zapata and then to kill him. The scheme was put into operation at once. Colonel Jesús Guajardo, one of González's subordinates in the Morelos campaigns, wrote to Zapata that he wanted to mutiny and to turn himself, some five hundred men, and all of their arms and ammunition over to the Zapatistas. Zapata demanded proof of Guajardo's sincerity, for tricks had been played in the past, and asked that several former Zapatistas, who had previously defected to the federal cause, be tried by court-martial and executed. Colonel Guajardo agreed and carried out the order. Zapata was still not fully convinced when news reached him from his own network of spies that Guajardo had captured the town of Jonacatepec in the name of the Zapatistas. Zapata at this juncture agreed to meet the defecting federal officer. A conference was set for April 10, 1919, at the Hacienda de Chinameca in Zapata's home territory. With only a few men accompanying him, Zapata rode into the hacienda in the early afternoon. A young eyewitness later described what happened.

6. Quoted in Fabela, ed., *Documentos históricos de la revolución mexicana*, 21: 305–10.

Ten of us followed him just as he ordered. The rest of the people stayed [outside the walls] under the trees, confidently resting in the shade with their carbines stacked. Having formed ranks, [Guajardo's] guard looked ready to do him honors. Three times the bugle sounded the honor call; and as the last note died away, as the General in Chief reached the threshold of the door . . . at point blank, without giving him time even to draw his pistols, the soldiers who were presenting arms fired two volleys, and our unforgettable General Zapata fell never to rise again.[7]

While Carranza had thus ridded himself of his most implacable adversary, he did not have much time left himself, as he would also die by the bullet. In 1920, when the president attempted to name his successor in the high office, Alvaro Obregón allied himself with fellow Sonorans Adolfo de la Huerta and Plutarco Elías Calles and declared himself in revolt. Under a new revolutionary banner, the *Plan de Agua Prieta*, a new army of northerners began marching on Mexico City. In May, Carranza was forced to flee the capital and, on his way into exile, was assassinated by one of his own guards in the squalid village of Tlaxcalantongo. The assassin was a loyal Obregonista, but evidence directly linking Obregón to the murder is scanty.

The Carranza regime has not yet received the type of careful historical evaluation it merits. When it is subjected to the tests of archival research it might very well prove to be the period of counterrevolution in the Mexican social upheaval. Carranza was so imbued with hatred for Victoriano Huerta, his predecessor, that he not only repudiated everything Huerta did but, in fact, nullified in the name of the Constitutionalist Revolution many of the more progressive measures undertaken by that dictatorship in the period 1913–14. Having determined that Huerta had raised teachers' salaries, Carranza reduced them to their former levels at the very time that inflation had pushed consumer prices up. Land that Huerta had begun to redistribute to the communal ejidos was restored to its Porfirian proprietors. While Francisco Madero had projected 7.8 percent of his total budget for education, and Huerta 9.9 percent, the figure under Carranza had slipped, by 1919, to an appalling .09 percent. Expenditures for all social programs dropped from 11.6 percent in 1913 to 1.9 percent in 1919.

While the counterrevolutionary thesis must remain a thesis pending further investigation, what is certain is that the social

7. Quoted in John Womack, Jr., *Zapata and the Mexican Revolution* (New York, 1968), p. 326.

revolution did not find a protagonist in the First Chief. Carranza would never have admitted that laissez faire could conflict with social welfare. One should not be misled by the fact that the socially oriented Constitution of 1917 was enacted during the Carranza years. Carranza was unhappy with its progressive articles and reacted to them by applying the old colonial maxim, *Obedezco pero no cumplo*. He simply failed to take into account the aspirations of the social reformers.

Mexico had finally rounded the corner by 1920. The violence was not yet completely spent, but generally the struggles in the post-1920 period became less chaotic and more deliberative as national politicians found more constructive releases for their energy and fervor. A gradual stabilization of the political order, coupled with a modest implementation of the new Constitution, would begin to change the contours of society in the 1920s. As the shock of carnage receded into the past, the goals of a better life began to be realized, but progress was slow and arduous. Not until the 1930s would Mexico inaugurate a president undeterred by centuries of tradition or by the vested interests.

Recommended for Further Study

Bailey, David C. "Alvaro Obregón and Anti-clericalism in the 1910 Revolution." *The Americas* 26 (1969): 183–98.

Braddy, Haldeen. *Pershing's Mission in Mexico*. El Paso: Texas Western College Press, 1966.

Brunk, Samuel. "Zapata and the City Boys: In Search of a Piece of the Revolution." *Hispanic American Historical Review* 73 (1993): 33–65.

Buffington, Robert. "Revolutionary Reform: The Mexican Revolution and the Discourse on Prison Reform." *Mexican Studies* 9 (1993): 71–93.

Chacón, Ramón D. "Salvador Alvarado and the Roman Catholic Church: Church-State Relations in Revolutionary Yucatán, 1914–1918." *Journal of Church and State* 27 (1985): 245–66.

Clendenen, Clarence C. *The United States and Pancho Villa: A Study in Unconventional Diplomacy*. Ithaca, N.Y.: Cornell University Press, 1961.

Coerver, Don M., and Linda B. Hall. *Texas and the Mexican Revolution: A Study in State and National Border Policy, 1910–1920*. San Antonio: Trinity University Press, 1984.

Cumberland, Charles C. *Mexican Revolution: The Constitutionalist Years*. Austin: University of Texas Press, 1972.

Garner, Paul. "Federalism and Caudillismo in the Mexican Revolution. The Genesis of the Oaxaca Sovereignty Movement (1915–20)." *Journal of Latin American Studies* 17 (1985): 111–33.

Gerlach, Allen. "Conditions along the Border—1915: The Plan de San Diego." *New Mexico Historical Review* 43 (1968): 195–212.

Gilderhus, Mark T. *Diplomacy and Revolution: U.S.–Mexican Relations under Wilson and Carranza*. Tucson: University of Arizona Press, 1977.

———. "The United States and Carranza, 1917: The Question of De Jure Recognition." *The Americas* 29 (1972): 210–31.

Hall, Linda B. *Alvaro Obregón: Power and Revolution in Mexico, 1911–1920*. College Station: Texas A & M University Press, 1981.

Harris, Charles H., and Louis R. Sadler. "The Plan of San Diego and the Mexican–United States War Crisis of 1916: A Reexamination." *Hispanic American Historical Review* 58 (1978): 381–408.

Hart, John M. *Revolutionary Mexico: The Coming and Process of the Mexican Revolution*. Berkeley: University of California Press, 1987.

Katz, Friedrich. *The Secret War in Mexico: Europe, the United States and the Mexican Revolution*. Chicago: University of Chicago Press, 1981.

Machado, Manuel A., and James T. Judge. "Tempest in a Teapot? The Mexican–United States Intervention Crisis of 1919." *Southwestern Historical Quarterly* 74 (1970): 1–23.

Martínez, Oscar J. *Fragments of the Mexican Revolution: Personal Accounts from the Border*. Albuquerque: University of New Mexico Press, 1983.

Meyer, Michael C. "The Mexican-German Conspiracy of 1915." *The Americas* 23 (1966): 76–89.

Monticone, Joseph R. "Pancho Villa and American Security: Woodrow Wilson's Mexican Diplomacy Reconsidered." *Journal of Latin American Studies* 13 (1981): 293–311.

Niemeyer, E. V., Jr. "Anti-Clericalism in the Mexican Constitutional Convention of 1916–1917." *The Americas* 11 (1954): 31–49.

———. *Revolution at Querétaro: The Mexican Constitutional Convention of 1916–1917*. Austin: University of Texas Press, 1974.

Quirk, Robert E. *The Mexican Revolution, 1914–1915: The Convention of Aguascalientes*. New York: Citadel Press, 1963.

Richmond, Douglas W. *Venustiano Carranza's Nationalist Struggle, 1893–1920*. Lincoln: University of Nebraska Press, 1984.

Sandos, James. "German Involvement in Northern Mexico, 1915–1916: A New Look at the Columbus Raid." *Hispanic American Historical Review* 50 (1970): 70–88.

Tate, Michael L. "Pershing's Punitive Expedition: Pursuer of Bandits or Presidential Panacea?" *The Americas* 32 (1975): 72–98.

White, E. Bruce. "The Muddied Waters of Columbus, New Mexico." *The Americas* 32 (1975): 72–98.

Womack, John, Jr. *Zapata and the Mexican Revolution*. New York: Knopf, 1968.

35

Society and Culture during the Age of Violence

The Impact of the Revolution on the Masses

The rapid changes in the presidential chair, the heated debates in Aguascalientes and Querétaro, and the redounding phrases of the Constitution of 1917 surely had little immediate meaning to the Mexican masses. It was the violence of that first revolutionary decade which most dominated their lives and left Mexico a country without charm or gaiety. For every prominent death—Francisco Madero, José María Pino Suárez, Pascual Orozco, Emiliano Zapata, or Venustiano Carranza—a hundred thousand nameless Mexicans also died. By any standard the loss of life was tremendous. Although accurate statistics were not recorded, moderate estimates calculate that between 1.5 and 2 million lost their lives in those terrible ten years. In a country with a population of roughly 15 million in 1910, few families did not directly feel the pain as one in every eight Mexicans was killed. Even Mexico's high birthrate could not offset the carnage of war. The census takers in 1920 counted almost a million fewer Mexicans than they had found only a decade before.

Some of the marching armies were equipped with small medical teams, and Pancho Villa even fitted out a medical train on which battlefield operations could be performed. But medical care was generally so primitive that within a week after a major engagement deaths of wounded often doubled or tripled losses sustained immediately on the battlefield. And in more cases than one likes to recount captured enemy prisoners, both federals and rebels, were executed rather than cared for and fed. Civilian deaths rose into the hundreds of thousands as a result of indiscriminate artillery bombardments and, in some cases, the macabre policy of placing noncombatants before firing squads in pursuit of some imperfectly conceived political or military goal.

It is axiomatic that war elicits not only the worst in man but often psychotic behavior in otherwise normal human beings. While Mexican history does not have names such as Andersonville, Dachau, Auschwitz, or My Lai to connote atrocity, the cumulative stress of exhaustion and constant exposure to death did produce its psychiatric casualties during the first decade of the Revolution and, on occasion, led to behavior that can only be termed sadistic. The inhumanity visited upon civilians by soldiers became legendary in the folklore of the Revolution. One could pass off stories of mutilated prisoners hanged from trees or telephone posts as exaggerations had not scores of eager photographers captured hundreds of horrifying scenes for posterity. Bodies with hands or legs or genitals cut off were a grotesque caricature of a movement originally motivated by the highest ideals.

A cost so outrageous and so cataclysmic exacted burning resentment and tremendous fear in the civilian population. An ap-

Execution without benefit of trial was common during the violent decade of 1910–20. Bodies were left hanging for weeks as object lessons.

proaching unit invariably meant trouble for poor, rural Mexicans. The best that could be hoped for was a small band demanding a meal. But often the demands were more outrageous as the war could not lend itself to decency or compassion. In northern Mexico tens of thousands of rural Mexicans joined their middle class and wealthy counterparts in seeking the security of the United States. On a single day in October 1913 some eight thousand refugees crossed the border from Piedras Negras, Coahuila, to Eagle Pass, Texas. While the vast majority left the country with the idea of returning once the situation stabilized, most remained in the United States. But in central and southern Mexico there was virtually no place to run, and the civilian population had no choice but to keep their heads low and resign themselves to the worst. The documentary evidence from the period suggests forcefully that the excesses of war cannot be attributed simply to one side or another. Both federals and rebels were guilty. An excellent community study of a village in Morelos corroborates the contemporary sources. Informants who had lived through the revolutionary period declared that both sides posed an equal threat in this war without scruple.[1]

Fear in the rural areas was challenged only by frustration. Two months spent clearing a field and planting crops under a burning sun could be wiped out in five minutes as an army of five hundred horsemen galloped through the carefully tilled rows of corn and beans. Then they might stop at the one-room hut and confiscate the one milch cow and four turkeys that held out some promise for a slightly less redundant diet in the six months to follow.

There is precious little published evidence upon which to assess the impact of the early Revolution on life in rural Mexico. But the findings of Professor Luis González, in his perceptive and beautifully written account of the Michoacán village of San José de Gracia (population about 1,200 in 1910) are probably not atypical. By 1913, when violence engulfed the region for the first time,

> Don Gregorio Pulido had given up taking local products to Mexico City, for bands of revolutionaries made the roads unsafe for travel. The San José area began to return to the old practice of consuming its own products. Trade declined. Padre Juan's goal of increasing prosperity receded in the distance. From 1913 on, increased poverty was the rule. . . . Everything in San José shifted into re-

1. Lola Romanucci-Ross, *Conflict, Violence and Morality in a Mexican Village* (Palo Alto, Calif., 1973), pp. 15–16.

verse. The revolution did no favors for the town or the surrounding *rancherías*. . . . Parties of rebels often came to visit their friends in San José, either to rescue the girls from virginity, or to feast happily on the delicious local cheeses and meats, or to add the fine horses of the region to their own. . . . They summoned all the rich residents and told them how much money in gold coin each was to contribute to the cause. In view of the rifles, no one protested.[2]

The "armies" the peones of rural Mexico saw and feared did not look much like armies. Standard uniforms were unheard of among the rebels, and weapons consisted of whatever could be found or appropriated. Sometimes makeshift insignias identified rank but gave slight clue as to group affiliation. Anonymity served rebel commanders well as it left them unconcerned with the niceties of accountability, but it caused problems for the rural *pacífico* wanting to respond correctly to the question, "Are you a Huertista, a Villista or a Carrancista?"

For Mexican women the Revolution often had a degrading personal meaning. With husbands, fathers, and sons serving somewhere in the ranks, they were subjected to the terror and indignity of wanton assault. But many did not mope or simply stay home to become the target of rape. Freeing themselves from the eternal task of grinding corn, thousands joined the Revolution and served the rebel armies in the capacity of spies and arms smugglers. So active were the women in smuggling ammunition across the border in Ciudad Juárez that the United States Customs Bureau was forced to employ teams of female agents to search the undergarments of suspicious, heavy-looking ladies returning from shopping sprees in El Paso.

Perhaps the most noteworthy role assumed by women was that of *soldadera*. The soldaderas were more than camp followers. They provided feminine companionship, to be sure, but because neither the federal army nor the rebel armies provided commissary service, they foraged for food, cooked, washed, and, in the absence of more competent medical service, nursed the wounded and buried the dead. Both sides were dependent upon them, and in 1912 a federal battalion actually threatened mutiny when the secretary of war ordered that the women could not be taken along on a certain maneuver. The order was rescinded. Not infrequently, the soldaderas actually served in the ranks, sometimes with a baby slung in a *rebozo* or a young child clinging to their

2. Luis González, *San José de Gracia: Mexican Village in Transition* (Austin, 1974), pp. 124–25.

Among the disparate revolutionary contingents in Mexico, the Yaqui Indians of Sonora figured prominently in the campaigns of the northwest.

skirts. Women holding officer ranks were not uncommon in the rebel armies.

The soldadera endured the hardships of the campaign without special consideration. While the men were generally mounted, the women most often walked, carrying bedding, pots and pans, food, firearms, ammunition, and children. Often the men would gallop on ahead, engage the enemy in battle, and then rest. By the time the women caught up, they were ready to move again, and the soldadera would simply trudge on. Losing her special "Juan" in battle, she would wait an appropriately decent period and then take on another, to prepare his favorite meal and share his bed. Not a few gave birth in makeshift military camps, and some even on the field of battle.

The hard life of the soldadera was a relative thing. A fascinating oral history of a Yaqui woman from Sonora who was deported to Yucatán, cut her hands raw on the henequen plants, and saw her babies die from lack of adequate care, reveals that she was thrilled to become a soldadera. She later recalled that "her personal misery decreased by impressive leaps and bounds. . . . At no point during the next several years did she view her life as anything but a tremendous improvement after Yucatán."[3]

While, with the protection of anonymity, men could treat women as virtual slaves, public displays were more often marked by the type of chivalric indulgence so long identified with the Hispanic tradition. One traveler to Mexico City in 1918 was especially amused by the sign he found posted in the streetcar:

> GENTLEMEN: When you see a lady standing on her feet you will not find it possible to remain sitting with tranquility. Your education will forbid you to do so.
>
> GENERAL MANAGER OF THE RAILWAYS[4]

In an oblique and unintended sort of way the Revolution contributed to the emancipation of the Mexican woman. As the shortage of adult males in the cities contracted the labor supply, women began to make some inroads into the business world. At first their contributions consisted of the simplest type of work in the stores, but once escaped from the confines of the house they would not be persuaded easily to return. In Yucatán, at least, a concerted policy of women's liberation was initiated by Governor Salvador Alvarado. A farsighted revolutionary, Alvarado de-

---

3. Jane H. Kelly, "Preliminary Life History of Josefa (Chepa) Alvarez" (mimeographed, 1970), p. 16.
4. Quoted in P. Harvey Middleton, *Industrial Mexico: 1919 Facts and Figures* (New York, 1919), p. 6.

Armies had to be fed, and the task of grinding corn for the daily supply of tortillas continued as it had for centuries.

A familiar sight between 1910 and 1920, the soldaderas experienced both the excitement and privations of life on the military campaign.

clared: "I have always believed that if we do not elevate the role of women we will find it impossible to build a country."[5] Not only did he lower the age of majority of women from age thirty-one to twenty-one, but he actively began placing women in open positions in state government. In 1916 he sponsored a Congreso Femenino in Mérida, Yucatán. Four major themes were discussed: the social means to be employed to remove the yoke of tradition; the role of primary education in women's liberation; the arts and occupations the state should support to prepare the women for a fuller life; and the social functions women should employ to contribute toward a better society.

The Revolution, to be sure, had different meanings to different Mexicans during those years of greatest violence. But a most recurrent theme is the fear of the leva, the institution that snatched away the male population for service in the military. One corrido, popular in 1914, capsulized the problem in the doggerel of the masses.

> La leva, la odiosa leva
> que sembró desolación
> en todo el suelo querido
> de nuestra noble nación.
> Al obrero, al artesano
> al comerciante y al peón,
> los llevaban a las filas
> sin tenerles compasión.[6]

Edith O'Shaughnessy, the wife of the United States chargé in Mexico City, described the leva in her memoirs.

> I was startled as I watched the faces of some conscripts marching to the station today. On so many was impressed something desperate and despairing. They have a fear of . . . eternal separation from their loved ones. They often have to be tied in the transport wagons. There is no system about conscription here—the press gang takes any likely looking person. Fathers of families, only sons of widows, as well as the unattached, are enrolled, besides women to cook and grind in the powder mills.[7]

Among those who suffered most were foreign residents of Mexico. Because the Revolution was in part a reaction against Díaz's coddling of foreign interests, not a few revolutionaries took out

5. Salvador Alvarado, *Actuación revolucionaria del General Salvador Alvarado en Yucatán* (Mexico, 1965), p. 49.
6. Quoted in Merle E. Simmons, *The Mexican Corrido as a Source for Interpretive Study of Modern Mexico (1870–1950)* (Bloomington, 1957), p. 121.
7. Edith O'Shaughnessy, *A Diplomat's Wife in Mexico* (New York, 1916), p. 58.

THE VIOLENCE TAKES A TOLL

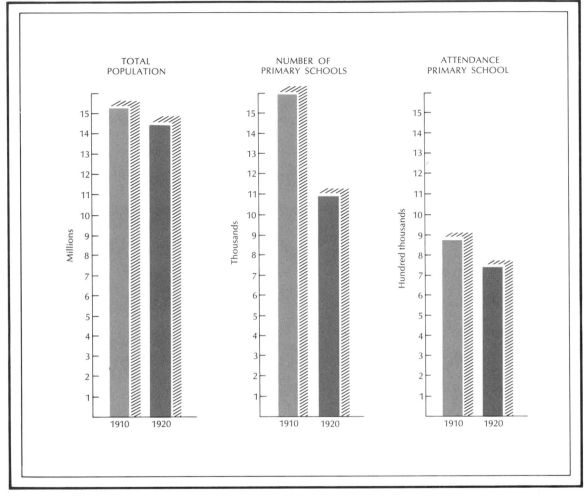

their wrath on the foreign community. Cast in the role of exploiters, foreign oilmen and miners were forced to pay not only taxes to the government but tribute to various groups of rebels and bribes to local bandits. But other frugal and industrious foreigners, without the slightest claim to exploitation, suffered worse. After a battle for control of Torreón in 1911 over two hundred peaceful Chinese residents were murdered simply because they were Chinese. A few years later Spanish citizens in Torreón were expelled from the country and their property confiscated by Pancho Villa. Colonies of United States Mormons in Chihuahua and Sonora were terrorized to such an extent that they finally packed up those belongings they could carry and left their adopted home.

City dwellers, too, were subject to the ravishments of war. Almost all of the larger cities in the country hosted battles at some time between 1910 and 1920, and some witnessed three or four major engagements and were turned into debris before the decade ran its course. The sight of burning buildings, the sound of wailing ambulances, and the nausea of mass burials brought home in tangible terms the most immediate meaning of the Revolution. Starvation reached major proportions in Mexico City, Guadalajara, and Puebla.

The construction boom of the Porfiriato ended shortly after the outbreak of hostilities. While a few unfinished public projects were completed, for the most part those workmen who could be spared from the ranks were kept busy clearing debris, repairing damaged structures, knocking down gutted buildings, and trying to put the railroad lines back in operation.

The early Revolution took a terrible toll in education. Hundreds of schools were destroyed and hundreds of others abandoned. In the Federal District alone the number of primary schools in operation declined from 332 in 1910 to 270 ten years later. The story repeated itself in city after city, town after town. Total primary school attendance in the country declined from 880,000 to 740,000 in the same ten-year period.

Intellectuals and Artists

The first decade of the Revolution, as violent as it was, nevertheless spawned a new generation of Mexican intellectuals and artists. During the last year of the Porfiriato a group of young thinkers had banded together to form the Ateneo de la Juventud. Among its charter members were a small group that would come to dominate early revolutionary thought: Antonio Caso, Alfonso Reyes, José Vasconcelos, and Martín Luis Guzmán. Meeting fortnightly, the members of the Ateneo began to formulate a philosophical assault on materialism in general and on positivism in particular. Impressed with Immanuel Kant and Arthur Schopenhauer, but most especially with Henri Bergson's masterpiece *L'Evolution créatrice* (1907), they lashed out against the científicos and launched a movement for ideological and educational reform based on a healthy respect for the humanities.

By 1912 the members of the Ateneo were ready to give some practical application to their antipositivist posture. Interested in moving into areas that Díaz had ignored, in December 1912 they founded a "people's university," the Universidad Popular Mexicana, and took their message to the factories and shops in Mexico's leading population centers. Mexico's future happiness, they preached, was not dependent upon commercial or industrial growth but rather upon social progress. The Universidad Popular Mexicana did not offer degrees; rather it tried to bring humanistic knowledge to those who would not otherwise receive it. Stressing lessons in citizenship and patriotism as well as practical instruction in hygiene and stenography, the *ateneístas* who constituted the faculty not only lectured but sponsored weekend tours to art galleries, museums, and historical and archeological sites. They all served without pay.

The winds of change shook the literary and artistic communities as well. A new age in the Mexican novel was born in 1915 when Mariano Azuela (1873–1952) wrote *Los de abajo* (translated as *The Underdogs*). A classic in twentieth-century Mexican literature, *Los de abajo* is a social novel and marked the beginning of a trend that would last for thirty years. Azuela was deeply concerned with the progress of the Revolution and through the character of Demetrio Macías probed its meaning. Historical novels were not new in Mexico, but Azuela added new ingredients. The story is related not in the sophisticated dialogue of the French school but in the colloquial language of the Mexican masses. Avoiding the intrusion of secondary plots, Azuela tells the story of real revolutionaries, not those who intellectualized the movement and coined its resounding phrases. Demetrio Macías is caught up in the struggle without really knowing why, yet when confronted with complex decisions is able to make proper choices with amazing spontaneity. Luis Cervantes, a middle-class federal deserter, joins Macías's guerrilla band and tries to articulate the revolutionary goals for him, but the uneducated Macías recognizes the shallowness and hypocrisy of Cervantes's explanations and the inherent opportunism in his actions.

The day-to-day dehumanizing realities of the Revolution are all there—pillage, looting, burning, destruction, theft, and general debauchery. Illustrative of the passion the Revolution evoked is Azuela's description of the battlefield after a struggle for control of Zacatecas: "The three-hundred-foot slope was literally covered with dead, their hair matted, their clothes clotted with grime and blood. A host of ragged women, vultures of prey, ranged over the tepid bodies of the dead, stripping one man bare, despoiling another, robbing from a third his dearest posses-sions."[8] The novel ends where it began—at the Canyon of Ju-chilpa. Demetrio Macías, by this time a general, is killed where he first ambushed a federal convoy. The circle has been com-pleted, and nothing has really changed. After all the suffering and killing, the Revolution seems to be back where it began. While social programs have been shunted aside and forgotten, the Revolution has become almost self-perpetuating—it just goes on and on. Shortly before he dies Demetrio's wife asks him why he must continue fighting. He answers by tossing a rock over a precipice and responding with a beautifully appropriate meta-phor: *Mira esa piedra cómo ya no se para* (Look at that rock—it just keeps rolling).

Mexican music, too, changed its tone as a new nativist move-ment was introduced by Manuel Ponce (1882–1948), a talented young pianist and composer from Zacatecas. Ponce decried that Mexican salons in 1910 should welcome only foreign music. He urged the acceptance of the native folk tradition and believed that the Revolution was already beginning to usher it in. In an essay he attacked the stodgy salons.

> Their doors remained resolutely closed to the *canción mexicana* until at last revolutionary cannon in the north announced the im-minent destruction of the old order. . . . Amid the smoke and blood of battle were born the stirring revolutionary songs soon to be carried throughout the length and breadth of the land. *Adelita, Valentina,* and *La Cucaracha,* were typical revolutionary songs soon popularized throughout the republic. Nationalism captured music at last. Old songs, almost forgotten, but truly reflecting the national spirit, were revived, and new melodies for new corridos were composed. Singers traveling about through the republic spread far and wide the new nationalistic song; everywhere the idea gained impetus that the republic should have its own musical art faithfully mirroring its own soul.[9]

Ponce was a major contributor to the movement he described. In 1912 and 1913 he composed his *canciones mexicanas*, includ-ing the famous *Estrellita*. And at approximately the same time

8. Mariano Azuela, *The Underdogs*, trans. E. Munguía (New York, 1963), pp. 80–81.

9. Quoted in Robert Stevenson, *Music in Mexico: A Historical Survey* (New York, 1971), pp. 233–34.

he was training the individual destined to become the most illustrious name in twentieth century Mexican music—Carlos Chávez.

Of all the intellectual and artistic groups in the country, Mexican painters showed themselves to be most restless. Having already embarrassed the Díaz regime at the centennial celebrations of 1910, these recalcitrant artists continued to scandalize staid society during the first decade of the Revolution. When neither interim President León de la Barra nor Francisco Madero was willing to remove the Porfirian director of the Art Academy of San Carlos, the artists took matters into their own hands. Not only did they go out on strike demanding the resignation of the director but on one occasion pelted the poor soul with rotten tomatoes. The desired change came with Victoriano Huerta, who named Alfredo Ramos Martínez, an impressionist, as director. Ramos Martínez reformed the curriculum, de-emphasizing the stifling classroom training in copying and formal portrait work that strived for photographic precision. Instead he encouraged the students to venture out into their Mexican world and paint what they saw and what they felt.

When the Constitutionalists came in, Ramos Martínez went out but his innovative ideas were not to be overturned. The new director, Dr. Atl (Gerardo Murillo), was even less conventional than his predecessor. Politically a loyal Carrancista but artistically a free spirit, Dr. Atl wanted to convert the academy into a popular workshop for the development of the arts and crafts. But when Pancho Villa marched his army into Mexico City following the Convention of Aguascalientes, the director and his loyal students, including José Clemente Orozco and David Alfaro Siqueiros, fled to Orizaba. The days of Mexican academic art were over.

The second decade of the twentieth century was still an experimental period for the Mexican artist. Diego Rivera spent most of his time in France and Spain, dabbling with some success in cubism. Siqueiros abandoned the brush for the gun and served in the Carrancista army for several years, storing up penetrating impressions of camp life, battles, and death, all of which he would later recreate. Orozco spent much of his time painting posters and sketching biting political cartoons and caricatures for Carrancista newspapers. In different ways these three giants of twentieth century Mexican art were preparing themselves for an artistic renaissance and the most important development in Latin American painting—the muralist movement of the 1920s and 1930s.

Social Change

Even during the chaos of violence certain unstructured social change was occurring in Mexico. Internal migrations took place, northerners and southerners came into more frequent contact with one another, and distinct regional language patterns began to yield to a more homogeneous national tongue. Increased travel, even that occasioned by the leva, provided a broader conception and a deeper appreciation of Mexico. Greater physical mobility brought about by the war tended to increase miscegenation and began to homogenize previously isolated zones. Thousands of Mexicans escaped obscurity and rose to positions of tremendous power in the various armies. Even though they did not always exercise their newfound influence with moderation, for them the Revolution was an agent of social change.

By 1920 a new kind of revolutionary nationalism had begun to emerge. The dead heroes had become martyrs to a young generation of Mexicans who did not always realize that their favorite protagonists had been killed fighting one another. The heroes loomed larger in death than in life, and their errors of judgment and human frailties could be overlooked. Madero became a symbol of democracy, Orozco of Mexican manhood, Carranza of law and justice, and Zapata of land for the humble. The newly developing revolutionary nationalism had its antiheroes as well: Porfirio Díaz, who had caused the holocaust; and Victoriano Huerta, the very incarnation of treachery and deceit.

In concrete terms, life for the great majority did not improve in the decade 1910 to 1920. In fact, because of the violence, it deteriorated in many ways. But the base of power in the republic had shifted into new hands, and the country was finally on the threshold of better times.

Recommended for Further Study

Azuela, Mariano. *The Underdogs.* Translated by E. Munguía. New York: New American Library, 1963.

Baldwin, Deborah J. *Protestants and the Mexican Revolution: Missionaries, Ministers and Social Change.* Champaign: University of Illinois Press, 1990.

Brushwood, John S. *Mexico in Its Novel: A Nation's Search for Identity.* Austin: University of Texas Press, 1966.

Charlot, Jean. *The Mexican Mural Renaissance, 1920–1925.* New Haven, Conn.: Yale University Press, 1967.

Flower, Elizabeth. "The Mexican Revolt against Positivism." *Journal of the History of Ideas* 10 (1949): 115–29.

Gonzáles, Luis. *San Jose de Gracia: Mexican Village in Transition.* Austin: University of Texas Press, 1974.

Guzmán, Martín Luis. *The Eagle and the Serpent.* Translated by Harriet de Onís. Gloucester: Peter Smith, 1969.

Innes, John S. "The Universidad Popular Mexicana." *The Americas* 30 (1973): 110–22.

Langford, Walter M. *The Mexican Novel Comes of Age.* Notre Dame: University of Notre Dame Press, 1971.

Macías, Anna. "Women and the Mexican Revolution, 1910–1920." *The Americas* 37 (1980): 53–82.

O'Shaughnessy, Edith. *A Diplomat's Wife in Mexico.* New York: Harper and Brothers, 1916.

Robe, Stanley L. *Azuela and the Mexican Underdogs.* Berkeley: University of California Press, 1979.

Romanell, Patrick. *Making of the Mexican Mind.* Lincoln: University of Nebraska Press, 1952.

Rutherford, John. *Mexican Society during the Revolution: A Literary Approach.* New York: Clarendon Press, 1971.

Salas, Elizabeth. *Soldaderas in the Mexican Military: Myth and History.* Austin: University of Texas Press, 1990.

Simmons, Merle E. *The Mexican Corrido as a Source for Interpretive Study of Modern Mexico (1870–1950).* Bloomington: Indiana University Press, 1957.

Sommers, Joseph. *After the Storm: Landmarks of the Modern Mexican Novel.* Albuquerque: University of New Mexico Press, 1968.

Stevenson, Robert. *Music in Mexico: A Historical Survey.* New York: Thomas Y. Crowell, 1971.

IX THE REVOLUTION: THE CONSTRUCTIVE PHASE, 1920-40

36

Alvaro Obregón Cautiously Implements the Constitution

Domestic Reforms

With the election of Alvaro Obregón to a four-year presidential term in 1920, Mexican politicians set to work on implementing the Constitution that had been drafted and promulgated at Querétaro in 1917. The war-torn country was closer to peace than it had been for a decade. Zapata had been killed, and, just a few weeks before Obregón assumed the high office, even the indomitable Pancho Villa had accepted a peace offering from the federal government. A good-sized hacienda, Canutillo, was given to him as an assurance that he would not again break the peace. The rigorous defender of the poor had grown tired, and he swallowed his pride to settle down in the comfortable role of an hacendado.

Obregón immediately turned his attention to the pressing problems of national reconstruction. A powerful and persuasive orator, he enjoyed a wide base of popular support. He was far from being a radical, but, unlike the nineteenth-century liberals, he was concerned with more than political reform. Unfortunately, the beginning of his administration coincided with the post–World War I economic slump. Prices of gold, silver, copper, zinc, henequen, and cattle were depressed. Unemployment was rampant in these industries, and the government's foreign exchange from these products fell off drastically. Hunger and general privation were more evident than they had been during the late Porfiriato. Only the price and demand for oil remained stable, and by 1921 Mexico was producing 193 million barrels, making it the world's third largest producer of petroleum. Oil

ARIZONA

NEW MEXICO

TEXAS

Mexicali

• Tucson

El Paso
Ciudad
Juárez

Nogales •
Agua Prieta •

• Cananea

SONORA

• Casas Grandes

CHIHUAHUA

Rio Grande

Piedras Negras
(Porfirio Díaz) •

COAHUILA

Nuevo Laredo

O Hermosillo

O Chihuahua

• Guaymas

C. Camargo •

Monclova •

Reynosa

Navojoa •

Jiménez •
Cuatrociénegas •

Saltillo

Monterrey

Los Mochis •
• Sinaloa

SINALOA

Gómez Palacio •
Torreón

O

NUEVO LEÓN

Ciudad
O Victoria

Culiacán O

DURANGO

O La Paz

Durango O

ZACATECAS

SAN LUIS
POTOSÍ

TAMAULIPAS

BAJA CALIFORNA NORTE

BAJA CALIFORNA SUR

Pacific Ocean

Mazatlán O

Fresnillo •
Zacatecas O

AGUASCALIENTES

O San Luis Potosí

Tam

NAYARIT

San Blas •
O Tepic

Guadalajara O
Atotonilco •

JALISCO

Colima •
Tuxpan •

Manzanillo •

MICHOACÁN

Chilpancingo O
GUERRERO
• Acapulco

Oax

México D.F. ✳

See inset map

INSET MAP

León •
O Dolores Hidalgo
San Miguel •

Guanajuato

QUERÉTARO

VERACRUZ

Papantla •

GUANAJUATO
O Querétaro
HIDALGO

Celaya •

O Morelia

Pachuca

Tlalnepantla •
Texcoco •
TLAXCALA
O Tlaxcala

MICHOACÁN

México D.F. ✳

O Puebla

Toluca O
Cuernavaca O
MEXICO
Yautepec •
Cuautla •
PUEBLA
Taxco •
MORELOS

INSET MAP

0   Miles   100

Miles

0   100   200   300

Gulf of Mexico

Progreso ●
○ Mérida
YUCATÁN
Cozumel ●

Campeche ○

QUINTANA ROO

Ciudad
Chetumal
○

CAMPECHE

os
co)
● Villahermosa ○
TABASCO

CHIAPAS
BELIZE

Gutiérrez ○   ● San Cristóbal
de las Casas

Tonalá ●

Tapachula ●
GUATEMALA
HONDURAS

✱ National capital
○ Capital cities

reserves, even with an inadequate taxation structure, sustained the administration and enabled the president to embark upon a modest implementation of the Constitution of 1917.

To implement Article 3 Obregón named José Vasconcelos, one of Mexico's most illustrious men of letters, to be secretary of education. Vasconcelos had been educated in Mexico City and received his law degree at the age of twenty-three. Late in the Porfiriato his antipositivist rebellion led him to join the Ateneo de la Juventud, and he shortly distinguished himself as one of the most brilliant minds in Mexico. An enthusiastic supporter of Francisco Madero, he became a Constitutionalist at the time of Huerta's coup and subsequently served in Eulalio Gutiérrez's Convention government. With the flight of Carranza from Mexico City in 1920, Vasconcelos briefly served as rector of the National University, but Obregón wanted him in the cabinet and he accepted the portfolio of education shortly after Obregón's inauguration.

If Nemesio García Naranjo, Huerta's secretary of education, had provided the initial impetus for the anticientífico revision of the curriculum, Vasconcelos was the patron of the rural school. With dramatically increased federal funds placed at his disposal, he sent dedicated teachers into hundreds of hamlets with a basic curriculum: reading, writing, arithmetic, geography, and Mexican history. Because the economic realities of rural Mexico dictated that children would attend only a few years of school, there simply was not much time for frills.

Vasconcelos had to inspire the teachers with a deep sense of national mission because life in rural Mexico, for many of them, was a type of cultural exile. Some of the villages were a two- or three-days' ride by horseback from the nearest railroad station, most lacked electricity, and few amenities of the comfortable life were to be found. In addition, the new teachers were not always welcomed with open arms. They often encountered deep hostility from villagers who did not want to change their traditional ways and from local priests who resented government encroachments into what they considered a church preserve. But the teachers did go into the hamlets and labored with dedication. Children attended during the day, while many adults consented to attend classes at night.

Vasconcelos's plan was designed not to segregate the Indian but through education to incorporate him into the mainstream of mestizo society. Vasconcelos would subsequently undergo a tremendous intellectual *volte-face*, but at this time he called for

FEDERAL EXPENDITURES FOR EDUCATION

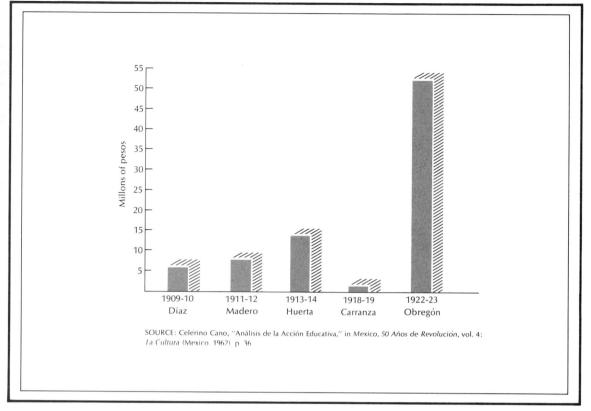

SOURCE: Celerino Cano, "Análisis de la Acción Educativa," in Mexico, *50 Años de Revolución*, vol. 4: *La Cultura* (Mexico 1962) p. 36

the incorporation of the Indians into a raza cósmica. In his memoirs he described the process as follows:

> I also set up auxiliary and provisional departments, to supervise teachers who would follow closely the methods of the Catholic missionaries of the Colony among Indians who still do not know Spanish. . . . Deliberately, I insisted that the Indian Department should have no other purpose than to prepare the native to enter the common school by giving him the fundamental tools in Spanish, since I proposed to go contrary to the North American Protestant practice of approaching the problem of teaching the native as something special and separate from the rest of the population.[1]

Over a thousand rural schools were built in Mexico between 1920 and 1924, more than had been constructed during the previous fifty years. To support the new endeavor, the secretary of education began a program of public libraries. Almost two thou-

1. José Vasconcelos, *A Mexican Ulysses: An Autobiography*, trans. William Rex Crawford (Bloomington, 1963), p. 152.

sand libraries had been established by 1924, most of them stocked with books designed to reinforce the humanist tradition of Mexico's new intelligentsia. Government presses printed millions of primary readers for both the schools and the libraries. A library set for a typical rural school consisted of about fifty books packed in special crates that could be transported on muleback.

Vasconcelos believed in the utility of informal education as well and employed some of Mexico's leading artists—Diego Rivera, José Clemente Orozco, and David Alfaro Siqueiros—to begin ornamenting the walls of public buildings with murals. The murals were designed for the people rather than for the art critics, but they received world acclaim as well. The themes were anthropological and historical for the most part and, with no shortage of polemicism, sought to instruct the literate and illiterate alike in the truths that the Revolution had come to hold dear.

Article 3 of the Constitution had stipulated, of course, that education should be secular and free, but President Obregón found this provision impossible to implement in full. The church was not removed entirely from the educational field because the state had neither the funds nor the teachers to educate all the children in Mexico. Both the president and the secretary of education opposed church education strongly, but, when confronted with an apparent impasse, they allowed that under guarded conditions it was preferable to no education at all. To assure that the church would not misconstrue the government's tolerant attitude toward Catholic education, however, Obregón encouraged the work of Protestant missionaries in Mexico. He openly endorsed the work of the YMCA (Asociación Cristiana de Jóvenes) and even supported its activities with state funds. The church naturally opposed this new development, but, with a few exceptions, open hostilities were avoided. Few realized in the early 1920s that church-state relations were undergoing a lull before a terrible storm.

Obregón's labor policy favored Luis Morones and the newly formed CROM. Because labor development had been so long stifled, Obregón leaned in the opposite direction, at least as far as the CROM was concerned. Nor did Luis Morones view the CROM as a government adversary. Realizing that Obregón had the power to crush the nascent labor movement if he wished, Morones worked to establish a balance between labor and capital rather than to attack the structure of the capitalist system. These modest goals were fully consonant with government policy, and, as a result, Morones and Obregón worked hand in hand and the

Alvaro Obregón (1880–1928). President of Mexico from 1920 to 1924, Obregón is shown here recovering from the amputation of his right arm following the battle of Santa Rosa (1915).

union offered the government stellar support. In turn, the administration financed the CROM's national labor conventions and provided free railroad passes for anyone who wished to attend. Blessed with government benevolence, membership in the union rose steadily from fifty thousand in 1920 to an estimated 1.2 million in 1924.

Other developing unions did not fare so well, however. Two radical labor groups, the Communist Federation of the Mexican Proletariat and the anarchist-led Industrial Workers of the World tried unsuccessfully to gain a foothold in the labor movement. In addition to the burdens of foreign leadership, which ran counter to the newly developing revolutionary nationalism, they both quickly incurred the strident opposition of the administration. Obregón expelled a number of foreign labor leaders from the country and declared strikes of the radical unions illegal. But it was not simply the radicalism of these unions that bothered the president; he was equally obdurate with the conservative Roman Catholic union movement.

Many Mexican labor leaders, however, had expected more because Obregón's followers had helped draft Article 123 and because the president had been sympathetic to labor's interests during his military career. But in his attempt to placate diverse interests in the country, labor often found itself shunted to one side. When asked to intervene in labor's behalf, the president time after time responded that the issue in dispute should be resolved at the state or local level. In states with progressive governors labor did not fare too badly, but in those with conservative administrations it languished. Obregón had decided that Article 123 of the Constitution would be implemented according to his understanding of Mexican reality, and he had decided that only the CROM represented legitimate workers' goals.

On the matter of agrarian reform Obregón again showed himself as a compromiser. He was aware that Mexican economy, for better or for worse, was still tied to the hacienda system and that a rapid redistribution of land would result in reduced agricultural productivity. The rural population would produce enough to feed itself but not enough to feed the nonagrarian sector of the society. On the other hand, Obregón had traveled in rural Mexico and had been touched by the abject poverty he had encountered there.

He decided not to declare all-out war on the hacendados of the republic. Rather, he moved with caution and deliberation, hoping that the modest redistribution he did sponsor would not be too disruptive. By the time his term expired in 1924 he had distributed some 3 million acres to 624 villages. The land went to the communal ejidos rather than outright to individuals, but the number of villagers directly benefiting was calculated at 140,000. The radical agrarianists, such as Antonio Díaz Soto y Gama, were understandably disappointed. They believed that the president's agrarian logic was specious. Luis Terrazas alone still owned as much land as the total distributed by the administration. Obregón had failed to strike while the agrarian iron was hot. It was true that he had multiplied by nine times the amount distributed by Carranza, but in 1924, seven years after the adoption of the Constitution, Article 27 had not yet benefited the overwhelming majority of rural Mexicans.

Why had Obregón not moved faster in the agrarian field? Without question he himself believed in the wisdom of a moderate course. In a speech made before the Congress he declared:

> We must act so carefully as to solve the problem without endangering our welfare and our economical interests. If we begin by destroying the big estates in order to create afterwards the small property, I sincerely believe we have made a blunder. . . . We must not destroy the big estates before creating the small one, as

an unbalanced state might follow leading us to dearth. I am of the opinion that we must act cautiously.[2]

Obregón was a cautious man but not simply as a matter of personal predilection. He felt it necessary to re-establish the political stability absent since the overthrow of Díaz. In addition, overshadowing many of his policy decisions was the specter of possible United States intervention to protect the interests of its citizens owning property in Mexico. The fears were not idle ones as United States troops had been in Mexico twice since the Revolution began, once in Veracruz and two years later in the north in the futile attempt to capture Pancho Villa.

Relations with the United States

Obregón's presidential term coincided with the Republican administration of Warren G. Harding in the United States. Supported by big business, Harding had won the presidency by a landslide and believed that his government's prime responsibility was the encouragement of private enterprise, both at home and abroad. Of all the corporate enterprises that dominated the Republican convention of 1920, none rivaled the oil interests of Harry F. Sinclair, Edward L. Doheny, and Jake Hammon. Within a couple of years the extent of petroleum influence in the administration would be exposed to the world in the scandal of Teapot Dome. But the petroleum interests were at work from the beginning.

For several years, through powerful lobby groups such as the National Association for the Protection of American Rights in Mexico and the Oil Producer's Association, under the chairmanship of Edward Doheny, American businessmen had been urging the United States government to become more active in the defense of their Mexican interests. Not encountering much success during the Wilson presidency, they found a much more receptive audience in President Harding and Secretary of State Charles Evans Hughes. Often working through Secretary of Interior Albert Bacon Fall (later arrested in the Teapot Dome scandal), they presented their case to the American president. Their Mexican oil properties, they contended, were about to be seized out from under them by Article 27, and, accordingly, the United States should not recognize the Obregón regime. Secretary Fall

2. Quoted in Eyler N. Simpson, *The Ejido: Mexico's Way Out* (Chapel Hill, 1937), pp. 87–88.

had long considered Americans living in Mexico as his special constituency and had won for himself, over the years, a reputation of being extremely well versed in Mexican affairs. When he wrote, "So long as I have anything to do with the Mexican question, no government of Mexico will be recognized, with my consent, which does not first enter into a written agreement promising to protect American citizens and their property rights in Mexico,"[3] President Harding was willing to be persuaded. From 1920 to 1923 Obregón was not recognized by the United States.

The United States oil interests, supported by the Harding administration and fully aware that any oil stoppage would cripple Obregón, argued that Article 27, if applied retroactively, would constitute an international wrong of the gravest proportions. Although Obregón needed the oil revenues, he could not buckle under to United States pressure; it would have been political suicide. The apparent impasse was averted by the Mexican Supreme Court. When, in September 1921, the Texas Company challenged the retroactive application of Article 27 in the Mexican courts, the Supreme Court handed down a decision propounding the doctrine of "positive acts." The oil lands could not be seized under Article 27 if the company in question had performed some "positive act" (such as erecting drilling equipment) to remove oil from the soil prior to May 1, 1917, the date on which the Constitution went into effect. If the company had not engaged in such a "positive act" prior to May 1, 1917, or if the concession had been granted after that date, Article 27 could be invoked at the pleasure of the state. This decision greatly relieved American oil interests, but, according to Mexican legal practice, five consecutive concurring decisions were necessary to establish a binding precedent. By the following year the four additional decisions had been rendered, and President Obregón then believed that he could enter into negotiations with the United States without being accused of treason.

In the spring of 1923 both countries named commissioners who agreed to meet on Bucareli Street in Mexico City during the summer. Under the terms of the agreements they reached, the Mexican government in essence agreed to uphold the doctrine of "positive acts" in its future relations with all the oil companies, and the Harding administration promised, in return, to extend diplomatic recognition. In addition, both countries agreed to establish a mixed claims commission to adjudicate the claims United

3. Quoted in John W. F. Dulles, *Yesterday in Mexico: A Chronicle of the Revolution, 1919–1936* (Austin, 1961), p. 159.

States citizens had brought against Mexico for damages suffered during the Revolution.

Political Tensions and Rebellion

At about the same time that the commissioners of the two countries were meeting on Bucareli Street in the capital, an extraordinary event occurred on Gabino Barreda Street in Parral, Chihuahua. The retired General Pancho Villa had just traveled from Canutillo to the little village of Río Florido to participate in the christening of an old comrade's baby son. After the ceremony Villa went on to Parral, where he decided to spend the night with a lady friend before returning to his famous hacienda. Early the following morning, surrounded by his bodyguards, he began the return trip to Canutillo. As his Dodge touring car turned onto Calle Gabino Barreda, eight men armed with repeating rifles burst out of a corner house and peppered the automobile. Within seconds Villa and several of his companions were dead.

Responsibility for the assassinations was not easy to fix; in fact, historians are not yet in complete agreement. Some contemporaries considered the murder to have been a personal affair in which a group of aggrieved citizens took vengeance for prior Villista depredations. But most believed that the murder was politically motivated, as Mexican politics had begun to heat up once again during the summer of 1923 and Villa had threatened to come out of retirement.

The assassination of Villa tended to exacerbate an already tense political atmosphere. The nationalists were unhappy with the Bucareli Agreements. Obregón, they contended, had truckled to the American oil men and their White House representatives. Their dissatisfaction was kept in check for a few months, however, until it merged with other disaffections in the Mexican community. The time was approaching when a decision had to be made concerning the presidential succession of 1924, and Obregón chose to support his fellow Sonoran and secretary of interior, Plutarco Elías Calles. This choice touched off political violence.

The revolution that began in Mexico in late 1923 combined the antagonisms of various interest groups. Many conservatives, including a number of wealthy hacendados and Catholic leaders, feared that Plutarco Calles was a genuine radical and sought to head him off before the upcoming elections. They were joined by military men, disgruntled at Obregón's reduction of the federal army for purposes of economy. Each carried important federal garrisons into the rebel ranks. But the rebellion was not simply an alliance of conservatives, as many ardent nationalists, unhappy with the Bucareli Agreements, pledged their support of the new movement, as did a number of labor leaders who had not been included within the ranks of the CROM. The opposition coalesced around still another leading figure from Sonora, Adolfo de la Huerta. De la Huerta was an experienced politician; he had served as interim president a few years earlier and had been Obregón's secretary of the treasury, a position he had managed—later charges notwithstanding—with rare aplomb.

In spite of the wide base of opposition, Obregón was not without his own sources of strength. Those unions under CROM control supported him unabashedly, as did a number of peasant organizations. Although some key army garrisons went over to the rebel side, many significant ones remained loyal to the government. But, most important, the recent diplomatic recognition by the United States provided Obregón's government not only with the moral support of Washington but also with an ample supply of war matériel. The war itself lasted only a few months, but it was a grueling episode for those who thought the days of violence had passed, and the toll of lives was tremendous. Some seven thousand Mexicans were killed before the rebels of de la Huerta admitted their defeat.

Obregón had been able to assert the dominance of the national government in the face of tremendous odds. Inheriting a country in financial peril and a citizenry with now-whetted aspirations, he emerged, if not unscathed by the political antagonisms of the day, at least with a good measure of dignity and respect, and his administration could take some pride in having put down a major antigovernment uprising. But, as the president neared the end of his term, some of the Mexican intelligentsia, indulging in self-criticism, realized that he had been slow to implement the reforms promised by the Constitution. They knew that through shrewd pragmatism he had co-opted the radical thrust of the Revolution, and, while occasionally yielding to the rhetoric of reform, he had not done much to alter the sustaining structure of society. On the other hand, many Mexican intellectuals, politicians, and journalists were willing to rationalize that in the early 1920s Mexican progress should be measured by Mexican standards. Since 1884 every Mexican president had been assassinated or driven from office by revolution. When Plutarco Calles won the presidential elections in 1924 and was inaugurated later that year, the ceremony marked the first time in forty years that the office was handed over peacefully from one chief executive to the next. Mexicans in their early sixties could perhaps remember that Manuel González had yielded peacefully to Díaz, but not a living soul could recall another instance. Political stability was returning to revolutionary Mexico, and with it Mexicans could not only afford the luxury of greater social experimentation but began to demand more from their leadership.

Recommended for Further Study

Beelen, George D. "The Harding Administration and Mexico: Diplomacy of Economic Persuasion." *The Americas* 41 (1984): 177–90.

Clark, Marjorie. *Organized Labor in Mexico*. Chapel Hill: University of North Carolina Press, 1934.

Dulles, John W. F. *Yesterday in Mexico: A Chronicle of the Revolution, 1919–1936*. Austin: University of Texas Press, 1961.

Gilderhus, Mark T. "Senator Albert Bacon Fall and 'The Plot against Mexico.'" *New Mexico Historical Review* 48 (1973): 299–311.

Haddox, John H. *Vasconcelos of Mexico*. Austin: University of Texas Press, 1967.

Hall, Linda B. "Alvaro Obregón and the Politics of Mexican Land Reform." *Hispanic American Historical Review* 60 (1980): 213–38.

Hansis, Randall. "The Political Strategy of Military Reform: Alvaro Obregón and Revolutionary Mexico, 1920–1924." *The Americas* 36 (1979): 197–232.

Lieuwen, Edwin. *Mexican Militarism: The Political Rise and Fall of the Revolutionary Army*. Albuquerque: University of New Mexico Press, 1968.

Ruiz, Ramón Eduardo. *Mexico: The Challenge of Poverty and Illiteracy*. San Marino, Cal.: Huntington Library, 1963.

Schoenhals, Louise. "Mexico's Experiments in Rural and Primary Education, 1921–1930." *Hispanic American Historical Review* 44 (1964): 22–43.

Scholes, Walter V. "Secretary of State Hughes' Mexican Policy." *Jahrbuch für Geschichte von Staat, Wirtschaft und Gesellschaft Lateinamerikas* 7 (1970): 299–308.

Tannenbaum, Frank. *Peace by Revolution: Mexico after 1910*. New York: Columbia University Press, 1966.

Vasconcelos, José. *A Mexican Ulysses: An Autobiography*. Translated by William Rex Crawford. Bloomington: Indiana University Press, 1963.

Wilkie, James W. *The Mexican Revolution: Federal Expenditure and Social Change since 1910*. Berkeley: University of California Press, 1967.

37

Mexico under Plutarco Calles, 1924-34

For a full decade beginning in 1924 Mexico found itself in the firm grip of General Plutarco Elías Calles. Though more popular among reformist groups in 1924 than Alvaro Obregón, ten years later his name was anathema to Mexican liberals. Born in Guaymas, Sonora, in 1877 to a poor family, Calles attended normal school in Hermosillo, did quite well in the classroom, and upon graduation, became a primary school teacher in the public school system. His political career began with the Revolution, and he served in a number of minor political and military capacities before becoming provisional governor of his home state in 1917. His loyal support of Obregón over a ten-year period won for him official endorsement for the presidency in 1924, and, with labor and agrarian support, he carried the election easily.

Calles's Domestic Program

Conservative elements in Mexico were far from elated by the election that year, for Calles enjoyed a liberal, even a radical, reputation. Landowners, both domestic and foreign, feared loss of property; industrialists anticipated higher wages for their workers; and church leaders recognized the new president as a confirmed anticleric. Each fear, it appeared, was grounded in understandable fact, and Calles soon let it be known that his domestic policy would not be characterized by the compromise and caution so typical of his predecessor. He was not only willing to ride the swelling tide of social revolution but sincerely believed, at least at the outset, that its course was inevitable. Better to be out in front, he conjectured, than to be dragged along.

Calles was the most strong-willed president since Díaz. He had an abiding faith in his own political instinct and, over his years in office, became increasingly domineering. Outspoken but often eloquent in public oratory, Calles was untormented by scruple when treating with his enemies. As the years passed he became less and less tolerant, more openly dictatorial, and relied heavily on the army to dispatch government foes. Deviation from presidential fiat was not tolerated during the Calles years. Political prisoners began filling the jails, and an alarming number "committed suicide." That the excesses were gross cannot be denied, but they were not, as enemies of the regime later charged, comparable to Jacobin or Stalinist purges following the French and Russian revolutions.

Calles inherited a more prosperous Mexico than had Obregón. The postwar economic slump was over and had given way to a sustained economic growth. Mexican raw materials were again in much demand from a recovered world economy. With a solid public treasury, Calles stepped up land distribution, just as the hacendados feared that he would do. Where Obregón had distributed some three million acres, Calles distributed eight million between 1924 and 1928. The vast majority of the land was granted to the communal ejidos rather than outright to individual heads of families. Because the uneducated peasant could not alienate his land through cheap sale, he was not subject to the machinations of the local land speculators. To try to stem a decline in agricultural productivity, the administration initiated a series of irrigation projects, established a number of new agricultural schools, and began to extend agricultural credit to the small farmer. While the radical agrarians had hoped that Calles would do still more, the pace of agrarian reform had accelerated demonstrably.

Calles's labor policy continued to favor Luis Morones and the CROM; in fact, Morones was brought into the cabinet as secretary of labor and quickly became the president's most intimate confidant. Other highly placed CROM officials served in the Congress, in the state legislatures, and even held state governorships. Hundreds of independent unions were brought into the CROM, and hundreds of new unions were organized. By 1928 CROM membership had reached 1.8 million, and the parent organization had affiliates in most of the states. The influence of the CROM became pervasive and its support of the government un-

A prosperous Luis Morones came to dominate the Mexican labor movement under
President Calles. At one time considered
a possible successor to Calles, charges of
corruption put an end to his political ambitions.

abashed. The confederation even prevented printers from type-
setting anti-Calles publications. The president returned the favors by supporting the CROM against employers and, more
important, against other unions. Wages rose gradually, though
never enough to constitute a serious burden to management. But
by 1928 many sincere labor leaders had begun to worry about
Morones. He was becoming a very wealthy man, and most believed that his diamond rings, new automobiles, and vast holdings in urban real estate had been acquired with union funds
and through various extortion schemes.

In the area of education Calles had inherited a new, well-
constructed foundation from Obregón and Vasconcelos. In 1924
there were approximately one thousand federally supported rural schools in operation. Calles and his able secretaries of education, José Manuel Puig Casauranc and Moisés Sáenz, continued
the emphasis of rural education. Before the presidential term
expired in 1928 they had added two thousand additional rural
schools. To facilitate the acculturation of the Indian, heavy emphasis was placed on the teaching of Spanish. Only if Spanish became the language of the village, they believed, could the Indian
be made a part of the national culture.

The government's health and sanitation program was built almost from scratch. When the Revolution broke out in 1910, sanitation conditions in Mexico were hardly better than they had
been during the colonial period. Calles was appalled and gave
his support to a newly organized Department of Public Health.

The department superintended the establishment of a new sanitary code designed to ensure cleaner markets and purer public milk supplies. For the first time in Mexican history major vaccination campaigns were undertaken. In 1926 alone over five million Mexicans were inoculated against smallpox. The government also began regular inspections of bakeries, butcher shops, dairies, cantinas, and barber shops. Those establishments that did not meet prescribed sanitary standards were closed down and their owners fined.

Relations with the United States

Relations with the United States still centered around oil. The Bucareli Agreements notwithstanding, United States Ambassador James Sheffield sought further assurances that foreign property interests would be protected. When Calles refused to go beyond the promises made on Bucareli Street, Sheffield started to bombard the U.S. State Department with Red scare dispatches. Gradually he convinced his superior, Secretary of State Frank B. Kellogg, that a Bolshevik plot was about to divest United States citizens of their just property rights. In the summer of 1925 Secretary Kellogg made a remarkable statement to the press. After reporting that an anti-Calles revolution was pending in Mexico, he continued:

> It should be made clear that this Government will continue to support the Government in Mexico only so long as it protects American lives and American rights and complies with its international obligations.
>
> The Government of Mexico is now on trial before the world. We have the greatest interest in the stability, prosperity, and independence of Mexico. . . . But we cannot countenance violation of her obligations and failure to protect American citizens.[1]

Calles expressed his strong displeasure with Kellogg's statement, for it appeared that the United States was once again nourishing aggressive designs. In a terse rejoinder the Mexican president declared that his government was well aware of its international obligations, but he rejected outright the inherent threat to Mexico's sovereignty in the secretary's pronouncement. He would never allow that any nation should create in Mexico a privileged position for its nationals.

1. Quoted in David Bryn-Jones, *Frank B. Kellogg: A Biography* (New York, 1937), p. 176.

In order to indicate that he would countenance no tampering with Mexico's sovereignty, Calles had his legislature enact a new petroleum law in December 1925. The legislation required all oil companies to apply to the government for a confirmation of their concessions. To determine whether or not to grant the confirmations, Mexico would apply the doctrine of "positive acts," as had been provided under the terms of the Bucareli Agreements, but the concessions would be granted only for a period of fifty years. As Calles began to enforce the new petroleum law, relations between Mexico City and Washington almost reached the breaking point.

In 1927 President Calvin Coolidge replaced Ambassador Sheffield in Mexico City with an old friend from Amherst College, Dwight Morrow, a partner in the famous financial firm of J. P. Morgan. Mexicans were, of course, convinced that the United States had sent yet another representative of Wall Street to press the case for the oil companies. But Morrow turned out to be a pleasant surprise. He did not make the Mexicans suspect that he was actually receiving his paychecks from Standard Oil. His first formal address in Mexico City presaged a more harmonious diplomatic atmosphere: "It is my earnest hope," he advised his Mexican audience, "that we shall not fail to adjust outstanding questions with that dignity and mutual respect which should mark the international relations of two sovereign and independent states."[2]

From the outset Morrow demonstrated a genuine interest in everything Mexican. He and his family lived in a Mexican-style house and shopped in the open marketplaces, marveling at native pottery and textiles. The ambassador visited the rural areas, taking special interest in new schools and irrigation projects and inquiring generally about the progress of the social revolution. He even began to study Spanish—not common for United States ambassadors in the 1920s—and invited Charles Lindbergh to Mexico on a goodwill tour. Morrow's relationship with Calles was unusually informal. The president and the ambassador began having breakfast together, and in this relaxed atmosphere, unencumbered by the bevy of official aides, they set to work on the sticky diplomatic problems besetting the two countries.

When the oil controversy first came up, Morrow did not warn that Mexico was on trial before the world; rather, in soft, diplomatic language he told Calles that he believed the issue should

2. Quoted in David C. Bailey, *Viva Cristo Rey: The Cristero Rebellion and the Church-State Conflict in Mexico* (Austin, 1974), p. 176.

be settled in the Mexican courts and expected no special consideration for United States citizens. Calles was impressed and quite possibly used his influence to see that the courts rendered a compromise decision. The Supreme Court ultimately held that the oil companies did have to apply for new concessions from the government, that the doctrine of "positive acts" would apply, but that the new permits would not expire at the end of fifty years. Both sides had given a little, but the genuine significance lay in the response of the U.S. Department of State. Remembering Calles's sensitivity to the question of sovereignty, an official release noted that the petroleum controversy had been resolved by the Mexican government and that any future controversies would also be resolved by the Mexican government without any interposition from the United States. For the first time Washington had formally recognized Mexico's full legal sovereignty, even when the interests of United States citizens were involved.

The Cristero Rebellion and the Assassination of Obregón

Calles's most serious problem turned out to be not with the United States but rather with the Roman Catholic Church. Whereas Obregón had turned his back on the anticlerical articles of the Constitution, Calles decided to enforce them. Although tensions had been building up gradually throughout the early 1920s, the event that triggered new hostilities was an interview José Mora y del Río, the archbishop of Mexico, gave to the press in February 1926. Reacting to the implementation of anticlerical provisions in a number of states, the archbishop argued that Roman Catholics could not in conscience accept the Constitution. Their opposition to it was stronger than ever, and their position was unshakable. The recalcitrant declaration served no purpose. Calles used the excuse to strike with both fists. He first disbanded religious processions, then began deporting foreign priests and nuns and closing church schools, monasteries, and convents. He also decreed that all Mexican priests had to register with civil authorities. The response of the church was both unique and unexpected. On July 31, 1926, the archbishop declared a strike, and on the following day, for the first time since the arrival of the Spaniards four centuries earlier, no masses were celebrated in Mexico.

The strike lasted for three full years; babies went unbaptized and the old died without receiving the last rites. It was not a peaceful strike. As Calles became more intemperate, gross, and even obscene in his denunciations of the clergy and the pope, Catholic leaders in Michoacán, Puebla, Oaxaca, Zacatecas, Nayarit, but especially in the backcountry of Jalisco, began organizing the masses to resist the godless government in Mexico City. To the cry of ¡Viva Cristo Rey! Anacleto González Flores, René Capistrán Garza, and Enrique Gorostieta led bands of Cristeros against government outposts. There were sordid excesses on both sides. The Catholic guerrillas burned down the new government schools, murdered teachers, and covered their bodies with crude banners marked VCR. In April 1927 the Cristeros dynamited a Mexico City–Guadalajara train, killing over a hundred innocent civilians. Not to be outdone, the government troops tried to kill a priest for every dead teacher, encouraged children to throw rocks through stained glass windows, looted churches, and took great pleasure in converting them into stables. Cristeros, or suspected Cristeros, were shot perversely without benefit of trial, some swearing to the last moment that an enemy had painted ¡Viva Cristo Rey! on their houses. The Cristeros could not withstand the military superiority of the federal army and gradually were worn down. But when Calles's presidential term expired in 1928, the rebellion was not yet completely suffocated.

The presidential election of 1928 and its immediate aftermath were shocking. The Constitution of 1917 had recently been amended to provide for a six-year presidential term and, with Alvaro Obregón specifically in mind, the possibility of re-election if it were not immediate. As the electoral process began to unfold, Calles threw his support behind the former president, no doubt thinking that Obregón would return the favor in 1934. Two opposition candidates also entered the fray: General Francisco Serrano, a former secretary of war, and General Arnulfo Gómez, a capable military man who had performed yeoman service in quelling the de la Huerta rebellion of 1923. Serrano and Gómez did not expend much energy attacking one another, they both concentrated their efforts on Obregón and attacked the principle of re-electionism. When Serrano and Gómez convinced themselves that the election of 1928 was not going to be fair, they rebelled against the government and the contemplated succession of Obregón. But within two months both of the opposition candidates had been captured and executed.

Obregón's victory brought no relief, however, for he never assumed office. On the afternoon of July 17, 1928, he attended a garden banquet in Mexico City's plush district of San Angel.

Many dignitaries whom he wanted to join the new administration were in attendance. While the guests were dining, a twenty-six-year-old artist, José de León Toral, sketched caricatures of those sitting at the head table. After showing some of his better drawings to several guests, he moved toward the head table to show the president his work. As soon as Obregón nodded his approval, Toral took a pistol from his pocket and fired five shots into the president-elect's head.

Some of the irate guests beat young Toral almost beyond recognition. That he was not killed on the spot by the hysterical mob reflected the good sense of several officials who immediately realized that the full circumstances behind the assassination had to be determined. At the police station following the assassination, Toral refused to answer any questions. Torture did not suffice to loosen his tongue, and only the threat of torture to his family elicited the desired information. In subsequent weeks, as the story began to unfold, it became increasingly apparent that this senseless act of violence was also an offshoot of Mexico's never-ending conflict between church and state.

Toral was a deeply religious man who lost touch with reality and became a mystic when the Cristero Rebellion broke out. A few months prior to the assassination he had been introduced to a nun, Sister Concepción Acevedo de la Llata, remembered in Mexican history simply as Madre Conchita. When the church declared its strike she offered spiritual consolation to the faithful in her own home, and it was in this capacity that her path crossed that of Toral. The young zealots who met regularly at Madre Conchita's house became increasingly militant as the rebellion grew more outrageous. They began manufacturing bombs and even discussed plans for killing Obregón. Finally Toral was chosen, or assumed responsibility, for implementing a mission they all considered to be divinely inspired. But just to make sure everything went as planned Toral began target practice in early July with a pistol borrowed from one of Madre Conchita's friends. Shortly after his confession, Madre Conchita and a number of others were arrested as well.

The trial, conducted in November, was a great public spectacle and undoubtedly the most sensational judicial inquiry since the trial of Maximilian. In a gesture of unparalleled magnanimity Obregón's widow asked the court to show Toral mercy, but the state was in no mood to turn the other cheek. The prosecuting attorney and the attorney general who testified in behalf of the state were warmly applauded by the gallery. On the other hand, the defense attorney, Demetrio Sodi, was heckled, disparaged, and shouted down with cries of "Death to the Assassin!" and "Death to the Prostitute Concha!" Jurors, fearful for their lives, came to the courtroom armed with pistols. Taunts of mockery and threats of lynching interrupted the proceedings, as did promises of reprisals to the jurors should they vote to acquit. The crowd became so agitated during the summation of Attorney Sodi that he was unable to conclude his defense. The court would not be used as a platform for Catholic views. The jury did not remain long in consultation. Toral's act, after all, had been witnessed by many; he implicated Madre Conchita during his testimony, and her denials were unconvincing. Toral received the death sentence, and Madre Conchita, because Mexican law forbade the execution of women, was given a prison sentence of twenty years.

The Maximato and the Shift to the Right

Obregón's assassination created a political vacuum, and only Calles commanded sufficient respect to fill it. He decided not to assume the presidential office himself but would control the nation's destiny as the power behind the scenes. The Congress, charged with choosing an interim president until new elections could be held, selected Calles's man, Emilio Portes Gil, a lawyer and former governor of Tamaulipas. Portes Gil proved to be the first of three puppets to fill out Obregón's term, but Calles, as "the Supreme Chief" (*Jefe Máximo*), clearly called the shots. By the time the election of 1929 occurred, Calles had organized a new, widely based political party, the Partido Nacional Revolucionario (PNR). Mexican presidents never again would be elected by temporary coalitions that would splinter soon after tasting the fruits of victory. The official party would change its name on several occasions, but its control over the Mexican political process would remain permanently intact.

When the special election occurred, Calles and his newly organized PNR ran Pascual Ortiz Rubio for the presidency. The opposition candidate, running under the rubric of the National Anti-Re-electionist party, was the more experienced and much better known José Vasconcelos. Vasconcelos directed his campaign against the Jefe Máximo rather than against Ortiz Rubio and argued that a vote for Ortiz Rubio was a vote for Calles. But the strategy was useless. When the government announced the results, Ortiz Rubio was declared the winner by the unbelievable margin of 1,948,848 to 110,979. He served only two years. Shortly after he attempted to oppose Calles on several policy decisions, he picked up a morning newspaper to read that he had resigned. On this occasion the Jefe Máximo picked General Abelardo Rodríguez, a man with less administrative talent than relish for power, as puppet number three of the *Maximato*.

In spite of the musical chairs played in the presidential office, the years 1928 to 1934 were not barren of accomplishment. An important step forward was made in professionalizing and de-politicizing the Mexican army. Calles had actually initiated the process during his own term in office, but the job was completed under the puppets. By giving the military a major voice within the PNR there was less reason for revolt in support of some disgruntled politician. While the army was by no means taken out of politics, it was co-opted by being brought into the political process. Military expenditures were curtailed during the six-year Maximato, but, since military men themselves participated in the decisions, they accepted the budgetary belt-tightening with admirable restraint.

Equally important to the political well-being of the nation was the resolution of the Cristero Rebellion. Ambassador Morrow played a major but unofficial role in the reconciliation as he arranged a series of meetings between Calles, Portes Gil and Father John Burke, a prominent Catholic leader in the United States. In early June 1929 Father Burke convinced the Mexican leaders that they should allow several exiled bishops to return to the country so that they, too, could participate in the negotiations. By late June a compromise had been hammered out. The church agreed that priests would have to register with the government and that religious instruction would not be offered in the schools. The government declared publicly that it had no intention of destroying the integrity of the church and even allowed that religious instruction would not be prohibited within the confines of the churches themselves. As a result, the hierarchy ordered the Cristeros to lay down their arms and the priests to resume religious services. Mexico's long-standing church-state controversy was not yet completely over, but it would never again reach the grotesque proportions of the Cristero Rebellion.

The Calles puppetship witnessed a dramatic shift of the Revolution to the right. The social reform programs that were conceived in the early Revolution, formalized in the Constitution of 1917, and gradually implemented during the years 1920 to 1928, were all but abandoned shortly after the assassination of Obregón. Land redistribution after 1928 slowed to a snail's pace. The state of Chihuahua affords a good example. The Terrazas family had been forced to sell most of its huge land holdings during the Obregón presidency but now was allowed to buy them back. Although the Terrazases paid a somewhat higher price than they had received earlier, they bought back only the best lands that they previously owned. The rural education program suffered, and the labor movement was abandoned as the government withdrew its support of the CROM. Luis Morones surely had profited at the public trough. While he might have been beneath contempt and above the law, his personal peculation scarcely justified the all-out attack on the labor movement itself. Other highly placed officials also dipped into the treasury with impunity. With handsome sinecures many bought luxurious homes in Cuernavaca on what the contemporary pundits labeled "the Street of the Forty Thieves." The honest revolutionaries were aghast at this new clique of "millionaire socialists," and the raconteurs celebrated their corruption with hundreds of sardonic anecdotes.

As the Revolution shifted to the right, the regime and its supporters grew more and more sensitive to any form of radicalism. Virtual war was declared on the small, inconsequential Mexican Communist party. The leaders were unceremoniously deported to the penal colony on Islas Tres Marías. The anti-Communist hysteria reached its apex in 1930 and 1931, years that witnessed the appearance of the Gold Shirts, a fascist-inspired organization of thugs whose self-appointed task was to terrorize all Communists and Jews.

The Revolution: An Assessment in the 1930s

Something drastic had happened to the Revolution and its leadership. Honest, idealistic men, dedicated to principles of social reform, had been not only diverted from tasks of high priority but corrupted as well. The phenomenon has never been adequately studied, but a provocative sociological hypothesis was posited by Professor Frank Tannenbaum.

> This period [1928-34] . . . is most perplexing. If it were possible to discover what had taken hold of the leadership of Mexico in those debased and clouded years, it would illumine much of Mexican history. Here was a group of new men, most of whom

had come from the ranks of the Revolution and had risked their lives in a hundred battles for the redemption of the people from poverty and serfdom. . . . and yet, at the first opportunity, each fell an easy victim to pelf and power. . . .

Their difficulty lay in the fact that they had come to power suddenly and without preparation, either morally, psychologically, politically, or even administratively. They were taken from their villages as barefooted youngsters who had slept on the floor and could barely read, and after a few years spent on the battlefields found themselves tossed into high office and great responsibility. This new world was filled with a thousand temptations they had not dreamed of. . . . Here, at no price at all, just for a nod, all their hearts desired was offered them in return for a favor, a signature, a gesture, a word.[3]

There is much to be said for Professor Tannenbaum's understanding of those perplexing years. While the hypothesis must remain tentative, it does have the ring of reality. At the same time, however, something more tangible was also involved—the Great Depression of 1929–32.

Mexico weathered the depression better than most Latin American countries, as the treasury had about 30 million pesos ($15 million) in cash reserves in 1930. But no country in the world emerged from the great crash unscathed. Important Mexican exports, especially oil and metals, reflected the structural weaknesses of the world market, and, as a result, national income from taxes declined and the value of the peso began to fall. While in 1930 two pesos bought a dollar, by 1932 the cost of the dollar was 3.50 pesos. The entire treasury surplus, and more, was used up in 1931, as government revenues fell 80 million pesos short of expenditures. As a result of the unhealthy economic atmosphere, capital began to flee the country in search of more secure investment fields elsewhere. Many industries were paralyzed because of monetary deflation and tight credit. Emergency tax measures helped the government a little, but programs had to be cut back in many areas. Government workers were fired, wage reductions averaged over 10 percent, and departments were ordered to reduce their expenditures. Given this dreary set of circumstances, the social revolution simply could not progress.

In a more general sense the depression discredited the set of revolutionary principles that had become sacrosanct to many. Poverty cut deeply, and government leaders decided to experi-

3. Frank Tannenbaum, *Mexico: The Struggle for Peace and Bread* (New York, 1956), pp. 69–70.

ment with new, shortsighted approaches. But the leadership had misread the economic indicators and gave up too easily to a slothful defeatism. The depression had not singled out Mexico; it was not partial to one or another ideology or economic system. The principles upon which the Revolution had been founded were still sound, and in 1934 a new, dynamic leader would give them the opportunity to run their course.

The Mexican revolutionary generation had not yet demonstrated any real political genius. In the Calles decade the question of presidential succession had continued to provoke violence, a president-elect had been assassinated, and the presidential chair had had three occupants in a single term. But by 1934 the worst was over. While day-to-day political conduct would not always be exemplary, Mexico had witnessed its last successful revolt. Mexican presidents would never again leave office without finishing their terms. There would be no more interim or provisional presidents. Presidents would never again try to succeed themselves in office and presidential succession would no longer occasion armed insurrection. In 1934 the political process would stabilize itself, and the social revolution would find a new protagonist.

Recommended for Further Study

Bailey, David C. *Viva Cristo Rey: The Cristero Rebellion and the Church–State Conflict in Mexico.* Austin: University of Texas Press, 1974.

Berbusse, Edward J. "The Unofficial Intervention of the United States in Mexico's Religious Crisis, 1926–1930." *The Americas* 23 (1966): 28–62.

Bernstein, Marvin D. *The Mexican Mining Industry, 1890–1950: A Study of the Interaction of Politics, Economics, and Technology.* Albany: State University of New York Press, 1964.

Carr, Barry. "The Mexican Communist Party and Agrarian Mobilization in the Laguna, 1920–1945: A Worker–Peasant Alliance?" *Hispanic American Historical Review* 67 (1987): 371–404.

Clark, Marjorie. *Organized Labor in Mexico.* Chapel Hill: University of North Carolina Press, 1934.

Dulles, John W. F. *Yesterday in Mexico: A Chronicle of the Revolution, 1919–1936.* Austin: University of Texas Press, 1961.

Levenstein, Harvey A. "The AFL and Mexican Immigration in the 1920's: An Experiment in Labor Diplomacy." *Hispanic American Historical Review* 48 (1969): 206–19.

Lieuwen, Edwin. *Mexican Militarism: The Political Rise and Fall of the Revolutionary Army.* Albuquerque: University of New Mexico Press, 1968.

Mabry, Donald J. "Mexican Anticlerics, Bishops, *Cristeros* and the Devout during the 1920s: A Scholarly Debate." *Journal of Church and State* 20 (1978): 81–92.

Miller, Barbara. "The Role of Women in the Mexican Cristero Rebellion: *Las Señoras y las Religiosas.*" *The Americas* 40 (1984): 303–24.

Quirk, Robert E. *The Mexican Revolution and the Catholic Church, 1910–1929.* Bloomington: Indiana University Press, 1973.

Ross, Stanley R. "Dwight Morrow and the Mexican Revolution." *Hispanic American Historical Review* 38 (1958): 506–28.

———. "Dwight W. Morrow, Ambassador to Mexico." *The Americas* 14 (1958): 373–89.

Ruiz, Ramón Eduardo. *Mexico: The Challenge of Poverty and Illiteracy.* San Marino, Calif.: Huntington Library, 1963.

Simpson, Eyler N. *The Ejido: Mexico's Way Out.* Chapel Hill: University of North Carolina Press, 1937.

Slawson, Douglas J. "The National Catholic Welfare Conference and the Church–State Conflict in Mexico." *The Americas* 47 (1990): 55–94.

Tannenbaum, Frank. *Mexico: The Struggle for Peace and Bread.* New York: Knopf, 1956.

Tuck, Jim. *The Holy War in Los Altos: A Regional Analysis of Mexico's Cristero Rebellion.* Tucson: University of Arizona Press, 1982.

Wasserman, Mark. "Strategies for Survival of the Porfirian Elite in Revolutionary Mexico: Chihuahua During the 1920s." *Hispanic American Historical Review* 67 (1987): 87–107.

Wilkie, James W. "The Meaning of the Cristero Religious War against the Mexican Revolution." *Journal of Church and State* 8 (1966): 214–33.

38

Cárdenas Carries the Revolution to the Left

Cárdenas

The many Mexicans impatient with the progress of the Revolution in 1934 were delighted with the election of Lázaro Cárdenas to the presidency in that year. His revolutionary career was typical of many who worked their way rapidly through the military ranks, ultimately reaching the grade of brigadier general by the end of the first violent decade. But Cárdenas was a civilian at heart. Not an imposing figure physically, he was attractive as a pensive, methodical man of principle and deep conviction. An avid reader, he was intensely interested in social reform and had that special charismatic quality of evoking passionate enthusiasm among many and strong dislike among some. And he was no run-of-the-mill politician. Supporting first Obregón and then Calles, he became, in the 1920s, a dominant force in his home state of Michoacán.

Cárdenas's governorship in Michoacán from 1928 to 1932 offered Mexicans a preview of what they might expect. The governor allowed himself to be confronted by the people and listened more than he spoke. He actually made important policy decisions, not on the advice of his confidants, but on the direct information received from the public. During years when the national government was shirking its educational responsibilities, Cárdenas opened a hundred new rural schools in Michoacán, inspected many classrooms personally, and made sure that the teachers received their salaries on time. He also encouraged the growth of labor and peasant organizations and even managed a modest redistribution of land at the state level. Throughout it all he continued to live modestly.

As the presidential elections of 1934 approached, Calles decided to throw his support behind Cárdenas, fully believing that the forty-year-old governor would be puppet number four. With the official endorsement of the Jefe Máximo, Cárdenas carried the 1933 PNR convention easily and was elected to the presidency in July of the following year. Immediately he broke with tradition as he cut his own salary in half and refused to move into the presidential mansion in Chapultepec. Instead, he kept his own modest home. Cárdenas had observed the six-year Maximato with some discomfort and once in office determined that he was going to free himself of Calles's domination, revitalize the Revolution, and carry it back to the left. Aware that Calles's control over Portes Gil, Ortiz Rubio, and Rodríguez had rested heavily on army support, the new chief executive assiduously began to cultivate promising junior officers. Not only did he raise salaries and benefits, but he also supported an improved system of education within the army and, in addition, sponsored a far-reaching internal reform of the entire military structure. Confident of the army by 1935, Cárdenas began to remove Calles supporters from the cabinet and other high governmental posts and even relieved Callista generals from their commands. When Calles discovered that he could not manipulate this president as he had the previous three, he began to speak out vociferously against the administration. By the spring of 1936 Cárdenas had had enough. He ordered that Calles and a few of his close supporters be arrested. They were placed aboard a special plane bound for the United States and informed that they should not return to Mexico.

Only once during his term was Cárdenas threatened with a serious internal revolt. Saturnino Cedillo, the conservative political boss of San Luis Potosí, withdrew recognition of the government and declared himself in open rebellion. Although Cedillo had the strong backing and financial support of conservative interests, both domestic and foreign, Cárdenas's army remained loyal and quelled the rebellion within a matter of weeks. The president would not be faced with similar problems again.

Once installed in the presidency Cárdenas did his utmost to keep close contact with the public. While cabinet secretaries and foreign dignitaries fidgeted fretfully in the presidential waiting room, Cárdenas would receive delegates of workers or peasants and patiently listen to their problems. A contemporary observer recounted that one morning the president's secretary laid before him a list of urgent matters and a telegram.

> The list said: Bank reserves dangerously low. "Tell the Treasurer," said Cárdenas. Agricultural production falling. "Tell the Minister of Agriculture." Railroads bankrupt. "Tell the Minister of Communications." Serious message from Washington. "Tell Foreign Affairs." Then he opened the telegram which read: My corn dried, my burro died, my sow was stolen, my baby is sick. Signed, Pedro Juan, village of Huitzlipituzco. "Order the presidential train at once," said Cárdenas. "I am leaving for Huitzlipituzco."[1]

The story is undoubtedly apocryphal; yet that it circulated in a sophisticated capital indicates the reputation the president enjoyed. More deeply committed to social reform than any previous Mexican head of state, Cárdenas came to the presidency at a time when a new, young generation of revolutionaries was beginning to displace the old veterans of the days of violence. Some of the familiar figures continued to serve in the national and state governments, but many names were heard for the first time. The younger generation had kept faith with the revolutionary principles enunciated in the years following the overthrow of the Díaz dictatorship but believed that it was finally time for a statist revolution to give them full rein.

Domestic Reforms

Agrarian reform more than anything else dominated the administration's concern during the first few years. Since the initiation of the land redistribution program some 26 million acres of land had been parceled out, but the figure appeared more impressive on paper than in Mexico's rural zones. Millions of Mexican peasants still owned no land at all and felt cheated by two decades of revolutionary rhetoric. Cárdenas early made up his mind to fulfill twenty years of promises. Unprepared to tarry leisurely, by the time his term expired he had distributed 49 million acres, about twice as much as all his predecessors combined. By 1940 approximately one-third of the Mexican population had received land under the agrarian reform program. In fact, most of Mexico's arable land had been redistributed. Only the large cattle haciendas on arid or semiarid land remained untouched.

1. Quoted in Anita Brenner, *The Wind That Swept Mexico: The History of the Mexican Revolution, 1910–1942* (Austin, 1971), p. 91.

PERCENTAGE OF LAND DISTRIBUTION BY ADMINISTRATION, 1915–40

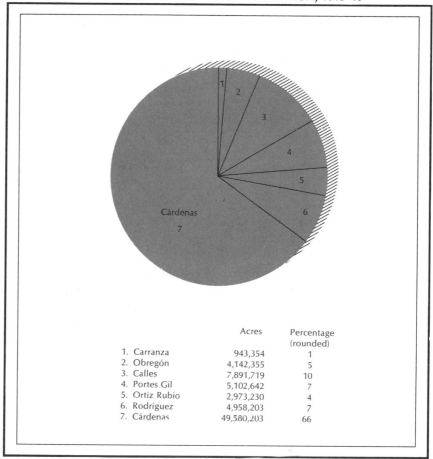

		Acres	Percentage (rounded)
1.	Carranza	943,354	1
2.	Obregón	4,142,355	5
3.	Calles	7,891,719	10
4.	Portes Gil	5,102,642	7
5.	Ortiz Rubio	2,973,230	4
6.	Rodríguez	4,958,203	7
7.	Cárdenas	49,580,203	66

The vast majority of the land distributed did not go to individuals or even heads of households but rather to the communal ejidos. The land was held in common by the communities, sometimes to be reapportioned to individuals for their use and sometimes to be worked by the community as a whole. The largest and most important of the ejidos dating from the Cárdenas redistribution was the huge Laguna cotton ejido, some eight million acres on the Coahuila-Durango border. The thirty thousand families that worked the Laguna ejido cooperatively engaged primarily in the cultivation of long-staple cotton but also grew large amounts of wheat, alfalfa, and maize for commercial sale. Most of the families also held small individual plots on which they grew their own subsistence crops. But the Laguna experiment consisted of much more than the mere redistribution of land. Government-supported schools were established, social services in the area were extended, and a modern ejido hospital was built in Torreón, in the center of the Laguna operation. Although the Laguna ejido was the biggest single cooperative land venture initiated by Cárdenas, other large ejidos were established as well. These ventures required large-scale financing, and for this reason the administration founded the Banco de Crédito Ejidal. During the Cárdenas years this agrarian bank made loans available to some thirty-five hundred ejidos.

The ejido was no economic or social panacea, however. A rapid population growth in rural Mexico tended to offset many of the gains, and the Banco de Crédito Ejidal did not possess sufficient capital to meet the continually growing demands. In addition, much favoritism and some corruption circumscribed the distribution of ejido loans. But more important yet, production of many ejidos, even the Laguna ejido, which received adequate loans from the agrarian bank, declined. Cotton production fell by almost nine thousand tons from 1936 to 1938, and henequen production on the new Yucatecan ejidos dropped by forty-five thousand tons during the same period.

Was the ejido program then a failure? The economists answered yes, but the administration was well aware that the redistribution of land would cause an initial decline in productivity. Cárdenas embarked upon the ejido program to meet a social, not an economic, need. The critics were harsh in their denunciation of cooperative agriculture, but what they could not deny was the unalterable fact that Cárdenas's dedication to agrarian reform spelled the demise of the traditional hacienda complex in Mexico. Millions of peasants were given a new faith in the revolutionary concept. While some argued with understandable conviction that the amount of land apportioned to each family under the ejido program was insufficient, and others suggested more theatrically that one form of peonage had simply replaced another, the fact remains that the type of servitude that had bound hacendado and peón for centuries was broken by 1940. Life in rural Mexico scarcely became idyllic as a result. Per capita income, infant mortality, and indeed life expectancy lagged behind that of the cities, but the gap in the quality of life between rural and urban Mexico began to be closed for the first time. If the ejido system was an economic failure, it was a political and social success.

Distributing more land than all of his predecessors combined, Cárdenas here assigns a land title to a group of peasants.

The relationship between the administration and the church was conditioned almost entirely by Cárdenas's determination to implement Article 3 of the Constitution. There was no doubt that the president was an anticleric; during his campaign he had attacked the church frequently. In the state of Tabasco he had declared, "Man should not put his hope in the supernatural. Every moment spent on one's knees is a moment stolen from humanity."[2] When the PNR met in 1933 to nominate Cárdenas for the presidency, it adopted a platform that, among other things, called for the teaching of socialist doctrine in the primary and secondary schools. A new curriculum had previously been developed by the secretary of education, Narciso Bassols. The church was already incensed, but, when the hierarchy learned that sexual education would be offered in the public schools, parents were threatened with excommunication should they send their children to the anti-Catholic schools. Secretary Bassols resigned his position during the controversy, and the administration backed down somewhat on sexual instruction but not on socialist ideals. That another church strike or Cristero Rebellion was avoided is testimony to the good sense of both Cárdenas and the archbishop of Mexico, Luis María Martínez. In an important pastoral letter the archbishop implored the Mexican clergy to show more concern for the socioeconomic welfare of the masses. At the same time Cárdenas allowed that socialist education should be positive—it need not encompass antireligious propaganda in the classroom. Education itself, he believed, would eradicate fanaticism.

The federal expenditure for education in 1936 surpassed 10 million pesos for the first time in Mexican history; by 1940 it had reached 11.3 million pesos. Cárdenas earmarked twice as much for rural education as any previous president. But although more Mexicans could read and write than ever before, illiteracy was not curtailed. Inflation coupled with a high rate of population growth outran the educational budget, and, as a result, in 1940 there were two million more illiterates in Mexico than there had been only a decade before.

President Cárdenas also worked hard to strengthen the organized labor movement and to dominate it. Annoyed at the deep-seated corruption that had beset organized labor under Luis Morones, the president supported Vicente Lombardo Toledano, a onetime CROM lieutenant, in his effort to form a new national union. Much more intellectually oriented than Luis Morones, Lombardo Toledano embraced the Marxian class struggle as best explaining Mexico's historical reality and called for the establishment of a dictatorship of the proletariat. But, while he held that man was excessively acquisitive and competitive, Lombardo

2. Quoted in Albert L. Michaels, "The Modification of the Anti-Clerical Nationalism of the Mexican Revolution by General Lázaro Cárdenas and Its Relationship to the Church-State Detente in Mexico," *The Americas* 26 (1969): 37.

Toledano was no orthodox Communist. He never completely abandoned the humanism he had learned at the feet of Antonio Caso, and when forced to accept an anti-Marxist position he would explain that Mexico's problems were so unique as to require Mexican solutions. While he might have preferred public ownership of all property, he was practical enough to realize that partial socialization was better suited to the Mexican situation in the 1930s.

Lombardo Toledano succeeded in joining together some three thousand unions and six hundred thousand workers to form the Confederación de Trabajadores de México (CTM). The CTM made Lombardo Toledano its secretary general, and although Cárdenas did not give the secretary general a government position, he pledged to support his efforts. Within two years the membership had passed one million.

The CTM in its capacity as spokesman for the workers engaged in many different activities. It sponsored health and sanitation projects and organized a series of sports and recreational programs. But, most important, it concerned itself with improving the wage structure of the country. A survey in 1930 had estimated that the minimum daily wage on which a head of household might adequately support his family was four pesos and revealed, at the same time, that the average minimum wage in Mexico was one peso, six centavos. As Lombardo Toledano sought to rectify the wage structure in the country, he found himself blocked at every step by both Mexican and foreign management. Only by concerted effort did he finally succeed in having a new minimum wage of three pesos, fifty centavos adopted on a nationwide basis.

Nationalization of Oil Companies

Without question Cárdenas's most dramatic encounter during his six-year presidential term was the oil controversy with the United States, a matter that had ostensibly been resolved by his predecessors. The dispute began, innocently enough, as a conflict between labor and management within the petroleum industry. In 1936 Mexican workers struck for higher wages and better working conditions. While the oil workers were paid quite well in comparison to other Mexican laborers, the oil companies were extracting huge profits from the country and refused to negotiate seriously with union representatives. Worse yet, company poli-

cies more often than not demeaned the Mexican worker. To
many, little had changed since the miners struck Colonel Greene's
Cananea Consolidated Copper Company in 1906. As the strike in
the oil industry began to weaken the Mexican economy, President Cárdenas ordered that the dispute be settled by an industrial
arbitration board. The board examined the records of the companies and the living conditions of the workers and issued a decision ordering an increase in wages by one-third and an improved
pension and welfare system. The companies, claiming that the
order meant an increase in operating costs of over $7 million,
appealed the decision to the Mexican Supreme Court, which ultimately upheld the original decision of the arbitration board.
When the foreign-owned companies refused to obey the Supreme
Court decision in its entirety, President Cárdenas held that they
had flagrantly defied the sovereignty of the Mexican state and
on March 18, 1938, signed a decree nationalizing the holdings
of seventeen oil companies.

The nationalization decree became an immediate *cause
célèbre*. Cárdenas received congratulatory telegrams from many
other Latin American heads of state and evoked the patriotism
of the vast majority of Mexicans. A few days after the decree was
signed, a huge celebration was held in Mexico City to honor the
stride for economic independence.

Cárdenas was reassured by the support he garnered, for he
realized that the reaction would be quite different in the United
States. Many United States newspapers expressed outrage, and
not a few politicians called for intervention to head off a Communist conspiracy on the very borders of the United States. But there
would be no intervention on this occasion, as Franklin D. Roosevelt had come to the United States presidency enunciating a new
policy of nonintervention in Latin America. His ambassador to
Mexico, Josephus Daniels, did his utmost to ensure that the oil
companies negotiated in good faith. The compensation issue was
fraught with difficulty, for the companies, led by Standard Oil
of New Jersey, bombarded the United States public with articles
and pamphlets vilifying Cárdenas and labeling the expropriation as common theft. While the companies claimed the value
of the expropriated properties to be in the neighborhood of $200
million (and the British companies claimed an additional $250
million), Cárdenas countered that, since the original investment had been recovered several times and since the subsoil
belonged to the Mexican nation, a just figure for the American companies was $10 million. Ultimately a mixed claims

Mexico's "Women's Workers' Army" supports the Cárdenas oil expropriation decree during the May Day celebration in 1938.

commission agreed upon a figure of almost $24 million, plus 3
percent interest effective from the day of expropriation.

A Change in Orientation

Shortly after the expropriation Cárdenas decided to alter the
structure of the PNR, which Calles had created in 1929. Realiz-

ing that Mexico was embarking upon difficult economic times, the president wanted an even more broadly based national party and for that reason established the Partido Revolucionario Mexicano (PRM), with representation from four sectors of society: the military, labor, agrarian, and popular. Much like its predecessor, the PRM was the official party and would encounter no serious opposition in either state or national elections.

In 1938 the leftist revolution began to lose some of its thrust, and, in retrospect, the oil expropriations climaxed the socialist and nationalist orientation of Cárdenas's program. The president's last two years were characterized by severe economic difficulty. Wealthy Mexicans, fearful of the establishment of a communist state, refused to invest in the Mexican economy, and foreign capitalists looked elsewhere for lucrative investment fields. Cárdenas created a government oil company, Petróleos Mexicanos (PEMEX), to run the industry, but, inheriting antiquated machinery and a lack of trained technicians, it got off to a shaky start. The situation worsened when Cárdenas learned that he could not buy spare parts in the United States. As oil revenues declined, the national debt rose and confidence in the government lagged. Worst of all, rampant inflation set in. Between 1935 and 1940 food prices alone rose by a staggering 49.39 percent.

The reform program—school construction, benefits for labor, agrarian reform—was expensive, and cuts had to be made somewhere. As early as 1936 the president abandoned his experiments with socialist education. Land redistribution slowed down markedly after 1938 as Cárdenas implemented agrarian reform only when he needed political support. At the same time, he became more and more sensitive to labor agitation and strikes. Almost imperceptibly, the Mexican Revolution was shifting into a new phase. The change in policy was formalized in 1939 when the recently formed PRM met to choose its presidential candidate. It was expected that Cárdenas would throw his support to his longtime political ally, Francisco Múgica, but instead the president, believing it was time to change the orientation of the Revolution, supported his secretary of war, Manuel Avila Camacho, a conservative. Cárdenas's support assured Avila Camacho of the nomination, and the nomination assured him of victory.

As the Mexican Revolution was about to embark on a new course not all of the old problems had been resolved, but the Cárdenas administration was remarkable, nevertheless, for what it had done. It saw the end of one age and the beginning of another. Cárdenas had finally broken the back of the hacienda system, had fostered an impressive program of rural education, had seen that the labor movement was cleaned up and that it was reorganized into a new, powerful union, and had struck a sharp blow for Mexican economic nationalism when he failed to be bludgeoned by the oil companies. He had demonstrated that reform could progress without bringing the church crashing to its knees and without resorting to strong-arm tactics. With most critics, persuasion, he learned, yielded greater dividends than coercion. But, perhaps most important, by avoiding pivotal mistakes and not sacrificing principles to expediency, he won a new respect for the office he held as well as the plans he espoused.

By 1940 most of the goals envisioned by the revolutionaries of 1910 had been reached, and they would have considered Cárdenas's efforts a vindication of their sacrifices. But just as societies are seldom static, revolutions, if they are to be worthy of the name, must be continuing. The thirty years intervening since 1910 had begun to leave a legacy of new problems, and it was now time to reorder priorities and seek new solutions.

Recommended for Further Study

Ashby, Joe C. *Organized Labor and the Mexican Revolution under Cárdenas*. Chapel Hill: University of North Carolina Press, 1967.

Becker, Marjorie. "Black and White and Color: Cardenismo and the Search for a Campesino Ideology." *Comparative Studies in Society and History* 29 (1987): 453–65.

Britton, John A. "Teacher Unionization and the Corporate State in Mexico, 1931–1945." *Hispanic American Historical Review* 59 (1979): 674–90.

Brown, Lyle C. "Mexican Church–State Relations, 1933–1940." *Journal of Church and State* 6 (1964): 202–22.

Cronon, E. David. *Josephus Daniels in Mexico*. Madison: University of Wisconsin Press, 1942.

Daniels, Josephus. *Shirt-Sleeve Diplomat*. Chapel Hill: University of North Carolina Press, 1947.

Hilton, Stanley E. "The Church–State Dispute over Education in Mexico from Carranza to Cárdenas." *The Americas* 21 (1964): 163–83.

Koppes, Clayton R. "The Good Neighbor Policy and the Nationalization of Mexican Oil: A Reinterpretation." *Journal of American History* 69 (1982): 62–81.

Michaels, Albert L. "The Crisis of Cardenismo." *Journal of Latin American Studies* 2 (1970): 51–79.

————. "Fascism and Sinarquismo: Popular Nationalisms against the Mexican Revolution." *Journal of Church and State* 8 (1966): 234–50.

————. "The Modification of the Anti-Clerical Nationalism of the Mexican Revolution by General Lázaro Cárdenas and Its Relationship to the Church–State Detente in Mexico." *The Americas* 26 (1969): 35–53.

Michels, Elizabeth F. "Standard Oil of New Jersey Fights Mexican Expropriation, 1938–1942." Occasional Paper no. 1, Georgetown University Latin American Studies Program, 1980.

Millon, Robert P. *Mexican Marxist: Vicente Lombardo Toledano.* Chapel Hill: University of North Carolina Press, 1966.

Rippy, Merrill. "The Economic Repercussions of Expropriation: Case Study, Mexican Oil." *Inter-American Economic Affairs* 5 (1951): 52–70.

Ruiz, Ramón Eduardo. *Mexico: The Challenge of Poverty and Illiteracy.* San Marino, Calif.: Huntington Library, 1963.

Townsend, William Cameron. *Lázaro Cárdenas: Mexican Democrat.* Ann Arbor: Wahr, 1952.

Weyl, Nathaniel, and Sylvia Weyl. *The Reconquest of Mexico: The Years of Lázaro Cárdenas.* New York: Oxford University Press, 1939.

Wilkie, James W. *The Mexican Revolution: Federal Expenditure and Social Change since 1910.* Berkeley: University of California Press, 1967.

39

Society and Culture
from Obregón to Cárdenas

Daily Life in Countryside and City

Between 1920 and 1940 the lives of average Mexicans changed more rapidly than they had in any previous twenty-year period. The population decline of the decade of violence stopped, and, with the greater political stability of the 1920s and 1930s, the number of people began to climb rapidly. When Obregón came to office in 1920 the total population of the country was slightly over 14 million, but when Cárdenas turned over the presidency to his successor twenty years later the total had almost reached 20 million.

Mexico was not yet an urban country when Cárdenas's term ended, although the percentage of population living in communities with fewer than twenty-five hundred people had slipped from about 70 percent in 1920 to some 65 percent in 1940. It was in the rural areas that the change in life-style was most dramatic. The percentage of people who wore neither shoes nor sandals declined markedly, as did the percentage of illiterates. By 1940 cultural anthropologists found it difficult to find many of those quaint Indians who spoke a native tongue exclusively.

The new *ejidatario* in rural Mexico, unlike his peón forefather, was no longer bound to the hacienda. He could travel as freely as his pocketbook allowed. It was no longer necessary to purchase daily necessities in the tienda de raya, but if he did shop in the ejido store he would likely find prices somewhat lower than those in the nearby community. The old mayordomos, of course, were gone, and in most cases ejido officials were elected by the ejidatarios themselves.

Thousands of families who had fled their villages in search of security during the early Revolution returned to find that some impressive changes were taking place. Blacktop highways began to supplant bumpy dirt roads, and buses rolled over them with more or less regularity. Bicycles began to push burros off the highways. Tractors challenged the ox-drawn plow. Gasoline engines, rather than mules or horses, turned the mills that ground the corn, and gasoline pumps drew the water from nearby streams. Electricity arrived even in some small towns.

Some of the major changes in Tzintzuntzan, Michoacán, in the 1930s were recorded by the anthropologist George M. Foster.

> The first major cultural impact of modern times occurred . . . in the spring of 1931. General Lázaro Cárdenas, then Governor of Michoacán, sent a Cultural Mission consisting of teachers who specialized in plastic arts, social work, music, home economics, physical education, and "small industries," and a nurse-midwife and an agricultural engineer. . . . Most villagers were reluctant to cooperate, to help find living quarters, and to aid staff members and rural teachers. . . . In spite of such difficulties, however, the Mission had a big effect. A number of the more progressive families agreed to whitewash their houses, to improve the appearance of the village, and the present plaza, then a barren wasteland with a few houses, was cleaned up, sidewalks were marked out, flowering jacaranda trees were planted, a fountain . . . was built . . . and place was cleared for a bandstand. At the end of the first month there was an open house exposition of arts, crafts, sports, and civic betterments, to which General Cárdenas came as guest of honor. . . . Changes now began to come more rapidly. . . . Electricity was brought in from Pátzcuaro in 1938 and running water . . . was installed about the same time. . . . By 1938 the road was graded, and in 1939 it was paved. Tzintzuntzan was now an hour from the state capital, Morelia, instead of a very long day's walk or ride. . . . In 1939 the new and modern *Escuela Rural 2 de Octubre*, named to commemorate the date of Tzintzuntzan's independence, opened its doors, and for the first time village children had ready access to the full six years of primary schooling.[1]

The rural school in the 1920s and 1930s became the focal point of village life. Economic and social activity centered on programs initiated by the rural teachers, and cultural life for the first time was dominated more by the school than the church. Daily tasks became somewhat easier, and, with the gradual extension of

1. George M. Foster, *Tzintzuntzan: Mexican Peasants in a Changing World* (Boston, 1967), pp. 26–29.

medical facilities into the village, life expectancy improved and the infant mortality rate dropped from 222 deaths per thousand in 1920 to 125 twenty years later. But by no means did all of the essentials of the good life come to rural Mexico between 1920 and 1940. Poverty continued to be the single most pervasive characteristic of rural life. Although it was no longer accurate to suggest that rural Mexicans continued to live as they had since the days of the Conquest, most had not yet really been incorporated into the mainstream of national life.

City life became more pleasant, at least, for some, as the amenities of technology became increasingly commonplace. Mexico's first commercial radio station began transmission in 1923, and scores huddled around each neighbor lucky enough to own or have access to a receiver. Two years later the Department of Education established its own radio station and began beaming educational broadcasts to primary schools recently equipped with receivers. By the mid-1930s the commercial cinema had begun to challenge the bullfight for pre-eminence in entertainment. The most interesting films were those of patriotic content depicting the glories of the Revolution, like Ezequiel Carrasco's *Viva México* (1934) and Luis Lezama's *El Cementerio de los Aguilas* (1938). But the greatest commercial success was Fernando de Fuentes's musical *Allá en el Rancho Grande* (1936), starring Tito Guízar and Esther Fernández. The extraordinary box office profits of this film led to a cinematographic genre of folk films, soon to be dominated by two towering figures of popular culture, Jorge Negrete and Pedro Infante.

Without question, it was the internal combustion engine that most changed the life style of the urban areas. The motor car had arrived in Mexico shortly before the outbreak of hostilities in 1910, but, because of the tremendous dislocations of that first revolutionary decade, it did not begin to transform Mexican life until after 1920. By 1925 fifty-three thousand motor vehicles were digesting thirty-five million gallons of gasoline annually; fifteen years later the number of vehicles had tripled and gasoline consumption had quadrupled. In the early 1920s the motor vehicle was still a prestige symbol, carrying a select few to and from their offices or their families on an occasional weekend outing. Later in the decade motor car racing became popular, and often left a toll of killed or injured. But by the 1930s, with a tremendous increase in the number of trucks and buses, the internal combustion engine had transformed commercial life as well as disrupted staid social patterns. Automobiles, trucks, and buses

As Mexico left the era of the silent film and moved into the age of sound Fernando de Fuentes's *Allá en el Rancho Grande* awoke world interest in the Mexican cinema.

required an expanded highway network, and Mexican engineers and day laborers completed several thousand miles of new, hard-surface roads during the twenty-year period.

The growth of Mexico City was nothing short of spectacular. The high national rate of population growth, coupled with an internal migration from rural to urban areas, gave Mexico City with a population of 1,726,858 in 1940, an increase of more than one million in only two decades. The dramatic growth yielded its share of social problems as neither the job market nor the school system could absorb the tremendous influx. Those fleeing to the capital in search of a better life were more often than not disappointed. Rapid growth in other cities also caused difficulties for tens of thousands of recent arrivals. While Mexicans laughed with derision at the prohibition experiment in the United States, alcoholic consumption rose sufficiently in Mexico in the 1920s to cause alarm in the medical and scientific communities,

Life for the Mexican woman was slow to change, and her special burdens inevitably evoked compassion from foreign visitors. Verna Carleton Millan, a North American, was appalled at what she found.

> The American woman who marries into a Mexican family has a gigantic task of readjustment before her; by the mere act of crossing the border, she slips into a world that has many features of the middle ages. . . . Her first psychological shock will take place

when she realizes that in Mexico women are still considered inferior beings, unfit to manage their own lives or assume any position of responsibility. . . . The Mexican woman of today, the woman of the towns and larger cities, has this enormous burden of race and tradition upon her shoulders; product of a mestizo culture, she is caught in the mesh of not one but two traditions, both equally repressive. The Spaniards brought to Mexico the strict Catholicism that has held women in a subjective, passive role for centuries. On the other hand, the Indian tribes since time immemorial have crushed the spirit of their women beneath ironclad taboos and repressions. . . . Within the home, the man reigns supreme, a heritage from the middle ages. The daughters are taught absolute obedience not only to their fathers but to their brothers as well. If there is a little money in the family, the sons are educated at the expense of the daughters. . . . Marriage is considered the supreme goal of every woman's life. The mother's marriage may have been a life-long tragedy, but she can conceive of no other fate for her daughters, on the theory that any kind of marriage is better than none because at least one thus fulfills the Christian command to multiply.[2]

The censure was essentially correct, but without the advantage of historical perspective Mrs. Millan could not have known that change, albeit almost imperceptible change, was taking place. More and more women were entering the worlds of business, education, government service, and medicine. Between 1920 and 1924 only 223 Mexican women received university degrees; ten years later the figure had doubled. By 1930 women were participating more actively in civic work than at any previous time, and hundreds of thousands had successfully rebelled against family-arranged marriages. In 1900 a woman in Mexico City would not have dreamed of carrying a placard of protest in a parade. By the time Cárdenas left office such activities were commonplace.

The feminist movement in Mexico was amorphous until 1935, when the United Front for Women's Rights was founded in Mexico City. With a membership of more than fifty thousand by 1940, the Front coordinated the efforts and defined the goals on a national basis. More important than anything else was the campaign to win for women the right to vote. Arguing the absurdity of disenfranchising women along with former convicts, fugitives from justice, and inmates of insane asylums, the Front assumed the offensive and, with Cárdenas's support, did manage to win the right to vote in a number of states. Woman's suffrage

2. Verna Carleton Millan, *Mexico Reborn* (Boston, 1939), pp. 148–58.

in national elections would have to wait a few more years, but the predisposition was clearly set by 1940.

The Intelligentsia of the Revolution

Mexican culture during the period 1920 to 1940 came to the service of the Revolution. The artistic, literary, and scholarly communities, with an abiding faith in the new thrust of Mexican life, supported revolutionary ideals by contributing their unique talents to awakening the consciousness of the new social order. The process is nowhere better illustrated than in the cultural achievements of Mexico's most famous painters.

The restlessness of Mexico's artistic community had been apparent during the late Porfiriato and during the first revolutionary decade, but Mexican art came into its own and won world acclaim after 1920. While secretary of education, José Vasconcelos commissioned leading artists to fill the walls of public buildings with didactic murals, and Mexico's artistic renaissance occurred in the process. Art was no longer directed to the privileged few who could afford to buy a canvas; it was for the public. If Mexico was not yet able to provide a classroom and a

A detail from Rufino Tamayo's *Allegories of Music and Song* (1933).

David Alfaro Siqueiros, *Head of an Indian.*

Juan O'Gorman, *Enemies of the Mexican People.*

seat for every child in the country, some measure of popular education could be provided by a muralist movement carried out on a scale grander than any the world had yet known.

Vasconcelos, while supplying the government subsidy, was too much the free intellectual to place any constraints on the artists. Coordinating his efforts with the artists' union, the Syndicate of Technical Workers, Painters, and Sculptors, he instructed the artist simply to paint Mexican subjects. To be sure, youthful enthusiasm carried some astray, but giants such as Jean Charlot, Rufino Tamayo, Juan O'Gorman, David Alfaro Siqueiros, Fernando Leal, and Roberto Montenegro emerged in the process as well. Two of the muralists began to dominate the movement and set themselves apart from their talented compatriots.

During the 1920s and 1930s Diego Rivera (1885–1957) became the most renowned artist in the western hemisphere and one of the most imposing artists of the twentieth century. A man of boundless talent and energy, he used the Indian as his basic motif. Rivera's realistic murals did not invite freedom of interpretation, and he depicted humanistic messages for the illiterate

masses on the walls of the Agricultural School in Chapingo, the
Cortés Palace in Cuernavaca, the National Preparatory School,
the Department of Education, and the National Palace in Mexico City. The Spaniard during the colonial period, and his criollo
offspring during the nineteenth century, had enslaved the Indian
and had kept him in abject poverty. It was now time to incorporate the Indian into the mainstream of society just as Rivera was
incorporating him into the mainstream of his murals. Although
Rivera was more interested in content than in form, he was without rival in technique. His symmetry was near perfect, but his
genius emerged even more clearly in his use of line and color.
The Indians were invariably depicted in soft, gentle lines, with
earthen red and brown tones, while the oppressors, white foreigners and white Mexicans, were portrayed in sharp lines and
harsh colors.

Rivera's greatest masterpiece was composed at the Agricultural
School at Chapingo, formerly the private hacienda of President
Manuel González. With esthetic originality and flamboyance,
Rivera spelled out his appreciation of the new revolutionary
ideology. Not only did his frescoes display the virtues of land

Details from Diego Rivera's mural in the Agricultural School at Chapingo.

Diego Rivera's *Awaiting the Harvest* (1923), a fresco in the Court of Labor, Department of Education.

Diego Rivera's *The Billionaires*, a mural in the Department of Education, satirizes international capitalism.

redistribution, but they instructed in the lessons of sociopolitical reality. On one wall he portrayed bad government—the peasants betrayed by false politicians, fat capitalists, and mercenary priests. But the opposite wall was one of revolutionary hope—a scene of agricultural cultivation, a rich harvest, and a liberated peasantry. Just in case the message might be lost, he painted over the main stairway of the building, "Here it is taught to exploit the land, not man."

Only slightly less famous than Rivera, but no less a genius, was José Clemente Orozco (1883–1949). As the violent decade passed, Orozco abandoned his career as a biting political caricaturist for mural art. Less a realist than Rivera, Orozco could be more forceful, expressive, and passionate. He was willing to experiment with new techniques as well as themes. His brutal and

José Clemente Orozco's *Modern Migration of the Spirit* (1933) from the fresco *Quetzalcóatl and the Aspirations of Mankind* was painted at Dartmouth College.

distorted Christs, grotesque depictions of God, and nude Madonnas pilloried all religious piety and brought forth a storm of protest. Some of his frescos were mutilated by angry crowds, but Vasconcelos did not interfere with Orozco's freedom of expression. Orozco's scenes of violence during the Revolution bring to mind Francisco Goya's *Horrors of War*, and he might well have had the Spanish master in mind when he conceived them.

Orozco had his tender moments too. During the 1920s, when he could see the first hesitant steps of social progress, some of his murals portray hope. His famous fresco, *Cortés and Malinche*, shows two nude and carnal figures sitting over the figure of the old, prostrate Mexico, and represents the miscegenation process, the biological and spiritual origin of the Mexican people. But in the 1930s, even as the pace of social reform began to accelerate, Orozco became increasingly disillusioned with the progress being made. After spending several years in the United States, he returned to his native Jalisco, and in the Instituto Cabañas in Guadalajara he decided to return to the theme of the Conquest. The new Cortés he portrayed was a powerful, violent conqueror in full armor and with sword in hand. The only hope held out is that the spirit whispering in Cortés's ear might convince him to use his power and technology for good rather than for evil.

The painters were not alone in transforming a national art into a nationalistic one. The literary community contributed as well with its novels of the Revolution. Two of the best came from the pen of Martín Luis Guzmán (1887–1976), who published *El águila y la serpiente* (translated as *The Eagle and the Serpent*) in 1928 and *La sombra del caudillo* the following year. The first constitutes a novelized personal memoir of the young Guzmán who left the comfortable life of a university student to join the Revolution and found himself a Villista. Captivated by Villa's personality, yet always afraid of his violence, Guzmán sketched the Centaur of the North most vividly in his discussion of revolutionary justice.

> This man wouldn't exist if his pistol didn't exist. . . . It isn't merely an instrument of action with him; it's a fundamental part of his being, the axis of his work and his amusement, the constant expression of his most intimate self, his soul given outward form.

José Clemente Orozco's fresco, *Cortés and Malinche.*

Between the fleshy curve of his index finger and the rigid curve of the trigger there exists the relation that comes from the contact of one being with another. When he fires, it isn't the pistol that shoots, it's the man himself. Out of his very heart comes the ball as it leaves the sinister barrel. The man and the pistol are the same thing.[3]

Villa did not turn out to be the ideal man Guzmán had hoped for. The intellectual simply could not communicate with the people's hero and ultimately took his leave. Guzmán never abandoned his revolutionary faith, but he began to wonder whether the goals could be attained without all the violence.

Guzmán's disenchantment with the politics of the Revolution is even more evident in *La sombra del caudillo*, a novel inspired by the presidential election of 1928, which saw opposition candidates Francisco Serrano and Arnulfo Gómez both dead by election day. Mexico's most powerful novel decrying dictatorship, *La sombra del caudillo* is written with truculence and righteous indignation. But even here Guzmán does not give up on the Revolution. To the contrary, the passionate condemnation was directed against Calles for having betrayed the ideals of the movement.

The Indianist novel of the Revolution reached its apex in 1935 with Gregorio López y Fuentes's *El Indio*. Without naming a single character or place, López y Fuentes is able to portray the Indian, not as the noble savage, but as a man beset with social problems that society can help to overcome. The plot is not intricate, as the author was more interested in atmosphere. He admirably succeeded not only in illustrating the wide chasm between Indian and white society but also in making intelligible the deepest suspicions of whites harbored in the Indian community. López y Fuentes was awarded Mexico's first National Prize for Literature for this perceptive novel.

The cultural nationalism focusing on the Indian was carried into the arena of music by Carlos Chávez (1899–1978). After studying in Europe and the United States, in his late twenties Chávez returned to Mexico to become director of the National Conservatory of Music and to begin a brilliant career as a conductor, pianist, musical scholar, and composer. His *Sinfonía India* (1935) and *Xochipili-Macuilxochitl* (1940) were scored for pre-Columbian instruments, but, realizing that not all performing orchestras would be able to acquire such esoteric accouterments as strings

3. Martín Luis Guzmán, *The Eagle and the Serpent*, trans. Harriet de Onís (Garden City, N.Y., 1965), p. 210.

of deer hooves, he made provision for modern substitutes. But both rhythmically and melodically the compositions were inspired by Mexico's aboriginal heritage. Though Chávez was Mexico's most distinguished musician, he, like the muralists, wanted to reach the people, and he composed two important works, *Llamadas* (1934) and *Obertura republicana* (1935), based upon familiar Mexican tunes. As a result, Chávez enjoyed a popular as well as a sophisticated audience.

Anthropologists led the way among social scientists in the redefinition of cultural values. With the publication in 1922 of Manuel Gamio's highly important three-volume *La población del valle de Teotihuacán*, Mexican archeologists, ethnologists, and social anthropologists began to take a new look not only at antiquities but at contemporary Indian problems as well. Rejecting theories of racial inferiority and the anti-Indian posture of many nineteenth-century intellectuals, they set out to depict the glories of the Indian past, to restore Indian arts and crafts, and in general to revitalize contemporary Indian culture. Their efforts were greatly facilitated in 1936 when the government established a Departamento Autónomo de Asuntos Indígenas and three years later the Instituto Nacional de Antropología e Historia.

While artists, novelists, musicians, and even anthropologists could mature and prosper with the overriding ideological assumptions of the Revolution, historians encountered problems in their quest for historical truth. Rejecting the positivist tradition that had permeated historical scholarship during the late nineteenth century, the historian of the 1920s and 1930s found no new ideological peg on which to hang his hat. As his discipline was called upon to serve as one of the many vehicles for the apotheosis of the Revolution, he was confronted with an apparently irreconcilable dichotomy: should he serve the interests of the movement or of historical scholarship in those cases in which reality suggested that the two did not converge? The overwhelming majority chose to be loved rather than candid.

Once accepting that the Revolution embodied all virtue, it was necessary to deprecate the real or imagined enemies of the movement in the most scathing terms. The pervading frame of reference thus became prorevolutionary, the historians disagreeing with one another only on the question of which of the many revolutionary protagonists was most orthodox in his revolutionary commitment. Crimes of the Revolution were dismissed on grounds of political necessity, while those of the opposition were portrayed as barbarisms of the worst kind. The Díaz regime, of course, was denounced in the harshest terms with scarcely a redeeming phrase offered in its defense. But the important questions of the day—the goals of the Revolution and the means of implementing these goals—were never brought into sharp focus. One must conclude that historical scholarship did not meet the standards of other cultural endeavors.

In spite of the mediocre record of Mexican historians from 1920 to 1940, the country's overall cultural production was remarkable during those two decades. With contempt for convention, the intelligentsia suffused the environment with a new confidence. The illiterate, the petit bourgeois, the pseudosophisticate, and the intellectual could all take genuine pleasure in the tremendous flowering of culture. It was no time for the romantic landscape, the vaporous abstraction, or the unintelligible dream-sequence novel. Art and literature, as well as the social sciences, had to come to the service of the Revolution, repudiating the traditions of the recent past, satirizing the heresies of the present, and commending the material and social conquests of tomorrow.

Unequaled in Latin America, those twenty years of cultural vitality and strength captured the Mexican spirit and yielded a sense of national purpose and pride. The intellectual community did not portray Mexico as an idyllic world or expect a perfect state to arise from imperfect men. But most agreed with the philosopher Antonio Caso, who suggested forcefully in his eloquent *Principios de estética* (1925) that a meaningful morality had to be based on sacrifice and love. The enthusiasm of the intellectuals rested with their realization that after centuries of indelible stigmata, Mexico had embarked upon a compassionate social experiment that drew its strength from the best of human instincts. Although tangible progress was admittedly slow, the system had not proved to be incorrigible. Self-assured by world acclaim, the Mexican intelligentsia could never again feel constrained to look toward Europe for hallowed cultural standards. But, more important, the revolutionary beneficence they portrayed penetrated Mexican society deeply. The fighting was now over, and from that sorrow and adversity something positive had been born.

Recommended for Further Study

Beals, Ralph L. "Anthropology in Contemporary Mexico." In *Contemporary Mexico: Papers of the IV International Congress of Mexican History*, edited by James W. Wilkie, Michael C. Meyer, and Edna

Monzón de Wilkie, pp. 753–68. Berkeley: University of California Press, 1975.

Brenner, Anita. *Idols behind Altars: The Story of the Mexican Spirit*. Boston: Beacon Press, 1970.

Brushwood, John S. *Mexico in Its Novel: A Nation's Search for Identity*. Austin: University of Texas Press, 1966.

Charlot, Jean. *The Mexican Mural Renaissance, 1920–1925*. New Haven, Conn.: Yale University Press, 1967.

Delpar, Helen. *The Enormous Vogue of Things Mexican: Cultural Relations Between the United States and Mexico, 1920–1935*. Tuscaloosa: University of Alabama Press, 1992.

Fernández, Justino. *A Guide to Mexican Art: From Its Beginnings to the Present*. Chicago: University of Chicago Press, 1969.

Folgarait, Leonard. *So Far From Heaven: David Alfaro Siqueiros' The March of Humanity and Mexican Revolutionary Politics*. Cambridge: Cambridge University Press, 1987.

Guzmán, Martín Luis. *The Eagle and the Serpent*. Translated by Harriet de Onís. Garden City, N.Y.: Doubleday, 1965.

Hale, Charles, and Michael C. Meyer. "Mexico: The National Period." In *Latin American Scholarship since World War II*, edited by Roberto Esquenazi-Mayo and Michael C. Meyer, pp. 115–38. Lincoln: University of Nebraska Press, 1971.

Johnson, William W. "The Tumultuous Life and Times of the Painter Diego Rivera." *Smithsonian* 16 (1986): 36–51.

López y Fuentes, Gregorio. *El Indio*. New York: Ungar, 1961.

Millan, Verna Carleton, *Mexico Reborn*. Boston: Houghton Mifflin, 1939.

Mora, Carl J. *Mexican Cinema: Reflections of a Society, 1896–1980*. Berkeley: University of California Press, 1982.

Reed, Alma. *Orozco*. New York: Oxford University Press, 1956.

Salmerón, Francisco. "Mexican Philosophers of the Twentieth Century." In *Major Trends in Mexican Philosophy*, edited by Mario de la Cueva et al., pp. 246–87. Notre Dame, Ind.: University of Notre Dame Press, 1966.

Siqueiros, David Alfaro. *Art and Revolution*. London: Lawrence and Wishart, 1975.

Sommers, Joseph. *After the Storm*. Albuquerque: University of New Mexico Press, 1968.

Stevenson, Robert. *Music in Mexico: A Historical Survey*. New York: Crowell, 1971.

Turner, Frederick C. *The Dynamic of Mexican Nationalism*. Chapel Hill: University of North Carolina Press, 1968.

Wolfe, Bertram D. *The Fabulous Life of Diego Rivera*. New York: Stein and Day, 1969.

X THE REVOLUTION SHIFTS GEARS: MEXICO SINCE 1940

40

From Revolution to Evolution, 1940-46

The Administration of Avila Camacho

To some, Mexico's presidential election of 1940 marked the end of the Revolution; to others that same political exercise was simply the harbinger of a new approach to problem solving. Many contemporary political pundits predicted that Cárdenas would give his support to Francisco Múgica, an aging radical with impeccable revolutionary credentials. The conservatives, terrified at the prospect of further socialization of the country, rallied behind Juan Andreu Almazán. A wealthy Catholic landowner who even attracted fascist support to his camp, Almazán won the endorsement of the Partido de Acción Nacional (PAN), a conservative party later to be dominated by urban industrialists. But the official party candidate supported by Cárdenas turned out to be not Múgica but Secretary of War General Manuel Avila Camacho, an honest moderate and scarcely a social revolutionary.

The Mexican citizenry knew little about Avila Camacho prior to the 1940 presidential campaign; in fact, he was nicknamed "the Unknown Soldier." Avila Camacho had joined the Revolution in 1914 and gradually worked his way up through the military ranks. His reputation in the army was one of a compromiser rather than a forceful leader. During the course of the campaign, when asked about his feelings toward the church, he answered with the words, *Soy creyente* (I am a believer). The candid response presaged things to come. It meant specifically, of course, that anticlericalism was not going to be a part of his administration, but more generally it meant that the orientation of the Revolution was about to undergo a fundamental change. No longer would the implementation of Articles 3, 27, and 123 be considered the touchstone of social progress. If the Mexican people were surprised that a candidate for the presidency dared to confess his faith so openly, the leaders of the PRM were not. The politicians who gave Avila Camacho the nomination knew that he was much more conservative than Cárdenas. With the war in Europe threatening the Mexican economy, they, like their leader, felt it was time to change the direction of the movement. Cárdenas himself had recognized the need to slow down during his last year and a half in office.

Official party nomination meant victory on election day. Avila Camacho defeated Almazán soundly and, on December 1, 1940, became the fifty-seventh president of Mexico. His inaugural address, read with United States Vice-President Henry Wallace attending the ceremony, suggested that the Revolution was over, that its tasks had been completed and that Mexico was moving from a period of revolution to a period of evolution. To be sure, he took pride in what had been accomplished since 1910, but Mexico could no longer afford to look backward. It was now time to look to the future. "Each new epoch," he instructed the nation, "demands a rebirth of ideas. The clamor of the entire republic now demands the material and spiritual consolidation of our social conquests in a prosperous and powerful economy. It demands an era of construction of abundant life, of economic expansion."[1]

Because the new president was determined to embark upon new programs, he began to phase out some of the old. Land redistribution did not stop entirely, but the pace certainly slowed. Whereas Cárdenas had distributed over 49 million acres, Avila Camacho parceled out fewer than 12 million. In addition, because he favored small, private ownership, emphasis was no longer placed on distribution to the ejido but rather to the heads of individual families.

Avila Camacho's educational program also reflected a change of direction. First of all, the ideology of the socialist school was abandoned, and great emphasis was placed on private initiative. Under the slogan "Each one teach one," the president and his secretary of education, Jaime Torres Bodet, had the Congress enact a law exhorting each literate Mexican to instruct one or more illiterates in the fundamentals of reading and writing. The program began amidst great fanfare with the president, his cabinet

---

1. Quoted in Betty Kirk, *Covering the Mexican Front: The Battle of Europe vs. America* (Norman, 1942), p. 320.

secretaries, and much of the federal and state bureaucracy setting aside an hour each day to give practical reading instruction. To encourage compliance, some public employees were fined for failure to cooperate. States initiated incentive plans of various kinds; Oaxaca promised a new school for the village that compiled the best record, and Michoacán reduced the sentences of prisoners who learned to read and write. Soon, however, the original enthusiasm lagged, and the program slacked off. Obviously, private initiative was not going to achieve what neither church nor state had been able to accomplish over centuries—the elimination of illiteracy.

The president replaced Marxist labor leader Vicente Lombardo Toledano with the much more conservative Fidel Velásquez. Lombardo Toledano's departing speech was caustic and indicated his anger at the recent turn of events. "I leave this office a rich man," he declared, "rich in the hatred of the bourgeoisie."[2] The press, for some time having portrayed Lombardo Toledano as inordinately egotistical, pointed out that he had used the word *I* sixty-four times in the farewell address and took the occasion to dub him "the Yo-yo Champion."

Under Velásquez's leadership, government support of the CTM was held to a minimum. Rejecting what he judged to be Communist domination of the confederation, Velásquez supported moderate elements within the union, and their requests to him were modest indeed. Although small increases in wages were won by the new labor leader, they did not keep pace with the rapidly growing inflation that engulfed the Mexican economy. All areas of the country were hit, but especially Mexico City.

COST OF LIVING IN MEXICO CITY
(Base year 1939 = 100)

Year	Food	Clothing	Services
1939	97.6	104.1	111.8
1940	97.0	114.4	102.9
1941	106.0	127.2	143.3
1942	119.1	156.4	153.9
1943	161.4	217.6	219.7
1944	188.8	241.9	235.7
1945	225.6	261.8	239.9

Source: Jorge Vera Estañol, *Historia de la revolución mexicana: Orígenes y resultados* (Mexico, 1967), p. 737.

2. Quoted in ibid., p. 90.

The entire philosophy of the union movement changed. Velásquez did not even protest vigorously when the administration
enacted measures limiting the use of strikes. Progressive and radical affiliates of the confederation were displeased with the new
leadership, and in 1942 workers from the textile and building
trades industries withdrew from the CTM. The most important
potential benefit to accrue to the workingman was the creation
of a social security agency, the Instituto Mexicano de Seguro Social (IMSS), in 1943, but the initial coverage was so limited
that only a small percentage of the workers fell under the program at this time. When Avila Camacho left office fewer than
250,000 workers were participating.

World War II

World War II broke out in Europe while Lázaro Cárdenas was in
the last year of his term, and the president left it to his successor
to define Mexico's position. After the Russo-German nonaggres-
sion pact of 1939, both the Mexican left, led by Lombardo Toledano and Múgica, and the right, led by Almazán, adopted a pro-
German position. But when in the summer of 1941 Hitler broke
his promises and ordered the Wehrmacht toward Moscow and
Leningrad, the Mexican left could no longer support the Axis
cause. President Avila Camacho enunciated an unmistakably
pro-Allied course of action, and only a few Mexican fascists and
neo-fascists failed to support him. One day after the Japanese attack on Pearl Harbor, Mexico broke diplomatic relations with
the Axis powers and Secretary of Foreign Relations Ezequiel Padilla took the lead in urging other Latin American countries to
support the Allies.

Most Mexicans were satisfied that breaking diplomatic relations was sufficient and that the ultimate step of declaring war
was unnecessary. The United States and Mexico appointed members to a joint defense board, and Avila Camacho deported German, Italian, and Japanese diplomats from Mexico. In March
of 1942, when the president participated in the opening of the
new Benjamin Franklin Library in Mexico City, he pointed to
the stark cultural contrast between free societies who valued
books and the Nazis who burned them. But Mexico would not
have entered the war had not Germany forced its hand. On the
night of May 14 a German submarine operating in the Caribbean torpedoed and sank the *Potrero de Llano*, a Mexican tanker

that was fully lighted and properly identified. Although a number of leftist organizations favored an immediate declaration of war, Avila Camacho instead sent an ultimatum to Germany demanding full satisfaction and proper indemnification. Germany's answer was forthcoming. On May 24 a second Mexican tanker, the *Faja de Oro*, was torpedoed. Thereupon the president went before the Congress and announced that, although Mexico had tried to avoid war, the country could no longer accept dishonor passively. He asked for and, without serious debate, received his declaration of war.

Many Mexican intellectuals were less shocked at being at war than they were embarrassed at being formally allied with the United States. But on September 16, 1942, on the 132nd anniversary of the Grito de Dolores, an amazing and unprecedented display of camaraderie occurred on the balcony of the National Palace. Six former presidents—Adolfo de la Huerta, Plutarco Elías Calles (invited to return from the United States), Emilio Portes Gil, Pascual Ortiz Rubio, Abelardo Rodríguez, and Lázaro Cárdenas—linked arms with Avila Camacho to indicate that past antagonisms had been forgotten and that Mexico was fully united in time of war.

Secretary of Interior Miguel Alemán was charged with eliminating subversive activity within the national boundaries. Once a stiff espionage act passed the Congress, he began seizing German, Italian, and Japanese properties including banks, drug firms, hardware stores, and coffee plantations to prevent them from being used as bases of propaganda or espionage. Several German agents, most notably Gestapo officers George Nicolaus and Karl Hellerman, were arrested, and Alemán's secret service also rooted out several enemy agents operating clandestine radio stations relaying instructions to German submarines in the Atlantic. Mexico's valuable oil fields and munitions factories were placed under strict military control. Some modernization of the Mexican army occurred as military supplies were received through the Lend-Lease program of the United States.

The Avila Camacho administration also moved to provide a small military contingent for service with the Allies. After consultation with the members of the joint defense board it was decided that an air force squadron—Squadron 201—should be prepared for duty in the Far East. The Mexican aviators and support personnel received their training in the United States and were assigned to the Fifth Air Corps in the Philippines. Squadron 201 participated in bombing and strafing raids in the Philippines

May Day demonstrators destroy a Nazi flag in front of a German-owned electric company.

Mexican nurses march in support of the war effort.

and Formosa in early 1945, and some Mexicans lost their lives. After the war the squadron received commendations from General Douglas MacArthur and a hero's welcome upon return to Mexico.

More important than token military support were the strategic war materials Mexico provided for the Allied war effort. Zinc, copper, lead, mercury, graphite, and cadmium flowed into United States war plants and were transformed into military products. The increased demand for these raw materials could have caused prices to soar, but the Mexican government instituted price controls as further testimony of its cooperation.

The most unique, and ultimately the most controversial, contribution to the war effort was the mutual decision made by Avila Camacho and Franklin D. Roosevelt to allow Mexican laborers (*braceros*) to serve as agricultural workers in the United States Southwest. The draft in the United States had depleted the work force, and the Mexicans in many ways picked up the slack as they began to harvest major crops. The terms of the agreement were carefully spelled out: the workers were to receive free transportation to and from their homes; they were not to displace United States workers or to be used to suppress wages; minimum wages were set at 46 cents an hour (later raised to 57 cents); and Mexican labor officials were authorized to make periodic inspections to certify that the rules were being enforced. By the spring of 1943, in spite of the opposition of organized labor in the United States, the program was expanded to include nonagricultural labor as well. When the war ended, the bracero program was well entrenched as some three hundred thousand Mexicans had worked in twenty-five different states, some as far north as Minnesota and Wisconsin. But innumerable difficulties had beset the program, for the regulations were not always enforced and the workers encountered deep-seated prejudices in the United States.

Industrialization

Although it would be an exaggeration to suggest that Mexico's support during World War II materially influenced the outcome, nevertheless its contribution was more substantial than that of any other Latin American country. Moreover, the war was of singular importance for Mexico's internal development. It marked improved relations with the United States and an end to

With thousands of men working as braceros in the United States, Mexican women were called upon to serve the country by working in industry, in the fields, and at home.

the intense and bitter factionalism that had been born with the Revolution. But most important, it contributed in a major way to the acceleration of the country's economic development.

Wartime shortages in the United States and Europe deprived Mexico of its normal source of imported manufactured goods and convinced even the doubters of the need for industrialization. The goal was not simply to meet the demands of the domestic market but to produce a surplus of manufactured goods for export to other Latin American countries. Even during the last years of the Cárdenas administration, Mexican social scientists had begun to argue the absurdity of dividing the same pie into smaller and smaller pieces. For the Revolution to realize its ultimate goal of providing a better life for the vast majority of the people, it was imperative that the country's economic base be expanded, and this could be accomplished only through a major program of industrialization. The program not only would provide additional employment for a rapidly growing population but, through increased productivity, would generate wealth and improve the standard of living for the masses.

To foster industrial expansion the Avila Camacho administration established the Nacional Financiera, a government-owned bank created primarily to provide loans to industry but also to oversee the industrial process. In each year of the administration the favorable loans of the Nacional Financiera increased dramatically, reaching a total of 286.8 million pesos by 1945.

In addition, other incentives, such as tax exemptions and tariff protection, persuaded potential investors that the risks were acceptable. With the CTM in the hands of moderate Fidel Velásquez, the wage structure of the country was not going to change markedly; in fact, Velásquez pledged his support to the new industrialists. Native Mexican capital did begin to pour into new industrial pursuits, but, because the program was such an ambitious one, in 1944 the Congress passed legislation allowing foreign participation in industrialization with the proviso that Mexican capital own the controlling stock in any mixed corporation. In spite of the oil expropriations of the previous decade, the wartime alliance seemed to have initiated an era of good re-

INDUSTRIAL LOANS OF THE NACIONAL FINANCIERA, 1940–45

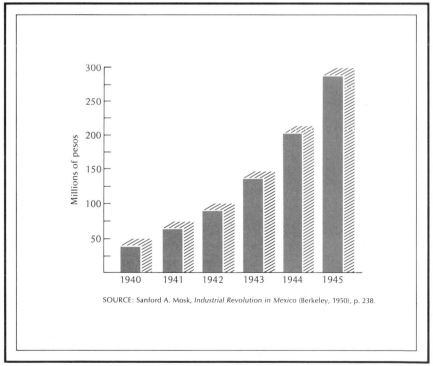

SOURCE: Sanford A. Mosk, *Industrial Revolution in Mexico* (Berkeley, 1950), p. 238.

lations, and some United States investors jumped at the opportunity. Credits were also extended through the Export-Import Bank in the United States.

The new and often young industrialists took it upon themselves to educate Mexican politicians, and indeed the public, in the virtues of industrial growth. In 1942 they founded the Cámara Nacional de la Industria de Transformación to develop an industrial consciousness in the country and to convince policy makers that without industrialization the masses were doomed to perpetual privation. During the Avila Camacho years industrialization became as important to the national self-conception as agrarian reform had been during the Cárdenas administration. Its lure was irresistible, and stories of new factories pushed political news off the front pages of the newspapers. The Cámara became not only an effective propaganda agency and lobby but, in essence, the recognized spokesman for the manufacturing industries.

There is no doubt that Cámara members convinced themselves that what was good for industry was good for the nation. Without it, they argued, Mexico would always be at the mercy of economic vicissitudes abroad. Their initial goal was to foster those industries which relied on Mexican raw materials, for example, cereal processing, edible oil from agricultural products, sugar, alcohol, and the manufacture of fibers and chemicals. The ultimate goal was to make Mexico completely self-sufficient in all manufactured goods consumed in large volume and to begin exporting these products as well.

The industrial revolution gathered momentum throughout the war years as a wide range of old industries were expanded and new ones initiated. The textile, food processing, chemical, beer, and cement industries grew rapidly. Pig iron production increased from 99,200 metric tons in 1930 to 240,300 metric tons in 1946, and during the same period steel increased from 142,200 metric tons to 257,900 metric tons. Electrical capacity rose by 20 percent, and the industrial proletariat grew steadily in size.

As predicted, industrialization generated much new wealth. The national income almost tripled, from 6.4 billion pesos in 1940 to 18.6 billion in 1945. Per capita income jumped from 325 pesos the year Avila Camacho was inaugurated to 838 pesos during his last year in office. As social critics quickly pointed out, however, increased per capita income does not necessarily mean a more equitable distribution of wealth or increased earning power for the poor. In fact, the middle class was growing in numbers and in earning power, but the large majority of the lower class was not benefiting fully from the improved economic indicators.

The emphasis of the Revolution had certainly changed. Those who had believed—and with some reason—that the semifeudal society inherited by the Revolution would be replaced by socialism had to re-examine their expectations. It now appeared increasingly certain that the post-Cárdenas period would be typified not by socialism but by industrial capitalism. The basic change in outlook became institutionalized in January 1946 when the PRM met to choose a candidate for the presidency.

For almost a decade the party had gradually been opened up. By 1946 it was no longer dominated by intellectuals, agrarian reformers, and ardent defenders of the labor movement. The business and industrial communities were now represented, as were economists and technicians. To symbolize that it endorsed the new thrust of the Revolution the party decided to change its name to the Partido Revolucionario Institucional (PRI). Of equal significance, to signify that the old Revolution was over, the official party for the first time endorsed a civilian, Miguel Alemán, as its presidential candidate. There would now be no turning back. Mexico's conception of modernity had been made synonymous with the industrial state.

Recommended for Further Study

Alvarez, José. "A Demographic Profile of the Mexican Immigrant to the United States, 1910–1960." *Journal of International American Studies* 8 (1960): 471–96.

Call, Tomme Clark. *The Mexican Venture.* New York: Oxford University Press, 1953.

Cline. Howard. *Mexico: Revolution to Evolution, 1940–1960.* New York: Oxford University Press, 1963.

———. *The United States and Mexico.* New York: Atheneum, 1963.

Galarza, Ernesto. *Merchants of Labor: The Mexican Bracero Story.* San Jose, Cal.: Rosicrucian Press, 1964.

Kirk, Betty. *Covering the Mexican Front: The Battle of Europe vs. America.* Norman: University of Oklahoma Press, 1942.

Leaming, George F., and Walter H. Delaplane. "An Economy of Contrasts." In *Six Faces of Mexico*, edited by Russell C. Ewing, pp. 209–43. Tucson: University of Arizona Press, 1966.

McWilliams, Carey. *North from Mexico: The Spanish-Speaking People of the United States.* New York: Greenwood Press, 1968.

Mosk, Sanford A. *Industrial Revolution in Mexico.* Berkeley: University of California Press, 1950.

Powell, J. R. *The Mexican Petroleum Industry, 1938–1950.* Berkeley: University of California Press, 1956.

Schuler, Friederich. "Germany, Mexico, and the United States During the Second World War," *Jarbuch für Geschichte von Staat, Wirtschaft und Gesellschaft Lateinamerikas* 27 (1985): 457–76.

Tannenbaum, Frank. *Mexico: The Struggle for Peace and Bread.* New York: Alfred A. Knopf, 1956.

Wilkie, James W. *The Mexican Revolution: Federal Expenditures and Social Change since 1910.* Berkeley: University of California Press, 1967.

41

The Institutionalized Revolution, 1946-58

For a dozen years following the Second World War, Mexicans were instructed by concrete example that the profound changes which had occurred with the Avila Camacho presidency were not to be transitory in nature but, in fact, had become institutionalized within the governmental structure. The next two chief executives, Miguel Alemán (1946–52) and Adolfo Ruiz Cortines (1952–58), both pledged to foster economic growth in general and large-scale industrialization in particular. That they were not diverted from this task is evidenced by the fact that Mexico's gross national product doubled during their twelve years in office. At the same time the agrarian revolution languished. Productivity on most of the ejidos had not lived up to expectations, and, as a result, government planners decided not to experiment further with communal agriculture.

The Presidency of Miguel Alemán

The election of Miguel Alemán, the first civilian president since Venustiano Carranza and the first to have played no illustrious role in the early Revolution, signified that the days of the soldier-politician were over. The new president reduced the military's share of the budget to less than 10 percent of the total for the first time in the twentieth century, and the generals accepted the decision, scarcely batting an eye. Over the years the military share of the budget had been gradually reduced, and, more suc-

PERCENTAGE OF MILITARY EXPENDITURE IN THE TOTAL BUDGET, 1917–52

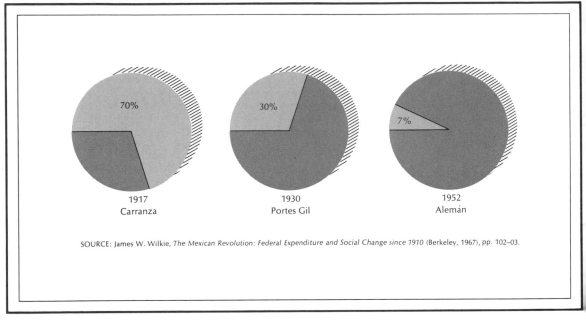

SOURCE: James W. Wilkie, *The Mexican Revolution: Federal Expenditure and Social Change since 1910* (Berkeley, 1967), pp. 102–03.

cessfully than its Latin American neighbors, Mexico curbed the problems of rampant militarism.[1]

With a healthy dollar reserve turned over to him by his predecessor, Alemán launched an impressive number of public works projects designed both to provide work for a steadily growing labor force and to meet a series of crucial developmental needs. Most important was the construction of dams to control flooding, increase arable land acreage, and supply ample power for the modernization impulse. The Morelos Dam on the Colorado River near Mexicali worked agricultural wonders in the northwest as some seven hundred thousand arid acres were reclaimed and converted into a rich truck-farming zone. In the northeast work was initiated, in cooperation with the United States, on the Falcón Dam in the lower Rio Grande Valley. Completed in 1953, the year after Alemán left office, the Falcón project yielded substantial agricultural benefits as well. The major project in the south was the harnessing of the Papaloapan River in the states of Puebla, Veracruz, and Oaxaca. Not only were tens of thousands of acres added to the agricultural base of the nation, but a series

1. The process is described in Edwin Lieuwen, *Mexican Militarism: The Political Rise and Fall of the Revolutionary Army* (Albuquerque, 1968).

of hydroelectric stations contributed to the tripling of Mexico's electrical output capacity by 1952.

Other large-scale public works centered on improving the communications network. In addition to modernizing the railway system, Alemán completed Mexico's segment of the Pan-American Highway in 1951. This all-weather road made possible automobile travel between the United States and Guatemala. Of equal importance commercially was the completion of the Isthmian Highway, which connected Puerto México and Salina Cruz across Tehuantepec. To cater to the tourist traffic, an increasingly important source of foreign exchange, Alemán ordered the construction of a four-lane superhighway between the capital and the Pacific resort town of Acapulco. In total, paved roads increased from about twenty-five hundred miles in 1946 to over ten thousand by 1952.

Postwar Mexico was prosperous and booming. If the working class did not share proportionately in the benefits of an expansive economy, the middle class continued to grow. Hundreds of small factories, not only in Mexico City but in Monterrey, Guadalajara, Puebla, and San Luis Potosí, took advantage of the cheap and abundant source of electric power and began to transform the economy and also the face of the nation. Low taxes and high rates of profit encouraged both Mexican and foreign capital to continue investing in the industrial sector of the economy. PEMEX expanded its activities; new pipelines and refineries, coupled with accelerated drilling, made it possible for the state-owned corporation to double its production between 1946 and 1952.

The most impressive construction project of all was the new University City built to house the National University of Mexico. Dedicated in 1952, the campus of three square miles was one of the most modern in the world. The architectural and artistic achievements at University City were unparalleled: the plans were conceived by leading artists such as Juan O'Gorman (1905–1982), the buildings designed by talented architects such as Félix Candela, and the walls adorned with anthropological and historical murals by Rivera and Siqueiros. Alemán considered the University a monument to his own presidency, and the first thing visitors encountered when entering the campus in the 1960s was a huge statue of Alemán himself.

Relations between the United States and Mexico continued to be cordial during the Alemán years. Accepting an invitation

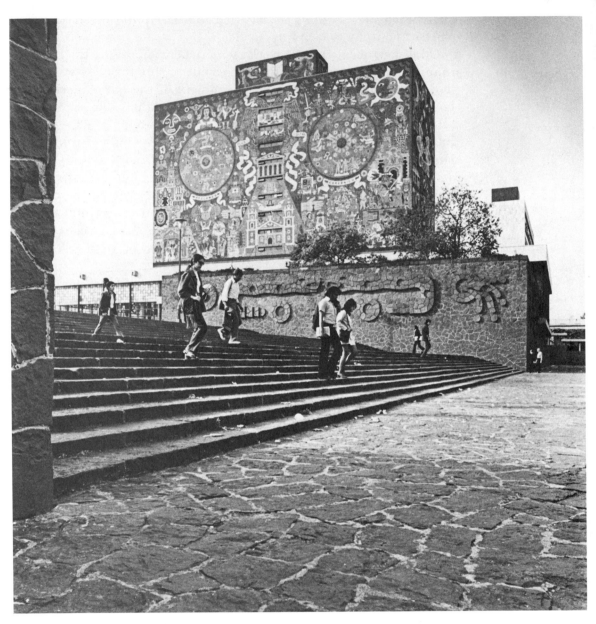

The main library at the National University of Mexico, University City.

from President Truman, Alemán became the first Mexican head of state to visit Washington, and Truman also called upon the Mexican president in Mexico City and delighted his hosts by placing a wreath at the monument of the Niños Héroes, the boy cadets who had fallen fighting United States troops a hundred years before. Both congresses voted to return all trophies of war sequestered in the middle of the nineteenth century. The outward manifestations of goodwill had practical effects as well. The United States was able to count on Mexican support in the cold war, and loans from the Export-Import Bank flowed into Mexico at an accelerated pace. United States tourists (over four hundred thousand in 1952 alone) left hundreds of millions of dollars in the country, and trade relations became more interdependent than ever before.

On the surface Mexico seemed healthier than at any time in her history. But, behind the showy façade Alemán had created,

A mural by José Chávez Morado at the Faculty of Science Building, University City.

President Harry S. Truman visits the Pyramid of the Sun during his trip to Mexico City.

serious problems had begun to sap the strength and vitality of his institutionalized Revolution. Corruption beset his administration, and many new millionaires emerged between 1946 and 1952.[2] The displays of sprawling mansions, yachts, and airplanes, paid for with bribes, brought to mind the venality of the days of Santa Anna. The library at the new University City, while a marvel to gaze at, was embarrassingly short of books. The row after row of empty shelves were symbolic of the building spree that failed to cope with basic issues and emphasized form rather than content.

While PRI politicians continued to mouth pleasant-sounding revolutionary euphemisms, the little man had been shunted aside. The labor movement was not crushed, but it was intimidated. Lombardo Toledano lamented to oral historians James and Edna Wilkie that under Alemán "the workers didn't dare to call large strikes because Alemán had embarked upon the cold

2. Estimates of dollars deposited in foreign banks by highly placed officials in the administration run between $500 million and $800 million. See William S. Stokes, *Latin American Politics* (New York, 1959), p. 390.

war and shared few sympathies with the working class."[3] While Lombardo Toledano cannot be considered an impartial observer, the facts nevertheless bear him out. When in April 1950 Secretary of the Treasury Ramón Beteta exhorted the industrialists of Monterrey to keep their costs down so that Mexican industry could become competitive, he was, in effect, inviting them to keep wages depressed. When petroleum workers struck, army troops were dispatched to patrol the fields and fifty union leaders were dismissed from their posts. In spite of John Maynard Keynes's revolution in economic theory, the Mexican worker was not yet to be confused with a consumer.

While new primary and secondary schools were built throughout the country, teachers' salaries were so paltry that it was almost impossible to staff them with qualified professionals. School attendance remained low. Of the 6 million schoolchildren in the age bracket six to fourteen, fewer than 2.25 million attended classes on a regular basis. In spite of the emphasis successive administrations since 1920 had placed on rural education, the 1950 census revealed that only .5 percent of rural children finished the sixth grade. Certainly it would be unfair to hold President Alemán responsible for all of the shortcomings of four decades of Revolution; yet his administration did not move in a direction suited to overcome them.

The Presidency of Ruiz Cortines

When PRI officials met to choose Alemán's successor, many believed it crucial to rekindle confidence in the integrity of the party. It would be necessary to repudiate the peculation of the Alemán administration by selecting as a presidential candidate one whose personal honesty and devotion to service were impeccable. Sixty-one-year-old Adolfo Ruiz Cortines fit the bill. During his governorship of Veracruz and tenure as secretary of interior under Alemán he had garnered a reputation for party loyalty, efficiency, and integrity. Although his campaign speeches enraptured nobody, with official party support he won over his leading opponent, Miguel Henríquez Guzmán, by a margin of almost five to one.

Ideologically much akin to his predecessor, the hard-working but unspectacular president did not disappoint those who had

3. Quoted in James W. Wilkie and Edna Monzón de Wilkie, *México visto en el siglo xx: Entrevistas de historia oral* (Mexico, 1969), p. 314.

urged a cleansing of bureaucratic corruption. He announced in his inaugural speech that he would demand strict honesty and ordered all public officials to make public their financial holdings. During the next several years he fired a number of notorious grafters. In an even more significant political reform he pushed through the Congress legislation fully enfranchising the Mexican woman. This long overdue measure culminated years of active campaigning by women's organizations throughout the country.

The Mexican economy remained dynamic during the Ruiz Cortines years as industry continued to receive government support and, in turn, established an entire series of new records for production. A devaluation of the peso in 1953 (to a rate of 12.50 to the dollar) helped stabilize the economy and prompt new foreign investment. United States capital, encouraged by the healthy economic indicators, poured into the country unhesitatingly, and United States visitors in the larger cities saw familiar signs advertising General Motors, Dow Chemicals, Pepsi-Cola, Coca-Cola, Colgate, Goodyear, John Deere, Ford, Proctor and Gamble, Sears, Roebuck, and other corporate giants who would not have dared to invest their stockholders' dollars in Mexico twenty years earlier. It was not easy to categorize the Mexican economy. Some observers viewed it as statist, some as socialist, and others as free enterprise. In reality it was a mixed economy comprising all three, and, in terms of development, it seemed to work.

Believing that Alemán had overtaxed the idea of public works, the new Mexican president did not initiate many grandiose construction schemes, but he did see hundreds of his predecessor's projects through to completion. Ruiz Cortines was content to serve the country by consolidating the gains made before he took office, and, as a result, many of the plaques he unveiled on public projects announced that they had been initiated during the presidential administration of Miguel Alemán. Whereas Alemán had built huge dams, Ruiz Cortines sponsored smaller projects; whereas Alemán had built superhighways, Ruiz Cortines paved two-lane roads to help the farmers get their products to a suitable market.

For the first time since its foundation in 1943, the IMSS expanded its coverage sufficiently to constitute an agency of genuine social importance. Ruiz Cortines's director, Antonio Ortiz Mena, not only obtained increased funding but moved the services into the countryside for the first time. The number of IMSS-sponsored clinics rose from 42 to 226 and hospitals from 19 to

105. Rural services did not yet approximate urban ones, but a beginning was at least made as about a hundred thousand rural persons received some kind of social security coverage for the first time. The basic issue of low wages was not resolved. Although salaries did rise by an average of 5 percent a year in the period from 1952 to 1958, the workers lost their increases to inflation, which rose annually at a rate of 7.3 percent.

Throughout his term of office Ruiz Cortines found himself caught up in a situation over which he had no direct control. Mexico's population was growing at a rate that began to alarm not only social scientists but also his political advisers. When Lázaro Cárdenas came to power the population of the country was only about 16 million. But by 1958 it had soared to more than 32 million. The population had doubled in only twenty-four years, and the dire consequences of this rapid and sustained growth were being felt for the first time. The population explosion was compounded by a concomitant trend toward urbanization. While the national growth rate had reached 3.1 percent a year by 1955 (as opposed to 1.9 from 1930 to 1940), the growth rate of the major cities approached 7 percent a year. The Federal District jumped from 3 million in 1952 to an amazing 4.5 million only six years later.

Drawn by the lure of industry, hundreds of thousands of rural Mexicans flocked to the cities in hope of a better life, but few found it. The industrial revolution required skilled, not unskilled, labor. The need for more jobs, schools, health services, sewage disposal plants, streets, and houses in the cities was now taxing even the extraordinary postwar prosperity. Although by 1958 a million and a half Mexicans were earning their living from industry, the laboring force was growing faster than industry could provide jobs. At precisely the time when the apparent thrust of the country was directed toward modernization, Ruiz Cortines found it necessary to order the use of hand labor rather than machinery on public works just to keep the new work force occupied. Allowing twenty men to work while an expensive machine stood idle seemed to meet a pressing social demand, but the scheme was directed toward the symptom rather than the disease.

The Revolution: An Assessment at Mid-Century

Ruiz Cortines considered himself a custodian of the Revolution as he announced repeatedly that he had full faith in revolutionary institutions. But surely his policies would have repulsed the heroes of the 1910 movement. The postwar generation of Mexican politicians had redefined priorities and concluded at mid-century that the programs of 1910 no longer had meaning. The burdens of industrial development fell most heavily on those who were least able to bear them. The president's economic advisers were aware of this problem, but they suggested that a temporary lack of equity constituted an important investment in the future. **These advisers had an abiding faith in the perfectibility of a system that would ultimately produce abundance. Mexico simply had to continue flexing its industrial muscles.**

From the very outset the Revolution had been criticized from both the left and the right. As it turned more conservative in the postwar years, however, the majority of the critics were isolated on the left. More wealth was being generated, but the proceeds were not being distributed. Mexican radicals were alienated by the new trends, but, more important, the moderate left was becoming increasingly apprehensive about the burgeoning population and the heavy emphasis on technology as the key to a more abundant life. If something were not done in the near future to arrest the tremendous rate of population growth, all discussion of the quality of life would be beside the point. For the first time in Mexican history social scientists began seriously to ponder the Malthusian theory of impending starvation. To be sure, the prophets of doom constituted only a small majority in 1958, but they addressed a serious problem that would concern more and more in the 1960s, 1970s, and 1980s.

On another important issue the left and right could agree. The official party, the PRI, had pre-empted the political life of the country. Party nomination was tantamount to election. Though the party itself was broadly based and incorporated many segments of society, its complete domination of the political process produced nothing less than a contradiction in terms—a one-party democracy.

When Mexico's distinguished political critic and respected scholar, Daniel Cosío Villegas, delivered his often-quoted Montgomery Lecture on Contemporary Civilization at the University of Nebraska, he provided a brilliant analysis of what was happening to the Mexican Revolution.

> The drive and energy of the Revolution were consumed much more in destroying the past than in constructing the future. As a result the past certainly disappeared, but the new present came

into being and began to develop haphazardly, so that, for lack of another image to imitate, it finally ended by becoming equal to the destroyed past. . . . The economy is sound, judged from a classical liberal point of view, so much so that it is often commented that Mexico has made phenomenal progress in recent years. . . . Strictly speaking the only problem of great magnitude is the rate at which the population and the national product grow. . . . It is possible that this population increase may very well strain the country's physical, human and economic resources, and that if energetic measures are not taken, it may present a very serious problem. . . . The political situation is decidedly less satisfactory. . . . The election [of the president, governors, and local authorities] is far from popular, being decided by personalist forces that rarely or never represent the genuine interests of large human groups. The economic and political power of the president of the Republic is almost all-embracing and . . . it is impossible for one man to know the special needs of each city or town and which person or persons are most suitable to resolve them.[4]

Ruiz Cortines's last message to the Congress was atypical of Mexican politicians of the twentieth century. He, too, had begun to hear the voices of criticism, and rather than exalt revolutionary successes, he took the occasion to pinpoint at least some of the shortcomings. The social imperfections of the system troubled him more than the deficiencies of one-party rule or executive dominance. The Mexican masses, the outgoing president conceded, had not benefited from the revolutionary process as much as he had anticipated. Many of the revolutionary promises were yet to be fulfilled. Illness, ignorance, and poverty had not been overcome. The desired balance between economic development and social justice had tipped in favor of the former.

PRI officials had to agree. The pace of the social movement had slowed and, since 1940, had almost ground to a halt. Perhaps a moderate shift to the left would mute government critics and reinstill some faith in revolutionary ideals. They were willing to give it a try.

4. Daniel Cosío Villegas, *Change in Latin America: The Mexican and Cuban Revolutions* (Lincoln, 1961), pp. 30–33.

Recommended for Further Study

Brandenburg, Frank. *The Making of Modern Mexico*. Englewood Cliffs, N.J.: Prentice-Hall, 1964.

————. "Organized Business in Mexico." *Inter-American Economic Affairs* 12 (1958): 26–50.

Call, Tomme Clark. *The Mexican Venture*. New York: Oxford University Press, 1953.

Cline, Howard. "Mexico: A Maturing Democracy." *Current History* (1953): 136–142.

————. *Mexico: Revolution to Evolution, 1940–1960*. New York: Oxford University Press, 1963.

Lewis, Oscar. "Mexico since Cárdenas." In *Social Change in Latin America Today*, edited by Richard N. Adams et al., pp. 285–345. New York: Vintage Books, 1960.

Mosk, Sanford A. *Industrial Revolution in Mexico*. Berkeley: University of California Press, 1950.

Padgett, L. Vincent. "Mexico's One Party System: A Re-evaluation." *American Political Science Review* 51 (1957): 995–1008.

Pérez López, Enrique, et al. *Mexico's Recent Economic Growth: The Mexican View*. Austin: University of Texas Press, 1967.

Ross, Stanley R., ed. *Is the Mexican Revolution Dead?* New York: Alfred A. Knopf, 1966.

Scott, Robert E. *Mexican Government in Transition*. Urbana: University of Illinois Press, 1959.

Taylor, Philip B. "The Mexican Elections of 1958: Affirmation of Authoritarianism?" *Western Political Science Quarterly* 13 (1960): 722–44.

Tucker, William P. *The Mexican Government Today*. Minneapolis: University of Minnesota Press, 1957.

Vernon, Raymond. *The Dilemma of Mexico's Development: The Roles of the Private and Public Sectors*. Cambridge, Mass.: Harvard University Press, 1963.

Wilkie, James W. *The Mexican Revolution: Federal Expenditure and Social Change since 1910*. Berkeley: University of California Press, 1967.

42

Adolfo López Mateos: The Lull Before the Storm, 1958-64

Prior to the presidential elections of 1958, some Mexican political analysts predicted that Luis H. Alvarez, the candidate of the
conservative, proclerical PAN, stood a good chance to make a
strong showing against the PRI candidate. For the first time in
Mexican history women were fully enfranchised, and the church
urged them not to follow the lead of their husbands blindly but
rather to consider carefully the qualifications of the conservative
opposition. The political temper of the country proved difficult to
measure, but in the end the Mexican people, both men and
women, were not about to turn the PRI out of office for a candidate who enjoyed the support of the church. The PRI nominee,
Adolfo López Mateos, the well-educated son of a small-town den-
tist, won the presidency with about 90 percent of the total vote.
The women's vote increased the total ballots cast but scarcely
changed the official party's margin of victory.

Domestic Policy

President López Mateos presented a stark contrast to his sixty-
seven-year-old predecessor. Only forty-seven at the time of his
election, he was dynamic, energetic, and personally attractive.
Having served as secretary of labor during the Ruiz Cortines administration, he had won a reputation as a liberal for his management of labor disputes; only a few of the thirteen thousand
cases he handled degenerated into strikes. He enjoyed the backing of Lázaro Cárdenas and seemed to be just the right man at

the right time. More intellectually oriented than presidents of recent vintage, he indicated during the campaign that he planned to nudge the Mexican Revolution back to the left. Hundreds of thousands of young Mexicans, disheartened with the slow progress in the social field since the Second World War, identified with López Mateos, much as the youth of the United States would, a few years later, identify with President John F. Kennedy. In fact, López Mateos was the last Mexican president to win the enthusiastic endorsement of the country's young.

Shortly after his inauguration the new president was asked to comment on his political philosophy and he answered with the words, "I am left within the Constitution." Mexican Communists, and other radicals whom he judged to be left *of* the Constitution, were not treated with kid gloves. López Mateos removed Communist leadership from the teachers' union and the railroad union and imprisoned Mexico's internationally known muralist and Communist, David Alfaro Siqueiros, on charges of "social dissolution," an amorphous kind of sedition. But just as local and foreign businessmen and industrialists sat back and relaxed, thinking that they had an unexpected friend in the presidential chair, López Mateos also began to demonstrate that he intended to depart markedly from the conservative, business-oriented policies of Manuel Avila Camacho, Miguel Alemán, and Adolfo Ruiz Cortines.

Land redistribution, almost forgotten as a revolutionary goal by the end of World War II, was stepped up once again, on both an individual and a collective basis. During his six-year term López Mateos parceled out some 30 million acres, more than any president except Lázaro Cárdenas. He also cleared and opened up new agricultural lands in extreme southern Mexico, which relieved land tension in the south.

State intervention in the economy accelerated from 1958 to 1964 as the administration purchased controlling stock in a number of foreign industries. In 1962, for example, the government gained control of the United States and Canadian electric companies and, not being able to divine a future in which energy would become a luxury, authorized huge, wasteful electric signs proudly announcing *La electricidad es nuestra* (The electricity is ours). At about the same time the government also purchased the motion picture industry, the production and distribution of which had been largely under United States domination. The president pledged to keep the price of tickets low so that all people could avail themselves of this medium of entertainment. So-

Even after the emphasis on agrarian reform programs, life for workers on the
maguey plantations of Yucatán remained
difficult.

cial welfare projects, most notably medical care and old age pensions, were expanded, and the IMSS program for rural Mexico
was stepped up markedly. By 1964 public health campaigns had
significantly reduced tuberculosis and polio rates, while malaria
was almost completely eliminated.

Like his predecessors, López Mateos continued to skirt the issue of birth control, even as a million Mexican babies were born
in 1962 and almost a million and a half in 1963. But he did recognize the tremendous dislocations occasioned by rapid urbanization. For the first time in history the government entered the
housing business on a large scale. Low-cost housing projects were
initiated in the major industrial cities, many of which had become encircled with shanty towns of indescribable misery and
poverty. One of the largest housing developments in Mexico City
covered some ten million square feet of a former slum, housed a
hundred thousand persons, and contained thirteen schools, four
clinics, and several nurseries. The rents were modest: $6.00 a
month for a one-bedroom apartment and $16.00 a month for a
three-bedroom unit. To be sure, it was impossible to build large,
multiple units rapidly enough to absorb the dramatically increasing population, but at least the problem had been acknowledged and a start made. To complement public housing, the
president also developed an incentive program designed to en-

A major campaign to eradicate malaria in 1962 and 1963 yielded positive results.

Curious villagers inspect the newly completed sewer system in the state of Chiapas.

URBAN-RURAL POPULATION DISTRIBUTION

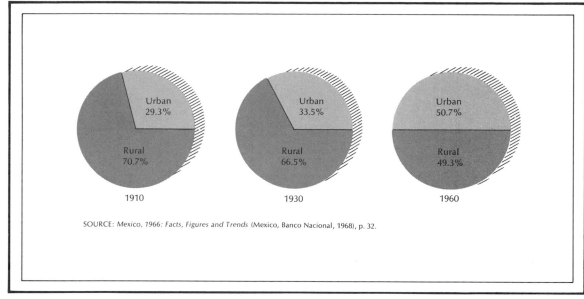

SOURCE: *Mexico, 1966: Facts, Figures and Trends* (Mexico, Banco Nacional, 1968), p. 32.

courage industry to stay away from the greater Mexico City environs. The emphasis on urban problems reflected a new reality in the demographic potpourri. In 1960, on the fiftieth anniversary of the Revolution, Mexico's urban population surpassed its rural population for the first time.

López Mateos's labor supporters were visibly shaken in 1959 when the president used federal troops to put down a major railroad strike. Arguing that the strike threatened to paralyze the country, he arrested a number of leaders, including Demetrio Vallejo, the head of the union. It was a bad start on the labor front. But the movement judged the new president too quickly and too harshly. His sympathies lay more clearly with the working class than any president since Mexico's industrial revolution began, and he set out to allay workers' fears. In an interesting move he decided to implement an almost forgotten article of the Constitution of 1917 that called for labor to share in the profits with management. In 1962 a special commission, the Comisión Nacional para el Reparto de Utilidades, was convoked to implement the profit-sharing plan. The formula agreed upon was complicated, dependent upon the amount of capital investment and the size of the labor force within each industry. But by 1964 many Mexican laborers were earning an extra 5 to 10 percent a year under the profit-sharing law.

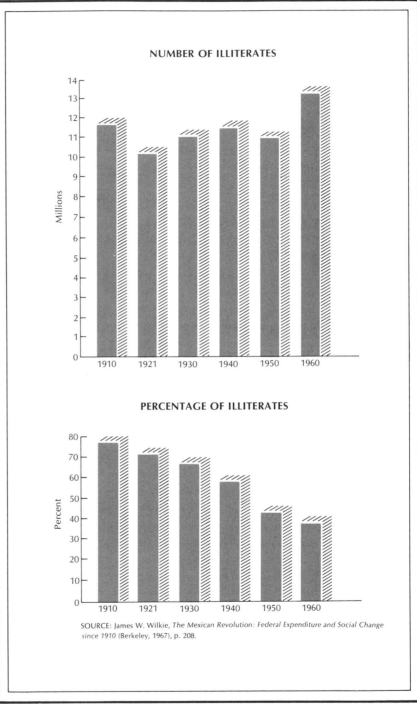

NUMBER OF ILLITERATES

Millions

1910 1921 1930 1940 1950 1960

PERCENTAGE OF ILLITERATES

Percent

1910 1921 1930 1940 1950 1960

SOURCE: James W. Wilkie, *The Mexican Revolution: Federal Expenditure and Social Change since 1910* (Berkeley, 1967), p. 208.

The educational policy of the López Mateos administration renewed the emphasis on the rural school. By 1963 education had become the largest single item in the Mexican budget, and the educational outlay was twice that allocated for national defense. The dramatic increase was made necessary by the revelation of some startling statistics in 1960. While the percentage of illiteracy in Mexico had been cut from some 77 percent in 1910 to less than 38 percent in 1960, the population explosion in a very real sense had nullified the results. In absolute numbers there were more illiterates in 1960 (13,200,000) than there had been at the time of the Plan de San Luis Potosí (11,658,000).

To attack illiteracy the president and his secretary of education, Jaime Torres Bodet, who had also served under Avila Camacho, launched a two-pronged assault. Through an ingenious system of prefabricated schools costing only $4,800 per unit, the number of rural classrooms increased rapidly. The government provided the building materials and the technical assistance, and the individual communities were called upon to provide the land and the actual labor. In this way villages were given a genuine stake in the educational process. Each unit contained unpretentious living quarters for the teacher, an important factor in convincing qualified teachers to venture into the rural areas.

Together with renewed emphasis on school construction, López Mateos decided to initiate a system of free and compulsory

In an attempt to reduce illiteracy, López Mateos revived the idea of adult reading classes.

textbooks. On this program he encountered opposition. Although
the books were prepared in consultation with some of the leading
scholars in the country, they did reflect the historiographical pre-
conceptions that had grown up with the Revolution, and the Roman Catholic Church took umbrage at the treatment afforded
many of its efforts throughout Mexican history. The National
Union of Parents Association, a conservative organization supported by the PAN and a number of leading clerics, led demonstrations against the books, insisting that their imposition on a
mandatory basis constituted a totalitarian act designed to stand-
ardize thought in the Mexican republic. At the same time radical
leftists opposed the textbooks because they exalted revolutionary
accomplishments and overlooked the shortcomings. But López
Mateos was not intimidated, and the books were adopted throughout the country over the protests.

If Mexico's rate of economic growth under López Mateos did
not quite keep pace with that under Miguel Alemán and Adolfo
Ruiz Cortines, the economy remained strong. British and French
capital poured into PEMEX's new petrochemical division. Private initiative constructed luxury hotels, and tourists came in
droves to Acapulco and the newly developed resort town of Puerto
Vallarta—and left behind millions of dollars that were put to
good use. By 1964 Mexico was self-sufficient in iron, steel, and
oil. Local capital no longer felt the need to seek investment fields
elsewhere and, indeed, purchased controlling stock in the Mexican telephone network. And in 1963 Mexican bonds were sold
on United States and European markets for the first time since
the Díaz regime. The country was still in its period of sustained
economic growth.

Foreign Policy

Mexico's foreign policy from 1958 to 1964 showed López Mateos
not unsympathetic to concerns of the left. Coming to the presidency only a few months before Fidel Castro's July 26 revolution
ousted rightest Cuban dictator Fulgencio Batista, López Mateos
occupied himself with defining the Mexican position on the most
crucial Latin American issue of the postwar period. To the chagrin of the United States, he opted for a policy of total nonintervention in Cuba's internal affairs. Arguing the national sovereignty and juridical equality of all states, Mexico refused to
condemn the Castro regime, voted against Cuba's expulsion from

the Organization of American States, did not endorse economic sanctions, and, most important, remained the only country in the Western Hemisphere to retain air service and diplomatic relations with Cuba. But the Mexican government was not prepared to accept dictates from Moscow either, and López Mateos condemned the Soviet Union in 1962 for placing offensive missiles in Cuba. Roll call votes in the United Nations verify that Mexico did not tie itself to either bloc but maintained an independent course. When French President Charles de Gaulle visited Mexico City in the spring of 1964 and was accorded the honor of being the first foreign head of state ever to speak from the presidential balcony overlooking the Plaza de la Constitución, the two leaders congratulated one another on escaping the tutelage of the superpowers. Mexico's independent foreign posture was a theme relayed in a series of trips that López Mateos and his close associates made to Yugoslavia, Poland, Indonesia, India, Canada, and a number of African countries.

By his own reckoning, López Mateos's greatest diplomatic victory concerned the final resolution of a century-old boundary dispute with the United States—the Chamizal controversy. At the end of the war with the United States the boundary had been set at the Rio Grande. But because of the sandy texture of the soil, especially in the area of El Paso, the river periodically shifted its bed. In 1864 it moved suddenly to the south, leaving some six hundred acres of Mexican territory north of the river in the state of Texas. Mexico, of course, claimed that this land, the Chamizal, was part of the national domain, but the various arbitration commissions had been unable to reach an accord suitable to the United States government. When President John F. Kennedy visited Mexico City in 1962, he was informed that the Chamizal continued to be a reminder of Yanqui imperialism and ordered the United States ambassador, Thomas Mann, to enter into new negotiations with the Mexican government for its final resolution. In the summer of 1963 the United States agreed to return the disputed territory to Mexico, to reimburse the El Paso residents for their lost property, and to share the costs of building a new international bridge and a concrete-lined channel to eliminate possible future disputes.

The Mexican public was elated when López Mateos appeared on a nationwide television news special to announce that "justice has come at last. . . . There is nothing left except to congratulate ourselves on the victory of law and reason."[1] An assassin's

1. Adolfo López Mateos, *El chamizal ya es Mexicano* (Mexico, 1964), pp. 47–51.

bullet took John Kennedy's life before he could sign the agreement, but his successor, Lyndon Johnson, met López Mateos at the Chamizal in September 1964 and formalized the arrangement amid sincere displays of goodwill. Through adroit diplomacy the Mexican president was considered a good friend of the United States—in spite of his failure to endorse a hostile policy toward Cuba, in spite of articulating an independent foreign policy, and in spite of his victories in the resolution of the Chamizal dispute.

Criticism of the One-Party System

Criticism of the PRI's monopoly on government continued to build during the López Mateos administration. His election in 1958 with 90 percent of the total vote marked thirty consecutive years of rule by the official party. The party not only had won every contest for the presidency but also had captured all of the senatorial and gubernatorial races. While electoral fraud might have contributed to some of the early victories, since 1934 there was no need to rig elections. The PRI had succeeded in identifying itself with the Revolution, and the Revolution was practically synonymous with the state. The PRI's colors—red, white, and green—were identical to those on the national flag; they appeared on its symbol on the ballot, and the lesson was not lost on even the illiterate. In addition, the party was able to mobilize bountiful resources to get its message across.

For many years Mexicans were willing to accept the PRI on its own terms, but by the early 1960s an increasingly sophisticated electorate began to question the bossism, favoritism, and corruption that had beset the PRI officialdom. A party without any genuine opposition was accountable to nobody. A party that could embrace the leftist policies of Cárdenas and the business-oriented policies of Alemán was ideologically bankrupt. How could it be expected to embark upon a meaningful redistribution of wealth designed to close the still gigantic gap between rich and poor? Alienation was broadly based, cutting across many class lines and most ideological persuasions. Effective democratization, in spite of potential obstacles, was deemed crucial. Properly conceived and skillfully channeled, it could lead to a developmental attitude that sought not only to increase the national product but to redistribute it. Pablo González Casanova, a distinguished Mexican social scientist, pinpointed this specific need when he argued in his perceptive *Democracy in Mexico:* "It is not enough to establish democratization formally in the under-developed countries in order to accelerate development, nor to imitate all of the specific forms of classic democracy in order to have democracy: democracy exists to the extent that the people share the income, culture, and power; anything else is demo-cratic folklore or rhetoric."[2]

López Mateos was not only willing to listen to criticism of the system; he was sensitive to it. Therefore he sponsored an amend-ment to the Constitution that altered the electoral procedures in the Chamber of Deputies. In order to broaden the opposition in the lower house of the legislature, his amendment provided that any party winning 2.5 percent of the national vote was entitled to five congressmen whether or not the candidates actually won their respective races. For every additional .5 percent of the vote these parties would receive an additional congressman, up to a total of twenty, each of whom would occupy a new seat, not re-place an elected congressman. Because of the new law the PAN received twenty congressional seats in the 1964 elections and the Partido Popular Socialista (PPS), ten seats. The electoral revi-sion by no means ended the debate on the shortcomings of Mex-ican democracy, but it did demonstrate a liberalizing tendency on the part of the presidential incumbent.

López Mateos is the most fondly remembered president of the postwar era. Like his contemporary in the United States, John F. Kennedy, part of his appeal undoubtedly lies in his style and charisma. But when the occasion demanded it, he exerted force-ful leadership. At the same time he was not doctrinaire and ap-preciated the value of compromise. Yielding to appeals and peti-tions, he made it a point to pardon muralist Siqueiros before he left office. Equally important to the favorable reputation he con-tinues to enjoy is the fact that he served his term at the right time, prior to the worldwide movement of social dissidence and student radicalism from which no head of state could emerge completely unscathed. Almost as soon as he left office he suffered a severe stroke and lay in a coma for six years until his death in 1970. He was eulogized as a nationalist who defended Mexican interests in the world community and a humane statesman who appreciated the concerns of the powerless masses at home. It is not difficult to agree on both counts. But Mexico in 1970 was a

---

2. Pablo González Casanova, *Democracy in Mexico* (New York, 1970), p. 194.

far different country from what it had been in 1964. In the post–
López Mateos years it was subjected to new tensions and the
spectacle of political violence once again.

Recommended for Further Study

Brandenburg, Frank. *The Making of Modern Mexico*. Englewood Cliffs,
    N.J.: Prentice-Hall, 1964.
Brown, Lyle C., and James W. Wilkie. "Recent United States–Mexican
    Relations: Problems Old and New." In *Twentieth Century Foreign
    Policy*, edited by John Braeman et al., pp. 378–419. Columbus: Ohio
    State University Press, 1971.
Cline, Howard F. *Mexico: Revolution to Evolution, 1940–1960*. New York:
    Oxford University Press, 1963.
Faust, John R., and Charles C. Stansifer. "Mexican Foreign Policy in the
    United Nations: The Advocacy of Moderation in an Era of Revolu-
    tion." *Southwestern Social Science Quarterly* 44 (1963): 121–29.
González Casanova, Pablo. *Democracy in Mexico*. New York: Oxford Uni-
    versity Press, 1970.
Hundley, Norris, Jr. *Dividing the Waters: A Century of Controversy be-
    tween the United States and Mexico*. Berkeley: University of Cali-
    fornia Press, 1966.
Johnson, Kenneth F. *Mexican Democracy: A Critical View*. Boston: Allyn
    and Bacon, 1971.
Liss, Sheldon. *A Century of Disagreement: The Chamizal Conflict, 1864–
    1964*. Washington, D.C.: University Press of Washington, D.C., 1965.
López Mateos, Adolfo. "Philosophy and Program of the Revolutionary
    Party." In *Is the Mexican Revolution Dead?* edited by Stanley R.
    Ross, pp. 169–74. New York: Knopf, 1966.
Machado, Manuel. *An Industry in Crisis: Mexican–United States Coopera-
    tion in the Control of Foot-and-Mouth Disease*. Berkeley: University
    of California Press, 1968.
Needler, Martin C. *Politics and Society in Mexico*. Albuquerque: Univer-
    sity of New Mexico Press, 1971.
Padgett, L. Vincent. *The Mexican Political System*. Boston: Houghton
    Mifflin, 1966.
Ross, Stanley R. "Mexico: Cool Revolution and Cold War." *Current History*
    41 (1963): 89–94, 116–17.
Schmitt, Karl M. *Mexico and the United States, 1821–1973*. New York:
    Wiley, 1974.
Vernon, Raymond. *The Dilemma of Mexico's Development: The Roles of
    the Private and Public Sectors*. Cambridge, Mass.: Harvard Univer-
    sity Press, 1963.

43

Sparks, Fire, and Smoldering, 1964–76

In spite of major breakthroughs in science and medicine and the space spectaculars that saw the United States place men on the moon, the late 1960s and early 1970s found a world full of tensions and hate. Modernization in general, and communications technology in particular, interlaced nations and dramatically shrank the globe. Word of Martin Luther King's assassination reached Angola only minutes after it reached Atlanta, and Robert Kennedy's assassination was known in Sao Paulo almost as soon as it was known in San Francisco. By the end of the 1960s the entire literate world knew that the United States had dropped a greater tonnage of bombs on Vietnam than the total dropped on all fronts during World War II. Massive marches for peace, for civil rights, and for the right of agricultural workers to organize were reported on the front pages of the world's press.

Mexicans in their living rooms, watching the evening news, saw the destruction of the black ghetto in Washington, the burning of Watts, and riots in Tokyo, Prague, and Berlin; they saw Parisian students pelting police on the Boulevard St. Michel and the senseless killing of students at Kent State University. Mexico's entire history demonstrates amply that Mexicans needed no foreign instruction in standing up for change or, if necessary, putting their lives on the line. And while the late 1960s did not witness any worldwide conspiracy of the young, there was a youthful commonality of interests that transcended national borders. The international pantheon of heroes, with a few national adaptations, included Che Guevara, Ho Chi Minh, Malcolm X, and Mao Tse-tung. The intellectually inclined devoured Herbert Marcuse, while others opted for the simpler, more doctrinaire answers of Fidel Castro. But, however an older generation might have been repulsed by the rebellion, shocked by its rhetoric, and disgusted by its tactics, many of the issues were real and deserved a fair hearing. In Mexico, as well as elsewhere, the sparks would soon begin to fly.

Díaz Ordaz and Political Discontent, 1964–70

When the PRI leadership chose Gustavo Díaz Ordaz as the presidential candidate for 1964, it badly misread the temper of the times. Díaz Ordaz had served as secretary of interior in the López Mateos cabinet and was badly tinged with policy decisions that reform-minded groups could not stomach. It had been he who applied the laws of "social dissolution" against David Alfaro Siqueiros and other radicals. Born in Puebla, the most Catholic state in Mexico, Díaz Ordaz was reputed to be the most conservative official party candidate of the twentieth century. But after winning the election by the customary official party margin, he pledged to carry out the policies initiated by his predecessor.

The electoral reform law that provided for minority representation in the lower house was interpreted to allow the seating of several minority parties in addition to the PAN—the PPS and, although it did not quite reach 2.5 percent of the vote, the Partido Auténtico de la Revolución Mexicana (PARM). But the PAN, the only genuine opposition party, received a very unfavorable ruling in the congressional elections. The congressional seats they actually won from PRI candidates would now be subtracted from the total of twenty they were allowed under López Mateos's constitutional amendment. The decision represented a rejection of the liberalizing tendency many hoped would continue to flourish. If there were any doubts about the trend, the sad and disappointing case of Carlos Madrazo removed them.

Shortly after coming to office, President Díaz Ordaz appointed Madrazo, a reform-minded liberal, to be president of the PRI. Championing a series of far-reaching innovations designed to promote internal democratization of the party, increase rank-and-file participation, reduce the vast power of local and state bosses, and bring more women into the organization, he ran headlong into the vested interests. In the spring of 1965, when Madrazo introduced new reforms designed to purify nomination procedures at the local level, the state political machines rose up in rebellion and, amid tremendous political uproar, prevailed upon Díaz Ordaz to fire him. That the president yielded to party pressure provided further testimony that the party liberalization urged by López Mateos was a thing of the past. As a matter of fact, just the opposite occurred. When PAN candidates won the mayoralties of Tijuana and Mexicali in Baja California, Norte, the government annulled the elections because of "irregularities." Opposition leaders who recalled that Díaz Ordaz had recently stated, "To us, political democracy is a living formula, even more, a way of life based on liberty,"[1] were once again reminded of the colonial maxim, *Obedezco pero no cumplo.* The official party, they contended, was stealing elections with total impunity. The party leadership had lost touch with the people and served simply as a vehicle for the realization of personal political ambitions.

The Olympic Games and Tlatelolco

Discontent with the official party was not limited to campaign headquarters. Campus after campus exploded with strikes and violence as local university issues merged with national political unrest. A massive strike at the National University in the spring of 1966 resulted in the resignation of the rector. Federal troops were dispatched to restore order on university campuses in Michoacán and Sonora. A major showdown was about to ensue, and the students picked their time very carefully. Mexico was planning its greatest extravaganza since the centennial celebrations of 1910.

When the International Olympic Committee accepted Mexico's bid to host the summer games in 1968, the world was informed that the Olympiad was to be held in Latin America and in a developing country for the first time. The challenge for Mexico was clear, for the Japanese had done a superb job in 1964 and it was incumbent upon the Mexicans to match their effort. Athletes, trainers, representatives of the press, and hundreds of thousands of visitors from the entire world would descend on Mexico and subject it to scrutiny. Construction of athletic facilities, hotels, housing projects, tourist facilities, and a new modern subway system preceded the games, and, amid some amazement, construction workers on round-the-clock shifts finished the

1. Quoted in Alfonso Corona del Rosal, ed., *Gustavo Díaz Ordaz: A Portrait of the President of Mexico for 1964–1970* (Mexico, n.d.), p. 32.

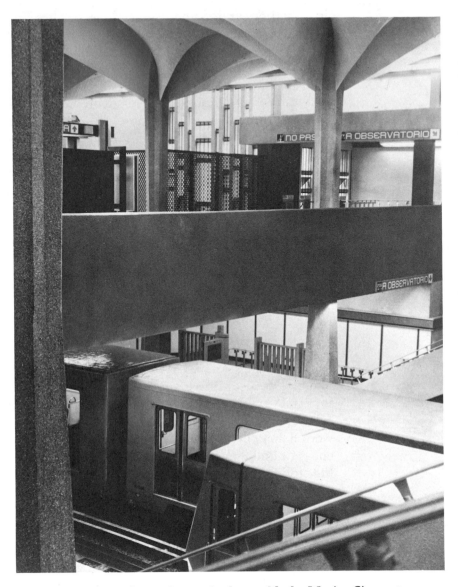

One of the most modern subways in the world, the Mexico City system was running to capacity and beyond within a few months of its completion. In 1990, more than 5 million Mexico City passengers were using the eighty-seven miles of the metro's double tracks every day. Plans to add an additional thirty-seven miles of track were cancelled because of financial exigencies.

Excavation for the subway uncovered hundreds of priceless pre-Columbian artifacts.

major installations on time. To add a unique flavor to the international sports spectacular, a cultural Olympics was scheduled simultaneously, featuring international art exhibitions, book displays, lectures, concerts, and plays. Early charges from critics that the costs were exorbitant for a country such as Mexico were fended off by administration spokesmen who argued that not only would the visitors leave behind tens of millions of dollars but the facilities themselves would be put to good use once the Olympic torch was extinguished. The party and the president were placing all their prestige on the line. The country, they insisted, would show itself as a prosperous and stable republic.

The trouble began almost innocently in July 1968 with a fight between the students of two Mexico City schools, a college preparatory school and a nearby vocational school. The principal of the high school called for police help, and the mayor of the Federal District, General Alfonso Corona del Rosal, erred badly in sending out the *granaderos*, a despised paramilitary riot force. The granaderos stopped the intramural fight but in the process politicized a large portion of the student population in Mexico City. A few days later, as leftist students gathered to celebrate the July 26 anniversary of the Cuban Revolution, they met the granaderos again, and on this occasion a full-scale street riot ensued. But nobody had yet been killed.

August 1968 was a very bad month in Mexico. As city workers were putting the finishing touches on the various construction projects, tensions between the students and the government reached the breaking point. Huge demonstrations were held on the campuses of the National University and the National Polytechnic Institute, and a National Student Strike Committee was formed. A list of demands accentuated tensions; students insisted that all political prisoners be released, that the chief of police be fired, that the granaderos be disbanded, and that the law of "social dissolution" be repealed. Secretary of Interior Luis Echeverría agreed to enter into private discussions with the student leadership, but when the students demanded that the dialogue be broadcast publicly on radio and television, negotiations broke down. On August 27 the National Student Strike Committee brought together in the Zócalo an estimated half a million people, the largest organized antigovernment demonstration in Mexican history. The rally lasted well into the night, and when the government moved tanks and armored cars into the downtown area, violence and the first verified student death resulted.

President Díaz Ordaz's State of the Union address on September 1, 1968, was not full of typical revolutionary platitudes. With the Olympic Games a little over a month away, he had to address himself to the issue of student unrest and respond to the demands.

> It is obvious that hands other than those of students were involved in the recent disturbances; but it is also a fact that . . . a good number of students took part in the affair. . . . I do not admit that there are "political prisoners." A "political prisoner" is one who has been deprived of his freedom *exclusively* because of his political ideas, without having committed any crime. Nevertheless, if I am informed of the name of any person who has been incarcerated without due process of law . . . orders will be given for his immediate unconditional release. . . . With regard to Articles 145 and 145b of the Penal Code, the first of which refers to the crime known as "social dissolution," the abolition of which is requested, let me make it clear that:
> The abolition of a law is not within the powers of the President. . . .
> We have caused Mexico to appear in the eyes of the world as a country in which the most reprehensible events may take place; for the unfair and almost forgotten image of the Mexican as a

violent, irascible gunman to be revived; and for slander to be mixed with painful truth in the same news reports.[2]

While some of the speech was conciliatory, most of it was hard line. The students were concerned with lack of freedom and the president with lack of security. The worst was yet to come. In the middle of September, with the capital bedecked with Olympic flags and signs of welcome and the students occupying the campus of the National University, Díaz Ordaz ordered ten thousand army troops, in full battle dress, to seize the campus. Some five hundred demonstrators were thrown into jail, and the new rector of the university, Javier Barros Sierra, resigned in protest of the army occupation of his campus. For two weeks, bands of disgruntled students and other malcontents who were in no way associated with the university roamed Mexico City streets, periodically seizing and burning buses, barricading streets, and pillaging. The climax came on October 2, 1968, at a place that will not be forgotten in Mexican history—Tlatelolco.

Strike organizers called for still another outdoor rally at the Plaza de las Tres Culturas in the District of Tlatelolco. The purpose was to berate the government for its failure to comply with the earlier demands. The rally was not large by recent standards, perhaps only five thousand, including many women, children, and innocent spectators. The speeches were emotional, but the demonstration was peaceful. At about 6:30 p.m., army and police units arrived in tanks and armored vehicles. When the demonstrators failed to disband as ordered, the granaderos moved in and began to disperse them with billy clubs and tear gas. What happened next will never be completely clarified. The government version, carried the next day in the Mexican press, claimed that terrorists in nearby apartment buildings began firing on the police. Others insisted that the police opened fire first and that only then did snipers in the buildings begin to shoot. At any rate, when the army units uncovered their high-caliber machine guns and other automatic weapons, thousands of innocent people were caught in the cross fire. Helicopters dropped flares into the crowds, and the troops, opting not to err on the side of safety, sprayed indiscriminately from short range. Official government statistics admitted first eight, then eighteen, and finally forty-three deaths, but few knowledgeable Mexicans accepted mortality figures under three or four hundred. Ambu-

2. Gustavo Díaz Ordaz, "State of the Union Address, September 1, 1968," in *Models of Change in Latin America*, ed. Paul E. Sigmund (New York, 1970), pp. 38–44.

The Plaza de las Tres Culturas, a tourist attraction for thousands, became a battleground for hundreds in October 1968. *Courtesy of James W. Wilkie.*

lances wailed through the night as hospitals and clinics filled beyond capacity with the wounded and dying. By the next morning, Mexico City jails held over two thousand new prisoners. The object lesson was clear. Political opponents were better eliminated than tolerated. One has only to recall the trauma that engulfed the United States after Kent State, a tragedy of much lesser proportion, to appreciate the anger and despair that Mexicans felt as the story was gradually pieced together over the next few days. But despair quickly gave way to recriminations as Carlos Madrazo attributed the killings to police brutality. The decision had been a political one, and it greatly altered public perception of the country's leadership.

The Olympic Games themselves were notably free of turbulence, and it appeared that the violence had spent itself. The year that followed was a period of reflection for many Mexicans. But in October 1969, on the anniversary of the tragedy at Tlatelolco, Mexicans became aware that urban guerrilla groups had been planning to renew their fight with the administration. Terrorist bombs ripped newspaper offices and government buildings. It was a bad omen as Díaz Ordaz neared the end of his term. The fire of Tlatelolco had been largely extinguished, but social smoldering would continue to choke the country for years. It would become increasingly apparent that much of the PRI's legitimacy had been eroded at the Plaza de las Tres Culturas.

Díaz Ordaz had fostered a number of important social and economic programs during his tenure as president. Federal expenditure for education reached over 26 percent of the total budget, one of the highest rates in the entire world. Urban renewal projects in the northern border cities catered to the tourist trade, and tourists left record amounts of money in Ciudad Juárez, Tijuana, Nogales, Piedras Negras, and Matamoros. The economy remained healthy, registering 6 percent annual increases in the gross national product. Mexico took the lead in international conferences, securing pledges that Latin America should be declared a nuclear free zone. Under other circumstances, Díaz Ordaz might have been remembered for these accomplishments, but, just as the administration of Richard M. Nixon will be remembered less for finally extricating the United States from Vietnam than for the shame of Watergate, the name of Díaz Ordaz will always be associated with the unpardonable tragedy at Tlatelolco.

The Presidency of Echeverría

The political atmosphere had not returned to normal when Mexico held its 1970 presidential election. PRI candidate Luis Echeverría had been secretary of interior during the recent Olympic trouble, and the Mexican left held him largely responsible for the government's overreaction. With a reputation for inflexibility and intolerance, he scarcely seemed the man to foster an atmosphere of national consensus. Echeverría decided to campaign vigorously, yet he failed to capture public imagination and left many wondering when he declared that Mexico, a country that had experienced an increase in population of some 14 million since 1960, had no need for family planning.

During the first year of his term, President Echeverría showed himself as a man of boundless energy; he put in long hours and demanded the same of those who surrounded him. He nurtured himself on face-to-face dialogue with farmers in dusty villages and workers in urban factories. Not nearly as inflexible as portrayed, he quickly began to counter his reputation by moving to the center and then to the left. To the chagrin of the conservative business community, he began renewing initiatives in rural Mexico and even announced that perhaps industrialization had to slow down. A major emphasis was placed on extending the rural road system and rural electrification. Caught in the worldwide inflation of the early 1970s, he tried to minimize its impact on the poor by ordering rigid price controls of basic commodities; at the same time, luxury items were hit with a new tax of 10 percent, and a 15 percent surtax was added to all bills in first-class restaurants and night clubs. Echeverría even moderated his stand on family planning and halfway through his administration gave a cautious endorsement to birth control. But Echeverría surprised his critics most when he released the majority of Mexico's student prisoners in early 1971.

The transition from Díaz Ordaz to Luis Echeverría seemed to be going well until in late 1971 and early 1972 Mexicans learned that the violent legacy of Tlatelolco was not yet over. A series of bank robberies in the fall were traced to the Movimiento Armado Revolucionario (MAR) when gunmen bragged that their exploits were in behalf of the coming revolution. Other robberies and political kidnappings followed: Jaime Castrejón, rector of the University of Guerrero, and Julio Hirschfield, director of the nation's airports, both fell into rebel hands. But there was still more to come. Terrance Leonhardy, United States consul general in Guadalajara, was kidnapped, as were the British honorary consul, Anthony Duncan Williams; Fernando Aranguren, a wealthy Guadalajara businessman; and Nadine Chaval, the daughter of the Belgian ambassador. A wealthy Monterrey industrialist, Eugenio Garza Sada, was killed during a kidnapping attempt, and a train carrying tourists was assaulted in southern Sonora, resulting in the deaths of four travelers. In the summer of 1974, President Echeverría's father-in-law, Guadalupe Zuno Hernández, a former governor of Jalisco, was captured and held for ransom by a group calling themselves the Fuerzas Revolucionarias Armadas del Pueblo (FRAP).

In the mountains of Guerrero, Lucio Cabañas, a flamboyant former schoolteacher, gathered a guerrilla army, had the police chief of Acapulco assassinated, and began attacking small army outposts stationed in the state. The eyes of the nation focused on Cabañas when guerrillas under his command kidnapped Guerrero senator Rubén Figueroa, at the time a candidate for governor. Ten thousand army troops were dispatched to Guerrero to capture the guerrillas, but it took them over a year to do the job.

Luis Echeverría (b. 1922). The most active president since Cárdenas, Echeverría was interested primarily in foreign policy, but his energies were directed to the country's serious economic woes.

Cabañas and twenty-seven of his men were killed in gun battles with the army, but most observers were convinced that another guerrilla leader would simply pick up his banner.

When United States ambassador Joseph John Jova told the Mexican Chamber of Commerce in September 1974 that "there is no large scale opposition to the federal government,"[3] one might have been reminded that in November 1910 Ambassador Henry Lane Wilson had made similar statements. But where Wilson was wrong, Jova was essentially correct. In spite of the headlines in the morning newspapers, Mexico was not yet falling apart at the seams. Pressures were building, but Echeverría had made major attempts to accommodate the interests of youth. He brought more young people into important positions in the government than any previous head of state. The voting age was lowered to eighteen, the age for holding a Senate seat from thirty-five to thirty, and for holding membership in the Chamber of Deputies from thirty to twenty-one. Other administration programs should have been well received by youth. Mexico granted diplomatic asylum to Hortensia Allende, widow of the murdered Chilean president. In 1972 the administration nationalized the tobacco and telephone industries. Echeverría's foreign travels opened new avenues of trade and, by extension, sought to lessen dependence

3. Joseph John Jova, "American Business and Mexican Development," address to the Mexican Chamber of Commerce, September 11, 1974 (mimeographed, 1974).

upon the United States. Yet all these measures were ineffectual palliatives.

Alienation had set it, and the roots went deep. To be sure, part of the problem could be attributed to the inflation rate, which topped 20 percent in both 1973 and 1974. But to ascribe the alienation simply to rate of inflation or even to the gradual demise of Mexico's postwar economic miracle would be to miss the point. In at least one sense some of the Revolution's successes, rather than its shortcomings, contributed to the growing tensions in Mexican society. As Stanley R. Ross noted in an article assessing the stresses in Mexico in the early 1970s:

> There is a fair amount of evidence which suggests that rapid economic growth may of and by itself adversely affect societal stability. Specifically it disrupts the existing social structure and increases the numbers who are gainers and losers. Rising literacy, exposure to mass communications, and other advances in integrating the nation produce rising demands on the political system. Equally important is the creation of rising expectations that soon outdistance the capacity of even a rapidly expanding economy to satisfy them.[4]

Other factors contributed to the alienation as well, and not least among them was the manner in which the Revolution had propagandized itself over the years. By the late 1960s and early 1970s, the young, sophisticated generation of Mexican students had absorbed an incredible amount of revolutionary rhetoric. A not untypical Sunday outing in Mexico City could include a car or taxi ride by the Monument to the Revolution and then on to Avenida 20 de Noviembre, where the book stores carried posters not of Sophia Loren and Farrah Fawcett-Majors but of Emiliano Zapata and Pancho Villa. Then, on Avenida Francisco I. Madero the walls would be plastered with billboards propagandizing the Partido Revolucionario Institucional. And on Sunday evening every radio station in the country carried "La Hora Nacional," a musical and cultural presentation interspersed with three- to four-minute orations on themes such as "The Pride of Being Mexican." "One Must Defend the Revolution," and "The March of Revolutionary Progress."

The spate of revolutionary euphemisms became more than the young intellectual could easily accept. Fewer and fewer Mexicans were content to look south toward Guatemala and beyond and, by comparison, to feel gratitude for their own Revolution.

4. Stanley R. Ross, "México: Las tensiones del progreso," *Latinoamérica* 4 (1971): 9–21.

Disquieting everyday realities denied the easy revolutionary platitudes. And when late in his term President Echeverría attempted to address a student convocation at the National University, he was driven off the campus by an angry, rock-throwing mob, calling for forceful action, not mindless rhetoric. But even in December 1975, Luis Echeverría most assuredly could not have realized that a year later he would leave office under a tremendous cloud of controversy. His successor would inherit a dispirited country, one in which cynicism had become a hallmark. The roots of the problem were economic, but they meshed with ideological postures and social realities to produce an unparalleled crisis of confidence.

The 1970s found Mexico suffering a large balance of payments deficit. The rate of industrial growth had been impressive, but it had rested on the foundation of government protection. Mexican industry was not cost effective and was not generally competitive on world markets. It was unable to turn the balance of payments tide. With imports outstripping exports by almost $3.5 billion in 1975 alone, Echeverría, currying Third World support in a bid for the secretary-generalship of the United Nations, ordered his ambassador in the world organization to cast two votes equating Zionism with racism. Since he had earlier made a speech comparing Yasser Arafat to Benito Juárez, the result shouldn't have surprised him. In early 1976 Jewish groups in the United States organized a tourist boycott of Mexico. Empty resort hotels dramatically testified that a substantial proportion of Mexico's tourist industry of $2.5 billion had been curtailed. Other factors, such as shortages of electric power, steel, and transportation facilities, contributed to a decline in the rate of economic growth. Echeverría had repeatedly lectured his citizenry on the need for democratization in Mexico and the value of a free press. As the economic situation deteriorated, however, he found himself attacked on all sides. When criticism from Mexico's largest daily newspaper, *Excelsior*, became too severe, the administration removed its editor, Julio Scherer García. By the summer of 1976, rumors were rampant that for the first time in twenty-two years Mexico would have to devalue the peso. The president's repeated assurances to the contrary did not prevent the flight of huge amounts of pesos as wealthy Mexicans exchanged their currency for dollars and investment in the United States and Europe. Capital flight in 1976 alone might have topped $6 billion. Mexican pundits quickly coined a new pejorative to deride their unpatriotic countrymen. *Sacadólares* (dollar extractors) would enter the day-to-day parlance.

The decision to devaluate came in September, and the peso fell from 12.50 to 20.50 to the dollar, a 60 percent devaluation. Once the initial shock subsided, Mexicans accepted the devaluation stoically, as they were assured that the resultant reduction of imports and growth of exports would combine to shore up the economy. But Mexican policy makers had not allowed the peso to float long enough to reach its true level. A month later a second devaluation of an additional 40 percent was announced in Mexico City. Psychologically, the second was more painful than the first, for it pointed up financial mismanagement of major proportions.

With the country still in shock, a serious old problem surfaced once again. Thousands of landless Sonora peasants moved onto privately owned lands in the rich Yaqui Valley and seized several hundred thousand acres from some eight hundred owners. Although the land seizures were being adjudicated in the Mexican Supreme Court, Echeverría, with not two weeks remaining in his presidential term, took matters into his own hands. He declared the seizures legal and gave the peasants 250,000 acres for communal development. The uproar could have been expected; Mexican industrialists and businessmen joined the former landowners in a huge protest strike. Yet to the more ardent agrarian radicals of the 1970s the presidential expropriation decree was disingenuous tokenism of the worst kind, a ploy to gain Echeverría a historical niche in the Cárdenas tradition.

The twelve years encompassed by the Díaz Ordaz and Echeverría administrations, 1964 to 1976, were difficult ones in Mexico's post–World War II experience. Since the onset of the institutional revolution in the early 1940s, Mexican confidence had been bolstered repeatedly by the country's political stability and remarkable economic success. Mexico seemingly had separated itself from the systemic problems of its neighbors to the south. But by 1975 and 1976, it was obvious to Mexicans and foreigners alike that the political system and economic structure had proved themselves to be quite fragile. This fragility would be severely tested in the years to come.

Recommended for Further Study

Anderson, Bo, and James D. Cockcroft. "Control and Co-optation in Mexican Politics." In *Dependence and Underdevelopment*, edited by James D. Cockcroft et al., pp. 220–43. Garden City, N.Y.: Doubleday, 1972.

Blough, William J. "Political Attitudes of Mexican Women: Support for the Political System among a Newly Enfranchised Group." *Journal of Inter-American Studies and World Affairs* 14 (1972): 201–24.

Cochrane, James D. "Mexico's New Científicos: The Díaz Ordaz Cabinet." *Inter-American Economic Affairs* 21 (1967): 61–72.

"Documents on the Student Revolt of 1968." In *Models of Political Change in Latin America*, edited by Paul Sigmund, pp. 33–44. New York: Praeger, 1970.

Eckstein, Susan. *The Poverty of Revolution: The State and the Urban Poor in Mexico*. Princeton, N.J.: Princeton University Press, 1977.

Erb, Richard D., and Stanley R. Ross, eds. *U.S. Policies toward Mexico: Perceptions and Perspectives*. Washington, D.C.: American Enterprise Institute for Public Policy Research, 1979.

Grindle, Merilee S. *Bureaucrats, Politicians, and Peasants in Mexico: A Case Study in Public Policy*. Berkeley: University of California Press, 1977.

Hansen, Roger D. *The Politics of Mexican Development*. Baltimore: Johns Hopkins University Press, 1971.

Johnson, Kenneth F. *Mexican Democracy: A Critical View*. Boston: Allyn and Bacon, 1971.

Liebman, Arthur. "Student Activism in Mexico." *Annals of the American Society of Political and Social Science* 395 (1971): 159–70.

Lomnitz, Larissa Adler. *Networks and Marginality: Life in a Mexican Shantytown*. New York: Academic Press, 1977.

Needler, Martin C. *Politics and Society in Mexico*. Albuquerque: University of New Mexico Press, 1971.

Paz, Octavio. *The Other Mexico: Critique of the Pyramid*. New York: Grove Press, 1972.

Pellicer de Brody, Olga. "Mexico in the 1970's and Its Relations with the United States." In *Latin America and the United States*, edited by Julio Cotler and Richard R. Fagen, pp. 314–33. Stanford, Calif.: Stanford University Press, 1974.

Ross, Stanley, ed. *Views Across the Border*. Albuquerque: University of New Mexico Press, 1978.

Schmidt, Samuel. *The Deterioration of the Mexican Presidency*. Tucson: University of Arizona Press, 1991.

Sepúlveda, César. "Student Participation in University Affairs." *American Journal of Comparative Law* 17 (1969): 384–89.

Shapira, Yoram. *Mexican Foreign Policy Under Echeverría*. Beverly Hills, Calif.: Sage, 1978.

Williams, Edward J. *The Rebirth of the Mexican Petroleum Industry*. Lexington, Mass.: Heath, 1979.

Womack, John, Jr. "The Spoils of the Mexican Revolution." *Foreign Affairs* 48 (1970): 677–87.

44

Mexico since 1976: The Tensions of Development and Democratization

José López Portillo and Petropolitics

On December 1, 1976, José López Portillo, the presidential candidate of the PRI, replaced Luis Echeverría in the Mexican presidency. While a few Mexicans evidenced optimism on that inauguration day, the vast majority found little cause for celebration. Sixty-six years had passed since Francisco Madero's Plan de San Luis Potosí, but many believed that the same old problems had emerged once again.

Prior to the famous Arab oil embargo in the early 1970s, the world thought little about energy, conservation, or the influence of petroleum and petroleum by-products on inflation and power politics. But these issues dominated the national and international press in the late 1970s and early 1980s. In some circles it became archaic to speak of the First, Second, and Third worlds. It seemed more appropriate to categorize nations as oil producers and oil consumers, and this, in turn, necessitated new conceptualizations of dependency and interdependency.

The large petroleum discoveries made in southeastern Mexico (primarily in the state of Tabasco and Chiapas and offshore in the Gulf of Mexico) antedated the inauguration of President José López Portillo in 1976, but their extent and influence grew markedly during his administration and came to overshadow every-

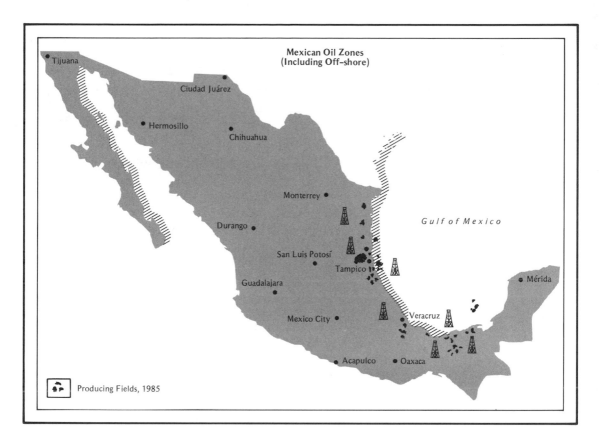

Mexican Oil Zones
(Including Off-shore)

Producing Fields, 1985

thing else. The figures for proven and probable reserves have varied tremendously since the discoveries were first announced in 1974. But in 1980, López Portillo verified that proven reserves topped 60 billion barrels, while probable reserves approached 200 billion.

From the outset, López Portillo followed a policy of gradual, not dramatic, daily increase. Although Mexico had the necessary capital and technology to increase production with great rapidity, it resisted pressures from the United States and other foreign powers to do so. The economic infrastructure was not prepared to digest suddenly huge infusions of foreign capital without negative side effects. More important, it then seemed obvious that the price of petroleum in the future was not doing to decline. Oil production rose steadily but sensibly during the López Portillo years, growing from about 800,000 barrels per day in 1976 to 2.3 million barrels a day in 1980. In 1981 Mexico became the world's fourth largest producer. The tripling of production during the administration did not reveal the whole story of how petroleum

influenced the Mexican economy. For two reasons, Mexico's earning of petrodollars rose much more rapidly than the increased
production figures would seem to suggest. First, a large percentage of the increase was destined for the international, not the
domestic, market. Even more important was the steadily spiral-
ing price of a barrel of crude. During the same period that production tripled, earnings from petroleum sales increased twelve-
fold, from $500 million in 1976 to about $6 billion in 1980.
Prospects for a healthy and dynamic economy never looked
better.

Mexican petroleum wealth had an incalculable impact on how
the country viewed itself and how it related to others in the international community. In an energy-hungry world, petroleum
production carried unusual international prestige. Mexico's new

GROWTH OF THE MEXICAN PETROLEUM INDUSTRY

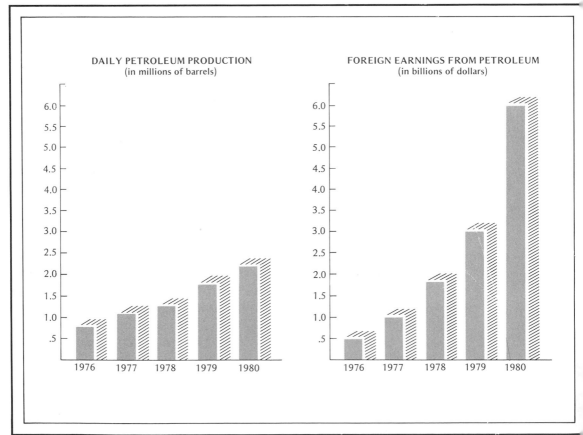

DAILY PETROLEUM PRODUCTION
(in millions of barrels)

FOREIGN EARNINGS FROM PETROLEUM
(in billions of dollars)

oil muscle was flexed repeatedly in its relations with the United States. Standing up to Washington and Wall Street, even in the face of threats, was nothing new in the history of the Mexican Revolution. What was different was the self-assurance Mexico carried into the international arena. The United States of Jimmy Carter had to learn that Mexico's support of foreign policy initiatives from Washington could not be taken for granted unless they were judged by Mexicans to be in Mexico's best interests. In a dramatic but symbolic gesture, López Portillo was one of the first Latin American heads of state to announce that his country could not support the Carter administration's boycott of the Moscow Olympics. When the United States and Mexico could not agree on the price of natural gas, the Mexican president simply decided to burn off excess gas rather than sell to the United States at a figure judged to be inequitable.

Mexico's new international posture was most graphically displayed during President Carter's goodwill visit to Mexico City in 1979. López Portillo, who never tired of berating his northern neighbor, used the occasion to chastise the United States for its historical record in Mexico, to criticize his guest for being insensitive to Mexican dignity, and to warn Carter against "surprise moves or sudden deceits." The new administration of Ronald Reagan quickly learned that outward manifestations of friendship and goodwill would not change Mexico's foreign policy. In 1981 Mexico joined France in a declaration recognizing rebel guerrillas in El Salvador as a representative political force. These incidents were less a new hostility than were they a reflection of the new petroleum equation in United States–Mexican relations.

Only the most naïve considered petroleum a panacea for Mexico's sundry social and economic problems, but few realized the dangers that petro-dependency portended for the future. The first indications of trouble were faint and subtle. By the late 1970s, López Portillo was faced with an unemployment rate of almost 25 percent and an underemployment rate of almost 50 percent of the country's work force. Petroleum was a capital-intensive, not a labor-intensive industry. With continuing increased production it could absorb perhaps 150,000 new workers each year, but by 1980, 800,000 Mexicans were entering the job market annually. Jobs would have to be created in other sectors of the economy.

Industry maintained healthy growth during the López Portillo administration, but agricultural production could not keep pace with the increase in population. Fearful that the newly found petrodollars could all be expended on food imports, in March

Between 1980 and 1982, Presidents José López Portillo and Ronald Reagan met on four occasions. The public cordiality of the visits notwithstanding, the two countries found it difficult to agree on important issues such as undocumented workers and the revolutionary turmoil in Central America.

1980 the president announced the formation of Sistema Alimentario Mexicano (SAM), the Mexican Food System. The first major coordinated effort to increase agricultural production in the postwar period, SAM's goals called for agricultural growth of 4 percent a year and self-sufficiency in basic grains by 1985. A few months after SAM was proclaimed, the World Bank approved a loan of $325 million, the largest loan that agency ever made, to help implement the program. SAM was an extremely important undertaking. Increased agricultural production not only promised to improve the standard of living in rural areas, but by eliminating the need for huge food imports would greatly improve Mexico's unfavorable balance of trade. The goals were certainly sound, but the success rate fell short of spectacular. Several years after López Portillo left office, Mexico was still importing about 10 million tons of food annually.

Mexico's 1980 census, conducted two-thirds through the López Portillo administration, revealed one very promising trend. In the early postwar years, the percentage of illiterates in Mexico was constantly reduced, but because of the population explosion, the absolute number of illiterates rose. The 1980 census documented not only a decline in the percentage of illiterates from 28 percent in 1970 to 17.1 percent in 1980, but a drop of 1.5 million in the absolute number of illiterates. The education efforts of all the postwar administrations had finally left their mark.

The Economic Slide Begins

López Portillo led Mexico on an unparalleled spending spree. Government construction, public works, social welfare projects, and government subsidies of consumer goods all meant an increased government participation in the economy. Although national income was insufficient to cover the costs, Mexico's vast petroleum reserves made the international banking community willing, indeed eager, to extend large loans. Mexico's massive deficit spending was predicated on the supposition that continuing rises in the price of oil would allow the country to generate new wealth and repay its foreign obligations. But contrary to all expectations, petroleum prices did not rise. Because of the world oil glut of the early 1980s, they began to decline, and this fact changed the nature of the Mexican political equation. López Portillo was forced to retreat from his assertive foreign policy and adopt a more moderate stance.

In 1982, during the last year of his administration, López Portillo found himself in a position which seemed similar to that of Luis Echeverría in 1976. Actually it was much worse. The Mexican rate of inflation greatly exceeded that in the United States, and the peso was again over-valued in relation to the dollar. As Mexican businessmen lost confidence in the economy, they began investing abroad and opening new bank accounts in the United States. To stop the monetary flight, in February the president ordered the Central Bank to stop buying and selling dollars and to allow the peso to find its true worth. Within a few days, it had lost one-third of its former value as it slipped from 26 to 37 pesos to the dollar, and by summer of 1982 had sunk to 100 pesos, marking the peso's lowest value ever. Concomitant price increases and tight currency controls created near panic in both business and government circles. It was only the tip of the iceberg.

In the last analysis, López Portillo applied the brakes too late, after he had first tried to squander Mexico into prosperity. The oil miracle had become the oil nightmare, and the president came under severe fire for mishandling the economy and demon-

strating a lack of judgment and leadership. His response was un-
anticipated as he accused the country's private banks of looting,
greed, and disloyalty for participating in the frenzied flight of
Mexican capital in the amount of $22 billion. He had found a
perfect scapegoat. In September 1982, without first soliciting any
advice from his cabinet, the president dramatically nationalized
fifty-nine of the country's banks. In a high state of exhilaration,
he lectured his countrymen: "A group of Mexicans, led, counseled, and aided by the private banks, has taken more money out
of the country than all the empires that have exploited us since
the beginning. . . . We cannot stand with our arms crossed while
they tear out our entrails."[1] The nationalization of the banks was
no economic elixir. Many of them were in bad financial shape
and assuming their burden was like putting chains on the national
economy. The presidential action proved only that clear thinking
seldom accompanies clenched fists.

As López Portillo's administration came to an end, Mexicans
were incensed to learn that the president, in spite of his pious
incantations about others, had taken care of himself prior to the
expiration of his term of office. He had constructed four large
mansions for himself and his family on prime land. The lofty site
of the López Portillo compound was dubbed "Dog Hill," a sarcastic reminder of the president's earlier remarks that he would
defend the peso "like a dog." As he departed Mexico for an extended vacation in Europe, he left behind Mexico's worst economic crisis of the twentieth century.

Miguel de la Madrid: From Crisis to Crisis, 1982–88

When forty-seven-year-old Miguel de la Madrid was told that
he had won the Mexican presidency, he reportedly quipped to
a friend, "Fraud, fraud!" If he did repeat those words, one could
scarcely have blamed him. He faced the sobering prospect of inheriting the leadership of a country beset with economic problems so serious that they threatened to disrupt the social order.

Educated at the Universidad Nacional Autónoma de México
and subsequently at Harvard University, Miguel de la Madrid's
rise to his country's highest office was nothing short of meteoric.
In spite of his relative youth, his formal education and previous
experience in public administration prepared him better for the

---

1. Quoted in Judith Adler Hellman, *Mexico in Crisis* (New York, 1983), p. 225.

Elected in July, 1982, Miguel de la Madrid succeeded López Portillo as president. He recognized that he would face difficult times but could not have predicted that the country was on the verge of economic collapse.

tasks that lay ahead than most of his twentieth-century predecessors. He had campaigned on a firm pledge of moral renovation, a promise to eliminate the corruption so endemic in the Mexican public sector. Those who accused him of political posturing were proven wrong. During his first year in office, revelations of corruption during the administration of López Portillo were carried in the front pages of the press almost on a daily basis. Although President de la Madrid did not prosecute his predecessor, he did strike out against other high-ranking government officials. In one spectacular case, Jorge Díaz Serrano, the former director of PEMEX, was indicted for embezzlement of $43 million. Serrano was convicted and sentenced to a ten-year jail term. Even more outrageous were the alleged crimes of Arturo Durazo, Mexico City's chief of police and a friend of López Portillo since childhood. "El Negro Durazo" was charged with fifty murders, trafficking in drugs, and extortion of superlative proportions. His luxurious residence in the coastal resort of Zihuatanejo was nicknamed "The Parthenon," to which it bore some resemblance. His palatial home near Mexico City came complete with its own discotheque, modeled after New York City's famous Studio 54. Weekend guests, flown to the $2.5 million estate in police helicopters, marvelled at Durazo's string of race horses, nineteen collector's automobiles, casino, gymnasium, and cellar of vintage wines. Not even the most shrewd businessmen, they opined, could have accumulated this kind of fortune on a government salary of $65 per week. But Durazo escaped prosecution by fleeing the country prior to the order for his arrest. United States law enforcement officials arrested him in Puerto Rico and sent him to Los Angeles to await extradition papers from Mexico City, but the process was delayed endlessly as the money in Durazo's foreign bank accounts, reported to total some $600 million, permitted him to hire one of the most prestigious law firms in California to fight the legal process. They delayed Durazo's extradition until the spring of 1986, when he was returned to Mexico and subsequently convicted.

The president received his share of accolades for his two highly publicized victories against the egregious dishonesty of Díaz Serrano and Durazo, but there was little euphoria as Mexicans knew that the battle against governmental malfeasance had scarcely been won. The country's comptroller general synopsized the issue perfectly when he stated that Mexican corruption was like garbage: it had to be removed daily. He was calling for a type of moral stamina that was difficult to find.

An equally persistent dilemma was the country's deepening economic crisis. The peso began to slip against the dollar in 1984 and then began a veritable plunge on the free market. Many stood in disbelief as it plummeted from 150 to 200, and then to 380 to the dollar during the summer of 1985, but the bottom had not been reached. By autumn 1986, currency houses and money brokers along the U.S.–Mexican border were exchanging the peso at an incredible 800 to 1. The year 1987 was even more catastrophic for the peso. When the year opened it took 950 pesos to purchase a dollar, but by December the exchange rate was an incredible 2,300 to 1. The relationship between the two countries' currencies was so out of kilter in the summer of 1987 that a U.S. tourist could ride the Mexico City metro over two thousand times for one dollar or make ten thousand calls on a pay phone for the same amount. The 20-centavo coins were worth so little that owners of hardware stores in Sonora drilled holes in their middles and sold them as washers.

Mexico's foreign debt under Miguel de la Madrid grew in geometric proportion. Although the president was able to arrange a rescheduling of payments on the debt, the pressure on him was tremendous. Political parties, peasant groups, and labor unions of the left, following the lead of Cuba's Fidel Castro, urged him to repudiate the debt or at a minimum to declare a unilateral

THE EXCHANGE RATE, PESOS TO THE DOLLAR, 1955-90

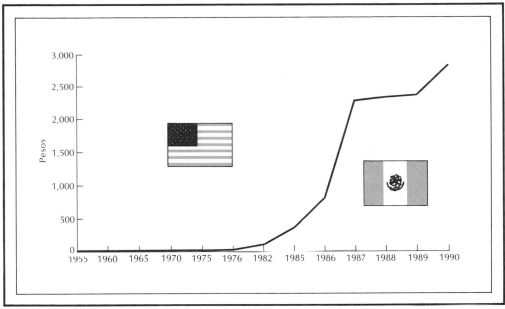

moratorium on repayment. The lessons of Mexican history cautioned against such precipitous action: a similar action in 1861, for no less dire reasons, had occasioned a foreign intervention and ultimately the establishment of a French empire in the valley of Anáhuac. And though de la Madrid feared no such intervention and undoubtedly agreed that the interest rates being paid on Mexico's debt were excessive, he did realize the necessity of rekindling some degree of confidence in the world's banking community and financial markets. He opted for economic austerity, not repudiation. It was a calculated risk: asking Mexico's beleaguered poor to tighten their belts once again was asking them to accept their miserable squalor.

Recognizing that government expenditures had to be drastically reduced, de la Madrid not only curtailed many new projects but also announced reductions in federal subsidies, the sale of inefficient and unprofitable state-owned enterprises, and a freeze on federal employment. Using the considerable influence of the presidential office, he did his best to limit the size of wage increases in the labor force. Finally in a bold move, the president eliminated some 51,000 federal jobs and cut back the salaries of other government employees whose positions could not be eliminated. The economic reforms seemed to be paying dividends, for in late 1984 the international banking community not only applauded his efforts but indicated that Mexico was dealing with the debt crisis more effectively than any other Latin American country. Progress had been made, and there was room for cautious optimism.

Then, suddenly, tragedy struck during the morning rush hour on September 19, 1985, as Mexico paid the price of sitting at the juncture of three of the earth's tectonic plates. An earthquake registering in excess of 8 on the Richter Scale devastated the capital, leaving more than eight thousand dead, many more injured, and damage estimated at $4 billion. This latest test for the Mexican citizenry was met with fortitude and heroism, but the calamity not only made payments on the foreign debt impossible, but presented dismal prospects for continued progress on the economic front.

The last years of the de la Madrid administration saw Mexico slip deeper and deeper into the economic morass. In addition to the collapse of the peso, inflation soared to unprecedented heights. Official inflation rates, released by Mexico's Central Bank, reported 63.7 percent in 1985, 105.7 percent in 1986, and 159 percent in 1987. The man on the street swore that the actual figures were even higher. Increases in the cost of gasoline, corn, wheat, and electricity led the assault on the consumer price index, but no product or service emerged unscathed. The only thing that could match the rapid rise in prices was the rapid growth of the foreign debt. When de la Madrid left office in December 1988, the Mexican government owed foreigners a whopping $105 billion in outstanding debts.

United States–Mexican Relations

Two major problems defying easy solution dominated United States–Mexican relations in the 1970s and 1980s. Both of them concerned movement across the common border, and both of them had national significance that transcended the international line that divides the two countries.

Since the 1950s, the United States–Mexican border region has witnessed one of the most profound demographic shifts in world history not conditioned by either war or epidemic disease. The result of a high birthrate and massive northern migration in Mexico and the equally telling Sunbelt phenomenon in the United States, the population has soared unremittingly on both sides of the border. In 1940, only about 16 million persons occupied the four U.S. states and six Mexican states that share

Damage in Mexico City was extensive, and the clean-up task monumental, after the earthquake of September 19, 1985.

For young and old alike, the chain-link boundary line separating Nogales, Arizona, from Nogales, Sonora, is little more than a daily inconvenience.

the international line. At the beginning of 1990, the estimated population of the same ten states was over 60 million. The swell has been so dramatic that it not only dominates day-to-day human relations of the region but drives international relations as well. The border between the countries is permeable, and not only to people. Disease, polluted water, contaminated air, to cite but a few examples, refuse to respect the artificial line drawn by nineteenth-century politicians to ratify the work of nineteenth-century generals.

Of the major problems growing out of a common international boundary, the most protracted one is that of the undocumented worker. Beginning in the 1970s unemployment, underemployment, persistent poverty, and the undeniable lure of the United States prompted hundreds of thousands of Mexican workers to cross the border illegally into the United States each year in pursuit of gainful employment. The number of undocumented workers in the United States at any given time cannot be calculated accurately, but most serious estimates range between 4 and 6 million.

The undocumented worker phenomenon is an emotion-charged topic that has precipitated much national and international debate. Everyone agrees that the United States has the right to enforce its immigration laws and to regulate entries into the country. But there is no consensus on precisely what should be done and how. Few United States citizens would feel comfortable living in a country that convinced itself that there was no alternative but to guard its southern boundary with mine fields, electrically charged barbed wire, or a human fence of soldiers stationed along that porous two-thousand-mile border at intervals of two hundred yards.

Realistic solutions are complicated by the fact that an undocumented worker mythology is current in the United States and is nurtured by vested interest groups. Contrary to popular opinion, the undocumented workers do not constitute a drain on social services. The best evidence suggests forcefully that most of them have federal and state taxes deducted from their wages but do not reap the benefits of the tax system for fear of being detected and reported to immigration authorities. In reality, undocumented workers subsidize social services and use them only infrequently. Equally evident is the myth that a great many displace United States workers and in a major way contribute to unemployment north of the international boundary. Undoubtedly some United States workers have been displaced, but the large majority of the undocumented fill positions that would remain vacant at wage levels falling below minimum scale. It is true that because many undocumented workers will accept jobs below the minimum wage they tend to depress the labor market. For this reason, a broad spectrum of labor organizations in the United States began calling for tighter controls while an equally broad spectrum of employers, in both rural and urban areas, favor the maintenance of the status quo.

A solution of sorts was reached in 1986 when the United States Congress passed the Immigration Reform and Control Act (the Simpson-Rodino Act). The main features of the legislation provided for a tighter enforcement of immigration policy, sanctions against those who knowingly employed undocumented workers, and an amnesty for those workers who could establish continued residence in the United States since 1982. But Simpson-Rodino did not solve the undocumented worker problem because it addressed only those factors that pulled the Mexican workers toward the United States, ignoring those that pushed them out of Mexico. The undocumented continued to come, albeit in smaller numbers, as there was no shortage of United States employers willing to offer work in spite of threatened sanctions. The fundamental problems remained. In 1989, Jorge Bustamante, Mexico's leading border specialist, reported that earnings sent back to

Mexico by undocumented workers totaled $1.25 billion annually, making this source of income the country's third largest source of foreign exchange.

If Mexican workers are performing useful labor, if they are able to earn money with which to support their families, if they are not contributing in a major way to unemployment in the United States, and if they do not constitute a burden on social services, why are they considered to be a problem? The answer in part rests with the plight of the undocumented workers themselves as revealed in the countless human tragedies that occur each year. Crossing the border illegally immediately converts a law-abiding citizen into a fugitive from justice with no protection from the varied forms of human exploitation. Those Mexicans, called *coyotes*, who contract with individual workers for surreptitious entry and transportation to a job have been known to collect their fees and deliver their human cargo to U.S. immigration authorities. United States employers have been known to set up two-week pay periods, and, after receiving thirteen days of labor from an entire work force, call in the border patrol, thus relieving themselves of the need to meet the payroll. In the Southwest, groups of vigilantes have taken "law enforcement" into their own hands and have terrorized and physically brutalized workers hungry for jobs as object lessons to those who would follow them. Unintended tragedies also abound as evidenced by two dozen undocumented workers asphyxiated in an air-tight van or thirteen more dying of dehydration trying to cross the Arizona desert by foot in the burning heat of summer. When thousands of sick people fear to go to a hospital or thousands of victims of assault and robbery fear to go to the police, when an entire group is made the scapegoat for a complicated potpourri of social ills, a compassionate society must be concerned.

The second and more serious problem that plagued the generally good relations between Washington, D.C., and Mexico, D.F., and that contributed to a politically charged atmosphere, was the unremitting flow of drugs across the United States–Mexico border. The smuggling of contraband between the two countries certainly was nothing new. Arms and ammunition, automobiles, trucks, agricultural equipment, household items, and scores of other products had long evaded the eyes, regulations, and taxing authority of the customs agents. What made the problem so volatile in the late 1980s was the especially insidious nature of the illegal cargo. The international drug traffic, both sides agreed, not only left its legacy of abuse and dependence, but also fostered an entire host of parasitic crimes, especially in the border region. Authorities from the two countries, however, agreed on little else. The public was soon treated to the most bizarre misapplication of the theories of the Scottish economist Adam Smith: United States officials found the problem to be simply one of supply, while their Mexican counterparts retorted that it was simply one of demand.

Following the murder of U.S. Drug Enforcement Administrative agent Enrique Camarena near Guadalajara, in 1986 and 1987 the United States Congress held formal hearings on terrorism and drugs. These hearings prompted the most intemperate statements on Mexico's alleged lack of cooperation on the drug issue in spite of indications to the contrary from the United States ambassador in Mexico City. By 1988, Mexico-bashing had become a favorite pastime of those who could think of no other reasons for the United States failure to win its much publicized war on drugs. In that year, the U.S. Senate failed to certify Mexico for economic assistance because it was not doing enough to intercept the flow of drugs before they crossed the border.

The strident rhetoric continued until early 1989 when crimes of violence became so outrageous in the border region that law enforcement officials on both sides had to stop shouting and start talking. In addition to many drug-related individual murders, execution-style killings in the spring of 1989 claimed six lives in Caborca, Sonora; four in Navojoa, Sonora; twelve in Agua Prieta, Sonora; five in Tucson, Arizona; and twelve in Matamoros, Tamaulipas. The binational cooperation in the investigation of these killings and the prompt extradition of suspects augured well for the future, but much remained to be done.

The Elections of 1988 and Mexican Democratization

The 1980s were a decade of democratization or redemocratization throughout much of Latin America. In most of the region, this phenomenon meant replacing military dictatorships with civilian governments chosen in an open or a relatively open electoral process. In Mexico, democratization was something very different. The army had ceased to call the political shots in Mexican politics decades earlier. Democratization in Mexico meant opening up the political system, recognizing that it had systemic weaknesses, and making it more responsive to the Mexican citizenry. The process was far from innocuous, for it meant that the influential political bosses in the country would have to share their power with others.

The basic problem was not new to the 1980s. Because of circumstances unique to Mexico's twentieth-century experience, one political party had gained almost absolute dominance. This official party, under different names, had won every election for president and every election for the thirty-one governorships since its foundation in 1929. If an occasional member of an opposition party could be found occupying a seat in the national Congress, it was probably not because he or she had won a congressional race but because Mexico's electoral law permitted the seating of a limited number of defeated candidates based on the percentage of votes cast for their respective parties in the last election. Mexican democracy had become increasingly diluted and deformed.

As the official party became almost synonymous with the government, and thus commanded huge resources as well as incredible patronage, elections became a farce. Mexico's democracy was a one-party system in which the citizens, for all practical purposes, were denied the element of choice, the most fundamental democratic right of all. In the 1980s, several opposition parties (conservative in the north and leftist in the south), capitalizing on increasing dissatisfaction with the performance of the official party, began to score some modest victories in state and local elections. With some regularity, the official party overturned the electoral results and had its own candidates installed in office. In this process, the PRI began to lose its sense of legitimacy. The growing challenges to the system were clearly evident in the presidential elections of 1988.

The conservative position was articulated by the PAN and its presidential candidate, Manuel Clouthier, a millionaire industrialist. Clouthier ran on a platform calling for a closer relationship with the United States, a more limited role for the government in the economy, a more vigorous private sector, and of course, an end to electoral fraud by the PRI. The leftist opposition came from Cuauhtémoc Cárdenas, the son of former president Lázaro Cárdenas and a former PRI governor of Michoacán. Cárdenas, who had harbored presidential ambitions for some time, broke with the official party over the issue of how presidential candidates were chosen from among those judged to be *presidenciable*. He ran on the Frente Democrático Nacional, a coalition that was able to temporarily unite a broad spectrum of leftist parties. Cárdenas agreed with Clouthier on one platform plank—the need to bring an end to the PRI's electoral fraud—but differed sharply

MEXICAN PRESIDENTIAL ELECTIONS, 1958–88
PRI CANDIDATES' PERCENTAGE OF VOTES

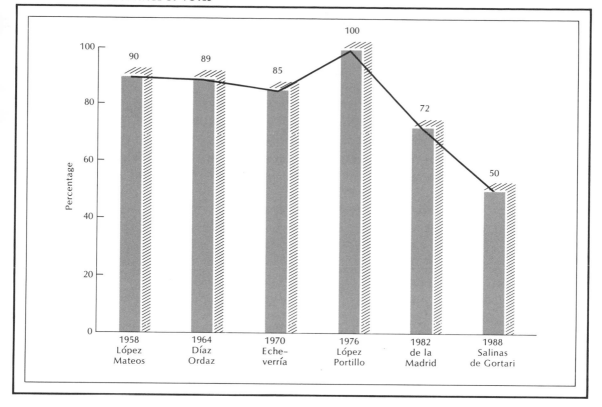

on other issues. He called for greater independence from the United States and indicated that if elected he would declare a moratorium on the repayment of Mexico's gigantic foreign debt.

The PRI candidate, Carlos Salinas de Gortari, was the epitome of the successful technocrat. He had earned a doctorate in economics from Harvard University and in the de la Madrid cabinet was secretary of planning and budget. Never having served in elective office, however, he was unaccustomed to political campaigning, and his effort in this regard was lackadaisical. Presaging things to come, his campaign speeches were less doctrinaire than those of his PRI predecessors. They were singularly free of commonplace Revolutionary rhetoric. For the first time in recent memory, the press gave extensive coverage to the opposition. Election day was a surprise even to the most astute political observers. The election was close enough for all three candidates to claim victory. Salinas ultimately was declared the winner, but his was the worst showing of an official party candidate since 1929. The political stock of PRI had fallen so precipitously that Salinas barely received a majority of the votes cast.

The democratizing process continued during the gubernatorial elections of 1989. In an electoral result that shocked everyone, PAN candidate Ernesto Ruffo won the governorship of Baja California Norte, and in the first test of his pledge to fair elections, President Salinas accepted the outcome. More change was to follow. In 1991 blatant electoral fraud cost PRI candidates two additional governorships in the states of Guanajuato and San Luis Potosí. The Chihuahua governorship also fell to PAN candidate Francisco Barrios, the former mayor of Ciudad Juárez in 1992. The president even endorsed a series of political reforms long called for by his political opposition. These included regulation of party finances, limits on campaign expenditures, and greater access to news outlets by opposition parties. Few now doubted that Mexican political culture was undergoing a remarkable metamorphosis.

Salinas Bids Adiós to the Revolution

The political education of Carlos Salinas de Gortari, like that of many recently elected heads of state throughout the world, was grounded in a new vocabulary and buttressed with concepts so shocking that politicians even a decade earlier would have considered them sheer madness. As notions of *détente* receded into the past, words like *glasnost* and *perestroika* became part of the common international parlance. The Berlin wall collapsed, as did the communist experiment in eastern Europe. The Soviet Union and Yugoslavia fell apart just as East and West Germany fell together. Fear of nuclear apocalypse no longer dominated political discourse. And most surprising of all, formerly socialist countries began to embrace what had previously been considered the capitalist demon. With changes so remarkable occurring elsewhere in the world, with the world in such tremendous flux, President Salinas decided that it was time for Mexico, too, to begin marching to a new cadence.

Throughout the entire post-World War II period Mexican politicians and intellectuals had asked themselves Is the Mexican Revolution dead? Some morticians had actually consigned the Revolution to an early demise in the 1940s, but other argued that it was only in a coma and called upon a variety of therapists to work with it, nurture it back to health, and instill a new vitality. Salinas left little doubt of his position. He would purchase a huge casket, nail down the lid securely, and inter the Revolution in such a deep grave that exhumation would be forever impossible.

Never articulating a leitmotif as captivating as Avila Camacho's "I am a believer," the president did begin to exorcise the ghosts of Mexico's anticlerical past. The process culminated with the president's memorable audience with Pope John Paul II and, in 1992, with the restoration of diplomatic relations between Mexico and the Vatican. Those relations had been severed for 130 years. Then came amendments to the Constitution of 1917. Public religious celebrations were legalized, the Church could again own property, it could operate religious schools, and foreign priests were welcome to preach on Mexican soil. While some Mexicans considered the relaxation of anticlericalism only as a symbolic gesture, others realized it was the harbinger of more substantive changes to come.

During his second month in office, Salinas struck out against the powerful oil workers' union and arrested its leader, Joaquín Hernández Galicia, who was better known by his pseudonym, La Quina. To labor's outrage, the president answered that La Quina and his two leading associates had been arrested because of fraud and corruption in union activities, but some saw the dramatic move as an object lesson to other union leaders who might demand more on the wage front than the government was willing to concede. Their fears did not prove idle. A few months later the president moved against the dock workers union in Veracruz. Not yet finished, in January 1992 Salinas ordered the arrest of labor leader Agapito González Cavazo, charging him with tax evasion. It seemed no accident that this arrest occurred only one day before González Cavazo's Union of Journeymen and Industrial Workers was scheduled to go on strike against thirty-three maquiladora plants owned mainly by United States interests. The picture now came into sharper focus: Mexican labor could no longer hide behind the protect provisions of Article 123 of the Constitution of 1917.

There was much more to come. Early in the administration the president began mild criticism of the ejido system, the sacred cow of agrarian reformers since the early 1920s. In one speech he had the temerity to call the ejidos unproductive and ultimately concluded that they had been a failure. They no longer represented the hope of a prosperous future for the nation's campesinos, rather they were the cause of rural poverty. They explained why Mexico in the 1990s was not yet self-sufficient in food production. They explained why rural income was only one-third that of the remainder of the country.

Land redistribution, for Salinas, was a bankrupt solution to a problem with roots in Mexico's ancient past. Before proposing his own solution in his third state of the nation message, the president assessed the problems of rural Mexico in historical terms.

> The land distribution established more than fifty years ago brought justice to the countryside. But to attempt in the present circumstances to continue along the path then followed no longer signifies prosperity for the country or justice for the campesinos. In the past, land distribution was a path of justice; today it is unproductive and impoverishing.[2]

New laws, unthinkable just a decade earlier, followed quickly. They provided for the private ownership of lands formerly owned by the ejidos. Not only were the campesinos given title to their land, but for the first time in the twentieth century, they could trade it, mortgage it, rent it, or even sell it. Salinas had again turned a venerable Revolutionary principle, agrarian reform, on its head.

All of the changes were predicated on a major reassessment of the proper role of government in addressing society's ills. As Mexico looked toward the twenty-first century, it was clear that the state would exercise a more constricted role than it had in the past. Salinas attributed much of Mexico's economic dilemma to an exaggerated statism, which had seen the government move into the private sector and acquire ownership and control of over a thousand private companies. These the president began to privatize. By early 1992, over 85 percent of these companies had been sold back to the private sector. Among the economic giants quickly purchased by consortia of private investors were BANAMEX (Banco Nacional de México) and BANCOMER (Banco de Comercio), Mexico's two largest banks, and TELMEX (Teléfonos de México), the country's only telephone company. Other investors grabbed up government steel companies, hotels, sugar refineries, steel mills, and mines. Only a few government concerns such as PEMEX, considered crucial to national security, were excluded from divestiture proceedings.

The shift to a free market economy enabled Salinas to lower Mexican inflation to a tolerable 10 percent by 1993 and to reduce Mexico's foreign debt by some 25 billion dollars. But it also served another purpose—it was an integral part of a calculated policy to foster a closer relationship with the United States. From the outset Salinas eschewed the nationalistic rhetoric of recent Mexi-

---

2. Quoted in "Salinas Prepares Mexican Agriculture for Free Trade," *The Backgrounder* (October 1, 1992), p. 7.

can heads of state because he believed that Mexico's economic malaise could best be addressed by the successful conclusion of the North American Free Trade Agreement (NAFTA) with the United States and Canada. This was not a view shared by old line Revolutionaries, whom Salinas dubbed "the new reactionaries." Their position was sadly tired and predictable: free trade would not only place Mexico at an economic disadvantage but would signal a loss of national sovereignty as well. Salinas and his supporters could not buy into that argument. They believed with certain justification that the agreement would herald more capital investment and as a result more well-paying jobs for Mexicans. Ultimately this position carried the day. Knowing that Europe would formally enter into its own common market on January 1, 1993, President Salinas, President George Bush, and Canadian Prime Minister Brian Muroney recognized that only a new, large, combined North American market would be competitive. The three initialed NAFTA just as Salinas reached the midpoint of his presidential term and shortly before President Bush turned over the White House to Bill Clinton. By the fall of 1993, free trade had become the centerpiece of the Salinas administration. It was a calculated risk because final passage by the United States Congress was far from certain. Rejection would be seen as a repudiation of Salinas's best efforts to draw Mexico closer to the United States. The sighs of relief were clearly audible when the United States Congress gave NAFTA its final approval in November 1993. The days of a nationalistic economy, suspicious of all foreigners now seemed to be over both in Mexico and the United States.

There was a substantial price to pay for declaring the Mexican Revolution dead. On January 1, 1994, a serious antigovernment rebellion broke out in the southern state of Chiapas. Led by a charismatic commander who called himself simply Sub-Comandante Marcos, a Maya Indian army, the Ejército Zapatista de Liberación Nacional, captured San Cristóbal de las Casas, the second largest city in the state. President Salinas sent army troops, rocket-equipped aircraft, and helicopter gun ships to engage the rebels, but ultimately negotiations conducted under the auspices of Bishop Samuel Ruiz—not military might—restored a tenuous peace. The rebellion focused national attention on an ethnic group and a region of the country unfulfilled by the promises of the Revolution.

A still greater shock to the Mexican body politic and to the country's self-image occurred in March 1994. The attractive and

Sub-Comandante Marcos, leader of the Chiapas rebellion in early 1994, is wearing the mask which was the emblem of the rebels. Unlike the original Zapatistas, these insurgents preferred the protection of anonymity.

energetic PRI candidate for president, Luis Donaldo Colosio, was assassinated during a campaign appearance in the border city of Tijuana. Conspiracy theories, reminiscent of those in the United States following on the heels of the assassination of John F. Kennedy thirty years earlier, surfaced everywhere: in the press, in television commentaries, in the classrooms, and in coffee shop conversation. While the best evidence suggested that a single deranged gunman, Mario Aburto Martínez, perhaps with the help of an accomplice bore responsibility, few were willing to rule out the possibility of a wider, politically motivated plot.

In the summer of 1994 it was still uncertain how the Chiapas rebellion and the assassination of presidential candidate Colosio would influence the Mexican political process. The PRI candidate chosen to replace Colosio, Ernesto Zedillo Ponce de León, pledged immediately to continue the policies of the Salinas administration. Although Zedillo was considered the front-runner, opposition candidates Cuauhtémoc Cárdenas and Diego Fernández de Cevallos used those portentous events to discredit the Salinas approach and to close the gap in the presidential race. The election returns showed that PRI candidate Zedillo won with slightly over 50 percent of the vote. It was a vote of confidence for Mexico's embrace of the free market economy and an early indication that the Revolution had not been prematurely entombed.

The Mexican Revolution: An Assessment for the 1990s

Why did President Salinas de Gortari signal that the Mexican Revolution had finally ended? Had it been a failure, a myth, a mere invention of historians? Throughout much of the post-World War II period, many alienated Mexicans responded in the affirmative. When U.S. scholar Ramón Ruiz synthesized the movement in a book published in 1980, he preferred not to use the word *revolution* and entitled it *The Great Rebellion: Mexico, 1905–1924*. By that time, some distinguished intellectuals argued forcefully that Mexico was in the throes of a neo-Porfiriato. The government had again become repressive, the scenario continued, and a small group was again enriching itself at the expense of the many. Social priorities, including the redistribution of land, had been laid aside in favor of economic development. Censorship, as evidenced in the celebrated *Excelsior* case, had become political reality once again. Economic exploitation in the form of the multinational corporation was even more pervasive than under the mining and petroleum companies of the early twentieth century. Bourgeois technocrats had replaced the científicos, but all the inadequacies of the closed society remained intact.

These judgments contain many truths, but many flaws as well; they obscure much more than they enlighten. While military force had been used irresponsibly and unpardonably at Tlatelolco, while the army had hunted down and killed Lucio Cabañas, and while political prisoners were taken at the time of the Olympic demonstrations, it is pure folly to imply that presidential tenure in the postwar period rested primarily or even largely on the force of arms, as it had under Díaz. Although private enterprise was flourishing, the state had intervened actively enough to challenge laissez faire economics. Can one imagine Porfirio Díaz, shortly after the turn of the century when rich oil fields were discovered in Mexico, telling a president of the United States "no special consideration for your consumers"? Yet this was precisely Echeverría's message to Gerald Ford when the two met on the Arizona–Sonora border in 1974. The United States would not use Mexico to weaken OPEC. In the 1980s, López Portillo and de la Madrid politely informed Ronald Reagan that Mexico's foreign policy, especially regarding Central America, would not be instructed from Wall Street or Pennsylvania Avenue. While some members of the intelligentsia had been co-opted with largess, in the 1970s Daniel Cosío Villegas could argue the neo-Porfirian theorem and excoriate the administration—indeed, the system— with neither a trip into exile nor a sojourn in a Mexico City prison. Had Díaz's father-in-law, Manuel Romero Rubio, been kidnapped in 1884 rather than Guadalupe Zuno Hernández ninety years later, many innocents would have perished in the search for information and the guilty would have been dispatched without even the formality of trial.

But all historical analogies tax intellectual sensibilities. The critics might do better to vent their displeasure on the obvious. The Mexican Revolution simply did not midwife the socialist state, nor did it usher in the millennium. The catalog of shortcomings was far from small. Poverty still abounded to all with open eyes. Several recent studies have concluded that the gulf between rich and poor widened rather than narrowed in the postwar years. Studies undertaken in the 1980s indicated that the lowest 20 percent of the population shared only 3 percent of the national wealth, whlie the upper 20 percent shared a whopping 54 percent. The manifestations of this stilted distribution of wealth were obvious. Millions were still illiterate; wages were low, and unemployment was high; housing was inadequate; medical care, especially in the rural areas, was grossly insufficient; and the industrial and vehicular smog of the Federal District choked the Mexican capital and threatened health problems of major consequences. One Mexico City barrio, Ciudad Nezahualcóyotl, with a population of 3 million, was the largest slum in the world. In the rural areas, a million peasants still worked plots too small to sustain themselves and their families. Only one-third of all Mexicans had access to running water in their place of residence. Real income declined in the 1980s as inflation consistently outran rises in the minimum wage. Worst of all, in 1987 the International Society of Public Health reported that 40 percent of all Mexicans still suffered from malnutrition.

But the Revolution had occurred; it had broken the back of neofeudalism, had eliminated the hacendado class, and had abolished the rurales. After ten years, it had yielded to a system of political stability without the daily use of force, to economic growth with a minimum of foreign participation, and to a broadened political base without the fragilities of traditional democracy or the repugnant liabilities of dictatorship. While the gulf separating the rich and the poor was as wide as ever, Mexico was no longer a country of two social poles. The caloric intake in the average diet doubled between 1910 and 1970; the infant mortality rate (deaths before the age of one year) fell from thirty deaths per hundred children to about five; and, concomitantly, life expectancy soared. The average Mexican lived only about thirty-six years in 1930; in 1990, life expectancy had reached seventy years, not much below that of the developed countries.

The overall goal of the Revolution had been to ensure a better life for the Mexican citizenry. In spite of persistent poverty and multiple imperfections in the system, in spite of many chores left half finished, more Mexicans were living better in the 1990s than ever before. Millions had ascended to the middle class and only to share the new bondage of middle-class cohorts throughout the western world: a mortgage on a house; large car payments; and a frightening debt occasioned by small plastic cards. It is naïve to expect that Mexico could completely eradicate the degradations of poverty. Nations that opened the twentieth century far ahead have not succeeded either.

The Revolution was brought to an end less because it failed than because it had finally served its purpose. The Mexican universe of Carlos Salinas de Gortari was totally different from that familiar to Francisco Madero and the revolutionaries of 1910. Recognizing that Mexico's revolutionary ideology was essentially bankrupt and inappropriate to new and constantly changing problems, Salinas had the courage to divorce Mexico abruptly from its twentieth century past. *Salinastroika* was not simply an act of political maturity. It was a remarkably bold departure from the political experience all Mexicans knew and understood. The Mexican president wanted his fellow citizens not to ponder the year 1910 but to envision a Mexican future beyond the year 2000, a future in which the country would at last emerge from the Third World and join the First. The Chiapas rebellion and the assassination of Luis Donaldo Colosio indicated that the path might be treacherous.

Recommended for Further Study

Brannon, Jeffrey, and Eric N. Baklanoff. *Agrarian Reform and Public Enterprise in Mexico: The Political Economy of Yucatán's Henequen Industry*. University: University of Alabama Press, 1987.

Domínguez, Jorge I., ed. *Mexico's Political Economy: Challenges at Home and Abroad*. Beverly Hills, Calif.: Sage, 1982.

Falk, Pamela, ed. *Petroleum and Mexico's Future*. Boulder, Colo.: Westview Press, 1987.

Fowerbaker, Joe, and Ann L. Craig, eds. *Popular Movements and Political Change in Mexico*. Boulder: Lynne Reinner Publishers, 1990.

Gentleman, Judith, ed. *Mexican Politics in Transition*. Boulder, Colo.: Westview Press, 1987.

Grayson, George W. *Oil and Mexican Foreign Policy*. Pittsburgh: University of Pittsburgh Press, 1988.

Hellman, Judith Adler. *Mexico in Crisis*. New York: Holmes and Meier, 1983.

Levy, Daniel, and Gabriel Székely. *Mexico: Paradoxes of Stability and Change*. Boulder, Colo.: Westview Press, 1983.

Martínez, Oscar J. *Troublesome Border*. Tucson: University of Arizona Press, 1988.

Middlebrook, Kevin J. "Political Liberalization in an Authoritarian Regime: The Case of Mexico." In *Elections and Democratization in Latin America, 1980–85*, edited by Paul W. Drake and Eduardo Silva, pp. 73–104. San Diego: Center for Iberian and Latin American Studies, University of California, 1986.

Morris, Stephen D. "Political Reformism in Mexico: Salinas at the Brink." *Journal of Interamerican Studies and World Affairs* 34:1 (1992): 27–58.

Purcell, Susan Kaufman. *Mexico in Transition: Implications for U.S. Policy*. New York: Council on Foreign Relations, 1988.

Reynolds, Clark W., and Robert K. McCleery. "The Political Economy of Immigration Law: Impact of Simpson-Rodino on the United States and Mexico." *Journal of Economic Perspectives* 2 (1988): 117–31.

Riding, Alan. *Distant Neighbors: Portrait of the Mexicans*. New York: Knopf, 1985.

Smith, Peter. *Mexico: The Quest for a United States Policy*. New York: Foreign Policy Association, 1980.

Thorup, Cathryn L., ed. *The United States and Mexico: Face to Face with New Technology*. New Brunswick, N.J.: Transaction Books, 1987.

Urquidi, Victor L. "Economic and Social Developments in Mexico." In *Mexico Today*, edited by Tommie Sue Montgomery, pp. 77–87. Philadelphia: Institute for the Study of Human Issues, 1982.

Velasco-S., Agustín. *Impacts of Mexican Oil Policy on Economic and Political Development*. Lexington, Mass.: Lexington Books, 1983.

Weintraub, Sidney. "US–Mexico Free Trade: Implications for the United States." *Journal of Interamerican Studies and World Affairs* 34:2 (1992): 29–52.

45

Society and Culture Since World War II

In the period after World War II, Mexico became more fully integrated into the international community than ever before. The country's charter membership in the United Nations at the close of the world conflict symbolized an end to the exclusive concern for parochial matters and a more profound interest in great world issues. Mexican presidents traveled widely carrying Mexico's message to Europe, Africa, Asia, and South America. They were determined to begin exerting leadership in the Third World. This new world outlook effected a basic change in self-image. The strident nationalism of the revolutionary era first gave ground and then surrendered to a new internationalism. Many perceived that the problems faced by the nation—rapid population growth, urbanization with its attendant social dislocations, persistent poverty, serious pollution, and ecological imbalance—were not only Mexican but global. Through science, technology, and economy the world had become increasingly interdependent, and solutions to these problems were scarcely possible within the confines of the national boundaries.

Population

The social and cultural changes of the postwar years were every bit as dramatic as those that had characterized the Porfiriato. The population growth was nothing short of fantastic, doubling in the twenty-three-year period between 1940 and 1963 and con-

MEXICAN POPULATION GROWTH, 1940–95

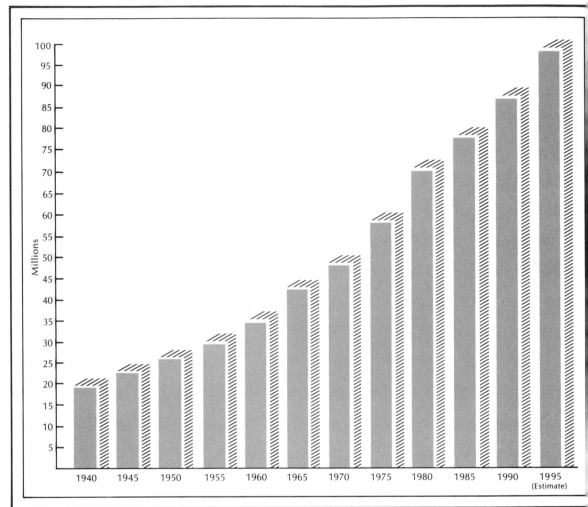

tinuing to burgeon in geometric proportion. At the end of World War II, the population of the country numbered some 22 million; by 1992, it had soared to about 90 million. At the current rate of growth (1.9 percent annually), Mexico will pass the 100 milion mark in 1998.

The capital had only 3 million inhabitants in 1950, but in 1993, according to some counts, greater Mexico City had swelled to a depressing 20 million. Like a giant magnet, it draws people from the countryside, adding hundreds of thousands to its population each year, and in the process becomes less uniquely Mexican and more like New York, Paris, or London. Those who enthusiastically approved of the changes argued that the nation's

Arguably the most congested city in the world, Mexico City streets, sometimes twelve lanes across such as the Periférico Norte pictured here, are often paralyzed by gridlock.

capital had at last become cosmopolitan; those who preferred the simplicity and charm of earlier days suggested that, as each colonial structure was torn down (in spite of protective legislation) to make room for a skyscraper or a freeway, as cellular phones, that quintessential yuppie symbol, rang during high mass at the main cathedral, the capital had—alas!—ceased to be Mexican. New elegant restaurants and ostentatious nightclubs catered to the thousands of tourists brought in each day by scores of jumbo jets. In 1985, the sprawling metropolis passed Tokyo for the distinction of being the most densely populated region on earth and had developed the most acute traffic and smog problems in the Western Hemisphere. In 1993, 3 million private vehicles; 46,658 mini buses; 200 trolley buses; and 58,877 taxicabs traveled the crowded streets of the Federal District, and the poisonous atmosphere caused over one hundred thousand deaths annually. Enterprising street vendors walked the sidewalks with tanks strapped on their backs selling individual doses of pure oxygen to sick-looking pedestrians. While some might have marveled at this creative therapy, it obviously did nothing to cleanse the noxious air. Blackouts, brownouts, inadequate telephone service, and low water pressure strained the nerves of virtually everyone. If pharmaceutical sales figures reflect reality, many *capitalinos* added Stresstabs (made in Mexico) to their shopping lists.

The huge working-class housing projects brought hundreds of thousands together into closer proximity than they would have imagined possible. Juvenile delinquency and adult crime rates soared. By 1988 Mexico City was recording 242 robberies and thirteen murders every day. Over one million youths belonged to street gangs (the Vikings, Sex Rats, Savages, Street Machine, and the like) that terrorized innocent passersby. With the thought of forestalling some Malthusian tragedy, Mexican urban planners began to consider seriously the building of an entirely new capital, much as the Brazilians had done in the late 1950s. But there was more talk than action as people rationalized that these costs of modernization were inevitable. Octavio Paz synopsized it well when he lamented that after centuries of struggle Mexico was finally a contemporary of all mankind.

In spite of the difficulties, Mexico City dominated the entire country as never before. Over 50 percent of the country's industries were located in the capital, and more than 70 percent of the country's daily banking transactions occurred there. Provincial Mexicans resented not only the exaggerated centralism emanating from Mexico City but also what they believed to be the arrogant attitudes of those from the nation's capital. They coined derogatory epithets for them, *Chilangos* and *guachos*, and in the state capitals decorated the walls of buildings with uncharitable graffiti inviting them all to go home.

While the provincial capitals were slightly more successful in retaining some of their local flavor, they, too, fell victim to the homogeneity of technological proficiency conditioned by electronic circuitry, pocket calculators, and large, sophisticated computers. One had to travel to the small village to encounter some of the charm of an age now past, but there, behind the façade of what seemed quaint to the foreign eye, the disabilities of underdevelopment remained stark. While more rural children were in school than ever before many of those schools had less than six grades and only one teacher. It would not be unusual for the children, at the end of the school's day, to return to hovels barren of comforts.

THE TEN LARGEST MEXICAN CITIES (1993 ESTIMATES)

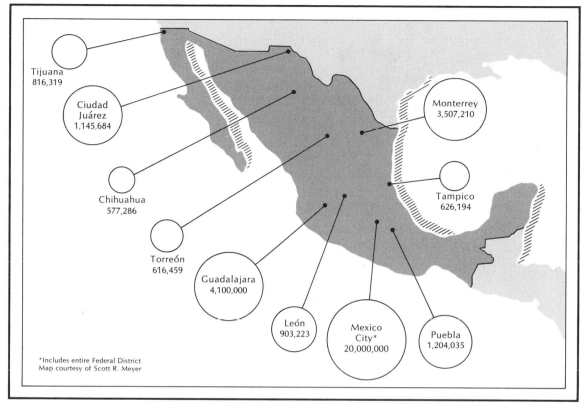

Tijuana
816,319

Ciudad
Juárez
1,145,684

Chihuahua
577,286

Torreón
616,459

Guadalajara
4,100,000

León
903,223

Mexico
City*
20,000,000

Puebla
1,204,035

Monterrey
3,507,210

Tampico
626,194

*Includes entire Federal District
Map courtesy of Scott R. Meyer

Mexican advocates of population control had their ups and downs in the postwar period. They were crushed by the 1968 papal encyclical banning all methods of artificial contraception because they recognized the awful truth in the quip that the rich get richer and the poor get children. During the presidential campaign of 1970, Luis Echeverría, the father of eight, announced that Mexico did not need to limit family size. In that same year, some six hundred thousand Mexican women underwent illegal abortions, and thirty-two thousand died. In 1972, in face of incontrovertible evidence, the Council of Mexican Bishops performed a remarkable *volte-face* and issued a pastoral letter declaring that Mexican couples should in good conscience make responsible decisions about the size of their families. The president agreed, and government-sponsored clinics began making birth control information available to those who requested it. The program began in a small way; the sell was very soft, but by 1980 López Portillo had earmarked over 500 million pesos annually for the family planning program and some dividends had been

THE TWO-CHILD FAMILY

La familia pequeña vive mejor
decida la suya . . .
(The small family lives better
decide on yours . . .)

Posters such as this, with an unmistakable message, became increasingly common in Mexican cities in the 1970s and 1980s.

recorded. A population growth rate that had hovered between 3.2 and 3.4 percent during the 1970s had been cut to about 1.9 percent in 1992. Over six thousand family planning centers, funded by the government, were in operation. There was no general rejoicing, however, as Mexican demographers expressed deep concern about the age distribution of the population. In 1990, fully 43 percent of Mexico's 87 million people had not yet reached fifteen years of age, and the female population about to reach childbearing age was enormous. In spite of the fact that more women than ever were visiting family planning clinics, some demographers predicted that the birth rate might actually begin to ascend once again.

The movement for women's rights built up steam during the postwar years. The full enfranchisement of women in 1955 was just the beginning. More important was the feminist victory scored in 1974. While the Equal Rights Amendment languished in the United States, President Echeverría sent a bill to the Congress asking that Mexican men give women their full stake in society. The law that passed promised women equal job opportunities, salaries, and legal standing. Beginning in the 1970s, the feminist movement began seriously to challenge laws and social practices denigrating the role of women. For the first time in its ninety-nine years, the prestigious Mexican Academy of the Language admitted a woman, Dr. María del Carmen Millán. Shortly thereafter Griselda Alvarez Ponce de León became governor of the state of Colima.

In 1984 and 1985, women were incorporated into various municipal police forces, not only because they could perform equally with men but also because they were thought to be less corruptible than their male counterparts. A few years later, Socorro Díaz, after establishing a brilliant record as a journalist, was elected to Congress and became the first woman to serve as president of the Chamber of Deputies. She was not alone in Congress. In 1988, ten of the sixty-four Mexican senators and fifty-five of the five hundred members of the Chamber of Deputies were women. The legal victories scored by the feminist movement were certainly impressive, but they were unable to seriously undermine the deeply ingrained cultural pressure of Mexican machismo. Behind a veil of anonymity, male attitudes toward women could be openly insensitive and degrading. The touching, grabbing, and verbal abuse suffered by women on the Mexico City metro became so intolerable in the 1980s that a radical solution was instituted. The Mexico City system became the only subway in the world where the individual cars were segregated by gender.

The Americanization of Mexico

Mass communication, and most especially television, changed not only patterns of leisure but the information level of the urban citizenry. By the mid-1960s, Mexican television was no longer the sole preserve of the middle and upper classes. Television antennas sprouted from the most decaying of urban slums and attested to the vastness of the audience. In the summer of 1969, millions of Mexicans watched in amazement as Neil Armstrong took his first tentative steps for mankind on the surface of the moon. And although some judged the telecast a gigantic hoax, most would soon have opinions about how nations, weak and strong, should allocate their limited resources. The great educational and cultural potential of the medium was approached no more in Mexico than elsewhere in the Western world, but the possibilities were so substantial that in the summer of 1985 the Mexican government contracted with NASA to carry Mexico's first television satellite into space. Successfully launched in an orbit 22,000 miles above the earth, *Morelos I* brought advanced telecommunications to the most remote parts of the country. It was followed shortly by *Morelos II*.

United States cultural influences overwhelmed Mexico in the postward period, occasionally for the better but generally for the worse. If anything, these new cultural inroads were more pervasive than those of the French during the late Porfiriato. Rodolfo

Stavenhagen, a distinguished Mexican sociologist, called it a steamroller. To the chagrin of those who prized traditional Hispanic values, advertisements and commercials assumed a distinct United States flavor, and hundreds of Anglicisms invaded the language. Somehow *el jit, el jonron, el extra inin* seemed more palatable, and certainly more understandable, than *okay, bay-bay, chance, jipi, biznes,* and *parquear.* Nobody could explain why Mexican teenagers began calling up their *suiti* for a date. Linguistic syncretism bequeathed its share of amusing redundancies, such as the cocktail lounge that displayed a sign reading "4:00–5:00, La Hora de Happy Hour" and the tourist restaurant whose menu proudly advertised "Chile con Carne with Meat." Quick lunches (*quik lonches*) and the coffee break (*kofi breik*) replaced heavy noon meals and afternoon siestas; beer supplanted pulque as the favorite alcoholic drink of the lower classes, while Scotch whisky took the place of cognac among the middle and upper classes. For the first time, Halloween, complete with plastic pumpkins and trick-or-treating, began to displace Mexico's traditional celebration of the Day of the Dead, and hand-carved folk toys lost favor to imported Tortugas Ninja.

American-style football did not really challenge the pre-eminence of soccer, but thousands of Mexicans became enthralled with professional football, telecast to Mexico City on Sundays. The January 1988 spectacular, Superbowl XX, between the Osos de Chicago and the Patriotas de Nueva Inglaterra seemed especially to captivate the Mexican sports fan. Mexican businessmen joined the Rotary and the Lions Club. Installment buying on Mexican version of Visa and MasterCard placed families in a new kind of debt but gave them the opportunity of acquiring furnishings and accouterments for the home that would have been unusual two decades before. *Supermercados* with plastic packaging and individually priced items began to replace the traditional marketplace in all the larger cities. Stocked with corn flakes, Campbell's soup, Heinz 57 Steak Sauce, Cap'n Crunch cereal, Van Camp's pork and beans, and Coca-Cola, Mexican supermarkets were distinguished from their North American counterparts only by the absence of huge parking lots.

Multinational chains carpeted Mexico City. Residents and tourists alike could rent a car from Avis, Hertz, Budget, or Thrifty and drive on Goodyear, Firestone, or Uniroyal tires to a fast food outlet called Denny's, Shakey's, or Pizza Hut. When the McDonald's chain opened its first restaurant on the southern edge of the sprawling capital in October 1985, eight Mexico City policemen

In spite of the anticlericalism embodied in revolutionary ideology, the faithful continued their pilgrimage to the Basilica de Guadalupe in the postwar period.

were kept busy for days directing traffic in front of the golden arches. United States music dominated most of Mexico City's twenty-four radio stations, while television audiences were treated to reruns of "Mannix," "Hawaii Five-O," "Los Dukes de Hazard," and "The Flintstones." Some cried understandably for spiritual independence, others more modestly for *taco si*, *hamburguesa no*. Another slogan would have been more appropriate. In January

1992, in the most bizarre example of gastronomical entrepreneurship, one United States corporation decided it could think of nothing better than to offer Mexicans an example of exquisite Mexican cuisine. Yes, Taco Bell opened its first Mexico City franchise!

What did it all mean? It was easy to simply label it all cultural imperialism but that ideologically loaded emblem explained little and resolved less. To the most thoughtful Mexicans the inherent problem was less Americanization than the type of Americanization. By this they meant too much Madonna and Rambo and too little Ernest Hemingway and Leonard Bernstein. But most realized that, in the absence of enveloping the country in a nationalistic cocoon, the process was lamentably inevitable. At the same time, they could take comfort in the obvious fact that the Mexican essence was scarcely imperiled by that process. Because tensions between Mexico and the United States had subsided, many Mexicans could now laugh at the absurdity of importing industrial tacos from the United States.

Literature, Art, and Scholarship

Mexico became a country of vibrant intellectual ferment in the forty-five years following World War II. Mexico City was clearly the cultural capital of the country and in 1985 could boast twenty daily newspapers and 250 periodicals. The television and film industries were based in the capital, as were the most outstanding art galleries and museums.

Throughout the postwar period, new literary journals and magazines of social protest provided the grist for healthy cultural debate. The postwar years saw the demise of both indigenismo and the novel of the Revolution as Mexican writers began their quest for the universal. While nobody could question the Mexicanidad of Octavio Paz, his writing revealed greater concern for ecumenical matters than for the heroes and apostates of the great Revolution. Born in Mexico City four years after the Revolution broke out, he was, by the 1950s, one of the most profound and prolific members of the new intelligentsia. As with many of the great intellects of the postwar period, it was often difficult to pinpoint where his philosophy ended and his literature began. In essays, in drama, and, above all, in poetry, he sought to link the Mexican experience with that of all humanity through the common denominators of suffering and tragedy. His most penetrating study, *El laberinto de la soledad* (translated as

The Labyrinth of Solitude) (1950), is a psychological study of the Mexican character but was conceived in the United States, where Paz was able to observe Mexicans in a foreign milieu. Solitude for Paz was a condition that Mexicans had to comprehend to understand themselves, but the inquiry into the Mexican psyche revealed his more basic interest in the human condition.

> Solitude—the feeling and knowledge that one is alone, alienated from the world and oneself—is not an exclusively Mexican characteristic. All men, at some moment in their lives, feel themselves to be alone. And they are. To live is to be separated from what we were in order to approach what we are going to be in the mysterious future. Solitude is the profoundest fact of the human condition.[1]

Paz's criticism of the Revolution was far from mundane. The intellectual paucity of the movement troubled him, especially the failure of the intelligentsia to relate the Mexican experience to the human enterprise at large.

While Octavio Paz broke out of the mold many considered properly Mexican, Juan José Arreola in a number of works turned his back on Mexican themes. Four years younger than Paz, Arreola developed a sharp, biting satire of the bourgeois values of postwar Mexican society. Culturally indebted to Bertolt Brecht and Albert Camus, he was sarcastic, irreverent, hyperbolic, humorous to the point of cruelty, and blatantly sexist. Arreola jabbed mercilessly at the pomposity and deceptions of his world. In one notably wicked short story, he invented a plastic woman and advertised her as would befit the merchandising practices of the new Mexico.

> Wherever the presence of woman is difficult, onerous, or prejudicial, whether in the bachelor's bedroom or in the concentration camp, the use of Plastisex is highly recommended. The army and the navy, as well as some directors of penal and teaching establishments, provide their inmates with the services of these attractive, hygienic creatures. . . . We will furnish you with the woman you have dreamed about all your life: she is manipulated by automatic controls and is made of synthetic materials that reproduce at will the most superficial or subtle characteristics of feminine beauty. Tall and slim, short and plump, fair or dark, redhead or platinum blonde—all are on the market. . . . The mouth, nos-

---

1. Octavio Paz, *The Labyrinth of Solitude: Life and Thought in Mexico*, trans. Lysander Kemp (New York, 1961), p. 195.

trils, inner parts of the eyelids, and other mucous regions are made of very soft sponge, saturated with hot, nutritive substances of variable viscosity and with different vitamin and aphrodisiac contents extracted from sea weeds and medicinal plants. . . .

Our Venuses are guaranteed to give perfect service for ten years—the average time any wife lasts—except in cases where they are subjected to abnormal sadistic practices. . . . Though submissive, the Plastisex is extremely vigorous, since she is equipped with an electric motor of one-half horse power. . . . Nude, she is simply unexcelled; pubescent or not, in the flower of youth, or with autumn's ripe opulence, according to the particular coloring of each race or mixture of races.[2]

Perhaps the most creative of the postwar writers was novelist Carlos Fuentes. Born in 1928 to a middle-class family, Fuentes took a law degree at the National University and then studied international law at Geneva. His most famous novel, *La región mas transparente* (*Where the Air Is Clear*), published in 1958, is a cynical story of disillusionment with the Revolution. But it is scarcely a novel of the Revolution in the classic sense. While those familiar with the outlines of Mexican history in the twentieth century might find it easier than others to comprehend, more than anything else it is a Marxist critique of human nature and a creative condemnation of capitalism. The names and the places are clearly Mexican, but the major themes—the abuses of power, the self-serving opportunism of the bourgeoisie, the pointless existence of the *nouveau riche*, and the tendency of the new society to accept all things foreign—clearly have an applicability transcending Mexico. The lesson of postwar Mexico for Fuentes was that it reflected the same degenerate bourgeois values that characterized most of the Western world.

The tragedy of Tlatelolco initiated a protracted national debate and spawned its own impressive body of literature in the 1970s. Tlatelolco litearture found expression in the essay, poetry, short story, and novel. While Octavio Paz and Carlos Fuentes dominated the outpouring of perceptive political essays searching for accountability, the fictional responses are best epitomized by Carlos Monsiváis's *Días de guardar* (1970), Arturo Azuela's *Manifestación de silencios* (1979), Elena Poniatowska's *La noche de Tlatelolco* (1971), Luis Spota's *La plaza* (1977), and Gonzalo Martre's *Los símbolos transparentes* (1978). No matter what the

2. Juan José Arreola, *Confabulario and Other Inventions*, trans. George D. Shade (Austin, 1974), pp. 134–39.

specific genre, the body of literature itself testified eloquently to the fact that the Mexican intelligentsia insisted that such an untoward episode should be neither repeated nor forgotten. When Poniatowska was awarded the Xavier Villarrutia Literary Prize for *La noche de Tlatelolco* she would not accept it, insisting that the only persons worthy of a prize were those who had given their lives at the Plaza de las Tres Culturas that fateful October evening in 1968. Tlatelolco, in essence, became not only a backdrop, not only a focus of literary discourse, but a major point of departure for the best Mexican literature published in the decade following the infamous events of 1968.

Mexican art in the postwar period also rejected—in fact, rebelled violently against—the nationalistic indigenismo. Although Mexican painters of the 1950s and 1960s never achieved the stature of the great revolutionary muralists, some of the new experiments with abstract expressionism and even op art were exciting to some and completely bewildering to others. Leading the *avant-garde* was José Luis Cuevas, who epitomized the rejection of traditional muralism when he stated that what he wanted for his country's art was "broad highways leading to the rest of the world rather than narrow trails connecting one adobe village to another."[3] Many of his contemporaries agreed, and the new generation, including Olga Costa, Jesús Reyes, Pedro Coronel, and Carrillo Gil, executed paintings that could have been conceived anywhere in the Western world. They did not believe it necessary to reaffirm their Mexicanidad or to instruct the masses. But it was Juan Soriano who depicted the movement best, and in 1957 a distinguished jury of artists at the Salón de la Plástica Mexicana gave him the first prize ever awarded to a Mexican abstract painting. Soriano later articulated his views on the new Mexican art to Elena Poniatowska in a celebrated interview.

> Siqueiros limits himself to one country—Mexico. And to one political idea. I'm interested in ideas that are much broader. . . . Siqueiros . . . wants to create a strongly nationalistic art. And I believe that his art is excellent because it expresses him. But I want, and have always wanted to be universal. . . . Those murals are only tourist bait. They're the same kind of thing as those gigantic posters of the travel agencies: *Visit Mexico*. Furthermore those murals reveal nothing. They're a chronicle and not a poetic creation. Diego Rivera created a completely bureaucratic art. He made himself a propagandist of the victorious revolution. . . . I

3. José Luis Cuevas, "The Cactus Curtain," *Evergreen Review* 2 (1959): 120.

reproach him for having completely prostituted the pictorial language, reducing it to little more than a caricature, vulgarizing it. Because, don't you see, the caricature is a creation of the bourgeoisie. . . . I'm not concerned with my nationality. I can assure you I don't carry it like a chip on my shoulder, nor do I have to remind myself daily that I'm a Mexican.[4]

To the amusement of some and to the shock of others, Mexican painting turned iconoclastic in the 1970s and 1980s. Artistic impiety was epitomized by the sacrilegious work of Rolando de la Rosa. His 1988 art exhibit featured the superimposed face of Marilyn Monroe on the image of the Virgin of Guadalupe and the face of actor Pedro Infante similarly substituted for that of Christ in his rendition of the Last Supper. A generation or two earlier this type of mocking materialism would have occasioned major outcries, but most viewers simply shrugged their shoulders. If the meaning of this anatomical frolicking was lost on some, no Mexico City resident was confused by the artistic celebration of Earth Day in 1992. The intensity was best captured perhaps by painter Roger von Gunten's depiction of colored smoke from a Mexico City factory. He entitled it *Rainbow of Death*. It reminded many of Carlos Fuentes' depiction of the capital in his latest novel, *Christopher Unborn*. He had dubbed it Makesicko City.

Historical scholarship had not fared well in the two decades prior to World War II, for historians often found it impossible to reconcile their faith in the Revolution with documentary evidence available to them. But in the postwar years historical scholarship came of age. Between 1940 and 1951, three important institutions—El Colegio de México, the Escuela Nacional de Antropología e Historia, and the Instituto de Historia of the National University—were founded and devoted major effort to improving historical training. Reacting against the blatant partisanship of the prorevolutionary school that had emerged in the 1920s and 1930s, the new generation of historians was much more concerned with methodology, archival research, careful bibliographical preparation, and documentary publication. The preparation of excellent regional histories and microhistories put the scholarly community on notice that in the future Mexico and Mexico City would not be considered synonymous terms.

Contributing to the maturation of historical scholarship were eight important conferences in which Mexican historians came

4. Quoted in Elena Poniatowska, "Interview with Juan Soriano," *Evergreen Review* 2 (1959): 144–49.

together with their United States and European counterparts. Meeting in Monterrey, Nuevo León, in 1949; in Austin in 1958; in Oaxtepec, Morelos, in 1969; in Santa Monica in 1973; in Pátzcuaro, Michoacán, in 1977; in Chicago in 1981; in Oaxaca in 1985; and in San Diego in 1989; historians from around the world who specialized in Mexican history, both established hands and young aspirants, submitted the fruits of their research to one another, tested new ideas, pinpointed lacunae, analyzed historiographical trends, disputed the latest trends in methodology, and

An architectural and anthropological achievement of gigantic proportions, the new Museum of Anthropology in Mexico City (above and on opposite page) became a prime tourist attraction in the 1970s.

published their proceedings. While the conferences were far from barren of vigorous controversy, polemical acrimony was noticeable mainly for its absence. The debates were healthy ones and augured well for the future of Mexican historiography.

One of the most remarkable historical endeavors undertaken in Mexico in the postwar era was the project of Daniel Cosío Villegas. In the late 1940s, he began work on an ambitious, multivolume history of modern Mexico. Twenty-five years later the ninth and final volume appeared, and the project had received acclaim as perhaps the most significant Latin American historical enterprise of the twentieth century. The *Historia moderna de México* covers the years from the restoration of the republic in 1867 to the outbreak of the Revolution, with separate volumes treating the political, economic, social, and international aspects of the period. Cosío planned the project with extreme care, founding in 1950 the Seminar on Modern Mexican History at El Colegio de México. This workshop brought together a group of talented researchers who, under Cosío's direction, prepared extensive bibliographies; compiled statistical data; searched out the major manuscripts, printed documentation, and newspapers; and cooperated in the production of the finished volumes.

Although thirteen scholars contributed sections, Cosío's conception of history permeated the entire enterprise and his guiding hand ensured a high quality. Eschewing the notion that history should be a tool for the apotheosis of the Revolution, Cosío did not find it necessary to excoriate Porfirio Díaz and his regime. He proposed that the birth of modern Mexico was properly attributable to the restored republic rather than to the Porfiriato. He held no special brief for the abuses of the Díaz dictatorship, but, in the tradition of classical nineteenth-century scientific history, he was content to let the facts speak for themselves. When conclusions were offered, however, they were clearly supported by the evidence. The picture that emerged was clear and objective, unflawed by the distortions of prorevolutionary presupposition. The historian Charles A. Hale prepared a penetrating view of Cosío's work in a long review essay. His conclusions are particularly appropriate:

> By breaking through the seemingly impenetrable ideological barrier thrown up by the Revolution of 1910, by eschewing the centennial impulse in historiography, and by basing interpretations on serious research, Daniel Cosío Villegas and his collaborators have given new life to the professional study of modern and contemporary Mexico, both within the country and abroad.[5]

It took a long time for the new scholarship to reach the public, but it did in dramatic fashion late in 1992. Mexico's mandatory school textbooks underwent a major revision. Porfirio Díaz emerged not as a despotic megalomaniac but as a positive actor in the creation of modern Mexico. The Revolutionary icons on the other hand, especially Emiliano Zapata, surfaced as rather less heroic, and not entirely free of warts. In general harmony with the post-Revolutionary political ethic, Mexico's serious national problems were no longer attributed to the imperialistic United States. The books were even silent on the American intervention in Veracruz in 1914. And of equal importance, for the first time Mexican school children were allowed to read a reasonable and accurate accounting of what happened on October 2, 1968, at Tlatelolco. They deserved to know. But the rearrangement of Mexico's history troubled many. Would Mexico become one of those countries where it was possible to predict the past?

5. Charles A. Hale, "The Liberal Impulse: Daniel Cosío Villegas and the *Historia moderna de México*," *Hispanic American Historical Review* 54 (1974): 498.

Mexico's post-Revolutionary cultural and intellectual community viewed the future with a mixture of skepticism and hope. Although some were visably uncomfortable with Mexico's new love affair with a free market economy and with the unembarrassed embrace of the United States, others were ready to watch and see. There had been little intellectual euphoria with the direction the Revolution had taken in the postwar period and even less faith in the beneficence of party leadership. The time for change had now come just as surely as it had in 1910.

Francisco Madero and his successors had evidenced the vision to launch Mexico on a grand experiment, which had served the nation well. At its best the Revolution enshrined an idealism that sought to feed the hungry and empower the dispossessed. Much had been accomplished, but six decades later a new world order had rendered the programs engendered by that idealism obsolete. President Salinas showed the political courage to redefine Mexico's identity, and notwithstanding the strong lure of Revolutionary nostalgia, the country would not turn back in its new approach to becoming a modern industrial state.

Recommended for Further Study

Alisky, Marvin. "Mexico versus Malthus: National Trends." *Current History* 66 (1974): 200–203, 227–30.

Arreola, Juan José. *Confabulario and Other Inventions.* Translated by George D. Shade. Austin: University of Texas Press, 1974.

Bailey, David C. "Revisionism and the Recent Historiography of the Mexican Revolution." *Hispanic American Historical Review* 58 (1978): 62–79.

Brody, Robert, and Charles Rossman, eds. *Carlos Fuentes: A Critical View.* Austin: University of Texas Press, 1982.

Brushwood, John S. *Mexico in Its Novel: A Nation's Search for Identity.* Austin: University of Texas Press, 1966.

Carr, Barry. "Recent Regional Studies of the Mexican Revolution." *Latin American Research Review* 15 (1980): 3–14.

Chavarría, Jesús. "A Brief Inquiry into Octavio Paz." *The Americas* 27 (1971): 381–88.

Cuevas, José Luis. "The Cactus Curtain." *Evergreen Review* 2 (1959): 111–20.

Duncan, J. Ann. *Voices, Visions and a New Reality: Mexican Fiction Since 1970.* Pittsburgh: University of Pittsburgh Press, 1986.

Fuentes, Carlos. *The Death of Artemio Cruz.* Translated by Sam Hileman. New York: Noonday Press, 1966.

———. *Where the Air Is Clear.* Translated by Sam Hileman. New York: Ivan Obolensky, 1960.

Goldman, Shifra M. *Contemporary Mexican Painting in a Time of Change.* Austin: University of Texas Press, 1981.

————. "Rewriting the History of Mexican Art: The Politics and Economics of Contemporary Culture." In *Mexico: A Country in Crisis*, edited by Jerry R. Ladman, pp. 96–115. El Paso: Texas Western Press, 1986.

Hale, Charles A. "The Liberal Impulse: Daniel Cosío Villegas and the *Historia moderna de México*." *Hispanic American Historical Review* 54 (1974): 479–98.

————, and Michael C. Meyer. "Mexico: The National Period." In *Latin American Scholarship since World War II*, edited by Roberto Esquenazi-Mayo and Michael C. Meyer, pp. 115–38. Lincoln: University of Nebraska Press, 1971.

Hayner, Norman S. *New Patterns in Old Mexico*. New Haven, Conn.: Yale University Press, 1966.

Langford, Walter M. *The Mexican Novel Comes of Age*. Notre Dame, Ind.: University of Notre Dame Press, 1971.

Lewis, Oscar. *The Children of Sánchez: Autobiography of a Mexican Family*. New York: Vintage Books, 1961.

Lipp, Solomon. *Leopoldo Zea: From Mexicanidad to a Philosophy of History*. Waterloo, Ontario: Wilfrid Laurier University Press, 1980.

Lorey, David E. *The University System and Economic Development in Mexico Since 1929*. Stanford, Calif.: Stanford University Press, 1993.

Meyer, Michael C. "A Venture in Documentary Publication: Isidro Fabela's *Documentos Históricos*." *Hispanic American Historical Review* 52 (1972): 123–29.

Paz, Octavio. *The Labyrinth of Solitude: Life and Thought in Mexico*. Translated by Lysander Kemp, New York: Grove Press, 1961.

Poniatowska, Elena. "Interview with Juan Soriano." *Evergreen Review* 2 (1959): 141–52.

Sáenz, Gustavo. "New Trends in Mexican Literature: A Response to Change." In *Mexico: A Country in Crisis*, edited by Jerry R. Ladman, pp. 116–31. El Paso: Texas Western Press, 1986.

Schmidt, Henry C. "Hector Aguilar Camín and the Interpretation of the Mexican Revolution." *New World* 1 (1986): 82–93.

Sommers, Joseph. *After the Storm*. Albuquerque: University of New Mexico Press, 1968.

Stabb, Martin. "The New Essay of Mexico: Text and Context." *Hispania/ Teacher* 70 (1987), 47–61.

Steele, Cynthia. *Politics, Gender and the Mexican Novel, 1968–1988: Beyond the Pyramid*. Austin: University of Texas Press, 1992.

Wilkie, James W. "Alternative Views in History: Historical Statistics and Oral History." In *Research in Mexican History: Topics, Methodology, Sources and a Practical Guide to Field Research*, edited by Richard E. Greenleaf and Michael C. Meyer, pp. 49–62. Lincoln: University of Nebraska Press, 1973.

————, Michael C. Meyer, and Edna Monzón de Wilkie, eds. *Contemporary Mexico: Papers of the IV Congress of Mexican History*. Berkeley: University of California Press, 1976.

Young, Dolly J. "Mexican Literary Reactions to Tlatelolco, 1968." *Latin American Research Review* 20 (1985): 71–85.

APPENDIX: MEXICAN HEADS OF STATE

The Aztec Empire

Tenoch	?
Queen Ilancueitl	1349–75
Acamapichtli and Queen Ilancueitl	1375–83
Acamapichtli	1383–96
Huitzilíhuitl	1396–1417
Chimalpopoca	1417–27
Itzcóatl	1427–40
Moctezuma Ilhuicamina (Moctezuma I)	1440–69
Axayácatl	1469–81
Tizoc	1481–86
Ahuítzotl	1486–1502
Moctezuma Xocoyótzin (Moctezuma II)	1502–June 1520
Cuitláhuac	June–October 1520
Cuauhtémoc	October 1520–August 1521

Immediate Post-Conquest Period

Fernando Cortés	1521–24
Crown Officials	1524–26
Residencia Judges	1526–28
First Audiencia	1528–31
Second Audiencia	1531–35

Viceroys of the Colonial Period

Antonio de Mendoza	1535–50
Luis de Velasco (the elder)	1550–64
Gastón de Peralta	1566–68
Martín Enríquez de Almanza	1568–80

Lorenzo Suárez de Mendoza	1580–83
Pedro Moya de Contreras	1584–85
Alvaro Manrique de Zúñiga	1585–90
Luis de Velasco (the younger)	1590–95
Gaspar de Zúñiga y Acevedo	1595–1603
Juan de Mendoza y Luna	1603–7
Luis de Velasco (the younger)	1607–11
Fray García Guerra	1611–12
Diego Fernández de Córdoba	1612–21
Diego Carrillo de Mendoza y Pimentel	1621–24
Rodrigo Pacheco y Osorio	1624–35
Lope Díaz de Armendáriz	1635–40
Diego López Pacheco Cabrera y Bobadilla	1640–42
Juan de Palafox y Mendoza	1642–48
Marcos de Torres y Rueda	1648–49
Luis Enríquez y Guzmán	1650–53
Francisco Fernández de la Cueva	1653–60
Juan de Leyva y de la Cerda	1660–64
Diego Osorio de Escobar y Llamas	1664
Antonio Sebastián de Toledo	1664–73
Pedro Nuño Colón de Portugal	1673
Fray Payo Enríquez de Rivera	1673–80
Tomás Antonio de la Cerda y Aragón	1680–86
Melchor Portocarrero Lasso de la Vega	1686–88
Gaspar de Sandoval Silva y Mendoza	1688–96
Juan de Ortega y Montañez	1696
José Sarmiento Valladares	1696–1701
Juan de Ortega y Montañez	1701
Francisco Fernández de la Cueva Enríquez	1701–11
Fernando de Alencastre Noroña y Silva	1711–16
Baltasar de Zúñiga y Guzmán	1716–22
Juan de Acuña	1722–34
Juan Antonio Vizarrón y Eguiarreta	1734–40
Pedro de Castro y Figueroa	1740–41
Pedro Cebrián y Agustín	1742–46
Francisco de Güemes y Horcasitas	1746–55
(subsequently first Count Revillagigedo)	
Agustín Ahumada y Villalón	1755–60
Francisco Cajigal de la Vega	1760
Joaquín de Monserrat	1760–66
Carlos Francisco de Croix	1766–71
Antonio María de Bucareli	1771–79
Martín de Mayorga	1779–83
Matías de Gálvez	1783–84
Bernardo de Gálvez	1785–86
Alonso Núñez de Haro y Peralta	1787
Manuel Antonio Flores	1787–89
Juan Vicente de Güemes Pacheco y Padilla	1789–94
(second Count Revillagigedo)	
Miguel de la Grúa Talamanca y Branciforte	1794–98
Miguel José de Azanza	1798–1800

Félix Berenguer de Marquina	1800–1803
José de Iturrigaray	1803–8
Pedro Garibay	1808–9
Francisco Javier de Lizana y Beaumont	1809–10
Francisco Javier de Venegas	1810–13
Félix María Calleja del Rey	1813–16
Juan Ruiz de Apodaca	1816–21
Francisco Novella	1821
Juan O'Donojú	did not assume office

Independence Period and Early Republic

Emperor Agustín de Iturbide	1822–23
Guadalupe Victoria (Félix Fernández)	1824–29
Vicente Guerrero	1829
José María Bocanegra (interim)	1829
Pedro Vélez, Luis Quintanar, and Lucas Alamán, triumvirate	1829
Anastasio Bustamante	1830–32, 1837–39, and 1842
Melchor Múzquiz (interim)	1832
Manuel Gómez Pedraza	1833
Antonio López de Santa Anna	variously from 1833 to 1855
Valentín Gómez Farías	1833, 1834, and 1847
Miguel Barragán	1835–36
José Justo Corro	1836–37
Nicolás Bravo	variously from 1839 to 1846
Javier Echeverría	1841
Valentín Canalizo	1844
José Joaquín Herrera (interim)	1844, 1845, and 1848–51
Mariano Paredes Arrillaga	1846
Mariano Salas	1846
Pedro María Anaya	1847 and 1848
Manuel de la Peña y Peña	1847 and 1848
Mariano Arista	1851–53
Juan Bautista Ceballos (interim)	1853
Manuel María Lombardini	1853
Martín Carrera (interim)	1855
Rómulo Díaz de la Vega	1855

The Reform and the French Intervention

Juan Alvarez	1855
Ignacio Comonfort	1855–58

Liberal Government

Benito Juárez	1855–72

Conservative Government

Félix Zuloaga	1858 and 1859
Manuel Robles Pezuela	1858

Miguel Miramón   1859–60
Ignacio Pavón   1860
Conservative Junta   1860–64
Emperor Maximilian von Hapsburg   1864–67

Post-Reform Period

Sebastián Lerdo de Tejada   1872–76
Porfirio Díaz   1876–80 and 1884–1911
Juan N. Méndez   1876
Manuel González   1880–84

Revolutionary Period

Francisco León de la Barra (interim)   1911
Francisco I. Madero   1911–13
Pedro Lascuraín (interim)   1913
Victoriano Huerta (interim)   1913–14
Francisco S. Carbajal (interim)   1914
Venustiano Carranza   1914 and 1915–20
Eulalio Gutiérrez (interim, named by   1914
  Convention)
Roque González Garza   1914
Francisco Lagos Cházaro   1915
Adolfo de la Huerta (interim)   1920
Alvaro Obregón   1920–24
Plutarco Elías Calles   1924–28
Emilio Portes Gil (interim)   1928–30
Pascual Ortiz Rubio   1930–32
Abelardo L. Rodríguez (interim)   1932–34
Lázaro Cárdenas   1934–40

Period of Institutional Revolution

Manuel Avila Camacho   1940–46
Miguel Alemán Valdés   1946–52
Adolfo Ruiz Cortines   1952–58
Adolfo López Mateos   1958–64
Gustavo Díaz Ordaz   1964–70
Luis Echeverría Alvarez   1970–76
José López Portillo   1976–82
Miguel de la Madrid   1982–88
Carlos Salinas de Gortari   1988–

Source: Adapted from Richard E. Greenleaf and Michael C. Meyer, eds., *Research in Mexican History: Topics, Methodology, Sources and a Practical Guide to Field Research* (Lincoln, 1973), pp. 221–24.

SOURCES OF ILLUSTRATIONS

We gratefully acknowledge the following persons and institutions for the photographs and illustrations in this book.

List of Abbreviations

AMNH	American Museum of Natural History, New York
AIA	Archaelogical Institute of America, New York
ASHS	Arizona State Historical Society, Tucson
BL	The Bancroft Library, University of California, Berkeley
HRC	The Humanities Research Center, The University of Texas at Austin
HL	Henry E. Huntington Library, San Marino, California
IADB	Interamerican Development Bank, Washington, D.C.
LC	Library of Congress, Washington, D.C.
MMA	The Metropolitan Museum of Art, New York
MNTC	Mexican National Tourist Council, New York
MNA	Museo Nacional de Antropología, Mexico
NA	National Archives, Washington, D.C.
NYPL	New York Public Library
OAS	Organization of American States, Washington, D.C.
SMM	The Science Museum of Minnesota, St. Paul
UAL	University of Arizona Library, Tucson

Chapter 1. p. 7, AMNH; 10, MNA; 11, LC; 12, left–Brooklyn Museum, lent by Mr. Robin B. Martin, right–MMA, Michael C. Rockefeller Mem. Coll. of Primitive Art. *Chapter* 2. p. 15, MMA, Rockefeller Coll; 19, above and lower left–AMNH, lower right–MMA, Rockefeller Coll; 21, MNTC; 22, AIA; 23, MNTC; 25, MNA; 26, Leslie Hewes; 28, Jeffrey House; 30, MMA, Rockefeller Coll; 32, above–AMNH, below–MNTC; 33, MNA; 34, left–MNA, right–Dumbarton Oaks, Washington, D.C. *Chapter* 3. p. 40, AIA; 42, above–NYPL, below–Alan Bates; 44, left– MMA, Rockefeller Coll, right–MNTC, below–MNA; 45, 46, Leslie Hewes; 47, above–AIA, below–Bradley Smith: 49, AMNH; 50, MNTC; 51, Thomas Laging. *Chapter* 4. p. 57, LC; 62, 64, AMNH. *Chapter* 5.

p. 68, OAS; 70, Biblioteca, MNA; 71, BL; 72, Dumbarton Oaks, Washington, D.C.; 77, LC; 83, 84, MNA; 88, AMNH; 90, left–Bradley Smith. *Chapter 6.* p. 97, above left–MMA, Rogers Fund, 1904, right–MMA, Gift William H. Riggs, 1913, below left–MMA, Gift Abraham Silberman, 1937, right–MMA, Rogers Fund, 1921; 100, Hospital de Jesús, México; 102, BL; 105, British Museum; 110, NYPL. *Chapter 7.* p. 119, above–Los Angeles County Museum of Natural History, below–MMA, Gift William H. Riggs, 1913; 123, NYPL; 125, Biblioteca, MNA; 127, above–after a model in the John W. Higgins Armory, Worcester, Mass. *Chapter 8.* p. 132, MNTC; 134, OAS; 141, from Justo Sierra, *Mexico, Its Social Revolution*, 1900; 144, BL. *Chapter 9.* p. 163, LC; 165, MMA. Gift William H. Riggs, 1913. *Chapter 10.* p. 171, Pan Amer. Development Foundation; 173, Weidenfeld & Nicolson, London; 175, NA; 178, upper left–Philadelphia Museum of Art, upper right and below–MMA, Gift Mrs. Robert W. de Forest, 1911; 179, from Carlos Nebel, *Viaje pintoresco y arqueológico sobre . . . la República Mexicana . . .*, 1839; 181, American Numismatic Society, N.Y. *Chapter 11.* p. 185, LC; 187, MNTC; 189, LC; 190, 192, Jeffrey House; 191, LC; Museo Nacional de Historia, México; 193, 196, 197, 198, Vicente Riva Palacios, *México a través de los siglos*, 1887–89; 194, LC; 200, Elsie Y. Haack. *Chapter 13.* pp. 222, 223, 226, from Justo Sierra, *Mexico, Its Social Revolution*, 1900; 228, 232, LC; 233, BL; 234, MNA; 235, Leslie Hewes; 238, 239, Hispanic Society of America, N.Y.; 242, from *México y sus Alrededores*, Editorial Valle de México, 1980. *Chapter 14.* p. 252, Bruckmann–Art Reference Bureau; 262, from *México y sus alrededores*, Editorial Valle de México, 1980. *Chapter 15.* p. 265, OAS; 266, LC; 267, from Carlos Nebel, *Viaje pintoresco y arqueológico sobre . . . la República Mexicana . . .*; 269, Weidenfeld & Nicolson, London; 271, Vicente Riva Palacios, *México a través de los siglos*, 1887–89; 272, The Brooklyn Museum; 273, BL; 280, MMA, Bequest Mrs. H. O. Havemeyer, 1929; 282, BL. *Chapter 16.* p. 287, LC; 291, Bettmann Archive. *Chapter 17.* p. 303, from *Gobernantes de México, 1325–1911, Artes de México* No. 175, año XXI, p. 59. *Chapter 18.* p. 317, from Justo Sierra, *Mexico, Its Social Revolution*, 1900. *Chapter 19.* p. 327, BL; 333, NYPL. *Chapter 20.* p. 341, BL; 349, NA. *Chapter 21.* pp. 359, 361, from Vicente Riva Palacios, *México a través de los siglos*, 1887–89; 363, 365, from B. Mayer, *Mexico, Aztec, Spanish and Republican*, 1852. *Chapter 22.* p. 377, BL. *Chapter 23.* p. 386, BL; 389, ASHS; 394, 400, from M. de los Torres, *El archiduque Maximiliano de Austria en México*, 1867. *Chapter 24.* p. 406, HRC; 409, NYPL; 411, HL. *Chapter 25.* p. 418, from Vicente Riva Palacios, *México a través de los siglos*, 1887–89; 420, BL; 423, from *México y sus alrededores*, Editorial Valle de México, 1980; 425, NYPL; 427, from Justo Sierra, *Mexico, Its Social Revolution*, 1900. *Chapter 27.* p. 441, HRC; 443, BL; 444, SMM; 447, ASHS. *Chapter 28.* p. 455, SMM; 456, UAL; 462, HL; 463, SMM. *Chapter 29.* p. 471, HRC; 472, ASHS. *Chapter 30.* p. 486, Hemeroteca Nacional de México; 489, BL. *Chapter 31.* p. 501, UAL; 504, HRC; 505, ASHS. *Chapter 32.* p. 512, HRC; 518, NA. *Chapter 33.* p. 525, HL; 533, LC. *Chapter 34.* p. 538, HRC; 540, 541, LC; 547, HRC. *Chapter 35.* p. 553, ASHS; 556, LC; 558, above–HL, below–HRC. *Chapter 36.* p. 575, HRC. *Chapter 37.* p. 584, NYPL. *Chapter 38.* pp. 601, 605, NA. *Chapter 39.* pp. 614, 615, LC; 616, Pan Amer. Development Foundation; 617, LC; 618, Dartmouth College Museum, Hanover, N.H.; 619, National Preparatory School, México.

Chapter 40. pp. 632, 634, NA.   *Chapter* 41. pp. 642, 643, Editorial Photocolor Archives; 644, NA.   *Chapter* 42. 653, MNTC; 654, OAS; 657, MNTC. *Chapter* 43. pp. 666, 667, MNTC; 670, James W. Wilkie.   *Chapter* 44. p. 682, Diego Goldberg/Sygma; 685, Secretaría de información y propaganda del Partido Revolucionario Institucional; 689, Alejandro Castañeda, Mexico D.F., 1985; 690, Photograph by David Burckhalter, *Journal of the Southwest* 32 (Spring 1990); Juan Miranda, Proceso.   *Chapter* 45. p. 702, David Mangurian, IADB, 1992; 708, OAS; 714, 715, MNTC.

INDEX